Dubai

timeout.com/dubai

Published by Time Out Guides Ltd, a wholly owned subsidiary of Time Out Group Ltd.
Time Out and the Time Out logo are trademarks of Time Out Group Ltd.

© Time Out Group Ltd 2007
Previous editions 2003, 2005

10 9 8 7 6 5 4 3 2 1

This edition first published in Great Britain in 2007 by Ebury Publishing
A Random House Group Company
20 Vauxhall Bridge Road, London SW1V 2SA

Random House Australia Pty Limited 20 Alfred Street, Milsons Point, Sydney, New South Wales 2061, Australia
Random House New Zealand Limited 18 Poland Road, Glenfield, Auckland 10, New Zealand
Random House South Africa (Pty) Limited Isle of Houghton, Corner Boundary
Road & Carse O'Gowrie, Houghton 2198, South Africa

Random House UK Limited Reg. No. 954009

For further distribution details, see www.timeout.com

ISBN 10: 1-84670-028-0
ISBN 13: 9781846700286

A CIP catalogue record for this book is available from the British Library

Printed and bound by Firmengruppe APPL, aprinta druck, Wemding, Germany

The Random House Group Limited makes every effort to ensure that the papers used in our books are made from trees
that have been legally sourced from well-managed and credibly certified forests. Our paper procurement policy can be
found on www.randomhouse.co.uk.

Time Out Guides Limited
Universal House
251 Tottenham Court Road
London W1T 7AB
Tel + 44 (0)20 7813 3000
Fax + 44 (0)20 7813 6001
Email guides@timeout.com
www.timeout.com

Editorial

Managing Editor Marcus Webb
Editor Matthew Lee
Sub Editor Ananda Shakespeare
Proofreader Anna Norman
Indexer Tom Lamont

Managing Director Peter Fiennes
Financial Director Gareth Garner
Editorial Director Ruth Jarvis
Deputy Series Editor Dominic Earle
Editorial Manager Holly Pick

Design

Designer Hiren Chandarana

Picture Desk

Picture Editor Jael Marschner
Deputy Picture Editor Tracey Kerrigan
Picture Researcher Helen McFarland

Advertising

Sales Director Mark Phillips
International Sales Manager Fred Durman
International Sales Consultant Ross Canadé
International Sales Executive Simon Davies
Advertising Sales (Dubai) Andy Baker, Gareth Lloyd-Jones

Marketing

Group Marketing Director John Luck
Marketing Manager Yvonne Poon
Sales and Marketing Director North America Lisa Levinson

Production

Group Production Director Mark Lamond
Production Manager Brendan McKeown
Production Coordinator Caroline Bradford
Production Controller Susan Whittaker

Time Out Group

Chairman Tony Elliott
Financial Director Richard Waterlow
Group General Manager/Director Nichola Coulthard
Time Out Magazine Ltd MD Richard Waterlow
Time Out Communications Ltd MD David Pepper
Time Out International MD Cathy Runciman
Group Art Director John Oakey
Group IT Director Simon Chappell

Contributors

Contributing Editors Chris Anderson, Dana El-Baltaji, Kaye Holland
Contributing Designers Mohammed Abu Salouk, Louise Browne, Philip Bunting, Dalton Butler, Catherine Warde

Introduction Marcus Webb. **History** Dana El-Baltaji, Marcus Webb. **Dubai Today** Conrad Egbert, Heba Elasaad, Jeremy Lawrence, Becky Lucas, Matt Slater, Marcus Webb. **Architecture** Caroline Cullern. **Culture & Customs** Dana El-Baltaji. **Where to Stay** Kaye Holland, Marcus Webb. **Urban Dubai** Dana El-Baltaji. **Further Afield** Dana El-Baltaji, Kaye Holland. **Guided Tours** Scott Walker. **Restaurants & Cafés** James Brennan, Matthew Lee. **Pubs & Bars** Andy Buchan, Matthew Lee. **Shopping** Matthew Lee, Sarah Murphy. **Festivals & Events** Heba Elasaad. **Children** Kaye Holland. **Film & Theatre** Arsalan Mohammad. **Galleries** Arsalan Mohammad. **Nightlife** Andy Buchan. **Spectator Sports** Becky Lucas. **Participation Sports** Becky Lucas. **Health & Fitness** Ananda Shakespeare. **Abu Dhabi** Matthew Lee. **Northern Emirates** Dana El-Baltaji. **East Coast** Kaye Holland. **Directory** Vicki Hughes.

Maps JS Graphics (john@jsgraphics.co.uk); maps are based on material supplied by Netmaps.

Photography Victoria Calaguian, Sevag Davidian, George Dipin, Francisco Fernandez, Valeriano Handumon, Khatuna Khutsishvili, Alejandro Rodriguez, Nemanja Seslija, Bernardino Testa, Paulo Vecina. Additional photography Louise Browne, Hiren Chandarana, Marcus Webb. Other photography courtesy of Arabian Courtyard Hotel, Al Bustan Rotana Group, Dubai Marine Beach Resort & Spa, Dubai Municipality, Dusit Hotels & Resorts, Emaar Properties, The Emirates Group, Hilton Hotels, Hyatt Hotels & Resorts, Jebel Ali International Hotels, The Jumeirah Hotels & Resorts, Kempinski Hotels, Mall Of The Emirates, One&Only Resorts, Radisson Hotels & Resorts, Al Raha Beach Hotel, Ramada Hotels, The Ritz-Carlton Dubai, Nakheel, Starwood Hotels and Resorts and Voyagers Xtreme. Pages 11, 199 Karim Sahib/Getty Images; pages 12, 15, 16 Ramesh Shukla/Blink; pages 21, 43 Nasser Younes/Getty Images; page 25 Rabih Moghrabi/Getty Images; page 29 James Law Cybertecture; page 34 Falcon City Of Wonders LLC; page 85 JD Dallet/Blink; pages 88, 293 Katarina Premfors/Blink; page167 Jimin Lai/Getty Images; page 194 Chris Jackson/Getty Images; page 219 Clive Brunskill/Getty Images; page 223 Shah Marai/Getty Images; page 225 Ezra Shaw/Getty Images; page 251 Robert Harding/Getty Images; pages 268, 276 Kami/Blink

The Editor would like to thank Greg Aris, Antonia Carver, David Donaghy, Kate McAuley, Georgie McCourt, Rob Orchard, Dinesh Rajan, Greg Wilson, Andrew Wingrove and other contributors to previous editions of *Time Out Dubai*, whose work forms the basis for parts of this book.

Contents

Introduction

In a city so fond of sound bites and self-promotion (the seven-star hotel, the man-made islands, the world's tallest tower), Dubai's most startling feature, its infancy, is often overlooked. Compared to most major cities, Dubai is in its formative years; but it's growing up fast.

In 1970, what is now a sprawling orgy of malls and hotels was little more than a sandy outpost, and even by the mid-1990s Dubai boasted few landmarks and even fewer tourists. But with the confidence that comes with youth, Dubai has burned itself on to the world's consciousness. Through a mixture of ambition, audacity and a swathe of mega-projects, the city has transformed itself into one of the most dynamic centres on the planet; a cultural and economic hub linking East and West.

This metamorphosis from sleepy pearl-diving village to one of the most talked about towns in the world has changed local people's lives beyond recognition. Where their grandfathers eked out a hand-to-mouth existence in the desert, many of today's Emiratis live in a world of luxury villas, flash cars and unbridled opportunities. They also find themselves a minority in their own city, as ever-greater numbers of people from around the globe are brought in to fuel Project Dubai. Meanwhile, a citywide army of cranes keeps the skyline in constant flux. New hotels, office blocks and residential areas are seemingly thrown up overnight and yet are still unable to accommodate the waves of tourists that continue to flood into the emirate.

And still they come. Despite suffering from overpowering heat and humidity during the summer months of May to September, the city attracted more than six million visitors in 2006 and expects to double that number by 2010. So what's the appeal? The answer is that Dubai takes the basics – sun, sea and shopping – and wraps them in layers of sumptuous luxury. Immaculate five-star hotels with white sand beaches line the coast, acres of shopping malls sate the hungriest consumer and the annual Dubai Shopping Festival in January and February brings in an average of 2.6 million spenders who leave some US$2.5 billion lighter. Add to that a vibrant nightlife scene and some truly outstanding restaurants, and the allure is obvious.

Many people question how long Dubai can continue to grow at this breakneck pace. Doomsayers talk of bubbles bursting, but the truth is that people continue to buy into the Dubai dream, and the city's PR machine has generated such a global buzz that those in search of winter sun who would never have previously considered the Middle East are now flocking to the City of Gold in droves.

So welcome to Dubai. It may be young, brash and at times vulgar, but that's half the fun. Prepare to be amazed.

ABOUT TIME OUT CITY GUIDES

Time Out Dubai is one of an expanding series of Time Out City Guides produced by the people behind London and New York's successful listings magazines. Our guides are written and updated by resident experts, in this case the same team that produces the weekly listings magazine *Time Out Dubai*. We have striven to provide you with all the most up-to-date information you'll need to explore the city, whether you're a resident or a first-time visitor.

THE LIE OF THE LAND

The city of Dubai is roughly divided in two halves by the Creek, forming the basic areas of Deira, to the north, and Bur Dubai, to the south. Many Dubaians refer to locations as being Deira-side or Bur Dubai-side respectively. Beyond Bur Dubai lies Jumeirah, the stretch of golden shoreline now home to opulent hotels and wealthy expats. Beyond Jumeirah is Dubai Marina, home to countless high-rises and the so-called 'golden mile' of five-star hotels, as well as the Palm Jumeirah development.

ESSENTIAL INFORMATION

For all the practical information you might need for visiting the city – including visa and customs information, emergency phone numbers, useful websites and the local transport network – turn to the **Directory** chapter at the back of this guide, it starts on *p293*.

THE LOWDOWN ON THE LISTINGS

Above all, we've tried to make this book as useful as possible. Addresses, phone numbers, transport information, opening times, admission prices, websites and credit card details are all included in our listings. And, as far as possible, we've given details

of facilities, services and events, all checked and correct at the time we went to press. However, since owners and managers can change their arrangements at any time, we always advise readers to phone ahead and check opening times and other particulars. While every effort has been made to ensure the accuracy of the information contained in this guide, the publishers cannot accept responsibility for any errors it may contain.

PRICES AND PAYMENT

We have noted whether venues such as shops, hotels and restaurants accept credit cards or not but have only listed the major cards – American Express (AmEx), MasterCard (MC) and Visa (V). Many businesses will also accept other cards and travellers' cheques.

The prices we've supplied should be treated simply as guidelines. Fluctuating exchange rates and inflation can cause charges, in shops and restaurants particularly, to change rapidly. If prices vary wildly from those we've quoted, please write and let us know. We aim to give the best and most up-to-date advice, so we always want to know if you've been badly treated or overcharged.

TELEPHONE NUMBERS

The international code for Dubai is 9714; the first three digits designate the country of the UAE, while the remaining '4' indicates the emirate of Dubai (each of the emirates – and other significant areas – have a corresponding number; international calls to Abu Dhabi, for example, should begin with 9712). Add '0' before this emirate-specific digit to create an area code (e.g. 04), but this is necessary only when dialling from one emirate to another. All phone numbers in the UAE have seven digits. For more on telephones, *see p308*.

MAPS

The street maps start on page 328; on them are pinpointed the specific locations of hotels (❶), restaurants and cafés (❶) and pubs and bars (❶) featured in this guide. There are also overview maps of the UAE on page 322, and Abu Dhabi on page 254. Maps date quickly in the UAE as it's such a rapidly expanding country.

LET US KNOW WHAT YOU THINK

We hope you enjoy *Time Out Dubai*, and we'd like to know what you think of it. We welcome tips for places that you consider we should include in future editions and take notice of your criticism of our choices. You can email your comments to us at guides@timeout.com.

Advertisers

We would like to stress that no establishment has been included in this guide because it has advertised in any of our publications and no payment of any kind has influenced any review. The opinions given in this book are those of *Time Out* writers and entirely independent.

There is an online version of this book, along with guides to many other international cities, at **www.timeout.com**.

In Context

Changing times: **Clock Tower Roundabout** in Deira, 1969.

History

With the focus on ground-breaking ventures, it's easy for visitors and residents to forget the emirate has a past.

With its gleaming skyscrapers, love of modernity and apparent lack of anything over ten years old, you'd be forgiven for thinking that Dubai is a mere child of a city, albeit one undergoing an incredible growth-spurt. While it's true that the city that headline writers know and love only really took shape over the last decade, settlements dating from the early fifth and sixth centuries AD have been found in what is now the modern suburb of Jumeirah. These relics indicate that with the advent of Islam, the Umayyad and the Abbasid Islamic dynasties, Dubai was already established as a stop-off point of business for the caravans serving Iraq – the Islamic epicentre of the day.

Until recently, the emirate hasn't been very good at preserving its historical sites. The widespread and almost hysterical construction boom that began in the 1990s, and which went into overdrive in 2003, has morphed Dubai into a bustling metropolis welding together Arab and Western cultures, sometimes successfully,

other times awkwardly, but almost always at the cost of its traditional architecture and old buildings. Consequently, there are precious few mementoes of Dubai's more distant past.

It was the lure of pearl trading that would put Dubai on the international map; Venetian jeweller Gasparo Balbi made the first written reference to 'Dibei' in 1580, during a search of the East to uncover a lucrative source of the precious stones.

TAMING THE GULF

Strategically located on a ten-kilometre (six-mile) creek, Dubai started its remarkable evolution from small, sleepy fishing village to dynamic city some time during the 18th century. The town was wedged between the two powerful clans who held sway over the lower Gulf, the Bani Yas of Liwa Oasis, who had gone on to settle in Abu Dhabi, the modern capital of the UAE, and the Qawasim, based in the northern emirates and parts of modern-day Oman.

The Qawasim's powerful navy had already triggered the ire of the British Empire's ruling classes, which led to the area becoming known as the 'Pirate Coast' owing to the agile, armed Arab dhows that plundered ships from the East India Trading Company. The disruption to British commercial interests prompted a show of superior naval power that brought the ruling families of this part of the Arabian coastline to their knees. Britain, fearing attempts from Russia and France to challenge its dominance of the region, then signed exclusivity treaties with the leaders of the 'Trucial States', offering protection and non-interference in local politics on the condition that leaders didn't even correspond with other global powers. Dubai and the rest of the Trucial Coast were now firmly within the sphere of British influence.

> ## 'The pearling industry thrived, and its wares were exported both to India and to Europe.'

MAKTOUM RULE

In 1833, the era of Maktoum family rule began, probably as a result of an internal quarrel among the Bani Yas of Abu Dhabi, when 'violent conduct' on the part of its leader, Sheikh Khalifa, prompted the emigration of around 800 members of the Al Bu Falasah branch of the tribe. There was little resistance in Dubai to Obaid bin Said and Maktoum bin Butti, who took over the then village-sized settlement along the Creek. With Obaid's death a few years later, Maktoum took the reins of power, ushering in the bloodline that continues to rule Dubai today.

The Maktoums based themselves in Shindagah, which provided easy access to the sources of Dubai's wealth: the Gulf for pearling and fishing and the Creek for trade. In 1820, Mohammed bin Hazza, then ruler of Dubai, signed the trading village's first preliminary truce with London, all too aware of the superior manpower of neighbouring Abu Dhabi and the Qawasim, who controlled much of the northern emirates and what is now Oman.

Under the protection of the British navy, which helped to stamp out the constant disruptions to trade caused by raids among the various tribes along the Trucial Coast, Dubai concentrated on making money. Like the other city-ports that went on to form the United Arab Emirates, Dubai evolved around its creek, an inlet from the sea. Like the other creeks along the northern coast, Dubai's suffered from

sandbars formed at its entrance by strong tides, but at least it was much longer than those of its neighbours, paving the way for the cargo ships that would make Dubai its fortune. Because the seas were pacified by sandbars, the pearling industry thrived, and its wares were exported both to India and to Europe. Trade with India and Persia encouraged more foreign traders to open up shop in the city-port; the town was already developing its reputation as being not only open for business, but as a place that warmly welcomed non-Arabs to take their share.

In the mid 19th century, Shindagah may have been the preserve of around 250 Arab homes, but the neighbouring Bur Dubai community was the base for almost 100 houses belonging to Indian traders. Across the Creek, Deira boasted 1,600 compounds, housing Arabs, Persians and Baluchis from what is now Pakistan. Deira souk was also thriving, with around 350 shops.

BUDDING DUBAI

It was the liberal, open-minded Maktoum bin Hashar, whose rule began in 1894, who capitalised on Dubai's emergence as a business and commercial centre. Foreshadowing a modern-day obsession with the tax-free environment, Dubai in the late 19th century exempted almost half of the men who worked in the pearling industry from taxes. Although more divers worked the pearl banks in Dubai than in any other Trucial State, the ruler ended up receiving only half the revenue of neighbouring Abu Dhabi.

No matter: Dubai's population exploded. As the pearl industry continued to bring more wealth to the town, Sheikh Maktoum deftly implemented business-oriented policies that attracted traders from Lingah, the Persian port on the other side of the Gulf. Run by the Qawasim family, Lingah had, through the 1800s, acted as the main entry point for goods coming into the Gulf. The Persians, desperate for tax revenue, wrested control of the port from the Arabs at the turn of the century, replacing Arab officials with Persians and then Belgians, whose rigid bureaucracy and high tariffs persuaded merchants to head off in search of cheaper trade environments on the Arab side of the Gulf.

As the 20th century began, Sheikh Maktoum made Dubai a free zone by abolishing commercial taxes. He also courted the big players in the Persian warehousing trade, offering important Indian and Persian traders cheap land. As he attracted these trade giants, others followed in their wake. In the first two decades of the 20th century, Dubai's population doubled to around 20,000, rapidly catching up with Sharjah, its larger neighbour and sometime trade rival.

Sheikh Zayed, architect of the UAE

The United Arab Emirates (UAE) stands as a model of success in a Middle East fraught with political tension, corruption and poverty. Two factors have thrust the union of emirates into the world consciousness. First, the speed with which the country has emerged from humble beginnings into a modern global citizen, and second, the reliance of that transformation upon the strength and vision of a single man, Sheikh Zayed bin Sultan Al Nahyan. Upon his death in November 2004, big business in the capital ground to a halt, the nation's newspapers hit the shelves without colour and even the awesome tourism machine of Dubai temporarily laid its profitable revelry to rest.

Sheikh Zayed's greatest gift to the UAE was arguably to inspire unprecedented unity, fashioning an economic powerhouse from a land with little industry bar a dying pearl trade and inhabited by fractious tribes. Where once the country boasted only 200,000 denizens, far-flung across a desolate landscape, its population today numbers over three million residents from all walks of life. Sheikh Zayed presided over visionary investment; since coming to power in Abu Dhabi in August 1966 it was his personal ambition that financed such civic projects as building roads, new hospitals, schools and water resources through the Trucial States Development Office. It was Sheikh Zayed who realised that only by leveraging the financial might of Abu Dhabi could the fledgling federal state be bound together, safeguarding the future of the United Arab Emirates. Today, the UAE's annual per capita GDP of Dhs74,300 is closer to that of the United States than to many of its neighbours in the Arab world.

Before the constitution, which officially created the UAE, was signed in 1971, Sheikh Zayed set off on a 'Unity Tour' through Dubai, Ajman, Umm Al Quwain, across the Hajar mountains to Fujairah and then to Sharjah. In each sheikhdom he promised to make money available to improve the electricity supply, even setting a low unified price by subsidising costs from his personal funds. The tour, and subsequent flow of electrical power, took on incredible significance, effectively symbolising a new national mindset. This sense of unification would be reinforced by many more national tours in the years of Sheikh Zayed's leadership.

Perhaps the key to Sheikh Zayed's ability to draw others to his cause was this capacity for, and demonstration of, understanding. He said that the key to leadership is 'retaining perspective'. No mean feat given the conflicting demands of traditional tribal life and those of a burgeoning modern state. Even during times of unprecedented highs in the UAE's growth, Sheikh Zayed maintained a hectic schedule, often meeting state ministers and Bedu tribesmen in the same afternoon. The infallible bond with his people was a trait that British explorer Wilfred Thesiger would identify in his book *Arabian Sands*, having met with Sheikh Zayed during a much earlier tour of the Trucial Coast. Thesiger wrote of Zayed: '...he had a great reputation among the Bedu. They liked him for his easy, informal ways and his friendliness, and they respected his force

Traders who had reckoned on a temporary sojourn in Dubai settled in the city once it became clear that taxes and regulations in Persia were there to stay. The pearling industry was now booming. Many people emigrated from the Persian district of Bastak, part of the Arab-dominated province of Lars, naming their newfound home on the Creek after their homeland; Bastakia soon became another thriving commercial area.

Sheikh Maktoum's power rose with the fortunes of his city-state. He began the process of building bridges between the rival sheikhdoms of the coast, calling a meeting of the Trucial leaders in 1905 that foreshadowed the creation of the federation that was to be agreed just under 70 years later.

THE BUBBLE BURSTS

After years of growing prosperity, Dubai and the rest of the Gulf fell prey to the worldwide recession of the 1930s, a warning to leaders that the trade-based city's fortunes would ebb and flow with the tide of global economic prosperity. The pearling industry first became a victim of the weak international demand for luxury goods, then the Japanese discovery of cultured pearls finished off the fragile trade, throwing thousands of pearl fishermen out of work.

In the final years of the trade, financiers were taking up to 36 per cent annual interest on the loans that captains needed to fit out boats and hire staff. As the pearling industry declined, traders redoubled their efforts in

of character, his shrewdness and his physical strength. They said admiringly, "Zayed is a Bedu. He knows about camels, can ride like one of us, can shoot, and knows how to fight."'

Sheikh Zayed's popularity and ability to connect would stand him in good stead when he was thrust into the upper echelons of power. Sheikh Zayed's father, Sheikh Sultan bin Zayed Al Nahyan, had no expectations of rule, but was called upon to assume leadership of the Al Nahyan family in 1922.

The devoted family man had four sons, Sheikh Shakhbut, Sheikh Hazza, Sheikh Khalid and Sheikh Zayed, the latter named after his grandfather, for half a century one of the most influential leaders on the Arabian Peninsula. One evening, on 4 August, 1925, Sheikh Sultan climbed the stairs to the roof of his palace where he would carry out the sunset prayer, when an assailant leapt from a hiding place, produced a gun and shot the ruler in his back. Sheikh Sultan died almost instantly.

Sheikh Zayed, staying at the family home in Al Ain, would never see his father again. Years later, in August 1966, power would devolve once more, this time to Sheikh Zayed from his reclusive elder brother, Shakhbut. The move was welcomed as much by the international community as by the adoring people of Abu Dhabi.

At the time of his death Sheikh Zayed had true stature as an international statesman, stature derived of something beyond the oil rigs and malls, the education system and housing. Ever an ambassador for Arabic and Islamic values he drew praise from leaders the world over. In the words of another famous international futurist, former United States President Jimmy Carter: 'A man can only express his admiration for Sheikh Zayed and his leadership. Without his skilful policy, the infrastructure and civil progress of the United Arab Emirates could not have been accomplished in such a brief period.'

black market trade with Persia, where tariffs continued to soar far higher than in those ports on the Arabian Peninsula.

The pearling industry continued to fall into decline. Dubaians with Persian connections built up their illicit cargo trade, making up for the city's lost revenue, but the increasing financial inequities between the traders and the recently unemployed Arab pearl divers amplified societal pressures. Further north in Kuwait, yearnings for political reform influenced the setting up of a parliament, giving the country the most developed political system in the Gulf.

Mirroring growing unease within Dubai society, splits within the royal family also emerged. The ruler's cousin, Mani bin Rashid, led the reform movement that challenged the ruling family's autocratic rule. Domestic slaves came closer to freedom, not because the British decided to enforce its ban on trading slaves, but because owners could no longer afford them. It wasn't until after World War II that the UK government started to enforce general manumission after having called a halt to the trading of slaves within the Gulf states a century earlier.

Against this background of social flux, events turned violent in October 1938. Sheikh Saeed and his followers set up their base in Dubai, while his cousins lined up against the ruler from across the Creek in Deira. After mediation from neighbouring sheikhs and the British political agent, or colonial ambassador,

Dubai Creek in 1967.

in Bahrain, Sheikh Saeed agreed to the setting up of a consultative council or *majlis* ('place of sitting'), heading up a cohort of 15 members, all of whom were proposed by leading members of the community who theoretically had the power to veto his decisions.

Sheikh Saeed was a reluctant leader and only attended the first few sessions, smarting at a system in which his office was allocated an eighth of the national budget, the remaining earmarked for the *majlis*'s projects. He still controlled the treasury and was hesitant to open up the state coffers for the council's projects, such as building state-run schools for the general populace, regulating the customs service and its payroll, adjusting tariffs and setting up a council of merchants to oversee the city-state's expanding commerce.

Six months after the council's foundation, Sheikh Saeed ordered some loyal Bedouin to storm and dissolve it. A strong believer in benign autocratic rule, he suspected that some of his royal rivals were exploiting the *majlis* for their own benefit. Though short-lived, Dubai's six-month flirtation with democracy nonetheless had lasting implications at the highest levels. It sounded the political death-knell for Sheikh Saeed: he devolved most of his authority to his son, Sheikh Rashid, who in time initiated many of the ideas of civic development proposed by the council's members.

POST-WAR DEVELOPMENT

Although spared the horrors that Europe and Asia endured during World War II, Dubai still struggled during those six tough years. The flourishing business of trade was brought to a near standstill and short supplies of rice and sugar caused hunger to grip parts of the city. The British government, which was landing seaplanes in the Creek throughout the conflict, imported food supplies that were to be rationed among the population. Never ones to miss a money-spinning trick, Dubai's traders began buying up some of these supplies and smuggled them to Iran's black market, where shortages were even more pressing.

Malnutrition was an even greater issue in the internal desert countryside, still ruled by autonomous nomadic tribes. Here there was almost constant warfare as the tribes fought for rations, and the leaders of Abu Dhabi and Dubai argued over the boundary between their territories. Open warfare between the two distant relatives, as well as among their allied and rival tribes of the hinterland, continued after World War II until the high level of casualties from Bedouin raids and counter-raids prompted the townsfolk and tribesmen to demand peace in 1948. The British authorities took it upon themselves to research the boundary dispute and draw the new frontier – London's first direct intervention in the internal politics of the Trucial States.

DUBAI STRIKES OIL

While trade remained at the core of Dubai's development, a revolutionary new prospect came the Trucial States' way in the early 1950s: oil. For a couple of decades, most petroleum engineers had concluded that large deposits would be found somewhere along the Trucial Coast. After all, massive reserves had been found across the Middle East and particularly in the Arabian Peninsula and the Gulf. Oil had first been discovered in Iran in 1908; Bahrain had started significant exports in 1936; and on the eve of World War II, neighbouring Saudi Arabia had found the first of its huge reservoirs. Companies began to explore across the region, frantically searching for more deposits of black gold. Petroleum Development (Trucial Coast), a British-owned company, won the concession to search for oil across the Trucial States and Oman.

But the war put a stop to the exploration, condemning the emirates to endure more years of poverty and encouraging thousands of locals to emigrate to neighbouring Kuwait and Saudi Arabia to work on the massive post-war oil development projects there. While a consortium formed by British Petroleum and France's Total found commercially viable oil deposits off the coast of Abu Dhabi in 1958, progress was limited in Dubai's onshore and offshore exploration blocks.

COMMERCIAL WHEELS TURN

Nevertheless, Dubai sought to capitalise on the massive trade opportunities brought by oil companies with huge equipment and manpower needs. Mortgaging Dubai with a huge loan from oil-rich Saudi Arabia and Kuwait of around Dhs3.1 million, an amount that far outstripped the city's yearly income, Sheikh Rashid had the Creek dredged by an Australian firm. The ambitious project, which allowed vessels of up to 500 tonnes to anchor there, greatly increased shipping capacity. The emirate's trade levels jumped by 20 per cent, outpacing the growth in neighbouring Sharjah, which had been snapping at Dubai's heels. Gold smuggling, which peaked in 1970, contributed to the new surge in business. The 3.5 per cent import levies imposed on dhows and steamers docking along its wharfage became the emirate's biggest revenue earner after the war; levies rose to 4.6 per cent in 1955, still lower than its regional rivals.

'In 1966, oil was discovered in an offshore field; exports began three years later.'

After seeing off Sharjah's maritime trade competition, Sheikh Rashid also took on his neighbour's airport. Sheikh Sultan of Sharjah had started levying taxes on gold arriving at Sharjah airport, which grew commercially on the back of the UK Royal Air Force base there. In 1960, Sheikh Rashid opened an airport, little more than an airstrip made from the hard sand found in Dubai's salt flats, which he expanded a few years later as demand for weekly flights to the UK grew. An open-skies policy allowed any airline to use the airport at a cheaper cost than any other in the region, triggering its eventual rise as an international passenger and freight hub.

Before then, however, Dubai too struck black gold. In 1966, oil was discovered in an offshore field; exports began three years later. The prospect of imminent oil exports, along with severe overcrowding of the Creek and the commercial centres around it, persuaded the government in 1967 to start building a Dhs367 million seaport, known as Port Rashid, which eventually opened in 1972 and was expanded again in 1978.

Trade and oil combined to give economic growth a massive injection. The petrodollar boom had finally arrived in Dubai, even though its oil reserves and revenues were minnow-like compared with its oil-rich neighbour Abu Dhabi. The population skyrocketed as migrant labour poured into the city to extract the oil and build and maintain the public services

that Sheikh Rashid, remembering the demands of the reform movement when he was being groomed for power, made a high priority for his government. In 1967, as the government planned Port Rashid, the population stood at 59,000. Five years later, in 1973, the city had doubled in size. By the end of the booming 1970s, 250,000 people lived in Dubai.

INDEPENDENCE

In 1967, Britain decided that its moment in the Middle East was over. London announced its intention to withdraw from its colonial outposts east of Suez, giving the Trucial States a departure date of 1971. Unlike in Aden, in southern Yemen, where years of insurgency showed a stark desire to see off the imperialists, the leaders of Dubai and the other Trucial States felt almost abandoned by the hasty nature of the British retreat. The Conservative opposition of the day also criticised the Labour government's decision to withdraw, arguing that British business exposure across the Gulf amounted to much more than the Dhs117.5 million annual cost of keeping British forces in the area, and that withdrawal would merely encourage new imperialists, such as the Soviet Union, to extend their influence over a strategic region of vital importance owing to its oil deposits.

Some Trucial leaders hoped the Conservative government, once it gained power, would reverse the decision to withdraw, but it wasn't to be. Sheikh Zayed of Abu Dhabi and Sheikh Rashid of Dubai met at the frontier between their two emirates and agreed to form a federation that would jointly decide foreign, defence and social policy. On the encouragement of the British, the rulers of the Trucial States Abu Dhabi, Dubai, Sharjah, Ajman, Umm Al Quwain, Ras Al Khaimah and Fujairah met in Dubai with the leaders of Bahrain and Qatar in February 1968 to discuss forming a joint federation. The leaders came up with an agreement expressing their intention to form a nine-strong federation, which met with broad regional approval, except from Iran, the Shi'a-led state that had a territorial claim on the majority Shi'a island of Bahrain.

The nine leaders of these islands, city-states and desert regions met on several occasions in the run-up to independence in 1971, discussing models of federation. Differences plagued the meetings, with Bahrain's larger, better-educated population suspicious of a federation in which political power would be spread evenly across the nine emirates, rather than being based on the population of each emirate. Bahrain, having ended border disputes with Iran, told the other prospective federation members that it would retain its independence, yoking its interests to its rich neighbour, Saudi Arabia. Qatar chose

Jebel Ali oil refinery – fuelling the economy.

the same path. In July 1971, with the British withdrawal approaching, the seven Trucial leaders met and hammered out a federal document. Six of them, excluding Ras Al Khaimah, signed the provisional constitution, which was then used to proclaim a federation in November 1971.

Ras Al Khaimah had felt undervalued in the negotiations and wanted to focus on three Gulf islands that Iran had occupied once the British forces left the area. But once the other emirates agreed to take on the issue of Abu Musa and the Greater and Lesser Tunb islands, it too acceded to the federation in February 1972. The federation was born, led by Abu Dhabi, owing to its disproportionate financial contribution to the federal budget, but with significant autonomy for all emirates in local affairs. Sheikh Zayed Al Nahyan became the country's first president; Sheikh Rashid, who through the 1970s pressed for more autonomy for his free-wheeling emirate, acted as Zayed's Vice President and Prime Minister.

THE 1970S: PETRODOLLAR BOOM
The 1970s were a decade of excess across the Gulf. Petrodollars flowed into the area as the world's seemingly unquenchable appetite for oil lapped up the region's exports. Oil revenues spiralled ever higher during the price shock of 1973 and 1974, triggered by the Arab producing states' boycott of nations supporting Israel in the third Arab-Israeli conflict. Dubai has never had the oil revenues that its rich cousin Abu Dhabi enjoys (by 1980, Dubai's annual oil income stood at US$3 billion compared with Abu Dhabi's US$15

billion), but these revenues went a long way towards helping Dubai to develop the infrastructure it needed to realise fully the potential of its core economic activity trade and commerce.

FAMILY FEUD
Questioning the unity of purpose between the country's seven emirates is something of a taboo in the United Arab Emirates (UAE). However, privately, historians recount stories of arguments between the leaders of all the emirates, especially the two powerhouses, oil-rich Abu Dhabi and commerce-friendly Dubai. Go back 50 years, and the two emirates were locked in all-out war, with the two leaders' Bedouin allies carrying out raids on the other's territory over three bloody years. Rivalries have cooled since the leaders of the seven Trucial States came together under one flag in the early 1970s. But even in those early days of unity, Dubai's Sheikh Rashid, while committed to the union, fought to give his emirate as much autonomy as possible.

Abu Dhabi's superior size and population has translated into greater political power. The discovery of huge oil reserves in Abu Dhabi gave Sheikh Zayed's emirate even more financial clout, as well as military muscle. When the UAE was formed, Abu Dhabi earned ten times more money from its oil revenues than Dubai, whose oil production has now fallen to an estimated 100,000 barrels a day. Meanwhile, Abu Dhabi is the world's fourth largest oil exporter while also earning more than Dhs73.4 billion a year interest on its huge investments in Western financial markets. The capital controls perhaps 90 per cent of the UAE's national wealth.

The federal government developed around Abu Dhabi's financial largesse. This helped the union's development, but sparked fears in Dubai and other poorer emirates, which were concerned that Abu Dhabi's bureaucrats, keen to control the disbursement of their funds, would whittle away at the emirates' close-knit tribal roots. In 1979, the UAE was in crisis, as Abu Dhabi pushed for more centralised authority than the other emirates would accept. The crisis abated as Sheikh Rashid accepted the post of UAE Prime Minister, while securing the rights of individual rulers to continue developing their emirates along their own lines.

The threat of international turmoil in the 1980s, as the Iran-Iraq War loomed large over the region, glued the emirates together. With Islamic Revolution boiling in Iran and civil shipping under attack in their own backyard, the seven emirates' petty squabbles paled into insignificance. Abu Dhabi continued to fund generous welfare systems for the entire country, especially the resource-starved northern emirates. Dubai got on with being Dubai: attracting businesses and allowing its liberal commercial attitude to flourish.

'By the 1990s, Dubai was busy reinventing itself as a tourist destination.'

Today, Abu Dhabi and Dubai are brothers with different characters. Many Abu Dhabians, more restrained and conservative than go-getting Dubaians, are frustrated at the international attention their precocious neighbour receives but they are also aware that the UAE is all the better for it. Dubai's entrepreneurial attitude has not always met with approval from traditionalists in the capital, but nobody is denying that the city's dynamic economy has also brought regional recognition and offers a blueprint for what Abu Dhabi might achieve as its oil resources dwindle.

THE RISE OF FREE ZONES
Sticking to Dubai's maritime heritage, the first major expansion beyond the Creek came with the completion of Port Rashid, near downtown Dubai, in 1973. On completion, the port had 16 berths for ocean-going vessels, rising to 35 after initial success allowed for expansion. Port Rashid itself had been regarded as overly ambitious, so when Sheikh Rashid announced the construction of a new port in Jebel Ali, 40 kilometres (25 miles) along the coast towards

Abu Dhabi from the centre of Dubai, the sceptics questioned the ruler's judgement.

By 1976, flush with petrodollars, Dubai ploughed Dhs9.2 billion into building the 66-berth port, the world's largest man-made harbour. Completed in 1983, Jebel Ali Port remained empty, seemingly Dubai's first white elephant and its ambition worrying even some of Sheikh Rashid's closest advisers. The massive port, along with the Jebel Ali Golf Resort & Spa hotel, stood alone in the vast expanses of desert.

But by 1985, spurred on by the construction of Jebel Ali Free Zone, business at the port boomed. The free zone was an idea borrowed from Sheikh Rashid's grandfather Sheikh Hasher, who'd lured Persian traders to Dubai at the beginning of the century with similar incentives. The port's fortunes were also helped by the bloody, extended war between Saddam Hussein's Iraq and the Islamic republic of Iran, which disrupted shipping as both sides started to attack tankers and oil facilities. With insurance rates sky-high in the northern Gulf, shippers looked for an alternative in the lower Gulf, turning to Jebel Ali.

DUBAI'S INDUSTRIAL REVOLUTION
Dubai, founded as a trade hub, quickly used growing oil revenues to diversify its economic base to include heavy industry. With abundant oil and gas resources, the emirates had a competitive advantage in large-scale industrial projects that require vast amounts of energy. Dubai's first great industrial project took the form of Dubai Dry Dock, constructed in 1973 as a ship repair yard, which Sheikh Rashid passed on to his third son and current ruler, Sheikh Mohammed. This venture, too, benefited from the outbreak of maritime war between Iran and Iraq, serving the steady stream of tanker war victims. Two years later, the Dubai Aluminium Co, or Dubal, was set up with an initial investment of Dhs5.1 billion, which took advantage of cheap oil to create one of the world's most profitable smelters. As well as industrial projects, the oil wealth of the 1970s brought modern infrastructure. By the end of the decade, another bridge and a tunnel complemented the original Maktoum Bridge linking Bur Dubai with Deira. Dubai's population rose to 207,000 in 1977, compared with 20,000 in the 1940s.

As Dubai grew from the 1950s, so did the number of roads, hospitals and schools. The police force, set up in 1956 under the command of British officers, came under local control in 1975. Immigrants started their own schools, complementing the state-run schools that catered for locals and expatriate Arabs.

If the 1970s spelt industrial development, the 1980s saw the arrival of big-time commerce. While strong global demand for oil under-pinned the soaring revenues enjoyed by oil-producing countries, Dubai continued to diversify. The World Trade Centre, opened in 1979, attracted some of the world's biggest companies to set up local or regional headquarters in Dubai. Once again, cynics whispered that the centre, today dwarfed by the high-rises of Sheikh Zayed Road, was too far from the central commercial district in Deira. But little did it matter, as foreign companies set up shop in a land free of bureaucracy, boasting political stability and liberal social mores. The economy further diversified, and the city kept booming through the 1980s; Dubai's population doubled to over half a million people.

THE AGE OF TOURISM

In the 1970s, businessmen travelling to Dubai were hard-pushed to find a single decent hotel. Sheikh Rashid even built a personal guesthouse for the trailblazing businessmen and women who visited in the early days. By 1975, the InterContinental had opened on the Deira side of the Creek, but never satisfied the growing hordes of travellers touching down at the new airport; executives even used to bunk up together in the rooms.

How times change. By the 1990s, after the death of Sheikh Rashid, Dubai was busy reinventing itself as a tourist destination. There were 42 hotels in 1985, jumping to 272 by 2002. The establishment in 1985 of Emirates, the Dubai-based international airline, helped the tourism sector flourish as the airline encouraged its passengers to stop over in the emirate en route to Asia, Africa or Europe. With initial start-up capital of Dhs36.7 million, the airline rapidly expanded, even staying profitable through the global travel slump following the terror attack of September 11, 2001.

With its oil reserves running out, Dubai has turned increasingly to tourism. International events such as the Dubai World Cup horse race, desert rally and golf, tennis and rugby tournaments helped fuel the boom. But it's Dubai's love affair with shopping that has sustained the emirate's industry. The Dubai Shopping Festival, launched in 1996, attracts around 3.5 million people to the city every year. A second shopping festival, Dubai Summer Surprises, was introduced in 1998, attracting Gulf visitors who are used to the soaring summer temperatures that put off many Western tourists. Combined with sea, sun and liberal attitudes to entertainment, annual tourist numbers have now reached around five million, five times the city's resident population.

Clock Tower Roundabout in Deira, May 2007.

BLACK GOLD TO WHITE COLLAR

Dubai's plan was, and continues to be, to attract professionals from across the globe. One of the emirate's most successful ventures to date is the formation of corporate free zones, where businesses in roughly the same industries are gathered in a corporate park, encouraging networking and new businesses. Dubai Internet City (DIC), announced in 1999, was the first such attempt to attract more professionals to the emirate. The venture was tailor-made to lure high-tech firms, offering tax-free 100 per cent ownership (outside free zones businesses need a local partner). DIC has since grown rapidly, enticing over 600 companies by 2005, although some critics say it's little more than a sales park as few products are actually created on the site. With Dubai International

Financial Centre (DIFC) open for business since early 2005 and set to expand massively in the next few years, the city finally has a financial centre ambitious enough to one day rival New York and London. The age of pearling and black gold is set to give way to an era of international investments and financial high-flying.

PROPERTY BOOM

Dubai's property boom, which exploded in 2003 with the introduction of freehold properties, is yet another reason why the emirate continues to make headlines across the globe. The repatriation of money from Western markets to the Middle East, especially the UAE, after September 11, 2001 gave Dubai's budding property industry a significant boost. Close to Dhs3.67 trillion poured into various sectors of the Middle Eastern market, a fair chunk of which went into Dubai's construction projects. Wealthy investors purchased dozens of apartments and villas, and small-time investors purchased an apartment or two at rock bottom prices.

Developments such as Emaar's the Greens (the first rent-to-own scheme) and the Marina sparked buying crazes from expatriates and investors interested in either making Dubai their home or a destination for holidays. Nakheel's record-breaking Palm islands and the World have attracted a number of heavyweight investors and celebrities who are as keen on owning a property in Dubai as they are about letting the world's media know about it. Local and international interest in Dubai's properties was, and still is, substantial, and no one has been prepared for the influx of cash into the budding, yet still immature, market.

Until recently, there wasn't a single law to safeguard foreign homeowners and their properties. Instead, investors nervously relied on the clauses in their contracts with developers, and hoped that the imminent law they heard so much about would give them the comfort they desperately needed. In March 2006, after months of speculation, the law was implemented. Foreigners now have the legal right to buy properties in designated areas across the emirate, and they can register the properties in their own names at the Dubai Land Department.

Even before the law was announced, Dubai's property market was one of the fastest-growing in the world. Since the emirate opened its doors to foreign homeowners five years ago, the market has been busting one financial ceiling after another. Those who bought properties off-plan in 2002 and 2003 have seen their investments more than double in value.

The UAE's power brokers viewing the **World**.

The property 'bubble', which is currently supported by a dangerously small supply of completed properties, is growing exponentially as more and more potential investors take the leap into home-ownership to escape rising rents. Some wonder if property prices, which rose by close to 30 per cent in the first half of 2007, are too inflated. Industry experts state that 71,800 homes are due for completion in 2007, 43,000 units in 2008 and 77,000 in 2009 – and suggest that such ambitious contruction may saturate the market, bringing prices down and forcing the market to correct itself abruptly. But this is all, of course, just speculation; as with other property markets around the world, it's difficult to predict. One thing that is currently certain, though, is that construction projects are continuing to attract overseas investors often willing to splash out on astronomically expensive apartments located on deserted back streets, with the (sometimes tenuous) hope that they'll be transformed into prestigious addresses in a matter of months.

A NEW ERA

In January 2006, following the death of Sheikh Maktoum bin Rashid Al Maktoum, Sheikh Mohammed, Sheikh Maktoum's younger brother, assumed power of Dubai. There was little doubt that he would be named leader. Accordingly, the transition between leaders was very smooth and any changes in government policy have been barely noticeable.

Clockwise from top left: **Sheikh Ahmad Attiya**, **Diyal Chand**, **Nadia Zaal** and **Deepak Ramrakhiani**.

Dubai Today

Dubai's polarisation of wealth makes for lives less ordinary.

Amid all the super-projects, luxury hotels and shopping malls, it's easy to forget that for 1.4 million people Dubai is simply home. The incredible influx of expats from all over the world has created not so much a melting pot as a salad bowl. This is still a city divided by class and creed, and a person's experience of Dubai today will depend very much on where they come from and what they do. Here, four very different Dubaians talk about their lives.

THE IMAM
Egyptian-born Sheikh Ahmad Attiya is the Imam at Malik Ibn Anas mosque in Jumeirah.
'Usually I wake up around 4.45am, wash, call the morning prayer, and read a bit from the Qur'an before sleeping again for a couple of hours. After reading from the Qur'an a second time and praying at the noon prayer, I eat lunch and read a few religious texts until Salat al Asr, the afternoon prayer, after which I give a lesson on a certain subject and read from the Qur'an to my congregation.

'Being an Imam, my work is to serve the community because I believe a community without religion is one without identity. Religion organises and saves society and I believe it is the base and foundation for that world. The people who sit in and listen to my speech are truly affected by these lessons.

'Dubai in general is a wonderfully civilised city to be in, with a large number of mosques, and the local people are really very nice. The only problem is the attendance of prayers is quite small. The reason is that most of the neighbourhood is made up of non-Muslims. With such a wide spectrum of residents, it's no surprise the West has an influence on the people here in the Emirates; it's no different from anywhere else. Dubai is an Arabic, Islamic society, but it also has different nationalities and religions and they definitely have an effect on the society. One of those influences shows clearly in the language, as English could almost be considered the city's first language. That language barrier doesn't help me much in trying to deliver my message.'

THE CONSTRUCTION WORKER

Diyal Chand hails from Punjab in India. The 24-year-old electrician has been working for a building maintenance company for two years and lives in Sonapur, the district of Dubai that literally translates into Hindi as 'the city of gold'.

'My bus leaves at 5.30am so by 4.30am I'm awake. As soon as we reach the site we start work. At 9am it's teatime for 15 minutes, then at noon we get a one-hour break and our final tea break is at 3pm. We don't get tea from the company; it's just called a tea break. If we want any refreshments we have to buy them ourselves. After working overtime, I get home at 7pm or 8pm. I have to cook as well – we don't get food from the company. By the time we finish cooking and bathing, it's about 11pm, so that's when we go to bed.

> ## 'I live with 13 people in my room. Work is too hard here, so it's not possible to be happy.'

'The only time we get to have some fun is on Friday when my friends come over. We eat together and spend time talking about how work and our lives are going. On this day, we get up a little later than usual, wash our clothes, bathe and shower, cook some food, eat, and then we just visit each other.

'I came to Dubai after I went to a recruitment agent and landed a job. I live with 13 people in my room. Work is too hard here, so it's not possible to be happy. To make it better here we need to have our salaries hiked and conditions improved. I haven't been able to save anything and I took a loan when I got here. In Dubai you can either enjoy life or save money but I haven't been able to do either. And I'm not alone in this situation – I'd say only two out of every 100 workers over here manage to save and then settle down.

'In Dubai, everything that is good is beyond our reach so it's best to be content with nothing. We get bored here because we can't afford anything – this place is built to cater to the rich. I think I'm going to be here for another year as my visa is for three years. When I go back home I will spend all the time I've lost with my family and maybe even get married. Maybe. My dream is to one day have a nice house and to be able to take care of my family so that they can depend on me.'

THE HIGH FLYER

Deepak Ramrakhiani was born in Mumbai, India. After three years studying in Australia, the 22-year-old came to Dubai last year to run a company started by his father, and has since settled into high society life.

'My average day starts at 9am. Although financially I definitely don't need to work, I enjoy what I'm doing. No offence to Dubai, but a lot of the guys over here who are my age just waste their time doing nothing. That high gets stale. My dad bought this villa for me and I live here on my own. After studying in Australia, I thought I'd come over and work for my dad.

'My father started the company, Emirates Vision, and now I'm running half of it. We work in events management, specialising in

Diyal Chand and fellow Indian co-workers work long hours under difficult conditions.

Indian expat **Deepak Ramrakhiani** is part of the high-society set.

them that is so nice. Their relationship with people is so different, so pure. When they like somebody they really like somebody. They will just have Dhs10 in their pocket, but they will buy you lunch. They're treated really badly here. I've seen what they are provided with and the way people treat them. It hurts. I've been there. I've done that kind of job. I've swept floors and picked up glasses. So I know how they feel.'

THE CEO

Nadia Zaal is the CEO of Al Barari, a mammoth accommodation and leisure complex in Dubailand. With projects being announced on a weekly basis, it is one of the most competitive industries in Dubai, but the Emirati says it is this challenge that makes her working day such an exciting one.
'A typical day begins with me making phone calls and checking emails over breakfast. I start reading the industry updates and research that will affect our company strategy. Afterwards, I structure my thoughts on paper following the reading session. I then always make sure that I have a personal discussion with members of staff and that is usually followed by hours of meetings – both internally and externally.

> ## 'I come from a family where summers were spent in internships.'

'Most days involve site visits and these are often followed by some meditation and yoga. I also often do meditation and yoga on potential sites as this helps put me in the right frame of mind to really get a feeling for the new site and its potential.
'My thought on Dubai is that it has emerged as the regional hub and now stands shoulder to shoulder with all the major cities in the world. It is beyond any doubt that it is an entrepreneur's dream. I have been entrusted with the role of CEO by the company's shareholders, who include some of the region's largest financial institutions. I find that I excel under pressure, which is good because Dubai is fiercely competitive, something that is especially true in the real estate industry.
'When I look back on how I got involved it is because I come from a family where summers were spent in internships and at lunches. We were all used as sounding boards to discuss issues facing the family businesses, so I suppose the core family business of real estate has always been in my blood.'

fashion shows around the world. When I do have free time I love going out dancing. I'm also really, really into cars. I recently bought a Chrysler 300cc – so I've got four cars now. I get to drive them fast when I go to Abu Dhabi or Bab Al Shams – that road is fantastic. I also drive down to the Jumeirah sands and listen to music to clear my head.
'Not all of my friends have the same financial status as me. Some of them are very high class, and then I've also got friends who are construction workers. They might be dirty or have dirty habits, but there's something about

Sheikh Mohammed, Ruler of Dubai

Equestrian, fighter pilot, poet and, above all, businessman, Sheikh Mohammed bin Rashid Al Maktoum is the leading force behind the emirate's lightning modern-day development. Acting as chief executive of the huge holding company that is the Dubai government, the crown prince is behind the strategic and day-to-day running of the emirate. Following the death of his elder brother, Sheikh Maktoum, during a visit to Australia in January 2006, Sheikh Mohammed officially became ruler of Dubai, although he had been considered the de facto leader for several years.

Sheikh Mohammed's boundless energy and unmistakable charisma propelled him into the role of crown prince of Dubai in 1995. He learned the trade of statecraft first under the watchful eyes of his famous grandfather, Sheikh Saeed, and then his much-adored and highly influential father, Sheikh Rashid, who as early as the 1960s was grooming his third son for power.

As UAE defence minister, he had to deal with international crises such as the Arab-Israeli war of 1973 and terrorist hijackings at Dubai airport. Then, as his father's health faltered in the 1980s, Sheikh Mohammed took a greater role in fostering Dubai's businesses and pro-business image. Most notably this included the oil industry, already in terminal decline, and the setting up of Dubai's airline, Emirates.

Today, 'Sheikh Mo', as he's affectionately nicknamed by expats, continues to develop and update the liberal policies of his Maktoum forefathers. Almost every month he announces a new scheme aimed at raising the emirate's business profile: 'Dubai doesn't need investors, investors need Dubai,' he once proclaimed. To achieve this goal, he has surrounded himself with the emirate's sharpest minds, drawing on the legions of nationals who have returned with qualifications from Western universities and business experience.

Yet while they advise, it is Dubai's clear lines of executive power, all of which end with Sheikh Mohammed, that have fostered the emirate's legendary clear-cut decision-making. A military man, trained in the arts of war by the British Army, Sheikh Mohammed knows the benefits of clear lines of command, which allow Dubai to follow through its plans with enviable efficiency. Senior employees across the spectrum of government say that just one phone call to His Highness can be enough to put a plan into action.

With so much power vested in a single pair of hands, the cult of personality runs deep. The sheikh's daily schedule receives in-depth, adoring coverage from a fawning press; his presence at public gatherings commands reverential respect. But Sheikh Mohammed has a common touch too: he drives himself around in a white Mercedes 4x4 (licence plate #1, of course). The Noodle House in the Emirates Towers is one of the crown prince's frequent lunch spots thanks to its no-nonsense attitude and speedy service.

Equestrianism is both a hobby and a business for Sheikh Mohammed, who says his love of horses runs through his veins. Raised on a diet of falconry and horse riding, his personal sporting forte lies in the equestrian world's version of the marathon, the punishing discipline of endurance riding, in which he has led UAE teams to many victories in international competitions. His fascination with horseracing, sparked as a young student in the UK, almost inevitably mutated into business. Set up in the mid 1990s, the royal family's stable, Godolphin, has quickly emerged as one of the world's top three equine operations, rivalled only by the Aga Khan and Ireland's Coolmore. The company's Dubai stables train their horses through the Gulf's pleasant winter months, before dispersing the steeds across the world for the spring racing season.

The sycophancy surrounding Sheikh Mohammed may seem excessive to Western visitors, brought up to regard politicians with deep cynicism, but in a region of under-achieving leaders, the never-ending adulation of Dubai's 'Big Man' is for once well placed.

Palm Jumeirah. *See p31.*

Architecture

A skyline permanently in flux.

With a hunger for innovative landmarks, and a peerless aptitude for publicising them, Dubai boasts multiple architectural feats to showcase its ambition and wealth to onlookers across the globe. When a *Vanity Fair* article hailed Dubai's 'skyline on crack', they weren't far off the mark; it seems that all new shopping malls, office spaces and residential estates must scale record-breaking heights, offer new dimensions in luxury or be architecturally bonkers for plans to be considered in the first place. Dubai, it can safely be said, is not the sleepy fishing town it was half a century ago.

Where once there was little more than sand and wind towers, billboards proclaim the imminent construction of the next mind-boggling creation with grandiose statements: the Burj Dubai is the 'most prestigious square kilometre on the planet', Falconcity of Wonders is 'beyond history', and Dubai Waterfront, we're told, is 'the ultimate spectacular liquid asset'. Yet look behind the buzzwords and the bombast and you'll discover that something quite extraordinary is taking place in this city. And while it's easy to scoff at the more outlandish projects it's impossible not to be impressed by the outside-the-box thinking, the enormous risk-taking, and, so far, the considerable rewards being reaped.

This building boom is a relatively new phenomenon. Unlike major cities like London or New York, Dubai's architectural history is astonishingly compressed: wind tower houses replaced palm-frond shelters in the early 20th century; following the oil boom, these were torn down to make way for concrete apartment blocks, which in turn were replaced by postmodernist skyscrapers. However, the city's design trend is seemingly turning full circle, with a penchant for Arabian-chic seeing architects re-incorporating wind towers into their designs for five-star hotels.

With the first exports of oil from the area taking place in the early 1960s, Dubai set about dragging itself into the 20th century with an almost religious zeal. The mantra of 'out with the old, in with the new', and the urgent need for mass housing, resulted in the razing of most of its old town and the rapid rise of towers and cheap apartment blocks. It wasn't until the 1990s that the government turned its attention to preserving and restoring what was left of the old town – and by then, for many historians, it was a case of too little, too late. Critics maintain that only Oman offers true examples of traditional Gulf architecture, but there are atmospheric pockets of authenticity left in early 21st-century Dubai in the Bastakia area.

> ## 'The debate still rages as to how to develop a local architectural language that references Dubai's past as well as its gleaming future.'

In terms of contemporary architecture, the audacious Burj Al Arab hotel became an instant icon upon its completion in 2000 and started Dubai's passion for breaking height records. The sleek lines of **Jumeirah Emirates Towers** continued the trend and Carlos Ott's **National Bank Of Dubai** and **Hilton Dubai Creek** are now widely admired. Meanwhile, international architects' drawing boards are stacked with plans for future Dubai cities-within-cities; the world's tallest tower (Burj Dubai) and first underwater hotel (Hydropolis) are scheduled for completion soon. Unsurprisingly, the debate still rages among architects as to how to develop a local architectural language that references Dubai's past as well as its gleaming future.

BACK IN THE DAY

It was the Bani Yas tribe – ancestors of the Bedouin – who first set up camp in the deserts and mountains of Abu Dhabi and Dubai in the 18th century. They split their time between animal hair and skin tents, ideal for winter wanderings, and *arish* or *barasti* (palm-frond shelters) for the summer months spent on date plantations. *Barasti* were also popular among fishermen, pearlers and traders.

Coastal areas featured blocky homes built from bricks of fossilised coral, bonded with *sarooj* (a blend of Iranian red clay and manure,

dried and baked in a kiln) or a lime mixture derived from seashells and plastered with chalk and water paste. Large courtyard houses built of *farush* (beach rock) and covered with lime plaster have been excavated in Jumeirah and dated back to the second century of the Islamic era (ninth century AD). When a branch of the Bani Yas – the Maktoums – settled by the Creek in the early 19th century, more permanent homes were built using *guss* (mud blocks) and roofed with palm fronds, materials that kept the temperature down. Rooms usually opened on to an airy central courtyard restricted to family use, and male guests were entertained in a separate *majlis* (meeting room). In many newer villas the *majlis* is in the main house, a layout which is still familiar to Dubaians living in villas built in the 1970s and 1980s.

Public buildings in the 18th and 19th centuries were mostly limited to stone forts, which doubled up as seats of government, and mosques. **Al Fahidi fort**, believed to be Dubai's oldest building, now home to Dubai Museum, was built around 1799 to guard landward approaches to the town. Parts of the old **Dubai wall**, built in the early 1800s, can also be seen in Bastakia.

As Dubai's pearling industry boomed in the late 1800s, Bedouin and mountain communities began to gravitate towards the coastal trading villages. The simple, outwardly minimalist homes they built were decorated inside with intricate rugs and wooden latticework on windows, and outside by elaborately carved doors – this tradition has continued in the brightly painted metal doors and gates on old villas by the beach, and there are some great antique wooden examples in Bastakia. Historians disagree on whether these decorations were traditionally Arab, based on Islamic designs, or inspired by Indian decorative principles. Homes were built close to each other, with shady *sikkas* (narrow alleys) running down towards the water.

By the late 19th century, spurred in part by a devastating fire in 1894, Deira's wealthy began to build their homes from coral stone and gypsum, although the poor still lived in *barasti* buildings. Today, *barasti* huts are constructed to shade farm workers in the desert, picnickers in villa gardens and cocktail drinkers at busy beach bars.

Sheikh Saeed Al Maktoum House (*see p76*) was built in 1896 on the southern bank of the Creek in Shindagha as a residence for the ruling family; it remained their home until Sheikh Saeed's death in 1958. Probably one of the first houses in the area to sport Iranian-inspired wind towers, it is a traditional coral-block structure built around a large central courtyard. The Emirati historian and architect Rashad Bukhash, who was formerly head of the Historical Buildings Section of Dubai Municipality, has described the Sheikh Saeed Al Maktoum House as 'the best example of traditional architecture, with all the wooden, decorative elements – such as carved latticework and teak doors – that were typical of the times.' The restored house now acts as a museum, displaying old photographs and historical documents.

By the mid 20th century, a village of around 50 compounds, each with a wind tower or two, had built up in Bastakia along the Bur Dubai side of the Creek. It remained more or less intact until the 1980s. A collection of wind tower shops still exists by the *abra* (boat) station; other fine examples open to the public are the **Majlis Gallery** and **XVA**, a restored café, gallery and guesthouse. Former residents of Bastakia today look back with fondness to less hurried times, when families were self-sufficient – with livestock kept and slaughtered at home – and a shopping trip involved taking a rowed *abra* to the souks of Deira.

A CITY IS BORN

Dubai's pace of urbanisation – like every other facet of life in what was then the Trucial States – was dramatically fast-tracked by the discovery of oil in the early 1960s, first in Abu Dhabi and then in Dubai. The city's skyline was transformed following the formation of the UAE in 1971, largely due to the explosion in Dubai's population.

The first house built from concrete blocks was constructed in Dubai in 1956, but much of the population continued to live in *barastis* until well into the 1960s. Typically, extended families grouped together into compounds separated by thin alleyways; transport was by donkey, camel or *abra* until the 1960s, when the first roads opened up.

Even before the oil days, Dubai's ambition was evident. Sheikh Rashid, who succeeded his father in 1958, spent his first few years in power setting up a Municipal Council, building and widening roads, constructing the first airport and bridging the Creek. The arrival of the car created the need for the establishment of a system of land management and ownership – after all, those losing half their compound to a widened road required compensation – and the concept of town planning was introduced. Working out who owned what in the tribal quarters of the city proved tricky but became essential as land value rose. Territory outside built-up areas and any reclaimed land (following the dredging of the Creek) belonged to the ruler – a decree that continues to this day.

International commentators were sceptical of Sheikh Rashid's grand plans, but there was no shortage of believers; Dubai's population doubled to 120,000 between the late 1960s and early '70s, and by 1981 had reached well over a quarter of a million. The few apartment blocks

Breaking new ground

Hydropolis

When the world's first underwater hotel opens in Dubai, the phrase 'sleeping with the fishes' will no longer be reserved for the Mafia. The completed hotel will consist of a wave-shaped land station and 220 suites in a jellyfish-shaped submarine leisure complex. Guests will be transported to their underwater room via a series of connecting tunnels, through which they will be propelled in a noiseless train.

Architect Joachim Hauser's ambitious project will be located 20 metres below the surface of the Gulf, just off the Jumeirah beach coastline. The original idea for creating an underwater hotel was born out of Hauser's curiosity with water and the sea. For Hauser, Hydropolis will be much more than just simply a tourist attraction; the architect believes that marine architecture is the key to the future

of city planning and that in the near future an entire city will be constructed underwater.

There's little doubt that Dubai's the perfect city for schemes that seem borrowed from *The Jetsons*, and the result for eager-eyed visitors should be spectacular. To put the size of the hotel into perspective, it will cover an area similar to that of London's Hyde Park, complete with restaurants, bars, meeting rooms and themed suites.

Sitting at the nerve centre will be the magnificent ballroom, whose large, petal-like roof will retract giving a beautiful view of the night sky. And that's not to mention the hotel's bubble-shaped suites, with clear glass comprising both the sleeping areas' walls and each room's bathtub.

The project has already been subject to delays and there are ongoing concerns about its impact on marine life, but the slated opening date is currently sometime in 2009.

The World, mapped out by around 300 man-made islands. *See p33.*

that sprung out of the desert around Deira's Clock Tower Roundabout (1963) in the 1960s weren't lonely for long and by the mid '70s, the Creek was lined with low and high-rise structures. Already soaring fortunes, built on increased trade, went stratospheric during the oil crisis of 1973, and the government began construction in earnest. Developing infrastructure took precedence – the **Shindagha tunnel** and **Al Maktoum Bridge**, the dry docks at **Port Rashid**, mosques, hospitals, schools and power stations all date from around the late '60s and early '70s. Sadly, however,

the need for build-'em-quick residential and office accommodation led to some entirely uncharismatic blocks being erected.

One exception is **Dubai Municipality** (1979), on the Deira side of the Creek, a building that's still widely admired for its abstract sensitivity – although the inner glass courtyard and water pools, which create a cool microclimate, weren't added until the 1980s. The **Dubai World Trade Centre** (DWTC), also built in 1979 and at the time the signature Dubai landmark and its highest building at 39 storeys, hasn't withstood history quite as well. Unmistakably 1970s, the

The Pad.

The Pad

The iPod changed the face of portable music entertainment, but will the Pad change the face of urban living? Apple's miniature music minx, in terms of both looks and innovation, has inspired plans for a residential tower. Designed by Hong Kong-based consultancy James Law Cybertecture, the multi-million dirham project is set to attract those looking for high-tech living. Each 'intelligent' apartment will be awash with gadgets and gizmos, such as the iReality, a real-time virtual projection of different locations around the world, which allows residents to change the city they see through their windows each morning. Interior decoration will be made easy with the iArt, whose server allows users to subscribe and upload art works from throughout history. In the two bedroom apartments, the living and dining area will rotate to give a *Continues overleaf.* ▶

DWTC is now dwarfed in size and stature by Jumeirah Emirates Towers and in function by the efficient Ibis and Novotel hotels, built to accommodate delegates to 2003's World Bank and IMF meetings.

Dubai's ritual building up and tearing down saw many of the smaller structures of the 1960s and '70s cleared to make way for skyscrapers. But tradition sat cheek by jowl with the shiny and new: timber for interiors and furniture was still imported to the Creek on wooden dhows and, even in the early 1980s, Bur Dubai was still a wind-tower village compared to Deira's burgeoning metropolis across the water.

By the end of the decade, Dubai's passion for the shock of the new began to soften slightly, perhaps owing in part to the emergence of the first wave of local architecture graduates. Rumour has it that Prince Charles, the UK's ambassador for architectural conservatism, expressed great enthusiasm for wind towers on a tour of Bastakia, encouraging Dubaians to start conservation projects. Meanwhile, the launch of Emirates airline in 1985 brought increasing numbers of tourists hungry for a taste of Arabia. The first restoration project, Sheikh Saeed's House, was completed in 1986, and through the 1990s another 70 buildings were saved. Architects began incorporating traditional or Islamic references into their designs. The thoroughly 1980s **Deira Tower**

(1980) in Baniyas Square, for example, features a distinctive circular white 'cap', like that worn by Emirati men under their *ghutra* (headdress).

INTO THE MILLENNIUM

Upon Sheikh Rashid's death in 1990, his sons, notably Sheikh Mohammed (*see p25* **Sheikh Mohammed**) set about furthering their father's plans to create the Hong Kong of the Middle East, with new buildings dedicated to commerce and tourism. Dubai's macho love affair with the tower became ever more fervent, while foreign architects' efforts to relate their buildings to the local environment ranged from the ultra-literal to the ultra-kitsch. Some managed to be both: visitors heading into the city from the airport can't miss the mock airplane hull of **Emirates Aviation College**. **Jumeirah Beach Hotel** (1997) represents a surfer's dream wave, and the unusually low-rise **Dubai Creek Golf & Yacht Club** (1993), the billowing sails of a dhow. Other architects' favourites include Ott's **National Bank of Dubai** building (1998), known locally as the 'pregnant lady'. Supported by two giant columns, the gold, glass and granite sculptural tower references the curved hulls and taut sails of *abras* and dhows, but in a subtly contextual manner. It's best viewed from an abra on a sunny day, when its curvaceous belly reflects all the nuances of the Creek. Ott is also

▶ ## Breaking new ground (continued)

changing view of the city. There's also the iClub, with its Jacuzzis featuring in-built television screens and underwater speakers. As if that's not enough there's also an 'ultrasonic' deckchair to sink into. Visit www.thepad.ae to find out more.

Sports City

Work is currently underway to create the world's first purpose-built sports city. The mammoth project will make up part of Dubailand, the world's largest theme park, and flaunt amazing sporting facilities. With a huge stadium capable of seating 60,000, a hockey field and both indoor and outdoor arenas, so that matches can be held come the super-hot summertime, the complex is set to stage major global sporting events. One of the biggest draws of Sports City will be the coaching facilities on offer. The Manchester United Soccer School will see some of the best coaches in the world hit the pitch to teach those hoping to be the football stars of tomorrow. With Sir

Alex Ferguson on board, the academy promises to lure United's squad members for training sessions in the sun. It's this weather that's helped tempt the International Cricket Council to permanently relocate from London to Dubai. The willow swingers will benefit from the new stadium to practise in and Dubai's proximity to the cricket-mad Indian subcontinent should help the city attract some major matches.

Burj Dubai

Any talk of groundbreaking builds in Dubai wouldn't be complete without acknowledging the world's tallest tower. Although the final height is still somewhat of a close-guarded secret, a certainty is that it will be substantially bigger than the current leader, the 509-metre 101 Tower in Taipei. Chicago-based architects Skidmore, Owings & Merrill designed the structure – which is expected to grow to around 800 metres – with three sections set around a central core that rises to a piercing spire. In an unsurprising twist, responsible for the nearby **Hilton Dubai Creek** (2001), a minimalist's dream.

Jumeirah Emirates Towers (*see p65*), currently the place to do business in Dubai, is equally sleek. The Australian design is frowned upon by some as 'anywhere architecture', but remains the city's most spectacular corporate buildings. The hotel tower rises up 355 metres (1,165 feet) – if you can dodge security (it's officially for hotel guests only), take a ride in the swooping *Charlie and the Chocolate Factory*-esque glass lifts. **Children's City** (*see p183*) in Creekside Park has a Duplo-style series of exhibition rooms, and is equally nashamedly modern and unusual in that it provides a spatial as well as a formal experience – as does the ultra-chic **One&Only Royal Mirage** hotel, which uses elements of traditional Islamic architecture. The impressive **Madinat Jumeirah**, a massive hotel and souk complex opened in late 2004, also harks back to the days of wind towers and coral block hues.

Of course, it was with Madinat's neighbour, the **Burj Al Arab** hotel (*see p50* **Jewel of the isle**) built in 2000, that Dubai really earned its reputation as an architect's playground. Tom Wright of Atkins aimed to build a 'state-of-the-art, almost futuristic building' that was 'Arabic, extravagant and super-luxurious'. The Burj became an instant icon and, upon its completion, the most recognised landmark in the city. Built some 300 metres (985 feet) off shore, it was the world's tallest hotel at 321 metres (1,053 feet) when it opened, and is supported by 250 columns descending 40 metres (130 feet) into the seabed. Rumour has it that sand from around the base has to be hoovered out each night to prevent subsidence, and that the tower sways by up to 30 centimetres (12 inches) at the top. Even if you can't afford a night's stay in the hotel, you can check out its 28 double-height floors of pure opulence by paying a Dhs200 entrance fee (this is redeemable in the bars and restaurants) and taking in the thrilling views from the Al Muntaha bar located in the oval pod that sits at the top of the 'mast'.

'Dubaians often wryly joke that they go to sleep alone only to wake up next to a skyscraper the next day.'

By the late 1990s, local architects were beginning to mutter about an identity crisis among Dubai's buildings. For some, the attempts by the likes of the Royal Mirage and intimate eco-retreat **Al Maha Desert Resort & Spa** to reference local or regional history

Burj Dubai, May 2007.

the main competitor to Burj Dubai's crown as king of the skies is likely to appear just down the road. Early reports suggest that Nakheel's Al Burj tower will be a neck-craning 1,200 metres tall and will be the centrepiece of the Dubai Waterfront development, another collection of man-made islands set to dwarf the Palm Jumeirah in size.

Palm islands

The Palm Jumeirah may be almost finished, but on the grand scale of things – and this is certainly a city for grand-scale things – the Palm Trilogy is only just beginning. The first offshore icon, Nakheel's Palm Jumeirah, will be home to thousands of sun-soaked residents and will soon be the prime location of a bounty of luxury hotels. But Dubai's conquering of the seas isn't stopping here: work is happening at a frantic pace on the Palm Jebel Ali (which will be part of the Dubai Waterfront Properties project) and the Palm Deira, which is expected to be bigger than Paris upon its slated 2015 completion. The three Palm island projects – which will be the three largest man-made islands in the world – will extend Dubai's coastline by over 500 kilometres (310 miles).

The sky's the limit

Think you've heard it all? You haven't. As if underwater hotels and the world's largest theme park weren't enough, even more outlandish projects may, or may not, be soon gracing Dubai. We assess their chances.

Dubai Sunny Mountain Ski Dome

Ambition: 4/5
If Willy Wonka were to be put in charge of designing a ski slope, it might end up looking something like Dubai Sunny Mountain. The plan is to feature real-life polar bears, the region's first Penguinarium, and – somewhat implausibly – a revolving mountain.
Plausibility: 4/5
The success of Ski Dubai at Mall of the Emirates suggests that snow and desert can mix well, but talk of building work at Sunny Mountain has gone a bit frosty of late and the late-2008 date for completion could be a little optimistic.

International Chess City

Ambition: 4/5
A whole city dedicated to chess? Blame the Republic of Kalmykia, a self-governing entity in Russia, which built its own chess city in their capital Elista and now wants to repeat the same trick in Dubai. Chess obsessive, self-proclaimed UFO abductee and Kalmykian leader Kirsan Ilyumzhinov unveiled plans in 2004 to develop 32 buildings in the shape of chess pieces on a giant board. The pawns are planned to house mid-range accommodation, while the rooks, knights and bishops will be five-star hotels and the kings and queens home to Burj Al Arab-style luxuriousness.
Plausibility: 1/5
Unsurprisingly, enthusiasm for a city solely dedicated to a fringe sport has hit a stalemate. The public relations company originally hired are no longer working on the project and there are no signs that any progress has been made since the initial announcement. It may be the case that the geek shall inherit the earth, but for the time being we can't see it happening in Dubai.

Falconcity of Wonders

Ambition: 4/5
Despite what the name suggests, this planned project isn't a homage to the great bird of prey, but instead pays respect to the architectural wonders of the world. The Eiffel Tower, the Grand Pyramid, the Taj Mahal and even the Hanging Gardens of Babylon are due to be replicated. The theme park will house shopping malls (surprise, surprise) as well as hotels, apartments and entertainment complexes.
Plausibility: 5/5
With construction already under way, Falconcity is a sure thing.

Burj Al Arabi

Ambition: 3/5
This might just be the most bizarre concept we've heard of yet. The proposed Burj Al Arabi project plans to represent an Arab man wearing national dress, with a special translucent fabric *kandura* suspended over what is planned to be the world's tallest concrete and steel realisation of the human form, at 140 metres (459 feet).
Plausibility: 1/5
When the planned building was announced in a local newspaper, no one was more surprised than Limitless, the company responsible for the Jumeirah Village project where the giant Emirati male was rumoured to be heading to. At the time of going to press, Limitless were saying that they hadn't submitted any plans for approval.

Falconcity of Wonders.

A home in Dubai

With new buildings springing up in Dubai at a ferocious pace, the city's property industry is one of the fastest growing and most exciting markets in the world. Billions of dirhams a year are being pumped into building a vast cityscape of record-breaking towers, elegant Spanish-inspired villas and almost everything in between. Until recently, the intrigued tourist wasn't able to get personally involved in the boom, but since March 2006, those not born in the UAE have been allowed to purchase freehold houses and apartments in Dubai, thanks to a new law.

The resulting onslaught of foreign money that flooded the market made prices spiral, and investors and buyers who got in early were able to reap huge rewards. After a period of instability, property prices are now starting to level off; investors are no longer making a quick buck, but they are buying with greater confidence that they aren't shelling out for an over-inflated price.

The property laws for foreigners are evolving all the time and potential buyers are advised to hire a lawyer and a surveyor to help ensure the developer is reputable and the property is structurally sound. Properties are usually cheaper when purchased off-plan, but then you're paying for something you can't live in and that might be subject to delays, which are becoming increasingly common as the city's electricity and water supplies are pushed to the limit.

Areas that have proven fruitful for investors in recent times usually offer easy access to the free zones off Sheikh Zayed Road and the relatively unclogged thoroughfare of Emirates Road – the Greens, Dubai Sports City and Dubai Silicon Oasis are particularly popular choices.

Prices are much higher than they were a few years ago but are still likely to look attractive to people from most European countries, especially the UK. It's too late to get a stupendous bargain, but the slowdown in the property frenzy isn't necessarily a bad change; it's a sign that Dubai's property market is finally maturing.

were key to creating a contextual and distinctive Dubai 'look'. For those who question the notion of 'Islamic architecture', these attempts amounted to mere pastiche: they say that Dubai's age-old position on the trading crossroads and its new-found identity as a global city necessitate universal buildings.

Dubaians often wryly joke that they go to sleep alone at night only to wake up next to a skyscraper the next day. Reflecting the transient and impatient nature of the new Dubai, many of the structures are impressive, but few of them are truly innovative, especially when it comes to environmental concerns (see *p34* **Green thinking**). Old-timers question why today's architects have yet to master the integrated use of cool air, shade and natural light perfected in wind tower houses. While European, American and Asian capitals patronise the new breed of superstar architects, Dubai tends to rely on faceless foreign corporations for its construction needs, and the public's imagination has yet to be grabbed by many cultural or public buildings. But the city has no problem grabbing the headlines with its commercial plans, and the ambition that saw Sheikh Rashid dredging the Creek back in the 1960s is more than evident today. A raft of projects such as the Palm Jumeirah and the World will come to startling fruition over the

next few years, making the construction of the Burj Al Arab seem like a walk in the park.

Dubai's new role as one massive real estate project has been facilitated by the launch of freehold property ownership for foreigners, enabling non-Emiratis to buy homes for the first time (*see above* **A home in Dubai**). Despite concerns over a lack of land and mortgage legislation, local and global investors have, so far, proved to be more than willing to partake in the Dubai dream. The city has displayed its usual marketing acumen, persuading several members of the England national football team to snap up luxury villas on the Palm Jumeirah, thus securing a series of headline-grabbing announcements.

In a decade's time, we can expect to find a million people living in futuristic cities-within-cities, alongside the world's biggest theme park, the world's tallest towers and grandest malls and entire archipelagos of man-made islands (*see p28* **Breaking new ground**). The bill for all these projects is somewhere in the billions, and there is also increasing concern about the environmental cost and the apparent human rights abuses taking place on construction sites. These are problems the authorities will have to deal with; as the mega-projects become a realisation, the emirate will be subject to increased scrutiny from the rest of the world.

Green thinking

The UAE is the not-so-proud owner of one of the largest ecological footprints in the world, so 'the emirates' and 'environmentally friendly developments' aren't terms that often figure in the same sentence. In the bid to become the blueprint for a 21st-century city, it seems that the damaging effects of creating man-made islands and energy guzzling skyscrapers have fallen by the wayside. In the 2006 *Happy Planet Index*, the UAE came 154th out of 178 countries in the ecological footprint category, meaning that the country consumes a huge amount of natural resources to sustain its lifestyle and culture, but barely creates any of these resources itself.

Environmentalists claim that offshore developments such as the World and the Palm islands are doing considerable damage to the region's marine life, with the digging up of the seabed suffocating it in a blanket of silt. While the intelligent design of wind towers cooled down traditional Dubai buildings, today's malls, hotels, offices and indoor ski slopes are heavily reliant on air-conditioning units to tackle the year-round hot weather, and this surplus of sun, so far, has not inspired many developers to consider solar power as a supplementary source of energy.

One of the few firms that has set its sights on sustainable design concepts is Glenn Howells. The British firm has proposed a rotating tower of apartments that uses solar power to help it revolve and recycle water for the irrigation system. Whether or not it's really necessary to live in a spinning tower – the developers boast that residents will be able to enjoy different views of the city each morning – is another matter entirely. Another eco-aware development is the Palisades, which claims to be the first big development in Dubai with environmental concerns at its heart. By recycling water and increasing design efficiency, the Palisades' buildings should have a smaller environmental impact than most others.

A project that can be lauded for its ecological efforts is the Dubai Desert Conservation Reserve. Situated 45 minutes out of town, the 225-square-kilometre landscape of preserved land will remain an untouched slice of the environment amid the surrounding building frenzy. With the goal of preventing the extinction of local wildlife while advocating the protection of the fragile desert ecology, it will remain a pristine wilderness.

Perhaps Dubai could pull a leaf out of Bahrain's book. Bahrain's new World Trade Center is formed of two main towers linked by three giant wind turbines, which will generate around 15 per cent of the building's energy through utilising the strong offshore winds. Environmentalists in the region hope that the groundbreaking building will inspire developers to work on similar projects in Dubai. It may be impossible to reverse the damage already done, but it does finally seem that this industrious emirate is becoming slightly more environmentally conscious.

The **Palisades** eco development.

Culture & Customs

For a gentle introduction to the culture and traditions of the Middle East, Dubai is the place.

Most cities are full of contradictions, but you'll be hard-pushed to find a city with so many apparent contradictions as Dubai. It promotes itself as the entertainment capital of the Middle East, where clubbers can find ample venues to night-crawl for weeks, yet the local population is generally very conservative. As devout Muslims, many UAE nationals continue to uphold the numerous religious practices Islam preaches, most of which have infiltrated local traditions and customs; yet, many of these practices also forbid them from indulging in the very entertainment services that the emirate is so keen to promote.

Dubai thrives on its image as an oasis amid a mysterious and largely unapproachable region. In the midst of the political dramas happening around it, Dubai is a luxury destination for the wealthy and hordes of nouveau riche; people who aren't willing to give up their social freedoms, such as drinking alcohol, while on holiday. Even mega-celebrities are flocking to party in Dubai's massive hotels and trendy bars, while the city's locals are left on the sidelines, watching expatriates and visitors party away at clubs and bars that are deemed inappropriate by Emirati society. But as long as the cash keeps flowing, it's an oxymoronic reality that Dubai seems willing to live with.

The result is an obvious dichotomy between foreigners and Emiratis – a rift so severe it physically separates most expatriates and visitors from locals; meeting and conversing with an Emirati is a special occasion rather than the norm. One of the drawbacks of this is the reinforcement of the expatriate bubble, in which foreigners forget or completely disregard the importance of adhering to and respecting local customs and traditions. No one's to blame; it's merely a consequence of Dubai's booming economy. The influx of foreigners, including an exorbitant number of Indian, Pakistani and Bangladeshi labourers brought in to build this city, has marginalised Emiratis and their way of life. Today, Emiratis only constitute around 20 per cent of the UAE's population, and the percentage of them living in the booming emirate of Dubai is much lower than that.

Scores of Emiratis have complained through the media that they feel like guests in their own nation, rather like cultural exiles within their palace walls. A natural consequence of this is a heightened sense of protectiveness over their culture and traditions. It is therefore advisable for visitors in Dubai to respect and adhere to the behavioural guidelines set by local custom, otherwise they risk offending Emiratis.

Urban myths

You can't drink

There are plenty of restaurants and bars serving alcohol – the only restriction is that they must be located within the confines of a hotel or sporting stadium. The letter of the law states that everyone drinking in the bar should be a guest of that hotel but this is never enforced and people are free to drink where they chose. Residents are free to drink in their own home providing they own a booze licence issued by the municipality. There are two alcohol distributors, a+e and MMI, which import alcohol and distribute it to bars and also sell it through their own shops to licence-holders. Tourists are free to bring limited amounts of alcohol into the country (*see p301* Customs). It is illegal to drink in the streets or in public places.

You can't eat pork

As with alcohol, pork is freely served in hotel restaurants. Many larger supermarkets have a pork section for non-Muslims. You do not need a licence to purchase pork.

Western women have to cover up

While it is still important to respect Islamic culture and dress appropriately, Western women are free to dress as they please and are not required to wear a veil or cover their shoulders in public. Visitors should dress more conservatively during the month of Ramadan (*see p176*).

Women can't drive

Women are subject to exactly the same driving laws as men.

Homosexuality is illegal

All sexual liaisons conducted outside of marriage are illegal in the UAE. As gay marriages are not recognised by Islamic law, all homosexual acts are illegal.

You are not allowed to enter the country if you are HIV positive

There is no test on entry to check if you are HIV positive. However, if you are found to be HIV positive during your stay you will face deportation. If you're applying for residency, you have to pass a medical proving you aren't HIV positive.

Couples need to be married to get a hotel room

Strictly speaking, it is illegal for an unmarried couple to share a hotel room. However, very few, if any, establishments will actually ask to see a marriage certificate – particularly if you are a Western couple.

You can't display affection in public

It is wise to moderate your behaviour in public. While hand-holding and kissing on the cheek is acceptable, more passionate displays of affection can result in fines and even arrests.

THE CITY OF IMMIGRANTS

Dubai's position at the crossroads of the Gulf, Indian subcontinent and Africa has always made it home – or at least port-of-call – for expatriates from the region and beyond, but its transformation from a pearl-diving town to an economic powerhouse over the past 70 years has brought about a dramatic change in the city's ethnic make-up.

However, in spite of the emirate's attempts to eradicate racism, there are marked distinctions between 'workers' and 'expatriates', the former consisting of labourers from the subcontinent and the latter a combination of skilled men and women from the Middle East, Europe, Australasia and South Africa. Even fly-by-night tourists can't fail to notice the busloads of workers who graft all year round, even in the heat of the summer, building Dubai's new luxury hotels and homes. There are over half a million construction workers in the city at any

time, living in what are openly called 'labour camps', and working long, round-the-clock shifts, for an average wage of US$175 a month. While capitalist enthusiasts argue that the workers are better off earning money for themselves and their families in the Gulf rather than struggling to find jobs back home, stories abound of construction workers arriving in Dubai under false pretences, collapsing in high summer temperatures and slaving away in dangerous conditions.

The city's service sector – the lower rungs of the tourist and entertainment industries, plus the maids and cleaners who look after local and expatriate families – tend to hail from the Philippines, Indonesia, East Africa and Sri Lanka. Dubai's labouring classes survive for years on end, sending money back via the informal *hawala* transfer system and visiting their families every two or three years. As every other taxi driver will tell you, many plan to come for a couple of years, but find themselves staying much longer; most can name the number of months and days until their next trip home.

Their obvious exploitation contrasts strongly with the city's penchant for brash consumer luxury; for professionals, life in Dubai is a different story. Companies sometimes include annual airline tickets and family memberships to beach clubs in their packages and, while rising rents and ever-increasing traffic mean that things aren't what they used to be, Dubai can still provide a classic expat lifestyle. But change is afoot: today's IT, media, tourism and property industries increasingly attract young Arabs, Iranians and Indians, as well as Brits, other Europeans, South Africans and Australasians, some of whom have an interest in the Middle East beyond its capacity for tax-free sunshine. The mantra is still 'work hard, play hard', but a new kind of sophistication is evident – and necessary, given Dubai's rapid pace of development.

DUBAI'S ARAB POPULATION

The Arab world's party people, the Lebanese, heavily influence Dubai's glamorous clubbing scene. The Lebanese tend to be Muslim or Christian and have always immigrated to far-flung lands; there are substantial numbers in Dubai. Joining them are Palestinians, Syrians, other Levantine Arabs and Iranians, many of whom have been educated in Europe, the US or other Gulf states.

As for Emiratis, it's their passion for sport, business and shopping that brings them together, and the Thursday horse racing nights at Nad Al Sheba attract huge crowds. But besides all things equine (racing, endurance riding, Arab horse racing and beauty contests), Emiratis are committed to their falconry – don't be surprised to see a row of hooded falcons coming through the airport's passport control, or in the gardens of the palaces in Jumeirah and Umm Suqeim. And finally, while shopping may be merely a pastime anywhere else in the world, here it's an obsession. Many families bond by hitting the mall every Friday afternoon, and with so many destinations to choose from, it's no wonder AA Gill observed that Dubai is the place where malls go on holiday.

THE ETHNIC FOOD CHAIN

Despite Dubai's generally harmonious and tolerant outlook, and its reputation as the most liberal of the emirates, some professionals do note a degree of racism – from the patronising attitude of some expatriates towards the service classes, to club bouncers sometimes refusing entry to groups of Indian men. At times, Dubai can seem to be made up of a collection of

different ethnic groups that keep themselves to themselves, living parallel but separate lives rather than side by side like in many mixed, multicultural societies in Europe. Certainly, the old order that places Emiratis at the top of the pile, followed by Europeans and then other Arabs, has shown staying power. But increasing numbers of professional Indians, the creation of democratically elected local councils, and new laws allowing – even encouraging – foreigners to own property could change this, creating new 'stakeholders' in Dubai society.

LOCAL RULE

While expatriates, particularly Westerners, might be highly visible, it's the local minority who define and rule the city. Many foreigners mistakenly believe that Emirati society is as uniform as its choice of dress, but dig beneath the surface and you'll find a complex, rapidly changing people. Young professionals, whose grandparents may have lived on camel milk and dates in the desert, deftly straddle Dubai's twin towers of capitalism and tradition. They are likely to combine an arranged marriage, the wearing of the *hijab* and other traditions with business acumen and an international education, plus an absolute respect for the ruling Sheikhs and a deep love of Hollywood. An active programme of 'Emiratisation' aims to get more Emiratis into all areas of employment, but for now they tend only to dominate the public sector.

THE WEEKEND

In September 2006, the government changed the official weekend days from Thursday and Friday to Friday and Saturday. Before the shift, private companies had different weekends to governmental organisations and schools, and these companies felt that the official weekend wasn't conducive to conducting business with companies in other countries. Either way, Friday, the Islamic holy day, remains sacred. Usually reserved for family time, many expatriates book large tables at an extensive Friday brunch, which has become a rather indulgent Dubai tradition. Between noon and 4pm, expatriates tuck into extraordinarily large buffets, complete with chocolate fountains and free flowing bubbly, until they can consume no more. As for the majority of Arabs and Emiratis, families gather at parks, beaches and homes to socialise and relax with loved ones, often until late in the evening.

THICKER THAN WATER

For Dubai's Emirati population – with only two generations of separation from tribal living – the extended family is of crucial importance, whether in business dealings and traditional

All that glitters: the **old gold souk**. *See p169.*

caving in. If a meal presents itself, expect vast amounts of delicious food, much of which will end up being left – a sign of your host's generosity. Eat only with your right hand, since the left hand is used for wiping the backside in the toilet.

Most Emirati men favour the traditional, practical *dishdasha* or *khandura* (a long, white shirt-dress), with *ghutra* (a white headdress) and *agal* (a black rope that holds the *ghutra* in place, traditionally used to hobble camels). In public, city women tend to wear an *abaya* (long black cloak) over a conservative dress, long skirt or tight designer jeans, with a *hijab* or *sheyla* (a scarf that either wraps around the face and hair, or covers the whole face). Older women sometimes wear a *burka* (a soft leather material that covers a woman's nose and lips) that just leaves the eyes exposed, or a traditional hardened linen mask that sits on the nose. While obviously influenced by the Islamic tenet for modesty, the clothes are also deeply practical, as anyone who's survived the biting sandy winds of a desert *shamal* (northerly wind) can testify.

gatherings or trips to the mall or the races. Names tend to define someone within their immediate family – as *bin* ('son of') or *bint* ('daughter of') – and within their tribe or extended family by the prefix *al*. Protocol dictates that respect and thanks should always be given to the older generations in each family, especially when it comes to official matters. The existence of *wasta*, the 'old boys' network' system of favours given to those with family and friends in high places, still happily resides alongside Dubai's new meritocracy.

KNOW YOUR HOSTS
Emiratis are known for their warm hospitality and politeness. Traditionally, every guest who entered a Bedouin's tent or home had to be unconditionally fed and given shelter for three days. Nowadays, this kind of generosity is not essential for survival, but old habits die hard. If you're lucky enough to meet and be invited by locals (or other Gulf Arabs) for tea or coffee, do accept. The ritual of making and presenting coffee – strong, espresso-sized cups – is prized, and you'll be offered refill after refill. If your heart can't quite take it, just gently shake your cup from side to side; your host will know not to offer you any more. If you are doing the entertaining, make sure you press more refreshments on your guest – they may well refuse a few times out of politeness before

'Once in the city, you're never more than 500 metres away from a mosque.'

As for Dubai's expatriate population, well, anything goes, but you're advised to dress to suit the occasion. Revealing or tight evening wear is tolerated in clubs, and a bikini is fine on the beach or by the hotel pool, but it's courteous (and advisable if you want to avoid getting stared at), to be more conservative when visiting heritage sites, the souks or anywhere in the city: no shorts is a good rule, and women should wear below-the-knee skirts and cover their shoulders. Beware that Sharjah (*see p268*) has 'decency laws', and be sure to dress conservatively on any day trips there.

Despite the flagrant exhibitionism of many expatriates, local police are quick to react to any complaints of harassment by men: should the generally harmless spectators at Jumeirah's public beaches become anything more disturbing, it is worth reporting them to the beach patrols.

KEEPING THE FAITH
The call to prayer is likely to greet you upon landing in Dubai; once in the city, you're apparently never more than 500 metres (a quarter of a mile) away from a mosque – expect the melodic intonations of the muezzin to define your day and remind you that you're in Arabia. Most mosques are packed for the Friday prayer,

expatriates a different set of rules, it's advisable to avoid being too informal. For example, wait for a member of the opposite sex to extend their hand before going to shake theirs. Better yet, place your palm on your heart as a sign of your warmth or gratitude. Ask before taking a photograph of an Emirati woman and steer clear of snapping any military sites. Chances are that even if you do make a blunder, your Emirati hosts will understand – their warm manner and good sense of humour will keep you blissfully unaware.

GENDER DIVIDE
Generally, in Emirati society, outside of the family and private sphere, unmarried men and women tend to lead separate lives – although, for young people, the advent of the mobile phone and the popularity of higher education, the cinema and mall, has facilitated a certain level of text message and other long-distance flirting. On public occasions, such as the horse races, it's rare to see Emirati wives accompanying their husbands; at weddings, women, dressed in all their designer finery, usually hold separate celebrations to the men; some areas of life, such as local football matches, are still off-limits to women. These traditions, which extend to ladies' days in parks, female-only beaches, and women being served first or separately in bank or other queues, sit alongside the rise of the Emirati businesswoman and the prominent role taken by some of the Sheikhas.

MIND YOUR LANGUAGE
Modern Dubai is effectively bilingual – road signs, maps, even several daily newspapers, are in English, and most Emiratis you'll meet will speak the language impeccably. Even if you're an Arabic speaker, many businessmen and women will prefer to converse with you in English. However, some public sector workers or those behind the scenes in Emirati businesses don't always have the same language skills; at some time during your stay, a public official is bound to say 'Yanni, give me passport' or 'I want form'. Combined with often unfathomable levels of bureaucracy, requiring bundles of passport photos and forms in triplicate, public offices can be a tad confusing, but keep your cool (and remember that it's much worse in most other Middle Eastern countries) and propriety will win through. It is also worthwhile trying to tune your ear to 'Hinglish' – a mix of Hindi or Urdu and English, or Indian English. The ethnic majority, Dubaians from the subcontinent, also manage their own unique blend of English plus a smattering of Arabic. Meeting them halfway is the least that you can do.

which is also broadcast from the minaret via loudspeakers, but Muslims can perform their five-times-daily prayers anywhere, from the side of the road to an office boardroom, as long as they are facing Mecca, to the west. Avoid walking in front of anyone praying, and don't stare; private yet public praying should be viewed as perfectly normal.

Compared to some other Gulf states, the UAE is tolerant and respectful of most other religions – and hosts a number of temples and churches – but active promotion is frowned upon. Likewise with the consumption of alcohol: while visitors and non-Muslim residents are welcome to buy duty-free products at the airport or have big nights out in clubs and hotel bars, the hard stuff is tolerated rather than celebrated. The nights before religious festivals are usually dry; there is virtually zero tolerance for anyone found drink driving; and members of Dubai's undercover CID tend to keep an eye on raucous parties. The two local importers – MMI and a+e – serve hotels, residents who hold liquor licences and, increasingly, big outdoor entertainment and sporting events, but their outlets are understated and windowless. You may see Gulf Arabs, whether local or visiting from Saudi and other strict states, propping up the bar in quieter establishments, but, generally, drinking is the preserve of expatriates.

Other *haram* (religiously forbidden) activities include the consumption of non-*halal* meat and pork products, which are sold to expatriates but from a separate 'pork shop' in supermarkets. Visitors should also resist public displays of affection between men and women – and be aware that hand signals (like beckoning with one finger and pointing directly, as well as the internationally recognised rude gestures) are offensive. Displaying the soles of the feet in someone's direction can also be insulting. Don't be fooled into thinking that the common sight of men holding hands is evidence of a burgeoning gay scene – among Indians, Pakistanis and Arabs, this is merely a sign of friendship.

While Emiratis are always forgiving of blunders, and tend to allow Western and Arab

EMBRACE THE ART
OF HOSPITALITY

DISCOVER A LUXURY WATERFRONT RETREAT ADJACENT TO THE
WORLD FAMOUS DUBAI CREEK GOLF AND YACHT CLUB. SITUATED JUST
MINUTES AWAY FROM THE CITY CENTRE, WORLD-CLASS SHOPPING
AND PRIME BUSINESS DISTRICTS, PARK HYATT DUBAI IS A
HAVEN OF TRANQUIL ELEGANCE AMIDST THE VIBRANT CITY OF DUBAI

PARK HYATT DUBAI°

DUBAI CREEK GOLF AND YACHT CLUB, PO BOX 2822, DUBAI, UAE
TELEPHONE + 971 4 602 1234 FACSIMILE + 971 4 602 1235 dubai.park.hyatt.com

Where to Stay

Where to Stay   **42**

Kempinski Hotel Mall of the Emirates.
See p64.

Where to Stay

Dubai's hotels may not be cheap, but you do get a lot for your money.

The iconic **Burj Al Arab** features the world's tallest atrium, at 180m (591ft). *See p50*.

Hotels in Dubai are far more than merely places to rest your head. Given that for the most part it's only hotels that can offer licensed restaurants and bars, they are the backbone of the social scene for both residents and tourists. It's entirely common for well-heeled visitors to spend more time relaxing in the ostentatious grounds of Dubai's finest resorts than exploring the city itself. More than simple exercises in luxury, several hotels embody the emirate's taste for architectural showmanship; such landmark hotels as the **Burj Al Arab** (*see p50* **Jewel of the isle**) and **Jumeirah Emirates Towers** (*see p65*) have become iconic symbols of the city, gaining international recognition. And more, much more, is still to come (*see p52* **New openings**). With the world's tallest tower, Burj Dubai, offering rooms with a view, the Palm Island promising 60 or so resorts and even the construction of an underwater hotel,

it seems that no space on land, sea or air is free from the relentless development of Dubai.

All this luxury comes at a price, however. Once upon a time Dubai's hotels were a steal, but today prices are comparable with Europe. That said, your money does go much further. A room in one of the chain hotels is likely to be far superior to its equivalent in London or New York. Competition between hotels means that unless you're visiting during a big event such as the Dubai World Cup, you shouldn't have to pay the 'rack rate'. For the best deals, visit the hotel websites – there's sometimes a substantial discount of up to 50 per cent to be had, particularly during Ramadan and Dubai's sizzling summer months (June to August).

The most interesting development in the hotel sector is the arrival of more budget chains. In the past, bargain bed hunters were forced into the less salubrious districts of Deira or Bur Dubai; now, with the opening of the Arabian Park Hotel and the promised arrival of a number of easyHotels, Holiday Inns and of Rotana's new Centro chain, in 2008 (*see p66* **Budget beds**), some lower rungs are at last being added to Dubai's hotel ladder.

> ❶ Green numbers given in this chapter correspond to the location of each hotel as marked on the maps. *See pp322-336.*

Distinguishing by district

Sheikh Zayed Road.

The first choice you should make when booking your hotel is deciding which part of town you want to stay in. In Dubai, geography largely dictates style, with prices generally dropping the further you get from the shore.

If it's the classic sun, surf and sand experience you're after, then Jumeirah – a loosely defined area that stretches from the start of Jumeirah Beach Road to just beyond the Burj Al Arab – or the Marina area further down the coast, are the districts you desire. Ritzy resorts dot Beach Road, but do make sure your wallet is well stocked. The accommodation here is mainly five-star (with the exception of the self-styled seven-star Burj Al Arab; *see p50* **Jewel of the isle**). These hotels are far from cheap, but you'll struggle to find one that doesn't have the wow factor – think stunning views, fine facilities and superlative service. It's worth bearing in mind, though, that when (or if) you tire of soaking up the sun's rays, it's a fair trek to the heritage sights that tend to be clustered around the Creek. The cloud-bothering Sheikh Zayed Road boasts the majority of the city's skyscrapers and will soon host the world's tallest building, the Burj Dubai. The main highway to Abu Dhabi is home to the bulk of the business hotels. Prices are as staggering as the architecture, but for location (it's strategically positioned between the beach and the Creek) and style, it's hard to beat.

Stretching from Creek to coastline, Bur Dubai offers some good value halfway houses between Jumeirah's polish and Deira's urban delights, and is also home to the **XVA** (*see p47*), one of the city's few genuine boutique hotels. But beware, while pockets of Bur Dubai such as Bastakia, Oud Metha, Satwa and Karama are some of the most charming in town, the central area is a heaving mass of high-rise towers. Good if you want to feel part of the action, but hardly conducive to a relaxing stay, especially when you factor in the frustrating taxi commutes during rush hour.

A colourful mix of souks, skyscrapers and shopping malls, Deira is one of the oldest areas of the city and a world away from the shiny new Dubai epitomised by the Marina. Hotels vary from high-class Creek-huggers such as the Sheraton to the cheap and less-than-cheerful establishments that line the rundown areas away from the water. Some way from the shoreline and near the airport, the area tends to be geared more to business than pleasure.

Those on a truly tight budget will struggle. Low-end options are not as prominent as the five-star excess dominating the Dubai hotel scene. YHA members would do well to check out the excellent **Dubai Youth Hostel** (*see p57*), while other economy-minded travellers will find that there are a few comfortable and cost-effective options to be had around Al Fahidi Street and Bank Street (Khalid Bin Al Waleed Road) in Bur Dubai. Here you can pick up a clean, if poky room, for a few hundred dirhams, but bear in mind that Bank Street is at the heart of the less salubrious end of Bur Dubai, where it's not unheard of for female tourists to be propositioned while popping into the supermarket in the middle of the day.

Across the Creek, the neighbourhood around Al Rigga Street in Deira is another reasonable hunting ground for cheap beds, but again suffers from less-than-squeaky-clean nocturnal activities. Fortunately there are plans in the pipeline for more budget beds (*see p66* **Budget beds**).

The **Arabian Courtyard Hotel**, in the heart of Bur Dubai's heritage area.

ABOUT THE LISTINGS

In this guide, the listings are divided up into the following categories: **Luxury** (Dhs1,500 and above); **Expensive** (Dhs1,000-1,499); **Moderate** (Dhs500-Dhs999) and **Budget** (below Dhs500). The categories indicate the average cost per night of a standard double room in high season (Oct-Apr), including ten per cent municipal tax and ten per cent service charge. Unfortunately, rates at Dubai hotels vary wildly, and booking a room can be like playing the stock exchange, with huge fluctuations within the space of a few days not uncommon. Don't be scared off by the high prices – bookings through travel agents and websites can be a lot cheaper than the rates listed here. Demand is always high in Dubai, so we recommend booking in advance.

For reviews of hotel beach clubs, health clubs and spas, *see pp237-249.*

Bur Dubai

Expensive

Grand Hyatt Dubai

Al Qataiyat Road (317 1234/www.dubai.grand.hyatt.com). **Rates** Dhs1,200-Dhs1,980 double. **Credit** AmEx, MC, V. **Map** p329 K3 ❶

With 674 rooms, the Grand Hyatt is an impressive exercise in hotel-based bombast. It also houses a running track, three outdoor pools, four tennis courts,

a spa, 14 busy restaurants and bars and (gulp) its very own indoor rainforest with four-tonne dhows hung overhead. Rooms are decorated with contemporary Arabic touches and bathrooms are on the small side, although the massaging shower and colossal tub – which could happily house three people plus the family pet – quickly subdue any spatial quibbles. A great deal of planning has gone into separating the business and pleasure areas, with secluded lounges and executive spaces ensuring the money-minded don't have to contend with children playing leapfrog. Big, bold and beautiful.

Babysitting. Bars. Beauty salon. Business services. Concierge. Gym. Internet (dataport). Limousine service. Minibar. No-smoking rooms. Parking. Pools. Restaurants. Room service (24hr). Telephone. Turndown. TV (satellite).

Moderate

Arabian Courtyard Hotel

Al Fahidi Street, opposite Dubai Museum (351 9111/www.arabiancourtyard.com). **Rates** Dhs530-Dhs1,300 double. **Credit** AmEx, MC, V. **Map** p330 H4 ❷

Set in the very heart of old Dubai, less than a stone's throw from the Creek and the Souk Al Kabir (Meena Bazaar), the Arabian Courtyard is so heavily themed on the heritage angle that you'll be surprised to discover it's one of the city's newer hotels. Spacious bedrooms, many of which have Creek views, make this a comfortable choice.

Babysitting. Bars. Beauty salon. Business services. Concierge. Gym. Internet (dataport). Laundry.

Limousine service. Massage services. Minibar.
Parking. Pools. Restaurants. Room service (24hr).
Sauna. Steam. Telephone. Turndown. TV (satellite).

Ascot Hotel & Royal Ascot Hotel

Khalid Bin Waleed Road (352 0900/www.ascothotel.
com). **Rates** Dhs600-Dhs800 double. **Credit** AmEx,
MC, V. **Map** p330 H4 ❸

The Ascot was the first upscale hotel to be built in
Bur Dubai; it's a homely place that is as inviting as
a fan in the Dubai heat. Rooms are Georgian in
style with green carpets and refreshing canary yellow walls. It might sound hideous, but somehow it
works. Those who believe in packing for every possible occasion will no doubt appreciate the large
wardrobes, while bathrooms are also spacious and
spacious. Staff are friendly and there are a number of restaurants and bars, including the ever-popular pub
Waxy O' Conner's (*see p133*). A couple of hundred
extra dirhams per night will bag you a more
upmarket room at the adjacent Royal Ascot Hotel;
the Ascot's new five-star sibling. While neither
hotel will blow you away, the Ascot's main asset is
its location. The Dubai Museum and Bur Dubai
souk are but a hop, skip and a jump away.
Business services. Minibar. Music hall. Pool.
Restaurants. Shuttle service to Jumeirah Beach. Spa.
Telephone. TV (satellite). Walk-in closet.

Capitol Hotel

Mina Road, Satwa (346 0111/www.capitol-
hotel.com). **Rates** Dhs720-Dhs870 double.
Credit AmEx, MC, V. **Map** p332 E7 ❹

A good alternative to Dubai's garish glitz, the
Capitol is a pleasantly basic affair with reasonably
sized standard rooms boasting huge beds but
banal views of built-up Satwa. Suites are large and
welcoming, with a well-decorated living space, and
can be extended through the use of an adjoining
twin room. Should the mood take you, you can
request one of three masseuses to perform treatments in your room. Sadly, the Capitol is let down
by its facilities; the rooftop is home to an underwhelming swimming pool and a lonely Lebanese
restaurant, the Chinese eatery is dismal and the
gym is poky. The hotel is situated close to both
Satwa's bustling streets and the beach, and nothing is more than a short taxi ride away. As such it
remains a popular choice for leisure travellers from
Eastern Europe, the Gulf States, China and India,
as well as more regular business guests.
Babysitting. Bars. Beauty salon. Business services.
Concierge. Gym. Internet (dataport). Massage.
Minibar. No-smoking rooms. Parking. Pools.
Restaurants. Room service (24hr). Telephone.
TV (satellite).

Dhow Palace Hotel

Bur Dubai (359 9992/www.dhowpalacehotel
dubai.com). **Rates** Dhs650-Dhs900 double.
Credit AmEx, MC, V. **Map** p333 G6 ❺

This relative newcomer on the block is shaped like
a ship, and all the staff wear sailing attire. Taste
has bypassed the lobby area too and reception staff
are sometimes less than helpful. Rooms, however
(there are 282 in total), are suitably spacious and
furnished in contemporary Arabic decor that does-
n't overly assault the senses. Not being by the
beach, the Dhow Palace is in need of a decent swimming pool; sadly its current one is surprisingly
small and suffers from a lack of tan-topping areas
and sun loungers. The gym and other leisure facilities are adequate enough – although hardly what
you would call five star. Situated slap bang in the
middle of the concrete jungle of Bur Dubai, the
Dhow Palace's location isn't a pretty one, but it is
conveniently close to several Dubai landmarks.
Babysitting. Business centre. Complimentary
beach/shopping mall shuttle service. Health club.
Internet. Laundry valet and dry cleaning. Minibar.
Personal safe. Plasma TV. Sauna. Swimming pool.

Four Points by Sheraton

Bur Dubai (397 7444/www.fourpoints.com/
burdubai). **Rates** Dhs630-Dhs1,450 double.
Credit AmEx, MC, V. **Map** p330 H4 ❻

The Four Points is a small and unremarkable hotel
in the centre of town that is geared towards the budget business traveller. With only 125 rooms and
basic services, it doesn't draw large crowds, which
is great if you're looking for somewhere quiet. The
decor of the bedrooms is a tad old-fashioned, but
rooms are clean and neat. The communal areas are
all a bit library-like but the Indian restaurant
Antique Bazaar and the Viceroy pub are both popular with local residents. All in all, it's not a bad base
for exploring Dubai's heritage area.
Babysitting. Beauty salon. Business services.
Concierge. Gym. Internet (dataport). Limousine
service. Minibar. No-smoking rooms. Parking. Pools.
Restaurants. Room service (24hr). Telephone.
Turndown. TV (satellite).

Jumeirah Rotana Dubai

Al Dhiyafah Road, Satwa (345 5888/www.rotana.
com). **Rates** Dhs700-Dhs1,320 double. **Credit**
AmEx, MC, V. **Map** p332 E8 ❼

The Jumeirah Rotana Dubai is cheekily and mis-
leadingly named: it is actually found in the shore-
free area of Satwa rather than beachy Jumeirah.
That said, this busy hotel has a casual atmosphere
and a 50/50 mix of business and leisure guests. The
spacious and light bedrooms come complete with
generously sized beds, plenty of wardrobe space
and entertaining views over the back streets. Decor
is typical bland Americana; although comfortable,
it's nothing to write home about. There's a shuttle
service to a beach club and nearby shopping centres. Guests can enjoy stretching their legs outside
on the ever-bustling Al Dhiyafah Road – home to
a number of pleasant alfresco eateries – but if you
have a romantic escape in mind, look a little
further towards Al Sufouh.
Babysitting. Bars. Beauty salon. Business services.
Concierge. Gym. Internet (dataport). Limousine
service. Minibar. No-smoking rooms. Parking. Pools.
Restaurants. Room service (24hr). Telephone.
Turndown. TV (satellite).

Bur Dubai's **Ramada Dubai** boasts the Middle East's largest stained-glass window.

Majestic Hotel Tower

Mankhool Road (359 8888/www.dubaimajestic.com).
Rates Dhs850-Dhs1,200 double. Credit AmEx, MC, V.
Map p330 H5 ❽

This relatively new hotel is well positioned for exploring the historical Bastakia Quarter and is only a short taxi ride away from the five-star strips of Sheikh Zayed Road and Jumeirah. There's not much to complain about, but there's not much to get overly excited about either. Rooms are spacious enough and Arabian accented – think varnished wooden floors and rich, opulent furnishings. Adding to the Majestic's appeal is a spacious pool area – you'll have no trouble finding a spot in the sun. Our main bugbear here is the dearth of lifts. Two lifts service 28 floors, so expect to queue and be prepared for it to take ten minutes to reach your room. Note also that the Majestic runs a tight ship; visitors aren't allowed in after 10pm. This aside, the place is a fine-enough option for those wanting to be based in Bur Dubai.
Business services. Hair & beauty salon. Internet. Minibar. Parking. Restaurants. Sauna & steam room. Room service. Shuttle service to beach & shopping centres. Swimming pool with sundeck. TV.

Mövenpick Hotel Bur Dubai

19th Street (336 6000/www.moevenpickburdubai. com). Rates Dhs720-Dhs1,150 double. Credit AmEx, MC, V. Map p329 J3 ❾

Comfortable without being stuffy, the Mövenpick has an inviting ambience. The panorama from the medium-sized rooms is all inner-city Dubai, but the beds are comfy and the furnishings adequate. The suites and executive rooms are a leap up from the standard ones, featuring Jacuzzis in the bathrooms. Business facilities are excellent, and fitness fanatics are well catered to with a gym and health club that offers innovative classes like power bhangra alongside the usual staples. Meanwhile, the rooftop boasts a large and lovely pool deck area and, strangely enough, a jogging track. It's a solid bet for access to the business districts and the odd shopping expedition.
Babysitting. Bars. Beauty salon. Business services. Concierge. Gym. Internet (dataport). Limousine service. Minibar. No-smoking rooms. Parking. Pools. Restaurants. Room service (24hr). Telephone. Turndown. TV (satellite).

Ramada Dubai

Opposite Jumbo Electronics, Al Mankhool Road (351 9999/www.ramadadubai.com). Rates Dhs660-Dhs1,100 double. Credit AmEx, MC, V. Map p330 H5 ❿

Proud owner of the largest stained-glass window in the Middle East, the four-star Ramada is just outside the more hectic heartland of the Golden Sands area. This and the hotel's shoreless location mean that most of its clients tend to be business folk. Rooms are spacious, although most overlook air-conditioning units, building sites or the busy streets below. There's a small pool, which only gets the morning sun. Good service, competitive corporate rates and decent sized rooms make this a sound choice for business guests, and in terms of class and value for money, it's streets ahead of its shabby sister hotel in Deira.

Hotels

For sleeping by the beach

Ritz-Carlton Dubai (see p62); **Le Meridien Mina Seyahi Beach Resort & Marina** (see p63).

For celebrity spotting

Shangri-La Hotel Dubai (see p65); **Fairmont Dubai** (see p65).

For guaranteed romance

One&Only Royal Mirage (see p61); **Park Hyatt Dubai** (see p51).

For overwhelming opulence

Burj Al Arab (see p50); **Grand Hyatt Dubai** (see p44).

For a taste of Arabia

Jumeirah Bab Al Shams Desert Resort & Spa (see p54); **Mina A'Salam** (see p59).

For sealing the deal

Hilton Dubai Creek (see p51); **Jumeirah Emirates Towers** (see p65).

For bargain beds

Dubai Youth Hostel (see p57); **Ibis** World Trade Centre Dubai (see p67).

For something a bit different

Al Maha Desert Resort & Spa (see p54); **XVA** (see right).

Babysitting. Bars. Beauty salon. Business services. Concierge. Gym. Internet. Limousine service. Minibar. No-smoking rooms. Parking. Pools. Restaurants. Room service (24hr). Telephone. Turndown. TV (satellite).

Rydges Plaza

Satwa roundabout, Satwa (398 2222/www.rydges. com/dubai). **Rates** Dhs550-Dhs1,020 double. **Credit** AmEx, MC, V. **Map** p333 F8 ⑪

Occupying a city centre location next to the Satwa roundabout, this old-fashioned nine-storey Australian hotel delivers far more in terms of comfort, style and facilities than its mundane exterior promises. The good position, attentive staff and faux-classical pool area attract a repeat clientele that's mainly made up of business travellers and elderly tourists. Bedrooms are spacious and comfortable, but the furnishings are, although in good condition, match the somewhat dated style of the hotel. Most rooms have a clear view of the bustling streets below, and there are complimentary beach and airport transfers to boot. The hotel outlets are fairly popular; Aussie Legends is a good choice if you're after simple pub grub.

Babysitting. Bars. Business services. Concierge. Gym. Internet (dataport). Limousine service. Minibar. No-smoking rooms. Parking. Pools. Restaurants. Room service (24hr). Telephone. TV (satellite).

XVA

Al Fahidi Roundabout, Bastakia, behind Basta Art Café (353 5388). **Rates** Dhs715-Dhs825 double. **Credit** AmEx, MC, V. **Map** p330 H4 ⑫

This stunningly attractive retro hotel is unique in Dubai. Built more than 70 years ago from coral and clay, it has been faithfully restored and reopened as a triple treat; it's a gallery (don't be surprised if you see an artist working on their canvas), café and boutique guest house. Nestled in the pocket of old Dubai known as Bastakia, this is one of a handful of wind tower-topped buildings holding out against the lightning modernisation of the city. There's currently a new surge of interest in looking after the last vestiges of pre-oil Dubai, and Bastakia is at the crest of the preservation wave; the care lavished on the building and the sense of time having slowed to a crawl within its walls making XVA one of the most interesting places to stay in town. The rooftop terrace is the place to swing in suspended rocking chairs looking out over the skyline of old buildings and mosques to the bright lights of Bur Dubai proper. XVA houses only a small number of guests at any one time, so book early. The special atmosphere here is only heightened by the incredibly competitive rates. In a city where five-star conformity rules, this place stands out as somewhere that little bit different, a little bit special. *Photo p49.*

Café. Concierge. Minibar. Restaurant.

Budget

Arabian Park Hotel

Near Wafi City, opposite Grand Hyatt Dubai (324 5999/www.arabianparkhoteldubai.com). **Rates** Dhs450-Dhs800 double. **Credit** AmEx, MC, V. **Map** p329 K3 ⑬

Think not of beautiful views – construction sites surround the hotel– but of convenience; the Arabian Park Hotel is close to the airport, the World Trade Centre and Wafi City Mall. Rooms – there are 318 in total – tend to be on the small side, but are comfortable and simply but tastefully decorated. The place also plays host to a decent-sized saltwater pool, a bar and a well equipped gym; although it can get crowded if more than four fitness fanatics decide to visit at any one time. Added attractions include a communal lounge on each floor, complete with a plasma TV, a mini library and friendly and efficient staff. Unfortunately, getting a taxi can be a bit of a nightmare and while the hotel has its own cars, these tend to cost more than normal metered cabs. Still, this is a good value contemporary three-star option that knocks spots off some of the city's dated four-star hotels. It's worth knowing that rates, while not expensive to start with, practically halve during summer months.

GRAND LEISURE

Set in 37 acres of landscaped gardens, Grand Hyatt Dubai is an oasis of tranquility
in the heart of the city. Relax and enjoy world-class leisure facilities
and an extensive choice of restaurants and bars.

FEEL THE HYATT TOUCH®

A break from the cutting-edge norm – the attractive **XVA** guest house. *See p47.*

Bar. Business facilities. Dry cleaning & laundry. Gym. Hairdryer. Internet. Mini bar. Pool. Restaurants. Shuttle bus to airport, beach & Wafi City. Room services. Tea/coffee making facilities. Telephone. Travel desk. TV.

Golden Sands Hotel Apartments

Off Bank Street (355 5553/www.goldensands dubai.com). **Rates** Dhs499-Dhs800 double. **Credit** AmEx, MC, V. **Map** p331 J5 ⑭
Comprised of a large number of sizeable and fully serviced self-catering flats, that range from one bedroom studios to three and four bedrooms, with additional services such as a gym, sauna and squash courts. Long-term visitors can extend their stay for up to a year, costing up to Dhs60,000 for an annual studio and Dhs90,000 for a two-bedroom apartment. *Gym. Housekeeping. Phone. Room service (24hr). Swimming pool. Sauna. Squash courts. Telephone. TV.*

President Hotel

Trade Centre Road, Karama (334 6565). **Rates** Dhs350-Dhs600 double. **Credit** AmEx, MC, V. **Map** p333 H7 ⑮
Sat on one edge of the bargain-heavy Karama markets, this 50-room, two-star hotel seems as happy to offer knockdown prices as the traders who have set up shop behind it. The dark and dimly lit hallways lead into similarly gloomy rooms, with views of surrounding buildings and the busy road out front. The beds themselves are quite small; the tiny bathrooms have equally small shampoo sachets.

Very cheap and centrally located, the President is a fair choice, but you're better off splashing out that bit more for the Jumeirah Rotana, Rydges Plaza or, if you can live without a pool, the Ibis. *Bars. Minibar. No-smoking rooms. Parking. Pools. Restaurants. Room service (24hr). Telephone. TV (satellite).*

Rush Inn

Bank Street (352 2235). **Rates** Dhs350-Dhs400 double. **Credit** AmEx, MC, V. **Map** p330 H4 ⑯
At this well-priced hostelry, the foyer is hung with slightly dismal snapshots of karaoke stars working the plethora of themed in-house bars (one Pakistani, one Filipino and one African – the wonderful Club Africana), but the rooms are none too shabby. If you're looking for a tranquil getaway, this place is not for you – the hotel's line-up of nightspots means it can be noisy until the wee small hours. *Air conditioning. Laundry. TV. 24hr room service.*

Deira

Expensive

Al Bustan Rotana Hotel

Casablanca Road, Garhoud (282 0000/www.rotana. com). **Rates** Dhs1,100-Dhs2,150 double. **Credit** AmEx, MC, V. **Map** p329 K2 ⑰
Located within striking distance of Dubai's airport, this Rotana has earned a reputation as a convenient business hotel. Not that it's all work and no play;

Jewel of the isle

The Burj Al Arab sits on its own artificial island.

Dubai's most famous hotel is every bit as extravagant and outrageous as you've been led to believe. The tallest hotel in the world when it was built back in 1999, the **Burj Al Arab** awarded itself two stars more than official ratings allow, and watched as the press inches, bookings and room rates rocketed.

The landmark building – whose sail-like structure recalls dhow-trading vessels as a tribute to the region's seafaring tradition – stands proudly on its own man-made island some 280 metres (919 feet) offshore, and is linked to the mainland by a slender, gently curving causeway. Taller than the Eiffel Tower at over 305 metres (1,000 feet), and only 61 metres (200 feet) shorter than the Empire State Building, it has its own helicopter pad on the 28th floor to receive guests who prefer to fly the 25 kilometres (16 miles) from Dubai's airport rather than ride in one of a fleet of 14 white Rolls-Royces across a bridge that shoots jets of flame to acknowledge the arrival of a VIP.

After the sleek and stylish exterior, the garish interior can come as something of a shock; it's definitely not a place for those with egalitarian sensibilities or an aversion to OTT gilding. A triumphant waterfall cascades into the lobby flanked by floor-to-ceiling aquariums so vast the staff have to don scuba gear to clean them. Bedrooms range from 170 square metres (1,830 square feet) to 780 square metres (8396 square feet), and 22-carat gold leaf covers columns, ceilings, panels and every tap. Huge golden pillars reach up into the atrium: greens, reds and blues all vie for prominence in a colourful reminder that style in Dubai is as much a question of volume as it is of taste.

However, if you have the cash to splash, a night here will earn you unlimited holiday bragging rights – after all, how many people

do you know of who have stayed in a (admittedly self-appointed) seven-star hotel? Each room at the Burj is a duplex suite and there are 202 in total, including two royal suites on the 25th floor. All are equipped with the latest technology: internet access, a 42-inch (107-centimetre) plasma screen TV, and, in keeping with the sheer decadence, a remote control allowing you to observe who's at the door and to let your guests in without having to leave the comfort of your armchair.

The management at the Burj Al Arab pride themselves on their hotel's highly personalised service, with an entire army of staff (1,200 no less) to tend to your every need. Each suite has its own butler and each floor has its own guest service desk. An unbeatable view of Dubai's coastline can be enjoyed from the Al Muntaha restaurant, which is suspended 200 metres (656 feet) above the Gulf and reached by an express panoramic lift travelling at six metres per second.

Be warned: treat yourself to a stay here and you may be reluctant to leave; the real world being too rude an awakening after such magnificence. If you can't afford a bed at the Burj (a standard room will set you back a whopping Dhs3,850 a night) but still want to see the obscene affluence of its interiors for yourself, then book yourself in for afternoon tea or cocktails. There's a minimum spend of Dhs250 per person, but the Burj is the closest Dubai has to an Eiffel Tower or an Empire State, so it's just about worth the extravagance.

Off Jumeirah Beach Road, Umm Suqeim (301 7777/www.burj-al-arab.com). **Rates** Suites from Dhs3,850. **Credit** AmEx, MC, V. **Map** p336 E1 ⑥
Hotel services *Babysitting. Bars. Beauty salon. Business services. Concierge. Dataport. Gym. Internet access. Limousine service. Minibar. No-smoking rooms. Parking. Pools. Restaurants. Spa.*

the hotel has a vast amount of leisure facilities, including a spacious swimming pool, an array of restaurants and a well-equipped, if poorly attended, gym. Standard bedrooms are reasonably sized with huge beds, but wardrobe space is limited and the bathrooms are dated. A handful of rooms come with their own private terraces facing the pool deck, which raises their appeal considerably. Executive club levels are a distinct improvement with larger rooms, a dedicated check in/out area, TV lounge, breakfast area and net access to boot.
Babysitting. Bars. Beauty salon. Business services. Concierge. Gym. Internet (dataport). Limousine service. Minibar. No-smoking rooms. Parking. Pools. Restaurants. Room service (24hr). Telephone. Turndown. TV (satellite).

Hilton Dubai Creek
Baniyas Road (227 1111/www.hilton.com). **Rates** Dhs1,050-Dhs1,770 double. **Credit** AmEx, MC, V. **Map** p331 L4 ⑱
One of Deira's classiest hotels, the Hilton Creek was designed by Carlos Ott; the brains behind the Opera de la Bastille in Paris. The hotel is also home to Gordon Ramsay's award-winning restaurant, Verre, sister restaurant the Glasshouse and some buzzy bars. Glide into the zen-like foyer where peaceful water features lap against glass and gleaming chrome and you enter a world of designer purity. Chances are you'll either love it or hate it. For some this exercise in modernism is just too cool, but if you want stylish urban chic, this is the place for you. The large rooms are statements in contemporary luxury, and the huge comfortable beds and ultra-cool black and white bathrooms prove there is substance beyond the style. This Hilton is an excellent choice if you need to stay in Deira. (*See also p63* Hilton Dubai Jumeirah.)
Babysitting. Bars. Beauty salon. Business services. Concierge. Gym. Internet (dataport). Limousine service. Minibar. No-smoking rooms. Parking. Pools. Restaurants. Room service (24hr). Telephone. Turndown. TV (satellite).

Hyatt Regency Dubai & Galleria
Deira Corniche (209 1234/www.dubai.regency.hyatt. com). **Rates** Dhs1,100-Dhs1,200 double. **Credit** AmEx, MC, V. **Map** p331 J1 ⑲
Built in 1980, this vast 400-room stalwart sits close to the mouth of the Creek in downtown Deira. Tried and tested, the Regency is an unashamed wooer of business guests, and a successful one at that. Dealmakers, in particular those from East Asia, arrive in droves, attracted by the veteran hotel's reputation, professionalism and plush suites. The out of the way location – around 7km (4 miles) from the city and about as far as you can get from Jumeirah's beaches and restaurants – has created something of a siege mentality, and the hotel has every leisure facility going, including a revolving restaurant, nightclub, cinema, ice skating rink, mini golf course and its very own (if paltry) shopping centre. The rooms are dominated by large glass windows offering fine views of

Dubai, the Corniche and Sharjah, with fresh flowers and plants to spruce the slightly dated furniture. It's a nice hotel, but its location proves off-putting to many, especially since the traffic outside its front doors is near-solid for much of the day.
Babysitting. Bars. Beauty salon. Business services. Concierge. Gym. Internet (dataport). Limousine service. Minibar. No-smoking rooms. Parking. Pools. Restaurants. Room service (24hr). Telephone. Turndown. TV (satellite).

JW Marriott Hotel Dubai
Al Muraqqabat Road (262 4444/www.jwmarriott. com). **Rates** Dhs1,260-Dhs2,750 double. **Credit** AmEx, MC, V. **Map** p329 K1 ⑳
Keeping in style with the Marriott brand, this is an elegant and grand hotel attached to the Hamarain shopping centre. Huge sofas and lush cushions all but engulf guests in the lobby and the enormous staircase is straight out of *Cinderella*. It's strange then that the classy ambience is undermined somewhat by an assemblage of plastic palm trees. Rooms are comfortable, offering an old-world formality that's rare in Dubai hotels, with signature Marriott beds ensuring you enjoy a deep slumber. As with most hotels in the Deira area, vistas are limited and there's little to please the eye in the neighbouring buildings or the busy main road. The pool and health facilities, aside from the massive gym and training area, are adequate if not incredible. Where the hotel's attention to detail really comes to the fore is in the daily beach-bound shuttle buses. Before they leave, passengers are presented with a beach bag that provides towels, water and sun lotion, and on return given cold face towels to calm the sunburn. It's a relaxing option that may go some way to compensating for the trek across town, although business travellers would do well to check out the Courtyard by Marriott (885 2222). Positioned in the Green Community, its location is handy for those sealing deals over at Media City.
Babysitting. Bars. Beauty salon. Business services. Concierge. Gym. Internet (dataport). Minibar. Parking. Pools. Restaurants. Room service (24 hr). Telephone. TV (satellite).

Park Hyatt Dubai
Dubai Creek Golf & Yacht Club (602 1234/www. dubai.park.hyatt.com). **Rates** Dhs1,200-Dhs2,160 double. **Credit** AmEx, MC, V. **Map** p329 K3 ㉑
Too good to leave only to golfers, this is also the destination hotel of choice for fashionistas; it's rumoured that Elle Macpherson, Tommy Hilfiger, Giorgio Armani and Diane von Furstenberg have all stayed at this drop-dead gorgeous hotel. The Park Hyatt oozes calm and luxury – from its white Moroccan low-rise architecture to the tasteful modern interior – and is one of the best hotels in the city for high-flying business travellers who won't miss the lack of a beach. The bedrooms are minimal but inviting and all boast designer bathrooms. The great setting means you can take a stroll along the Creek and lust after the boats moored at the

New openings

More than six million people visited Dubai in 2006, and the government's target is to up the figure to 15 million by 2012. To cope with the influx, an abundance of new five-star hotels are due to open before the end of 2009, including a new **InterContinental** (www.ichotelsgroup.com) and **Crowne Plaza** (www.dubaihotels. crowneplaza.com), a second **One&Only** and the emirate's first **W**, **Four Seasons** and **Raffles** (www.dubai.raffles.com) hotels.

Fashion heavyweights **Armani** and **Versace** are also getting in on the hotel act. Armani's first slumber station (www. armanihotels.com) is due to open in 2008 inside the world's tallest building – the Burj Dubai. Nearby, a new Sofitel hotel called the **Palace**, will open before the end of 2007. Meanwhile the Versace brand's second hotel venture – the 215 room **Palazzo Versace** (www.palazzoversace. com) – will open on Dubai Creek.

Elsewhere, Donald Trump – New York's infamous property magnate – is so entranced by the emirate that he is developing a 48-storey, gold tulip-shaped hotel and apartment block on the Palm Jumeriah, while the Hard Rock group is rumoured to be planning a hotel to go with their restaurant. Simon Woodroffe, the creator of Yo! Sushi, has plans for a **Yotel**; its Japanese-style capsule rooms should provide a very different take on business hotels.

In the long-term, there's **Hydropolis** (see p27) – the much-hyped underwater hotel which promises guests the chance to 'sleep with the fishes' – and the Dhs100 billion Las Vegas-style **Bawadi** project to look forward to. The latter is to be constructed over eight years on a six-mile stretch of desert and will have 35 hotels as well as 500 restaurants and 100 theatres. Among the hotels will be the five star **Al Maghreb Resort & Spa**, with its Moroccan-themed restaurants and spa.

marina. Facilities include a 25m (82ft) pool, an exclusive gym and one of the best spas in town, with treatment rooms that lead onto courtyards with outdoor rain showers.
Bars. Business centre. Concierge. Gym. Internet (dataport). Limousine service. Minibar. No-smoking rooms. Parking. Pools. Restaurants. Room service (24hr). Spa. Telephone. Turndown. TV (satellite).

Sheraton Dubai Creek
Baniyas Road (228 1111/www.sheraton.com/dubai). **Rates** Dhs1,100-Dhs1,980 double. **Credit** AmEx, MC, V. **Map** p331 K4 ㉒
Stunning from the outside, with its tower and thrusting waterfront extension, the Sheraton is slick but straightforward businesslike within. A huge escalator leads the way up to the dimly lit foyer, where a number of restaurants are located. There are numerous room options, some with amazing Creek views (for which you pay extra). Rooms are comfortable, and while they don't exactly ooze character you can cheer yourself with the fact that they're excellent value for money. The key advantage for the more adventurous tourist is the hotel's location – although the Sheraton is far from the beach, it is a short skip away from the likes of the abra station and gold and spice souk.
Babysitting. Bars. Beauty salon. Business services. Concierge. Gym. Internet (dataport) access. Limousine service. Minibar. No-smoking rooms. Parking. Pools. Restaurants. Room service (24hr). Telephone. Turndown. TV (satellite).

Taj Palace Hotel
Between Al Maktoum Street & Al Rigga Road (223 2222/www.tajpalacedubai.ae). **Rates** Dhs1,000-Dhs1,560 double. **Credit** AmEx, MC, V. **Map** p331 L3 ㉓
A haven of extravagance in downtown Deira, the Taj Palace Hotel is a grand mass of glass and steel. Decked out with regal curtains, plush sofas and deep carpets, it is keen to uphold traditional Arabian ideals, and as such no women work past 11pm and it's one of only two top-end hotels in the city not to serve alcohol. These values have made the Taj hugely popular with visitors from Gulf countries, and in particular Saudi Arabian businessmen. The rooms are unusually large – and we mean large – combining wooden floors and stylish furnishings to comforting effect. Health facilities are unisex, and the rooftop pool and tranquil and stylish Ayoma Spa are deservedly popular. It's an excellent option for those who are happy to forego location and a glass of wine with dinner. And if you do decide to dine in, try the hotel's Indian restaurant, Handi.
Babysitting. Beauty salon. Business services. Concierge. Gym. Internet (dataport). Limousine service. No-smoking rooms. Parking. Pools. Restaurants. Room service (24hr). Telephone. Turndown. TV (satellite).

Moderate

Coral Deira
Al Muraqqabat Road (224 8587/www.coral-deira.com). **Rates** Dhs700-Dhs1,000 double. **Credit** AmEx, MC, V. **Map** p331 L3 ㉔
Amid Deira's bustle lies the Coral hotel. A short drive from the airport, it dominates Al Muraqqabat Road and is one of only two five-star hotels in Dubai that doesn't serve alcohol (the Taj Palace being the

Le Meridien Dubai, housed in Le Meridien Village, comes alive at night.

other). As such, the Coral is popular with visitors from the Gulf countries, particularly businessmen from Saudi Arabia. Get past the unconvincing exterior purple lights and the hotel is relatively stylish in appearance and warm in atmosphere. Modern-day comforts include Villeroy & Boch bathrooms with elongated tubs, while excellent business facilities include two conference rooms and a well-equipped business centre. There's even a florist on site. The courtesy coach service and travel reservations are handy if you're pressed for time. *Babysitting. Beauty salon. Business services. Concierge. Gym. Hairdressing salon. Internet (dataport). Limousine service. No-smoking rooms. Parking. Pools. Restaurants. Room service (24hr). Telephone. Turndown. TV (satellite).*

Le Meridien Dubai
Airport Road, Garhoud (282 4040/www.lemeridien. com). **Rates** Dhs720-Dhs1,260 double. **Credit** AmEx, MC, V. **Map** p329 L2 ㉕
A large, low-lying, two-storey hotel situated near the airport, but away from the flight path, the Meridien caters mainly to shotgun visitors in Dubai for a quick shop or on an en-route layover. Rooms could be described as 'grandma chic', with dated decor and ageing white sofas. However, peer through the nets and you'll be greeted with some surprisingly pleasant views of the gardens and pool area; add the health club, terrace balcony rooms and swim-up bar, and this hotel is a popular choice with older

American and European tourists and businessmen. The grounds house Le Meridien Village, a culinary tour de force with a throng of eateries set in their own walkwayed gardens. The place comes alive at night, with people eating and drinking alfresco into the early hours. The steep room rates are a turn-off, although depending on the month of your visit, you might be able to secure yourself a special deal. *Babysitting. Bars. Beauty salon. Business services. Concierge. Garden. Gym. Internet (dataport). Limousine service. Minibar. No-smoking rooms. Parking. Pools. Restaurants. Room service (24hr). Telephone. Turndown. TV(satellite).*

Marco Polo Hotel
Off Al Muteena Street (272 0000/www.marcopolo hotel.net). **Rates** Dhs500-Dhs1,200 double. **Credit** AmEx, MC, V. **Map** p331 K2/L2 ㉖
This homely hotel has 126 rooms that are due a sprucing up. The Marco Polo does, however, boast a smattering of decent dining options, including one of the city's finest Indian restaurants, and a swimming pool and gym, which are much better than many in this range. While there is nothing particularly distinguishing about this hotel, it's nevertheless a relaxed place with no pretensions. For a four-star hotel, we can't help feeling the Polo is a tad overpriced, but consistently high occupancy rates mean they must be doing something right. *Ballroom. Business centre. Cable TV. Minibar. Nightclub. Reception (24hr). Restaurants.*

Desert resorts

If you have the time and money, a stay at one of Dubai's sublime desert hotels is a must.

Al Maha Desert Resort & Spa

Part of the Dubai Desert Conservation Reserve, Al Maha Desert Resort & Spa opened with the mission statement that 'the United Arab Emirates' rich natural heritage must be protected and conservation made a priority.' Up went a perimeter fence around 225sq km (87sq miles) of desert, ringing in and protecting the natural wildlife and shutting out dune-bashers and construction firms. Bordered only by Fossil Rock, Jebel Rawdah and a handful of camel farms, this isolated spot is the single largest conservation area in the country.

Go to this luxurious eco-resort – which is run by Emirates Holidays – and expect to be greeted by a boisterous desert guide, who will be your personal host during your stay – there to answer any questions you might have about flora, fauna and wildlife while also arranging desert jaunts. Next you'll be golf-buggied over to your standalone

Jumeirah Bab Al Shams.

tent-roofed suites; all of which have chilled private pools and unrivalled views of dunes dotted with the white oryx antelope, which the hotel is named after. This is the true delight of Al Maha – the opportunity to get a personalised experience of Arabian nature, and with only 40 suites and two royal suites available at any one time (private vehicles, visitors and children aren't allowed), privacy is at a premium.

Early birds can wake at 5am for coffee and muffins in the library, before being driven out into the heart of the dunes as the sun rises to uncover the secrets of the desert. The sands are surprisingly fertile: patches of dune grass spring up overnight if there's the slightest whiff of water in the air, and the reddish desert is a world apart from the spoilt sands closer to town. For those looking to restore body and soul, the Jamilah Spa is on hand for all your pampering needs. Whatever you do, don't forget to book in for the sunset camel ride, a deservedly popular 20-minute trip into the gathering dark. *Between Dubai & Al Ain (303 4222/ www.al-maha.com).* **Rates** for a Bedouin suite start at Dhs5,885 – inclusive of three meals and two activities.

Jumeirah Bab Al Shams Desert Resort & Spa

A cheaper but less exclusive alternative to Al Maha, Bab Al Shams is a luxury hotel in the middle of the dunes. This grid of low-rise buildings made from pre-scratched, crumbling mock-sandstone is filled with hidden corridors and secret stairwells: rooms open directly onto the sands, while a swimming pool, spa and four restaurants cater to guests' needs. The range of activities isn't as extensive as at Al Maha (and mainly revolves around desert excursions), but there is a well-equipped children's centre, which should keep your ankle-biters entertained. At night, enjoy a sunset shisha at Al Sarab bar or try out the Al Hadheerah desert restaurant, which offers a Disneyfied Arabian experience complete with belly dancer, band and some fairly potent shisha. *(832 6699/www.jumeirahbabalshams.com).* **Rates** double rooms start from around Dhs1,800 per night.

Sit back with a drink in the **Metropolitan Deira Hotel** – a calm retreat in hectic Deira.

Metropolitan Deira Hotel

Dubai Clock Tower Roundabout (295 9171/
www.habtoorhotels.com). Rates Dhs850-Dhs1,000
double. **Credit** AmEx, MC, V. **Map** p331 L3 ㉗
This mid-market hotel was built back in 1998 and
despite occupying a central position in busy downtown Deira, an air of calm and peace prevails inside.
The hotel is a little past its sell-by-date, though; the
lobby has recently been refurbished yet still looks
as though it is desperately in need of a facelift.
Meanwhile, the rooms may be comfortable and
clean, but they're also slightly tired, while the
rooftop swimming pool is somewhat shabby. Other
facilities include a gym and a few restaurants. The
Metropolitan's main draw card is its location;
adjacent to the famous Clock Tower Roundabout,
it's close to the Creek, corniche and Deira City Centre
shopping mall. The hotel offers a daily complimentary shuttle bus service to the latter as well as to the
Habtoor Grand Resort & Spa (*see p62*), where guests
get to use the beach facilities at a discounted rate.
All in all, the Metropolitan Hotel is nothing to write
home about, but while you won't come away wowed,
neither should you come away broke.
Bar. Beauty salon. Business centre. Gym. Internet.
Laundry service. Minibar. Pool. Restaurants. Room
service (24 hr). Telephone.

Millennium Airport Hotel

Casablanca Road, Garhoud (282 3464/www.
millenniumhotels.com). Rates Dhs840-Dhs1,100
double. **Credit** AmEx, MC, V. **Map** p329 K2 ㉘

As you'd expect from the name, this comfortable
crash pad is within spitting distance of Dubai's main
airport terminal and attracts a great deal of fleeting
business from European suits and airline crew.
Kenny G muzak aside, the marble-heavy hotel foyer
is elegant and inviting, while the large swimming
pool and banks of green grass make it a low-key
family favourite. Rooms are large (a twin share
could easily sleep four adults), airy and have pleasant garden views. Wardrobe space and beds are
both ample, while a subtle Arabic touch runs
throughout the decor and furnishings. The hourly
airport bus service makes it an obvious choice for
business travellers, but leisure visitors will also find
the hotel a perfectly comfortable place at which to
stay – although it's a long way from the beach.
Babysitting. Bars. Beauty salon. Business services.
Concierge. Internet (dataport). Minibar. No-smoking
rooms. Parking. Pool. Restaurants. Room service
(24hr). Telephone. Turndown. TV (satellite).

Radisson SAS Hotel, Dubai Deira Creek

Baniyas Road (222 7171/www.radissonsas.com).
Rates Dhs720-Dhs1,860 double. **Credit** AmEx,
MC, V. **Map** p331 J3 ㉙
Almost as old as the UAE itself, this 1970s mono-
lith was Dubai's first five-star and is the grand-
daddy of the hotel scene. While impeccable service,
brilliant restaurants and interesting decor still
make the Radisson SAS (formerly known as the
InterContinental) a fine place to stay, you can't

escape the feeling that time has taken its toll. On the plus side, recent renovations have updated the place a little and the furnishings, although plain, are very tasteful. Views are of either the large hotel pool or the majestic Creek, and are stunning regardless of the way your window faces. The black marble-walled executive club is a little cold, but is a popular spot for businessmen to sit and take in the colourful corniche views. It's a fair option for travellers who want to experience the city rather than baste themselves on the beach, but the Radisson is no longer the leading light it once was.

Babysitting. Bars. Beauty salon. Business services. Concierge. Gym. Internet (dataport). Limousine service. Minibar. No-smoking rooms. Parking. Pool. Restaurants. Room service (24hr). Telephone. Turndown. TV (satellite).

Renaissance Dubai Hotel
Salah Al Din Road (262 5555/www.marriott.com). **Rates** Dhs960-Dhs1,740 double. **Credit** AmEx, MC, V. **Map** p329 K1

The Renaissance, owned by the Marriott Group, is a relatively luxurious hotel in a downtrodden part of town. The rooms are a tad old-fashioned but comfortable, but the suites leave a little to be desired. Although the hotel is pleasant, its location lends itself more to business travellers than visitors in search of sun and sand. However, Deira is an interesting location for those after more than a tan, as the spice, textile and gold souks are all nearby. The facilities here are modern and in good condition, but the rates are quite expensive for this part of town, considering the few facilities on offer.

Babysitting. Bars. Beauty salon. Business services. Concierge. Gym. Internet (dataport). Limousine service. Minibar. No-smoking rooms. Parking. Pools. Restaurants. Room service (24hr). Telephone. Turndown. TV (satellite).

Al Sondos Suites by Le Meridien
Opposite Deira City Centre mall (294 9797). **Rates** Dhs780-Dhs1,200 double. **Credit** AmEx, MC, V. **Map** p329 K2

These pleasant suites combine self-catering convenience with five-star service, making the place popular with long-term guests. Handily located opposite the City Centre mall and a short hop from the Creek, Al Sondos will satisfy businessmen, although it is not really suited to the tourist trade. Getting a taxi can be difficult and you're some way from the beach. There's an impressive burnt-orange lobby and the tiled rooms are clean, spacious and stylishly comfortable. Facilities include daily shoe-shining, turn-down services and high-speed internet facilities.

Beauty salon. Business centre. Doctors. Gym. Housekeeping. Internet. Laundry. Phone. Restaurant. Room service (24hr). Swimming pool. Telephone. Turndown. TV (satellite).

Sun & Sand Hotel
Near Dubai Clock Tower, off Maktoum Road (223 9000). **Rates** Dhs700-Dhs1,200 double. **Credit** AmEx, MC, V. **Map** p331 L3

Radisson SAS Hotel. *See p55.*

One of the better options in this neck of the woods, the small, reasonably well-equipped Sun & Sand Hotel includes a pool, gym and shuttle services to the shopping malls, airport and beach. Don't be fooled by the hotel's name, because you're some way from the shore, although you can always soak up the rays of the sun by the hotel's rooftop pool. The decor is somewhat dated – think gilt-edged sofas and chairs and marble floors – but amenities are fairly good and the staff are friendly.

Airport pick-up. Babysitting. Business Services. Café (24hr). Fitness centre. Health spa. Internet (dataport). Laundry services. Minibar. Porter service (24hr). Reception (24hr). Room service (24hr). Swimming pool. Telephone. Turndown. TV (satellite).

Budget

Dubai Youth Hostel
Ousais Road, near Al Mulla Plaza (298 8161/ www.uaeyha.com). **Rates** Dhs170-Dhs200 double. **Credit** AmEx, MC, V.

More of an upmarket boarding house than a hostel, Dubai Youth Hostel is deservedly popular. Dormitories are offered alongside spruce, well-maintained family rooms for travellers with kids,

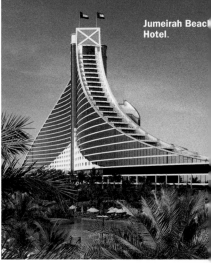
Jumeirah Beach Hotel.

while the new wing has single and double rooms. Facilities are good for a hostel – a pool and gym are juxtaposed alongside a Jacuzzi, spa, sauna and tennis court. But bear in mind, that Dubai Youth Hostel is a little way from the action, and any dirhams saved on accommodation could quite easily be spent on taxi fares. Make sure you book well in advance and if you've youth hostel membership, you can get a discount.
Gym. Housekeeping. Laundry. Restaurant. Swimming pool. Telephone. TV

Al Mamzar Apartments
Sharjah border (297 2921). **Rates** Dhs250-Dhs500 double. **Credit** AmEx, MC, V.
This complex boasts modest but fully furnished apartments, plus a swimming pool and gym that can be used for a small surplus charge. Although slightly away from the town centre, its location is within easy reach of the delightfully peaceful Al Mamzar beach; unlike the calm Jumeirah waters, they have waves perfectly suited to bodysurfing and boast far fewer tourists.
Air conditioning. Gym. Housekeeping. Room service (24hr). Swimming pool. Telephone. TV.

Nihal Hotel
Near Clock Tower Roundabout (295 7666/ www.nihalhoteldubai.com). **Rates** Dhs400-Dhs750 double. **Credit** MC, V. **Map** p331 L3 ③③
This three-star cube-shaped hotel is well positioned in the heart of Deira, making it a good choice when it comes to shopping and checking out Dubai's heritage areas. It's not the most impressive hotel in the looks department, but at these prices you can't complain. Although the rooms are basic and there's certainly nothing lavish about the bathrooms, they're reasonably clean and comfortable and possess more character than most in this price bracket (although watch out for the plastic covering on the bed headboards). The pool is small and an odd shape – forget any thoughts of doing laps and lengths – but at least it's there, alongside dilapidated sun loungers. If you're serious about swimming and soaking up the sun's rays, take advantage of the complimentary shuttle service to Al Mamzar beach park – quite possibly Dubai's best public beach.
Airport transfers. Jacuzzi. Laundry services. Minibar. No-smoking rooms. Parking. Pool. Restaurants. Room service (24h). Shuttle service to beach & shopping malls. Telephone. TV.

Jumeirah

Luxury

Dar Al Masyaf
Al Sufouh Road (366 8888/www.madinatjumeirah. com). **Rates** Dhs3,160-Dhs3,790 double. **Credit** AmEx, DC, MC, V. **Map** p336 D2 ③④
These exclusive summerhouses, which include seven royal villas named after the seven emirates, offer the best of both worlds. You get the privacy

of secluded surroundings as well as access to the rest of the Madinat's extensive facilities. With one pool to every three villas and a 24hr butler service, the palatial villas are wonderfully indulgent. Assuming you can stretch to the hefty price tag, the two-storeyed quarters with their lush, intimate settings and intricately landscaped gardens will excite even the most blasé of holidaymakers.
Babysitting. Bars. Beach. Beauty salon. Boutiques. Business services. Concierge. Internet (dataport). Gym. Limousine service. Minibar. No-smoking rooms. Parking. Pools. Restaurants. Room service (24hr). Spa. Telephone. Turndown. TV (satellite). Water sports.

Jumeirah Beach Hotel
Jumeirah Beach Road (348 0000/www.jumeirah beachhotel.com). **Rates** Dhs2,100-Dhs3,600 double. **Credit** AmEx, MC, V. **Map** p336 E1 ③⑤
A Dubai landmark, the wave-shaped Jumeirah Beach Hotel is the city's best-known piece of architecture after the Burj Al Arab. For all its outer grandeur, however, it's a down-to-earth hotel patronised in the main by young European families in search of a spot of winter sun. In the shadow of its arching blue glass walls there's a decent children's club and a family adventure playground; just across the road lies the Wild Wadi flume park (*see p188*), home to aquatic tomfoolery on an epic scale. The hotel's beach hosts Beit Al Bahar, a series of luxury villas that offer an idyllic Gulf-side retreat, overlooked by the towering hulk of the Burj. Whether you choose to stay in the spacious, colourful rooms of the main hotel or in the refined chic of Beit Al Bahar, you'd be crazy not to tool up at the hotel's dive centre and pay a visit to the man-made coral reef just off shore.
Babysitting. Bars. Beauty salon. Business services. Concierge. Gym. Internet (dataport). Limousine service. Minibar. No-smoking rooms. Parking. Pools. Restaurants. Room service (24hr). Telephone. Turndown. TV (satellite).

Mina A'Salam

*Al Sufouh Road (366 8888/www.madinatjumeirah.
com).* **Rates** Dhs1,800-Dhs2,900 double. **Credit**
AmEx, MC, V. **Map** p336 E1 ③⑥

The Mina was the first hotel completed as part of
the Madinat Jumeirah resort. Built around 3km (2
miles) of Venetian-style waterways filled with
abras that ferry guests around the resort, the Mina
has a more laid-back look than its neighbour – the
iconic Burj – and successfully marries Dubai's
modern-day opulence with its old-world architecture. The sand-coloured buildings are topped with
legions of wind towers and the interior is palatial.
Each of the 292 sea-facing rooms at this 'harbour
of peace' are styled in keeping with the Arabian
theme: heavy studded doors give way to Moorish
arches hung with ornate lanterns, and the beds are
piled high with exotic dark blue, red and gold fabrics. The real hooks, however, are the large terraces
jutting out towards the water, ideal for sitting and
sipping a leisurely drink as the sun goes down.
With walkways along the harbour, alfresco restaurant terraces, the extremely convivial Bahri Bar
and a souk full of lavish boutiques, Mina has a distinctly villagey feel to it – albeit a village full of the
obscenely affluent.

*Babysitting. Bars. Beauty salon. Business services.
Concierge. Garden. Gym. Internet (dataport).
Limousine service. Minibar. No-smoking rooms.
Parking. Pools. Restaurants. Room service (24hr).
Telephone. Turndown. TV (satellite).*

Al Qasr

*Al Sufouh Road (366 8888/www.madinatjumeirah.
com).* **Rates** Dhs1,800-Dhs3,480 double. **Credit**
AmEx, MC, V. **Map** p336 D1 ③⑦

More stately and ostentatious than its sister, Mina
A'Salam (*see above*), Al Qasr was designed to
reflect the royal summer residence while providing
the 'jewel in the crown' of the Madinat resort. It's
certainly grandiose; the huge lobby with Arabian
lanterns and plump cushions leads to an opulent
cigar lounge, continuing the theme of the Mina
A'Salam, although the bedrooms here are larger
than those in its sister hotel. What makes Al Qasr
stand out, however, is its 24-hour butler service (not
quite the Burj – here you have to share your Jeeves
with 11 other rooms), its 2km of private beach and
its proximity to the Talise Spa (*see p248*), one of
the most sensational spas in the Gulf. There are
club executive (kid-free) lounges and a kids' club
as well as a separate pool, so although Al Qasr is
family friendly, you can also have an adults-only
break without much intrusion. Transportation
through the immense resort is through both water
taxis and golf buggies.

*Babysitting. Bars. Beach. Beauty salon. Boutiques.
Business services. Concierge. Gym. Internet
(dataport). Limousine service. Minibar. No-smoking
rooms. Parking. Pools. Restaurants. Room service
(24hr). Spa. Telephone. Turndown. TV (satellite).
Water sports.*

The Palm islands

When it comes to hotel rooms, demand
greatly outstrips supply in Dubai. So, in
this sense, it's a good thing that the sea
is rapidly being colonised to allow for a
glut of new hotels and resorts. The Palm
Jumeirah – one of the three largest
man-made islands in the world, under
construction off Dubai's coast – is set
to become a major tourism hotspot with
around 25 beachfront hotels opening
over the coming years.

Right now the hype is all about the
Trump International Hotel & Tower
(the centrepiece of the island, due for
completion in 2009), and the 1,539
room ocean-themed **Atlantis**. However,
other hotels to take up a tenancy include
the **Taj Exotica Resort & Spa**, which will
boast the biggest spa in the world, the
Fairmont Palm Hotel & Resort and the
Kempinski Hotel Emerald Palace Dubai.
With enough rooms for about 25,000
hotel guests or one million visitors a year,
the arrival of these Palm pads could and
should go a long way to help meet Dubai's
desperate need for more hotel rooms.
Check out www.thepalm.ae for the latest
developments on the Palm project.

Expensive

Dubai Marine Beach Resort & Spa

*Jumeirah Beach Road (346 1111/www.dxbmarine.
com).* **Rates** Dhs1,450-Dhs2,000 double. **Credit**
AmEx, MC, V. **Map** p332 D9 ③⑧

Situated at the beginning of the Jumeirah Beach
Road in the built-up area of Jumeirah, the Dubai
Marine Beach Resort & Spa is the beachfront hotel
closest to the action. The resort's great location,
small but attractive beach, lush gardens and two
swimming pools make it an ideal leisure venue,
while its proximity to the city gives it the edge for

Experience the serenity, discover the desert

This 'Gateway to the Sun' is a magical Resort far removed from the ordinary and every day, where history walks hand in hand with tomorrow's dreams. Let this desert oasis retreat comprising 115 rooms and suites offer you the luxuries that benefited the noblemen of a bygone era. The dining experience at Bab Al Shams Desert Resort & Spa reflects world-class standards in both cuisine and service, complimented by culturally rich Arabic festive entertainment.

BAB AL SHAMS
DESERT RESORT & SPA

Tel. +971 4 832 6699, Fax: +971 4 832 6698, e-mail: JBASinfo@jumeirah.com or visit us at Jumeirah.com

Life's a beach and then you fry, at **Dubai Marine Beach Resort & Spa**. *See p59*.

beach-loving business travellers. Accommodation is scattered in 33 low-rise villa-style buildings spread throughout the resort, with each villa containing only six suites. The quiet, green gardens and a sun-drenched stretch of sand make Dubai Marine a perfect chill-out spot; if you do want to get active there are tennis courts on site. While the rooms themselves could do with a facelift, the complex as a whole is a great place to relax before hitting the onsite buzzing bars (try Sho Cho, *see p135*) and restaurants when night falls.
Babysitting. Bars. Beauty salon. Business services. Garden. Gym. Internet (dataport). Limousine service. Minibar. No-smoking rooms. Parking. Pools. Restaurants. Room service (24hr). Spa. Telephone. Turndown. TV (satellite).

The Marina

Luxury

Le Royal Meridien
Al Sufouh Road (399 5555/www.leroyalmeridien-dubai.com). **Rates** Dhs1,500-Dhs3,000 double. **Credit** AmEx, MC, V. **Map** p336 B1 ⑲
Roses are a big deal at Le Royal Meridien. In the rooms are finger bowls of water topped with petals in which to dip the digits; rose residue scatters the bed, and the bathroom has more blooms than a florist on 13 February. Such in-your-face opulence is typical of Le Royal Meridien, and the pools, gardens and

great stretch of sand have been sculpted in a timelessly classic style. All of the rooms are sea facing, large, bright and comfortable, with balconies from which to enjoy the view down the beach or over the Gulf. Sexy European clients flitter around the upmarket all-beige coffee spaces and bars, and it is doubtful that the pool has seen a full swimsuit since the place opened. For more decadence, head over to the lovely Caracalla spa (*see p244*).
Babysitting. Bars. Beauty salon. Business services. Concierge. Garden. Gym. Internet (dataport). Limousine service. Minibar. No-smoking rooms. Parking. Pools. Restaurants. Room service (24hr). Spa. Telephone. Turndown. TV (satellite).

One&Only Royal Mirage
Al Sufouh Road (399 9999/www.oneandonlyresorts.com). **Rates** Dhs1,750-Dhs2,400 double. **Credit** AmEx, MC, V. **Map** p336 C1 ⑳
Styled on an Arabian fort, the Royal Mirage is still Dubai's most romantic resort, despite some stiff competition from Madinat Jumeirah. It's composed of three hotels: the Palace, the Arabian Court and the Residence, each one plusher and more expensive than the last. While many of Dubai's landmarks owe their success to a degree of shock and awe, the Royal Mirage presents an illusion of days gone by with welcome subtlety. The complex's simple low-rise architecture holds sumptuous interiors of rich fabrics and intricate woodwork. Iron lanterns throw patterned candlelight onto sand

coloured walls, and pockets of rooms are interspersed with Moorish arches and verdant gardens. Add the delicate use of gold and warm tones throughout, and the scene is set for the ultimate romantic getaway. The hotel is never more beautiful than at night, when couples emerge to take quiet strolls down past the pool and on to the beach before ending the night up on the Roof Top (*see p136*) for drinks. Deluxe rooms are sensibly sized and packed with wonderful examples of attention to detail, from the slippers by the bed to the hand towel artfully folded into the shape of a swan. Every inch of the Royal Mirage seems designed to make you feel good about life; we'd happily hole up here permanently (budget permitting, of course).

Babysitting. Bars. Beauty salon. Business services. Garden. Gym. Internet (dataport). Limousine service. Minibar. No-smoking rooms. Parking. Pools. Restaurants. Room service (24hr). Spa. Telephone. Turndown. TV (satellite).

Ritz-Carlton Dubai

Al Sufouh Road (399 4000/www.ritzcarlton.com). **Rates** Dhs2,150-Dhs3,500 double. **Credit** AmEx, MC, V. **Map** p336 B1 ④

The most classically stylish of Dubai's hotels, the Ritz-Carlton is immaculately presented with a grand marble lobby and gigantic windows offering uninterrupted views of white sands and the lapping Gulf. Too traditional for those who get off on Arabian chic, the hotel is all about formal European luxury. The wooden-beamed tea lounge is a sophisticated stopoff, while the terrace is a delight at sunset. There's a separate adults-only pool offering peace for couples, and even the family dip-pit is large and languid. Most of the generous-sized rooms look out to sea and enjoy private balconies and sumptuous soft furnishings; the bathrooms again are an exercise in comfort, with vast, glass-fronted showers and deep baths to lounge in. For a relaxed stay with some old-world charm, the Ritz ticks all the right boxes. Make sure you visit for afternoon tea and check out the in-house spa that offers both Asian and Arabic-inspired treatments.

Babysitting. Bars. Beauty salon. Business services. Concierge. Garden. Gym. Internet (dataport). Limousine service. Minibar. No-smoking rooms. Parking. Pools. Restaurants. Room service (24hr). Spa. Telephone. Turndown. TV (satellite).

Expensive

Grosvenor House West Marina Beach Dubai

Dubai Marina (399 8888/www.grosvenorhousedubai.com). **Rates** Dhs1,200-Dhs2,520 double. **Credit** AmEx, MC, V. **Map** p336 B1 ④

The lobby to this landmark hotel – the first to open in the Marina – is small and swish, with dozens of staff to greet and direct you. With 45 storeys, you're pretty much guaranteed an excellent view, whether of the sea or the Dubai skyline. Rooms are spacious, furnished using a brown and cream colour palette, and

Self-catering apartments

A cost-effective alternative to staying in a hotel is to rent an apartment, the majority of which tend to be situated in Bur Dubai. The **Golden Sands Hotel Apartment** chain (355 5553) is a reasonable option if you're prepared to do without room service. Offering spacious and fully-serviced self-catering flats from Dhs500 per night, Golden Sands has a range of clean, furnished rooms stretching from one bedroom studios to three and four bedroom apartments. As a rough guide, prices start from around Dhs3,500 per week for a studio in one of the better value apartments, although you should be able to negotiate a better rate if staying for longer than one week. A full list of apartments is available at www.dubaitourism.ae.

come complete with the essential plasma TV. An excellent choice for business travellers, Grosvenor House's rooms have high-speed internet access, and if you want a formal or informal meeting there are plenty of meeting rooms and classy cafés and bars. There's a small spa, and after unwinding you can relax even more by heading up to Bar 44 for an aperitif while watching the sun set over the Gulf. If you want to ensure full holiday bragging rights, the Grosvenor is a good choice; it's not such a good option if you want to walk out of your room and onto the beach. To feel the sand between your toes, guests can take the shuttle to Le Royal Meridien's beach resort (*see p61*).

Babysitting. Beauty salon. Business services. Gym. Internet (dataport). Limousine service. Minibar. No-smoking rooms. Parking. Pools. Restaurants. Room service (24hr). Spa. Telephone. Turndown. TV (satellite).

Habtoor Grand Resort & Spa

Dubai Marina (399 5000/www.grandjumeirah. habtoorhotels.com). **Rates** Dhs1,260-Dhs2,520 double. **Credit** AmEx, MC, V. **Map** p336 B1 ④

The Habtoor serves both beach-bound holidaymakers and business travellers well, but at rather hefty prices. There's an impressive stretch of beach as well as two floodlit tennis courts and a well-equipped gym to work out in. The rooms are quite conservative, but the bathrooms are ornate, decked out in green mosaics and those tiny glass sinks that were fashionable a few years ago. If you fancy some pampering, the Elixir Spa has a good range of treatments on offer. Like most Dubai hotels, the Grand also caters for business travellers and tends to get the

Le Meridien Mina Seyahi Beach Resort & Marina – paradise for sun worshippers.

details right; if you want a fax machine installed in your room, flights booked or travel arrangements confirmed, consider it done.
Babysitting. Beauty salon. Business services. Concierge. Dataport. Gym. Limousine service. Minibar. No-smoking rooms. Parking. Pools. Restaurants. Room service (24hr). Spa. Telephone. Turndown. TV (satellite).

Hilton Dubai Jumeirah
Al Sufouh Road (399 1111/www.hilton.com). **Rates** Dhs1,170-Dhs1,800 double. **Credit** AmEx, MC, V. **Map** p336 B1 ㊹

A classic resort hotel, the Hilton Jumeirah is more package than out-and-out luxury: the decent-sized rooms are comfortable and functional rather than decadent, with cute little balconies affording views of the Gulf. The hotel's large pool has a swim-up bar with underwater stools on which to sit and slurp your cocktail. Pleasant terraced gardens lead down to the white sandy beach where a number of water sports are available, and a decent health club and gym add to the list of facilities on offer. While being family friendly, the hotel is also a great spot for couples, with sophisticated restaurants and pleasant grounds. If you can get a room for the advertised rate or below then you really must: this is a bargain for the beachfront.
Babysitting. Bars. Beauty salon. Business services. Concierge. Gym. Internet (dataport). Limousine service. Minibar. No-smoking rooms. Parking. Pools. Restaurants. Room service (24hr). Telephone. Turndown. TV (satellite).

Le Meridien Mina Seyahi Beach Resort & Marina
Al Sufouh Road (399 3333/www.lemeridien-minaseyahi.com). **Rates** Dhs1,080-Dhs2,280 double. **Credit** AmEx, MC, V. **Map** p336 B1 ㊺

With a gem of a beach for sun worshippers, the Mina retains a casual ambience that's at odds with its rather more formal big brother, Le Royal Meridien (*see p61*). Rooms are simple but comfortable, with beachside balconies overlooking the Palm Jumeirah (request a room with a view when you book). Bathrooms are fairly ordinary but include nice little touches like an in-room radio. It is outside where the Mina really comes into its own. With over 850m (2,800ft) of golden sands, the hotel boasts more beach than any other in Dubai. And it utilises every inch of it with excellent water sport facilities (including a PADI-certified dive centre), a stunning pool area, and one of the best beach bars in Barasti Bar (*see p135*). The children's facilities, including the Penguin Club and dedicated pools, ensure the sprogs don't interfere with tan topping time, while the glass-fronted gym allows you to look out to sea while working out. The hotel was undergoing some fairly major construction work at the time of going to press, but normal service should be resumed by the end of 2008.
Babysitting. Bars. Beauty salon. Business services. Concierge. Garden. Gym. Internet (dataport). Limousine service. Minibar. No-smoking rooms. Parking. Pools. Restaurants. Room service (24hr). Telephone. Turndown. TV (satellite).

Dusit Dubai.

Currently the furthest beach hotel from the city, the Sheraton is a stylish resort with a good stretch of sand, decent beach club, spacious gardens and a fine swimming pool. Popular with European package tourists, the hotel blurs the five star lines with the overall feel more comfortable than lavish. Rooms are large and overlook either the sea and resort area or the rather less pleasing building sites of the developing Dubai Marina and Jumeirah Beach Residence. Still, it's a great-value place for those looking to escape the trappings of inner-city vacations, which is just as well as a taxi ride into town will set you back a fair whack.

Bars. Beauty salon. Business services. Garden. Gym. Internet (dataport). Limousine service. Minibar. No-smoking rooms. Parking. Pools. Restaurants. Room service (24hr). Spa. Telephone. Turndown. TV (satellite).

Oasis Beach Hotel

Al Sufouh Road (399 4444/www.jebelali-international.com). **Rates** Dhs1,050-Dhs2,340 double. **Credit** AmEx, MC, V. **Map** p336 B1 ⑯

The Oasis is the only four-star hotel on the beach (all the others are five-star), but it has two cards up its sleeve: lower prices and one of the best beach clubs in town. These elements are enough to make it fiendishly popular with package holidaymakers looking for a week on the sand. While the public areas are a touch rough and ready, the rooms are surprisingly attractive, decked out with a hint of oriental style. When booking, ask for a shore-side room; the others overlook a noisy and ever-expanding building site. Private balconies offer tropical views over the palms and the pools, with the occasional jet skier cutting up the waves in the mid-distance. Look out for regular price promotions.

Babysitting. Bars. Beauty salon. Business services. Gym. Internet (dataport). Limousine service. Minibar. No-smoking rooms. Parking. Pools. Restaurants. Room service (24hr). Spa. Telephone. Turndown. TV (satellite).

Radisson SAS Hotel, Dubai Media City

Dubai Media City (366 9111/www dubai.radisson sas.com). **Rates** Dhs1,200-Dhs1,500 double. **Credit** AmEx, MC, V. **Map** p336 B2/C2 ⑰

The Radisson is a mid-range hotel that is clearly after business travellers, although it's not that far from the beach or Mall of the Emirates. Room-wise, the decor is modern with dark wood furnishings, and there's a well-equipped gym and a Wellness Centre.

Babysitting. Bars. Beauty salon. Business services. Gym. Internet (dataport). Limousine service. No-smoking rooms. Parking. Pools. Restaurants. Spa. Room service (24hr). Telephone. Turndown. TV (satellite).

Sheraton Jumeirah Beach Resort & Towers

Al Sufouh Road (399 5533/www.starwoodhotels.com). **Rates** Dhs1,260-Dhs2,400 double. **Credit** AmEx, MC, V. **Map** p336 A1 ⑱

Sheikh Zayed Road

Luxury

Kempinski Hotel Mall of the Emirates

Mall of the Emirates, Al Barsha Interchange (341 0000/www.kempinski.com). **Rates** Dhs2,100-Dhs3,200 double. **Credit** AmEx, MC, V. **Map** p336 D2 ⑲

The Kempinski is attached to the biggest shopping mall outside of North America, which is home to the only indoor ski slope in the UAE (*see p235*). So if your idea of a holiday centres on bagging as many designer labels as you can and fitting in a spot of skiing in-between, then the Kempinski is very much the place for you. Once you've shopped till you've dropped, you can take some time out at the hotel's Wellness Centre and spa where the emphasis is on ayurvedic treatments. And if you can't bear to be far from the ski slope for long, you can stay in one of the 15 chalets that overlook the slope. The chalets and hotel rooms come with all

Kempinski Hotel Mall of the Emirates.

mod cons, including flatscreen TVs and DVD players. The decor is homely yet modern and top-class service is guaranteed.
Bars. Beauty salon. Business centre. Concierge. Gym. Internet (dataport). Limousine service. Minibar. No-smoking rooms. Parking. Pools. Restaurants. Room ervice (24hr). Spa. Telephone. Turndown. TV (satellite).

Shangri-La Hotel Dubai

Sheikh Zayed Road (343 8888/www.shangri-la.com). **Rates** Dhs1,740-Dhs1,980 double. **Credit** AmEx, MC, V. **Map** p335 E12/F12 ⑳

The Shangri-La towers above its more established competitors both literally and figuratively. The chic and serene foyer is immaculate and has welcomed many celebrities, and the breathtaking views it offers out over the magnificent structures of Sheikh Zayed Road are incomparable. The stylish, spacious standard rooms impress with their minimalist chic, and the Aigner-equipped bathrooms feature separate tub, shower and toilet spaces. Business facilities are state-of-the-art and secluded, while the suites dazzle with their luxurious fittings and Bang & Olufsen entertainment centres. The hotel also boasts several top eateries, including the wonderful French-Vietnamese restaurant Hoi An and the seafood-heavy fine dining of Amwaj. You'll sleep happily here.
Babysitting. Bars. Beauty salon. Business services. Concierge. Gym. Internet (dataport). Limousine service. Minibar. No-smoking rooms. Parking. Pools. Restaurants. Room service (24hr). Spa. Telephone. Turndown. TV (satellite).

Expensive

Crowne Plaza Hotel Dubai

Satwa side (331 1111/www.ichotels.com). **Rates** Dhs1,100-Dhs2,400 double. **Credit** AmEx, MC, V. **Map** p333 G10 ㉑

This Sheikh Zayed Road stalwart does a nice sideline in the tourist trade. Owing to its prime location at the Creek end of Sheikh Zayed Road, guests are only a short drive from the beach, the malls or indeed from anywhere in the city. The grand lobby area, which is reached via steep and skinny escalators, has aged well on the whole, although the once-swish decor is looking a little tired. Standard rooms are on the small side, while the itsy-bitsy bathrooms are dated. The views, however, are as good as any in Dubai. It's the range of facilities that keep business and leisure tourists alike loyal to the Crowne Plaza. Both the health club and pool are spacious and casual, and the club floor features an executive lounge allowing VIP visitors to eat away from the chattering masses.
Babysitting. Bars. Beauty salon. Business services. Concierge. Gym. Internet (dataport). Limousine service. Minibar. No-smoking rooms. Parking. Pools. Restaurants. Room service (24hr). Telephone. Turndown. TV (satellite).

Dusit Dubai

Trade Centre side (343 3333/www.dubai.dusit.com). **Rates** Dhs1,200-Dhs2,400 double. **Credit** AmEx, MC, V. **Map** p335 F12 ㉒

One of the most striking buildings on the street, the Dusit is a bow-legged colossus of glass and steel. Its Thai-style decor is evident throughout, from the Asian-chic rooms to the smart sarong-wearing staff. Rooms are lovely, with rich browns and sweeping views. Guests can work out in the well-stocked gym with its bird's-eye city views or laze in the 36th floor open-air pool, before heading to the mini spa to beautify themselves for a night out on the town. This used to be the closest you'd get to a high-class bargain on Sheikh Zayed Road, but prices have risen in recent times.
Babysitting. Bars. Business centre. Gym. Hair salon. Internet (dataport). Limousine service. Minibar. No-smoking rooms. Parking. Pools. Restaurants. Room service (24hr). Telephone. Turndown. TV (satellite).

Fairmont Dubai

Satwa side (332 5555/www.fairmont.com). **Rates** Dhs1,000-Dhs1,800 double. **Credit** AmEx, MC, V. **Map** p333 G9/G10 ㉓

An elegant beast of a hotel, the Fairmont juggles the requirements of both business and leisure guests with some style. Set directly across from the Trade Centre, it has four illuminated turrets that change colour throughout the week and have taken on a unique place in Dubai's cityscape. At the hotel's centre is a massive foyer graced with groovy velvet sofas and a huge atrium, its walls splashed with every tone of colour to head-spinning effect. Bedrooms are spacious, with large beds, huge windows and well-chosen furnishings – although again they suffer from the 'more is more' approach to colour. The minimalist bathrooms, though large, will seem sterile by comparison. A keen eye for detail is evident in the two pool areas on either side of the building – the sunset and sunrise decks – decorated with pretty mosaics to reflect their respective themes. There's an impressive health club, plus the first-rate Willow Stream Spa (*see p249*). Since the hotel is situated as close to town as the Sheikh Zayed Road will allow, its lively restaurants – especially the superb Exchange Grill (*see p131*) – pick up a lot of local trade.
Babysitting. Bars. Beauty salon. Business services. Gym. Internet (dataport). Limousine service. Minibar. No-smoking rooms. Parking. Pools. Restaurants. Room service (24hr). Telephone. Turndown. TV (satellite).

Jumeirah Emirates Towers

Trade Centre side (330 0000/www.jumeirah.com). **Rates** Dhs1,000-Dhs3,000 double. **Credit** AmEx, MC, V. **Map** p328 H4 ㉔

The third Dubaian landmark (although some way behind the Burj and the Jumeirah Beach Hotel in the postcard stakes), Emirates Towers dominated Sheikh Zayed Road's skyline until the arrival of the Burj Dubai. Occupying the taller of the two towers

Jumeirah Emirates Towers. *See p65.*

Budget beds

While Dubai has developed a reputation for its glitzy, luxury hotel developments, what it hasn't had – until now – is bijou accommodation on a budget. But change, it seems, is afoot. Leisure group Whitbread recently announced a franchise deal to take its Premier Travel Inn chain to Dubai, while **Rotana Hotels** has unveiled a new brand, **Centro**, aimed at the budget-conscious business traveller – the first two hotels will open in 2008.

Centro is a departure from the group's Rotana Hotels, Rotana Resorts and Rotana Suites brands, which are predominantly five star. The new brand will offer three star and above hotels in the Middle East, starting with two in Dubai in 2008.

Meanwhile, irrepressible entrepreneur Stelios Haji-Ioannou – the man who revolutionised air travel in Europe – is bringing over **EasyHotel**. From pizzas to insurance and men's toiletries to mobile phones, his range of products has grown in every direction, and he is now set to make his mark on Dubai's hotel industry. His tangerine-tinted low cost hotel accommodation is due to hit Karama in early 2008. As yet, pricing hasn't been confirmed, although insiders anticipate that rooms will start somewhere in the region of Dhs250-300 per night. Another chain planning to deliver budget accommodation to Dubai is **Holiday Inn**, which plans to open several of its Express hotels here over the coming years.

(the other being the most desirable office block in town), the hotel is geared principally to work trippers and is arguably the best business hotel in the Middle East. A sophisticated lobby lounge – a top people-watching spot – and acres of atrium dominate the ground floor, while the glass lifts that shoot up and down the 52 storeys are a vertigo-inducing delight. Rooms are sizeable, with attractive dark wood tables, bright soft furnishings, and panoramas that would blow the socks off the most seasoned of travellers. Despite being business focused, the Towers does boast its own large swimming pool, spa, complimentary shuttle and entry to Wild Wadi water park (*see p188*).
Babysitting. Bars. Beauty salon. Business services. Gym. Internet dataport. Limousine service. Minibar. No-smoking rooms. Parking. Pools. Restaurants. Room service (24hr). Telephone. Turndown. TV (satellite).

Al Manzil Hotel
Burj Dubai Boulevard (428 5888/www.almanzil hotel.com). **Rates** Dhs1,300-Dhs1,500 double. **Credit** AmEx, MC, V. **Map** p335 F14 ⑯
Dubai has an outstanding new four-star hotel in Al Manzil. Although views are currently of a construction site, when the work is completed guests will be treated to vistas of the Burj Dubai – aka the tallest building in the world. The decor of the rooms is contemporary Arabic and all rooms boast a unique – if unusual – open style bathroom with a rainfall shower and gigantic oval-shaped bath in which you can wallow like a hippo and watch a film on the rotating plasma TV. Days can be spent

chilling out by the large, rectangular pool or taking advantage of the complimentary shuttle bus to both the beach and shopping malls. A 50-shop souk and number of restaurants are scheduled to open adjacent to the hotel, which may push the price up, but for now at least this is a gem of a hotel which represents fantastic value for money; no wonder it's already got a loyal following.
Business centre with complimentary internet access. Complimentary in-room internet access. Fitness centre. Flat screen TV. Mini bar. 24hr parking. Restaurants. Room service (24hr). Shuttle service to beach and shopping centres. Swimming pool.

Al Murooj Rotana Hotel & Suites Dubai
Al Saffa Street, off Sheikh Zayed Road (321 1111/ www.almuroojrotanaholeldubai.com). **Rates** Dhs1,300-Dhs2,280 double. **Credit** AmEx, MC, V. **Map** p335 F13 ⑯

Towers Rotana Hotel: stylish, airy and with great views to boot.

Tucked behind the Sheikh Zayed Road and surrounded by a moat-like manmade lake, the Al Murooj Rotana offers the convenience of being close to Dubai's main thoroughfare without the traffic noise. The hotel is in the shadow of the rapidly rising Burj Dubai, but with this privilege sadly comes the ongoing drone of construction work, for the time being anyway. The rooms are comfortable and contemporary, the pool area pleasant, and there's a well-equipped gym and spa at which to purge your sins. The hotel is principally geared towards business travellers, with its excellent meeting and conference facilities, but leisure travellers not excited by the beach should be more than happy. One word of warning: the second floor rooms are near the perenially busy and noisy Double Decker pub (*see p137*), so avoid if you're a light sleeper.
Babysitting. Beauty salon. Business services. Concierge. Dataport. Gym. Limousine service. Minibar. No-smoking rooms. Parking. Pools. Restaurants. Room service (24hr). Spa. Telephone. TV (satellite).

Moderate

Novotel

Behind World Trade Centre (318 7000/www. novotel.com). **Rates** Dhs675-Dhs725 double. **Credit** AmEx, MC, V. **Map** p333 G10 ⑰
Built to house the World Bank and IMF meetings held in Dubai back in 2003, the no nonsense Novotel proves that budget accommodation need not be boring or basic. The lobby – all dark wood, open space and ordered sophistication – is suitably stylish, while rooms, although small, aren't at all cramped. The hotel holds little appeal to sun-seekers, offering only a small pool and gym, but it will score highly with businesspeople and those operating along Sheikh Zayed Road. The central location will also probably save you a bundle on taxi fares.
Bars. Business services. Concierge. Gym. Internet (dataport). Minibar. No-smoking rooms. Parking. Pools. Restaurants. Room service (24hr). Telephone. Turndown. TV (satellite).

Towers Rotana Hotel

Satwa side (343 5111/www.rotana.com). **Rates** Dhs750-Dhs1,400 double. **Credit** AmEx, MC, V. **Map** p335 F12 ㊳
Surrounded by grander, and considerably more expensive five-stars, the Towers Rotana has a minimal design style and a younger clientele than its neighbours. Rooms are average size, but are very comfortable, and the views over Jumeirah will wobble the knees of most tourists. Decor is light and airy in the bedrooms, and there's a large pool space and gym situated in a separate wing of the building. While pitched predominantly at business travellers, the Rotana is seconds away from the nightlife of the Sheikh Zayed strip, although the hotel houses its own popular boozer, Long's Bar, which is busy both at the weekends and during the week. Overall this hotel is a good option for holidaymakers who can't afford the lavishness of Jumeirah, yet want to avoid the congested roads of Deira.
Bars. Beauty salon. Business centre. Gym. Internet. Limousine service. No-smoking rooms. Parking. Pools. Restaurants.

Budget

Ibis World Trade Centre Dubai

Behind World Trade Centre (318 7000/ www.ibis hotel.com). **Rates** Dhs395-Dhs575 double. **Credit** AmEx, MC, V. **Map** p333 G9 ㊴
The ever-popular Ibis is a fuss-free affair; there's no pool and facilities are minimal, but the hotel has invested its time and energy into the fundamentals, developing a sophisticated feel for a three star. The lobby is elegant, simple and dotted with Philippe Starck furniture, although the rooms, at 20sq m (215sq ft), are small – and offer pretty drab glimpses of the Dubai World Trade Centre apartments. Nonetheless, it's a sound choice for the shoestring traveller who has no desire for fancy extras and is fantastic value for money, which is difficult to find in Dubai.
Bars. Internet (dataport). No-smoking rooms. Parking. Restaurants. Telephone. TV (satellite).

The new V8 Vantage now at Al Habtoor Motors, Dubai. Electrifying performance and outstanding agility sprung taut into a truly exhilarating sports car. Its signature 4.3-litre V8 engine churns up 380 bhp of refined power to send this handcrafted beauty racing

V8 Vantage. No flight plans. No control tower. Co-pilot optional.

ASTON MARTIN

Power, Beauty and Soul

up to 280 km/h, in full song. Supreme balance and thoroughly tested safety systems team up with manual gears to make the V8 Vantage a picture of controlled aggression. Come. Hit the new high in driving pleasure.

Sightseeing

Introduction

Often forgotten amid the glitz and glamour of five-star Dubai are the fascinating parts of the city packed with culturally rich hidden gems.

Dubai Creek.

In most cities, sightseeing might involve roaming through an ancient castle, investigating a historical fort, or wandering round galleries and museums. Things are a little different in Dubai. While there's a scattering of historical buildings concentrated in the area by the Creek, most visitors to the emirate focus on touring a series of five-star, record-breaking hotels and their restaurants.

Dubai's main attractions were all built in the last ten years, and, like in Las Vegas, most visitors don't come here to explore historical monuments. Instead, they're here to take advantage of every over-the-top service the emirate is so keen on providing. For visitors in search of glamorous nights out and spectacular meals, finding the perfect venue is simply a matter of picking a five-star hotel, but for those few tourists who'd care to explore Dubai's past, culture and traditions, the search for a 'real' Dubai is a search indeed. With a little forward planning and some perseverance, however, you'll find yourself exploring impressive historical buildings, revelling in the local culture and experiencing the city's many hidden treasures.

GATEWAY TO THE GULF

Dubai sits on the Gulf, a body of water that is key to the city's success today and has been a source of both food and trade for centuries. Historically Dubai was made up of two settlements built on either side of the Creek, a 15-kilometre (9.5-mile) inlet around which the city's trade developed. Deira is a catch-all term for the area to the north of the Creek and Bur Dubai refers to the south. The terms 'Deira side' and 'Bur Dubai side' are still used to differentiate between the areas north and south of the Creek. Further along the coast, Bur Dubai merges with Jumeirah, where residential and tourist developments stretch for some 15 kilometres (9.5 miles) southwards. The recommended sights mentioned in these pages are categorised by these areas.

When petro-dollars began to flow into the emirate in the 1960s, Deira and Bur Dubai developed rapidly, the former becoming the trade centre and the latter the residential area. Today, however, all the major developments in the city (with the exception of Dubai Festival City) are taking place on the Bur Dubai side, with projects such as Dubai Knowledge Village and Dubai Media City springing up alongside Sheikh Zayed Road. This thoroughfare runs from Abu Dhabi, the UAE's capital, to Bur Dubai and feeds Deira with traffic via three bridges: Garhoud Bridge, named after a district, Al Maktoum Bridge, after the ruling family, and the Business Bay Crossing, which opened in 2007. When driving from one end of the city to another, Sheikh Zayed Road is a faster if less scenic option than Jumeirah Beach Road.

GETTING AROUND

Dubai is not yet well served by public transport. The first sectors of the Dubai Metro, which will be the longest fully automated metro system in the world upon its completion, will open in 2009. Until then, options are limited to the city's bus network. The best way to get around the city is by car and, as a result, traffic problems are increasing. Dubai's road network is mostly new and generally easy to navigate, but many additions to the network are under construction, which causes further congestion. *See also p295-298.*

NAVIGATION

Taxis are the best way of getting around if you want to see Dubai's most rewarding sites. The government recently allowed independent companies to set up business in this previously state-run service, and the effect has been a dramatic improvement in quality. Drivers are generally courteous and knowledgeable, and all cars have meters. A growing number of taxis accept credit cards. You should have no problem getting a taxi outside any major hotel, mall or tourist attraction, but you might face problems in more secluded locations or very late at night – call Dubai Transport (208 0808) to book a taxi. For more on taxis, *see p296-297.*

Choosing to drive yourself means dealing with other road users. Drivers used to roads in the Middle East or the Indian subcontinent will find driving in Dubai a breeze, but those arriving from the West will be alarmed by the weaving motorists who drive too fast, then too slow, too close to each other and rarely with the use of indicators. For more on driving, *see pp297-298.*

Dubai's lack of effective street addresses will also become painfully obvious. Residents offer and receive directions according to landmarks such as parks, banks, malls and hotels. It pays to have a well-known spot in mind if you're looking for somewhere off the beaten track. For more on addresses, *see p299.*

LOOKING BEYOND

What Dubai lacks in historical sites it makes up for in character and ambition; in the shadow of proud hotels and office structures nestle heaving

The best Sights

For historic settlements

The oasis town of **Hatta**, deep in the foothills of the Hajar mountains, boasts glorious Arabic architecture and crystal clear rock pools (*see p83*).

For a mosque tour

Get an introduction to Islam at the **Jumeirah Mosque** courtesy of the Sheikh Mohammed Centre for Cultural Understanding (*see p80*).

For traditional crafts

Witness a day in the life of early weavers and pearl divers at the **Heritage & Diving Village** (*see p76*).

For seven-star overindulgence

Stop for afternoon tea at the **Burj Al Arab** (*see p50*).

For pre-skyscraper architecture

Wander around **Bastakia** (*see p75*) and stop by the **Dubai Museum** (*see p75*).

For the kitchen

Get your bearings, plunge into Deira and enjoy the colours and aromas of the **Spice Souk** (*see p147*).

For a bumpy ride

Have a qualified driver take you on a **desert tour** into the dunes for a barbecue and belly dance (*see p90*).

For ornithologists

Great white egrets, spoonbills and greater flamingos are just some of the thousands of species that can be seen at **Al Khor Wildlife Sanctuary** (*see p86*).

souks and forlorn shipyards, a glimpse of the small fishing village that was swallowed up by the big city forever. While it may be tempting to cling to the beached splendour of Jumeirah, a trip downtown to the Creek is not to be missed.

Further afield are unspoiled beaches, wadis and water holes easily explored in a day. While dune bashing requires a masterful hand, those not yet skilled can turn to nearly any local tour operator for a 4x4 safari, with a barbecue and belly dancing thrown in for good measure. For weekend excursions, Dubai's sister emirates (*see pp251-291*) are sleepier, but prettier, with opportunities to walk along deserted shores or laze at the feet of cool mountains.

Sightseeing

Urban Dubai

Dubai's old districts provide the sights and sounds of the city.

Snapshots of city life along the Creek, where the old and the new meet.

It's surprising how little evidence there is in Dubai to suggest that it's ever been anything other than the entertainment playground it is today – and more surprising still when you consider that UAE nationals value tradition and history very highly. However, the government's recent drive to protect the handful of landmarks that remain has given visitors a chance to experience old Dubai. There are a few historical sights scattered across the city, most of which have been developed in recent decades with tourism in mind. Visiting these will give you a perspective of how much Dubai has evolved in such a short period of time.

Bur Dubai

As Dubai was settled, a residential area developed along the sandy southern banks of the Creek and became known as Bur Dubai. It's here that the emirate's rulers made their home in sea-facing fortifications, and the district remains the seat of the Diwan (the Ruler's Office), Dubai's most senior administrative body. As the city grew, the area became home to embassies and consulates, creating an atmosphere of diplomatic calm, with commercial activity centred on the mouth of the Creek. Today the situation is changing fast and, while the banks of the Creek are still free from development, Bur Dubai has sprawled inland, with tower blocks springing up on practically every available inch of sand.

As the residential community has grown, so commerce has developed to support local residents. The once tiny souk has expanded dramatically, supermarkets and shopping malls have opened and highways traverse the area. **Dubai Museum** (*see p75*) makes a good starting point for exploration of Bur Dubai, and visitors with cars can park in the adjacent space. From the museum, make your way northwards towards the Creek and enjoy the **Bur Dubai souk** on foot. A curious mixture of old and new, it lacks the traditional charm of **Deira's old souk** (*see p147*) but does boast a vast array of goods. At worst, this lesser-known area could be described as tacky and cheap; at best it would be fair to say it's a haphazard market-style collection of shops.

Be sure to pass through the **textile souk** (*see p147*). This is a great place to buy traditional Arab clothing, Pakistani and Indian saris and *salwar kameez*, the traditional baggy shirt and trouser outfits worn by women in Pakistan, Afghanistan, and, to a lesser degree, India. These can be tailored from the fabric of your choice in a matter of hours. Streets filled with fabric and tailoring shops lead you to the covered area of the Bastakia souk, which is filled with Arabic curios and souvenirs. The best bargains are to be found in the less attractive streets beyond the renovated centre.

A walk through the covered area ends at the abra crossing station, where a left turn will lead you to the collection of shops known as the watch souk. Hefty doses of caution are advised, but some of the watches on display are genuine and prices are hard to beat. If you head west from this point you will reach the electrical souk (also known as **Electrical Street**, *see p152*), a great place to buy camera and video equipment or white goods. As with most souks, the boundaries are hazy, but those in search of computers, software or games would do well to explore its southern streets.

Bur Dubai sprawls southwards to merge with the coastal development of **Jumeirah** and westwards to **Port Rashid** on the coast, but the most rewarding sights are to be found where it all began: along the Creek.

Abra Crossing Point

End of Al Seef Road, close to entrance of Bastakia souk, Dubai Creek. **Map** p330 H3.
The cheapest way to view the Creek is by *abra* (traditional wooden water taxis), which cross the Creek day and night. These seemingly rickety but watertight boats have been ferrying residents and traders across the Creek since Dubai was first settled; originally they were rowing boats, but today they're powered by smelly diesel engines. Even now, approximately 15,000 people still cross the Creek by *abra* every day.

The *abras* are commuter vehicles for manual and low-paid workers, and boarding can be chaotic at peak times when hundreds of workers jostle for space on the stone steps where the boats pull up. You are likely to find yourself pulled across the decks of several boats by helpful *abra* captains, who are quick to extend welcoming but rather soiled hands to anyone hesitating or looking for a space on the bench seating.

The basic crossing allows you to take in the atmosphere of the Creek and gives a great insight into how the city operated in the past. For a more comprehensive tour of the Creek, it's well worth hiring your own *abra* – simply ask a boat captain and agree a price and the length of the tour before you set out. A journey up and down the Creek should cost no more than Dhs50.

Dubai Museum proves the city has a history.

Bastakia

Between Al Fahidi Street & the southern bank of the Creek. **Map** p330 H3.
One of Dubai's most picturesque heritage sights, Bastakia is being carefully renovated and turned into a pedestrianised conservation area. The name Bastakia comes from the first people to settle the area, who were traders from Bastak in southern Iran. The ruler of Dubai encouraged such immigration in the early 1900s by granting favourable tax concessions. Many came and most stayed, which explains why so many Emiratis are of southern Iranian descent. Stepping into the narrow alleyways of Bastakia is to walk into Dubai's past. Many older UAE nationals tell of summers spent in Bastakia when entire families would gather to sleep outside on raised platforms in order to escape the heat of indoor rooms.

Dubai Museum

Al Fahidi Fort, Bastakia (353 1862/www.dubai tourism.co.ae). **Open** 8.30am-8.30pm Sat-Thur; 2.30-8.30pm Fri. **Admission** Dhs3 adults; Dhs1 children aged 4-6; free under-4s. **No credit cards.** **Map** p330 H4.
Considered by many residents to be a must for visitors, Dubai's museum is well worth a visit. The Al Fahidi Fort was built in 1787 as Dubai's primary sea defence and also served as the ruler's residence. In 1970, it was renovated so the museum could be housed within its walls. Inside, the displays are

creative and imaginative, allowing you to peek into an Islamic school, walk through a 1950s souk, watch traditional craftsmen at work and even to experience the tranquil beauty of a night in the desert.

Grand Mosque
Al Mussalla Road, nr Dubai Museum,
Bastakia. **Map** p330 H3.
While it may look like a historical building that's been restored recently – like a good portion of the structures in the area – the Grand Mosque was built only a little over ten years ago. However, it was constructed and styled to resemble the original Grand Mosque. Built in around 1900 in the same location, the earlier mosque doubled as a religious school. Sadly, the first Grand Mosque was torn down in the 1960s and replaced by another smaller one. While non-Muslims are not allowed inside, the exterior and beautiful minaret makes it worth the short walk from Dubai Museum (*see p75*).

Heritage & Diving Village
Al Shindagha (393 7151/www.dubaitourism.co.ae).
Open 4.30-10.30pm Sat, Fri. 8.30am-10.30pm Mon-Thur, Sun; **Admission** free. **Map** p330 G3.
This pleasant 'living' museum by the Creek, staffed by guides, potters, weavers and other craftspeople, focuses on Dubai's maritime past and depicts the living conditions of original seafarers, who harvested the waters of the Gulf for pearls and fish to trade. Static but entertaining displays chart the history of Dubai's pearling industry, and a tented village gives a glimpse into the Bedouin way of life that remained unchanged until well into the 20th century. During religious holidays, such as Eid Al Fitr and Eid Al Adha, and throughout the Dubai Shopping Festival (Jan-Feb; *see p142* **Consumer Culture**), traditional ceremonies are laid on, including sword dancing and wedding celebrations. At these times old pearl divers are often on hand to recount tales of adventure and hardship.

Krishna Mandir
Bastakia (No phone). **Open** only during prayer times (usually 6.30am, 8.30am, 10.15am, 5pm & 6pm). **Admission** free. **Map** p330 H4.
Nestled in the winding alleyways of the Bastakia district, this Hindu temple (somewhat strangely) seems right at home in this Islamic city. To go in, slot your shoes in one of the outdoor shoe racks and keep your camera well hidden; worshippers don't take kindly to snap-happy tourists.

Sheikh Saeed Al Maktoum House
Al Shindagha (393 7139/www.dubaitourism.co.ae).
Open 7.30am-9pm Sat-Thur; 3-10pm Fri. **Admission** Dhs2; Dhs1 concessions; free under-7s. **No credit cards.** **Map** p330 G3.
Built in 1896 out of coral covered in lime and sand plaster, this traditional house was the home of Dubai's former ruler until his death in 1958, hence its strategic position at the mouth of the Creek. Now restored and converted into a museum, it displays small exhibitions of old documents, stamps, currencies

Krishna Mandir – Bastakia's Hindu temple.

and a collection of old photographs of Dubai and its ruling family. Guided tours are available.

Deira

Deira is a bustling, chaotic, dusty commercial hub where plate-glass office blocks tower over the single-storey buildings of the old souks. It is an area best explored on foot. Broadly speaking the word 'Deira' is used to describe everything north of the Creek that, in reality, is an amalgam of sub-districts. The most exciting part for the visitor, however, is the original 'Deira' alongside the Creek – the heart and soul of old Dubai.

The best way to start to discover Deira is to walk along the Creek, where old meets new with full force. Five-star hotels such as the Sheraton Dubai Creek and Radisson SAS Hotel Dubai Deira Creek are situated just yards away from wharfs that haven't changed in the past 60 years. On the roads, limousines and 4x4s jostle for space with pick-up trucks, while sharp-suited businessmen and women wait at zebra crossings alongside sarong-clad workers from the subcontinent pushing handcarts, and fishermen in work-stained *kandouras*. Traditional dhows still line the Creek wharf and, day and night, seamen unload goods destined for the many tiny shops that make up Dubai's oldest trading area.

It's here that you'll find **Deira old souk** (**Map** p330 H3), sprawling around the mouth of the Creek on the north shore, where the waterway widens at the entrance to the Gulf. The area is best explored during late afternoon or evening, when temperatures are lower and the traders are at their busiest. The entrance to the old souk stands under renovated buildings

with traditional wind towers. Like most markets, it has evolved into sections defined by the goods sold in each, and criss-crossed by alleyways. The areas are known individually as the **spice souk**, **antique souk** and **textile souk** (*see p147*).

Step into the spice souk and you instantly breathe in the scents of Arabia and the East.

Mosque matters

Mosque building in the UAE reached a peak in the 1970s and 1980s as the population and wealth of the emirate grew, but there are a few examples of older structures. One of the oldest mosques in the UAE – the **Ottoman Mosque** – is in Badiyah village, Fujairah, along the road between Khor Fakkan and Dibba. A study dates the simple structure to around the end of the 15th century; some say that it was built by a fisherman grateful for the discovery of an oversized pearl.

Other notable mosques include the modestly designed **Grand Mosque** (*see p76*; pictured) in Bastakia (probably the oldest in the city), the more elaborate **Ali Ibn Ali Taleb Mosque** (also in Bastakia), the intricately tiled **Iranian Mosque** (*see p79*) in Satwa, and – for modern aesthetics – **Bin Madiya Mosque** near Al Nasr Square in Deira, built in the late 1980s by Greek architects. If you're taking a trip to Abu Dhabi, you can't miss its **Grand Mosque**, located just outside the city. Currently under construction, when finished it'll be one of the grandest mosques in the world and possibly the largest built in modern times. At the other end of the scale are tiny, prefab, roadside mosques that closely resemble the kitschy alarm clock versions you can snap up for Dhs10 at the Bur Dubai or Deira souks.

Most mosques in the UAE feature a simple, open space for praying, generally roofed over, that includes a *mihrab*, from which the imam leads prayer, and a *minbar*, a kind of pulpit that often features a minaret. The floor is covered in mats, and worshippers leave their shoes at the door. There is sometimes a separate area for women to pray.

The UAE does not allow non-Muslims to enter mosques – with the exception of the **Jumeirah Mosque** (*see p80*) on Jumeirah Beach Road. While nothing like the spectacular examples to be found in Syria or Iran, the Jumeirah Mosque is grand, reflecting Egyptian fatimid design and modelled – as are most mosques in the UAE – on an Anatolian structure, with a massive central dome. The Sheikh Mohammed Centre for Cultural Understanding conducts interesting and informative tours of the mosque on Thursdays and Sundays at 10am. Young guides from the non-profit-making centre, set up to bridge the gap between the different cultures in the UAE, are on hand to explain the mosque's layout, describe the five pillars of Islam, and take questions. Visitors should dress conservatively (no shorts) and women should bring a headscarf; children under five are not usually admitted.

Chillies, cardamom and saffron are piled high outside spice shops; ornately decorated glass-stoppered bottles line shelves in traditional perfume shops; and the sweet aroma of frankincense fills the air. At one time more valuable than gold, frankincense (a gum resin obtained from trees of the genus Boswellia) remains one of Arabia's most prized perfumes and is the base for some of the world's most expensive scents. Traditionally, crystals are placed in a frankincense burner and heated over a flame, allowing the resulting aromatic smoke to waft through clothes and rooms. Shopkeepers are happy to demonstrate the custom, and both frankincense crystals and the burners can be bought at very good prices throughout the souk.

The original coral-stone shops have been renovated and much of the dusty charm of the souk has been lost, but it is now a far cleaner place to visit. Take the time to make your way through the myriad of alleyways to explore the shops selling Arabic curios and antiques. Once you reach the antique shops you know that you are approaching the renowned **gold souk** (*see p169*). Its centre is a wide alley covered by a roof and supported by carved wooden pillars, but the souk extends into the adjoining streets. It's worth venturing beyond the main plaza-like

area to explore the outer alleys where many specialist shops trade in silver, pearls and semi-precious stones. Bargaining or haggling is expected in all souks; don't be afraid to leave a shop to try the competition next door if you cannot reach a price that you consider reasonable. Most shopkeepers will offer tea, coffee or cold drinks while a deal is being made – a sign of traditional hospitality and an indication that negotiations are progressing smoothly.

What Deira lacks in refinement it makes up for in atmosphere and character. And to experience it first hand, simply walk along the corniche that borders the Creek. Bear in mind that Deira is by no means pristine: despite the Dubai Municipality's efforts, litter abounds and noisy spitting in the street is distressingly commonplace.

Al Ahmadiya School & Heritage House

Nr Gold House building, Al Khor Street, Al Ras (226 0286/www.dubaitourism.co.ae). **Open** 8am-7.30pm Sat-Thur; 2-7.30pm Fri. **Admission** free. **Map** p330 H3.

Established in 1912, this was the first school in Dubai and was renovated as a museum in 1995. Next door is the Heritage House, a traditional house with

Walking tour

There are only a handful of neighbourhoods in Dubai in which you can take a stroll; Bastakia is the most historic area to head to and as it's fairly small, will just take around an hour to explore.

Over a hundred years ago, Iranian traders settled in this district and built homes out of corals, topped with wind towers that served

as natural air-conditioning units. Today, the wind towers are merely decorative, but in the past Dubai's dwellers occasionally hung wet cloths in the towers when the summer was especially cruel: the wet cloths would cool the air before it entered the home, giving inhabitants some much-needed respite from the heat.

Aside from the wind towers, this district is home to some of the city's best art galleries and a host of quaint outdoor cafés. Start your walk at the the **Majlis Gallery** (*see p201*) on Al Fahidi Road, which houses a wonderful collection of local art, including paintings, illustrations, sculpture, silverwork and Arabian trinkets. You can comfortably browse the entire collection in half an hour, and leave anything you buy with the owners for picking up later. Step out of the Majlis, turn right and a few metres down you'll see the **Basta Art Café** (*see p96;* pictured left), a beautiful courtyard eaterie. After checking out their limited range of local crafts, snag a table in the shade of the central tree and order some super-healthy pitta wraps or salads, washed down with lime and mint juice.

interiors from 1890. Guides and touch screens take you through the tour of these two small – and ever so slightly dull – museums.

Dhow Wharfage

Alongside the Creek. **Map** p331 L4.
Set along the Creek where the towering National Bank of Dubai building curves over Dubai's watery artery, the Dhow Wharfage is a testament to Dubai's lively past. The many dhows that dock alongside each other on the Creek, bringing in spices, textiles and other goods from neighbouring countries, are more than just vessels. In many cases, the seafarers who brave the Gulf and the Indian Ocean live in these colourful wooden beauties, turning each one into a makeshift home. A stroll along this end of the Creek yields a plethora of opportunities for great holiday snaps.

Iranian Mosque

Al Wasl Road, in front of the Iranian Hospital. **Map** p332 E9.
One of the most ornate structures in the city, the Iranian Mosque's intricate, predominantly blue decor, which is inspired by Persian art, stands out in this largely beige Jumeirah neighbourhood. Across the street from the mosque is the Iranian Hospital, which is equally colourful. However, staff and patients might find it a little creepy if you walk around the hospital gawking at the detail. The management is more than happy to allow tourists to take snapshots of the structure, however, so long as you don't get in the way of business.

Jumeirah

Just half a century ago, Jumeirah was a fishing village set several kilometres outside of Dubai. Today it is one of the most high profile areas of the city and residents often refer to it, with tongue placed firmly in cheek, as the Beverly Hills of Dubai. A few original villas survive and are much sought after by expatriate residents as (almost) affordable beachside homes. The area commonly referred to as Jumeirah – although Jumeirah is only a part of it – stretches along Dubai's southern coast for some 16 kilometres (ten miles), incorporating the suburb of Umm Suqeim. It is serviced by two main roads: the Jumeirah Beach Road that runs along the coast and the Al Wasl Road that runs parallel a few blocks inland. A haphazard network of streets lined with luxury villas links the two.

Jumeirah developed southwards from Satwa's borders, and the oldest part, known as Jumeirah 1, remains one of the most desirable addresses in Dubai. It is here that the first chic malls and coffee shops grew up, and it is still a popular choice today for residents in search of a

Once you're fully refreshed, continue the heritage walk by turning right down the narrow alleyway that separates the Majlis Gallery and Basta Art Café. At the end of the alley you'll see the backside of **XVA Gallery** (*see p203*), an idyllic slice of old Arabia hung with white fabric and home to regular exhibitions. Climb up to the roof and you'll get a view over the

area's wind towers, minarets and cobbled streets. Check out the contemporary art and the local jewellery, clothing and magazines in the store before stopping for lunch in the courtyard. Leaving XVA, head out of the wind tower quarter and down towards the Creek, and you'll emerge next to the **Bastakia Mosque**, near a clutch of abras for hire.

Turn left along the waterfront and walk along the boulevard until you hit the **textile souk** (*see p147;* pictured). Weave through this network of cloth-pushing salesmen and you'll rejoin the Creek. From here it's a ten-minute saunter to Al Shindagha, the other remaining pocket of Old Dubai, where you can take a trip around **Sheikh Saeed's** childhood home (*see p76*), the **Heritage Village** (*see p76*) and end up on the terrace at **Al Bandar** restaurant (393 9001) for a leisurely shisha and lashings of mint tea. And when you've had your fill of lounging about, head to **Leena Beauty Salon** (353 8828/9.30am-10pm daily), a ladies only henna parlour behind the Dubai Museum. There you can get a traditional henna tattoo for a fraction of the price charged by tourist traps in hotels and malls.

latte or manicure. At this end of the Jumeirah Beach Road, the **Jumeirah Mosque** (*see p80*) is one of the city's most picturesque and the only one to welcome non-Muslims, via a guided tour.

Along the Jumeirah Beach Road are various shopping malls (one of which, Mercato Mall, can boast Dubai's most fashionable clientele), the shameful **Dubai Zoo** and several public beaches. The shoreline runs from Jumeirah 1 to the far end of Umm Suqeim, where the **Jumeirah Beach Hotel** (*see p59*) and **Burj Al Arab** (*see p50*), next to **Wild Wadi** water park (*see p188*), mark the beginning of the resort strip. It's extremely likely that if you're heading to the beach for the day, you're heading to Jumeirah.

Dubai Zoo

Jumeirah Beach Road, Jumeirah 1 (349 6444).
Open 10am-5pm Sat-Mon, Wed-Fri. **Admission** Dhs3. **No credit cards**. **Map** p332 C10.
The animals at Dubai Zoo are the survivors, and progeny, of a private collection now owned by the Dubai Municipality. The zoo has been heavily criticised for the fact that animals are caged and enjoy little freedom. There were allegedly plans to move it to a more spacious site out of town but, despite promises over several years, there has been little action. The range of species is surprisingly wide and includes lions, tigers, giraffes, bears, reptiles and birds, but it's up to your conscience to decide whether it's worth a visit.

Gold & Diamond Park Museum

Gold & Diamond Park, Interchange 4, Sheikh Zayed Road (347 7788/www.goldanddiamondpark. com). **Open** 10am-10pm Sat-Thur; 4-10pm Fri.
Admission free. **Map** p336 E2.
The Gold & Diamond Park features examples of Arabian, Italian and Indian jewellery and conducts guided tours of the manufacturing plant, showing how diamonds are cut and how gold is produced. There are lots of opportunities to make purchases, although you'll probably get a better deal in the souks.

Jumeirah Mosque

Jumeirah Beach Road, Jumeirah 1. **Map** p332 D9.
Arguably the most beautiful mosque in Dubai, the Jumeirah Mosque stands at the northern end of Jumeirah Beach Road. Non-Muslims are not normally allowed inside mosques, but the Sheikh Mohammed Centre for Cultural Understanding (344 7755/smccu@emirates.net.ae) organises visits to the Jumeirah Mosque at 10am on Sundays and Thursdays. You'll get a chance to walk through the mosque with a small group of fellow sightseers before putting questions to your guide about the mosque and the Islamic faith. You must wear modest clothing (no shorts) and women should put on a headscarf. Both men and women will be asked to remove their shoes before entering. A worthy destination in its own right, this also makes a good starting point from which to explore Jumeirah.

Jumeirah Mosque.

Majlis Ghorfat Um Al Sheef

Jumeirah Beach Road, Jumeirah 4; look for the brown heritage signposts when nearby (394 6343). **Open** 8.30am-1.30pm, 3.30-8.30pm Sat-Thur; 3.30-8.30pm Fri. **Admission** Dhs2. **No credit cards. Map** p334 A15.
Built in traditional style from coral and stone, the two-storey Majlis was used by the late ruler of the city, Sheikh Rashid bin Saeed Al Maktoum, founder of modern Dubai. *Majlis* means 'meeting place' in Arabic and is traditionally where matters of business or other importance were discussed. Thankfully, the Dubai Municipality has carefully preserved this particular *majlis*, located in a quiet part of Jumeirah. The ground floor is an open veranda, and the first floor room is furnished with cushions and Arabic antiques. The rooftop terrace was used for sleeping, as the height ensures the platform enjoys a stiff sea breeze. The fact that many of the visionary plans for modern Dubai were probably hatched in such a simple structure, by a man who had known nothing of 20th-century luxury for most of his life, is remarkable. A visit to the Majlis highlights the dramatic development and the extent of the changes that Dubai has undergone in just a matter of decades, particularly as you can see the Burj Al Arab hotel from the rooftop. That said, it only really merits a fleeting visit: although fascinating as a contrast between old and new Dubai, it should not be rated as a significant cultural experience.

Bird's eye view

Due to its extreme youth, Dubai is almost entirely lacking in historical landmarks. However, when viewed from above, this modern metropolis can be a breathtaking sight, a steel and concrete oasis springing from the desolate desert. To get your view from on high, call **Lama Desert Tours & Cruises** (334 4330/ www.lamadubai.com), which offers a helicopter ride over the city every Saturday for Dhs4,000 per group (3-4 people). The helicopter takes in Jumeirah Emirates Towers and the Burj Al Arab before zipping across to the Palms project to witness the birth of the huge new islands.

A considerably cheaper option is the cable car at **Creekside Park** (336 7633), which offers charming views over the water. Okay, so it's a bit creaky – and there's inevitably a point when you're convinced you're about to plummet to earth and crush a tribe of merry picnickers – but once you've quelled your fears you'll have a ball. Entry to the park is Dhs5 and it's a further Dhs25 (Dhs15 for concessions) to ride the wire.

Dubai's skyscrapers also offer opportunities to check out the city from above. Vu's Bar on the 51st floor of **Jumeirah Emirates Towers** (*see p65*; pictured) offers stunning views from a classy setting. There is a strict dress code in force – those wishing to drink in the clouds must be wearing a collar and smart shoes.

Sightseeing

Cruise control

With the Creek dividing up the city as dramatically as it does, it's no surprise that tour operators and hotels run dinner cruises on it. Tourist traps they may be, but these cruises are ideal for exploring Dubai's skylines on either side of the Creek. Most cruises (with the exception of Bateaux Dubai) take place on traditional dhows, and a predictable buffet, band and belly dancer are included in the price. But the food's not really important, since you'll be getting a ride along the city's most interesting attraction, and a chance to see the dichotomy between old and new Dubai.

Bateaux Dubai

A dinner cruise on the Creek couldn't be enjoyed on a better vessel (pictured) – the boat's huge glass windows offer superb views of the city's skyline. During Dubai's scorching summer months, the air-conditioned interior of this boat offers the most comfortable way to enjoy the sights along the Creek. The dinner cruise costs Dhs275 per person, which is significantly more pricey than its competitors, but on Bateaux Dubai you get a non-alcoholic drink upon arrival, canapés and a four-course à la carte meal cooked on-board. There's even an on-board pianist and violinist, making Bateaux Dubai by far the most sophisticated option on the water. Boarding begins at 7.30pm and the boat departs at 8.30pm daily, from opposite the British Consulate.
Call 399 4994 for reservations.

Danat Dubai Cruises

In addition to running dinner cruises on a traditional dhow, where an Arabic and international buffet is served (Dhs175 per person), Danat Dubai also organises cruises on its catamaran (Dhs200). Rather than sailing down the Creek, the catamaran is taken to the open sea, from where Dubai's famous skyline can be better appreciated while tucking into an international buffet. Boarding time is 8pm and the boats depart at 8.30pm daily from directly opposite the British Consulate.
Call 351 1117 for reservations.

Lama Desert Tours & Cruises

Lama's traditional dhow departs from the Creek opposite the Dubai Municipality or the Radisson SAS Hotel. The services offered on this dinner cruise are almost identical to other cruises, except Lama Tours has a pick-up and drop-off option for an extra Dhs40. For Dhs180, you can ravage an international buffet, guzzle unlimited soft drinks and listen to a live band as you cruise the Creek. Boarding is at 8pm, and the boat departs at 8.30pm daily.
Call 334 4330 for reservations.

Al Mansour Dhow

With an onboard oud player, this cruise is extremely popular. The lulling sounds of this Arabian instrument, which provides the soundtrack while you feast on a reasonably good Arabic and international buffet, give this Dhs175 cruise an edge over the competition. The dhow belongs to the Radisson SAS Hotel in Deira, which also serves as the meeting point. Boarding is at 8pm, and the dhow departs at 8.30pm daily.
Call 205 7333 for reservations.

Further Afield

Get out of the city to experience the customs and traditions of the UAE.

Top hotels, fine dining and designer shops help Dubai hold its own against tourist destinations the world over. But there is plenty of life beyond the glittering city – although it moves at a much slower pace. Quieter times and no less stirring sights await the more adventurous traveller; hit the road and you'll find towering desert dunes and cool mountain pools are yours for the savouring.

These next few pages feature recommended sights beyond the city boundaries – all an easy ride away. Unfortunately, Dubai's lack of public transport makes driving the only viable option. Taxis – while cheap within Dubai – are not cost-effective over longer journeys (across to Hatta, for example), not to mention the impracticality of hailing a cab for the return journey. Hiring wheels, preferably a four-wheel drive, for excursions during your stay is a much better idea (see p298).

Hatta

Snugly tucked between Dubai and the mountains of Oman is the oasis town of Hatta, where the pace of life is reminiscent of a bygone era, before development and mass tourism hit the country. Although only an hour's drive from Dubai, the area benefits from its mountain seclusion, where the natural springs and streams have created a lush green landscape, dotted with luminous yellow wild flowers and plenty of wildlife. It isn't uncommon to see mountain goats and camels roaming across the roads without a care in the world. As such, it's a popular day trip for tourists with wheels, offering plenty of off-road action and just a dash of heritage.

From Sheikh Zayed Road, Dubai, take either the Trade Centre roundabout, or Interchange 1 or 2, and turn inland. From here you will see signs to Hatta. As you continue along the highway, you will notice the landscape change colour slowly, from a washed-out pale yellow to a rich red ochre. It's the iron oxide present in the sand that gives it this unusual warm glow; in the right light it can be spectacular.

Shortly after the village of Madam (expect a large roundabout and little else) you will pass through a small patch of Oman. Be aware that most hire-car insurance will not cover trips outside of the UAE and you will be uninsured

for this section of road should you have an accident, even though there are no official border posts to notify you. The views are stunning and the layers of jagged peaks fading off into the distance across the gravel plains and the acacia trees gives the area something of an African air.

Soon you will reach the town of Hatta, considered to be the oldest village in the emirate of Dubai. The town is overlooked by two defensive towers built in the 1880s and boasts an old-world country charm. Its tranquil setting in the foothills of the Hajar Mountains, the rocky range that spans the eastern flank of the UAE (see p278 **Scaling the Hajar heights**), is compelling, and the location offers numerous routes to explore on foot, by mountain bike or 4x4, plus wonderful natural rock pools.

Big Red

About 30 minutes outside Dubai, in the direction of Hatta, you will come to a huge sand dune on your right-hand side affectionately known by expatriates as Big Red. It's a majestic, looming sight, a fiery orange-red mass set against a brilliant blue sky. But if you've made it this far, don't sit lovingly by the roadside in your 4x4. Big Red is a playground for big kids with big engines: by far the best way to enjoy this stretch of desert is to get stuck right in. Nearby is a popular quad biking centre, which is great fun but somewhat chaotic, making accidents worryingly commonplace. You have a choice of 50cc, 80cc and 200cc bikes. Prices range from Dhs15 for 15 minutes on a 50cc to Dhs200 for an hour on the 200cc bike. You can even hire a Land Cruiser for Dhs50 per 30 minutes for a shot at getting to the summit of Big Red itself. Rentals operate from 8am to sunset daily. Should you require sustenance, a supermarket and a restaurant are on hand.

Most tour operators run trips to Hatta via Big Red but you can always set your own schedule and hire a 4x4. One of the best places to do so is **Budget** (285 8550), which offers Toyota Land Cruisers fully kitted out and complete with steel bumpers and roll bar for Dhs750 per day, including insurance. If you choose to drive yourself, remember that it is not safe to venture off-road with just one vehicle; get someone else to hire another vehicle and accompany you. Mobile phone coverage is poor in the mountains and you are likely to be out of touch. To be safe, be sure to carry at least one full cool-box of water for every two people (10-12 litres), a good supply of food, a first-aid kit, some tow rope and a shovel.

Hatta Fort Hotel

Hatta (852 3211/www.hattaforthotel.com). **Rates** rooms from Dhs685; Dhs1,440 suites. **Credit** AmEx, MC, V.

One of the country's oldest hotels, this is the only place to stay in Hatta and well worth a stop-off for a sundowner even if you're not planning to settle down for the night. The building houses two eating options, Café Gazebo, whose terrace has great views over the mountains, and the slightly more formal Jeema Restaurant.

The 50 individual chalet-style abodes each have a private balcony overlooking the rolling green lawns of the 80-acre property. The grounds are home to a teeming wealth of birdlife: keep an eye out in particular for the brilliant turquoise flash of the elusive Indian roller. If you want a touch of luxury, the hotel has two villas in its grounds, each boasting its very own Jacuzzi to relax in after a day of sightseeing. Other facilities include two swimming pools, a nine-hole 'fun' golf course, golf driving range, jogging track, tennis court, archery and camel rides around the grounds. Experienced guides are also happy to conduct 4x4 excursions to the Hatta Rock Pools. Alternatively, if you aren't the active type, head to the Elemis spa to have your muscles soothed and knots masterfully worked away.

Dinner is included in the basic rate, with breakfast priced at an extra Dhs65 per person. There are excellent promotions on rooms during the summer months, with rates substantially lower than the norm. But be warned: while the mountains escape the humidity endured by coastal areas, temperatures can still rise above 50 degrees centigrade.

Hatta Rock Pools

The Hatta Rock Pools are the main draw to the area, which in the summer months attract masses of sweaty Dubaians trying to escape the heat of the city. The pools are situated 20 kilometres south of Hatta in the rock crevices that have developed along the floor of the dried-out riverbeds known as wadis. The pools are safe to swim in, as are the two waterfalls; however, an eye should be kept on children, as in some parts the pools can change from shallow to deep quite quickly. The pools suffer from the same problem as other beauty spots in the UAE – the unwelcome attention of litter louts and vandals. Although it isn't necessary to hire a 4x4 for the trip to the rock pools, you will need one if you are going to do a bit of *wadi* bashing (driving through the rocky dried out river beds) or heading past Hatta to the town of Al Ain.

Hatta trick

Getting to Hatta Pools from Dubai

● From Dubai take route 44 until you reach Hatta
● At the Fort Roundabout go right (first exit) and head through the town
● Take the turning to the left, signed Hatta Heritage Village
● At the next junction turn left
● Take the next right and travel over the multiple speed bumps
● Continue straight for approximately 4km travelling through a small village where the tarmac will end
● Take the gravel track heading towards Buraimi, an Omani border town
● After the Al Bon sign, take the well-used track off to the left. This will take you in the direction of the Wadi and a makeshift car park where you can leave your vehicle, and then make the rest of the way by foot

Heritage Village

Hatta (852 1374). **Admission** free. **Open** 8am-5pm daily.

A great way to get an impression of how Hatta, the oldest town in the emirate, once looked, is to pay a visit to the Heritage Village. The complex is ordered by two round towers built to protect the town from attacks during the rule of Sheikh Hasher bin Maktoum bin Butti in the late 1880s. As you stroll in, a group of UAE nationals enjoying the quietude of village life will greet you at the entrance. Although the place is hardly a hive of activity, the traditionally built stone and mud houses and fort offer a fascinating insight into what life was like before electricity and modern construction took over. Head to the Hatta House to see how homes in the area were designed just a few decades ago. Visitors will get a glimpse of traditional folklore inside the poet's *majlis*.

One fascinating construct of traditional life is the falaj system, the ancient method of irrigation. Heritage Village has one of the few working falaj in the country, as most were replaced with modern irrigation systems. In its heyday falaj were used to supply water to agricultural plots and date palm plantations, which required a constant stream of water to prevent them dying in the harsh heat of the summer. In Heritage Village, they are still used to maintain a small patch of date palms, as well as the goats and chicken that playfully frolic about inside the enclosure. To drive to the Heritage Village, turn at the Fort roundabout and follow the brown signposts.

Hatta.

Jebel Ali

Jazira Beach Club
After Jebel Ali, take the 399 exit off the highway
signposted Ghantoot Polo & Racing Club. Follow
signs for the bungalows (02 562 9023).
Jazira Beach Club is an absolute gem of a find for
beach lovers disillusioned with the sprawling developments closer to town. A mere ten minutes' drive
past Jebel Ali, you'd be forgiven for thinking you
were miles from Dubai. When you reach the new
club – it only opened its doors in February 2007
– you'll find all the rustic charm that has disap-
peared from much of the city. There's three quarters
of a kilometre of coastline, a sheltered bay, a swimming pool and more activities than you could
squeeze into an entire winter, including wakeboarding, diving, water skiing, kayaking, paintballing and quad biking. There's also a bar with live
music at the weekend if you stay on after sunset.
Expect to feel as though you've stepped back in time
ten years to an earlier Dubai era, especially when
you see the price – Dhs75 for adults from Thursday
to Saturday and a mere Dhs35 during the week.

Jebel Ali Beach
Sheikh Zayed Road, between Jebel Ali
Hotel & Ghantoot.
Dubai's most remote and unspoiled beach lies some
40 minutes' drive south of the city, towards Abu
Dhabi, and stretches, unencumbered by development, for some 15km (9.5miles) to the Abu
Dhabi/Dubai border. This expanse of unbroken
sand represents Dubai's only remaining 'natural'
beach, yet there are strong rumours that, despite
the fact that it is a nature reserve, development
plans are underway. The area is likely to be affected
by the Jebel Ali Palm and there are fears that this
valued area will soon be damaged or lost forever.
A favourite with beach-loving residents and
kitesurfers, who relish the freedom of the emirate's
longest free stretch of coastline, the beach is open
to all, but those who wish to camp on the sand,
which comes highly recommended, must apply for
a permit from Dubai Municipality.
To get there, take the exit signposted for the Jebel
Ali Hotel, off the Sheikh Zayed Road. Turn left at
the roundabout before the hotel and follow the tarmac road that runs along the coast behind the dunes.
Pick your spot and turn right towards the sea – the
beach is straight ahead. A 4x4 is essential to get on
to the beach itself, although hard-packed sand tracks
enable two-wheel-drive vehicles to reach the northern edge. There are showers (not all of which work)
and barasti (palm-leaf) sunshades, but no other
amenities; this is not a beach for those who enjoy
luxury or need facilities to be close at hand.

Jebel Ali Golf Resort & Spa
Jebel Ali (883 6000).
The Jebel Ali complex is the elder statesman of
beach-front hotels. Refined, elegant and less showy
than its newer five-star rivals, it makes for an ideal
day out of town. It's true that construction work in
the area has made this area less serene than it used
to be, but the sprawling grounds are big enough to
offer seclusion from the worst of the activity.
Entrance is Dhs200 from Thursday to Saturday,
including a barbecue on Friday and a buffet spread
on Thursday and Saturday. During the week, entry
costs Dhs120 (excluding lunch), but you're advised
to book a week in advance. If you tire of the beach,
the complex has myriad activities on offer, including water sports, squash courts, horse riding and a
golf course, though you'll have to pay extra for these
and, again, it's best to book in advance.

Jebel Rawdah

The main activity at this part of the emirate,
known as Death Valley, is scaling the imposing
hulk of Jebel Rawdah – a 4km (2.5mile) trek
from the base. The views en route to the
summit are spectacular, looking out over the
varied landscape of the area, and there is also a
plethora of plants and desert animals. If you've
got a four-wheel drive, you'll be able to travel

Sightseeing

Flamingos at the **Al Khor Wildlife Sanctuary** – a twitcher's paradise.

far higher up the valley to check out the large number of wadis in and around the mountain. Death Valley appropriately offers solitude, peace and the chance to forget about the sights and sounds of the city. When you set out to explore the area, have a look for the camel bones scattered around the area. Death Valley got its name because this is the place that camels come to die. It's a strange but nonetheless intriguing sight. To get there, head towards Hatta, going over the Madam roundabout east of Lahbab. Eleven kilometres (seven miles) past the roundabout, just past a mosque on your left-hand side, look for a sign that says Al Barwani Crushers. Turn left and then take the next right. At the next junction turn left on to a gravel track, then turn right at the next junction, and drive along the outskirts of a farm. After 2.5 kilometres (1.5 miles), you'll be at the base of Jebel Rawdah.

Al Khor Wildlife Sanctuary

Ras Al Khor industrial area (223 2323). **Open** 9am-4pm Sun-Thur. **Admission** free. **Map** p329 J4.
Managed by WWF (formerly World Wildlife Fund) and the Emirates Wildlife Society, Al Khor Wildlife Sanctuary is the only urban protected area in Dubai

and one of only a handful in the world. Located at the beginning of the Creek, the marshy ground is home to thousands of flamingos, waders and other birds, many of which migrate to Dubai seasonally. The area was once closed to the public, but the WWF – with the help of the National Bank of Dubai – opened three hides a few years back, affording twitchers spectacular views of the birds against a backdrop of the Dubai skyline. The first viewing area, aptly dubbed 'Flamingo', is located opposite the Emarat garage on the Oud Metha road and offers great views of the pink birds in all their glory. From here it is a short walk to the Lagoon sanctuary, a quieter hide that looks back across the marshes. If you return to the Oud Metha Road and travel away from the city before taking the left turn to Ras Al Khor, you'll find the Mangrove Hide – located behind the Dubai Exiles Rugby Football Club. Although further from the wildlife, this wooden shack boasts superb views back across the wetlands towards the city and shows the sanctuary's star-tlingly close vicinity to the skyscrapers. Admission to the hides is free but a maximum of ten people are permitted in a hide at one time and groups larger than four must apply for an entry permit from the Municipality (206 4240). Forms can be downloaded from their website: www.environment.dm.gov.ae.

Mushrif Park

On the airport road towards Al Khawaneej, near Mirdif (288 3624). **Open** 8am-11pm daily. **Admission** *Park* Dhs3; Dhs10/car. *Swimming pool* Dhs10; concessions Dhs5. *Train* Dhs2. **Map** p327 F4. The park is approximately ten minutes' drive out of town, close to the residential suburb of Mirdif. It is so huge that you can drive around it or take the miniature train that tours every afternoon. The variety of themed displays include miniature houses from around the world. Camel and pony rides are available in the afternoons. Wildlife such as deer and gazelles roam the farthest corners of the park, where landscaped gardens give way to sand dunes covered with indigenous vegetation. Dogs are strictly not allowed in the park.

Nad Al Sheba

The Nad Al Sheba area, a ten-minute drive inland from Dubai, is home to two sports at the heart of Arab heritage: horse racing and camel racing.

Nad Al Sheba Racecourse

Nad Al Sheba (332 2277). **Map** p327 D4. Home of the world's richest horse race, the Dubai World Cup (*see p181*), the Nad Al Sheba Club used to incorporate a golf course as well as a racecourse. (Sadly for golf enthusiasts, the 18-hole golf course shut in May 2007.) The racing stables are still here however, and house some of the world's most valuable bloodstock. Between November and March the club hosts race meetings on Thursdays and Saturdays, the most prestigious of which are the Dubai Racing Festival meets – held over nine weeks, starting in January.

Nad Al Sheba Camel Racetrack

Opposite the splendour of the horse racecourse you will find a less glamorous, but no less spectacular activity going on: camel racing. Also known as the 'ships of the desert' and prized by locals, camels might have earned a reputation for trudging miles without water in the harshest of environments, but there's nothing plodding about a racing camel. They can reach surprisingly high speeds at full gallop, and some fine specimens are even worth as much as their equine counterparts.

Since the child jockey ban back in 2005, the sport of camel racing has gone from strength to strength. The sport is no longer shielded from the eyes of the outside world, but is embracing visitors who travel to see the races for themselves. (Note that the season runs from September to March.)

At the time of going to press, work on a new camel racing track was well underway, and is slated to be ready for the start of the season in September 2007. Conveniently, this new complex is being built very near to the old Nad Al Sheba venue – just off the Dubai-Al Ain Road – and is set to stage three to four fixtures every week. The schedule of camel races has always been frustratingly erratic, with fixtures subject to change at the last minute. However, as a rough guide, races should take place every Tuesday, Wednesday and Thursday between 6am and 7am and 2pm and 3pm. There is also racing on alternate Mondays and occasional meetings on Fridays.

New Falcon Market

New Falcon Market, Nad Al Sheba (336 3766). **Open** 9am-6pm daily. Falconry has long been regarded as a noble art in the UAE, with ownership symbolic of high birth (*see p88* **Flight of fancy**). If you want to get up close and personal with a feathery falcon, head to the Falcon Heritage & Sports Centre. Surrounding the enclosed courtyard are a multitude of shops selling a wide range of falcons priced from Dhs8,000 to the million dirham mark. Although tours aren't available, visitors are more than welcome to stroll around and take a look at the bizarre sight of hooded falcons perching en masse. The cooing crew are happy for you to have a stroke; just steer clear of their sharp beaks and monster talons.

One hump or two?

The Arabian camels found in the UAE are known as dromedary camels and have one hump. Only the Bactrian camels of Africa and Asia have two humps. Contrary to popular belief, the hump doesn't store water, but is in fact a mass of fatty tissue from which energy is drawn at times when food is hard to come by. Most of the camels you will see on your visit will have a firm, hard hump as they are well fed and rested, but if you do happen to come across a saggy-looking beast this means it has been drawing energy from its bumpy reserve.

Sightseeing

Flight of fancy

Shield your eyes from the intense desert sun and you may catch a glimpse of a majestic falcon as it soars across the tower-lined horizon. In the past, falconry was a way of life and a means of sustenance for the nomadic desert dwellers of the UAE. Bedouin tribes used falcons for hunting houbara and hare to supplement their meagre diets with much needed protein. However, the winged hunters are not just humble dinner providers; throughout history these magnificent birds of prey have been regarded as status symbols. Falconers were, and still are, regarded as authority figures because of their ability to master these wild creatures.

The skill of a falconer is initially tested when they have to capture their mighty bird. Once the falcon has been caught, it's time for the falconer to tame and train the bird, a skill that requires plenty of patience and bucketloads of bravery. Leather hoods (*al burqa*) are used to cover the falcons' eyes to keep them calm.

By day, the bird perches on the tamer's sleeve and by night the falcon is tied to a wooden perch (*al wakr*), being occasionally released to hop around and get comfortable in its surroundings. Throughout this process, the tamer talks and calls to the bird, which results in a voice recognition over great distances, vital for getting the birds to return after they have made a catch. Slowly the trainer will feed the falcon from his own hand to build up trust and to get the bird used to perching on the leather clad arm.

Contrary to popular belief, falcons are not keen flyers. For this reason, flight training involves the falconer sending the bird on short flights, rewarding it with a tasty chunk of meat after each burst. In this way the birds begin to connect taking flight with filling their belly. Gradually they are made to fly greater distances until they are encouraged to swoop on other birds. The falconer's ultimate success in training is to get the bird to return to his arm without having to offer up a reward. By this point the falcon understands that as long as it completes its day job, dinner will be waiting afterwards.

Until around 40 years ago, the point of falconry in the Gulf States was to put food on the table. However, today hunting is illegal throughout the UAE and as a result falconry is becoming more of a tourist attraction as owners display their birds' skills to the public rather than out in the desert.

Guided Tours

Explore the emirate – from sand dunes to city centre.

Two things Dubai isn't short of are 4x4s and sand – a perfect combination for some heart-stopping adventures in the desert. But don't try and take on the emirate's toughest sand dunes in a hire car – heading off the beaten track without knowledge of the area is a recipe for disaster. Instead, leave the car at home and book yourself on to one of the many affordable desert safaris. This way you'll have an experienced driver who can take you on a fairground-like ride across the sand dunes in a safe manner.

Although there's a focus with many tours on 4x4s and sand, there are plenty of other options on offer too. Operators run an array of organised trips from relaxing city tours and dhow cruises to the more exhilarating sand boarding and dune buggy safaris. We've listed some reliable tour operators (*see p90* **Tour operators at a glance**), but be warned: as with anywhere, you'll always find some companies who employ inexperienced and ill-equipped guides.

City tours

Most tour operators run a variety of trips, including different city tours as well as the more daring desert adventures. With such a wide range of options, it's a good idea to hop on a bus early on in your trip and get an overview of what Dubai has to offer. These organised jaunts usually last half a day and generally focus on landmarks and sites that define the city's heritage and development. The **Burj Al Arab** is often the first port of call, with visits to the Palm Jumeirah – the world's largest man-made islands (until the Palm Deira is finished) – residences of former sheikhs, mosques, the Creek and the spice and gold souk other likely stop-off points. Excursions to Al Ain, Abu Dhabi, Sharjah and Ajman are also available.

Shopping tours are very popular and combine high-street names in ultra-modern malls with the simple pleasures of traditional souks. These tours last a few hours and run during the day and into the evening.

Bus tours

It's no surprise, in a city that has developed so quickly, that the **Big Bus Company** (324 4187/ www.bigbus.co.uk) has conquered these shores;

Hop on, hop off, with a **Big Bus** tour.

since 2002, Dubai has had its own fleet of double-decker buses (imported from London), and these operate every day of the year and offer fine views of the city from the open-top decks. As with all the company's tours worldwide, you have the hop on, hop off option at all 23 stops so that you can explore in your own time. The Big Bus Company is now also offering the option to take the two-hour beach tour at no extra cost. You'll have live and informative commentary in English on every bus. The distinctive vehicles leave from outside Biella restaurant at Wafi City on the hour every hour from 9am to 5pm but you can join the tour at any of its stops. Ticket prices (Dhs150; Dhs100 concessions; Dhs400 families) include entry to **Dubai Museum** (*see p75*) and **Sheikh Saeed Al Maktoum House** (*see p76*), plus a cruise on an Arabian dhow.

London sent over double-deckers, while New York sent over the amphibious **Wonder Bus** (359 5656/www.wonderbusdubai.com). This slightly more surreal look at the city offers a road trip around Dubai's landmarks before splashing headlong into the Creek to take in the city's sites from the water. The two-hour trip (Dhs125; Dhs85 concessions; Dhs390 family), complete with on-board TV, leaves from the **BurJuman Centre** (*see p143*) and takes in Wafi City Mall, the Grand Hyatt hotel and Creekside Park before hitting the Creek by Garhoud Bridge. Gimmicky, yes, but plenty of fun.

Desert tours

Nothing can quite justify the outrageous number of gas-guzzling 4x4s on Dubai's roads, but when you consider the vast playground the desert provides to expats, UAE nationals and tourists alike, it begins to make a little more sense. It goes without saying that knowledge is the key to driving in the desert, so it's highly recommended that you travel with an experienced guide to avoid the potential dangers of being stranded. There's only so much help a camel can provide.

It's an absolute must for visitors to take a trip to the desert. This adventure park can be breathtakingly beautiful and there is tremendous fun to be had in the rolling dunes. Of course, the freedom to roam Dubai's dunes has its downside. The region's eco-structure is suffering as a consequence of the increasing number of tours and much of what should be pristine wilderness is heavily littered – and, as yet, little is being done to clean up the mess.

A few tour operators run desert driving schools, quad biking and dune buggying, but the majority simply run a selection of desert safaris, comprising half-day and full-day trips or overnight stays. Experienced desert drivers will collect you from your hotel in an immaculate 4x4 and whisk you 45 minutes inland. Here, the gold of coastal sands gives way to deep red, originating from the rock of the Hajar mountains that run from north to south across the country.

Tour operators at a glance

Arabian Adventures
(303 4888/www.arabian-adventures.com).
Tours include: dhow cruise (Sept-May Dhs305, June-Aug Dhs280), camel riding and sand skiing safari (Dhs230) and breakfast stable tours (Dhs230; Dhs165 concessions).

Arabian Desert Tours
(268 2880).
Tours include: desert safari (Dhs180; Dhs150 concessions), quad biking (Dhs300; Dhs200 concessions) and city tour (Dhs120; Dhs70 concessions).

Desert Rangers
(340 2408/www.desertrangers.com).
Tours include: dune buggy safari (Dhs525), Hatta pool safari (Dhs325; Dhs230 concessions) and sand boarding safari (Dhs195; Dhs135 concessions).

East Adventure Tours
(355 5677/www.holidayindubai.com).
Tours include: Bedouin evening desert safari (Dhs160; Dhs100 concessions), quad bike safari (Dhs550; Dhs250 concessions) and exclusive city tour (Dhs150; Dhs100 concessions).

Good Times Tourism
(335 5120/www.goodtimesdubai.com).

Tours include: overnight safari (Dhs320; Dhs200 concessions), shopping tour (Dhs120; Dhs70 concessions), dune safari (Dhs300).

Lama Tours
(334 4330/www.lamadubai.com).
Tours include: dune safari (Dhs220; Dhs150 concessions), Hatta trek (Dhs260; Dhs200 concessions) and various city tours (Dhs90-Dhs170; Dhs60-Dhs100 concessions).

Net Tours
(266 6655/www.netgroupdubai.com).
Tours include: desert safari (Dhs275; Dhs200 concessions), city tour (Dhs110; Dhs75 concessions) and Hatta trek (Dhs355; Dhs315 concessions).

Off-Road Adventures
(405 2917/www.arabiantours.com).
Tours include: desert safari (Dhs160; Dhs120 concessions), VIP Arabian night safari (Dhs650, min 4) and Hatta mountain trip (Dhs300; Dhs225 concessions).

Voyagers Xtreme
(345 4504/www.turnertraveldubai.com).
Tours include: dhow dinner cruise (Dhs210; Dhs105 concessions), Hatta safari (Dhs260; Dhs185 concessions) and city tours (Dhs120-Dhs180; Dhs55-Dhs90 concessions).

Sightseeing

The desert adventure typically begins close to an outcrop known as **Fossil Rock** that rises above the desert some 30 kilometres (20 miles) from the Dubai-Hatta road. A brief stop allows the driver to deflate the vehicle's tyres (think 'high heels on grass'; fully inflated tyres sink into soft sand, whereas partially deflated ones pass over all but the softest surfaces). Your journey will then take you past ramshackle camel and goat farms, over small scrub-covered dunes and into the red desert. Make sure you're feeling on good form for a desert safari. It's a bit like a fairground ride, whizzing up and down the dunes – nail-biting but exhilarating.

After a roller coaster ride up and down more demanding dunes, you will visit a purpose-built campsite for lunch or a barbecued dinner and, depending on the length of your tour, a range of entertainment. This is likely to include belly dancing and the chance to smoke shisha and ride a camel – if only for 20 metres or so. It's all good fun, but staged purely for tourists and bearing little resemblance to traditional Emirati life. In fact, the camel handlers are normally Sudanese, while the bellies energetically shaking in front of you usually belong to Russian or Lebanese women.

Tour operators normally require a minimum of four people to embark on a trip, and will often group couples and individuals together with others in order to make up the numbers. Typically (with the exception of full day tours), safaris begin in the afternoon as temperatures drop towards the end of the day. Many overnight safaris will combine a desert tour with a wadi-bashing mountain trip the next morning. Wadis are river beds that are dry for the majority of the year and form wonderfully rugged tracks which can be followed in a 4x4 – an act known to expats as 'bashing'. In some places pools of water remain all year round and it can even be possible to swim in them.

Expect to pay in the region of Dhs450 for an overnight desert safari. Normally all food and drink is included, but check before you set out. In the UAE you are never far from a main road, and mobile phone coverage normally extends everywhere but the most mountainous areas. Tour groups rarely travel without back-up vehicles too, but it is still wise to take a few precautions. Carry at least a small bottle of water with you and a few basics such as plasters and sunscreen. Long, loose clothing is recommended (long shorts are acceptable for both men and women) and you should take a hat. The most practical headgear is the traditional Arab headdress (*ghutra*), which both protects from the sun and can be wrapped Bedouin-style around your face to keep off blowing sand. If you are staying overnight it's wise to take a jumper as the desert can cool rapidly when the sun goes down. To tackle the hot desert sand, opt for boots over flip-flops or sandals.

Activity tours

If your heart isn't lodged firmly enough in your mouth already, most tour operators also offer supervised alternatives for the most hardcore of adrenaline junkies (*see p90* **Tour operators at a glance**). This way, *you* can be at the controls; it's worth having a go at quad biking, sand skiing (essentially snowboarding but on sand) and dune buggying to experience even more thrills the desert has to offer.

Mountain & wadi tours

If you've got a head for heights, the Hajar mountains are a popular tourist attraction. Often referred to as the 'backbone of the Arabian peninsula', the range lies towards Dubai's eastern border with Oman, running from the Empty Quarter across the length of the UAE before rising to its zenith in the north in **Musandam** (*see p280*), above the Strait of Hormuz. Tours usually take in deep wadis and tracks and venture through abandoned settlements. Some companies will also provide tailor-made guided trekking, hiking and rock climbing tours based on individual fitness, ranging from two to eight hours. The more expensive tours can cost up to Dhs400 and usually include lunch.

Traditionally, Dubai's ruling Al Maktoum family would escape the coastal humidity of the summer in the oasis mountain village of Hatta, close to the Omani border. Today, **Hatta** (*see p83*) still boasts some of the most dramatic scenery in the emirate. Even before you get there, watch out for Big Red – the huge, fiery orange sand dune – along the way. Storms can lash the mountains at any time of year creating flash floods that turn wadis into raging torrents. Over the centuries, water has carved paths into the limestone and Hatta is perhaps best known for its crystal clear freshwater pools. Mountain and wadi tours explore this charming, desolate region over a full day, and include visits to the 16th-century Hatta Fort and heritage clay village, with lunch either eaten picnic-style in the mountains or in the **Hatta Fort Hotel** (*see p84*) during the unbearably sticky summer months. As with the desert, boots are preferable to beach footwear. Sunscreen, a hat and a supply of water are essential, and if you fancy a dip in the Hatta pools, don't forget your swimming gear. Expect to pay up to Dhs400 for a mountain and wadi tour including lunch.

Sightseeing

Eat, Drink, Shop

Restaurants & Cafés

From street shawarmas to world-class curries and fine dining,
Dubai's eating scene is as diverse as its population.

Traditional Arabian hospitality at **Bastakiah Nights**.

Hungry? If so, you've certainly come to the right place. Dubai is unabashedly eager for more and more places to eat out and there isn't a nook in this blossoming city that doesn't house an eaterie of sorts to cater for the multitude of nationalities that have settled in this booming emirate. You can find food from just about any country in the world here, ranging from Ethiopian to Sri Lankan. It's one of the many privileges of visiting or living in Dubai.

However, people don't come here to sit on the floor of an authentic Yemeni restaurant; they usually come here for a taste of the good life and that means exquisitely tasty gourmet food in five-star settings. In Dubai, glitz and glamour are very affordable; you don't have to take a second mortgage to eat at the best

restaurants in town. And for those residents and tourists who are looking to woo their taste buds with top quality grub, Dubai has more than its fair share of options.

With over 40 five-star hotels in the emirate, each offering a throng of restaurants, finding a special place where you can enjoy unadulterated class both on and off your plate isn't hard. In fact, plenty of Dubaians and tourists believe that eating out beyond the walls of Dubai's top-end hotels is hardly worth the trouble. But in doing so they're missing some culinary diamonds in the rough. There are plenty of out-of-the-way eateries in Dubai at which you can eat like a sheikh for under Dhs50 a head. The only drawback to these cheap independent places is that they are not allowed to sell alcohol. However, they're still worth bursting that bubble of luxury for.

For independent and opinionated reviews of over 500 of the emirate's restaurants, pubs, bars, cafés and shops, buy the *Time Out Eating Out* guide (Dhs20), available in bookshops and supermarkets across the city.

> ❶ Purple numbers given in this chapter correspond to the location of each restaurant or café as marked on the maps. *See pp322-336.*

Bur Dubai

Arabic & Persian

Awtar

Grand Hyatt Dubai, Oud Metha (317 1234).
Open 12.30-3pm, 7.30pm-2am Sun-Fri. **Average**
Dhs400. **Credit** AmEx, MC, V. **Map** p329 K3 ❶
Although there's an à la carte menu, the set menu is always recommended by the smiling staff. Go on, indulge, but you should know that you're in for a feast of epic proportions. After huge quantities of excellent cold mezze you'll receive bowlfuls of delicious hot dishes, after which you'll be stuffed. So it'll be something of a horror when after only a token pause, waiters will stride over with fresh platters, laden down with kebabs and seafood, more plates of salad and bread baskets. The feast is grand in scale and quality. But unleash the set menu at your peril; it will require a loosening of the belt (and the wallet – nothing is particularly cheap here) and no food plans should be made for the next three days. Stick to that, and you'll be amply rewarded.

Bastakiah Nights

Bastakia, Bur Dubai (353 7772). **Open** 12.30-11.30pm daily. **Average** Dhs300. **Credit** AmEx, MC, V. **Map** p330 H3 ❷

Step inside this restaurant and prepare for your romantic Arabian fantasies to be realised. The flickering torches and grand, heavy wooden doors – intricately carved and studded with vast iron nails – immediately transport the unsuspecting guest into old-world Arabia. Although, sadly, the service and food don't quite live up to the setting. Truckloads of mezze and grilled meats arrive when you order the set menu, but nothing really stands out, and service can be slightly grumpy. But the ambience is unbeatable.

Al Mallah

Al Dhiyafha Road (398 4723). **Open** 6am-4am Sat-Thur; noon-4am Frit. **Average** Dhs50. **No credit cards**. **Map** p333 F8 ❸
An old stalwart on the bustling Al Dhiyafah Road scene, Al Mallah is the place to go for simple Arabic fast food. Skip the mezze, which is better elsewhere, and munch on their winning shawarmas and falafel sandwiches. The lamb and chicken shawarmas are small but among the tastiest in the city, while the falafel drips with tahini and isn't too oily. The Al Mallah Special fruit cocktail, which comes with huge quantities of sliced fruit and nuts, is a must-try. It's a prime people-watching point, especially on weekend evenings, when young men drive in circles around Satwa showing off their cars.

The essentials

The restaurants in this chapter have been grouped by area: Bur Dubai, Deira, Jumeirah (which covers all of Jumeirah Beach Road and goes as far as Madinat Jumeirah), the Marina, Sheikh Zayed Road and Out of Town. We've also subdivided them by broad cuisine categories and have included the average price of a meal. This is the typical price of a three-course dinner for two with drinks: a glass of house wine per person if the restaurant is licensed, a glass of juice or a soft drink if it isn't.

You'll find that all restaurants have air-conditioning, and that in fine dining places dress codes are less stringent than in many Arab and Western countries. While you won't be welcome in top-end restaurants in shorts and a T-shirt, only the Burj Al Arab insists on jackets and no jeans for dinner. Reservations are essential when eating in hotels, both because popular restaurants get incredibly oversubscribed and because they have an annoying habit of changing their opening hours on a near-weekly basis.

During Ramadan (falling in early September in 2007, *see p176*), you'll find that most restaurants aren't open for lunch and many have different opening times in the evenings. You will, however, be able to indulge in the pleasures of the fast-breaking tents where expats and UAE nationals congregate to eat mezze, nibble dates, slug back coffee and puff on shishas over a game or two of backgammon. During the month of Ramadan eating in public during daylight hours is not only considered disrespectful, but is also illegal and can result in fines.

When dining out, be mindful that water is routinely served prior to a meal and often without your consent. You will be charged for it unless you make a point of turning it down. If you want the cheapest water available, ask for local water – a brand such as Jeema, Masafi or Aquafina. Otherwise you might end up with the kind of expensive imported water restaurant staff are told to subtly force on you.

Wherever and whenever you eat in Dubai, don't forget to tip good service: ten to 15 per cent is standard, although most hotel restaurants simply add a charge of ten per cent to the bill.

Eat, Drink, Shop

Sidra

Al Dhiyafah Road, Satwa (345 3044). **Open** 24 hrs
daily. **Average** Dhs100. **Credit** AmEx, MC, V.
Map p332 F8

Sidra's mezze is temptingly arranged behind the
first counter, while warm, small and fluffy bread is
baked in the corner, near where kebabs are grilled
to perfection. On Sidra's terrace overlooking
Dhiyafah Road you can sit down to bowls of houmous beiruti (blended with onions, garlic and herbs),
a *fattoush* low on oil and high on fresh, crisp greens,
and a *zaatar* salad, with strands of tangy, potent
thyme and chopped olives. The food's usually fantastic, but the mezze chef is prone to drizzling his
food in tons of oil, so if you want to eat healthily it's
best to speak out at the time of ordering.

Cafés

Basta Art Café

Bastakia (353 5071). **Open** 8am-10pm
daily. **Average** Dhs130. **Credit** AmEx, MC, V.
Map p330 H4

At the far end of Dubai's historic Bastakia quarter,
twinkling fairy lights lead to a courtyard shaded by
leafy trees and decorated with chirruping fountains
and Arabian lanterns. Basta Art Café has long been

a favourite lunch spot with residents and visitors,
offering healthy dishes and romantic surroundings.
Unfortunately, the quality of the food doesn't quite
do justice to the setting and the service, but wash it
all down with a tangy pot of Moroccan tea and a
delightful plate of Arabic sweets, and spending the
afternoon relaxing on cushions in the shade really
doesn't seem so bad after all.

Other location: Arabian Ranches (362 6100).

XVA Café

Al Fahidi Roundabout, Bastakia (353 5383). **Open**
9am-9pm Sat-Thur; 9am-6pm Fri. **Average** Dhs150.
Credit AmEx, MC, V. **Map** p330 H3/H4

XVA's clandestine hiding place in the middle of
Bastakia makes it one of the most atmospheric
places in the city. And with trees unfolding and
canopies billowing to keep the outdoor courtyard
in a calm shade, XVA must be the prettiest art
gallery in town. It's also home to a little café.
The open-faced *magalumi* sandwich is a great
lunchtime bet. Strands of haloumi cheese, grilled
to golden brown perfection, sit on top of a mound
of roasted aubergine and courgette on a thin slice
of brown bread. Prices are high, but where else can
you find a historic courtyard, an art gallery, regular film nights and a great location, all a stone's
throw from the Creek?

Buns in the oven at **Sidra** – a good choice for mezze.

Eat, Drink, Shop

Eat, Drink, Shop

Basta Art Café's shaded courtyard is a favourite lunch spot with residents and visitors.

European

Andiamo!

Grand Hyatt Dubai (317 1234). **Open** 12.30-3pm, 6-11.30pm daily. **Average** Dhs250. **Credit** AmEx, MC, V. **Map** p329 K3 ⑦

Clad with vibrant mosaics, the interior of Andiamo!, with its explosions of colour, is far removed from the calm verdant canopy of the faux-rainforest outside its doors. Choose from ocean fare such as king prawns, mussels and calamari, or team your choice of salads with a range of freshly carved cold meats. A word of warning though – the chef might persuade you to try a slice of exotic white meat called *lardo*. Be careful: it's lard, taken from below a pig's skin. Most importantly, remember to leave room for the tiramisu, which attains a lofty level of pungent creaminess that even a hardened Sicilian grandma would be softened by.

Bateaux Dubai

Al Seef Road, opposite the British Embassy (399 4994). **Average** Dhs600. **Credit** AmEx, MC, V. **Map** p331 J3 ⑧

At nightfall the Creek comes alive with boats lit by fairy lights offering dinner cruises to suit any budget, and Bateaux Dubai is the king of them all. The red-carpet welcome creates the mood for top-notch hospitality and *amuse-bouches* before some excellent mains. The glazed duck breast is smothered in a black truffle and cassis jus, which adds a pleasingly sharp sweetness to the rich meat. With vistas of Bur Dubai's wind towers and Deira's skyscrapers passing beyond immense glass windows, and gentle live jazz murmuring in the background, it's equally suited to a romantic dinner for two or alternatively a lively group of friends.

Medzo

Wafi Pyramids (324 0000). **Open** 12.30-3pm, 7.30-11.30pm daily. **Average** Dhs350. **Credit** AmEx, MC, V. **Map** p329 J3 ⑨

Wafi's much-loved Mediterranean restaurant continues to show off its considerable strengths. The food is very good, the decor is spot-on and the service is excellent. The lobster soup with porcini mushrooms arrives with a freshly whisked froth in a white china cup like a mid-morning cappuccino, and the soft mushrooms balance the sweetness of the seafood with a pleasant bitterness that ably prevents the soup from becoming too sickly. With its cool monochrome prints, soft leather chairs, billowing white tablecloths and affable, unimposing staff, Medzo has got the formula just right.

Troyka

Ascot Hotel, Bank Street (352 0900). **Open** 12.30-2.45pm, 8pm-2.45am daily. **Average** Dhs250. **Credit** AmEx, MC, V. **Map** p330 H4 ⑩

In between slices of beef, chicken breast and pineapple, the 'Troyka steak' contains a surprise

The best Restaurants

For Dubai's very best food
Tang (*see p121)*; Pisces (*see p117)*;
Verre (*see p105)*.

For that one special meal
Eau Zone (*see p120)*; Majlis Al Bahar
(*see p112)*; Pierchic (*see p117)*.

For lunchtime bites
Boardwalk (*see p104)*; Bussola
(*see p119)*; Legends (*see p109)*;
Lime Tree Café (*see p111)*.

For the best global cuisines
Ashiana (*see p107)*; Handi (*see p108)*;
Khazana (*see p100)*; Kiku (*see p106)*;
Al Qasr (*see p109)*; Ravi Restaurant
(*see p101)*; Shabestan (*see 102)*;
Zheng He's (*see p114)*.

ingredient – a cow's tongue. This bovine munching mechanism is moderately tasty, although some diners may not find it very tasteful. The borscht is also fine, as purple as Jimi Hendrix's loon pants and packed with subtly crunchy onion and soft potato. But while Troyka is hardly a superpower for culinary expertise, its eccentric cabaret floor show is a riot of music and dance. Don't expect great food, but for sheer jaw-dropping entertainment, Troyka simply can't be licked.

Far Eastern

Lemongrass
Near Lamcy Plaza, Oud Metha (334 2325).
Open noon-11.30pm daily. **Average** Dhs150.
Credit AmEx, MC, V. **Map** p329 J3 ⓫
One of the most reliably authentic and tasty Thai restaurants in the city, Lemongrass offers a rare experience in urban dining escapism. A tasteful interior blocks out the smog and traffic, creating the illusion that the restaurant is in New York or Paris, or anywhere where restaurants aren't usually tethered to hotels. It's awash in sleek yellow and dark wood, spaciously and moodily appointed with carved Thai antiques and reed vases, resulting in a sleek yet immensely warm and welcoming atmosphere. The food is exquisite – heady aromas normally only found in Bangkok leap off dishes laden generously with peppercorns, lime leaves and other such Thai essentials. Try the stir-fried prawns, the tamarind-drenched fish or the perfect *tom yam koong*.

Peppercrab
Grand Hyatt Dubai (317 1234). **Open** 7-1am Sat,
Fri; 7pm-midnight Sun-Thur. **Average** Dhs700.
Credit AmEx, MC, V. **Map** p329 K3 ⓬

The pepper crab here is fantastic – a good thing really, because going to Peppercrab and not ordering the eponymous dish is like going on holiday to Agra and skipping the Taj Mahal. Skilled knifemen split the shell and pull apart the legs, meaning all the diner needs to do is put on an apron, seize the nutcrackers and scraping scalpels and locate the meat. Flakes of the sweet meat fall from the bone and should be lapped up with crusty white bread, seafood fried rice, pak choi and the restaurant's signature pepper sauce. The rest of the menu doesn't reach the heights of the main event, and a single mud crab will cost around Dhs400, so if your wallet isn't well stocked or you aren't crazy about crab, best give this restaurant a miss. But for the best-tasting crustaceans in the business, Peppercrab fits the bill.

Thai Chi
Wafi Pyramids, by Wafi City Mall, Oud Metha (324 0000). **Open** 12.30-3pm, 7pm-midnight daily. **Average** Dhs220. **Credit** AmEx, MC, V. **Map** p329 J3 ⓭
With tasteful decor, an impressively varied menu and friendly, attentive service, Thai Chi is a solid bet for good Thai and Chinese food. Once you've navigated the bridge over the burbling river and ducked underneath the pagoda, there's a range of rooms to sit in, so you can either enjoy a private meal or savour the bustling atmosphere. Highlights from the Thai menu include the chicken wrapped in pandan leaves and the *goong thirapod* – tiger prawns accompanied by a delicious sweet and sour sauce. The wok-fried beef with oyster sauce, zingingly laden with mushrooms and spring onions, is the pick of the Chinese list.

Indian subcontinent

Aangan
Dhow Palace Hotel (359 9992). **Open** 12.30-3.30pm,
7.30pm-1am daily. **Average** Dhs350. **Credit** AmEx,
MC, V. **Map** p333 G6 ⓮
The flurry of fussy attention that greets you as you set foot in the dimly lit, wood-finished restaurant can be overwhelming, but persevere. Start with the *jhinga kandhari*, with its absurdly giant yet torrentially juicy tiger prawns, seared to unworldly perfection with a crimson explosion of harmonious tandoori spices. The main courses are also excellent, especially the *saag gosht* with tender lamb pieces bathed luxuriously in a phenomenally rich sauce of puréed baby spinach, lush coriander and smoky onions. Considering that it only opened in the autumn of 2006, it is impressive that Aangan already ranks as one of the city's finest restaurants. *Photo p101.*

Antique Bazaar
Four Points by Sheraton (397 7444). **Open**
12.30-3pm, 7.30pm-2am daily. **Average** Dhs150.
Credit AmEx, MC, V. **Map** p330 H4 ⓯
Walk into Antique Bazaar and you're likely to find a restaurant full of diners rapt by the colourful musicians performing atmospheric Indian music on a

Dinner and a jaw-dropping cabaret show at **Troyka**. *See p97.*

See p97.

lambent stage. The audience will probably also be enjoying its food. The shami kebab appetisers are tidy packages of soft minced lamb and chickpeas infused with boldly flavoured coriander; and the dark, rich minced lamb of the *hyderabadi kheema* makes for a fine main course – the flavour of the soft, juicy meat is every bit as pleasing as its appearance. Which is why Antique Bazaar is a reliably good mid-range restaurant.

Asha's
Wafi Pyramids, by Wafi City Mall (324 0000).
Open 12.30-3pm, 7.30pm-12.30am daily. **Average**
Dhs350. **Credit** AmEx, MC, V. **Map** p329 J3 ⑯
The first branch of music icon Asha Bhosle's planned global chain is getting better all the time, although in a city blessed with an abundance of great Indian restaurants, it's not yet quite at the top of the league. Start with the wonderful *murg*

tikka chaat, which sees chicken tikka mixed up with onions, green chilli and coriander in tamarind chutney. And for mains, the *machli masala* is delicious, with perfectly cooked hammour in onion and tomato gravy. There's no doubt it's good fun dining at such an atmospheric and friendly restaurant – the food just needs a little more edge and it'll be a serious contender.

Gazebo
Near Dhow Palace Hotel, Kuwait Street (359 8555).
Open noon-3.15pm, 7-11.45pm daily. **Average**
Dhs120. **Credit** AmEx, MC, V. **Map** p333 G6 ⑰
Gazebo's lengthy menu focuses on dishes from Lucknow and Hyderabad, such as the excellent *tawa masala*, with chunks of succulent lobster stir-fried in a curry of spring onion, tomato and black pepper. The *achari gosht* is another winner; tender, juicy cubes of lamb fired up by a sauce of tamarind,

Tandoori meets tapas at Indian restaurant **Iz**.

Eat, Drink, Shop

fennel and sun-dried tomatoes. You'll be wowed by the intensity of the flavours, the lingering warmth of the spicing, the tantalisingly fruity aromas on the nose and the dazzling colours of the dishes. Unfortunately, the service isn't great and you should expect lengthy waits, but it's a clean, smart, functional and contemporary restaurant, with dark wood fittings, reddish-brown shades, a few Indian arts and crafts and, most importantly, some of the city's best Indian food.

Govinda's

Karama (396 0080). **Open** noon-3pm, 7pm-midnight Sat-Thur; 1.30-3pm, 7pm-midnight Fri. **Average** Dhs100. **Credit** AmEx, MC, V. **Map** p331 J5 ⑱
This Karama restaurant serves Jain food (no meat, no fish, no garlic, no onions) and is a firm favourite among the Indian community. As a result you might find yourself waiting for a table here, but it's well worth staying in line for. Inside, Govinda's is a cosy joint with soft lighting, religious paintings and a not particularly appealing fake tree. The yellow dahl with spinach is wholesome and the vegetable *haridwar* is a creamily satisfying dish. Wash this excellent food down with fresh juices and you'll be hooked.

Iz

Grand Hyatt Dubai (317 1234). **Open** 12.30-3pm, 7-11.30pm daily. **Average** Dhs550. **Credit** AmEx, MC, V. **Map** p329 K3 ⑲

The concept at this new Indian restaurant involves picking a number of small tandoori dishes from the menu, which arrive in the order they are cooked – something like Indian tapas. After a deluge of warm and wondrous mini naan breads of various hues, try the sensuous masala sauce with a fine catch of podgy prawns. The salmon tikka, meanwhile, is a spice-infused celebration of dewy flakes that disintegrates with aplomb in the mouth. Then there's the vegetable biryani with apricot, cashew nuts and figs, and the raan leg of lamb, which is intensely flavourful. It's early days yet, but Iz has all the makings of a very fine restaurant.

Khazana

Al Nasr Leisureland (336 0061). **Open** 12.30-2.30pm, 7-11.30pm daily. **Average** Dhs250. **Credit** AmEx, MC, V. **Map** p329 J3 ⑳
The trouble with Indian celebrity chef Sanjeev Kapoor's Khazana is summoning up the willpower to depart. That's because the tandoori chicken legs, as only one example of the wondrous food here, render mere words redundant – they're perfectly tender, and by the time you've sucked the deliriously juicy meat from the bones they'll be as smooth as ice. Best of all, the bill is likely to be surprisingly good value, given the high quality of the food. All this means that Khazana is one Indian restaurant that you'll be returning to on a regular basis – if you are able to bring yourself to leave in the first place.

Finely tuned Indian food and music at **Aangan**. *See p98.*

Ravi Restaurant

Opposite Rydges Plaza Dubai, Satwa (331 5353).
Open 5am-3am Sat-Thur; 1.30pm-3am Fri. **Average**
Dhs40. **No credit cards. Map** p333 F8 ㉑
The swanky restaurants of Jumeirah might pull
out all the stops to keep you entertained, but they'll
put a dent in your wallet the size of the Burj. The
simple Pakistani food and unintentional street
drama at Ravi's can be just as compelling – at a
fraction of the price. Sit outside, watch the tireless
tide of humanity sweep along the Satwa Road and
enjoy a tender *bihiri* kebab alongside a feisty mut-
ton *palak* in a rich curry swamp spiked with chilli,
or an aggressive chicken *sukha* in a rich quicksand
of spice. You'll struggle to spend more than Dhs50
for two people and the food is excellent, which
might explain Ravi's near legendary status.

Seafood

Fish Basket

*Opposite Mövenpick Hotel Bur Dubai, Oud Metha
(336 7177).* **Open** 10am-12.30am daily. **Average**
Dhs120. **Credit** AmEx, MC, V. **Map** p329 J3 ㉒
In a city where many restaurants will happily strip
you of Dhs200 (plus a cooking charge) for an
overcooked slab of salmon, here you can feast like
a king for Dhs60 per person. Diners can either
choose their own fish from the market or be guided
by the knowledgeable staff. Feast on fresh bread,
salads and yoghurt dips, before getting stuck into
a tray of grilled hammour, battered calamari,
anchovies, some super fresh crab and a couple of
stately king prawns. It's not the place for a long
lingering lunch, and it's a disastrous choice for a
date, but dirham for dirham, the Fish Basket
destroys most of the opposition.

Steakhouse

Manhattan Grill

Grand Hyatt Dubai (317 1234). **Open** 12.30-3pm,
7-11.30pm. **Average** Dhs350. **Credit** AmEx, MC, V.
Map p329 K3 ㉓
The steaks remain Manhattan Grill's biggest
draw: mighty fine Nebraskan cuts served on the
bone that melt like sorbet in the summer sun.
They're very expensive, and MG's price tag may
scare off a few, especially when side dishes at
Dhs25 a pop must be added to supplement the 'just
the meat' mains. The decor – a strange mismatch
of booths, grand tables, side rooms and a mini
veranda – may also not be to everyone's taste;
think impressive business dinners rather than
romantic soirées, but the staff are all knowledgeable, polite and welcoming to a tee.

Shabestan dishes up great Persian food, and views over the Creek.

Deira

Arabic & Persian

Golestan
Next to Computer College, Garhoud (282 8007).
Open 12.15pm-midnight daily. **Average** Dhs120.
Credit AmEx, MC, V. **Map** p329 L3 ㉔
From the painstakingly carved dark wooden divides
and beautifully arranged mosaic finishes to the wonderfully evocative music, this low-key Persian restaurant gets everything right. Start with a huge gathering
of garden-fresh green leaves, sweet and juicy tomatoes, crumbly feta cheese and midnight-black olives,
before moving on to a superb mixed grill, an icy *faloo-
da* (a vermicelli-based Persian dessert) and a platter
of traditional Iranian sweets. Excellent.

Al Mijana
Le Meridien Dubai, Garhoud (282 4040). **Open**
noon-3pm, 8pm-12.30am daily. **Average** Dhs270.
Credit AmEx, MC, V. **Map** p329 L2 ㉕
From the dramatic wooden ceiling to an open kitchen
and wine cellar, Al Mijana is reminiscent of the
classy but understated restaurants perched on the
edge of Lebanon's striking mountains. Here you can
gorge on wonderful *fattoush*, raw minced lamb and
a note-perfect mixed grill, before sipping Turkish
coffee and letting the oud player's tear-jerking tunes
take you back to Lebanon's glory days.

Sarband
Century Village, Garhoud (283 3891). **Open** 11am-
2am daily. **Average** Dhs130. **Credit** AmEx, MC, V.
Map p329 L3 ㉖

The contemporary Mediterranean decor, along
with the recently expanded outdoor terrace, is more
than pleasant, but what keeps people so interested
in Sarband is the excellent Persian food. The *kashk-
o-bademjan*, a grilled aubergine dip made with
whey and caramelised onions, is smooth and full
of kick, while an order of green olives marinated in
crushed walnuts and pomegranate is a perfect way
to begin a wonderful meal. And then there's the
hearty, smoky and torrentially juicy mixed kebab
combo with prawn and hammour marinated in saffron, and the *ghormeh sabzi*, a thick lamb stew of
mixed herbs, kidney beans and lime served with
buttery saffron rice. Recommended.

Shabestan
Radisson SAS Hotel, Dubai Deira Creek (222 7171).
Open 12.15-3.15pm, 7.15-11.15pm daily. **Average**
Dhs300. **Credit** AmEx, MC, V. **Map** p331 J3 ㉗
Shabestan is a beautiful, spacious Persian eaterie.
Illuminated by sunlight and with great views of the
Creek during the day, by night it's a moody,
romantic affair with live entertainment from a trio
of accomplished musicians. The hot flatbread
cooked by a friendly gent at the back of the restaurant should be used to scoop up delicious dips
including *nargesi* (fresh spinach served warm and
topped with a fried egg), and *mirza ghasemi* (a
piquant garlic and aubergine dish). The *cholo*
kebabs are superb, especially the enormous *soltani*
version – two types of beautifully marinated lamb
and a huge pile of saffron rice. Finish with the
Iranian ice cream, which is imbued with the taste
of saffron and pistachio, and savour the plate of
peanut brittle, heart-shaped shortbread and maca-
roons that comes with the bill.

A spot of afternoon tea

Cast aside that cappuccino. Leave the latte alone. Tea is brewing up a storm. Yes, the charming, relaxed ritual of afternoon tea is back in fashion. In the busy, bustling city of Dubai, where sometimes there hardly seems time to breathe, it's no surprise that the mid-afternoon meal is proving to be such a hit. For a quintessential afternoon tea experience, head to one of Dubai's smarter hotels to indulge in the ritual of a formal tea. It can be costly and you'll have to dress up, but when everything is as it should be – fresh and interesting sandwiches, rivers of refreshing teas and extravagant cakes – this is a great way to while away an afternoon. Here we list the best spots in town.

Leaves

There are various packages to suit your taste and budget at this impressive Chinese-themed tearoom. The Grosvenor House option features finger sandwiches, scones, a plethora of pastries, coffee and tea for Dhs95 per person.
Grosvenor House, West Marina Beach Dubai (399 8888). **Tea served** 3-6pm daily.

Lobby Lounge

Afternoon tea – sandwiches, scones, pastries and tea for two – at the Jumeirah Emirates Towers is fantastic value at Dhs80 for two people.
Jumeirah Emirates Towers (319 8088). **Tea served** 3-7pm daily.

Lobby Lounge

The Ritz-Carlton's excellent Dhs88 afternoon tea is served in the lounge area; expect the full panoply of silver teapots, tip-top pastries and sandwiches. If you can't wait for cocktail hour, take the Dhs175 champagne package with flutes of bubbly to accompany your freshly baked scones.
Ritz-Carlton Dubai (399 4000). **Tea served** 2-6pm daily.

Lobby Lounge Palace

Traditional afternoon tea (Dhs80 per person) nets you the complete old-style spread (*pictured, bottom*) on a pleasant veranda overlooking the sea in what is arguably Dubai's most romantic resort.
One&Only Royal Mirage, Dubai (399 9999). **Tea served** 3-6pm daily.

Sahn Eddar

If you want to see inside the Burj Al Arab, taking afternoon tea at Sahn Eddar (*pictured, top*) is a lovely way to do it. It's not cheap (Dhs250 for the regular offering or Dhs350 for the indulgent tea, which includes a glass of champagne), but you will be waited on hand and foot and as a one-off treat, we reckon it's worth it. Go on, spoil yourselves.
Burj Al Arab (301 7600). **Tea served** 3-5pm & 5-7pm daily.

Al Samar

Good-value afternoon tea presented on the finest bone china is what's on offer at this classy Madinat Jumeirah hotel. Traditional high tea is priced at Dhs95, while the deluxe tea costs Dhs125.
Mina A'Salam, Madinat Jumeirah (366 8888). **Tea served** 3-6pm daily.

Eat, Drink, Shop

More really does offer more. A good choice for breakfast, lunch or dinner.

Cafés

More

Behind Lifco supermarket, Garhoud (283 0224).
Open 8am-11pm daily. **Average** Dhs170. **Credit**
AmEx, MC, V. **Map** p329 K2 ㉙
Whether you go to its Garhoud or Al Murooj branch,
More's a good choice for breakfast, lunch or dinner.
If you're there before work, try the glorious eggs
benedict, and if you're there at lunch, grab the
Brazilian tandoori sandwich with its spicy and radi-
antly orange fragments of chicken marinated in
yoghurt and coriander sauce. In the evening, try one
of the main courses (be warned, the starters are big
enough to fill you up), such as the fish of the day
with rice and grilled vegetables, the delicious
lasagne or the tagine with pieces of tender beef
cooked in a clay pot with tangles of spinach, chickpeas and a spicy sauce. Service can be slow, but
More is still one of the city's best cafés.
Other locations: Al Murooj Rotana complex
(343 3779).

European

Boardwalk

Dubai Creek Golf & Yacht Club (295 6000).
Open 8am-midnight daily. **Average** Dhs150.
Credit AmEx, MC, V. **Map** p329 K3 ㉙

The Boardwalk, which enjoys perhaps the best
lunchtime location in the city, has come on leaps and
bounds in recent times. If you've got the appetite,
the burger plates are safe choices – the meat is tasty
and tender, and the vegetables are fresh and crisp.
Although the food is nothing to write home about,
we're delighted that this place is on the rise because
the location is so appealing. Built on a wooden terrace over the Creek, the restaurant lets diners take
in a gorgeous marina view while *abras* – and some
more ostentatious sea crafts – chug by.

Café Chic

Le Meridien Dubai (282 4040). **Open** 12.30-2.45pm,
8-11.45pm daily. **Average** Dhs550. **Credit** AmEx,
MC, V. **Map** p329 L2 ㉚
The return of Chef Pierrick Cizeron to Café Chic signals a new chapter in the cultured French bistro's
success story. With its airy open kitchen, spacious
feel and impeccable service, it seems like business
as usual. For starters, a teeming arrangement of
barigoule has crunchy artichokes, beans, stuffed
squid and smoked salmon jostling for position. The
Tasmanian salmon fillet is persistently flavourful,
pleasingly moist and cooked beautifully. Desserts
are excellent too – try the scrumptious bitter chocolate cannelloni with caramelised custard ice cream
and *guanaja* chocolate sauce. Café Chic doesn't quite
have the wow factor to put it among the city's very
best restaurants, but it's consistently good.

Dine at **Focaccia** for fine Italian food with coastal views.

Focaccia

Hyatt Regency Dubai & Galleria (209 1100). **Open** 12.30-3.30pm, 7-11.30pm daily. **Average** Dhs250. **Credit** AmEx, MC, V. **Map** p331 J1 ③①

When Italian decor is attempted anywhere other than Italy, the result usually goes one of two ways: wonderfully cosy or downright tacky. Focaccia manages the first, with only the odd sprinkling of the second. With the view onto the palm-fringed promenade, it's exceedingly pleasant watching Dubai dwellers doing what very few of them ever do here – walk. The menu is an eclectic mix of Italian staples like gnocchi with four cheeses, with some experiments thrown in such as the beetroot risotto with hammour. All in all, this is a charming restaurant in which to have a relaxing meal, followed by a leisurely stroll along the corniche.

Traiteur

Park Hyatt Dubai (602 1234). **Open** noon-3.30pm, 7pm-midnight daily. **Average** Dhs600. **Credit** AmEx, MC, V. **Map** p329 K3 ③②

With a colossal open kitchen – replete with a large wine cellar, meat-ageing room and kinetic kitchen staff – the restaurant is a pleasant exercise in understatement, with an amiable terrace where you can watch the boats bob along the Creek. But having showed initial promise, the food doesn't

always live up to its lodgings. The pan-fried cod fillet, for instance, is a proud hunk in mother of pearl, but the accompanying claggy lentils let it down. If Traiteur's menu can recapture some of the majesty it once displayed this would be a wonderful restaurant, but for now there's plenty of room for improvement.

Verre

Hilton Dubai Creek (227 1111). **Open** 7-11pm daily. **Average** Dhs950. **Credit** AmEx, MC, V. **Map** p331 L4 ③③

Consistent excellence has defined Verre since its explosion onto Dubai's restaurant scene in the most unlikely of locations in 2001. Unlikely because the slick, understated minimalism of Gordon Ramsay's Creek-side restaurant in Deira is hardly the setting one would expect for food so dependably superb. The Menu Prestige showcases everything Verre does brilliantly. The vine tomato minestrone with basil pesto is astoundingly fresh and zingy, while the incomprehensibly tender roasted sea scallops with caramelised pork belly is tempered majestically by the gushing coolness of the pan-fried watermelon and the mellow twist of the ginger emulsion. Which is why our position hasn't changed over the years – Verre is unwaveringly outstanding. *Photo p106.*

You can swear by Gordon Ramsay's Dubai outpost, **Verre**. *See p105.*

Vivaldi

Sheraton Dubai Creek (228 1111). **Open** 6.30am-
1.30am Sat-Thur; 6.30am-4pm, 7pm-1.30am Fri.
Average Dhs300. **Credit** AmEx, MC, V.
Map p331 K4

Maybe it's due to its Deira location, or perhaps its
tacky mock-Venetian wall paintings, but Vivaldi
rarely gets the plaudits when the city's best Italian
restaurants are mentioned. Yet it deserves to. The
carpaccio starter is faultless, with circles of melt-in-
the-mouth beef drizzled in lemon oil. The grilled beef
tenderloin with foie gras, potato skins and masala
wine sauce is stunning. PETA might reconsider
their stance on inconveniencing geese if they sampled the foie gras (or maybe not), and the meat is
wonderfully tender too. Nab a seat on the terrace,
and you can enjoy fine Italian food while the Creek
chugs merrily along in the background.

Far Eastern

China Club

Radisson SAS Hotel, Dubai Deira Creek (205 7333).
Open 12.30-3pm, 7.30-11pm Sat-Thur; 11.30am-3pm,
7.30-11pm Fri. **Average** Dhs450. **Credit**
AmEx, MC, V. **Map** p331 J3

When you open a steaming basket of *siew mai dim*
sum under the fading 1970s-style lampshades
circling the ceiling, you might start considering
full-time membership of this particular club. After
the Peking duck has been ceremoniously shredded
and wrapped at your table, the deep-fried cod
arrives in dark crispy curls and a sultry black pepper sauce. And the boiled lamb in Szechuan sauce
offers substantial slices of fine-spun flesh that fall
apart like a lover spurned. Which is why we like
the China Club – there's no membership fee and
no initiation ceremony, and it's open to everyone
who appreciates fine Chinese food and great service in a relaxed atmosphere.

Kiku

Le Meridien Dubai (282 4040). **Open** 12.30-2.45pm,
7-11pm daily. **Average** Dhs250. **Credit** AmEx, MC,
V. **Map** p329 L2

Kiku is a fantastic Japanese restaurant, and if you
don't want to take our word for it, trust the huge
throng of Japanese people that populate the place
on a nightly basis. The excellent, authentic and

Sukhothai leads the pack.

well-priced food dished up by friendly and efficient staff really leaves its mark. The starters, such as the grilled squid and elegantly sauced fried aubergine, are exquisite and perfect for sharing, while for mains it's hard to pass up one of the set menus. The sushi gozen bento comes equipped with generous, extraordinarily well-prepared portions of traditional sushi and sashimi.

Miyako
Hyatt Regency Dubai & Galleria (209 1100). **Open** 12.30-3pm, 7-midnight daily. **Average** Dhs350. **Credit** AmEx, MC, V. **Map** p331 J1 ⑦
Miyako is an intimate, tidy and tranquil restaurant of light oranges and browns – a perfect place for the quiet contemplation of life over a bento box. The menu is extensive – we recommend the cook-it-yourself *shabu shabu*, a boiling broth with Chinese cabbage, juicy mushrooms, chunks of tofu and thinly sliced raw beef. Alternatively, the sushi and sashimi are made from the freshest possible ingredients, while the teppanyaki dishes are among the finest in town. It's a mellow, welcoming restaurant that dealing with the endless traffic outside the Regency's doors seems like a minor inconvenience.

Sukhothai
Le Meridien Dubai (282 4040). **Open** 12.30-3.30pm, 7.30pm-12.30am daily. **Average** Dhs400. **Credit** AmEx, MC, V. **Map** p329 L2 ㊳
With a majestic wood panelled interior that captures the spirit of Thailand without being excessive, Sukhothai has been one of the leading Thai restaurants in Dubai for many years, with unquestionably authentic food. Viscous flower-shaped crabmeat dumplings explode with flavour in the mouth, and chubby prawns are enveloped in tight jackets of dried noodles. You can't go wrong with the red and green curries either, made with the perfect balance of coconut cream, kaffir lime leaves, lime, lemongrass, ginger and chilli. It's very clear why Sukhothai has been winning over Dubai's hearts since its inception.

Thai Kitchen
Park Hyatt Dubai (602 1234). **Open** 7pm-midnight Sat-Thur; noon-4pm, 7pm-midnight Fri. **Average** Dhs370. **Credit** AmEx, MC, V. **Map** p329 K2/K3 ㊴
Elegant Arabesque arches, candlelit walkways, the gentle lapping of the Creek in the background and the restaurant's sleek minimalist decor all point to great things. The menu is divided into different sections (wok, clay pot, chargrilled, salads, noodles and steamed), and the dishes are served in tapas-sized portions. The food's slightly hit-and-miss, but standout dishes include the zesty roast duck curry, a hearty and succulent helping of braised pork shank, and grilled fish in a banana leaf combining lemongrass and ginger to heady effect. The best time to visit is on Friday lunchtimes, when you can order as much as you want from the menu and drink unlimited wine for Dhs159 per person.

Indian subcontinent

Ashiana
Sheraton Dubai Creek (228 1111). **Open** 12.30-3.30pm, 7.30-1.30am Sat-Thur; 7.30-1.30am Fri. **Average** Dhs350. **Credit** AmEx, MC, V. **Map** p331 K4 ㊵
As cross-legged musicians bounce mysterious vibes off the dark wooden flourishes and soft fabric finishes, tuck into the *gosht boti* kebab, which offers monolithic boulders of tender, pink spice-infused lamb that fall apart like a fake football shirt after an economy wash. But even that's trumped by the *murg barrah* kebab, which crowds a plate with an aromatic mountain range of yoghurt-lashed chicken that crashes onto the taste buds in an avalanche of bold flavours. Ashiana has had some ups and downs over the years, but now it's flying. The food is heavenly, the atmosphere is fantastic and service is top-notch.

Bombay
Marco Polo Hotel (272 0000). **Open** 12.30-2.30pm, 7.30pm-12.30am daily. **Average** Dhs250. **Credit** AmEx, MC, V. **Map** p331 K2 ㊶

Eat, Drink, Shop

The biryani is a speciality at elegantly furnished **Handi**.

The Marco Polo Hotel, where the Bombay is located, is no Burj Al Arab, but its off-the-beaten-track location proves that sometimes you have to dig a little deeper to find the most valuable treasures. Here, the fish tikka *lahsooni* with chunks of pomfret coated with garlic marinade flakes alluringly, and the butter chicken makes for a deliciously creamy and a subtly spiced main course. When going for an Indian meal in Dubai, it's easy to plump for cheap and cheerful or go to the other extreme and opt for luxury and high prices. Somewhere in between the two, the Bombay is a mid-range discovery that Marco Polo himself would have been proud of.

Handi

Taj Palace Hotel Dubai (223 2222). **Open** noon-3.30pm, 7-11.30pm daily. **Average** Dhs350. **Credit** AmEx, MC, V. **Map** p331 L3 ㊷
We've always been mightily impressed by the Taj Palace Hotel's Indian restaurant. The chef – who belongs to the Qureshi dynasty, and whose ancestors once worked in the Royal Court – has an impressive pedigree that manifests itself in a dazzling panoply of deliciously exotic dishes. The house speciality is biryani, and the chicken option is excellent.

The fluffy basmati rice and rocks of chicken huddle under a crusted dome of baked bread, which cracks open to an explosion of prickly steam like a miniature spice volcano. If you're looking for good Indian food in an atmospheric and beautifully finished restaurant, you should pay Handi a visit.

Steakhouses

JW's Steakhouse

JW Marriott Hotel Dubai (262 4444). **Open** 12.30-3.30pm, 7.30-11pm daily. **Average** Dhs650. **Credit** AmEx, MC, V. **Map** p329 K1 ㊸
JW's Steakhouse has an exclusive gentlemen's club feel, yet to join the flesh-chomping fraternity here you don't have to belong to the old boy network – you just have to be willing and able to part with a significant sum of cash. The brass nameplates on each table are earned by visiting JW's a belt busting 24 times in six months – and proof there are plenty who are willing to do this regularly. And who can blame them? The steaks are tender, wonderfully marbled and big enough to fill a cannibalistic cow and the thick, crispy fries suitably soak up the creamy béarnaise and hollandaise

Al Qasr is the place for a banquet and a belly-dancing show.

sauces that accompany them. It's not perfect – starters and desserts are nothing special – but we're sure that the brass nameplates on JW's tables will continue to appear.

Legends
Dubai Creek Golf & Yacht Club (295 6000).
Open 7pm-midnight daily. **Average** Dhs350.
Credit AmEx, MC, V. **Map** p329 K3 ㊹
Sat overlooking the palm trees and lush greens of the golf club in one direction, and the Creek in the other, this eatery consistently serves legendary meals at very attractive mid-range prices. The main event here is steak. From the tenderness of a perfectly cooked 14oz New Zealand rib-eye to the succulent US prime Angus tenderloin, these cuts are stirringly juicy, slice like butter and melt in the mouth. It's well worth investigating its early bird deals, which consist of three-course meals with wine for around Dhs160 per person. If it's not too hot, make sure you bag a candlelit table outside on the terrace for a leisurely meal.

Palm Grill
Radisson SAS Hotel, Dubai Deira Creek Hotel (205 7333). **Open** 7.30pm-1am daily. **Average** Dhs750.
Credit AmEx, MC, V. **Map** p331 J3 ㊺
The fireplace here is fake – but the dancing flames in the kitchen are determinedly real. The view into the kitchen, and of chefs using huge quantities of butter and cream in many of the dishes, will affirm you're in for a calorie-busting feast. The Australian filet mignon steak is magnificent. An initial prod into the brownish surface reveals its slice-like-butter tenderness, while further investigation unveils a perfect pinkness and then a bloody red centre. A downpour of juiciness accompanies every memorable bite. On most nights of the week a talented jazz pianist performs, making this a fine spot for a romantic, if rather pricey, dinner.

Jumeirah

Arabic & Persian

Al Khayal
Jumeirah Beach Hotel (348 0000). **Open** 7pm-2am daily. **Average** Dhs400. **Credit** AmEx, MC, V.
Map p336 E1 ㊻
Waiters with attitudes are rife in Lebanese eateries, and sadly they've given the cuisine an unfortunate reputation. So when a restaurant offers not only excellent food and a classy setting, but also welcoming and friendly service, it deserves a salute. OK, so the tabbouleh is too parsley-heavy and the spicy potatoes are a bit oily, but other dishes make up for these shortcomings: the baba ganoush is exquisite, and the mixed grill is a tasty array of grilled lamb, beef and chicken. If you can manage more, the *mouhalabiya* is a sweet combination of milk, rose water and pistachios, and is a light and delicious end to a fantastic meal.

Al Qasr
Dubai Marine Beach Resort & Spa (346 1111).
Open 12.30-3.30pm, 7.30pm-2am Sat-Wed, Fri; 12.30-3.30pm, 7.30pm-3am Thur. **Average** Dhs300.
Credit AmEx, MC, V. **Map** p332 D8/D9 ㊼
Al Qasr doesn't do things by halves. Opt for the set menu and a dizzying deluge of mezze arrives with all the commotion of a flash flooding, covering every available square inch of your table. The no-holds-barred banquet continues with a verdant tabbouleh, *kibbeh nayeh* (raw lamb), lamb sausages, *sambusak* with melted cheese, and a tremendous mixed grill. While the band plays and the belly dancer does her thing, you should finish with a mountainous stack of fresh fruit, cakes and shisha. You might not be able to stand up after an evening here, but it's fantastically good fun.

Eat, Drink, Shop

Contemporary design, contemporary Lebanese cuisine at **Shu**.

Shu

Jumeirah Beach Road (349 1303). **Open** 10am-4am Sat-Thur; 10am-3am Fri. **Average** Dhs250. **Credit** AmEx, MC, V. **Map** p334 A15 ⓭

With its eccentric red and grey fascia, lizard-eye oval window and splashy fountain, this contemporary Lebanese restaurant looks like the humble abode of one of Roger Hargreaves' *Mr Men*. Among the offerings from the Yann Arthus-Bertrand-inspired menu, which features stunning photographs from the *Earth from the Skies*, are delicious *fatayer* pastries, fresh-tasting and vibrant stuffed vine leaves and a brilliant signature dish – fried sparrow drizzled in pomegranate syrup.

Cafés

Fudo

Next to Mercato Mall, Jumeirah Beach Road (349 8586). **Open** 9am-3am daily. **Average** Dhs150. **Credit** AmEx, MC, V. **Map** p334 C12 ⓭

One of the most eccentrically, and inappropriately designed places in Dubai, Fudo places large images of war refugees and African children alongside chandeliers, goldfish in uncomfortably tiny bowls and cosy colourful sofas. A something-for-everyone

approach results in an eclectic menu spanning several continents and offering hundreds of dishes, most of which are fairly good. The Thai appetiser plate is a safe place to start, with tender battered cuttlefish and a garlicky chicken skewer, while the goods from the sushi bar are well sliced and impressively fresh.

Lime Tree Café

Near Jumeirah mosque, Jumeirah Beach Road (349 8498). **Open** 7.30am-6pm daily. **Average** Dhs100. **Credit** AmEx, MC, V. **Map** p332 D9 ⓮

The front courtyard of the Beach Road branch, with its leafy plants, trickling water and shady upstairs balcony, offers some of the most sought-after seating in the Emirates. The menu changes daily and the food is fresh, wholesome and well priced. For a light lunch you can't go wrong with the olive-studded focaccias, healthy wraps, and chunky, tasty salads. The dairy-free smoothies and fresh juices are also excellent and the huge slices of carrot cake are legendary. At busier times you may have to queue to place your order, and sometimes it's tough to get a table, which is all testament to Lime Tree's enduring popularity. *Photo p112.*

Other location: Ibn Battuta Mall (362 1900).

Eat, Drink, Shop

Lime Tree Café: fresh food in a fresh atmosphere. *See p111.*

THE One Café

*Next to Jumeirah mosque, Jumeirah Beach Road
(345 6687).* **Open** 9am-9.30pm Sat-Thur; 2-9.30pm
Fri. **Average** Dhs130. **Credit** AmEx, MC, V.
Map p332 D9 ⑤

We've yet to be disappointed by the fresh and inventive food served at the café of this popular furniture store. Given THE One's reputation for wackiness, we expect nothing less than innovative dishes like the purple blueberry tofu ice-cream and the Caribbean coconut chicken salad of prawns, tropical fruits, cashew nuts and beetroot vermicelli. We're also fans of the stylishly oversized crockery and the equally stylish staff – all of whom are attired in quirky T-shirts.

European

Der Keller

Jumeirah Beach Hotel (348 0000). **Open** 6pm-1am
daily. **Credit** AmEx, MC, V. **Average** Dhs350.
Map p336 E1 ⑤

Thankfully, Der Keller isn't one of those German establishments that trumpets its existence with maddening oom-pah music. There are no waiters in lederhosen, heartily plonking frothing beer steins on to your table. Instead, it's so unpretentiously German it's like being a schnitzel's throw from the Rhine. The potato soup, with its chunks of pork and slices of fried black pudding, is gloriously thick and comforting, while the pan-fried pork chop is magnificently pink and tender, and rests on a dollop of creamy mashed potato with kale cabbage. In the best traditions of German *schadenfreude*, there's a clear message for everybody who laughingly shuns German food – the joke is on you.

Majlis Al Bahar

Burj Al Arab (301 7777). **Open** 7pm-midnight
daily. **Credit** AmEx, MC, V. **Average** Dhs1,200.
Map p336 E1 ⑤

If the first bite is with the eye then Majlis Al Bahar offers a full eye-candy banquet before you've even taken your seat. Flickering candles and up-lit palm trees fringe the alfresco eaterie while the Gulf and its bobbing clientele of yachts, tankers and cruisers glisten in the moonlight beyond. The Burj Al Arab completes the visual, proudly displaying its chameleon-with-a-complex light show. The food might be unremarkable and hugely expensive, but for the coo-inducing setting and the chance to eat at the Burj, you can just about justify the cost.

Emirati eats

If you think you can just saunter into a restaurant and expect to find Emirati cuisine, you might be disappointed. Visitors generally don't know much about UAE food, but they soon find out that it's not readily available, and that Emiratis like to keep it that way. Nothing personal, it's just part of life in Dubai – visitors and UAE nationals don't mix very often.

It's hard to find Emirati eats worth recommending. UAE nationals tend to eat their own cuisine at home and it's almost unheard of for Emiratis to leave the house for a family meal. When they do go to restaurants for Arabic food, it'll usually be Lebanese mezze on their plates. According to Samira, owner of Cooking Sense (361 6117; call for details on their Emirati cooking classes) and an Emirati food aficionado, that's not as strange as it sounds. 'Emirati food is normally cooked in big quantities,' she says. 'If it isn't, then the dish won't taste right. It has something to do with the way the spices mesh together and the methods of cooking. So for a restaurant, which needs to make small quantities of everything, it doesn't make sense to offer authentic Emirati food when the taste will be off if it's not cooked in small portions, and if the restaurant makes big quantities of everything it'll lose money.'

The issue with quantity, in fact, isn't just a matter of taste, but it's rooted in Emirati culture. Samira explains: 'If you look at the quantity of the food cooked in a traditional UAE home, you'd think the amount would be enough for an army. But what many people don't understand is that the woman of the house takes into account the possibility of having at least one walk-in guest. That happens often in UAE culture.'

In spite of their legendary hospitality, it's a rare treat to be invited to an Emirati home for a traditional meal. If you're only in Dubai for a few days and want to sample the cuisine, a few Emirati restaurants do exist. Expect lots of heavy dishes of meat and rice, such as *harees* (a bland blend of meat and barley with the consistency of porridge), *ouzi* (a goat baked with rice, onions and eggs) and *tharid* (an ancient dish made with vegetables, meat and bread, slow-cooked into a tasty stew). Not all of the following restaurants serve Emirati food exclusively; several, such as Al Hadheerah, serve Emirati food alongside the better-known Lebanese dishes.

Al Areesh
Al Boom Tourist Village, near Garhoud bridge (324 3000). **Open** noon-4pm, 7pm-midnight daily. **Average** Dhs120. **Credit** AmEx, MC, V.

Bastakiah Nights
(353 7772) **Open** noon-10pm Sat-Thur; 3-10pm Fri. **Average** Dhs350. **Credit** AmEx, MC, V. **Map** p330 H3. *See p95.*

Bin Eid Traditional Restaurant
Near Dubai Hospital, Hamriya, Deira (266 3644). **Open** 8am-1am daily. **Average** Dhs50. **No credit cards. Map** p329 K1.

Al Hadheerah
Jumeirah Bab Al Shams (832 6699). **Open** 8-11pm daily. **Average** Dhs700. **Credit** AmEx, DC, MC, V. *See p131.*

Local House
Bastakia, Bur Dubai (338 5775). **Open** 7.30am-1pm, 4-8pm daily. **Average** Dhs250. **Credit** AmEx, MC, V. **Map** p330 H3.

Al Shangdaga Restaurant & Kitchen
Al Hudaba Road, opposite Satwa Electricity Company, Bur Dubai (398 5776). **Open** 11am-11pm daily. **Average** Dhs60. **No credit cards. Map** p332 F7.

Eat, Drink, Shop

Al Muntaha

Burj Al Arab (301 7600). **Open** 12.30-3pm, 7pm-midnight daily. **Average** Dhs1,400. **Credit** AmEx, MC, V. **Map** p336 E1 (54)

Al Muntaha's location, at the peak of the Burj Al Arab, with sweeping views of man-made archipelagos and skyscraping towers, demands you dress up to the nines. And serious cash is needed to buy Burj soup. At around Dhs150 for a tiny portion, you'd expect the supernaturally tasty meat of an endangered species, not a white bean and celeriac broth of preternatural plainness. The grilled *wagyu* steak might not fare much better, and a wonderfully ethereal passion fruit soufflé and a trio of sweets made with Grand Cru chocolate might be too little too late. The words 'tourist' and 'trap' may spring to mind, but there's still nowhere quite like this for sheer, crazy indulgence.

Segreto

Malakiya Villas, Souk Madinat Jumeirah (366 8888). **Open** noon-3pm, 7-11.30pm daily. **Average** Dhs550. **Credit** AmEx, MC, V. **Map** p336 D1 (55)

It's clear that the folks here are going all out for the lovers' dirham; there's even a cheeky Petrus on the wine list for couples prepared to blow Dhs40,000 on celebrating their love. But sadly, Segreto seems to over-fuss its food and end up with frustratingly inconsistent results that don't justify such high prices. The tagliatelle with wild mushroom ragoût is a highlight, although the tiny spoonful of caviar on top is unnecessary. Segreto impresses in terms of originality and presentation, and the setting is beautiful, but doesn't always hit the heights it promises.

Villa Beach Restaurant

Jumeirah Beach Hotel (348 0000). **Open** noon-4.30pm, 6.30-10.30pm daily. **Credit** AmEx, MC, V. **Average** Dhs750. **Map** p336 E1 (56)

Some of the most postcard-perfect views in the emirate can be found at this beachside restaurant – those of the Burj, in all its alien-like glory, flickering in the night sky. Unfortunately, too many of the tables at this restaurant don't offer a view, which can make a visit here a bit of an anticlimax. The pick of the menu is a wondrously tender beef fillet with a bovine bundle of oxtail served with wild mushroom mash and green peppercorn sauce. Ultimately it's a solid experience, but if you haven't got the view it's difficult to justify the big bucks in the cheap seats.

Far Eastern

Pai Thai

Al Qasr, Madinat Jumeirah (366 8888). **Open** 7-11.30pm daily. **Average** Dhs450. **Credit** AmEx, MC, V. **Map** p336 D1 (57).

Accessible through contrived waterways on an inauthentic-looking *abra*, Pai Thai is a wonderfully peaceful restaurant serving good Thai food. Starters such as the king prawns wrapped in egg noodles, and main courses like the deep-fried hammour with sweet and sour chilli sauce thrill the taste buds, before a sublime deep-fried *pandan* ice-cream provides a sensational denouement. It's one of Dubai's more expensive restaurants, but worth it for the romantic location and superb cuisine.

Fire your appetite at **Zheng He's**.

Zheng He's

Mina A'Salam, Madinat Jumeirah (366 8888). **Open** noon-3pm, 7-11.30pm daily. **Average** Dhs650. **Credit** AmEx, MC, V. **Map** p336 E1 (58)

Beyond the neat stacks of gleaming dinner plates and racks of polished glasses opens a window on to a bustling kitchen. And beyond this restaurant's inimitable sense of style there is substance in abundance. The squid ink dumplings are succulently meaty, and the hot and sour soup is as crowded as an *abra* at rush hour. But the stunning tenderloin beef with wild mushrooms, glowing in the crimson drizzle of a sweet red wine fermentation, massages every taste bud in a surge of masterful flavours that makes time stand still while you savour its intensity. It's evidence enough that Zheng He's has the culinary prowess to match its beautifully elegant interior.

Global

Maria Bonita's Taco Shop

Near Spinneys Umm Suqeim, Al Sheif Road (395 4454). **Open** noon-11.30pm daily. **Average** Dhs150. **Credit** AmEx, MC, V. **Map** p326 C2 (59)

Pierchic is the most romantic restaurant in town. *See p117.*

After several years as Dubai's only authentic taqueria, Maria Bonita's keeps on hitting the spot with its fresh, traditional Mexican food, relaxed atmosphere and reasonable value for money. To the sound of chirping parrots and Mexican pop music, dunk crispy tortilla chips into fiery salsa dips before moving onto gooey cheese quesadillas laced with mushroom and onion. Then try the burritos, which are the best in Dubai by some distance. Kick back with a pitcher of iced *horchata* (a cinnamon drink made with rice milk), put up with the squawks of the resident birds and soak up the uniquely laid-back atmosphere.
Other locations: Green Community, near Courtyard Marriott (885 3188).

Seafood

Flooka
Dubai Marine Beach Resort & Spa, Jumeirah Beach Road (346 1111). **Open** noon-midnight Sat, Fri; noon-3am, 7pm-midnight Sun-Thur. **Average** Dhs350. **Credit** AmEx, MC, V. **Map** p332 D8 ⑩
All contemporary pine finishes, tastefully clean lines and nautical rope adornments, this Lebanese seafood restaurant is a pleasant place for an evening of feasting. The mezze is simple, yet impressively innovative with its use of fish. The *makanek samak* are spicy little sausages made of fish; the *kibbeh samak* emit gusts of fishy flavour from their crispy

wheat shells, and the *samke nayeh* consists of fragile morsels of hammour carpaccio that disintegrate in the mouth. The main courses are straightforward but excellent – huge quantities of grilled, oven-baked or deep-fried fish. Flooka is a major hit with the city's seafood eaters.

Al Mahara
Burj Al Arab (301 7600). **Open** 12.30-3pm, 7pm-midnight daily. **Average** Dhs1,500. **Credit** AmEx, MC, V. **Map** p336 E1 ⑪
Al Mahara, the Burj's seafood restaurant, is a restaurant with a difference. For starters, there's the submarine. While you don't actually move through the sea – and the visuals and sound effects are outrageously corny – it's all part of the fun. But the real action begins when you enter the restaurant. An aquarium filled with freaky-faced fish, sharks, turtles and even eels greets you upon arrival, and midmeal a diver feeds the fish, which might just distract you from a fantastic if bankrupting dinner. There are several different menus: classic (think saline-fresh fin de claire oysters baked in the shell with champagne *sabayon*), modern (deliciously frothy blue swimmer crab milkshake with Asian soft shell crab tempura), 'Arabic adventure' (perfectly succulent Omani lobster), and 'seafood experience' (brawny, juicy grilled tiger prawns). Eating here costs a small fortune, but it's a dining experience you won't quickly forget. Reservations are essential.

Eat, Drink, Shop

wagamama

delicious noodles | rice dishes
freshly squeezed juices | salads

wagamama crowne plaza
sheikh zayed road | tel • +971 (0) 4 305 6060

wagamama the greens
tel • +971 (0) 4 361 5757

wagamama al fattan
al fattan towers | jumeirah road

positive eating + positive living
wagamama.ae

uk | ireland | holland | australia | uae | belgium | new zealand | denmark | turkey | usa

Marina Seafood Restaurant

Jumeirah Beach Hotel (348 0000). **Open** noon-3pm,
6pm-1am daily **Average** Dhs850. **Credit** AmEx, MC,
V. **Map** p336 E1 ㉜
The view from the Marina Seafood Restaurant, surrounded as it is by its wave-shaped hotel – the Burj
Al Arab – and countless man-made islands, should be
magnificent, but at night the reflective glass windows
offer little more than a view of your companion's back
and the restaurant's central fish tank. It's a brilliant
location, but the viewless, rather unromantic reality is
slightly disappointing. This is a shame because the
offerings on the fish-heavy menu are extremely good.
The sea bass sashimi dissolves gently on the tongue;
the pan-fried scallops are light and buttery, and the
tuna steak is sturdy and grey on the outside, reddish
pink and rare in the centre, and absorbed with spices.
We're happiest recommending Marina as a lunch or
Friday brunch option, so you can actually see something on the other side of the window.

Pierchic

Al Qasr, Madinat Jumeirah (366 8888). **Open**
noon-3pm, 7-11.30pm daily. **Average** Dhs800.
Credit AmEx, MC, V. **Map** p336 D1 ㉝
If you can get a seat on the terrace, Pierchic is
Dubai's most romantic restaurant bar none. After a
gentle meander down the pier, leaving the lights of
Madinat Jumeirah behind, you can dine under the
stars and with an uninterrupted view of the neon
Burj Al Arab sails, the Palm Jumeirah and the
Madinat kingdom. The seared sea scallops are a particularly good starter, with tender melting flesh complemented by crispy pancetta, while the main
courses are dominated by marine life. A standout is
the wild sea bass, which has a delicate saffron cream
blanketing the artichoke ravioli, carrots and baby
onion. For a special occasion or for the first meal
after payday, this is an excellent option; however,
be prepared for your wallet to be seriously pillaged
– it's an expensive restaurant. *Photo p115.*

Pisces

Souk Madinat Jumeirah (366 8888). **Open** noon-3pm,
7-11.30pm daily. **Average** Dhs800. **Credit** AmEx,
MC, V. **Map** p336 D1/D2 ㉞
You won't walk into Pisces; you'll drift in with the
tide. Beyond the burnished chrome and glass staircase that gushes down to the reception, a lambent
glow flickers against a furrowed wall where streams
of sculpted waves sweep customers inside. The
ambience is placid, liquid, flowing. The food is glorious. The black eden mussel marinière is a haul of
tiny, tender molluscs in a half-shell under a sizzling
spume of flavourful foam, while the pan-fried sea
scallops and foie gras with sautéed spinach, wild
mushrooms and truffle jus crashes over tongues in
a tsunami of intense flavours. For dessert, the crêpes
brûlée raviolis yield candied agrume and a potent
jus citronelle that jab at your taste buds with all the
power and majesty of Neptune's trident. Pisces has
scrupulously smoothed the exact science of fine dining down to a fine art.

P²

Souk Madinat Jumeirah (366 8888). **Open** noon-
3pm, 7-11.30pm daily. **Average** Dhs620. **Credit**
AmEx, MC, V. **Map** p336 D1 ㉟
This informal outdoor brasserie opened in the spring
of 2007 and is every bit as good as you'd expect the
younger sibling of Pisces (*see above*) to be. The oysters are fresh and wonderfully saline, while the duck
confit is delicately crisped yet moist, and the crème
brûlée is joyously light and fluffy. Diners will
inevitably draw comparisons between the food
downstairs and the fare at this algebraically named
restaurant, but it's easy to do the maths – P^2 fits
perfectly into the Pisces equation. *Photo p119.*

Steakhouse

La Parrilla

Jumeirah Beach Hotel (348 0000). **Open** 12.30-3pm,
6.30pm-1am daily. **Average** Dhs750. **Credit** AmEx,
MC, V. **Map** p336 E1 ㊱
The tango show at this Argentinean restaurant is
full of red-blooded passion, but the real drama
unfolds on your plate. The 500g tenderloin is outstanding, coming perched between bowls of fries
and beans like a sacrificial virgin offered to King
Kong. And there are other Latin American offerings
too; warm up with the succulent Havana chilli
prawn and sweetcorn nuggets with guacamole and
salsa. Then go for the superb flambé margarita
– which is tossed in a flaming commotion of strawberries and crêpes at your table. It'll make you want
to open the windows and loudly extol La Parrilla's
virtues from the 25th floor.

MJ's Steakhouse

Al Qasr, Madinat Jumeirah (366 8888). **Open**
7-11.30pm daily. **Average** Dhs700. **Credit** AmEx,
MC, V. **Map** p336 D1 ㊲
In its previous incarnation as a contemporary
American restaurant, visits to MJ's were charac-
terised by good, but not great dishes. But now, as a
carnivorously committed steakhouse, things have
improved. Unfortunately, in all the kerfuffle of name
changing and menu revamping, some of the decor
problems haven't been cleared up as succinctly. The
high ceilings and bright lights mean the atmosphere
remains cold, and the giant *Alice in Wonderland*-
esque chairs only add to an imposing feel.
Thankfully, the menu rethink is far more successful
– start with amazing oysters and move on to steaks
that cut at the mere suggestion of a fork.

The Marina

Arabic & Persian

Tagine

One&Only Royal Mirage Dubai (399 9999).
Open 7-11.30pm Tue-Sun. **Average** Dhs370.
Credit AmEx, MC, V. **Map** p336 C1 ㊳

Eat, Drink, Shop

Middle Eastern cuisine

Arabic cuisine is far from the sophisticated fare you'll get in France and Italy, but that has much to do with its history. Created and developed by nomadic tribes across Arabia, the cuisine is based on a number of transportable foods, like stock or dried fish, and that recipes depended entirely on what was available. Tribes would migrate from one region to the next, searching for water sources throughout the Middle East, and as they travelled they gathered and used more ingredients in their cooking. Unsurprisingly, tribes from different parts of the Middle East have recipes that suit the vegetation and livestock of each country, but the spices, which kept for long periods, are fairly standard throughout.

However, the intricacies of each Arab country's cuisine aren't immediately obvious to visitors to the region. One of the biggest reasons is that Lebanese food is often misrepresented as the basis of Arabic cuisine. Although restaurants across Europe, the United States and even Dubai pass off Lebanese food as the epitome of Middle East cuisine, the reality is that other Arab nations have their own renditions of stews, salads, shish kebabs and coffee;

the person who lumps the Middle East's cuisine into a single category is misguided.

Historically, the Turks are responsible for many of the Levant's dishes, including such staples as *kibbeh nayeh* (raw lamb), houmous and shawarma. Throughout their reign (1299-1922), the Ottomans introduced a number of cuisines to their subjects, often forcing the Arabs to learn their favourite dishes. Consequently, the Turks heavily influenced Arabic cuisine throughout the Levant, which explains why it's common to find a number of variations of houmous, some with garlic and others with parsley. In many cases, the differences are slight, but for larger dishes like Moroccan tagine (a meat dish) and *Syria fatteh* (a yoghurt and chickpea dish), the disparities are palpable.

The first step to figuring out the differences between each Arab nation's cooking is to stop lumping them all together and recognise that each country's unique history has shaped its particular cuisine. The next step is to be open to trying new dishes, even if the thought of nibbling on lamb brains and stuffed intestines doesn't instantly appeal to you. Be adventurous; there's more to Middle Eastern cuisine than tabbouleh and shawarma.

P2. *See p117.*

From the instant you enter the great wooden gates of this Moroccan paradise, you'll know you're in for a rare Dubai treat: excellent surroundings, exquisite food and not a hint of cheesy *Arabian Nights* paraphernalia in sight. The mezze, which includes beetroot salad, a carrot concoction and a courgette mix, is exquisitely served in tiny blue and white ornamental plates. For mains, try the lamb tagine with ginger, parsley and a host of other flavours, a generous portion of juicy soft lamb and vegetables served with justifiable pomp. Tagine is a thoroughly classy establishment and perfect for a romantic evening out.

European

Bice
Hilton Dubai Jumeirah (399 1111). **Open** noon-midnight daily. **Average** Dhs550. **Credit** AmEx, MC, V. **Map** p336 B1 ⓭
With its colonial-style high ceilings, wood panelling and huge windows, Bice is one of the more elegant places in which to enjoy Italian food in Dubai. By and large the food is as grandiose as the surroundings – dishes are built around well-to-do meats and hulking seafood, and even the simpler pasta dishes are studded with truffles or wild mushrooms. The

results are rich and satisfying – the tortelli offers a smattering of dense ricotta and spinach parcels cuddled in a creamy white truffle sauce. For a stately celebration of high-class Italian eats (with price tags to match), Bice is a treat.

Bussola
Le Meridien Mina Seyahi Beach Resort & Marina (399 3333). **Open** 9am-2am daily. **Average** Dhs400. **Credit** AmEx, MC, V. **Map** p336 B1 ⓰
Customers are lured to Bussola by the promise of a gentle sea breeze drifting romantically through their locks, the stars lighting up the night sky and the gentle swish of the sea from the beachside terrace. They're also attracted by some of the most impressive Italian food in town. The sea scallops wrapped in courgettes are soft, succulent and juicy, and the accompanying polenta cakes are interspersed with a winning peach, leek and dry martini concoction. Even better, the oversized ravioli with lobster in a prawn bisque is generously portioned and combines the fishy and creamy flavours beautifully.

Certo
Radisson SAS Hotel, Dubai Media City (366 9111). **Open** noon-3.30pm, 7pm-midnight daily. **Average** Dhs350. **Credit** AmEx, MC, V. **Map** p336 C2 ⓱

Mezzanine stands out in the Dubai scene thanks to a precious commodity: space.

It may be situated in a nondescript corner of a business hotel, in the most corporate of all Dubai's 'cities', but Certo serves far too good Italian fare to be wasted on the occasional business diner. True, the atmosphere and high-ceilinged design are a little cold, but when you're wrapped in the warm culinary embrace of the hearty lasagne, enjoying the *agnello alla brace* (with wonderfully tender lamb) or demolishing a plate of balsamic-soaked strawberries with cracked black pepper, you can forget your own name let alone your surroundings.

Eau Zone

One&Only Royal Mirage (399 9999). **Open** noon-3.30pm, 7-11.30pm daily. **Average** Dhs650. **Credit** AmEx, MC, V. **Map** p336 C1 ⓬

The blissful, lambent netherworld of Eau Zone is a wonderfully romantic spot, and the food, skilfully concocted by a talented Mauritian chef, is very good too. The duck liver terrine with deep-fried liver confit comes with a scoop of bracing *kumquat* chutney to balance its richness, while the beef ribs have the heady aroma of mulled wine – spicy and fruity with strong overtones of anise and cinnamon. A Dubai must-eat, the Eau Zone tiramisu is a light but rich mocha-flavoured whipped cream potion that is out of this world. Such pleasures don't come cheap, but for romantic soirées or special occasions, it can't be surpassed.

Mezzanine

Grosvenor House West Marina Beach Dubai (399 8888). **Open** 7.30pm-midnight Sat-Wed, Fri; 7.30pm-1am Thur. **Average** Dhs900. **Credit** AmEx, MC, V. **Map** p336 B1 ⓭

From its high ceilings to its uncluttered floors, Mezzanine's airy, expansive dining room welcomes guests with a commodity that's sadly all too rare in Dubai's restaurants – space. Crimson explosions of flowers, flamboyant candelabras and chromatic armchairs punctuate the cool white canvas, colourfully quashing the spectre of sterility. The food hasn't been quite as animated lately, but at the time of going to press the kitchen was set for an overhaul by British celebrity chef Gary Rhodes, so we can look forward to a brand new menu of contemporary British cuisine.

Ottomans

Grosvenor House West Marina Beach Dubai (399 8888). **Open** Sat, Mon-Fri 8pm-1am. **Average** Dhs450. **Credit** AmEx, MC, V. **Map** p336 B1 ⓮

Beyond a candlelit marble water feature, there's a plush dining area with well-spaced tables, languid curtains and a slumber party of cushions. Resist the temptation to curl up in a ball and you'll be well rewarded with shrimp in pistachio, featuring a pair of prawns as big as a sultan's slippers, encased in spirited, crunchy batter shells on an unmade bed of sweetened onion and bell pepper shavings. Also recommended is the stuffed chicken, which is expertly crammed with sprightly wild rice and accompanied by creamy mash and ferric spinach. With its serene ambience and comfortable food, dining out here feels like a cosy night in.

Tang
Le Meridien Mina Seyahi Beach Resort & Marina (399 3333). **Open** 7-11pm Sun-Fri. **Average** Dhs750. **Credit** AmEx, MC, V. **Map** p336 B1
The experiments in molecular gastronomy at Tang take you places. Far removed from the restaurant's exclusionist high-backed seats or the tennis courts next door. The chocolate cognac and tobacco dessert, for example, takes you to the cool crumpled leather of a Chesterfield armchair – brandy swirling in one hand, cigar smouldering in the other. It is audacious, surprising and unreasonably tasty. There is simply nowhere in Dubai that offers food as challenging as Tang. But since it has the atmosphere of a furniture showroom next to a leisure centre, what else is there to do but taste the food, close your eyes and enjoy the journey.

Far Eastern

Buddha Bar
Grosvenor House West Marina Beach Dubai (399 8888). **Open** 8pm-2am daily. **Average** Dhs700. **Credit** AmEx, MC, V. **Map** p336 B1
A favoured haunt of Dubai's ostentatious in-crowd, this Buddhism-themed bar/restaurant is a faithful recreation of the Parisian prototype: candlelit tables buzz with chatter and well-trained staff mill about unobtrusively serving up excellent food that is good and occasionally brilliant. The sushi appetisers are fresh, light and clean on the palate and the lacquered Chinese duck is light, grease-free and covered with caramelised fruit compote, which tempers the gamey taste of the meat. Other dishes, such as the seafood bouillabaisse, aren't as successful, but then who said the path to celestial perfection was going to be straightforward?

Indian subcontinent

Indego
Grosvenor House West Marina Beach Dubai (399 8888). **Open** 7.30pm-midnight Sat-Wed, Fri; 7.30pm-1am Thur. **Average** Dhs650. **Credit** AmEx, MC, V. **Map** p336 B1
This beautiful restaurant, full of bronze statues, exotic masks and antique Indian shoes, is tucked away in a hushed corner of Grosvenor House's sweeping mezzanine lobby. Try the tubby tandoori prawn starter, pricked with devilish spice with snappy fresh onion and a stub of creamy-chunky potato. And the impossibly moist and yielding meat of the lamb shank rogan josh departs from the bone like a kicked-off slipper after a hard

Molecular gastronomy at **Tang**.

day's table service. It's the most expensive Indian restaurant in Dubai, but it is also one of the best.

Nina
One&Only Royal Mirage Dubai (399 9999). **Open** 7-11.30pm daily. **Average** Dhs450. **Credit** AmEx, MC, V. **Map** p336 C1
Over the years, this large, inviting and usually very busy restaurant has delivered some of the most innovative and exciting food in Dubai. As interesting as the menu is, it hasn't changed much in recent times. So the savoury tasting plate, which throws together a range of starters usually including the masala dosa, is always a good place to begin. A good main course is the lamb dumplings, which are tender, warm and gorgeously spiced, while the tomato butter chicken is stunningly smooth and silky.

Seafood

Beach Bar & Grill
One&Only Royal Mirage Dubai (399 9999). **Open** noon-3.15pm, 7-11.30pm daily. **Average** Dhs450. **Credit** AmEx, MC, V. **Map** p336 C1
This beachfront restaurant boasts one of the best locations in town, with low-lit lanterns, wooden walkways over the sand and an uninterrupted view of the Palm island. Considering the restaurant's speciality is seafood, the shellfish dishes are a bit hit-and-miss, but the pan-fried red snapper with clams and roasted fennel is deliciously delicate and is accompanied by a barely detectable but divine rose

The **Grand Grill**, for juicy rare treats.

and pistachio sauce. Alternatively, investigate the grill selection, which boasts generous cuts of beef, including *wagyu*. In keeping with the seductive location, the desserts are equally as tempting; we recommend the warm chocolate cake with espresso ice-cream for a decadent end to the evening.

Steakhouse

Grand Grill
Habtoor Grand Resort & Spa (399 5000). **Open** 1-4pm, 7pm-midnight daily. **Average** Dhs600. **Credit** AmEx, MC, V. **Map** p336 B1 ③⓪
This South African steakhouse, with its bustling open kitchen adjacent to the entrance, and serene dining room that's half wine cellar, half Oxbridge library, ticks all the decor boxes for a fine steakhouse. The brawny 500g Aussie rump steak is magnificent, taking the prize for sheer size and flavour. This slab of meat is so big and bouncy that even after eating half of it, you could curl up and sleep on the remainder, and the tender, rare flesh isn't so much cooked as impassioned. It's a shame the non-beef options, such as the seafood esperada, aren't as good, but even if you bust the top button on your trousers, it's worth stuffing yourself here.

Sheikh Zayed Road

Arabic & Persian

Almaz by Momo
Harvey Nichols, Mall of the Emirates (409 8877). **Open** 10am-midnight Sat-Thur; 10am-1.30am Fri. **Average** Dhs230. **Credit** AmEx, MC, V. **Map** p336 D2 ③①
With its multicoloured low-hanging lamps, a ceiling that glitters like a desert sky and a soundtrack of frantic zithering beats, the dusky Almaz isn't short on atmosphere. The food is impressive too: tiny, golden nuggets of lamb *kibbeh*; visceral, aromatic pan-fried liver; prickly, spicy merguez sausages, and a zesty, fresh Moroccan salad are menu highlights. Almaz arrived here in 2006 courtesy of restaurateur Mourad 'Momo' Mazouz, whose Momo's outlet in London, with its hugely popular celebrity clientele, provides the blueprint for what seems sure to be a Dubai success.

Marrakech
Shangri-La Hotel Dubai (343 8888). **Open** 6.30pm-1am Sat-Thur. **Average** Dhs300. **Credit** AmEx, MC, V. **Map** p335 F12 ③②

Elegant Lebanese staples at **Al Nafoorah**.

This upmarket Moroccan joint is effortlessly elegant. The decor is clean-cut North African – lots of graceful arches, subdued lighting, plenty of pottery and an imposing, tiled and tomb-like central feature bedecked with artfully arranged twigs. Two gentlemen in *burnouses* sit in an alcove, one with an oud, the other toting a violin, making soulfully sung folk. The food is a perfect match, with a huge pigeon pastilla, mountainous couscous dishes, and note-perfect lamb and chicken tagines. With an atmosphere of snug conviviality, Marrakech just needs to pep up the service to allow us to recommend it wholeheartedly for a splendid evening of feasting.

Al Nafoorah

Jumeirah Emirates Towers (319 8088). **Open** 12.30-3pm, 8pm-midnight daily. **Average** Dhs350. **Credit** AmEx, MC, V. **Map** p328 H4 ⑬

Nestled at the base of the Emirates Towers, Nafoorah welcomes steady streams of discerning foodies through its elegant doors. The Lebanese staples are excellent: light and fluffy houmous, which is dive-bombed by squadrons of folded flatbread; a busy baba ganoush salad of aubergine, tomatoes, onion and fragrant herbs; and a lipstick-pink mound of *kibbeh* – a thick carpet of minced raw lamb with ground bulgur wheat. For mains, the grilled hammour is an excellent choice. Nafoorah offers good food in the stately surroundings of the charming restaurant, or alternatively on the beautiful terrace in the long shadow of the skyscrapers above.

Cafés

Shakespeare & Co

Al Attar Business Tower (331 1757). **Open** 7am-1am daily. **Average** Dhs150. **Credit** AmEx, MC, V. **Map** p335 F12 ㉞

A world away from the soulless, facsimiled coffee empires that are taking over the world, Shakespeare & Co – with its granny chic interiors (all lacy doilies and fussy table clothes) mix-and-match furniture and stunning outdoor terrace – radiates warmth. The terrace somehow manages to shut out the noise of cars, while the clever use of billowing sheets and Sartre-deep sofas creates intimate nooks in which to enjoy your mint soda. The food is reasonable rather than impressive (try the mushroom soup) and the service is very erratic, but they could be serving up stewed tea and scones that bounce and we'd still return just to soak up the languid ambience. **Other locations**: Al Wasl Road (394 1121), Gulf Towers, Oud Metha Road (335 3335), the Meadows (360 8886), Village Mall, Jumeirah Beach Road (344 6228).

Zyara

Behind Al Salam Tower (343 5454). **Open** 8am-1am daily. **Average** Dhs140. **Credit** AmEx, MC, V. **Map** p335 F12 ㉟

Exuding bohemian sensibilities, Zyara is strewn with a hodgepodge of pastel-toned floral patterns, 1960s swirls and the grandmotherish features of pink rose porcelain and doily tissue holders. The amiable staff

Eat, Drink, Shop

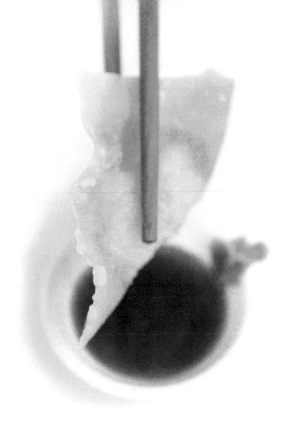

Shang Palace

Only at Shangri-La

our food speaks for itself
[...even if it is Cantonese]

Enjoy the best of the Orient in all its splendour. Fine Cantonese specialities and seasonal dim sum prepared using only the freshest ingredients. Guaranteed to leave your tastebuds speechless.

Taste the difference, discover Shangri-La

For reservations call 04 405 2703 or email f&breservations.sldb@shangri-la.com

Tall orders: **Vu's** offers fine food from the Emirates Towers' 50th floor.

whisk smoky espressos from a golden machine crowned with a winged lion, and also serve an excellent menu of Lebanese mezze as well as fresh salads and tasty sandwiches. At cooler times of the year, Zyara's large patio is a great place to smoke shisha.

European

Nineteen
Montgomerie Golf Club (390 5600). **Open** 7pm-midnight daily. **Average** Dhs550. **Credit** AmEx, MC, V. **Map** p336 B2 🇬🇧

It's not often that you find a good restaurant at a golf club. But Nineteen, a contemporary European restaurant with a decidedly Asian swing, is definitely on the ball. Order the surf and turf main and each meaty ball of sweet lobster will go down your hole in one, while a dewy pink hunk of tenderloin steak seeps its juices into a rich black-bean sauce. Or hack divots out of an oven-baked red snapper, which is moist, firm, boneless and delicious. Golfers and non-golfers alike will be delighted to hear that at Nineteen excellent food, great service and a relaxing and informal atmosphere are all very much par for the course.

Vu's
Jumeirah Emirates Towers (319 8088). **Open** 12.30-3pm, 7.30-11.30pm daily. **Average** Dhs750. **Credit** AmEx, MC, V. **Map** p328 H4 🇬🇧

From up here, on the 50th floor, you can look down on some of Dubai's most famous buildings. And with young Aussie chef James Viles under its belt, the food at Vu's is well on the way to becoming a star attraction of its own. His menu is loaded with quality ingredients and imaginative combinations. For example, the risotto with a half shell of Scottish razor clam – resembling a ride at Wild Wadi – is delicious, with a kick from a Mexicanising scattering of chipotle pepper. Be warned, the dress code at Vu's is fairly strict, prices are high and it's not a place to take the kids, but it offers one of the city's finest dining experiences.

Far Eastern

Hoi An
Shangri-La Hotel Dubai (343 8888). **Open** 6.30pm-1am daily. **Average** Dhs400. **Credit** AmEx, MC, V. **Map** p335 F12 🇬🇧

World class shopping
Award winning restaurants
Sheer self-indulgence

Experience Dubai's favourite shopping and leisure destination.

With a choice of the world's finest brands and a wide variety of award-winning restaurants,
it's no wonder that a visit to Wafi is a perfect way to experience the best of Dubai.
At Wafi, we're offering a range of special benefits and discounts for new visitors -
ask at Customer Service about our special Wafi Welcome to find out more.

WAFI CITY
www.waficity.com
Tel (04) 324 4555

Sushi, sashimi and Sapporo beer at **Sakura**.

Hoi An offers customers a wily fusion of French and Vietnamese cuisine. Spring rolls burst apart with crab and shiitake mushrooms; tender beef skewers gleam with chilli sauce, and a tasty filling of chicken and shrimp pushes against the constraints of a rice paper wrap. And then there's the fillet of salmon with a tamarind-infused crispy skin. The atmosphere can be cold, literally, due to the strong air-conditioning, as well as the predictable new-age Asian music, but nevertheless Hoi An offers a fascinating and impressive dining alternative.

Noodle House
The Boulevard at Jumeirah Emirates Towers (319 8757). **Open** noon-midnight daily. **Average** Dhs150. **Credit** AmEx, MC, V. **Map** p328 H4 ⑥⑨
Few restaurants can claim such a loyal following. Turn up to any of the branches of the Noodle House for lunch or dinner, and there's a good chance you'll have to wait for a seat. There are simple reasons for this – the food is reliably good, service is cheery, the atmosphere is buzzing, and prices are very reasonable. The menu breezes through the cuisines of the Far East, offering everything from an Indonesian *bakmi goring* to Singaporean noodles and Szechuan spiced beef. A great bet for a quick eat.
Other locations: Bin Hendi Mall, Deira City Centre (294 0885); Souk Madinat Jumeirah (366 8888).

Sakura
Crowne Plaza Hotel Dubai (331 1111). **Open** noon-3pm, 7-11.30pm daily. **Average** Dhs240. **Credit** AmEx, MC, V. **Map** p333 G10 ⑨⓪
The Japanese restaurant at the Crowne Plaza is great fun, with clangs of knives, clatters of saltshakers and roars of laughter greeting guests upon arrival. The food's a little hit-and-miss, although the wonderful *samurai teppanyaki* – which is tossed, twirled and juggled about with the dexterity of Forrest Gump playing table tennis – makes up for rather average sushi and sashimi. A real advantage of dining at Sakura is the option to pay Dhs60 and add unlimited quantities of Sapporo beer to your meal.

Shang Palace
Shangri-La Hotel Dubai, Sheikh Zayed Road (343 8888). **Open** 12.30-3pm, 8pm-midnight daily. **Average** Dhs450. **Credit** AmEx, MC, V. **Map** p335 F12 ⑨①
Deftly prepared with the discipline of a *wushu* sword ritual, the Beijing duck at Shang Palace offers contrasting textures and flavours that surpass all the ceremony of its preparation. The main courses are also superb – the beef tenderloin with green peppers in black-bean sauce is excellent, and the scallops are tender and as light as dandelion spores. Yet while the staff tend to be friendly and helpful, the restaurant is nudged into the corner of

Eat, Drink, Shop

Spectrum On One.

the mezzanine floor overlooking the cold marble foyer, and suffers from a lack of atmosphere as a result. Even so, Shang Palace is comfortably one of Dubai's best Chinese restaurants.

Tokyo@TheTowers

Jumeirah Emirates Towers (319 8088). **Open** 12.30-3pm, 7.30pm-midnight Sat-Thur; 1-3pm, 7.30pm-midnight Fri. **Average** Dhs400.
Credit AmEx, MC, V. **Map** p328 H4 ❷

The food at Tokyo is very expensive, although this isn't our main gripe. The restaurant is laid out in such a way that some diners end up eating in the none-too-atmospheric corridor that leads from the entrance, past the private rooms, to the teppanya-ki table and sushi bar at the back. Thankfully the food is superb. The oyster *ponzu* consists of some plucked shellfish ingeniously deep-fried, the saba sashimi are tiny but potently smoky slices of blanched mackerel, and the sushi is always perfectly fresh. It's one of the city's best Japanese restaurants; just be sure to request one of the better tables in the main room.

Global

Spectrum On One

Fairmont Dubai (332 5555). **Open** 6.30-11.45pm Sat-Thur; noon-3pm, 6.30-11.45pm Fri. **Average** Dhs450. **Credit** AmEx, MC, V. **Map** p333 G9 ❸

The appeal of Spectrum On One lies in its sheer variety – although it does have a touch of the upmarket cruise ship about it. The chefs at each cooking station communicate via Madonna-esque headphones and microphones, coordinating every table's meal to within five seconds of each other, regardless of whether the dishes hail from the mountains of India or the heart of rural France. Most of them are very good, such as the *ebi gyoza* sautéed prawn dumplings. The staff provide the culinary journey – all of them, from the wine waiter to the cheery chap who changes the cutlery for each course, address customers by name.

Teatro

Towers Rotana Hotel (343 8000). **Open** 6-11.30pm daily. **Average** Dhs350. **Credit** AmEx, MC, V. **Map** p335 F12 ❹

The Friday brunch

After a tough working week, Dubaians let their collective hair down every Thursday night and miss the following morning's breakfast. This explains why brunch has become an institution in Dubai, and why gallons of inclusive champagne are guzzled every Friday lunchtime. Here are some of our favourites:

Andiamo!
Grand Hyatt Dubai (317 1234). **Brunch served** 12.30-4pm Fri. **Price** Dhs175 (with alcohol); Dhs95 (soft drinks).
Hearty Italian food – a great choice for lunch with friends.

Beachcombers
Jumeirah Beach Hotel (348 0000). **Brunch served** 12.30-4.30pm Fri. **Price** Dhs150; Dhs35 children.
Pan-Asian eats at the ultimate family brunch.

Cellar
Aviation Club (282 9333). **Brunch served** 11.30am-4pm Fri. **Price** Dhs89.
À la carte brunches in a neo-gothic restaurant.

Certo
Radisson SAS Hotel, Dubai Media City (366 9111). **Brunch served** noon-4pm Fri. **Price** Dhs160 (with alcohol); Dhs120 (soft drinks); Dhs60 (children).
Excellent food in the heart of New Dubai.

JW Marriott
JW Marriott Hotel Dubai (607 7977). **Brunch served** noon-midnight Fri. **Price** Dhs235 (with alcohol); Dhs178 (soft drinks).
A 12-hour brunching marathon – a real Dubaian experience (*pictured above*).

Mediterraneo
Shangri-La Hotel (343 8888). **Brunch served** noon-3pm Fri. **Price** Dhs250.
Wonderful Mediterranean buffet with inclusive bubbly.

Mina A'Salam
Mina A'Salam, Madinat Jumeirah (366 6730). **Brunch served** 12.30-3pm Fri. **Price** Dhs295.
A gloriously indulgent celebration of excess.

Planet Hollywood
Wafi Pyramids (324 4777). **Brunch served** noon-3pm Fri. **Price** Dhs85.

The kids' favourite – expect dubious celebrity endorsements all round.

Al Qasr
Al Qasr, Madinat Jumeirah (366 8888). **Brunch served** 12.30-4pm Fri. **Price** Dhs295; Dhs150 children.
Eating on a grand scale, with inclusive booze added in to the mix.

Spectrum On One
Fairmont Dubai (311 8316). **Brunch served** noon-3pm Fri. **Price** Dhs340.
Near-legendary brunch with free-flowing Moët – book in advance.

Spice Island
Renaissance Dubai Hotel (262 5555). **Brunch served** noon-3pm Fri. **Price** Dhs135 (with alcohol); Dhs121 (soft drinks).
A boozy brunch with global fare.

Splendido
Ritz-Carlton Dubai (399 4000). **Brunch served** 12.30-3.30pm Fri. **Price** Dhs288 (alcohol); Dhs188 (soft drinks).
Top-notch Italian fare, to be enjoyed on the sun-drenched terrace.

Thai Kitchen
Park Hyatt Dubai (602 1234). **Brunch served** noon-4pm Fri. **Price** Dhs159 (alcohol); Dhs109 (soft drinks).
Excellent à la carte Thai food with alfresco dining options.

Yalumba
Le Meridien Dubai (282 4040). **Brunch served** 12.30-3.30pm Fri. **Price** Dhs333.
A hugely popular, and occasionally boisterous, champagne brunch.

Eat, Drink, Shop

Amwaj.

Eat, Drink, Shop

A permanent fixture on Dubai's restaurant leaderboard for over five years, Teatro consistently works its magic on the hearts and taste buds of a loyal crowd of regulars. The choice of food is excellent, with options from around the globe: Thailand, China, Italy and India. They even have a sushi menu and the standard is consistently high. Lately, the service has greatly improved and Teatro remains a fun, buzzy and friendly place for an evening meal. Furthermore, the early bird offer is one of the most attractive deals in Dubai – dine between 6pm and 8.30pm (last order 7.15pm) and your food bill will be cut in half.

Seafood

Amwaj

Shangri-La Hotel Dubai (343 8888). **Open** noon-3pm, 7pm-midnight Sun-Fri. **Average** Dhs700. **Credit** AmEx, MC, V. **Map** p335 F12 ⑮

The arrival of chef Matthias Diether has turned Amwaj into a gastronomic heavyweight. Ghosting around the open kitchen without making a sound, Diether and his team collaborate to create delicious creations. The raw *wagyu* beef with asparagus is tremendous, the diver scallops with lemongrass-sauce is cooked to perfection and the foie gras and veal tenderloin is astoundingly tender and tasty. The chink in Amwaj's armour is its setting – one of the few Dubai fine dining restaurants without any view. However, it's home to a chef talented enough to let the food satisfy all the senses.

Salmontini

Mall of the Emirates (347 5844). **Open** noon-midnight daily. **Average** Dhs340. **Credit** AmEx, MC, V. **Map** p336 D2 ⑯

The second Salmontini – the original is in downtown Beirut – is a refined and elegant restaurant where diners can watch pre-school kamikazes hurtling down snowy inclines in miniature dinghies at Ski Dubai. And it specialises, not surprisingly, in the preparation, presentation and degustation of salmon. Whether it's royal, red, pink or silver, smoked, poached, grilled or cured, Salmontini can leap to the task. The smoked heart of salmon is the pick of the menu, consisting of five substantial strips of firm, fresh fish that look like pink piano keys and dissolve in the mouth with a smooth density made all the more intense by a herby cream cheese. The intriguingly named 'unilateral salmon' is fascinating, as one side of an impressive fillet is grilled and the other left intentionally raw. A dedicated salmon restaurant with a view of an indoor ski slope? Only in Dubai, as they say.

Steakhouse

Exchange Grill

Fairmont Dubai (311 5999). **Open** 7pm-midnight daily. **Average** Dhs650. **Credit** AmEx, MC, V. **Map** p333 G9 ⑰

With its masterful combination of great service, brilliant food and relaxing ambience, the Exchange Grill is one of the region's finest steakhouses. When your food arrives it looks almost as excited to be meeting you as you are to have ordered it. The dishes are lovingly prepared, with bold flavours and superb ingredients brought to the fore. Start with the freshly shucked oysters or a refined and elegant duck bouillon, and follow up with a filet mignon steak – an utterly luscious slab of beef, alive with flavour and bursting with character. Teamed up with delicately steamed asparagus and some exquisite steak fries, it's a poem of a meal. The restaurant won the best steakhouse category at the 2007 *Time Out Dubai* Restaurant Awards.

Nezesaussi

Al Manzil Hotel, Burj Dubai Boulevard (428 5888). **Open** 1pm-2am Sat, Fri; 3pm-1am Sun-Thur. **Average** Dhs350. **Credit** AmEx, MC, V. **Map** p335 F14 ⑱

The name may be unpronounceable, but Nezesaussi is usually buzzing with animated punters. The curved bar is normally populated by sports fans, and the restaurant full of favourite dishes from New Zealand, South Africa and Australia. The 'Ref's Advocate' offers three giant skewers of tender beef, juicy chicken and flavourful lamb, while the Australian CAAB steak is gushing, butter-soft and as rare as tartan paint. This relatively new eaterie is so successful that hotel guests happily dine in for days on end. And who cares if the name sounds like an inebriated Glaswegian's sneeze, or that it's surrounded by construction until the Downtown area is completed? Get your hard hat on and check it out.

Out of town

Al Hadheerah

Jumeirah Bab Al Shams Desert Resort & Spa (832 6699). **Open** 7pm-midnight daily. **Average** Dhs650. **Credit** AmEx, MC, V.

Capitalising on just about every cliché in the book – Arabian horses, bumpy camel rides, henna tattoos, belly dancers, falconry, an Arabic band and shisha are all present and correct – Al Hadheerah is as much a theme park as it is a restaurant. But it's a success. A huge range of food from across the Middle East is cooked to order, including the traditional lamb ouzi, sharwarmas, fresh fish, kebabs and plenty of Lebanese mezze. It's extremely expensive for a buffet meal that doesn't include alcohol, and service can be slow, but it's a great location for a Disneyesque night of Arabian food fun and just about worth the long drive out of the city to the picturesque Bab Al Shams.

Think pink at **Salmontini**.

Eat, Drink, Shop

Pubs & Bars

Despite being an Islamic city, Dubai has some great alfresco bars and plush cocktail joints, as well as more down-to-earth pubs.

You will never go thirsty in Dubai. Despite alcohol consumption being discouraged – it's taxed heavily and is restricted to hotels and major sports clubs – the city is awash with pubs, bars and lounges. By confining its drinkeries to hotel premises, Dubai may have robbed itself of charming 'locals' or low-key beach bars, but in their place you have some sumptuous alfresco booze-pushers, sleek designer bars and, rather less impressively, facsimile copies of the West's worst chains.

As Dubai expands, the range of drinking options grows at an increasingly fast rate. Some of the larger hotels have several pubs and bars while the grand resorts, like Madinat Jumeirah, house enough watering holes to challenge the most hardened pub crawlers. Over in Bur Dubai and Deira, meanwhile, there are plenty of one- and two-star hotels whose raison d'être is seemingly to serve alcohol – some of these places almost have as many bars and nightclubs as they have rooms.

There are numerous English, Irish and Australian venues in Dubai to cater for the large population of Western expatriates, and the city's work-hard-play-hard culture (a nine-to-five workday is a rarity in this city) ensures that bars aren't short of customers in the evenings. Don't expect the pubs here to be brimming with character; expect instead, with a few notable exceptions listed here, stereotype-riddled boozers incongruously tacked on to hotel lobbies.

Pubs open around noon and stay open until around 1am on weeknights, 2am on the weekends. The bars, meanwhile, tend to open their doors around 4pm and close between 1am and 3am. The distribution of alcohol in the UAE is handled by just two companies, a+e and MMI, and this, combined with the difficulty and expense of importing stock, means that the big brands rule, while your favourite real ale, wheat beer or organic cider probably won't be behind the bar. Don't make

The Anglophile **Double Decker**. See p137.

plans to sample the local tipple – no alcoholic drinks are legally produced in Gulf countries.

The so-called 'haram' (forbidden by Islam) tax adds 50 per cent to the cost of your drink, so despite plenty of competition, drinking in Dubai is an expensive business. By law, every bar or pub has to be housed in a hotel or hold a special licence, usually only awarded to social clubs or large sporting grounds, which means that most outlets are in effect tourist traps already. This means paying top whack for pick-me-ups. You'll struggle to find a tipple below Dhs15, and in classier joints you'll pay up to Dhs40 for a bottle of beer. On average, expect to pay Dhs20-25 for beers, wine and spirits, and when you add in taxi rides, admission prices and post-club munchies you're looking at a hefty bill for a night out.

> ❶ Pink numbers given in this chapter correspond to the location of each bar as marked on the maps. See pp322-336.

Irish Village.

Bur Dubai

Boston Bar
Jumeira Rotana Hotel, Al Dhiyafah Road (345 5888/www.jumeirarotana.com). **Open** noon-1.30am Sat; noon-1.30am Sun-Mon; noon-2am Tue-Fri. **Credit** AmEx, MC, V. **Map** p332 E8 **❶**
Based on the bar in *Cheers*, the Boston is an unpretentious expat boozer that's typically full of Brits. It can get very lively during football matches, and dancing on the bar frequently breaks out during the ladies' night every Tuesday.

Ginseng
Pyramids, Wafi City, Oud Metha Road (324 8200/ www.ginsengdubai.com). **Open** 7pm-1am Sat-Mon; 7pm-2am Tue-Fri. **Credit** AmEx, MC, V. **Map** p329 J3 **❷**
A cosy Asian-themed venue that can't quite work out whether it's a bar, a restaurant or a nightclub. Ginseng has a large array of fierce cocktails, and while it's stylish, it's not as pretentious as many similar bars in the city. They also, at the time of going to press, slice a massive 50 per cent off your total bill if you dine before 9pm.

Vintage
Pyramids, Wafi City, Oud Metha Road (324 4100/ www.waficity.com). **Open** 6pm-1.30am Sat-Wed; 4pm-2am Thur, Fri. **Credit** AmEx, MC, V. **Map** p329 J3 **❸**
There's something about Vintage's chic interior and stupendous cellar that soothes the soul. The wine bar is constantly buzzing with sophisticated chatter and there's a good cheeseboard to hand to help you soak up the excess alcohol.

Waxy O'Conner's
Ascot Hotel, Khalid Bin Al Waleed Road (Bank Street) (352 0900/www.ascothoteldubai.com). **Open** noon-2am Sat, Tue, Fri; noon-1.30am Sun, Mon, Wed. **Credit** AmEx, MC, V. **Map** p330 H4 **❹**
In no way affiliated to the popular UK chain, Waxy's is a bustling Irish pub on the equally frantic Bank Street. The reason for the sun-starved pint pit's success is simple: the proprietors have lined up a deluge of deals to entice in the budget-conscious boozer.

The biggest bargain is the Friday brunch, at which Dhs50 will get you a full Irish breakfast, five drinks and a second buffet further down the line.

Deira

Dubliners
Le Meridien Dubai, Airport Road, Garhoud (282 4040). **Open** noon-2.45am daily. **Credit** AmEx, MC, V. **Map** p329 L2 **❺**
An intimate Irish bar serving decent pub grub and some of the biggest pies in town, Dubliners is a jovial place for a pint. The decor incorporates dark wood, the obligatory Guinness posters and the back end of a truck, alongside acres of Celtic paraphernalia. It's a good bet for televised sports and its proximity to the airport makes it worth a punt if you've only got a few hours in town and aren't feeling adventurous.

Irish Village
The Aviation Club, Garhoud (282 4750/www.irish village.ae). **Open** 11am-1am daily. **Credit** AmEx, MC, V. **Map** p329 K3 **❻**
While the Irish Village hardly stands out from any of the billion other Irish hooch houses from Dubai to Derby, it's a great option if you're looking for a pint, a nibble and a crowd to enjoy them with. The major draw during winter months is the fantastic outside terrace that hugs a duck pond, yet the vast assortment of draught beers available – including old country favourites Guinness and Kilkenny – keep people flooding in all year round.

QD's
Dubai Creek Golf & Yacht Club, off Garhoud Road (295 6000/www.dubaigolf.com). **Open** 6pm-2am Fri-Wed; 5pm-2am Thur. **Credit** AmEx, MC, V. **Map** p329 K3 **❼**
In the cooler months, the setting at QD's is as atmospheric as any in the city. As wafts of fruit-tinged shisha whisper through the air, lazy dhows chug by against the twinkling backdrop of the Creek at twilight. The food certainly isn't anything to write home about – it's passable bar grub presented without any real flair, and QD's biggest problem remains the inattentive and unreliable service. But

Eat, Drink, Shop

Stir crazy

In a city with so much cash to splash, it's no surprise to find some truly outstanding cocktail offerings. From tobacco-infused rum drinks to heady champagne concoctions (amid some truly unique molecular creations) there are plenty of tempting treats to make the mouth water. Here's our pick of the city's cocktail bars.

Après
For listing, see p136.
To discover the difference between a barman and a mixologist, go to Après. Not only do staff serve all the classics, but they have also created the most inventive cocktails in the city, using ingredients such as thyme and lemon vodka, for instance. There's enough to suit all tastes and wallet sizes, but if you fancy something lavish, the tobacco cocktail features a seven-year-old Havana Club rum that's been infused with Cuban tobacco leaves. And if you're feeling particularly flush then the Mojito Gold is one of the most extravagant cocktails in the city, although at a whopping Dhs250 (the Moët is what you're paying for) you might not want to buy a big round of them. It's the perfect spot for a drink after a hard day's shopping. For a new take on people-watching, get one of the window seats – the bar overlooks the crashes at the bottom of Ski Dubai (see p224).

Ginseng
For listing, see p133.
With dim lighting, non-intrusive music, friendly staff and good Asian food, a visit to this Wafi bar is a treat. The cocktails are among the best in Dubai. The berry sour has been known to wean hardened lager drinkers off the malt and hops for life, while the lemongrass martini and plum caipirissima are also excellent. But frankly, if you shut your eyes and stick a pin in the menu you're almost guaranteed to pick a winner. Leave the flip-flops at home as the door staff can be a bit fussy, but when they're mixing drinks as good as these, putting on some decent clobber is the least you can do for them.

Skyview Bar
For listing, see p135.
Try your best to ignore the garish 1970s-inspired carpets and furniture, because this bar on the top floor of the Burj Al Arab has

much to offer. Skyview isn't your average watering hole: here the staff create your cocktails from scratch based on your specifications. And rather than go to the bar, the fully operational mobile bar comes to you. Stellar custom-made cocktails and incredible views of the sea and Dubai are what define this world-class bar. Prices are accordingly sky-high.

Vu's Bar
For listing, see p139.
Vertiginously located on the 51st floor of the Jumeirah Emirates Towers, Vu's lives up to its name with panoramic views over the Gulf. However, with an extensive new cocktail menu boasting over 200 liver-pickling concoctions, there's plenty to distract you should the view start to pall. Vu's is putting its stock in tailored cocktails such as the Vox'tini (a heady brew of grape vodka, wine and melon liqueur) and the gastronomically molecular pearl bellini (a sumptuous blend of champagne, peach schnapps and pearl balls, frozen using liquid nitrogen). As you'd expect, such high-end cocktails aren't cheap, but with excellent views and knowledgeable staff, Vu's provides an excellent start or finish to your night.

pricing is fair and the setting is quite wonderful, with some of the seats right next to the water.

Terrace

Park Hyatt Dubai, off Garhoud Road (317 2222).
Open noon-1am daily. **Credit** AmEx, MC, V.
Map p329 K2/K3 ❽
Blessed with year-round sunshine and baby blue skies, Dubai demands a spot for an alfresco drink or two, and the sumptuous Terrace bar is one of the best places to see the light of day. The cocktail list is almost as impressive as the panoramic views that take in the Creek-side marina – replete with envy-inducing 60ft schooners – and Dubai's haphazard skyline.

Jumeirah

BarZar

Souk Madinat Jumeirah (366 6197/www.madinat jumeirah.com). **Open** 5pm-2am Sat-Thur; noon-2am Fri. **Credit** AmEx, MC, V. **Map** p336 E2 ❾
BarZar's languid waterside terrace is one of the most popular drinking spots in the city. Set in the Madinat's bustling souk, the bar pulls in punters with a variety of drink deals and promotions. The place is huge with two indoor floors plus the aforementioned patio. Big screen TVs play a mix of muted MTV and sports events.

Dhow & Anchor

Jumeirah Beach Hotel (348 0000/www.jumeirah beachhotel.com). **Open** noon-midnight daily.
Credit AmEx, MC, V. **Map** p336 E1/E2 ❿
Falling somewhere between an old-fashioned British boozer and a Mediterranean taverna, the Dhow & Anchor is a lively place where residents and tourists alike throw back drinks and talk nonsense at an increasing volume. However, beyond the fog of cigarette smoke is a snug dining room and a lovely open terrace where decent Anglo-centric pub fare can be sampled reasonably cheaply.

Left Bank

Souk Madinat Jumeirah (368 6171/www.mmidubai. com). **Open** noon-2am daily. **Credit** AmEx, MC, V.
Map p336 E1/E2 ⓫
Neon lighting, low seating and minimalist decor is the order of the day here. Left Bank's All Bar One-esque interior won't be to everyone's taste, but the bar's waterside terrace is worthy of a visit – if you are able to get a seat that is.

Sho Cho

Dubai Marine Beach Resort & Spa, Jumeirah Beach Road (346 1111/www.dxbmarine.com).
Open 7.30pm-3am daily. **Credit** AmEx, MC, V.
Map p332 D8/D9 ⓬
With a gorgeous terrace overlooking the Gulf and manga movies projected on to the fish tank-studded walls, Sho Cho is a super-hip Japanese-themed bar. Sophisticated, classy and dead trendy, this is where the beautiful people go to play, pose and look pretty: you will not see an ounce of spare body fat in the place. Tuesday and Sunday nights

Barasti Bar is a shore thing.

are rammed, but phone ahead for reservations or arrive as a couple as the door policy is notoriously anti-single males. *Photo p139.*

Skyview Bar

Burj Al Arab (301 7777). **Open** 7pm-2am daily.
Credit AmEx, MC, V. **Map** p336 E1 ⓭
Certainly not the place for a swift one (there's a minimum spend of Dhs250 per person, reservations are essential and the strict dress code's not open for discussion), the Skyview's position atop the famous seven-star hotel ensures its popularity. The bar's decor is garish to say the least – think chameleon-with-an-identity-crisis carpets and broken Casio calculators on the wall – but the views are superb, and the bragging rights on your return home help to justify the cost.

The Marina

Bar 44

Grosvenor House, Dubai Marina (04 317 6871/ www.grosvenorhouse-dubai.com). **Open** 6pm-2am daily. **Credit** AmEx, MC, V. **Map** p336 B1 ⓮
There's a plethora of classy venues in Dubai, but the vertiginous Bar 44 – so-called as it proudly stands on the 44th floor of the Grosvenor House – has plenty to elevate its standing. The views across new Dubai are exceptional, while the exquisite cocktail menu will have you revisiting the bar time and time again. Add in efficient and knowledgeable service – nearly any cocktail can be engineered to your tastes – and you have a classy, if expensive, bar that stands head and shoulders above the majority of its neighbours.

Barasti Bar

Le Meridien Mina Seyahi Beach Resort & Marina, Al Sufouh Road (318 1313/www.starwood-hotels.com).
Open 11am-2am Sat-Wed; 11am-3am Thur, Fri.
Credit AmEx, MC, V. **Map** p336 B1 ⓯

Time for a cold one? **Après** overlooks the only ski slope in the UAE.

Permanently packed, this wood-decked, sun-drenched beach bar almost doubled in size during its 2006 refit, but you'll still struggle to find a table, particularly at the weekend. Alongside the usual alcoholic treats, the bar does a nice sideline in shisha pipes and offers the perfect setting for a puff overlooking the sea. Despite being set in one of the more touristy locations, Barasti still generates a cheery local ambience. *Photo p135.*

Roof Top

Arabian Court, One&Only Royal Mirage, Al Sufouh Road (399 9999/www.oneandonlyresorts.com). **Open** 5pm-1am daily. **Credit** AmEx, MC, V. **Map** p336 C1 ⑯

A sedate sipping station, the Roof Top remains one of the most magnificent drinking venues in the city. The views, which take in the serene Gulf and the bizarre Jumeirah Palm, can't be beaten, and the soundtrack of commercial chilled beats peppered with the odd classic is perfectly judged. Drinks certainly aren't cheap here, but the setting is unbeatable. The Roof Top is an excellent launch pad for that special romantic evening.

Sheikh Zayed Road

Agency

Jumeirah Emirates Towers, Sheikh Zayed Road (319 8780/www.jumeirah.com). **Open** 3pm-3am Sat, Fri; noon-1am Sun-Thur. **Credit** AmEx, MC, V. **Map** p328 H4 ⑰

An upmarket wine bar, the Agency attracts affluent, well-dressed, well-behaved thirtysomethings looking to drink away the stresses of the day. The bar's chilled-out interior – a blend of dark wood and crimson velvet furniture – is made for conversation. It's a crying shame then that the exterior is so uninspiring – sat on patio furniture and flanked by potted plants, you gaze out towards a pair of escalators. If it's alfresco ambience you're after, the branch at Souk Madinat Jumeirah is a better bet, although it's practically impossible to get a seat there on most nights of the week.
Other location: Souk Madinat Jumeirah (366 8888).

Après

Mall of the Emirates (341 2575/www.mmidubai. com). **Open** noon-1am daily. **Credit** AmEx, MC, V. **Map** p336 D2 ⑱

Après is a huge ski-lodge-meets-DJ-bar-meets-Ikea kind of place that manages to find an unlikely compromise between alpine resort and contemporary nightspot. Armed with every conceivable drink under the sun, the staff claim to be able to make a cocktail to suit anyone's tastes. And with connoisseur choices made from ingredients as diverse as cucumber, tobacco-infused rum, sage and coriander, the fussiest of taste buds should be tickled. The food is reasonably good too – try the spectacularly tasty fondue. The sight of cartwheeling skaters through the large slope-facing windows, along with the cocktail waiters' impressive juggling, should keep you entertained.

Blue Bar

Novotel, Sheikh Zayed Road, behind Dubai World Trade Centre (332 0000). **Open** 2pm-2am daily. **Credit** AmEx, MC, V. **Map** p333 G10 ⑲
The Blue Bar has carved itself a bit of a live music niche thanks to its regular jazz nights on Thursday evenings, which invariably have the place packed. Located on the ground floor of the business-like Novotel, the place combines fashionable decor, chilled out vibes and an unusually good selection of draught Belgian beers to potent effect. On regular nights, a bevy of TV screens churn out the usual middle of the road pap and the place resembles the hotel bar it is, but it's still a nice enough place to enjoy a quality lager or two.

Cin Cin

Fairmont Dubai, Sheikh Zayed Road (332 5555). **Open** 6pm-2am daily. **Credit** AmEx, MC, V. **Map** p333 G9/G10 ⑳
Curved around an enormous central pillar, this horseshoe-shaped wine-pusher is a favourite among the post-office crowd. The floor to ceiling wine racks house over 250 different varieties, while the sporadic use of lighting, languid soundtrack and adjoining cigar bar all impress. A bar for grown-ups, with prices to match.

Double Decker

Al Murooj Rotana Hotel & Suites Dubai, Defence Roundabout, near Dusit Dubai (321 1111/www. almuroojrotanahoteldubai.com). **Open** noon-3am daily. **Credit** AmEx, MC, V. **Map** p335 F13 ㉑
As British as launching complaint after complaint about the weather while bemoaning the lack of buses, Double Decker is an unashamed Anglophile of a bar. From the grandiose coats of armour adorning the walls to the hordes of sunburnt punters parading around, it's a home away from home for the expat crowd. It might not harbour the most adventurous atmosphere, but with excellent service and a resident DJ armed with party tunes, it's a frequently packed pub. The Friday brunch followed by a raucous karaoke contest will either be your idea of heaven or hell. *Photo p132.*

Harry Ghatto's

Jumeirah Emirates Towers, Sheikh Zayed Road (330 0000/www.jumeirahemiratestowers.com). **Open** 8pm-3am daily. **Credit** AmEx, MC, V. **Map** p328 H4 ㉒
People can be split into two camps: those who love karaoke and those who hate it, but secretly wish they were up on stage crooning 'Suspicious Minds'. If you have accepted your inner diva, then Harry Ghatto's is the best place in Dubai to belt out a few classics. Nestled in the back room of the Tokyo@The Towers sushi restaurant, the can't-swing-a-cat cosiness and twin microphone set-up inspires a brothers-in-song ambience. Dutch courage comes courtesy of extremely expensive imported Japanese beers and saké, but don't worry if you're still a little nervous: the staff are always on hand to show you how it's done.

Long's Bar

Towers Rotana Hotel, Sheikh Zayed Road (312 2231/www.rotana.com). **Open** noon-3am daily. **Credit** AmEx, MC, V. **Map** p335 F12 ㉓
Long's is one of those places ruddy-faced expats refer to, with a crinkly grin, as being a 'Dubai institution'. Certainly, some of the punters here could do with being removed to a facility of some sort, but the reason it's such a longstanding favourite is because it's a fairly authentic reproduction of a spit 'n' sawdust British pub. Expect TV football, good value drinks and predictable if tasty food.

Lotus One

World Trade Centre, near Novotel, Sheikh Zayed Road (329 3200). **Open** noon-3am daily. **Credit** AmEx, MC, V. **Map** p333 G9/G10 ㉔
A swanky Thai fusion restaurant/bar/club, Lotus One is a popular weekend hangout. Occasionally slow bar service and plenty of knocks and nudges from sunglass-toting posers can make it a little frustrating, but with suspended decks and chairs, cow-print leather cushions and a glass floor showcasing a river and rubble scene underneath, there's plenty to keep your eyes busy.

Scarlett's

Jumeirah Emirates Towers, Sheikh Zayed Road (330 0000/www.jumeirahemiratestowers.com). **Open** noon-5pm, 6-11.30pm daily. **Credit** AmEx, MC, V. **Map** p328 H4 ㉕
Another of Dubai's three-in-one specials, Scarlett's is a popular bar/restaurant/nightclub with a Dixieland theme. It has become a bit of a Dubai institution with its young, mostly affluent and invariably well-dressed crowd spending its time drinking and attempting to strike up conversations with members of the opposite sex. It follows that Tuesday's ladies' night is particularly popular.

The best Venues

For a pint under the stars
Irish Village *(see p133),* **QD's** *(see p133),* **Barasti** *(see p135),* **Roof Top** *(see p136).*

For dizzying views
Skyview Bar *(see p135),* **Bar 44** *(see p135),* **Vu's Bar** *(see p139).*

For a fine vintage
Vintage *(see p133),* **Agency** *(see p136),* **Cin Cin** *(see p137).*

For the big match
Waxy O'Conner's *(see p133),* **Double Decker** *(see p137),* **Boston Bar** *(see p133).*

THE PALACE

THE OLD TOWN

A PALATIAL HERITAGE

Classical themes and Arabian tradition are combined to create The Palace -
managed by Sofitel Luxury Hotels, the centrepiece of The Old Town,
Downtown Burj Dubai

The Palace is a beautifully proportioned hotel with an enchanting Middle Eastern
theme, rich in colour and regional textures. Hosting an array of international
restaurants featuring fine cuisine; with recreational facilities including a luxury
spa and pool. We welcome you to visit our palatial heritage set amidst the world's
most spectacular destination.

The Old Town Island, Downtown Burj Dubai, P.O. Box 97
Dubai, UAE. Tel +971 4 428 7888 Fax +971 4 428 7999
E-mail: thepalacesales@emaar.ae
Website: www.sofitel.com

Opening 2007

Trader Vic's

Crowne Plaza Hotel Dubai, Sheikh Zayed Road (331 1111/www.tradervics.com). **Open** 12.30-3pm, 6.30-11.30pm daily. **Credit** AmEx, MC, V. **Map** p333 F10/G10 ②

Trader's combination of a jolly Polynesian-style band and some of the most potent cocktails in the UAE creates a wonderfully carefree atmosphere. Seating is limited and the bar is often crowded, so arrive early if you want to take the weight off your feet and make the most of the happy hours (when prices drop from astronomical to merely expensive). **Other locations**: Souk Madinat Jumeirah (366 5646).

Vu's Bar

Jumeirah Emirates Towers Hotel, Sheikh Zayed Road (330 0000/www.jumeirahemiratestowers.com). **Open** 5pm-2am daily. **Credit** AmEx, MC, V. **Map** p328 H4 ②

Laid-back elegance at premium prices has well-heeled punters heading up to this swanky 51st-floor bar, which boasts one of Dubai's finest views. Arrive early in the evening to watch the sun go down and the lights come on across the city – an experience made all the sweeter thanks to the bar's mouth-watering cocktail list. Wear a collar and shoes or the fashion police who guard the doors won't let you in. A change in hotel policy means that you can no longer enjoy the spectacularly speedy glass elevator ride from the lobby to the bar (now only available to the fortunate few with room keys).

Sho Cho: for the beautiful set. *See p135.*

Authorised alcohol

The sheer number of bars, pubs and clubs in Dubai might suggest otherwise, but the UAE is a Muslim country and the consumption of alcohol by non-Muslims is tolerated rather than encouraged or celebrated. Here's the low-down on legal drinking.

Bringing it in

It is fine to bring alcohol into the UAE – in fact, once you're through passport control the first thing you'll see is a duty-free shop. At present you're limited to four items per person. After leaving Dubai Duty Free it's advisable to keep your purchases bagged up until you reach your destination. (For more on Customs, *see p301*.)

Buying it here

Dubai residents can buy alcohol from one of the city's two suppliers, MMI (209 5000) and a+e (222 2666), providing they have a valid alcohol licence. Only one licence is awarded per household and the amount you can purchase is dependent on your salary.

The law demands that all bars be housed within hotels or private clubs, although many establishments will have their own entrances away from the hotel lobby. It is illegal for drinking establishments to serve Muslims alcohol, but don't be surprised to see this law being quite openly flouted.

Drunk and disorderly

Public displays of drunkenness are frowned upon and there is zero tolerance when it comes to the city's strict underage drinking and drink-driving countermeasures. You must be 21 to purchase or consume alcohol, and many bars will require photo ID before they serve baby-faced boozers. Drive with the faintest whiff of alcohol on your breath and you can expect to do some time in one of Dubai's prisons as well as pay a small fortune in punitive fines. (It is worth bearing this in mind the morning after a heavy night – stay off the road until the last traces are out of your system.) Dubai isn't really geared up for walking from pub to pub so opt instead for one of the city's inexpensive taxis.

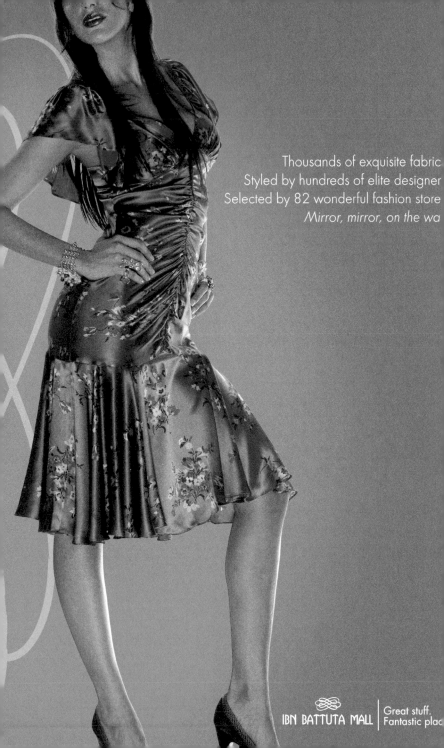

Thousands of exquisite fabric
Styled by hundreds of elite designer
Selected by 82 wonderful fashion store
Mirror, mirror, on the wa

IBN BATTUTA MALL | Great stuff.
                   Fantastic plac

Shops & Services

While independent shops and souks can be found, Dubai is best
suited to the mall-minded.

**Boulevard at Emirates
Towers.** See p146.

Eat, Drink, Shop

Dubai is all about the three 's's: sun, sea and
shopping. Tourists flock to the sandy city to
see if the rumours are true – are there really
over 100 shopping malls? Well, yes and no.
The sizzling heat of half the year means that the
environment isn't right for strings of stores in
the open air. To pull in the punters, top shops
amalgamate in the air-conditioned safety of the
malls. But don't expect every shopping centre
to be a hotbed of great labels and well-known
brands; there are around a dozen malls (*see
pp143-147*) worth jumping in a taxi for – the
others serve day-to-day needs and have only
basic stores on offer.

The **Mall of the Emirates**, the biggest
shopping centre in the Middle East, is so large
that a simple shopping trip can become a feat
of endurance if you park at the wrong entrance,
yet two even larger structures dedicated to
consumption are on the way. The **Dubai Mall**,
which will feature an Olympic-sized ice rink, a
huge aquarium and a gold souk, is expected to
be declared the world's largest mall when it
opens in 2008; the almost-as-big **Mall of Arabia**
is slated to open the following year. Tax-free
Dubai's shops may be, but if you're expecting
rock-bottom prices, you might be disappointed.
While certain brands are considerably cheaper,
on the whole you'll pay similar amounts to
those you'd pay in other major cities. That said,
you can pick up more than a bargain or two at

the **Dubai Shopping Festival** that takes
place annually from December to February
(*see p142* **Consumer culture**) – a much-hyped
extravaganza that shopaholics might want their
trips to coincide with. Away from the malls,
there is the infamous district of Karama, Dubai's
treasure trove of small shops brimming with
knocked-off goods, from bags to watches
and games (*see p145* **Instant Karama**).

In terms of variety and colour, the shopping
experience is a long way off New York's Fifth
Avenue, but Dubai is upping the ante year
after year, introducing more great outlets
opening bigger malls. And, thanks to changes
in legislation, independently-owned boutiques
are flourishing. When it comes to souks (*see
p147*), this may be the Middle East, but if you
have vivid images of bustling thoroughfares
similar to those in Egypt or Syria, you'll be
surprised – most are covered markets – but
you can still haggle to your heart's content
and walk away with glittering gold, beautiful
silks and bags of fragrant spices.

Frittering away money is a national sport
in the UAE, so you can splash your hard-earned
cash late into the night. Typical shop opening
hours are from 10am until midnight, with stores
opening later on Fridays, usually at around
2pm. So with all that in mind, arrive with a
wallet full of cash and credit cards, and prepare
to leave laden with goodies.

BARGAINING

Haggling is a tradition in Dubai's souks, and it really is rare to pay the full price on the tag – if there is one. Most shopkeepers will quote you a figure saying that it is the price 'before discount'. Even 'best price' isn't necessarily as low as you can go. The trick to haggling is to take your time, be polite and to decide what you are happy to pay for the item. A common rule is to offer half the quoted price at first. If you can't get the price down, simply walk away; many shop assistants will literally chase you out into the street to secure a purchase. Bargaining isn't common practice in malls, although it doesn't hurt to ask for a discount, especially if you're paying cash.

SHIPPING

To export goods home contact a cargo or shipping agency directly (*see p300*) or consult the *Yellow Pages* under 'Shipping'. A good agency will give you a quote for shipping bulk items home, and most operate globally. The price of exporting things varies depending on the item (electronic goods can be more expensive) and quantity. In the end, visitors may find it isn't worth the money to ship items home, as export tax makes the process very expensive.

REFUNDS

Visitors used to generous return, exchange and refund policies found in Europe and the United States should be aware that consumers don't have as many rights in Dubai. At present there is no body to protect consumer rights and a large number of stores, even global franchises, will not offer cash returns, and in some cases exchanges aren't available either. When exchanges are available, rather than having weeks to take your purchase back, the norm here is between three to seven days. Be sure to ask what a store's policy is before making your purchase to avoid unwanted stress on your holiday.

Consumer culture

Along with sun, sea and sand, the annual **Dubai Shopping Festival** helps explain the lure of Dubai to holidaymakers throughout the world. Started in 1996, the event is going from strength to strength, with bigger and better offers and seemingly every Tom, Dick and Harry of the retail world jumping onboard. The city comes to life with nearly every mall, individual stores and souks partaking in the events, with eye-catching displays, discounts, promotions and competitions. Big stores often slash their price tags by up to 75 per cent, and if you rock up early on in the festival, you'll definitely find bargains (leave it too late and you'll be left riffling through last year's tat). On top of the bargains, the festival brings together music shows, art exhibitions, dancers and plenty more to spice up your Dubai visit.

Those less inclined to part with well-earned cash might be more interested in Global Village – the festival's most bizarre element. It's a celebration of cultural diversity, and of the UAE population's hopeless addiction to spending money, with displays of dance, handicrafts and music. The concept is admirable, but it's always been a hit-and-miss affair; for every gem you'll unearth from the markets of Afghanistan or Yemen, you'll find countless examples of global tat – vegetable peelers, teddy bears and numerous dubious weight-loss devices.

The festival usually attracts more than three million visitors, a figure that is set to rise significantly in future years. You can discover all about the stores taking part, and the events and exhibitions taking place, at the official website: www.mydsf.com.

Tailor made

We're not all lucky enough to have the cash to splurge on an Armani suit, but luckily for penny pinchers there is a plethora of tailors around town to prevent you resorting to off-the-peg fashions. Always go with a good idea of what you're after, ideally with magazine clippings to help prevent confusion. Here are the tailors we can recommend.

Century Tailoring

Shop No.25, Block C, Karama (337 6610). **Open** 9am-10.30pm Sat-Thur; 9-11.30am, 4-10.30pm Fri. **No credit cards. Map** p329 J2. These tailors in the Karama market area specialise in men's suits, trousers and shirts. It takes two days to make up the clothes, with one fitting. Prices start at Dhs30, but you're generally getting a bargain across the board.

Coventry Tailoring

Next to Deepak's material shop, Al Hudaiba Road, Satwa (344 7563). **Open** 9.30am-1pm, 4-9.30pm Sat-Thur. **No credit cards. Map** p333 F8. Satwa tailors with a fine reputation in an area swamped with cloth-cutters. The workmanship is second to none, and staff are pretty quick, usually knocking out a well-crafted copy and a pair of trousers in about a week.

Diamond Palace Tailors

Near Rigga Road, Deira (269 4071). **Open** 9.30am-1.30pm, 3.30-10pm Sat-Thur; 4-8pm Fri. **No credit cards. Map** p331 L3. Diamond Palace's showroom is manned by Saleem, the owner, and two wizened old men on ancient sewing machines. For around Dhs700, Saleem and his cracking team will create a dapper and charming suit.

Dream Girl Tailors

Opposite Emirates Bank International, across from Satwa roundabout, Satwa (349 5445). **Open** 10am-1.30pm, 4-9.30pm Sat-Thur; 6-8pm Fri. **No credit cards. Map** p333 F8. This place is so popular you may have to wait a couple of weeks for a garment, but they can courier it to you. Bring in a pair of your favourite trousers, and they will make perfect copies. **Other locations**: Bur Dubai (352 6463).

Gents Tailors

Near the Astoria Hotel, Al Fahidi Street, Bur Dubai (353 1460). **Open** 9am-1pm, 4-10pm Sat-Thur; 4.30-10.30pm Fri. **No credit cards. Map** p330 H4. At Gents Tailors, stick figures scrawled on scraps of paper are swiftly transformed into beautiful fitting, good-value clothes – staff can carbon copy anything you bring along.

Kachins Tailors

Meena Bazaar, opposite Cosmos Lane, Bur Dubai (352 1386/www.kachinsdubai.com). **Open** 9am-1.30pm, 4-10.30pm Sat-Thur; 4-10.30pm Fri. **Credit** MC, V. **Map** p330 H4. Kachins has a good reputation for turning out smart suits at smart prices. Tailoring for a two-piece is about Dhs600; shirts start from Dhs40.

Royal Fashions

Souk Madinat Jumeirah (368 6192). **Open** 10am-11pm daily. **Credit** MC, V. **Map** p336 D1. Located at the Souk Madinat Jumeirah, Royal Fashions will put together a suit for you from some of the best fabrics sourced out from England, France, Italy and Switzerland. **Other locations**: Jumeirah Beach Hotel (348 6878).

Malls

Bur Dubai

BurJuman Centre

Trade Centre Road (352 0222/www.burjuman.com). **Open** 10am-10pm Sat-Thur; 4-10pm Fri. **Map** p331 J5. Much improved following an extension, BurJuman is a subdued, chic mall with plenty of designer barns, including Burberry, Donna Karan, Christian Lacroix and Tiffany & Co, as well as a good selection of high street stores such as Zara, Mango, Diesel and Massimo Dutti. Saks Fifth Avenue makes it stand out from the crowd. There are plenty of upmarket cafés to rest at in between a splurge.

Al Ghazal Mall

Al Dhiyafah Road (345 1434). **Open** 10am-10pm Sat-Thur; 4-10pm Fri. **Map** p332 F8. It's not one of the city's hottest shopping haunts, but this quiet mall is ideal for a laid-back roam, with its decent cross-section of stores. There's a well-stocked La Senza and a handful of quirky independent brands such as Pilgrim and Dethar.

Lamcy Plaza

Oud Metha (335 9999/www.lamcyplaza.com). **Open** 9am-midnight Sat, Thur, Fri; 9am-10pm Sun-Wed; **Map** p329 J3. Seemingly abandoned in a strange time warp, Lamcy Plaza certainly doesn't strive to keep up with other malls' obsession with cutting-edge modernity.

No white elephants at **Ibn Battuta Mall**.

Festival Waterfront Centre & Festival Power Centre

Dubai Festival City, Garhoud (375 0505/232 5444/ www.dubaifestivalcity.com). **Open** 10am-10pm Sun-Wed; 10am-midnight Thur-Sat. **Map** p329 L3.

These connected centres opened in early 2007 to a cavalcade of hype, a whopping 500 stores and a fantastic location by the water. The spacious corridors are bathed with natural light and several good restaurants are scattered along the waterfront. Few malls offer so much variety – there's Marks & Spencer, Kenzo, Lacoste, Mark Jacobs, Calvin Klein and an enormous Ikea to boot. The picturesque Festival Square at the heart of the venue offers a regular programme of entertainment too.

Al Ghurair City

Al Rigga Road, Deira (222 5222/www.alghurair city.com). **Open** 10am-10pm Sat-Thur; 2-10pm Fri. **Map** p331 K3.

This veteran mall (the oldest in Dubai) combines Arabic decor with modern design. Popular outlets include Nine West and Paris Gallery. The mall is a bit of a maze and spread over two floors, with corridors branching out at all angles, but it's worth persevering; tucked in the alleyways are excellent speciality stores selling everything from Arabic jewellery and rugs to South African beauty products.

The interior is dated, there's a bizarre and tacky replica of Tower Bridge and an unrealistic-looking waterfall. But if you're looking for bargains this might just be the perfect mall for you. Stock up on cut-price clothes from Fashion Factory and handy Dhs5-10 knick-knacks at the extraordinary Japanese discount store Daiso. Before you go, grab a cheap curry at Thai Express.

Deira

Deira City Centre

Deira/Garhoud area (295 1010/www.deiracitycentre. com). **Open** 10am-10pm Sat-Thur; 2-10pm Fri. **Map** p329 K2.

Once the jewel in Dubai's shopping crown, Deira City Centre has had to work hard to fight off stiff competition from the likes of Mall of the Emirates and Ibn Battuta Mall. It's putting up a good fight, and having introduced a whole flood of new titles to its portfolio, including Club Monaco, H&M and New Look to name but a few, it's still a shopping heavyweight. There's also a massive branch of French hypermarket Carrefour, the amusement centre Magic Planet and a multiplex cinema.

Jumeirah

Ibn Battuta Mall

Between Interchange 5 & 6, Sheikh Zayed Road (362 1900/www.ibnbattutamall.com). **Open** 10am-midnight Sat, Thur, Fri; 10am-10pm Sun-Wed. **Map** p336 A2.

Inspired by the adventures of the intrepid Arab traveller Ibn Battuta, this mall is one of the most eclectic in town. It's divided into six themed courts, each with corresponding architecture: Andalusian, Tunisian, Egyptian, Persian, Indian and Chinese. There are streams of great shops, so check out the Apple Centre and the vast branch of Debenhams.

Jumeirah Centre

Jumeirah Beach Road, Jumeirah (349 9702/ www. gmgdubai.com). **Open** 10am-9pm Sat-Thur; 4-9pm Fri. **Map** p332 D9.

This attractive mini-mall is popular with local residents and has compact outlets interspersed over its two floors. Benetton, the Nike Store and the Body Shop all feature, as well as Blue Cactus, which sells discounted designer gear. At the handicraft store Sunny Days, you can splash out on beautiful textiles and Persian rugs. Alternatively sit back in one of the alfresco cafés with a cappuccino and relax.

Jumeirah Plaza

Jumeirah Beach Road, Jumeirah (349 7111). **Open** 10am-10pm Sat-Thur; 5-10pm Fri. **Map** p332 D9.

There are no big brands to be found here, but this pretty centre is home to several smaller outlets, including gift shop Susan Walpole and the excellent second-hand bookshop House of Prose. For

Instant Karama

The shopping heart of the residential district of Karama, in Bur Dubai, is a network of narrow alleys lined with stores selling absolutely everything, from clothing and bed sheets to furniture and DVDs. This is the place to visit for those exceptionally tacky (and cheap) camel and falcon souvenirs you just have to have. Just make sure you're prepared for a bombardment of shopkeepers lying in wait to avidly advertise their wares – you can barely walk ten yards without being offered a 'best price' on fake Rolex watches and Gucci handbags or pirate DVDs. Meanwhile, bargain-hungry tourists clutch grey plastic bags, evidence that they've been busy spending, with their new purchases virtually indistinguishable from the real designer goodies. Many shops here have 'secret' back doors or attic rooms crammed with products the law does not allow them to show off.

Most of the outlets follow traditional shop opening hours, meaning that your best bet is either to arrive early in the morning or late in the afternoon. Remember to use your bargaining skills – you'll have to haggle for good prices.

City Shoes
Near Karachi Darbar restaurant/Emirates Bank (335 0821). **Open** 9.30am-10.30pm Sat-Thur; 4.30-10.30pm Fri. **Credit** AmEx, MC, V. **Map** p333 J7.
One of the few places in Karama that sells authentic merchandise. City stocks Skechers and Timberland among other brands, and has a few lesser-known names and older collections too. The place holds frequent sales.

Expect to find CAT shoes for under Dhs300 and JanSport bags for around the same price.

Gifts & Souvenirs
Near to Lulu supermarket, Karama (337 7884). **Open** 9am-10pm Sat-Thur; 4-10pm Fri. **Credit** AmEx, MC, V. **Map** p333 H7.
The main branch of this cleverly named store is clean, well stocked and staffed by a helpful and well-informed crew. Everything from pretty cushion covers to 'Real Bug' key chains are sold, but the real prize is the woodwork. A gorgeous wooden cabinet with metal rings is priced at a surprising Dhs1,600, and a lovely chess set, made with a special drawer compartment for pieces, sells at Dhs150.

Ibn Al Saada
Near Lulu supermarket (336 7309). **Open** 9am-10.30pm Sat-Thur; 4-10.30pm Fri. **Credit** AmEx, MC, V. **Map** p333 H7.
While most things in this functional souvenir shop aren't exactly stunning, there are a few interesting items, like the fun Arab nesting dolls, complete with *abaya* and *dishdasha* go for around Dhs20; unique-looking shisha pipes with East Asian designs; and very pretty glass and metal cups, perfect for tea lights.

Top Gain
Near Karama Fish Market (050 846 3637). **Open** 9am-11pm daily. **Credit** MC, V. **Map** p329 J2.
If you're looking for the knock-offs Karama's famous for, try this eclectic outlet. Billabong trousers are very cheap here, and you'll be able to buy lots of fun Rastafarian bits and pieces that you won't find in the other stores.

creatives out there, there is a T-shirt design shop, and for interior fanatics, a few well-stocked craft shops situated upstairs.

Mall of the Emirates
Interchange 4, Sheikh Zayed Road (409 9000/ www.malloftheemirates.com). **Open** 10am-midnight Sat, Thur, Fri; 10am-10pm Sun-Wed. **Map** p336 D2.
Staggeringly big and horrifically busy at weekends, this mall is Dubai's main hive of shopping activity, bringing together designer, high street, boutique and craft outlets under one enormous roof. The ground level is lined with high street names and a huge Carrefour, while the upper level caters for the exclusive brands. Take time out and catch a movie at the multiplex or cool off after all that window-shopping by getting on the piste at the ski dome. There are also oodles of cafés and restaurants – some licensed

to serve alcohol – to keep you well fuelled. And thanks to the arrival of the Dubai Community Theatre & Arts Centre, on some nights you can catch a bit of live entertainment too.

Mercato Mall
Jumeirah Beach Road, Jumeirah (344 4161/www. mercatoshoppingmall.com). **Open** 10am-10pm Sat-Thur; 2-10pm Fri. **Map** p334 C12.
Italian designed and inspired, Mercato is a light and airy mall decorated with stonewash murals and alleys. While there is not quite the choice you'll find in bigger malls, there's a good mix of stores, including Mango, Massimo Dutti, Virgin Megastore and Topshop. There are also a few little boutiques worth checking out, including funky swimwear and lingerie store Moda Brazil, and the *Sex and the City*-inspired Fleurt.

Souk Madinat Jumeirah recreates the old Arabian shopping experience.

Palm Strip

Jumeirah Beach Road, Jumeirah (346 1462). **Open** 10am-10pm Sat-Thur; 4-10pm Fri. **Map** p332 D9.
Set by the beach, this whitewashed mall is one of the very few open-air shopping strips in the city. Shops are set back from the road and arranged over two levels. The lower level is dominated by eateries, including Starbucks and Japengo Café, in addition to a well-stocked branch of Zara Home. Upstairs you can opt for a bit of preening in the N.Bar nail salon, browse through a few home stores and check out a great haunt for mothers, Favourite Things Mother & Child.

Souk Madinat Jumeirah

Al Sufouh Road (366 6546/www.madinatjumeirah. com). **Open** 10am-11pm daily. **Map** p336 D1.
One of Dubai's most popular spots, the Madinat's souk has been created to resemble a traditional Arabian marketplace. With its maze of dimly lit identical corridors, it's easy to find yourself walking in circles while meandering past colourful outlets selling arts, crafts, homeware, jewellery and plenty of souvenirs. While there are a handful of branded stores including Bonpoint and Ounass, the majority of shops here cater mainly to tourists, and prices are accordingly high. Connected to a huge hotel complex, the mall has plenty of licensed bars and restaurants, which means it's always bustling with bags of atmosphere. Head to the man-made waterways to dine alfresco and people-watch under the eye of the Burj Al Arab.

Town Centre

Jumeirah Beach Road, Jumeirah (344 0111). **Open** 10am-10pm Sat-Thur; 5-10pm Fri. **Map** p334 C12.
Nestled next to Mercato Mall, this boxy centre seems slightly dated. At least Feet First offers top-notch reflexology, the S.O.S salon provides affordable beauty treatments and Kaya Skin Clinic is a high-tech centre that will help tackle any skin woes. Visiting families should check out the innovative Café Céramique, where you can paint your own crockery while snacking on healthy food.

Village

Jumeirah Beach Road, Jumeirah (342 9679/ www. thevillagedubai.com). **Open** 10am-10pm Sat-Thur; 4-10pm Fri. **Map** p332 D9.
Attracting boutiques rather than high street outlets, the Village is an avant-garde shopper's dream. S*uce is a girly fashionista's treasure, Luxecouture is packed with New York's finest designer pieces and Ayesha Depala's boasts some wonderful chi chi designs.

Sheikh Zayed Road

Boulevard at Emirates Towers

Sheikh Zayed Road (330 0000/ www.jumeirah emiratestowers.com). **Open** 10am-10pm Sat-Thur; 4-10pm Fri. **Map** p328 H4.
Nestled at the base of the Jumeirah Emirates Towers office block, this swanky mall offers a sophisticated

Duty calls

It's not uncommon for tourists to arrive at Dubai airport especially early for their flight home, such is the near-mystical appeal of Dubai Duty Free. The tax-free store boasts a vast array of cosmetics, perfumes, music, electronics, tobacco and alcohol, although the range of clothes is more limited. Upon arrival in Dubai, each passenger is allowed to purchase up to four items of alcohol (be it bottled spirits, wine or a case of beer) and two cartons of cigarettes. (For more on Customs, *see p301*.)

spread of designer stores over its two floors. Gucci, Giorgio Armani, Yves Saint Laurent and Bottega Veneta dominate the ground floor, while upstairs you'll uncover Jimmy Choo.

Souks

Dubai's markets provide a lifeline for local traders. You won't find the colourful bazaars seen in some Arabian cities, but prices can be cheaper than those in the malls (*also p169* **The gold rush**).

Fish market
Deira, opposite Hyatt Regency Dubai & Galleria. **Open** 9am-1pm, 4pm-10pm Sat-Thur; 4-10pm Fri. **Map** p330 H2.
An army of men in blue uniforms rush around boxing, weighing and carving up the day's catch in this huge hall with stall upon stall of fish. While splashing your path past the stalls – this is not a place for flip-flops – expect to see black hammour, koffer, kingfish, safi, shark and plenty of brawny king prawns.

Fruit & vegetable souk
Deira, opposite Hyatt Regency Dubai & Galleria. **Open** 9am-1pm, 4-10pm Sat-Thur; 4-10pm Fri. **Map** p330 H2.
If you enter here from the adjoining meat market, it's like dying and being reborn. Bright, colourful and fragrant with an upbeat aura, it's a fun place to look around even if you have no intention of

stocking up on fresh goods. Pick up some ice-cold coconut water to keep you refreshed as you ogle everything from bog standard bananas to more intriguing buys, including bitter gourds, custard apples, dragon fruits and mangosteens.

Meat market
Deira, opposite Hyatt Regency Dubai & Galleria. **Open** 9am-1pm, 4-10pm Sat-Thur; 4-10pm Fri. **Map** p330 H2.
It's unlikely you'll want to invest in half a lamb carcass while on holiday, but for those with an interest in food, the meat market will be fascinatingly repulsive. Duck behind the huge carcasses that swing from intimidating meat hooks while butchers busy themselves by hacking away at cow heads – watch out for flying jaws as fragments are thrown in various buckets. If that hasn't put you off, meat eaters can find plenty of bargains here.

Spice souk
Between Al Nasr Square and the Creek, near Gold Souk, Deira. **Open** No set opening hours, but most stalls open between 8am-1pm & 4-9pm Sat-Thur, & 4-9pm Fri. **Map** p330 H3.
Postcard-pretty sacks of aromatic ingredients line the small shop fronts at this colourful souk. Expect to find frankincense, nutmeg, cardamom, star anise, vanilla pods and saffron imported from Iran. This is one of the most atmospheric souks in town and gives you a glimpse into the old Dubai, but don't expect a leisurely stroll – getting through the area without being lured into several shops is hard work.

Textile souk
Al Fahidi Street, Bur Dubai. **Open** 9am-1pm, 4-10pm Sat-Thur; 4-10pm Fri. **Map** p330 H4.
The shops on this street house an enormous range of designs from the simple to the intricately elaborate. The majority of the material comes from the Indian subcontinent and at most stores you're free to haggle for a great price. If you intend to get something made up by a tailor, it's worth asking them how much material you will need to avoid any unnecessary revisits. Rivoli (352 5448) comes highly recommended; it's split into men's and women's floors, and you can find a good selection of materials here.

Antiques & curios

Antique Museum
Third interchange, Al Quoz Industrial Area (347 9935). **Open** 9am-8.30pm Sat-Thur; 9-11am, 3-8.30pm Fri. **Credit** AmEx, MC, V. **Map** p336 E3.
Although Al Quoz may appear to be a deserted industrial estate, tucked away behind the bleak exteriors are some of Dubai's best antique haunts. Although not an actual antique museum, this warehouse is a diamond in the rough: once past the giant wooden doors you are transported into a secluded cave of lost riches. The narrow aisles are packed with a wide range of handicrafts, shisha pipes, pashmina shawls, furniture and the odd belly-dancing costume.

Eat, Drink, Shop

Sculpture-vultures head to **Majlis Gallery**.

Creative Art Centre

*Behind Choithram supermarket, Jumeirah Beach
Road, Jumeirah (344 4394).* **Open** 8am-6pm
Sat-Thur. **Credit** AmEx, MC, V. **Map** p332 D10.
Spanning two pristine villas, this centre brings
together souvenirs, art and antiques. As a result,
it's a haunt for people who want to add a splash of
panache to their homes as well as a great spot for
visitors to find some interesting keepsakes from
their trip. Among the array of Arabic knick-knacks
are several collector's items including wooden
chests, old Omani doors turned into coffee tables
and plenty of Bedouin silver.

Gallery One

Mall of the Emirates (341 4488). **Open** 10am-
midnight daily. **Credit** AmEx, MC, V. **Map** p336 D2.
With its beautiful bold prints and one-offs, this compact exhibition space is rapidly gaining popularity
among the art lovers of Dubai. The outlet features an
eclectic mix of oil prints and photography, including
limited edition original prints of the Beatles, Bob
Marley and Jimi Hendrix among others.

Kani Home

Ibn Battuta Mall (368 5408). **Open** 10am-midnight
Thur, Fri, Sat; 10am-10pm Sun-Wed. **Credit** AmEx,
MC, V. **Map** p336 A2.
Kani Home stocks Kashmiri goods, including handmade silver jewellery, brightly dyed silk kaftans,
elaborate bedspreads, genuine pashminas, beautifully detailed rugs and antique Jamava shawls.

Majlis Gallery

*Al Fahidi Roundabout, Bastakia, Bur Dubai
(353 6233/www.majlisgallery.com).* **Open** 9.30am-
1.30pm, 4.30-8pm Sat-Thur. **Credit** AmEx, MC, V.
Map p330 H4.
With its appealing location in Bastakia, Dubai's old
town, this is a great place to stop off for a coffee
and a bit of shopping as you wander the winding
alleyways. Step back in time through the chunky
wooden doorway to find yourself in a serene courtyard surrounded by a series of exhibition rooms
displaying work from local and international
artists. Small sculptures and Arabian ornaments
are often on display and if you don't mind paying
top dirham, the gallery has a deserved reputation
for its original on-canvas creations.

Showcase Antiques, Art & Frames

Jumeirah Beach Road, Jumeirah (348 8797).
Open 9am-8pm Sat-Thur. **Credit** AmEx, MC, V.
Map p336 E2.
Three storeys of antiques, artefacts and art make
Showcase a store well worth a visit. There are plenty of items hailing from Oman – you can pick up a
rosewood chest from around Dhs1,800 and 19th century firearms from Dhs900. The beautiful Arabic
pots that line the stairs are hard to resist and will
set you back around Dhs700 a piece. A range of
framed tribal jewellery, knives and khanjars dating
back 100-odd years will appeal to customers looking to purchase a small slice of history.

Total Arts

*The Courtyard, between Interchange 3 & 4, Sheikh
Zayed Road, Al Quoz (228 2888/www.courtyard-
uae.com).* **Open** 8am-1pm, 4-8pm Sat-Thur.
Credit AmEx, MC, V. **Map** p336 E3.
A welcome surprise in the middle of dreary Al Quoz,
the Courtyard is a self-enclosed street reminiscent of
New York's Soho district. It offers an eclectic hotch-
potch of impressive art stores and cafés. Tribal weav-
ings and rugs from Iran are also available, and every
piece is clearly labelled with details of age and origin.

Books

The state of play for Dubai's book lovers has
improved greatly in recent years. Until not
long ago, it was extremely difficult to find
contemporary fiction beyond the bestseller list,
but new Jashanmal and Magrudy's bookstores,
the expansion of Virgin's stores and the arrival
of Borders means that the range of books on
sale is broader than ever. However, censorship
laws still mean that all books coming into the
country are checked; off-limits subjects include
Israel and Judaism, gay and lesbian interest,
alcohol, drugs and sex, while nudity and
anything controversial regarding Islam is
also likely to be blacklisted. International
magazines are painstakingly leafed though
and anything deemed indecent is blacked out

Book Corner.

Eat, Drink, Shop

using a marker pen. While books are sold at roughly the UK/US price, imported magazines can double in price by the time they've reached Dubai's shop shelves.

Book Corner

Al Dhiyafah Road (345 5490/www.bookcorner.ae). **Open** 10am-10pm Sat-Thur; 2-10pm Fri. **Credit** AmEx, MC, V. **Map** p332 F8.

A sleek, modern affair, with an exceptional non-fiction section. The cookery section upstairs is also one of the best in town, while on the lower level you'll find fantastic books on subjects such as interior design, architecture and art.

Book World

Al Hudaiba Street, Satwa (349 1914). **Open** 10am-1.30pm, 5-9.30pm Sat-Thur; 4.30-9.30pm Fri. **Credit** AmEx, MC, V. **Map** p333 F7.

Crammed with over 45,000 used books and thousands of magazines, this store operates on a pile-them-high-sell-them-cheap policy. Everything from gluts of Ian Rankin to the odd Khaled Hosseini is available, and few items cost over Dhs25.

Other locations: Karama, behind Pizza Inn (396 9697).

Borders

Mall of the Emirates (341 5758/www.bordersstores.com). **Open** 10am-midnight daily. **Credit** AmEx, MC, V. **Map** p336 D2.

One of the world's biggest bookshop chains; Borders opened with a bang in November 2006, offering perhaps the widest selection of titles in town. The range of fiction is second-to-none in Dubai, and the children's section and choice of Arabic-language books are also extremely impressive.

House Of Prose

Jumeirah Plaza, Jumeirah Beach Road, Jumeirah (344 9021). **Open** 10am-10pm Sat-Thur; 5.30-8pm Fri. **Credit** AmEx, MC, V. **Map** p332 D2.

This Dubai institution has a simple policy: you buy any one of the reasonably priced books, read it, then keep it or return it and get 50 per cent of your money back. So the books stay in circulation, you save money and you get to see what the bookworms of Dubai are reading. Rummage around for long enough and you'll discover there's something for everyone. **Other locations**: Ibn Battuta Mall (368 5526).

Jashanmal

Mall of the Emirates (266 5964/www.jashanmal-uae.com). **Open** 10am-10pm Sat-Thur; 2-10pm Fri. **Credit** AmEx, MC, V. **Map** p336 D2.

Meticulously neat and well stocked, Jashanmal outlets make an effort to stock all the new releases available in the region. The biography section is excellent too, and for those with families there's a well-stocked kids' area. The store holds regular events, including in-store author appearances.

Other locations: Village Mall (344 5770).

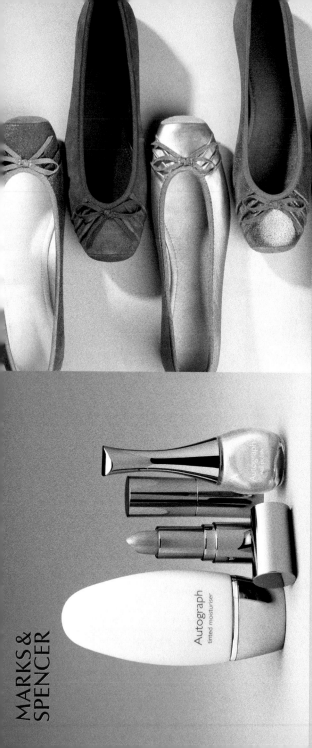

Harvey Nichols.

Magrudy's
*Jumeirah Plaza, Jumeirah Beach Road (344 4193/
www.magrudy.com).* **Open** 10am-10pm Sat-Thur;
2-10pm Fri. **Credit** AmEx, MC, V. **Map** p332 D9.
A Dubai institution, Magrudy's now has shops
throughout the city, although this original outlet on
Jumeirah Beach Road remains its spiritual home.
The chain's had to improve to keep up with the likes
of Borders and Virgin, but it's holding its own with
particularly impressive education, business and children's sections and a good selection of audio books.
Other locations: BurJuman Centre (295 3323);
Deira City Centre (295 7744); Ibn Battuta (366 9770).

Virgin Megastore
Mall of the Emirates (341 4353/www.virgin.com).
Open 10am-midnight daily. **Credit** AmEx, MC, V.
Map p336 D2.
Virgin may specialise in DVDs and CDs, but their
range of books is impressive too. New releases, best-
sellers and self-help titles dominate the shelves, but
you'll also find a large collection of art, design and
photography books, Arabic-language titles and
Penguin classics. Virgin's range of contemporary fic-
tion is second to none.
Other locations: Deira City Centre (295 8599);
Mercato Mall (344 6971).

Department stores

Bhs
BurJuman Centre (352 5150/www.bhs.co.uk).
Open 10am-10pm Sat-Thur; 2-10.30pm Fri.
Credit AmEx, MC, V. **Map** p331 J5.
While not exactly an exclusive haunt in its native
Britain, Bhs does a roaring trade in Dubai. Cheap
prices with plenty of wardrobe basics make it a one-
stop shop for families. Unlike its sister stores in the
UK, here you'll find the focus on children's wear
rather than adult clothing.
Other locations: Al Ghurair City (227 6969); Ibn
Battuta Mall (368 5404); Lamcy Plaza (335 8334).

Debenhams
*Mall of the Emirates (340 7575/www.debenhams.
com).* **Open** 10am-midnight daily. **Credit** AmEx,
MC, V. **Map** p336 D2.
The Dubai branch of Britain's popular department
store won't disappoint and stocks a comprehensive
range of goods from cosmetics to homeware.
Concessions are this store's forte, and you can find
up-to-the-minute fashion from collections by John
Rocha, Jasper Conran, Matthew Williamson and
Pearce Fonda. The lingerie section is particularly
strong and includes lines by Triumph, Chantelle
and, for the bigger busted, Freya.
Other locations: Deira City Centre (294 0011);
Ibn Battuta Mall (396 5900).

Harvey Nichols
*Mall of the Emirates (409 8888/www.harveynichols.
com).* **Open** 10am-midnight daily. **Credit** AmEx,
MC, V. **Map** p336 D2.
The third venture for Harvey Nichols on foreign soil
after Riyadh and Hong Kong, this store filled a big
gap in Dubai's shopping market. With high-end
brands, luxury accessories and the cult cosmetic
haven Fushi, the department store is unsurprisingly sleek with a clientele to match.

Jashanmal
Wafi City Mall (324 4800/www.jashanmal-uae.com).
Open 10am-10pm Sat-Wed; 10am-midnight Thur,
Fri. **Credit** AmEx, MC, V. **Map** p336 D2.
The UAE's answer to the UK's John Lewis, this
home-grown store has a fine selection of well-kitted
out departments. The household section is particu-
larly strong. Here you'll find everything from
Disney sandwich boxes to kettles, vacuum cleaners,
Le Creuset pans, bedding and crockery.
Other locations: Al Ghurair City (227 7780); Mall
of the Emirates (347 1715).

Marks & Spencer
*Waterfront Centre, Dubai Festival City (206 6466/
www.futtaim.com).* **Open** 10am-10pm daily.
Credit AmEx, DC, MC, V. **Map** p329 L3.
Dubai's largest branch of the British high street
favourite stocks plenty of off-the-peg suits and family-friendly clothing essentials, and is home to a fantastic lingerie department. The health and beauty
section is particularly well stocked too, and there's

Eat, Drink, Shop

Saks Fifth Avenue – for fine threads.

also a food department that stocks frozen meals, freshly baked goods and plenty of crisps and nuts. **Other locations**: near Al Ghurair City, Deira (222 2000); Wafi City Mall (324 5145).

Saks Fifth Avenue

BurJuman Centre (351 5551/www.saksfifth avenue.com). **Open** 10am-10pm Sat-Thur; 2-10pm Fri. **Credit** AmEx, MC, V. **Map** p331 J5.
The epitome of New York chic, this store has not lost any of its sassiness in its transplant to the Middle East. Over two levels you'll find an array of top-end labels including Prada, Alberta Ferretti, Philosophy and Dior. You can also splurge on Manolo Blahnik here.

Salam

Wafi City Mall (324 5252/www.salams.com). **Open** 10am-10pm Sat-Wed; 10am-midnight Thur; 2.45pm-midnight Fri. **Credit** AmEx, DC, MC, V. **Map** p329 J4.
With D&G, Moschino, Escada and Lacoste all in supply, this department store will have your whole family decked in designer gear – the children's section even has plenty to choose from too.

Electronics

The malls are full of chain stores such as Jacky's, Jumbo Electronics and Plug-ins, but for the best deal in town on electronics, head to Computer Street, a flurry of shops just off Khalid Bin Al Waleed Road (Bank Street) in Bur Dubai. Start where the road intersects with Mankhool Road and you'll soon see the large Computer Depot store (355 1515), an open-plan showroom that stocks PCs and peripherals from all the big brands. From here you'll discover about a mile of shops squeezed along one side of the road with their small glass fronts stacked with the latest computers, printers, scanners and almost every other conceivable networking toy.

Just a blip away on your GPS system lies Electrical Street, which shares space with the textile souk on Al Fahidi Street. In the evenings its shopfronts blaze with fluorescent and flashing lights, proudly proclaiming such manufacturers as Sharp, Sony, Panasonic and Philips. There's a vast range of electrical goods to choose from, and over-eager shop assistants will do their best to entice you in. Take your time and look for the best deal. On the whole prices are competitive, owing to the number of places offering the same or similar products, so you should be able to pick up a bargain DVD player, digital camera or stereo if you haggle hard. It makes sense to plug in your purchase in the shop to make sure it works properly. Most shops close for prayers between 1pm and 4pm and open again in the late afternoon until 11pm.

It pays to do a little research before heading out to hunt for electrical goods here, as shop attendants are not always knowledgeable about their stock. If you are planning to take your item back home with you, check that you are buying a model that will operate in your home country (TVs are set to operate at different frequencies in different parts of the world, and DVD players are restricted to play discs from a certain region, so what works in Dubai won't necessarily work in London and Lahore).

Carrefour

Deira City Centre, Garhoud (295 1600/ www.carrefouruae.com). **Open** 9am-midnight Sat-Thur; 10am-midnight Fri. **Credit** AmEx, MC, V. **Map** p329 K2.
A supermarket may not seem the ideal place to pick up electronics, but Carrefour has a bastion of bargains waiting to be snapped up. Alongside the cameras and music systems are plenty of cheap, high-quality household items. The staff may not be as knowledgeable as those working in specialist stores, but you're almost certain to get the best price in town here, if you're prepared to deal with the queuing and the crowds.
Other locations: Mall of the Emirates (409 4899).

CompuMe

Near Dubai Tennis Stadium, Zalfa Building, Garhoud (282 8555/www.compume.com). **Open** 9am-9pm Sat-Thur; 4-10pm Fri. **Credit** AmEx, MC, V. **Map** p329 K3.

CompuMe includes a PC clinic, where repairs and upgrades are carried out while you wait, and sells specialist software programs, computing magazines and books. You'll also find good-value laptops, cheap and cheerful PCs, pocket-sized PDAs and photo-quality printers. HP, IBM, Dell and Toshiba are among the brands on sale here.
Other locations: Mall of the Emirates (341 4442).

Jacky's

Deira City Centre (294 9480/www.jackys.com). **Open** 10am-10pm daily. **Credit** AmEx, MC, V. **Map** p329 K2.

One of the giants of the electrical scene in Dubai, Jacky's has come a long way since opening its first store in 1988. Now with seven outlets in the emirate, the city centre location goes head-to-head with fellow superpower Jumbo Electronics next door. A vast selection of fridges, freezers, washers and dryers is complemented by an assortment of kitchen and household essentials such as blenders, toasters, kettles and irons.
Other locations: BurJuman Centre (352 1323); Mall of the Emirates (341 0101); Al Mankhool Road, Bur Dubai (352 3555); Wafi City Mall (324 2077).

Jumbo Electonics

Deira City Centre (295 3915/www.jumbocorp.com). **Open** 10am-10pm Sat-Thur; 2-10pm Fri. **Credit** AmEx, MC, V. **Map** p329 K2.

This popular shop is one of the largest Sony distributors in the world, and has 16 outlets scattered around the city. But the shop also boasts an enviable supporting cast of all the other leading international brands. The store layout is very customer orientated and aims to be interactive, meaning that

Apple picking at the **Mac Store – Apple Centre**. *See p154.*

you can road test potential buys, like the PlayStation3 or the PlayStation Portable (PSP).
Other locations: BurJuman Centre (352 1232); Mall of the Emirates (341 0101); Al Mankhool Road, Bur Dubai (352 3555); Wafi City Mall (324 2077).

LG Digital Centre
Al Sayegh Brothers Building, Port Saeed Road, Deira (262 2770/www.lgcommercial.com). **Open** 8.30am-1.30pm, 2-6.30pm Sat-Thur. **Credit** AmEx, MC, V. **Map** p329 K2.
Given its location, where haggle-hard, sell-it-quick traditions still pervade, this store is a welcome haven from the bustle outside its doors. Products by the Korean electronics giant LG dominate, of course; expect plenty of a/c units, washing machines, ovens, fridges and mobile phones.

Mac Store – Apple Centre
China Court, Ibn Battuta Mall (366 9797/www.apple.com). **Open** 10am-noon Sat, Thur, Fri; 10am-10pm Sun-Wed. **Credit** AmEx, MC, V. **Map** p336 A2.
Make sure you have your sunglasses at the ready before entering this gleaming sheen of whiteness. The very latest electrical products are available and the staff are well trained up on computing know-how. As well as the likes of the 15-inch MacBook and the TVMicro there are G5s, iMacs and plenty of iPods stocked, plus audio speakers and natty little optical mice. *Photo p153.*

VV&Sons
Al Fahidi Street, Bur Dubai (352 2444/www.vvsons.com). **Open** 9am-1pm, 4.30-9.30pm Sat-Thur; 4.30-9.30pm Fri. **Credit** AmEx, MC, V. **Map** p330 H4.
This is the shop for the serious audiophile. A vast range of speakers are displayed at the back of the store, catering for anything from home cinema to outdoor gigs. Upstairs there's a selection of high quality DVD players and amps for heavy-duty home cinema. In terms of names, lesser-known brands such as Jamo and Sherwood Electronic Labs sit next to international favourites like JBL.
Other locations: Nasser Square, behind HSBC bank, Deira (221 8077).

Fashion

Beachwear

Aqua Beachwear
Al Ghazal Mall, Dhiyafah Road (345 3490/www.aquabeachwear.com). **Open** 10am-10pm Sat-Thur; 4-10pm Fri. **Credit** AmEx, MC, V. **Map** p332 F8.
Finding a bikini that flatters your figure can be an infuriating process, but this store comes to the rescue, with a wide selection of styles to suit all shapes and sizes. The bright designs are eye-catching, and you'll be able to match them with accessories such as sarongs, bags and towels.

Goldenpoint
Mall of the Emirates (341 0834/www.goldenpoint online.com). **Open** 10am-midnight Sat-Thur; noon-10pm Fri. **Credit** AmEx, MC, V. **Map** p336 D2.
Sporty labels from Speedo and Rip Curl are stocked here. As well as more frivolous styles, avid sporty types will be able to pick up items that won't get ripped off in the crashing waves.

Heat Waves
Town Centre Mall, Jumeirah Beach Road, Jumeirah (342 0445). **Open** 10am-midnight Sat-Thur; 5pm-midnight Fri. **Credit** AmEx, MC, V. **Map** p334 C12.
For straightforward swimsuits and bikinis in a range of plain and flattering colours, head to Heat Waves. Most of the swimwear on offer leans towards the conservative end of the market, but if you're prepared to have a root through, you'll come across more fashionable styles.
Other locations: Jumeirah Plaza (344 9489).

Moda Brazil
Mercato Mall, Jumeirah Beach Road, Jumeirah (344 3074/www.modabrazil.com). **Open** 10am-midnight Sat-Thur; 2-10pm Fri. **Credit** AmEx, MC, V. **Map** p334 C12.
This lush Latino boutique stocks one of the widest selections of fashionable beachwear in town, from racy cut-out swimsuits to tropical-coloured bikinis. Sizes are on the small side, but designs are cutting edge and will make you feel as if you've just stepped off the catwalk.

Praias
Mall of the Emirates (341 1167). **Open** 10am-midnight Sat-Thur; noon-10pm Fri. **Credit** AmEx, MC, V. **Map** p336 D2.
The fashion-conscious will love this store. With the sexiest bikinis in town, there is something for everyone. It's not just for model-esque figures, since a good handful of the bikinis are underwired and offer excellent support.

Childrenswear

½ Pint
Organic Foods & Café, Mankhool Road, Satwa (398 6889). **Open** 8.30am-6.30pm Sat-Thur; 10.30am-3pm Fri. **Credit** MC, V. **Map** p333 F8.
1/2 Pint sells handmade casual clothes for children aged up to eight. The range is designed by Mariam El-Accad, who only uses natural fabrics to create practical and comfortable clothes.

Armani Junior
Mercato Mall (342 0111/www.armanijunior.com). **Open** 10am-10pm Sat-Thur; 2-10pm Fri. **Credit** AmEx, MC, V. **Map** p334 C12.
Armani Junior boasts a colourful range of kids' clothing that caters to boys and girls from the age of two to 14. As well as T-shirts, hats and jeans, denim separates for girls are available along with trousers and jackets for cooler climes. For the

Small-minded high fashion at **Bonpoint**.

A store with its finger firmly on the fashion pulse, Bonpoint has cornered a niche market showcasing a children's collection inspired by high fashion and celebrity culture. Thoughtfully laid out, Bonpoint's collection features cute, yet terribly chic outfits.

Favourite Things Mother & Child
Palm Strip Mall, Jumeirah Beach Road (345 2725/ www.favouritethings.com). **Open** 10am-10pm Sat, Fri; 9am-10pm Sun-Thur. **Credit** AmEx, MC, V. **Map** p332 D9.
This recently opened store is a boon to those Jumeirah Janes who were growing a tad bored with the neighbourhood's other offerings. With a safe indoor play area, a party room and a coffee shop for mums, this all-encompassing shop is bound to keep both mother and child entertained for hours. The novelties boutique is great for finding original birthday gifts, and they'll even cater for parties.

Iana
Ibn Battuta Mall (368 5518). **Open** 10am-midnight daily. **Credit** AmEx, MC, V. **Map** p336 A2.
Devotees of casual chic Italian garb need look no further than Iana for colourful, pint-sized and laid-back attire. The chain's brand of no-nonsense, candy-coloured cottons are aimed at babies to pre-teens.

I Pinco Pallino
Wafi City Mall (324 4944/www.ipincopallino.it). **Open** 10am-10pm Sat-Thur; 5pm-midnight Fri. **Credit** AmEx, MC, V. **Map** p329 J3.
This upmarket Italian brand's formal range includes pastel gowns in luxurious natural fibres with coordinated accessories, clothes for babies and casual wear. But I Pinco doesn't come cheap and Park Avenue princesses-to-be can expect to shell out a small fortune.

Osh Kosh B'gosh
Mall of the Emirates (341 3040/www.oshkoshbgosh. com). **Open** 10am-midnight daily. **Credit** AmEx, MC, V. **Map** p336 D2.
This cute store offers everything a preppy little New Englander could want, with a vast selection of cords and shirt combos for boys, as well as precious embroidered dresses, skirts and hats for mini madams.

Patchwork
Mercato Mall (349 6060). **Open** 9am-10pm Sat-Thur; 2-10.30pm Fri. **Credit** AmEx, MC, V. **Map** p334 C12.
Patchwork perfectly illustrates that you are never too young for a bit of bling. Top names such as GF Ferré, Miss Sixty and Energie are all stocked, with sizes to fit children aged four to 14 years.

Tape à L'oeil
Mall of the Emirates (341 0480). **Open** 10am-10pm Sat-Thur; 2-10pm Fri. **Credit** AmEx, MC, V. **Map** p336 D2.
If your children fancy themselves as Monte Carlo high rollers, then this fashion brand from France is the perfect choice to suit their needs.
Other locations: BurJuman Centre (352 3223).

label-conscious young man, a range of trousers, hoodies and trainers complete the collection.

B Bush
Souk Madinat Jumeirah (368 6212). **Open** 10am-11pm daily. **Credit** AmEx, MC, V. **Map** p336 D1.
Aspiring surfers and boarders will feel at home in this urban store. It stocks a range of trendy clothes including sweatshirts, trousers, shorts and T-shirts, so you'll leave with the coolest kids on the block.

Bambu Beach
Ibn Battuta Mall (368 5214). **Open** 10am-10pm Sun-Wed; 10am-midnight Thur-Sat. **Credit** AmEx, MC, V. **Map** p336 A2.
Offering fashion for the whole family, this Dubai-based label was created with the UAE lifestyle in mind. Children from three to 12 are catered for with linen, cotton and silk separates, swimwear and accessories all available. Think butterfly prints and polka dots for girls and brightly patterned shorts for boys.

Bonpoint
Souk Madinat Jumeirah (368 6212/www.bonpoint. com). **Open** 10am-11pm daily. **Credit** AmEx, MC, V. **Map** p336 D1.

Eat, Drink, Shop

Bershka.

Designer

For bespoke suits, *see p143* **Tailor made**; for independent boutiques, *see p161* **State of independence**.

Ayesha Depala
The Village, Jumeirah Beach Road (344 5378). **Open** 10am-10pm Sat-Thur; 4-10pm Fri. **Credit** MC, V. **Map** p332 D9.
This talented young Indian designer's first boutique in Dubai is awash with silk, chiffon, tulle and lace, all in soft, serene colours. Her collections are the epitome of femininity – as is the store itself. With lilac walls, sparkling chandeliers and a chic chaise longue, browsing is a treat. From long evening gowns, baby-doll dresses and delicate cardigans, each garment is beautifully cut and timelessly stylish.

Boutique 1
The Boulevard at Jumeirah Emirates Towers (330 4555). **Open** 10am-10pm Sat-Thur; 3-10pm Fri. **Credit** AmEx, DC, MC, V. **Map** p328 H4.
Formerly known as Villa Moda, Boutique 1 boasts over 150 brands, from established names like Missoni and Chloé to emerging designers. With a bountiful supply of jeans and eveningwear, plus everything in between, it combines luxury with youthful energy.

Burberry
BurJuman Centre (351 3515/www.burberry.com). **Open** 10am-10pm Sat-Thur; 2-10pm Fri. **Credit** AmEx, MC, V. **Map** p331 J5.
At Burberry, customers can wander across acres of plush carpet to lay their hands on cashmere scarves, desirable updates on the classic Burberry trench, and plenty of chequered tartan on bags, skirts and accessories.

Carolina Herrera
Mall of the Emirates (341 5095). **Open** 10am-10pm Sun-Wed; 10am-midnight Thur-Sat. **Credit** AmEx, MC, V. **Map** p336 D2.

With scented candles scattered around, this store feels like a chic living room. Herrera's gowns are popular on the red carpet and, should you have the funds, are well worth investing in.
Other locations: Dubai Festival City (232 6030).

Chanel
Wafi City Mall (324 0464/www.chanel.com). **Open** 10am-10pm Sat-Thur; 5-10pm Fri. **Credit** AmEx, MC, V. **Map** p329 J3.
This shop is the epitome of chichi French chic and has a small but select range of the label's latest collections. In among the classy suits there are a few gems from the eveningwear couture range. There is also a good selection of affordable accessories for those finishing touches.

Christian Lacroix
BurJuman Centre (352 7755/www.christian-lacroix.fr). **Open** 10am-10pm Sat-Thur; 2-10pm Fri. **Credit** AmEx, MC, V. **Map** p331 J5.
This hoity-toity designer range has a small but wildly elegant selection in its Dubai branch. With plenty of eccentric pieces, this is the place for people who view fashion as art.

Donna Karan
BurJuman Centre (351 7554/www.donnakaran.com). **Open** 10am-10pm Thur-Sat; 2-10pm Fri. **Credit** AmEx, MC, V. **Map** p331 J5.
At Donna Karan's first-floor BurJuman outlet you'll find many of her signature tailored pieces, as well as plenty of sumptuous coats and to-die-for red dresses. For dressed down – and more affordable – clothing, look at the ground floor DKNY diffusion range.

Fleurt
Mercato Mall (342 0906). **Open** 10am-10pm Sat-Thur; 2-10pm Fri. **Credit** AmEx, DC, MC, V. **Map** p334 C12.
A selection of the highly desirable and glam Dina Bar-El dresses, colourful leather handbags and stylish modern jewellery is what's on offer at this sassy little store. We defy you to leave empty handed.

Giorgio Armani
The Boulevard at Jumeirah Emirates Towers (330 0447/www.armani.com). **Open** 10am-10pm Sat-Thur; 4-10pm Fri. **Credit** AmEx, MC, V. **Map** p328 H4.
A slick store that oozes style thanks not only to the fashion but also to the minimally decked out surroundings. Sparkling black marble floors, dark walls and spotlights draw you to the colourful rails of clothes. Women will find a mind-boggling range of flattering skirts, smart jackets and funky party pieces, while men will leave in perfectly fitting suits.

Gucci
Al Maktoum Street, Deira (221 5444/www.gucci.com). **Open** 10am-11pm Sat-Thur; 5-9.30pm Fri. **Credit** AmEx, MC, V. **Map** p331 L3.
Gucci has long been synonymous with high-octane glamour and sex appeal, and this has been maintained despite Tom Ford's departure a few years back. You'll find the best of the best in this two level outlet. The womenswear, menswear and accessory departments are all brimming with luxurious but expensive buys.
Other locations: The Boulevard at Jumeirah Emirates Towers (330 3313); Mall of the Emirates (341 0669).

Hermès
BurJuman Centre (351 1190/www.hermes.com). **Open** 10am-10pm Sat-Thur; 2-10pm Fri. **Credit** AmEx, MC, V. **Map** p331 J5.
Liberally sprinkled in the credits of all the major fashion magazines, Hermès has become known as a long-standing symbol of Gallic elegance and style. Push through the somewhat intimidating doors and you'll find scarves of every hue and design, a great range of glamorous tote bags and purses made from the skins of a variety of deceased exotic animals.

Hugo Boss
Mercato Mall (342 2021/www.hugoboss.com). **Open** 10am-10pm Sat-Thur; 2-10pm Fri. **Credit** AmEx, MC, V. **Map** p334 C12.
Among the more expensive brands out there, Hugo Boss shirts do give you real quality for the extra cost. Almost 84 years on from the company's birth, Boss has branched out from formalwear and now makes some of the softest and most comfortable jeans around, as part of the casual Boss Orange label collection. The Boss Green collection is the sportier side of the brand. Great for top-class hoodies and sportswear that you won't want to get dirty by actually playing sports in.
Other locations: BurJuman Centre (355 7845); Deira City Centre (295 5281); Mall of the Emirates (341 0630).

Max Mara
BurJuman Centre (351 3140). **Open** 10am-10pm Sat-Thur; 2-10pm Fri. **Credit** AmEx, MC, V. **Map** p331 J5.
If there is one thing Max Mara does well, it's coats. Not wildly flamboyant ones, but simply good quality classics. The Italian fashion house has a long-standing reputation for creating couture lines. You'll also find SportMax stocked here too, a slightly cheaper line of knits and outdoor wear.

Ounass
Souk Madinat Jumeirah (368 6167/www.altayer.com). **Open** 10am-11pm daily. **Credit** AmEx, MC, V. **Map** p336 D1.
The best thing about Ounass is the fact it brings together an eclectic mix of labels and styles from Hale Bob and Juicy Couture, alongside sleek lingerie, pretty dresses and a great footwear selection.

Tiger Lily
Wafi City Mall (324 8088). **Open** 10am-10pm Sun-Thur; 5-10pm Fri. **Credit** AmEx, MC, V. **Map** p329 J3.
Shopping here is akin to rummaging through a stylish celebrity's wardrobe. Draping rails filled with flowing, feminine dresses vie for your attention, while kitsch accessories catch the eye. Look for pieces by Australia's hottest exports sass & bide as well as UK favourite Julian MacDonald.

Versace
Al Maktoum Street, Deira (355 1845/www.versace.com). **Open** 10am-10pm Sat-Thur. **Credit** AmEx, MC, V. **Map** p331 L3.
Figure-hugging dresses, the skinniest of trousers, leather jackets and lashings of fur and gold are the order of the day at this store. Alongside the ostentatious creations are lots of very wearable clothes.
Other locations: BurJuman Centre (351 7792); Wafi City Mall (324 7333).

Yves Saint Laurent
Mall of the Emirates (341 0113). **Open** 10am-10pm Sun-Wed; 10am-midnight Thur-Sat. **Credit** AmEx, DC, MC, V. **Map** p336 D2.
Yves Saint Laurent's modern collection ranges from expensive jackets right down to reasonably priced dress shirts, and while it's not cheap, you should consider that in 1999 Gucci bought the YSL brand, so the standards will be high, but the prices still are cheaper than their parent company.
Other locations: The Boulevard at Jumeirah Emirates Towers (330 0445).

High street

Benetton
Mall of the Emirates (341 4646/www.benetton.com). **Open** 10am-10pm Sun-Wed; 10am-midnight Thur-Sat. **Credit** AmEx, DC, MC, V. **Map** p336 D2.
The 1980s knitwear giant is still going strong, the famous sweaters and cute Ts in a hue of rainbow colours are still in store, but have been joined by lingerie, loungewear and sleepwear. The store also stocks some great basics for a working wardrobe.
Other locations: Deira City Centre (295 2450); Jumeirah Centre (349 3613).

Bershka
Mercato Mall (344 8645/www.bershka.com). **Open** 10am-10pm Sat-Thur; 2-10pm Fri. **Credit** AmEx, MC, V. **Map** p334 C12.

Eat, Drink, Shop

Diesel – it's in the jeans.

Bershka produces an exciting collection of funky casual clothes and sassy going out gear. Thumping trance accompanies customers around the store and gets them in a foot-stomping festival mood. *Photo p156.* **Other locations:** Deira City Centre (295 8440); Mall of the Emirates (341 0223).

Blue Cactus
Jumeirah Centre, Jumeirah Beach Road, Jumeirah (344 7734). **Open** 10am-9pm Sat-Thur; 4.30-9pm Fri. **Credit** AmEx, DC, MC, V. **Map** p332 D9.
Quality not quantity is what's on offer at Blue Cactus. The store may be small, but the stock consists of top-notch chain-store labels and designer womenswear. Expect to find Kay Unger dresses, Prada short-sleeve shirts and entire outfits by DKNY at a fraction of their usual retail price. *Photo p156.*

Club Monaco
Deira City Centre (295 5832/www.clubmonaco.com). **Open** 10am-midnight Sat-Thur; 10am-10pm Sun-Wed. **Credit** AmEx, MC, V. **Map** p329 K2.
Two decades after its birth, Club Monaco has finally reached the Middle East. This store is home to chic essentials aimed at urban men and women. With plenty of A-list fans, Club Monaco's a great alternative if you can't afford high fashion labels. Colours tend to be subdued, so you won't find any garish creations here.

Diesel
BurJuman Centre (351 6181/www.diesel.com). **Open** 10am-10pm Sat-Thur; 2-10pm Fri. **Credit** AmEx, MC, V. **Map** p331 J5.
Chock-full of hipster must-haves that ooze attitude, this is a veritable warehouse of du jour jeans and accessories. Well cut jeans and retro tops will leave you looking too cool for school.

Other locations: Deira City Centre (295 0792); Mall of the Emirates (341 1395); Mercato Mall (349 9958).

Fashion Factory
Lamcy Plaza, Oud Metha (336 2699). **Open** 9am-10pm Sun-Wed; 9am-midnight Thur-Sat. **Credit** AmEx, DC, MC, V. **Map** p329 J3.
Don't let Fashion Factory's location deter you from visiting. Lurking at the back of Lamcy Plaza, it's also easy to miss, but with nearly every item in the store priced at under Dhs100, make it your mission to seek it out. There are bargains to be had on major high street brands, including Monsoon, Camaïeu and more.

H&M
Mall of the Emirates (341 5880). **Open** 10am-midnight Sat, Thur, Fri; 10am-10pm Sun-Wed. **Credit** AmEx, DC, MC, V. **Map** p336 D2.
H&M has opened two shops in Dubai. If you like jumble sales, you'll love H&M, which sells cheap clothes across the age/sex spectrum, as well as cosmetics, accessories and underwear. This is the place to pick up serviceable basics for a snip.
Other locations: Deira City Centre (295 7549); Ibn Battuta Mall (364 9819).

Mango
BurJuman Centre (355 5770/www.mango.com). **Open** 10am-10pm Sat-Thur; 2-10pm Fri. **Credit** AmEx, MC, V. **Map** px331 J5.
Dubai's Mango outlets are as well stocked and as reasonably priced as those in Europe. As well as the usual range of well-picked, stylish clothes, expect some bejewelled and flowing styles to fit in more with local tastes.
Other locations: Deira City Centre (295 0182); Mall of the Emirates (341 4324); Mercato Mall (344 7195).

Massimo Dutti
Deira City Centre (295 4788/www.massimodutti.com). **Open** 10am-midnight Sat, Thur, Fri; 10am-10pm Sun-Wed. **Credit** AmEx, MC, V. **Map** p329 K2.
Stacks of sophisticated suits, crisp cotton shirts, rugged leather jackets, ultra-glam eveningwear, well-finished accessories and catwalk-savvy shoes make Dutti one of the city's most popular shops. The store is a boon for men and women of all ages – the clothes effortlessly exude class and don't have sky-high price tags.
Other locations: BurJuman Centre (351 3352); Mall of the Emirates (341 3151); Mercato Mall (344 7158).

New Look
Deira City Centre (295 9542/www.newlook.co.uk). **Open** 10am-10pm Sun-Wed; 10am-midnight Thur-Sat. **Credit** AmEx, DC, MC, V. **Map** p329 K2.
This huge shop opened its doors in 2006 and has been the destination for bargain-loving fashionistas ever since. The season's top trends are always on offer, as well as all the basics such as jeans and T-shirts. Head to the back of the store and you're surrounded by endless rows of pumps and points. The lingerie and accessories departments are also fantastic.

Eat, Drink, Shop

Topshop.

Aimed at younger customers, the majority of this store's stock is suited to teenagers. Big on bright colours, Lycra, short skirts and funky extras, it's certainly an eye-catching space. The shoe and bag selection is impressive too.
Other locations: Mall of the Emirates (341 3999).

Topshop
Mercato Mall (344 2677). **Open** 10am-10pm Sat-Wed; 10am-11pm Thur-Fri. **Credit** AmEx, DC, MC, V. **Map** p334 C12.
Leggings, stretch minis, layered Day Glo tops, leg warmers, plastic jewellery, vest dresses, boob tubes, studded belts, coloured court shoes, neon fishnets, lashings of bling – the high street darling of the fashion pack has got it all. The collection changes with the whimsical speed of high fashion, but you'll always be sure to find a wide range of cheeky underwear.
Other locations: Deira City Centre (295 1010), Ibn Battuta Mall (368 5948).

Lingerie

There are plenty of shops selling luxury lingerie in Dubai, but expect lots of frilly numbers put together with little erotic flair. No nonsense, everyday underwear is also difficult to come by, and prices are often marked up heavily. Nonetheless, the following stores fight the good fight against mediocrity.

Agent Provocateur
Inside Saks Fifth Avenue, BurJuman Centre (351 5551/www.agentprovocateur.com). **Open** 10am-10pm Sat-Thur; 4-10pm Fri. **Credit** AmEx, MC, V. **Map** p331 J5.
Agent Provocateur serves up decadent sauciness without descending into sleaze. As a brand, it's a well-executed and well-oiled machine from the packaging and perfume to the lingerie itself. Also a good place to pick up stockings.

Inner Lines
Deira City Centre (295 0627). **Open** 10am-midnight Sat-Thur; 10am-10pm Wed-Sun. **Credit** AmEx, MC, V. **Map** p329 K2.
At Inner Lines you'll find a small but attractive selection of Calvin Klein underwear, encompassing knickers and bras in every colour of the rainbow. Other brands stocked include BodySlimmers and the Princesse Tam Tam range, which supports and flatters the fuller figure.

Nayomi
Mercato Mall (344 9120/www.nayomi.com). **Open** 10am-10pm Sat-Thur; 4-10pm Fri. **Credit** AmEx, MC, V. **Map** p334 C12.
One of the leading Middle Eastern retailers of quality lingerie, Nayomi stocks lacy dressing gowns and rather less sexy nightdresses for around Dhs300.
Other locations: Al Ghurair City (227 3887); Ibn Battuta Mall (366 9832); Mall of the Emirates (341 4377).

Promod
BurJuman Centre (351 4477/www.promod.com). **Open** 10am-10pm Sat-Thur; 2-10pm Fri. **Credit** AmEx, MC, V. **Map** p331 J5.
This Spanish store's vibe is definitely Bohemian. There's a vast range of daywear and covetable extras like beaded necklaces, bangles, hats, scarves and bags. With Promod's casual rather than dressy clothes, you can rejuvenate your wardrobe without breaking the bank.
Other locations: Deira City Centre (295 7344); Mall of the Emirates (341 4944); Mercato Mall (344 6941).

Reiss
Mall of the Emirates (341 0515/www.reiss.co.uk). **Open** 10am-10pm Sun-Wed; 10am-midnight Thur-Sat. **Credit** AmEx, MC, V. **Map** p336 D2.
This is a gorgeous shop where the clothes have a designer feel. There are full and pleated skirts with unusual stitching details and abstract patterns in the weave, plus cotton tops in contemporary shapes and plenty of well tailored suits. It's more expensive than your average chain, but worth the extra splurge.

Stradivarius
Deira City Centre (295 1221). **Open** 10am-midnight Sat, Thur, Fri; 10am-10pm Sun-Wed. **Credit** AmEx, MC, V. **Map** p329 K2.

Sport meets fashion at **Adidas**, in the BurJuman Centre.

Sportswear

Adidas

BurJuman Centre (359 0995/www.adidas.com).
Open 10am-10pm Sat-Thur; 4-10pm Fri. **Credit**
AmEx, MC, V. **Map** p331 J5.
Adidas is one of the rare sports brands that also succeeds as street fashion, and at their Dubai stores you can find plenty of old-school styles alongside gym essentials. This store boasts a massive range of trainers, tracksuits, shorts and T-shirts, as well as a selection of Adidas watches.
Other locations: Adidas Factory Shop (282 5868); Deira City Centre (295 0261); Al Ghurair City (228 9733); Ibn Batutta Mall (366 9777); Mall of the Emirates (347 7007).

Golf House

BurJuman Centre (351 9012). **Open** 10am-10pm
Sat-Thur; 4-10pm Fri. **Credit** AmEx, MC, V.
Map p331 J5.
Catering for the flourishing golf scene in Dubai, Golf House is a good stop-off before you hit the green. With top of the range clubs, clothes and all the essentials, there is plenty to keep both the novice and the seasoned professional happy here.
Other locations: Deira City Centre (295 0261); Ibn Batutta Mall (366 9895); Lamcy Plaza (334 5945); Mall of the Emirates (341 0511).

Go Sport

Ibn Batutta Mall (368 5344). **Open** 10am-midnight daily. **Credit** AmEx, MC, V. **Map** p336 A2.
The items available at this French megastore include clothing and equipment for almost every sport you can think of, including biking, riding, golf, weights, boxing and fishing.

Nike

BurJuman Centre (351 5376/www.nike.com).
Open 10am-midnight Sat-Thur; 2-10pm Fri.
Credit AmEx, MC, V. **Map** p331 J5.
The sizeable Nike store ticks all the right boxes thanks to well-stocked shelves and helpful staff. Besides the latest tracksuits, trainers, sports and gym clothing, this outlet boasts an excellent collection of sunglasses and futuristic-looking watches.
Other locations: Al Ghurair City (227 5758); Ibn Batutta Mall (366 9777); Mall of the Emirates (341 0933).

Rage

Mall of the Emirates (341 3388). **Open** 10am-midnight daily. **Credit** AmEx, MC, V. **Map** p336 D2.
This shop boasts the best selection of skateboards in the city. And the place is full of personality too; expect to find edgy punk tunes blasting out, and smashed-up boards decorating the ceiling. Whether you're after a pair of Etnies trainers, a funky bikini or the latest Flip skateboard, you won't leave disappointed.
Other locations: Dubai Festival City (336 9007).

Sun & Sand Sports

Khalid Bin Al Waleed Road (Bank Street), Bur Dubai (351 6222/www.sunandsandsports.com).
Open 10am-10pm Sat-Thur; 2-10pm Fri. **Credit**
AmEx, MC, V. **Map** p330 J5.
One of the biggest sports shops in Dubai, Sun & Sand Sports stocks everything from tennis gear to gym equipment. Prices are reasonable, and although you won't find the best selection of footwear in town, the sheer quantity of everything else more than makes up for this flaw.
Other locations: BurJuman Centre (351 5376); Deira City Centre (295 5551); Ibn Batutta (366 9777).

State of independence

Dubai's Achilles heel as a shopping city is that the chain names dominate at the expense of quirky and independent boutiques. This is partly down to the fact that in the past a non-UAE national who wanted to open a shop was required by law to have an Emirati sponsor, which isn't always straightforward when Emiratis make up such a small percentage of the population. However, in 2006 regulations changed, allowing UAE residents to open up businesses without relying on the help of a national. Slowly but surely, more independent stores are opening that will fill the shopping void, and hopefully these outlets will bring in fashion influences from all over the world. Here's the best of the current flock of independent boutiques.

Boom & Mellow

Mall of the Emirates (341 3993). **Open** 10am-10pm Sat-Tue; 10am-midnight Wed-Fri. **Credit** AmEx, MC, V. **Map** p336 D2.
This is the Aladdin's cave of the accessory world with bags lining the walls, chunky necklaces hanging temptingly from silver pegs and crystal-encrusted earrings sparkling alluringly behind glass cabinets. Look out for the cool vintage creations from the likes of Madame Rêve.

Dethar

Al Ghazal Mall (345 4403). **Open** 10am-10pm daily. **Credit** MC, V. **Map** p332 F8.
Dethar is a unique shop, with its entire collection hailing from a handful of artisans

S*uce.

from Lebanon. The pretty embellished bags are the highlight, but the equally appealing metallic pumps, crochet cardigans and the plethora of costume jewellery are all hard to leave behind. Bring a big bag.

Five Green

Behind Aroma Garden Caffe, Oud Metha (336 4100/www.fivegreen.com). **Open** 10am-10pm Sat-Thur; 4-10pm Fri. **Credit** AmEx, DC, MC, V. **Map** p329 J2.
The perfect antidote to the acres of identikit boutiques and mall stores that smother the city, Five Green is an elegant and tasteful repository of loveliness. Part clothes store, part art space, part music store (think Soul Jazz Records and Jazzanova releases), it stages art shows while stocking styles from the likes of 2K, Aei:Kei, Paul Frank, Gsus, Tsubi and Upper Playground, alongside fashion by Dubai-based designers.

IF Boutique

IF Boutique, Umm Al Sheif Street, Jumeirah (394 7260). **Open** 10am-9pm Sat-Thur. **Credit** MC, V. **Map** p332 D9.
With its art deco-like façade and front terrace of iron cast statues, it's no surprise this store is home to labels such as Comme des Garçons, Emma Hope, Undercover and Milia M. One of the few boutiques to move out of the malls and into the outside world, it's in the ideal location nestled beside a string of cafés and within walking distance to the beach.

Luxecouture

The Village, Jumeirah Beach Road (344 7933). **Open** 10am-10pm Sat-Thur; 4-10pm Fri. **Credit** AmEx, DC, MC, V. **Map** p332 D9.
Stocked with chic New York labels, this compact shop focuses on niche designers and classic rather than frivolous items. You can find everything here from slick work attire to breathtaking gowns.

S*uce

The Village, Jumeirah Beach Road (344 7270/www.shopatsauce.com). **Open** 10am-10pm Sat-Thur. **Credit** AmEx, DC, MC, V. **Map** p332 D9.
S*uce is a true fashion cocktail of cutting-edge and flirty cult labels including sass & bide, Isabella Capeto and 3.1 philip lim. As well as a mishmash of colourful dresses, handmade jewellery, and spangly belts and bags, there's a well-stocked gift section.

Eat, Drink, Shop

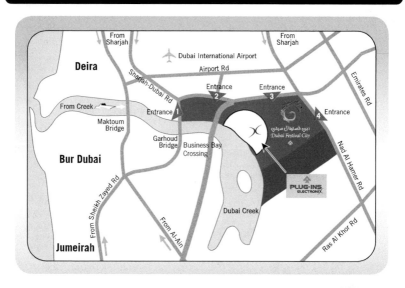

Fashion accessories

Hats

Sunny Days

Jumeirah Centre, Jumeirah Beach Road, Jumeirah (344 7737). **Open** 9.30am-9pm Sat-Thur; 5-9pm Fri. **Credit** AmEx, MC, V. **Map** p332 D9.

Local milliner Lynn Holyoak caters to the smart set, yet her prices are surprisingly reasonable. Expect to pay around Dhs400 for a stylish head-turner.

Jewellery

For gold jewellery, *see p169* **The gold rush**.

Accessorize

Mall of the Emirates (341 0479/www.monsoon.co.uk). **Open** ; 10am-midnight Sat, Thur, Fri; 10am-10pm Sun-Wed. **Credit** AmEx, MC, V. **Map** p336 D2.

This high street accessories chain is an offshoot of Monsoon, which accounts for the subtle ethnic flavour of many of its ranges. A haven for boho fans, this store offers plenty of beaded, bobbled and embroidered goodies.

Other locations: Ibn Battuta Mall (341 3993); Lamcy Plaza (335 7375).

Glitter.

Cartier

The Boulevard at Jumeirah Emirates Towers (351 3332/www.cartier.com). **Open** 10am-10pm Sat-Thur; 5-10pm Fri. **Credit** AmEx, MC, V. **Map** p328 H4.

This branch of Cartier is packed to the brim with dazzling charms, links and delicate paves.

Other locations: BurJuman Centre (355 3533).

Damas

Deira City Centre (295 3848/www.damasjewel.com). **Open** 10am-midnight Sat, Thur, Fri; 10am-10pm Sun-Wed. **Credit** AmEx, MC, V. **Map** p329 K2.

The most advertised and popular jeweller in the Middle East prides itself on its high-quality gold creations – and there's not a knuckleduster in sight. Damas caters for women of all ages, and the Lebanese singing sensation Nancy Ajram is currently the face of the brand.

Other locations: The Boulevard at Jumeirah Emirates Towers (330 3262); Al Ghurair City (296 0063); Ibn Battuta Mall (366 9944); Lamcy Plaza (335 5177); Mercato Mall (349 8833); Souk Madinat Jumeirah (344 0111); Wafi City Mall (323 4555).

Dazzle

Al Ghazal Mall, Dhiyafah Road (345 3163). **Open** 10am-10pm Sat-Thur; 4-10pm Fri. **Credit** AmEx, MC, V. **Map** p332 F8.

Subtlety isn't Dazzle's strength. From huge chandelier ear adornments to chunky rings Mr T would blush over, the small boutique shamelessly revels in attention-seeking accessories. Look closely and you will uncover some pretty and more delicate dazzle with which to lift your outfit.

Glitter

Ibn Battuta Mall (368 5582). **Open** 10am-midnight Thur-Sat; 10am-10pm Sun-Wed. **Credit** AmEx, MC, V. **Map** p336 A2.

You don't have to blow your budget to get seriously fashionable, just take a trip to Glitter and check out the Crislu collection of crystal rings and pendants. With the platinum-coated bands ranging in price from Dhs750 to Dhs1,000, you'll still have dirhams in your purse to splash out on the elegant pendants at Dhs500.

Other locations: Deira City Centre (295 4012); Al Ghurair City (229 3978).

Tiffany & Co

Deira City Centre (295 3884/www.tiffany.com). **Open** 10am-midnight Thur-Sat; 10am-10pm Sun-Wed. **Credit** AmEx, MC, V. **Map** p329 K2.

The aura of Audrey Hepburn glamour will always linger around the legendary Tiffany's. This outlet may be small in size, but it still squeezes in a flabbergasting selection of classy jewellery, chic accessories and gift items. Check out the highly coveted engagement rings and signature heart chains. It's worth asking for a discount if you're buying something expensive – it may just save you a dirham or two.

Other locations: BurJuman Centre (359 0101); Mall of the Emirates (341 0655).

MAC.

Shoes

For **City Shoes**, *see p145* **Instant Karama**.

Aldo

BurJuman Centre (359 3375/www.aldoshoes.com).
Open 10am-10pm Sat-Thur; 2-10pm Fri. **Credit**
AmEx, MC, V. **Map** p331 J5.
This Canadian shoe emporium is hard to beat for
sheer choice, boasting a dazzling array of styles for
men and women at surprisingly cheap prices. Aldo
are pretty hot on the heels of the latest trends, and
a selection of bags, belts and beads is also available.
Other locations: throughout the city.

Jimmy Choo

The Boulevard at Jumeirah Emirates Towers
(330 0404/www.jimmychoo.com). **Open** 10am-
10pm Sat-Tue; Wed-Fri 4-10pm. **Credit** AmEx,
MC, V. **Map** p328 H4.
The king of shoemaking has a swanky branch in the
sleek Jumeirah Emirates Towers. You can load up
on ornate sandals, strappy kitten heels, spectacular
evening shoes and leather books.

Nine West

Deira City Centre (295 6887/www.ninewest.com).
Open 10am-10pm Sat-Thur; 2-10pm Fri. **Credit**
AmEx, MC, V. **Map** p329 K2.
Nine West can be a bit hit-and-miss with catwalk
looks, but for everyday basics it consistently delivers
the goods. It's also one of the few shoe shops in Dubai
to offer large sizes, and prices are reasonable.
Other locations: BurJuman Centre (351 6214);
Al Ghurair City (221 1484); Ibn Battuta Mall (368
4097); Mall of the Emirates (341 0244); Mercato
Mall (349 1336).

Pretty FIT

Mercato Mall (344 0015/www.prettyfit.com).
Open 10am-10pm Sat-Thur; 2-10pm Fri. **Credit**
AmEx, MC, V. **Map** p334 C12.
Pretty FIT is a reliable shop selling flats, heels,
strappies and slip-ons in a variety of colours. Styles
are often adorned with stripes, polka dots, checks or
flowers that may not be to everyone's taste, but there
are some beautifully simple styles that will work
with any outfit. Prices are an absolute bargain too.
Other locations: Deira City Centre (295 0790); Mall
of the Emirates (341 3666).

Vincci

BurJuman Centre (351 7246). **Open** 10am-10pm
Sat-Thur; 2-10pm Fri. **Credit** AmEx, MC, V.
Map p331 J5.
This upmarket store stocks one of the city's finest
ranges of footwear. The quality of the shoes is excellent, and there are some interesting details in the
mainstream styles. Delicate pumps sit alongside
suede slouch boots and glam sky-high heels.

Food shops

Chocoa

Al Barsha, behind Mall of the Emirates (340 9092).
Open 10am-midnight Sat-Thur; 4pm-midnight Fri.
Credit AmEx, MC, V. **Map** p336 D2.
Wonderful chocolate-covered dates and dried apri-
cots are piled high in this sugary-scented showroom.

Jeff de Bruges

Mall of the Emirates (341 0960/www.jeff-de-
bruges.com). **Open** 10am-midnight daily.
Credit AmEx, MC, V. **Map** p336 D2.

Chocolate lovers will worship the scrumptious offerings here. With the finest Belgian chocolates on sale this side of Wallonia, the place is chock-full of truffles, marzipan, fruit jellies, ganaches and pralines.

Oil & Vinegar
Harvey Nichols (409 8961/www.oilandvinegar.com).
Open 10am-midnight Sat, Thur, Fri; 10am-10pm Sun-Wed. **Credit** AmEx, MC, V. **Map** p336 D2.
Ordinary bottles of oil and vinegar might suit you fine, but if you've got a fine taste in condiments and you're a sucker for nice packaging, you'll find solace here. Situated on the top floor of Harvey Nichols, Oil & Vinegar offers an elaborate selection of oils from olive to truffle.
Other locations: Madinat Jumeirah (368 6178).

Patchi
Souk Madinat Jumeirah (368 6101/www.patchi.com).
Open 10am-10pm daily. **Credit** AmEx, MC, V. **Map** p336 D1.
Renowned for its selection of high quality chocolates, Patchi, a Lebanese brand, is undoubtedly the Rolls-Royce of chocolates in the region.
Other locations: Mercato Mall (349 1188); Wafi City Mall (324 4030).

Wafi Gourmet
Wafi City Mall (324 4433). **Open** 9am-1am daily.
Credit AmEx, MC, V. **Map** p329 J3.
At the heart of this Egypt-themed mall, Wafi Gourmet is a temple of temptation for any food-loving pharaoh. The shop is filled to the rafters with Arabian cheeses, sweets, olives, truffles and dates. There's a café in the corner, so you can enjoy your purchases from the deli counters without having to wait until you get home.

Health & beauty

Cosmetics & perfume

Ajmal Perfumes
Deira City Centre (295 3580/www.ajmalperfume.com).
Open 10am-10pm Sat-Wed; 10am-midnight Thur, Fri. AmEx, MC, V. **Credit** MC, V. **Map** p329 K2.
Ajmal is a swanky Arabian perfumer at which you can pick up strong scents from the region. A word of warning to the uninitiated – Arabian scents are much headier and spicier than Western perfumes.
Other locations: BurJuman Centre (351 5505).

Arabian Oud
Souk Madinat Jumeirah (368 6586/www.arabian oud.com). **Open** 10am-10.30pm daily. **Credit** AmEx, MC, V. **Map** p336 D1.
This Saudi perfumer's Eastern ambience is balanced by its contemporary interior and an unlimited range of authentic oils and potions. You can create your own mix and then choose the intricate bottle it will end up in. A popular destination for the uninitiated as well.
Other locations: BurJuman Centre (352 6767); Ibn Battuta Mall (368 5638).

Areej
Mall of the Emirates (340 5223/www.altayer.com).
Open 10am-midnight daily. **Credit** AmEx, MC, V. **Map** p336 D2.
As well as plenty of designer names including Dior and Chanel, you'll find funkier labels like Smashbox at branches of Areej. New fragrances tend to arrive here very promptly, meaning you're bound to find the latest products.
Other locations: The Boulevard at Jumeirah Emirates Towers (330 3340); Ibn Battuta Mall (366 9985); Mercato Mall (344 6803).

Body Shop
BurJuman Centre (351 1335). **Open** 9.30am-10pm Sat-Thur; 2-10pm Fri. **Credit** AmEx, MC, V. **Map** p331 J5.
The Body Shop continues to sell divine products that have been going for years, like the mango body butter and excellent Amlika leave-in conditioner, alongside their newer cranberry and orange ranges. Those with a conscience will be pleased to know that even in Dubai you can take any of your old products in for recycling and that along with having a fair trade policy, the Body Shop continues to champion animal and human rights issues.
Other locations: Deira City Centre (295 0701); Al Ghurair City (228 9494); Jumeirah Centre (344 4042); Ibn Battuta Mall (368 5456); Mall of the Emirates (341 0551); Wafi City Mall (324 5435).

Boots
Ibn Battuta Mall (368 5936/www.boots.com/ www.alshaya.com). **Open** 10am-10pm Sun-Wed, 10am-midnight Thur-Sat. **Credit** AmEx, MC, V. **Map** p336 A2.
When this famous British healthcare and pharmaceuticals brand announced it was spreading its wings to the Middle East, there was a collective jump for joy among British expatriates. Fill your basket with items from the No 7 make-up range, pamper your complexion with creams from Skin Kindly and Botanics, and for something to help you unwind, check out the Sanctuary's excellent product range.
Other locations: Mall of the Emirates (340 6880); The Village (349 9112).

Faces
BurJuman Centre (352 1441). **Open** 10am-10pm daily. **Credit** AmEx, MC, V. **Map** p331 J5.
Beauty magazines come to life when you step inside this shop. With a mixture of designer fragrances, cosmetics and mid-range brands like Bourjois, Urban Decay, Hard Candy, Pout and Benefit, it's a favourite with twenty- and thirtysomething women.
Other locations: Dubai Festival City (232 5747); Ibn Battuta Mall (368 5594); Mall of the Emirates (347 1225).

MAC
Deira City Centre (295 7704/www.maccosmetics.com).
Open 10am-10pm Sun-Wed, 10am-midnight Thur-Sat. **Credit** AmEx, MC, V. **Map** p329 K2.
MAC is used by professional make-up artists around the globe, and it's no wonder with its plethora of

foundations, glosses and beauty tools, and show-stopping bright and glitter eye shadows. The staff are helpful and on hand to give you a makeover and make-up tips. *Photo p164.*
Other locations: BurJuman Centre (351 2880); Ibn Battuta Mall (368 5966); Mall of the Emirates in Harvey Nichols (409 8931); Mercato Mall (344 9536); Wafi City Mall (324 4112).

Paris Gallery
Deira City Centre (295 5550/uae-parisgallery.com).
Open 10am-midnight Sat, Thur, Fri; 10am-11pm Sun-Wed. **Credit** AmEx, MC, V. **Map** p329 K2.
This stalwart of the UAE's beauty industry invokes the ambience of a Parisian boudoir. Staff can be overeager, but most international brands are stocked, with products tantalisingly displayed on carousels. There's also a spa on the upper level.
Other locations: BurJuman Centre (359 7774); Al Ghurair City (221 1166); Ibn Battuta Mall (368 5500); Lamcy Plaza (366 2555); Wafi City Mall (324 2121).

Pixi
Mall of the Emirates (341 3833/www.pixibeauty.com).
Open 10am-midnight Sat, Thur, Fri; 10am-11pm Sun-Wed. **Credit** AmEx, MC, V. **Map** p336 D2.
A treasure trove of cosmetic variety, Pixi is bursting with rainbow coloured make-up, natural skincare and all the beauty tools you need to keep immaculately groomed. As the name suggests, the vibe is fun, cheeky and definitely quirky.

Rituals
Deira City Centre (294 1432/www.rituals.com).
Open 10am-midnight Sat, Thur, Fri; 10am-10pm Sun-Wed. **Credit** AmEx, MC, V. **Map** p329 K2.
The face, body and hair ranges at Rituals, a Dutch lifestyle brand that embraces Eastern philosophies, are a little more expensive than your regular toiletries, but the quality is superb.

Salons

Franck Provost
Burj Al Arab (301 7249/www.franckprovost-dubai. com). **Open** 10am-10pm daily. **Credit** AmEx, MC, V. **Map** p336 E1.
It's hard to get a booking at this salon for two very good reasons: the stylists actually know what they're doing, and when you have an appointment, you get to go into the Burj Al Arab without the usual hassle. Considering the location, prices are surprisingly affordable (Dhs300 for a cut). They also offer great packages of cut, colour and blow-dry combos, with prices starting at Dhs550.
Other locations: Dubai Marina (362 9865); Dubai World Convention Centre (331 0801); Mall of the Emirates (341 3245), Ritz-Carlton Dubai (318 6141).

N.Bar
Ibn Battuta Mall (339 4801). **Open** 10am-10pm daily. **Credit** AmEx, MC, V. **Map** p336 A2.
N.Bar is light and airy with white walls and chrome fittings, although it stops just short of being clinical. The staff are friendly, helpful and efficient to a tee.

Minimalism reaches the Middle East: **Ikea**.

Treatments include waxing, massage, manicures, pedicures, acrylic, silk, gel and fibreglass nail enhancements, plus a number of luscious-sounding treatments for pampered hands and feet.
Other locations: The Boulevard at Jumeirah Emirates Towers (330 1001); BurJuman Centre (359 0008); Dubai Internet City (390 9535); Al Ghurair City (228 9009); Grosvenor House (399 9009); Palm Strip Mall (346 1100).

Toni&Guy
Jumeirah Emirates Towers (330 3345/www.toni guy.com). **Open** 10am-10pm Sat-Thur; 4-8pm Fri. **Credit** AmEx, MC, V. **Map** p328 H4.
Don't expect to find bog-standard hairdressers at Dubai's Toni&Guy branches; these guys are no less than hair technicians, and each one has worked their way up through the T&G ranks. A visit here is not cheap (a wash, cut and blow-dry will cost you between Dhs195 and Dhs275), but you know you are in safe hands.
Other locations: Grand Hyatt Dubai (324 4900).

Home furnishings

Ikea
Dubai Festival City (263 7555/www.ikeadubai.com).
Open 10am-10pm Sat-Fri. **Credit** AmEx, MC, V.
Credit AmEx, MC, V. **Map** p329 L3.

Eat, Drink, Shop

Ikea has flat-packed itself all the way to the Middle East with its 25,400sq m outlet offering miles and miles of inspiration to nest builders. Expect self-assembly kitchen, bedroom and bathroom furniture and accessories in abundance, designed to Scandinavian standards and tastes. Clean minimalist lines, homely wooden frames, and cute but curious Swedish names are the order of the day. *Photo p167*.

Kas Australia
Mercato Mall (344 1179/www.kasaustralia.com.au). **Open** 10am-10pm Sat-Thur; 2-10pm Fri. **Credit** AmEx, MC, V. **Map** p334 C12.
Kas Australia is a master purveyor of the soft, fluorescent and frilly. Citrus-coloured pillows plump up against extravagantly textured throws and brightly coloured fabrics in this snug Aussie outlet. **Other locations**: BurJuman Centre (349 0503); Ibn Battuta Mall (366 9386).

One
Jumeirah Beach Road, Jumeirah (345 6687). **Open** 9am-10pm Sat-Thur; 2-10pm Fri. **Credit** AmEx, MC, V. **Map** p332 D9.
This Dubai company is almost as famous for its colourful ad campaigns and frequent publicity stunts as it is for its frequently splendid contemporary furniture. The secret to its success is its design-led product range, which neatly marries ethnic accessories (think incense burners, Buddha heads and textured photo frames), with bold, contemporary items of furniture that wouldn't look out of place in any budding interior designer's home. **Other locations**: BurJuman Centre (351 4424); Mall of the Emirates (341 3777); Wafi City (324 1224).

Zara Home
Mall of the Emirates (341 4184/www.zarahome.com). **Open** 10am-10pm Sun-Wed; 10am-midnight Thur-Sat. **Credit** AmEx, MC, V. **Map** p336 D2.
Just like the clothing range, Zara Home caters for fans of hip urban chic, with a country twist. There is a mix of styles to suit every design taste, from ethnic animal print and vibrant Indian batik to kitsch paisley and modern cream hues. **Other locations**: BurJuman Centre (359 9988).

Rugs

Dubai offers a vast range of rugs, from contemporary to traditional, antique to new, and cheap to expensive. They come from a number of countries, including Iran, Turkey, Pakistan and Central Asia. If you're planning on purchasing an antique rug, you should check its reverse side. The more knots there are on the underside, the better the rug's quality and the longer it's likely to last. On the whole, silk is more expensive than wool, and rugs from Iran are generally more expensive than the equivalents from Turkey or Kashmir. Be sure to visit the Dubai Shopping Festival (*see p142* **Consumer culture**) for Afghan, Iraqi and tribal designs at low prices at Global Village.

Life's a bed of roses, at **Kas Australia**.

Music

Disco2000
Spinneys Centre, Al Wasl Road, Umm Suqeim (394 0139). **Open** 9am-9.30pm Sat-Thur; 10am-9.30pm Fri. **Credit** AmEx, MC, V. **Map** p332 E9.
With every passing year, the name seems less hip and more retro, but buried deep in the heart of the Spinneys complex lies Disco2000, a store that brims with DVDs. They have an excellent supply of US television dramas, so if you're after the likes of *Desperate Housewives, Prison Break, 24* or *The Sopranos*, this is a good bet.

JS Music
Ibn Battuta Mall (366 9715). **Open** 10am-midnight daily. **Credit** AmEx, MC, V. **Map** p336 A2.
Whether you are looking to crash and burn as the next Keith Moon or strum-diddley-dum your hippy tunes, you should find the appropriate instrument in here. There's a good range of instruments in store, and all the additional bits of kit that you'll need to start you on your way to Carnegie Hall.

The gold rush

The malls may be home to the likes of Tiffany & Co, Cartier and Damas, but to find true jewellery bargains you can't beat a trip to the gold markets, like the old gold souk. Investing in gold may be a centuries-old practice, but it's still a major factor in the UAE's economy. Like anywhere in the world, gold's value is not dependent on its rarity, but rather the process involved in extracting it from the ground. It's valued according to its carat – the amount of gold in the mixture – that falls into four categories: 22, 18, 14 and nine.

Gold prices are based on a standard rate per gram that changes very frequently. Typical rates in Dubai are around Dhs60 per gram of 18 carat gold, Dhs75 for 22 carats, and 24 carats at around Dhs80. What makes the difference is the work that has gone into the piece of jewellery, and most stores charge a workmanship fee of approximately 10 to 20 per cent. The gold market in Dubai has stringent laws in place to ensure that all gold is valued and labelled correctly, and government officials regularly check these markings, helping maintain the city's popularity with bargain hunters who are only after the genuine article.

Old gold souk

Nr Baladiya Street, Deira. **Open** 7am-noon, 5-7pm Sat-Thur; 5-7pm Fri. **Map** p330 H3.
When you're dropped off, don't get confused and wander into the shopping complex called the Gold Centre. The old gold souk is an entirely different open market further down a wide alley. But don't worry too much about getting lost – the souk's actually not that hard to find, framed by a wooden monster of an entrance welcoming visitors in bright lights and scrolling text to the Dubai City of Gold. The souk is a crazy collection of walkways lined with jewellery stores with windows full of all manner of exotic, mind-boggling pieces. If you get bored with all the glitter, there are a few hidden spots where you can find clothing for sale, while there's also a vendor selling

Omani halwa, a warm and madly fattening traditional sweet. There are also plenty of alleyways leading off to little shops where you can haggle over a shisha (the Arabian waterpipe), a backgammon set or even a voluminous black *abaya*, so allow plenty of time for exploration. Towards the eastern end of the old gold souk, there's the perfume souk – a small collection of stores specialising in scents from both Europe and the Middle East. It's a good place to stock up at very competitive prices.

Where to shop in the souk

Kanz Jewels

(226 5639). **Open** 8.30am-11pm Sat-Thur; 8.30am-12.30pm, 2.30-11pm Fri. **Credit** AmEx, MC, V. **Map** p330 H3.
Kanz is another big name in the business, with more than one outlet in the old souk. The pieces that stand out here are the traditional Gulf necklaces; delicate, draping gold chokers with inlaid gems from all over the region. The store also boasts a collection of UAE-made chokers that tie with a traditional red chord costing around Dhs11,000 each.

Ruby Damas

(226 3648). **Open** 9am-10pm daily. **Credit** AmEx, MC, V. **Map** p330 H3.
This UAE-based company has stores all over the world, so it's not surprising that there are more than just a few in the old gold souk. This particular branch is the only one also carrying the name of Ruby Jewellers, an Indian jeweller bought by Damas. Take a look at the tempting diamonds, mainly coming in from Italy, and wide selection of fashionably modern gold accessories, but make sure you don't miss their pearls. The Arabic pieces include a simple strand of Bahraini pearls for around Dhs27,000.

Sona Jewellers

(226 6012). **Open** 9am-2pm, 4-9pm Sat-Thur; 9-11.30am, 4-10pm Fri. **Credit** MC, V. **Map** p330 H3.
Sona Jewellers is the only spot in the souk that showcases an interesting collection of gold statuettes. The elaborate mini models, which are hollow and made from mould casts in Asia, are based on mythical figures and Hindu gods. Each piece is priced differently, with glistening Ganeshas priced at around Dhs150 per gram.

Eat, Drink, Shop

Ohm Records.

Virgin Megastore.

Music Chamber

Crowne Plaza Shopping Centre (331 6416). **Open** 10am-11pm Sat-Thur; 5-10pm Fri. **Credit** AmEx, MC, V. **Map** p330 G10.

The concept of the Music Chamber is 'musicians, not merchants'. This philosophy means that prices are kept low on instruments, from handmade guitars to pianos, and that all the little bits of kit that Dubai's musicians have traditionally had to order over the internet (sax, reeds, trumpet oil, guitar strings) are now all to hand. There are also 15 practice rooms that you can hire to play the piano or rehearse with your band. Lessons are also available: choose from violin, percussion, singing, sax, flute, trumpet, piano, oud, kanoun and guitar, and pay Dhs540 for four one-hour lessons, plus a one-off registration fee of Dhs100.

Ohm Records

Opposite BurJuman Centre (397 3728/www.ohm records.com). **Open** 2-10pm daily. **Credit** AmEx, MC, V. **Map** p331 J5.

Ohm Records was the first record shop in the Middle East to sell vinyl shipped in from overseas. It prides itself on introducing the masses to innovative electronic music, and all its records come from independent labels, with not a mainstream tune in sight. Professional and bedroom DJs gather at the weekends to play on the decks for free. The shop also sells record bags and a small line of streetwear, as well as processors and turntables.

Virgin Megastore

Mall of the Emirates (341 4353/www.virgin.com). **Open** 10am-midnight daily. **Credit** AmEx, MC, V. **Map** p336 D2.

Virgin's vast range of music, movies, multimedia, games, computers, mobile phones, consumer electronics and books is the most impressive in town, although those with eclectic tastes might struggle to find their CD or DVD of choice – the selection focuses on the mainstream. There's also an in-store café for coffee buffs, a quirky game zone for PlayStation2 and XBox fanatics, as well as the store's ever-popular listening stations.

Other locations: BurJuman Centre (351 3358); Deira City Centre (296 8599); Mercato Mall (344 6971).

Opticians

Most malls have an optician; eye tests are often free if you buy glasses or contacts.

Bahrain Optician

Wafi City Mall (324 2455/www.bahrainoptics.com). **Open** 10am-10pm Sat-Thur; 4.30-10pm Fri. **Credit** AmEx, MC, V. **Map** p329 J3.

Not only does this store make an effort to stock the latest designs and change its collection each season, but also the service is quick and reliable. You can go from eye test to final fitting in just a couple of days.

Barakat Opticals

Beach Centre, Jumeirah Beach Road (329 1913). **Open** 10am-10pm Sat-Thur; 4.30-10pm Fri. **Credit** AmEx, MC, V. **Map** p332 D10.

If you're looking for a quick optical fix, then you should be satisfied with the service here. Barakat Opticals is a straightforward glass-pusher with a reasonable if unexciting spread of frames. Service is friendly and efficient.

Bavaria Optics

Al Dhiyafah Road, Satwa (345 1919). **Open** 9am-1pm, 5-9.30pm Sat-Thur; 5- 9.30pm Fri. **Credit** AmEx, MC, V. **Map** p333 F8.

One of a barrage of great opticians on the Al Dhiyafah Road (the equally good Yateem Opticians is just down the road; 04 345 3405), Bavaria Optics sells a great range of specs while the eye tests are extremely thorough.

Al Jaber Optical Centre

Deira City Centre (295 4400). **Open** 10am-10pm Sat-Thur; 2-10pm Fri. **Credit** AmEx, MC, V. **Map** p329 K2.

At Al Jaber you'll find shades by practically every luxury brand under the sun, although the glasses section is a little skimpy. Featured brands include Montblanc, Hugo Boss, Giorgio Armani, Cartier, Oakley, Burberry and Nike.

Outdoor equipment

Al Boom Diving Club

Le Meridien Mina Seyahi Beach Resort (399 2278/www.alboomdiving.com). **Open** 9am-5pm daily. **Credit** AmEx, MC, V. **Map** p336 B1.

Al Boom offers both diving lessons and all the equipment you'll need to get started. They offer unbeatable facilities (including a swimming pool for beginners), a full range of PADI courses, full equipment rental and a shop stocking the latest from the top brands in diving equipment.

Al Boom Marine

Ramool showroom, before Mirdif, turn right at the Coca-Cola sign (289 4803/www.alboommarine.com). **Open** 8am-8pm Sat-Thur; 4-8pm Fri. **Credit** AmEx, MC, V. **Map** p329 L3.

Stockists of the coolest beach and outdoor clothing in Dubai, Al Boom is the exclusive distributor

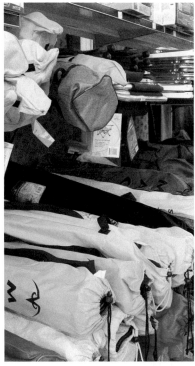

Camp it up, at **Picnico**.

for brands such as Bombardier, Oakley, O'Neill, Rip Curl and Hurley, so this is the place to head to for boards, bikinis and beanies as well as respectable brands of surf- and wakeboards.

Other locations: Al Bahar showroom, Jumeirah 3, Jumeirah Beach Road (394 1258).

Dubai Desert Extreme

Beach Centre, Jumeirah Beach Road (344 4952/ www.dubaidesertextreme.com). **Open** 10am-8pm Sat-Thur. **Credit** AmEx, MC, V. **Map** p332 D10.

This is where the skate kids get their decks, trucks, wheels and spare rails to grind. If you're looking for some skate fashions, this is a good bet, with T-shirts from Shorty's and Independent the pick of the bunch.

Picnico

Al Bahr Marine, Jumeirah Beach Road (394 1653). **Open** 9am-9pm Sat-Thur; 4.30-9pm Fri. **Credit** AmEx, MC, V. **Map** p334 C11.

Picnico is an eclectic camping emporium located on Jumeirah Beach Road (on the edge of the petrol station forecourt). It's better suited to seasoned rather than inexperienced campers, specialising in GPS systems as well as tents, sleeping bags, gas stoves and barbecue sets.

Eat, Drink, Shop

www.sony-mea.com

SONY

Shoot true to life images while recording movies

Your Hard Disk Handycam™ captures close to life movies and photos thanks to the new ClearVid™ CMOS Image sensor that gives you higher picture resolution and allowing you to take 6.1 Mega Pixel still images. Take pictures and record movies simultaneously with the Dual Rec feature. Never miss a moment.

SR300
- 6.1 Mega Pixels Still Image Recording
- 5.1 Ch Surround Recording
- 1/2.9" ClearVid CMOS Sensor
- 40 GB Hard Disk memory
- Stamina Battery (Longer recordings)
- One touch DVD Burn
- Hard Disk protection

SR200
4 Mega Pixel
40GB

SR82
1 Mega Pixel
60GB

SR62
1 Mega Pixel
30GB

SR42
40x Optical Zoom
30GB

SR300

HDD
HARD DISK DRIVE

HANDYCAM.

like.no.other™

Arts & Entertainment

Jam Jar. *See p191.*

Arabian Desert Tours

affiliated to Ahlan Dubai Experience

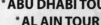

* DESERT SAFARI
* QUAD BIKES
* OVERNIGHT SAFARI
* DUNE DRIVE AND SAND SKIING
* DUBAI CITY TOUR
* SHARJAH / AJMAN TOUR
* ABU DHABI TOUR
* AL AIN TOUR
* EAST COAST TOUR
* HATTA MOUNTAIN TRIP
* FISHING TRIP
* SHOPPING TRIP
* DHOW DINNER
* HELICOPTER TOUR
* LUXURY YACHT / CRUISES TOUR
* OMAN / KHASAB TOUR
* BURJ AL ARAB RESERVATION
* HOTEL RESERVATION
* VISA ARRANGEMENTS

Tel: +971 4 2682880,   Fax: +971 4 2682881
PO Box 93349 Dubai U.A.E
E-mail: arabian7@emirates.net.ae
Website: www.adtuae.com
For 24 hours reservation: +971 50 7588911 & +971 50 8465565

Festivals & Events

Sports fans will jump for joy at the line-up; culture vultures, on the other hand, might find themselves disappointed.

Dubai Desert Rock Fest. *See p180.*

It's hard to believe that a couple of decades ago a person moving to Dubai would have qualified for a hardship allowance from their employer – financial compensation for having to live and work in such a hot, boring place. Things have certainly changed. The climate may be as inhospitable as ever, but Dubai's calendar is now packed with numerous festivals and events to lure in visitors and hopefully persuade some of them to settle here.

Dubai's ambition to make such events world-class is more than matched by its spending power. Golfing phenomenon Tiger Woods turns up annually to compete in the **Dubai Desert Classic**; Roger Federer and Maria Sharapova can be spotted most years mingling around the Irish Village; rock stars like Chrissie Hynde have been spotted wandering the gold souk, and Frankie Dettori usually leads the field in the city's most prestigious spectacle, the **Dubai World Cup**. To many, this latter event is all about the fabulously absurd hats, champagne and fashion contests rather than the horse racing, although you're sure to find plenty of serious equine enthusiasts and wealthy Emirati horse owners at the edge of their seats watching some of the finest breeds in the world.

While Dubai excels at producing high-profile sporting events in the winter months, it's been criticised in the past for treating the idea of art and culture as just another dutiful tick on the what-makes-a-city checklist. But it's been rapidly injecting art into its development plans, and not only in the form of naff-sounding residential projects like Culture Village. The city's now home to an international film festival, major Christie's auctions, the **Dubai Desert Rock Fest** and the **DIFC Gulf Art Fair**, which, in its inaugural year, brought in pieces and prints from contemporary artists like Damien Hirst, as well as a handful of Picassos and Warhols.

If you're after a truly Emirati experience, then the holy month of Ramadan, either of the two major Eid celebrations or the exuberant festivities during the **UAE's National Day** on 2 December, are the events you need to witness. Similarly, Dubai's 'ethnic majority', the Indian population, makes the most of the Hindu religious holiday **Diwali** by dressing up apartment blocks with bright lights and candles and partying in the streets and restaurants of neighbourhoods such as Karama and Satwa. As well as cultural events, you'll find more lightweight fare offered by the **Dubai Shopping Festival**; Dubai is obsessed with shopping, so the event's popularity should come as no surprise. Yet what other city in the world would dare, with a straight face, to put on a month-long festival – albeit an incredibly profitable one – dedicated to the art of consumption?

The big events are crammed into the high season from September to May when the climate is bearable, although events like the elaborate **Dubai Summer Surprises** festival make those unruly heat waves a little more attractive.

The dates listed below are subject to change. For more information on these events and other one-off events in the city, pick up a copy of *Time Out Dubai* magazine. Tickets are available from the venues listed below or from the Time Out ticketline (800 4669/ www.timeouttickets.com).

Autumn

Ramadan
Various venues. **Date** 12 Sept-11 Oct 2007 & 2 Sep -1 Oct 2008 (depends on the lunar calendar).
The Muslim holy month is dedicated to the practice of fasting from sunrise to sunset, an imperative extended to non-Muslims in public settings. But as soon as the sun goes down and the imam calls for prayer, the calm is replaced by a lively and elaborate cultural event. The major attraction for tourists here is the *iftar* feast, something most restaurants and five-star hotels take full advantage of. Expect to be offered an array of plump dates and milk, a common way to break the day's fast, followed by *Arabian Nights*-worthy samplings of some of the region's most popular cuisine. If you're not lucky enough to be a guest at an Emirati family's *iftar* dinner – an invitation that means nothing less than a full night (and early morning) sitting – catch the Ramadan experience by trying an *iftar* buffet dinner at the popular Lebanese restaurant Al Nafoorah at the Emirates Towers (*see p123*), the Iranian set menu at the Radisson SAS Hotel's Shabestan in Deira (*see p102*) or one of the many shisha-serving Ramadan tents across the city, such as the Ritz-Carlton's stunning Bedouin village. It is important that tourists behave respectfully throughout this month. Drinking alcohol in public is unacceptable and live or loud music is considered offensive.

Eid Al Fitr
Various venues. **Date** 11-13 Oct 2007 & 1-3 Oct 2008 (depends on the lunar calendar).
As Ramadan comes to a close, excitement starts to build as Muslims wait for a lunar sign that it's time for Eid Al Fitr – 'Feast of Breaking the Fast'. The three days after the month-long fast are among the

Ramadan rules

Ramadan is Islam's holiest month, one of prayer, self-restraint and spirituality. Accordingly, there are a few things visitors should keep in mind during this month:

● Make sure you don't eat, drink or smoke in public after sunrise and before sunset, the period when Muslims are required by Islam to fast. This includes chewing gum and eating anything in your car or a taxi.
● Dress conservatively throughout the month; public displays of affection are a definite no-no.
● Don't swear in public.
● At the *iftar* table, Muslims are allowed to break their fast at the sound of the *adhan*, or call to prayer. If you're invited to an *iftar* meal, you shouldn't eat before that point.
● Don't play loud music or keep your television volume high, particularly during times of prayer, and loud behaviour in public is frowned upon.
● Don't try to convince a Muslim to break the fast and never buy a Muslim alcohol. The latter is legally forbidden at all times of the year, though it is enforced with graver consequences during Ramadan.
● Don't walk on a prayer mat or pass in front of a Muslim who is praying, and always ask permission before entering a mosque.
● Don't photograph or point and stare at Muslim or Emirati women.

most vibrant in the Islamic calendar, with celebrations culminating in an elaborate daily show of fireworks, traditional music and festivities.

Desert Rhythm
Dubai Country Club (333 1155/339 0550/ www.desertrhythmfestival.com). **Map** p329 L5. **Date** 26-27 Oct 2007.
Desert Rhythm, a two-day festival of world music, is Dubai's answer to WOMAD. The line-up in 2007 was promising although not particularly adventurous, with John Mayer, Wayne Wonder, Khaled and Karen Zoid performing. Attendances were disappointingly low, yet the promoters are planning a second bash in late 2007; tickets are Dhs200 a day or Dhs300 for the weekend.

UAE Desert Challenge
Various venues (www.uaedesertchallenge.com). **Date** 27 Oct-2 Nov 2007.
The second largest motor sport event in the Middle East, the Desert Challenge pits the world's finest endurance riders and cross-country drivers against each other. The last round of both the FIA Cup and FIM World Championship for cross-country rallies, the UAE Challenge is the final shakedown before January's Paris-Dakar Rally. The five-day drive starts in Abu Dhabi, cutting through the Liwa Oasis, and on to the finish line at the Dubai International Marine Club (DIMC).

Camel racing
Nad Al Sheba camel racetrack, off the Dubai-Al Ain Road (338 2324/338 8170). **Map** p327 D3. **Date** Oct-Mar.
Whether it's the 'sport of kings' connotation or the ungainly efforts of the 'ships of the desert' that grab you, a visit to a camel race is an interesting cultural experience; they attract all strata of UAE society plus a fair number of visitors. The season's races usually take place on Thursdays and Fridays at around 7am; you can watch training sessions most mornings at around 10am and later from 2pm to 5pm. The season reaches its peak in March, with prize races attended by the ruling families. Responding to international criticism, the UAE recently replaced child jockeys under 16 years of age (some of whom were as young as five) with robot jockeys. A new track down the road from Nad Al Sheba is slated to open at the end of 2007.

Diwali
Various venues. **Date** 9 Nov 2007 & 28 Oct 2008.
The Hindu 'Festival of Lights' – the equivalent of the Western New Year or the Muslim Eid Al Fitr – is celebrated during the month of Ashwin, and normally falls between mid October and mid November. There's a focus on colour and the local Indian population make sure there's no shortage of vibrant shades and bright lights around the city. Entrances to villas, restaurants and shops are decorated with rangoli designs (symmetrical images depicting gods, goddesses, dancers and other

Nad Al Sheba – home to some fine fillies.

figures) and candles to welcome Lakshmi, the goddess of wealth and prosperity, and drive away evil spirits. Come evening time, kids race down from apartment blocks to let off homemade firecrackers, and communal fireworks parties take place all over town. For five days or so, the streets are filled with lively music and drumming, while tons of sweets and desserts fill the homes of those celebrating. You might manage to wrangle an invitation to a party; if not, soak up some of the atmosphere in one of Dubai's Indian neighbourhoods, preferably over a cheap-as-chips meal in one of Karama or Satwa's many curry houses.

Horse racing
Nad Al Sheba Racecourse, off the Dubai-Al Ain Road (336 3666/332 2277/www.nadalshebaclub.com). **Map** p327 D4. **Date** every Thur from 7pm (9pm during Ramadan) from Nov-Mar.
Horse racing is such a big part of Emirati society that many smaller towns and villages have their own racetracks. The country's principal venue for the sport is in Dubai at Nad Al Sheba, where local and international steeds and their jockeys compete through a winter season that culminates with the Dubai World Cup in March. In accordance with Islam, gambling is not allowed, although various competitions, such as the 'pick 6' race card, have cash prizes.

Arts & Entertainment

THE BIG BUS COMPANY® DUBAI

- Magnificent views from an open top, double-decker bus
- One ticket covers two exciting routes
- Ticket valid for 24 hours
- Hop on and Hop off at all major sights in Dubai
- Guided English commentary or choice of 8 digitally recorded languages
- Buses operate 7 days a week from Wafi City main entrance
- No Advance booking necessary
- Free daily Arabian Dhow Cruise
- Free Walking tour daily from Oct -April
- Free entry to Dubai Museum and Sheikh Saeed Al Maktoum's House
- Free Wafi City Advantage Card (Up to 20% discount at selected outlets)

infodubai@bigbustours.com

www.bigbustours.com

+971 4 324 4187

Dubai Rugby Sevens – a sporting highlight of the Dubai calendar.

Winter

Dubai Rugby Sevens

Dubai Exiles Rugby Football Club, 6km (4 miles) east of Dubai on the Al Awir Road (321 0008/ www.dubairugby7s.com). **Map** p329 D4. **Date** 29 Nov-1 Dec 2007.
The IRB World Sevens Series features 16 world-class international teams and huge quantities of local and regional teams competing for a variety of trophies over three days. The tremendously popular event, which attracts up to 30,000 spectators a day, is a sporting and social highlight for residents and overseas visitors alike.

Dubai International Rally

Dubai International Marine Club, Le Meridien Mina Seyahi Beach Resort & Marina, Al Sufouh Road, Jumeirah (399 4111/228 4019). **Date** 29 Nov-2 Dec 2007. **Map** p336 B1
Following the UAE Desert Challenge (*see p177*) comes the International Rally championships, the final leg of the FIA Middle East events held throughout the region. Starting in the UAE in January, the competition then makes its way through Qatar, Bahrain, Jordan, Syria, Oman, Lebanon and Cyprus. Dubai's very own Mohammed Bin Sulayem is the most successful driver in FIA history, so expect the crowds to be cheering him on. Snap-happy visitors should take their cameras to this event for some great photo opportunities.

National Day Festival

Various venues. **Date** 2 Dec 2007.
The UAE's Independence Day sees the whole country turn into one jammed street, packed with noise, toys, beautiful cars and enough silly string to cover the Palm Jumeirah. All the major monuments and tourist attractions are open to the public and in the evening there are fireworks displays and concerts featuring some of the region's biggest names.

World Offshore Powerboat Championship

Dubai Marine Club, Le Meridien Mina Seyahi Beach Resort & Marina, Al Sufouh Road, Jumeirah (399 4111). **Date** 6-8 Dec 2007. **Map** p336 B1
The UIM Class 1 World Offshore Powerboat Championship takes place over two days in December and is a part of the international championships, which take place in cities from southern Europe to the Gulf. Top teams from around the world compete for a place on the podium in 42-foot, five-tonne powerboats that travel at over 160mph.

Dubai International Film Festival

Various venues (www.dubaifilmfest.com). **Date** 9-16 Dec 2007.
While Dubai cinemas rarely stray from a popular mix of Hollywood blockbusters and corny action flicks, the increasingly popular DIFF showcases cinema that is otherwise impossible to see in the UAE. *See also p194.*

Arts & Entertainment

Eid Al Adha

Various venues. **Date** 20 Dec 2007, depending on the lunar calendar.

The second Eid takes place on the tenth day of the last month of the Islamic calendar, Dhul-Hijjah. The Festival of the Sacrifice, marking the period after the pilgrimage to the holy city of Mecca, begins with Muslims gathering for the Eid prayer. Although only the pilgrims in Mecca can participate fully, other Muslims all across the world join with them by also celebrating on the correct days. In Dubai there is a four-day holiday. No alcohol is served on the day that precedes Eid Al Adha.

Dubai Shopping Festival

Various venues (www.mydsf.com). **Date** Jan-early Feb 2008.

A month-long festival of bargain hunting, with various bits of shopping-related entertainment thrown in (*see p142* **Consumer culture**). The festival coincides with the launch of Global Village.

Dubai Desert Golf Classic

Emirates Golf Club, off Interchange 5, Sheikh Zayed Road (295 6440/www.dubaidesertclassic.com). **Date** 31 Jan-3 Feb 2008. **Map** p336 B2.

Every winter the Emirates Golf Club welcomes the finest swingers in the world to its pristine greens to compete for an impressive prize purse of US$2.4 million. Dubai-based Swede Henrik Stenson won the 2007 tournament to the delight of a partisan crowd, and South African Ernie Els is the most successful competitor in the tournament's history, with three victories to his name.

Dubai Tennis Championships

Dubai Tennis Stadium, Aviation Club, Garhoud Road (282 9166/www.dubaitennischampionships.com). **Date** mid Feb-early Mar 2008. **Map** p329 L3.

Why miss a chance to see what Roger Federer does best – that's win tournaments, of course – in a laid-back, sun-drenched venue? The Dubai Open is a fantastic opportunity to see the world's top players, such as court superstars Rafael Nadal and Maria Sharapova, slamming it out at the Aviation Club, home to the Irish Village pub where strawberries and champagne are served for the event. Ticket prices start at a bargain Dhs30.

Dubai International Jazz Festival

Dubai Media City, off Sheikh Zayed Road (391 1196/www.chilloutproductions.com). **Date** 28 Feb-1 Mar 2008. **Map** p336 B2.

It's hardly Montreux, but the Dubai International Jazz Festival has been a huge crowd-puller since the first event in January 2003. It's been able to attract musicians such as Stanley Jordan, Mike Stern, Jamie Cullum and – controversially – Toto, while the pleasant outdoor setting helps create a good vibe.

Dubai Desert Rock Fest

Dubai Country Club (333 1155/www.csmentertains. com). **Date** 7-8 Mar 2008. **Map** p329 L5.

This moshfest of extreme proportions is the most important event on any respectable headbanger's calendar. The successful inaugural event saw The

Arts & Entertainment

Global Village – part of the **Dubai Shopping Festival**.

Darkness, Sepultura and Machine Head thrill the city's surprisingly large rock contingent and the organisers, CSM, haven't disappointed since. The 2007 gig featured Iron Maiden, Incubus and the ever-popular The Prodigy, and for the fifth year anniversary of Desert Rock in 2008, CSM say they've got big things planned. Day tickets are around Dhs200, while a weekend ticket's about Dhs300. *Photo p175*.

Gulf Art Fair
Madinat Arena, Madinat Jumeirah, next to Wild Wadi on Jumeirah Beach Road (366 8888/www.madinat jumeirah.com). **Date** 19-22 Mar 2008. **Map** p336 D1.
The first major international art fair in Dubai came to fruition in 2007, and although it had the likes of Desert Rock and the jazz festival to compete with, it still managed to make some waves. A number of big names in the art world came in to show off some impressive works, including an Andy Warhol 'Dollar Sign'. A forum on contemporary art in the region also took place.

Dubai World Cup
Nad Al Sheba stadium, off the Dubai-Al Ain Road (332 2277/336 3666/www.dubaiworldcup.com). **Date** late Mar 2008. **Map** p327 F4.
The US$6 million Dubai World Cup is the richest horse race in the world and draws in thousands of enthusiasts every year. But it's not just a sporting event – it's the biggest date in the city's social calendar, and a boom time for milliners as the emirate's womenfolk compete to sport the most fanciful hat. All facets of UAE society attend, in all manners of dress and levels of sobriety, and the atmosphere in

the free stands can be pretty electric – never more so than when a member of Godolphin (the royal family's stable) romps home first, ridden by beloved celebrity jockey Frankie Dettori. The attached (and fully licensed) International Village resembles the largest wedding reception in history.

Jumeirah – A Festival of Taste
Various venues (366 8888). **Date** See www.madinatjumeirah.com for an up-to-date schedule.
A week-long excuse to live and eat extravagantly, the Festival of Taste sees top chefs from around the world descend on the Madinat Jumeirah to host gala dinners, talks and classes. The 2007 event saw top chefs like Gary Rhodes, James Martin and Jean-Christophe Novelli do their thing.

Summer

Dubai Summer Surprises
Various venues (www.mydsf.com).
Date Jun-Aug 2008.
A three-month effort to draw in the crowds over Dubai's stifling summer, DSS features the odd bargain and an endless stream of free children's entertainment, which mainly takes place in the city's shopping malls. DSS is presided over by the irksome Modhesh, a bright yellow cartoon character that appears in 'person' in the various malls and in caricature at every street corner and roundabout. A shopping festival may seem an unusual concept, but in 2006 1.87 million people turned up for the event and spent Dhs2.57 billion.

Arts & Entertainment

ESCAPE EVERY DAY

SKI DUBAi
an unforgettable snow experienc

Children

With a plethora of beaches, activity centres and theme parks, keeping the kids entertained in Dubai is child's play.

Children are revered in this part of the world, so it should come as no surprise that Dubai has plenty of attractions to keep kids occupied and entertained – be they tots or teens. With its bountiful selection of safe beaches and array of children's clubs at the major hotels, Dubai is one of the most child-friendly destinations in the world – perfect for parents in search of a worry-free winter getaway between the months of October and May. Active youngsters looking to expend energy will be in their element with scuba diving, sports parks and water sports widely available across the city.

The summer months can be a tad more trying with the sky-rocketing temperatures and humidity. During this time, many families find themselves hiding from the heat (not to mention the congestion) in the city's gigantic shopping malls. In the knowledge that the hot weather forces families inside, all the major malls offer dedicated play and entertainment areas.

The city's restaurants and cafés generally welcome children, particularly those in hotels and malls, and have dedicated children's menus. However, they aren't always equipped with high chairs so it's worth making enquiries in advance. Streetside independent restaurants are often kitted out with 'family rooms' and are also always welcoming. Many Friday brunches (*see p129* **The Friday brunch**) are aimed at families and come complete with clowns, face painters and other such child-pleasers. Pubs don't tend to be so child-friendly; your best bet for an outing is to head for alfresco venues that also serve food such as the **Irish Village** (*see p133*) and the perennially popular beachfront **Barasti Bar** (*see p135*).

Heritage centres such as the Dubai Museum don't tend to be particularly child-oriented, but Dubai does boast the fantastic, dedicated **Children's City**, a colourful construction in Creekside Park billed as the world's fifth-largest 'infotainment' facility. Little ones will love it, although older children might not be quite so enthusiastic.

In fact, the town's older kids and teenagers are less well catered for generally, and Dubai's offerings are limited to sports activities, arcade games centres and shopping; the clothes stores in Karama and Satwa are full of imitation designer gems for the teenage shopper. For

Get a leg-up, at **Al Safa Park**. *See p188.*

mid to late teens, there are occasional 'rain parties' and other non-alcoholic raves as well as a few local bands that play in unlicensed venues around town. Sadly these events are few and far between; check the weekly *Time Out Dubai* magazine for listings.

Essentially, Dubai is an astonishingly safe city where the beating sun and teeming traffic are the only potential pitfalls for parents. The importance of keeping kids covered up, sunscreened and away from the busy roads cannot be overstated at any time of year.

If you are planning a trip to Dubai, be sure to ask your hotel in advance about babysitting services and kids' clubs. If you're stuck for ideas during a holiday visit, need advice or are planning a longer stay, the local community group **Expat Woman** (www.expatwoman.com) and **Dubai Kidz** (www.dubaikidz.biz) will be of invaluable help.

Customer care

With a bewildering array of shops and malls spread around the city, you're spoilt for choice when it comes to splashing the cash. But if you've got kids in tow, things could get a little tricky. Or so you might think. Luckily, practically all of Dubai's major malls offer some sort of entertainment for kids. These centres are all well staffed and safe, with most offering a 'drop and shop' option to allow you to get some spending done in peace. Most feature secure gates and staff who take your mobile phone number so you can be reached immediately in the case of any problem.

Toby's Adventure Land (355 2868) at BurJuman Centre offers a great respite for younger children while allowing harassed parents to grab a coffee after shopping. The staff are friendly and experienced, which makes it a great place to meet mothers with children of a similar age. The larger malls have broader options. For a mall that's vibrant, fun and diverse, **Lamcy Plaza** (335 9999) is a good choice. The climbing clown in the foyer provides entertainment as soon as you arrive, while **Lou Lou Al Dugong's Play Centre** looms large to the left of the entrance. Probably best for children under ten, it features slides, ball-shooting galleries and rides, as well as sand and paint play areas for younger children. The mini-arcade next door has cheap fun and games for the kids before you drag them back to the shops to snap up some bargains. It's gated, and the staff are wonderfully welcoming.

Fun City at Mercato Mall (344 4161) again features friendly staff and the usual range of activities, including some quieter ones such as painting. **Magic Planet** (341 4000) at Mall of the Emirates (with a smaller outlet at Deira City Centre) is possibly the loudest activity centre in Dubai. Packed with video games, simulators and even bowling to complement the usual slides and rides, it's a total screamathon, and guaranteed to entertain kids of all ages.

Exploring the city

Bastakia & the Creek

Dubai's heat, hard edges and multi-lane roads can make urban exploring with children a nightmare. There are, however, spots where you can leave the highways behind and take off on foot, interspersing your journey with brief taxi rides. The **Creek**, with its *abra* stations and dhow wharfage, plus **Children's City** (*see p189*), makes for an ideal half-day family wander.

While energy levels are high, begin at **Dubai Museum** (*see p75*) in Bastakia, Bur Dubai. Some displays of artefacts can be a little tedious for younger kids – although older ones might enjoy the traditional weaponry – but the mock souk situated halfway through the museum is spooky enough to grab the attention of wandering minds, and the pearl-diving display is also interesting. Entrance costs a mere Dhs1 for children (under-fives free; adults Dhs3).

Further round on the Bur Dubai side is the **Heritage & Diving Village** (*see p76*), particularly worth visiting in the winter evenings, when children can take donkey and camel rides and watch traditional singing and dancing. The Heritage & Diving Village can be sleepy during the summer and some weekday evenings: phone in advance (226 0286) to check whether special activities are taking place.

A five-minute walk from the museum down to the Creek will take you to the *abra* stations – kids will love packing on to the water taxis with Dubai's workers and chugging across to the Deira side (for a bargain Dhs1), although little ones will need to be kept on a tight rein as there's not much protection. *Abras* can be hired for longer trips (around 30 minutes) up and down the Creek; this is a fun way to check out the Deira cityscape, Bastakia wind towers, and dhows packed with goods bound for Iran. You have to haggle for the cost of the trip but you shouldn't be paying much more than Dhs50.

Teenagers will enjoy sauntering around the souks in Deira, but you may be better off catching the *abra* back again with younger ones and heading upstream to the lush, green **Creekside Park** (*see p187*) and Children's City, an interactive centre aimed at five- to 15-year-olds. Highlights include the giant, open-backed computer and larger-than-life internal phones. There's also the odd kids' book launch.

Further upstream, just before Garhoud Bridge, is **Wonderland Theme & Water Park** (*see p189*), a kids-oriented leisure centre that includes

Arts & Entertainment

a 'Desert Extreme' skate park, funfair rides, karting, paintballing and Splashland, complete with nine water rides and several pools. It's good clean fun but – compared to Children's City – is beginning to show its age.

Jumeirah & Umm Suqeim

Jumeirah, with its long strip of public and private beaches, is not only Dubai's best-heeled neighbourhood but its seaside lifestyle and residential, family-oriented atmosphere make it an ideal base for holidaying with children. Jumeirah's public beach can fill up quickly at weekends; an alternative is to head up the coast to Umm Suqeim beach – or pay the Dhs5 entrance fee (Dhs20 per vehicle) to **Jumeirah Beach Park** (see p238). Dubai's favourite beach park boasts showers, picnic tables, a children's play area, a food kiosk and some shady areas for when you need to escape the heat, but note that Mondays are for women and children only.

Dubai Zoo (see p80), on Jumeirah Beach Road, is long overdue a transfer to more spacious grounds in the desert. For now, the animals are crammed into small cages. These cramped conditions, which can make for unpleasant viewing, have justifiably provoked much anger, yet it remains a popular distraction for some families. The various malls along the Jumeirah Beach Road – **Mercato Mall**, **Palm Strip**, **Town Centre Jumeirah** and **Beach Centre** – all offer fast food, coffee bars and other refreshment options, plus shopping and some games centres for kids.

Arty visitors might prefer to indulge in a spot of painting over at **Café Céramique** (see p190), where kids and adults alike can pick a ceramic bowl, plate, mug, piggy bank or other item, and paint and glaze it. Children can be left for a couple of hours if booked into a workshop, and there's a great terrace with sea views where you can while away the hours and enjoy a light lunch while your kids get creative. Jumeirah is also home to the **Dubai International Art Centre** (see p190), which has classes in everything from pottery to marble mosaics for children, teenagers and adults – although classes do need to be booked in advance. While your little one is scribbling away, you can pass the time at its gallery.

Heading up the coast to Umm Suqeim – next to Dubai's most recognisable landmark, the Burj Al Arab – is **Wild Wadi** water park (see p188). With both scary and sedate rides, a wave pool, several eateries and a shipwreck, this is a day's activity in itself – and the kids will no doubt pester you to return afterwards.

Tee time

To many, golf is a sport associated with business meetings and long Saturday afternoons. But it's also a sport that offers families a chance to spend some quality time together. It gives children the opportunity to improve their coordination and their balance as well as giving them plenty of exercise in both anaerobic and aerobic forms. From a very young age, motor skills (developing the use of the limbs) are a key aim for all children, and golf can help to refine and focus these.

It's probably not advisable to start kids on formal tuition before the age of six or seven. The UGA (UAE Golf Association) has a junior development programme that's offered at most courses in Dubai. This course consists of eight one-hour sessions; children have to pass a session to progress to the next one. All courses have professional coaches who are members of the PGA (Professional Golfers Association) and highly qualified. Timings vary from club to club, and an eight-session course costs around Dhs700.

The **Emirates Golf Club** (380 2222/ www.dubaigolf.com) features the manicured lawns and beautifully maintained grounds you'd associate with any world-class venue. For those serious about the subject, it also hosts the Peter Cowan Golf Academy. **Dubai Creek Golf & Yacht Club** (295 6000/www.dubaigolf.com) is equally well maintained. Along the course, the two 'comfort stations', which offer a pause for refreshments, are a perfect way to break up the day for younger children. The Creek Golf Club also offers 'Sundowner' golf on weekdays after 3pm, but if you're taking children, they need to have a handicap of less than 28, so it's more suitable for older children than beginners.

If you're based in new Dubai and don't fancy straying too far away from home or heading into town, **Arabian Ranches Golf Club** (366 3000/www.thedesertcourse.com) is another good choice. Due to its location, there's a big focus on families and a range of golfing options is available to suit all ages.

Arts & Entertainment

Al Mamzar Beach Park – a haven of peace and calm.

Outdoor fun

While those few nasty months of soaring temperatures see Dubai's residents desperately dive for air-conditioned environments, the sun-drenched city does normally offer excellent opportunities to get outdoors. Many an expatriate parent will tell you that their child's ability to play outside almost all year round is reason enough to relocate to Dubai. Adults can enjoy immaculate beach parks (*see p237*) and various water sports (*see p235*), but there are plenty of activities for kids too.

Parks & play areas

Creekside Park

Between Maktoum & Garhoud bridges, Umm Hurair (336 7633). **Open** 8am-11pm daily. **Admission** Dhs5. **No credit cards.** **Map** p329 K3.
Creekside has everything you could possibly want from a park. There are rolling hills, an amphitheatre,

picnic areas, playgrounds and a cable car offering some of the very best views in the city. At any of the entrances, you can hire tandem tricycles for Dhs30. On the food front, ice-cream vendors on bikes regularly trawl the length of the park, and there are a number of Malik Burger outlets for those craving a fast food fix. The main draw card is Children's City (*see p189*). *Photo p190.*

Al Mamzar Beach Park

Al Mamzar Creek, by the Sharjah border (296 6201). **Open** 8am-11pm daily. **Admission** Dhs5. **No credit cards.** **Map** p331 K1.
Looking out over a blue lagoon to the emirate of Sharjah, this grassy park has three beaches and plentiful barbecue areas, providing one of the most entertaining places for children in the city. There is also an impressive large wooden fort and an amphitheatre that regularly lays on family shows. On Fridays the park has a fantastic laid-back atmosphere, and is filled with Indian and Arab families enjoying barbecues and celebrating their day off by singing and playing drums.

Arts & Entertainment

Mushrif Park

Al Awir Road, past Dubai Airport (288 3624).
Open 8am-11pm daily. **Admission** Dhs10 for cars.
Swimming fee is Dhs10 (adults) and Dhs5 (children).
No credit cards.
The dilapidated charm of Dubai's oldest park might
not appeal to all, but the fairground should keep kids
happy. There's also the World Village, a rather odd
collection of mini houses from different countries,
and a small aviary with a moody resident turkey.

Al Safa Park

Near Choithram supermarket on Al Wasl Road,
Jumeirah (349 2111). **Open** 8am-11.30pm daily.
Admission Dhs5. **No credit cards**. **Map** p328 G5.
Al Safa Park, a firm favourite with the prosperous,
villa-dwelling Jumeirah crowd, has large stretches of
grass that are perfect for games of football or cricket, plus plenty of shady areas and trees to relax
under. Weekends are often extremely busy with bar-
becuers and sauntering couples, and the amusingly
bouncy tarmac path running around the perimeter
attracts pre- and post-work powerwalkers and jog-
gers in their droves. The tiny boating lake, miniature
funfair (with a small Ferris wheel) and play areas dotted around are perfect for children. The slightly rundown but ludicrously cheap tennis courts are handy
for older kids, but you may well have to wait your
turn before actually getting on to one. *Photo p183*.

Umm Suqeim Park

Near Jumeirah Beach Hotel, off Jumeirah Beach
Road (348 5665). **Open** 8am-9.30pm Sat, Thur, Fri;
8am-8pm Sun-Wed. Ladies & children only on Sat
& Wed. **Admission** free. **Map** p334 A15.
This small oasis of greenery offers an unbeatable
location to while away an hour or two. It's very family orientated with access for women and children
only on Wednesday and Saturday. Take a walk along
the beach, and then stop for a drink in the delightful
and surprisingly homely café. Here you can sip tea,
let the children play on the slides and look out over
the park to the turquoise ocean beyond.

Za'abeel Park

Sheikh Zayed Road (398 6888). **Open** 9am-11pm
Sat-Thur; 9am-11.30pm Fri. **Admission** Dhs5.
No credit cards. **Map** p333 H9.
Located at the Creek end of Sheikh Zayed Road,
Za'abeel Park is Dubai's newest open space. It's vast,
so it's well worth noting which gate you came in at
if you want to avoid getting lost. The landscaping is
hugely impressive and because it's so new, everything is shiny and clean – from the toilet facilities to
the kiosk and cooking areas. On one side of the park,
there's a large lake where you can hire a boat at
Dhs40 for 20 minutes. On the other side, the huge
amphitheatre features built-in steps/seats on one side
and a rolling expanse of green on the other. The
adventure playground is also great fun, and the play
areas in the park are all equipped with state-of-the-
art designer equipment that'll keep children entertained for hours and hours.

Scuba diving & snorkelling

Al Boom Diving

Near the Iranian Hospital, Al Wasl Road, Satwa
(342 2993/www.alboomarine.com). **Cost** varies;
call for details. **Credit** MC, V. **Map** p332 E9.
If your offspring see themselves as Ariel – aka *The
Little Mermaid* – hotfoot it to Dubai diving institution Al Boom. This long established diving centre runs the PADI Bubblemaker courses (a 60 to 90
minute basic introduction to diving for over-
eights), PADI Seal courses (basic principles for
over-eights, 12 hours) and PADI Junior Open Water
courses (ten years and over, 30 hours) in two fully
equipped classrooms and a swimming pool. Prices
range from Dhs250 to Dhs2,000 depending on the
course. All are extremely popular.

Scuba Arabia

Le Meridien Mina Seyahi Hotel, Al Sufouh Road,
Jumeirah (399 3333/2278). **Cost** varies; call for
details. **Credit** AmEx, MC, V. **Map** p336 B1.
Eight- to ten-year-olds can become PADI Seal team
members and discover the thrill of underwater diving in the safety of the hotel's Club Mina pool.
Over-tens can move on to the Open Water course
(they must be accompanied by an adult), which
earns them a certificate that allows them to dive
anywhere in the world.

Theme & water parks

Luna Park

Al Nasr Leisureland, Oud Metha (337 1234). **Open**
9am-10.30pm daily. **Admission** (Leisureland, incl
Luna Park) Dhs10; Dhs5 under-10s. **Credit** AmEx,
MC, V. **Map** p329 J3.
Luna Park is a permanent funfair offering a range
of rides suitable for four-year-olds upwards, including bumper cars, go-karts and a roller coaster.
Leisureland also includes an ice rink, bowling alleys,
a giant outdoor pool with three-foot-high waves and
a tiled 'beach', plus six slides and a water playground with water cannons (although admission to
the pool will involve dropping some more dirhams).

Wild Wadi

Next to Jumeirah Beach Hotel, Jumeirah Beach
Road (348 4444/www.wildwadi.com). **Open**
Winter 11am-6pm daily. *Summer* phone for times.
Admission Dhs140; Dhs120 concessions; free
under-3s. **Credit** AmEx, MC, V. **Map** p336 E1.
Dubai's Arabian-themed water park has around 30
fun-filled rides for kids and adults. Wind your way
in leisurely fashion around Whitewater Wadi, pro-
pel yourself up Summit Surge, then fly down the
33m-high (108ft) Jumeirah Sceirah (read 'scarer').
Don't forget to hold on to your shorts. Plenty of lifeguards are on hand to make sure that you and your
rubber ring don't part company. Kids love the shipwreck with its squirting cannons, and there are
plenty of fast-food restaurants at which they can

Water babies will be splash happy at **Wild Wadi**.

stuff their little faces afterwards. Parents, meanwhile, can take it in turns to chill out in Breaker's Bay.

Wonderland Theme & Water Park

Creekside Park, near Garhoud Bridge, Garhoud (324 1222). **Open** *Theme park* 10am-10pm daily. *Splashland* 10am-6pm daily. **Admission** *Whole park* Dhs95 adults; Dhs85 4-12s; Dhs25 under-4s. *Splashland only* Dhs70 adults; Dhs60 4-12s; free under-4s. **Credit** AmEx, MC, V. **Map** p329 K3.
Wonderland has a little of everything for the youngsters, including a theme park, a water park (Splashland) and the Desert Extreme skate park. The latter has half-pipes, trick boxes, rail slides and ramps for BMXers, skateboarders and inline skaters (over-fives only); helmets are compulsory and all equipment can be hired. Besides Splashland, with its nine water rides and activity pools, there's a huge variety of indoor and outdoor rides, food outlets, paintballing, go-karting and, for the less active, camel rides. Timings are liable to change, so do phone ahead before setting out.

Indoor fun

Activity centres

Children's City

Creekside Park, entrance on Riyadh Road (334 0808). **Open** 9am-10pm Sat-Thur; 4-10pm Fri. **Admission** Dhs15; Dhs10 concessions. **Credit** AmEx, MC, V. **Map** p329 K3.

Children's City is a huge Duplo-esque centre situated in Creekside Park, a brightly coloured blocky building that boasts myriad educational zones, designed to stimulate the curiosity of toddlers and teenagers alike. These areas of 'edutainment' include the Toddler area, the Discovery Space section, the Physical Science zone, the Computer & Communication Gallery, the Way We Live area and the Nature Centre, plus culture blocks dedicated to the history of the UAE and profiles of Arab intellectuals, a planetarium and an amphitheatre. The displays are imaginative, interactive and also highly entertaining (our favourite is the giant computer with a rideable mouse). The centre also features a Malik Burger joint, a library and an early-learning shop.

Encounter Zone

Level 3, Wafi City mall, Oud Metha Road (324 7747). **Open** 10am-midnight Sat, Thur, Fri; 10am-11pm Sun-Wed. **Admission** *Galactica* Dhs30/hr. *LunarLand* Dhs25/hr. *All zones* Dhs45/day. **Credit** MC, V. **Map** p329 J3.
Encounter Zone has two parts: LunarLand, for the pre-teens, with its Snow Capsule, Komet roller coaster and the slides and tunnels of Skylab; and, for everyone else, the excellent Galactica. The latter has network games, an indoor skate park, a 3-D cinema, an anti-gravity racing simulator and the mentally challenging Crystal Maze with its medieval, future and ocean zones. Kids can be left at the drop 'n' shop babysitting service.

Arts & Entertainment

Magic Planet

Deira City Centre mall, Garhoud (295 4333). **Open** 10am-midnight daily. **Admission** free; rides & games from Dhs5. **Credit** AmEx, MC, V. **Map** p329 K2.

Whizzing and whirring, Magic Planet is possibly the noisiest of Dubai's indoor play areas. It boasts literally dozens of arcade games, fairground rides (including a Ferris wheel, a traditional carousel, bumper cars and a small train, which snakes its way through the 'planet') as well as sand art and pinball stations, so you'll have a tough time tearing kids away. The easily accessible food court allows you to watch over your children in the large, soft play cage, but the place is generally unsupervised, so don't expect any babysitting service. There's also a ten-pin bowling centre.

Peekaboo!

The Village Mall, Jumeirah Beach Road (344 7122). **Open** 9am-8pm daily. **Admission** Dhs30/hr. **Credit** AmEx, MC, V. **Map** p332 D9.

Children aged up to seven years can learn through role-play in the Kitchen and Book Corner. There's also the usual quota of soft play apparatus. Other activities include face painting, music classes and colouring. Note that an adult must accompany children under three at all times.

Toby's

Level 3 Food Court, BurJuman Centre, Trade Centre Road, Bur Dubai (355 2868). **Open** 10.30am-10pm Sat-Tue; 10.30am-11pm Wed-Thur; 2-10.30pm Fri. **Admission** Dhs25. **No credit cards. Map** p331 J5.

At Toby's, tots under the age of four get to romp in their own colourful ball pit and soft play area, while bigger kids can frolic in a larger zone of slides, punch bags, space hoppers and swinging inflatables. There's a cafeteria, where parents and minders can grab a coffee while simultaneously keeping an eye on the tinies themselves, or the mall and food court just outside if they would prefer to leave over-fours in the capable hands of the staff – the play pit is gate-controlled so there's no chance of any escapees.

Arts & crafts centres

In recent years Dubai has seen a new wave of child-friendly craft workshops open their doors to the city's young and young at heart. The concept is simple: gather together art utensils and materials (usually attached to a coffee shop) and for a flat rate plus the price of materials patrons are free to indulge their inner Picasso.

Café Céramique

Town Centre Jumeirah, Jumeirah Beach Road (344 7331/www.cafeceramique.com). **Open** 8am-midnight Sat-Thur; 10am-midnight Fri. **Admission** Studio fee Dhs25; Dhs15 concessions. **Credit** AmEx, MC, V. **Map** p334 C12.

This is indeed a café, but the name gives a hint as to its raison d'être: customers, both adult and children, are encouraged to select an unpainted item of ceramic crockery from the hundreds displayed and decorate it with their own designs. Staff then glaze and fire your handiwork, which is ready for collection a couple of days later. There is a great winter terrace with sea views, plus a programme of kids' workshops and activities. Studio fees are Dhs25 for adults and Dhs15 for concessions. Items start at Dhs10 while the studio fee is reduced by 50 per cent on weekday mornings.

Other locations: Mall of the Emirates (341 0144).

Dubai International Art Centre

Jumeirah Beach Road (turn right towards the sea opposite Commercial Bank of Dubai) (344 4398/ www.artdubai.com). **Open** 8.30am-6.30pm Sat-Wed; 8.30am-3.30pm Thur. **Admission** *School holidays* Dhs75-Dhs150 per workshop. *Term-time* phone for membership details. **Credit** AmEx, MC, V. **Map** p332 D9.

This arts centre has a well-deserved reputation for recruiting friendly, professional teachers. Hands-on classes cover mixed media, ceramics, photography, silk painting, dressmaking and calligraphy.

It's all smiles at **Creekside Park**. See p187.

Café Céramique should get the kids all fired up.

Jam Jar
Near Gold & Diamond Park & the Dubai Garden Centre, exit 39 off Sheikh Zayed Road (341 7303/ www.jamjardubai.com). **Open** 10am-9pm Sat, Mon-Thur; 2-9pm Fri. **Credit** MC, V. **Map** p336 E2.
The excellent Jam Jar is a hands-on arts studio that allows visitors to create their own art masterpieces. The place itself is fairly big; an open, warehouse-like location, littered with easels and dressed with paintings suspended from the high ceiling. A three-hour session, inclusive of all supplies, is priced at Dhs170 for adults and Dhs85 for children with the Jam Jar providing everything necessary to get you started on your masterwork. Firstly you choose your canvas, from the sweetly small to the wall-hoggingly mammoth. Then you help yourself to the giant tomato ketchup-style dispensers, filled to the brim with globules of richly coloured acrylic paints, before picking from an array of bristling brushes and sponges. Once you're happy with your work, it's time to take it home and proudly display it in your living room.

Cookery

Minichefs
Entrance B, Loft 3 building, Dubai Media City (361 6117/www.cooking-sense.com). **Cost** *One-off classes* Dhs60. **Map** p336 B2.
Give your kids a head start at becoming culinary geniuses with the wide range of recipes taught by Minichefs, where the chefs hail from all over the world. Classes are for children aged six to eight or nine to 11 years and there are no more than 12 kids in a class. If you're finding your kids a bit unruly, you can always send them to a Minichefs etiquette class.

Education

Mad Science
Al Khaleej Building, Za'abeel Road (337 7403/ www.madscience.org/uae). **Map** p333 J7.
Mad Science offers entertaining and educational science lessons and birthday parties for children aged three to 12 years. Themes include lasers, sound modulation, space and indoor fireworks.

Haircuts

Finola's Salon
Opposite Beach Centre, Jumeirah Beach Road (344 4757). **Open** 9am-7.30pm Sat-Thur. **Map** p332 D10.
A friendly, independent salon that's housed within a villa in Jumeirah. A children's haircut costs between Dhs40 and Dhs50.

Kutz For Kids
Bin Sougat Centre, Rashidiya (285 8311). **Open** 10am-10pm Sat-Thur; 4-10pm Fri. **Map** p327 F4.
A colourful studio that has helpful staff and even a special play area for little ones.

PURSUIT GAMES.
PAINTBALL DUBAI

Come rumble with some of the best Paintball this side of Earth.....we've eliminated the competition

For bookings call: **050-6514583**
                                04-3244755

www.paintballdubai.com

Film & Theatre

Local talent is on the rise, but the mainstream still dominates.

Screenings galore at Dubai's **Grand Megaplex** in Ibn Battuta mall. *See p195.*

See p195.

Film

Cinemas are extremely popular in Dubai. From the huge multiplexes found in most of the city's major shopping malls to the network of small Indian cinemas dotted about the place, most Dubaians enjoy a trip to the flicks on a regular basis. The soaring summer temperatures, combined with the fact that many Dubaians eschew bars and clubs for religious reason, means that the cinemas continue to have a strong and loyal audience.

Despite the diverse nature of Dubai audiences, Western films remain the most popular, with mainstream Hollywood blockbusters filling auditoriums for weeks on end. A cursory glance at a week's listings will reveal a decided taste for lowbrow comedies, inoffensive rom-coms, an endless parade of horror flicks and the occasional low-budget martial arts title all jostling for attention. There is no real art house scene to speak of, apart from a few dedicated individuals who hold free screenings around town in clubs and galleries. Yet, as the population expands, so does the breadth of material available. The annual **Dubai International Film Festival** has achieved much in its short lifespan, bringing some seriously impressive and eclectic international programming for an all-too-brief week every December. A regional forum, the **Emirates Film Competition** aims to serve Emiratis with an amateur film community, while the newly developed **Dubai Studio City** hopes to attract world-class production talent to the region.

In recent times, we've seen films such as *Code 46*, *Syriana* and *The Alchemist* utilising Dubai's unique backdrops, which serve directors equally well whether they are after a rolling desert landscape or a futuristic cityscape. Dubai Studio City's long-term objective of hosting first-rate production facilities should see an increasing number of big-budget productions heading this way.

While Dubai's release dates for Western titles are frequently completely out-of-kilter with other major territories, Bollywood releases play to large and appreciative audiences pretty much on schedule with Indian release dates, and often a few days in advance. The Indian film community enjoys healthy links with the subcontinent, and many Bollywood producers have chosen to shoot in Dubai in recent years, a trend that looks set to continue.

Arts & Entertainment

Perhaps unsurprisingly, given the diversity of audiences here, film distributors tend to play it safe when it comes to programming, opting for sure-fire mainstream Hollywood fare (horror and comedy is perennially popular) over the more cerebral or contemplative. This lowest common denominator approach occasionally irks residents, but keeps cinemas packed all year long. Films open on a Wednesday, often with a midnight showing for bankable titles. While the big blockbusters tend to open at the same time as the rest of the world, more unusual films and non-US English-language titles can make it onto the distributor's schedule at any time, with some even appearing months after the DVD release.

Don't expect to enjoy your film in silence; for many cinemagoers, especially teenagers, films serve merely as a backdrop to frenzied text-messaging and mobile phone conversations, garrulous socialising, the noisy consumption of malodorous snacks and, in some cases, bouts of prolonged snoring. A few well-aimed tuts are usually about as far as anyone goes in combating the problem of noisy cinemagoers. Further occasional discomfort comes from over-enthusiastic air conditioning, which can make auditoriums feel like wind tunnels after a while – remember to take a light wrap or pullover.

Dubai boasts an **IMAX cinema** for full-on surround sound and vision extravaganzas at **Grand Megaplex** (*see p195*) at the Ibn Battuta mall, which is especially popular on weekends – so always call ahead should you

wish to crane your neck around the latest visual spectacular. Another popular innovation is the **Gold Class Cinema** at **CineStar Mall of the Emirates** (*see p195*), where, for a Dhs100 ticket, you can stretch out in a luxury recliner, enjoy table service and view a film in far more convivial surroundings than the usual bear pits. It's advisable to call ahead and check availability here, especially on weekends.

Time Out Dubai magazine lists and reviews the week's screenings, but distributors and cinemas can change the programme with little warning, so it's always best to phone and check in advance. If taking children with you, do also check with the cinema for the rating that has been assigned to the film: G (General), PG (Parental Guidance), 15 (aged 15 and above) and 18 (18 and over); while the UAE uses a similar certificate system to the USA and UK, it sometimes gives the film a different category or age bracket.

CENSORSHIP

Until recently, all films released for public screening were censored at a central office in Abu Dhabi. Now each emirate has been granted autonomy to cut and filter releases as they see fit – but in reality, there is very little variance between what gets through and what doesn't. Broadly speaking, the Dubai Department of Censorship will cut any nudity and overt sexual references as well as any homosexual scenes. Scenes of drug taking are also

Festival fever

In 2004, Dubai launched the inaugural **Dubai International Film Festival** at the Madinat Jumeirah complex. Attracting stars such as Morgan Freeman, Diana Kruger, Laurence Fishburne and Oliver Stone in the past few years, the festival has succeeded in crossing cultural boundaries with exemplary line-ups of Arab, Indian, Far Eastern and Western films, alongside meet-and-greet forums, educational programmes and, naturally, plenty of parties. The vast majority of films are screened at the Mall of the Emirates' multiplex cinema (*see p195*), while gala screenings take place at the Madinat Souk auditorium (*see p146*). The 2006 event saw some inspired programming and a hugely enthusiastic public response to the screenings, but the festival is still very much in its infancy and, despite the hype, will have to work hard to convince the star names it craves to travel over from Hollywood in the middle of December.

Madinat Jumeirah.

forbidden. Political comments relating to Arab governments or anything deemed defamatory towards Islam is also out, as is anything that comes close to recognising Israel. These cuts can be heavy-handed, with films lurching awkwardly past the offending scene. Films that are deemed to be too contentious for exhibition will simply be dropped altogether, although this is quite rare. The general message seems to be a willingness to accommodate the public as far as possible within the framework of the country's culture and customs, in a display of tolerance and compromise on both sides.

DVD PIRACY

Take a stroll through the Karama district, and it won't be long before you hear the hiss of a furtive-looking gentleman muttering 'DVD? DVD?' in varying tones of insistence. If you give the nod, you will most likely find yourself in a sweltering cubby-hole a few minutes later, sifting through piles of counterfeit DVDs, ranging from the latest Hollywood releases to American TV shows and sometimes even pornography. Residents often don't even have to leave the house to find their dodgy discs, with peddlers of pirated goods often going door-to-door in search of custom.

DVD piracy is endemic in Dubai, as in many parts of the world, and while authorities claim that the Arabian Anti-Piracy Alliance (AAA) is leading the way in the region in the war against fakes, local film distributors and legitimate vendors are united in exasperation at the rapidly escalating black market. However, many agree that given the delays and censorship requirements bona fide releases are subjected to, it is inevitable that film fans will sometimes gamble on a 'dodgy DVD'.

LOCAL TALENT

Dubai's Emirati minority, who have watched their once tiny city boom and grow over the past few decades, have a few stories of their own they want to tell – and as video technology and hardware becomes cheaper, more and more UAE nationals are turning to film to document and chronicle their lives.

While the UAE's feature films can still be counted on the fingers of one hand (the first such example is *Al Hilm* from 2005), the grassroots amateur film industry is thriving under the aegis of the Emirates Film Competition, which now acts as a focal point for dozens of local amateurs. The competition itself is held each March, and the standard of films – is rapidly improving, with growing sophistication from both the production side of things, and the scripts.

Multiplexes

The following venues all show similar programmes of English-language (mainly Hollywood) films, with a smattering of Arab, Egyptian and Hindi blockbusters. Hollywood and Bollywood films will carry Arabic subtitles.

CineStar
Deira City Centre mall, Garhoud (294 9000). **Tickets** Dhs30. **Screens** 11. **Credit** AmEx, MC, V. **Map** p329 K2.

CineStar at Mall of the Emirates
Mall of the Emirates (341 4222). **Tickets** Dhs30 (Dhs100 Gold Class). **Screens** 14. **Credit** AmEx, MC, V. **Map** p336 D2.

Grand CineCity
Above Spinneys supermarket in Al Ghurair City mall, Al Rigga Road, Deira (228 9898). **Tickets** Dhs25-Dhs30. **Screens** 8. **Credit** AmEx, MC, V. **Map** p331 K3.

Grand Cineplex
Next to Wafi City mall, Garhoud (324 2000). **Tickets** Dhs25-Dhs30. **Screens** 10. **Credit** AmEx, MC, V. **Map** p329 J3.

Grand Megaplex
Ibn Battuta mall (366 9898). **Tickets** Dhs30 (Dhs50 IMAX). **Screens** 20 plus 1 IMAX screen. **Credit** AmEx, MC, V. **Map** p336 A2.

Grand Mercato
Mercato Mall, Jumeirah Beach Road (349 9713). **Tickets** Dhs30. **Screens** 7. **Credit** AmEx. **Map** p334 C12.

Grand Metroplex
Metropolitan Hotel, Interchange 2, Sheikh Zayed Road (343 8383). **Tickets** Dhs30. **Screens** 8. **Credit** AmEx, MC, V. **Map** p328 G5.

Local cinemas

The following cinemas show a mix of Malayalam, Tamil and Hindi films, usually with Arabic (but not English) subtitles.

Galleria Cinema
Hyatt Regency Dubai & Galleria, Al Khaleej Road, Deira (273 7676). **Tickets** Dhs20. **Screens** 2 (Malayalam & Tamil films). **No credit cards**. **Map** p331 J1.

Lamcy Cinema
Next to Lamcy Plaza mall, Oud Metha (336 8808). **Tickets** Dhs20. **Screens** 2 (Hindi films). **No credit cards**. **Map** p329 J3.

Plaza Cinema
Opposite Bur Dubai taxi stand, Al Ghubabai Road (393 9966). **Tickets** Dhs20. **Screens** 1 (Hindi, Malayalam & Tamil films). **No credit cards**. **Map** p330 G4.

Cirque du Soleil.

Theatre

Dubai isn't renowned for its domestic theatre scene. There are a couple of full-sized auditoriums around town – the **Madinat Theatre** and the **Dubai Community Theatre & Arts Centre** (DUCTAC) – as well a few smaller enterprises, but, on the whole, quality drama and Dubai are yet to form a meaningful and long-term relationship.

Just five years ago, one would be hard-pressed to find anything other than the occasional production, largely staged by cheery expat British amateur dramatics groups. Today, while those genial amateur exercises continue apace, there is a growing market for international productions that cater to the general public and effortlessly sell out. Shows such as *Mamma Mia!*, *Chicago* and *Simply Ballroom*, for instance, have all packed out Dubai theatres recently.

Theatre schedules at the Madinat Theatre tend towards a crowd-pleasing blend of cabaret-style acts and mainstream dramas. Over at the relatively new, purpose-built theatre at DUCTAC, a more multicultural programme is in place, showing occasional flashes of inspiration; giant Iranian puppet shows and traditional folk dancing have all been seen here. DUCTAC has also hosted productions by the **Al Ahli Theatre Club**, a small but dedicated troupe of performers who seek to promote Arabic-language theatre; productions range from self-penned plays to progressive renditions of work by writers ranging from Shakespeare to Arthur Miller.

Streetwise Fringe is a group actively seeking to stage quality productions for appreciative audiences. Sourcing performers predominantly from an annual trawl through the Edinburgh Festival, the group stages regular shows at the Crowne Plaza Hotel Dubai (*see p65*) throughout the year, as well running a popular annual youth theatre school.

The largest company to visit Dubai in recent times was **Cirque du Soleil**, which held a month-long residency in a purpose built tent at the start of 2007. The run was so successful that Cirque has announced plans to have a permanent venue and show at the Palm Jumeirah by 2010.

Still, despite such advances, there is very little chance of, say, a season of Sarah Kane or Mark Ravenhill productions in Dubai at present. Yet, given time, financial support and the efforts of the emirate's small but enthusiastic drama-lovers, there is every chance the city will be sustaining a lively and inventive theatrical scene in the not-too-distant future.

OTHER PERFORMING ARTS

Public performances of Emirati poetry, song and dance are mainly limited to ceremonial occasions and traditional displays at the **Heritage & Diving Village** (*see p76*). While the strong tradition of poetry and storytelling, sometimes set to music, is handed down from nights around the campfire, many of the songs derive from days on the pearling dhows, when team spirits would be buoyed through sea shanties based on each task, led by a *naha'an* (professional song leader).

At Eid and other celebrations, you're also likely to see *ayyalah* performances, which re-enact battles and hunting expeditions with groups of men beating sticks, and hurling swords high up into the air. Dressed in the bright *abayas* (cloaks) of the desert, groups of women engage in separate *na'ashat* dances, swinging their long hair and swaying to music. Local bands are made of players of *tubool* and *rahmani* (drums), *daf* (tambourine) and *nai* and *mizmar* (wind instruments). As for international dance, there are some ballet schools and a lively salsa scene, but performances of Western classical dance are rare.

The city's classical scene is still in its infancy: local musicians play in the **Dubai Chamber Orchestra** (www.dubaiorchestra. org) and there are some enthusiastic amateur choirs, but the really dedicated travel to Abu Dhabi for international concerts, often held at the **Cultural Foundation** (*see p257*). Consult the monthly *Time Out Abu Dhabi* magazine for performance details.

Mamma Mia! – mainstream shows dominate the Dubai theatre scene.

Theatres

Dubai Community Theatre & Arts Centre

Mall of the Emirates, Level 2, Magic Planet entrance (341 4777/www.ductac.org). **Open** 9am-10pm Sat-Thur; 2-10pm Fri. **Credit** AmEx, MC, V. **Map** p336 D2

A welcome addition to the Dubai cultural scene, DUCTAC, as it's known, opened with great expectations in 2006, complete with two purpose-built auditoriums, art galleries, studios and classrooms. They have a reasonably consistent programme of events, taking in a wide and diverse range of productions, aiming at all times to fulfil their remit of serving the city's multi-ethnic population with relevant and contemporary cultural events.

Madinat Theatre

Souk Madinat Jumeirah (366 6546/www.madinat jumeirah.com/events). **Open** times vary. **Credit** AmEx, MC, V. **Map** p336 D1.

Set amid the extensive Madinat Jumeirah complex, the Madinat Theatre provides a busy mix of light and accessible entertainment. Recent productions have seen the likes of Mark Little (ex-*Neighbours*), *The Complete Works of William Shakespeare (Abridged)*, *One Man Star Wars* and *The Sound Of Music* packing in the hordes. The theatre excels in commercial and family-friendly fun and is consequently consistently popular, especially among the expat crowd.

Theatre companies

Al Ahli Club Experimental Theatre

Al Quasais (298 8812).
The Al Ahli Club Experimental Theatre has been running since 1981 and exists to promote a lively and progressive programme of Arabic-language productions. Having established itself within the UAE, the team frequently travel abroad, performing at fringe festivals and international drama events. At home, it runs workshops and summer schools for local children, encouraging a broad and progressive approach to drama.

Dubai Drama Group

(333 1155/www.dubaidramagroup.org).
Flying the flag for amateur dramatics in the UAE, the DDG keeps going on a blend of enthusiasm, fun and passion for drama. With over 30 years experience, the group generally serve up decent quality fare that's reliably accessible and ranges from the frothy fun of *Joseph and the Amazing Technicolor Dreamcoat*, *Treasure Island* and *Run For Your Wife!* to Shakespeare. They can be found plying their trade at a number of venues around town, including Madinat Theatre and Dubai Community Theatre & Arts Centre (for both, *see above*).

Rangmanch Theatre Company & Academy

Office 21, Block 13, Knowledge Village, near Interchange 4, Sheikh Zayed Road (391 3441). **Map** p336 C2.
Rangmanch runs mini theatre festivals throughout the year, featuring theatre companies from India at various venues. All the plays are in Hindi.

Streetwise Fringe Theatre

(050 652 6920/www.streetwisefringe.com).
The long-running Streetwise Fringe collective imports plays, musicals and one-man shows from the UK, including pre-London runs and hits from the Edinburgh fringe. The company also runs a popular youth theatre workshop in the summer.

Quintessential Spice.

Experience the real taste of Mughal life on a plate at our award winning HANDI,
the best Indian Restaurant in the Emirate.

Daily from 12:00 noon – 3:00 pm and 7:00 pm – 11:00 pm
Lobby Level; Ext.: 3045

Handi
Indian Restaurant

TAJ
Luxury Hotels

فـنـدق تـاج بـالاس دبــي
TAJ PALACE HOTEL Dubai

Galleries

Despite continued censorship, it's boom time for art in Dubai.

Looking out over the transient, ever-shifting skyline of Dubai, along the vast swathes of construction lining the coastlines and deep into the desert around the city, the frenetic progression of the emirate can't help but impress in its sheer audacity and scale. Yet in this city of shopping malls, high-rise apartments, new cash and lurid, materialistic dreams, it would seem that you've come to the wrong place for art. And certainly, until a few years ago, that was very much the case.

All that is now changing as Dubai, along with neighbouring emirate Sharjah and big brother Abu Dhabi, has designs on making itself a regional centre for artistic achievement, while also striving to attract art dealers and businesses. The past few years have seen dozens of commercial galleries springing up throughout Dubai, displaying contemporary and traditional work from across the Middle East and beyond. There are now two informal art 'quarters' in the city, one in **Al Quoz** and the other in **Bastakia**. What's more, on the doorstep is the cerebral **Sharjah International Art Biennial** (*see p269*), which is packed with works by international artists every two years.

Back in Dubai, the inaugural **DIFC Gulf Art Fair** in March 2007 showcased works from all over the world. The city has also been hosting record-breaking auctions courtesy of Christie's, while the capital is set to become home to Guggenheim and Louvre franchises. As if that's not enough, there's a billion-dollar Culture Village planned in Dubai, which will intriguingly mix luxury apartments with artfully aged courtyards and wind towers in an attempt to become a hub for the region's artistic activities. Clearly Dubai is serious about staking its claim in the art world. But while this hubbub of activity looks promising and bodes very well, the city is presently still in the process of developing a cohesive and unique artistic identity.

Given that the vast majority of Dubai's residents are foreigners, the nature of the work to be seen across the city is a wide and diverse mix. Those seeking genuine Emirati art will probably find themselves disappointed – aside from tourist-friendly knick-knacks to be found dotted in malls around the city, there is precious little contemporary Emirati art to uncover outside of the infrequent yet

Arabic calligraphy at the **DIFC Gulf Art Fair**.

fascinating local student shows. You're far more likely to go home with an oil painting of a horse or falcon, and if that's all you're after, this is the town to find it in. Indian art is extremely popular and well served by establishments such as **1x1 Art Space** and **Bagash Gallery**, which manage to put on diverse and exciting shows of contemporary work from across the subcontinent, ranging from installation and conceptual pieces to retrospectives of luminaries such as **M F Husain**. The **Red Gallery**, meanwhile, revives a long-standing Dubaian love affair with Far Eastern work, with a focus on Vietnamese art.

Younger art lovers tend to head towards the contemporary galleries in the Al Quoz area, a desolate industrial estate behind the Mall of the Emirates. Here, you'll find professionally curated shows in renovated warehouses, with art of a high standard sourced from across the Middle East and North Africa. For contemporary painting, photography and installations, it doesn't get much better than

Five Green hosts quirky exhibitions inside its Oud Metha boutique.

the **B21** and the **Third Line** galleries. Located within minutes of each other, they offer a rich palette of work and act as the city's lightning rod for responsive and occasionally ground-breaking work. Nearby, you'll also find the **Courtyard**, run by Iranian expat **Dariush Zandi**, who regularly sources and shows some of the best in modern Persian work, alongside a bustling, pleasingly chaotic little street filled with all manner of arts and crafts. Further away from the main drag, there's a new addition to the Al Quoz scene in the shape of the **Meem Gallery**, which is bringing the cream of contemporary Arabic art to the region, mixing up old and new in exciting and hugely instructive exhibitions dedicated to Islamic and pre-Islamic pieces.

Down by the Creek lies the historic Bastakia district, home to the **Dubai Museum** and the few relatively old buildings left standing. Here, among the wind towers and coral and stone buildings, the **XVA** and the **Majlis Gallery** hold frequent shows by contemporary and also more traditional artists. A visit to this district is a must for any tourist in Dubai and these two excellent art spaces, while more geared for the casual visitor than the Al Quoz establishments, also contribute to the city's artistic development. Other smaller galleries are starting to crop up in this area too.

In general, this wide variety of work on display across town reflects the cosmopolitan make-up of the city, rather than pushing the boundaries of contemporary art. As with all cultural affairs in Dubai, there are guidelines that can't be crossed and boundaries that mustn't be transgressed. Some would argue that art of any value cannot exist in such a pre-determined environment, that local art should challenge local issues and subjects and generate debate. This is unlikely to happen. As with the films being shown in the megaplexes down the road, there will be no nudity, no anti-religious sentiment and no criticism of Dubai and its leaders through the medium of art. Many artists and gallerists will tell you they don't wish to challenge these limits and are happy operating within them – certainly for the many artists arriving from the heavily policed artistic communities of Tehran or Saudi Arabia, Dubai is a relative oasis of freedom and possibility. In spite of the restrictions, things are definitely changing and as an increasing number of younger artists, Emirati or expatriate, grow in confidence, we can expect art in Dubai to start resonating with even more meaning and substance. With a young, wealthy, cosmopolitan market pushing the art market forward, expansion and enthusiasm remains boundless and invigorating.

Galleries

1 x 1 Art Space

Villa 1023, Al Wasl Road (348 3873/onexone@ emirates.net.ae). **Open** 11am-8.30pm Sat-Thur. **Admission** free. **Map** p326 C3.

This Jumeirah-based enterprise is dedicated to showcasing some of the best contemporary Indian art around. Recent exhibitions have seen the hugely ambitious ideas and concepts of Chittrovanu Mazumdar spilling over into a disused warehouse, and a retrospective of work by the venerable painter M F Husain.

Art Space

9th Floor, Fairmont Dubai (332 5523/www.art space-dubai.com). **Open** 10am-8.30pm Sat-Thur. **Admission** free. **Map** p333 G9.

Situated on the ninth floor of the Fairmont, Art Space is a clean and functional spot that excels in sourcing work from young female artists from across the Middle East and subcontinent.

Bagash Art Gallery

Kuwait Street, nr Centrepoint Apartments, Bur Dubai (351 5311/www.bagashartgallery.com). **Open** 10am-7pm Sat-Wed. **Admission** free. **Map** p331 J5.

Bagash is a small yet vibrant space that regularly shows fresh and challenging exhibitions from the subcontinent and Far East. The gallery was set up by an art collector, Ali Bagash, who wanted to share his passion for art with the Dubai community and promote art in the region.

B21

Al Quoz 3, nr the Courtyard (340 3965/www. b21gallery.com). **Open** 2-5pm Sat; 11am-6pm Sun-Thur. **Admission** free. **Map** p326 B3.

Run by the Palestinian-born painter and local iconoclast Jeffar Khaldi, B21 is the place for provocative, in-your-face and, as much as the term can be applied to Dubai, cutting-edge art. Khaldi's own Expressionist-influenced visceral paintings are usually lurking around too, adding some much needed vim and vigour to the occasionally docile local scene.

Five Green

Behind Aroma Garden Caffé, Oud Metha Road (336 4100/www.fivegreen.com). **Open** 10am-10pm Sat-Thur; 4pm-10pm Fri. **Admission** free. **Map** p328 J3.

Although this Oud Metha boutique isn't technically a gallery, it frequently plays host to quirky exhibitions by local and visiting artists and cultural activists. Aside from the unique range of haute streetwear, music and trainers, Five Green acts as a meeting place for the city's young art mavens.

Majlis Gallery

Al Fahidi roundabout, Bastakia, Bur Dubai (353 6233/www.majlisgallery.com). **Open** 9.30am-8pm Sat-Thur. **Admission** free. **Map** p330 H4.

Set amid the gorgeous alleyways and shady courtyards of the Bastakia district, Majlis is one of the oldest commercial art spaces in Dubai. Less cutting-edge than some of its contemporaries, the gallery instead focuses mainly on more traditional styles, including plenty of landscapes and calligraphy shows.

The colour of money

Dubai's art market has been booming in recent times. As more and more investors gain confidence in the business of buying art from around the region, there has been a commensurate influx of business to support and nurture this growth. Previously, the handful of local galleries used to rely mainly on local businesses and hotels – looking to top up their in-house decor with some choice pieces – for their main source of income. However, if the events of the past few years serve as a reliable indicator, art collecting in the region is becoming big business. In May 2006, the auctioneers Christie's came to town, and in their inaugural sale of contemporary art – which saw Arab, Indian and Iranian art next to Western pieces – made a whopping US$7.9 million. Successive auctions have maintained healthy sales and there's been a positive knock-on effect, with local contemporary art galleries reporting increased sales.

Perhaps buoyed by this success, a London gallerist, John Martin, was encouraged to establish the first Gulf Art Fair in 2007, which saw over 40 galleries worldwide set up camp in the Madinat Jumeirah for a three-day sale of modern art, from a handful of Picassos and ever-popular Warhols, to a smörgåsbord of established and up-and-coming names selected from international galleries. While there was a consensus regarding the excellent standard of work shown, there were some grumbles about local collectors failing to engage with contemporary Western art with the same enthusiasm as regional work. While this is to be expected – especially among older collectors, who look askance upon Damien Hirst, or with polite indifference to the Chapman brothers – the fact that 2008's Art Fair is going to be twice the size of the first event shows that the assault on the region's art aficionados is only just getting underway.

Arts & Entertainment

Meem Gallery

Umm Suqeim Road, heading towards Arabian Ranches from Interchange 4 (347 7883/www. meem.ae). **Open** 9.30am-6.30pm Sat-Wed; 9.30am-2pm Thur. **Admission** free. **Map** p336 D2.
A new face on the Al Quoz scene that aims to offer – in lieu of a proper art museum in the city – some idea of the rich history of Arabic and Islamic art. Part-owned by a prominent local businessman and patron of the arts and a London-based Islamic art dealer, the gallery is an essential visit for anyone interested in learning more about quality Arabic art or indeed those looking for a regional purchase.

Red Gallery

Villa No.833b, Al Wasl Road, Umm Suqeim 1 (395 5811/050 655 7210). **Open** 4-8pm Sat; 10am-8pm Sun-Thur. **Admission** free. **Map** p326 C3.
An exciting new gallery that aims to showcase the best in Vietnamese and Far Eastern art.

Third Line

Al Quoz 3, nr the Courtyard, between Marlin Furniture & Spinneys (341 1367/www.thethird line.com). **Open** 11am-8pm Sat-Thur. **Admission** free. **Map** p326 B3.
Slick and professional, the Third Line ties with B21 as the destination of choice for those seeking radical and ground-breaking Middle Eastern art in a cool and contemporary setting.

XVA

Behind the Majlis Gallery, Bastakia, Bur Dubai (353 5383/www.xvagallery.com). **Open** *Summer* 9am-9pm Sat-Thur. *Winter* 9am-9pm Sat-Thur; 9am-6pm Fri. **Admission** free. **Map** p330 H4.
Now in the hands of the vibrant 9714 crew (the team behind various edgy happenings in town), this Dubai institution has revitalised itself with a number of strong shows in recent times, focusing on contemporary work from artists across the Middle East and subcontinent. A definite must-see, this picturesque space also boasts a café and a tiny, romantic guesthouse.

Art classes

Dubai International Art Centre

Villa 27, Street 75b, behind Town Centre Jumeirah mall (344 4398/www.artdubai.com). **Open** 9am-6.30pm Sat-Tue; 9am-5pm Wed; 9am-4pm Thur. **Map** p334 C12.
DIAC is the oldest art institution in Dubai, having been around in one form or another since 1976. As well as an excellent programme of evening classes covering ceramics, crafts, drawing and design, the centre has its own gallery, Gallery 76, which displays work by its members.

Third Line.

Nightlife

Live music may be thin on the ground, but Dubai boasts the most vibrant clubbing scene in the region.

Trilogy.
See p209.

Dubai's nightlife scene acts as the perfect mirror for this rapidly expanding dichotomous city. With over 140 nationalities living side-by-side, there are enough clubs and events here to suit almost everyone. The big-spender looking to hang out in his own private cage suspended 20ft above the dancefloor should look no further than **Trilogy** (*see p209*). And for those who want to sample an eight-piece Congolese band free-rap while wading through acres of fake foliage, then simply head down to **Club Africana** (*see p206*).

Things haven't always been so vibrant. In the 1980s, visitors and expats were stuck with a smattering of British-style boozers and little else, but the 1990s saw the arrival of the Lebanese and with them the ostentatious partying of Beirut. Cue swanky venues with stunning light and sound systems, over-dressed, over-coiffured clientele and wall-to-wall house music. Other clubbing communities followed suit, and these days, whether you're in the market for buckets of lager and cheesy disco or wallet-busting cocktails and roomfuls of wafer-thin girls, there's a scene for every taste.

Most bars and clubs are open until 3am, but patrons are always fashionably – and often frustratingly – late, meaning places don't get going until 1am, allowing for two hours of mayhem before bedtime. Dubai's clubbers are a notoriously fickle crowd, and one month's 'in' place is passé almost before the paint's dry. The result is a cynical and cyclical, hedonistic and invariably expensive club scene: a night at one of the city's top clubs can easily come in at over Dhs700 when entrance fees, extortionately priced drinks and taxis are factored in. It's this high-end market that dominates the city's vibrant nightlife scene, and for a place that prides itself on being the biggest and best, it's no surprise to see superstar deck-heads DJ in the city on a regular basis. Paul Oakenfold, Pete Tong, Tiësto and Carl Cox have all spun here in recent years, while if you cast your eye over the big clubs' listings, you'll see a long list of top-class DJs, no doubt handsomely paid for their two hours of work.

While this has undoubtedly created something of a DJ utopia where international brands flock to the big spending city, it's also brought with it several downfalls. Budding local DJs are rarely afforded the chance to shine because big names are inevitably preferred, while it's also had an impact on the local music scene. If one guy with his box of records can pack out a 3,000-capacity venue, then why bother paying for the extra flights and hotel rooms a whole band and its entourage require?

There are signs, however, of a grassroots movement. While some major mainstream rock and pop tours continue to hit our shores – Aerosmith, Iron Maiden, The Prodigy and Shakira have all got UAE stamps in their passports – there has been a marked upturn in the number of local bands making an impact. Rockers Juliana Down, soul-funk four-piece Abri and Bahraini group Brothermandude have all made inroads in the international market having cut their teeth on Dubai's gestating scene. Local event organisers have spotted this trend too, with the **Dubai Original Music Festival**, a two-day event showcasing around 20 local and original groups and musicians. Held at the start of every March, the **Dubai Desert Rock Fest**, (see p180) is now a true Dubai institution with thousands of metal-heads emerging for the two-day rockathon. Recent headliners have included Iron Maiden, Robert Plant, the Prodigy, The Darkness and Megadeth. If you're more of a jazz fan than a metal-mosher, then the annual **Dubai International Jazz Festival** (see p180) might be up your musical alley. Don't expect Ornette Coleman or Cecil Taylor though – this is a very mainstream affair, with recent acts including Toto, ELO, Jamie Cullum and Dee Dee Bridgewater.

If you're looking for a little bit of everything, then head to the Madinat complex where you'll find a conglomeration of more than 40 bars and restaurants. From hip supper clubs boasting impressive blues musicians (like JamBase, see p209) to larger-than-life super clubs, here you should find your fix. If you are commuting between drinks, cabs are cheap and plentiful, although the rather erratic driving can prove troublesome if you're feeling a little worse for wear.

The rise of the city's nightlife has resulted in some out-of-this-world venues to host the major players. First among them has to be **360°** (see p208) at Jumeirah Beach Hotel. Located on its own stonewalled pier 200 metres out to sea, and with a stunning Burj-side location, it offers panoramic views of Dubai's ever-expanding skyline. Factor in some excellent resident DJs, not to mention the long-running Friday nights that showcase the finest in underground electronica, and you have the best bar Ibiza never built.

Equally fantastic but rather more secluded is **Après** (see p136) at the Mall of the Emirates. Overlooking the indoor ski slope, it's a DJ bar-cum-Swiss alpine lodge that offers the best cocktails in town. They don't come cheap (the Moët-laced mojito gold is a hefty Dhs250, but almost worth it), but owning to the unique location, relaxed atmosphere and some very decent grub, the place has become a very popular hang-out with both tourists and residents.

Unsurprisingly, weekends see the biggest events take place, with Thursdays dominated by the gargantuan outdoor venue that is **Chi Club** (see p207), where you can expect a soundtrack of house, hip hop and R&B. Fridays are governed by **Peppermint** (see p211), which regularly pulls in over 2,000 punters, while Deep Nights at **Trilogy** (see p209) offers an entertaining alternative.

While the big nights are predominantly at the weekend, you can also amuse yourself during the working week. Tuesday night, for example, is a citywide ladies' night, which means free drinks at most bars for the fairer sex. The schedule of touring DJs also sees big-league beat merchants playing at various venues midweek, with **Zinc Bar & Club** (see p211) the most popular hangout.

Although the majority of bars and clubs are based in hotels, some venues have a separate entrance to keep well-oiled patrons away from hotel guests. Entry to most bars and pubs is free, but be prepared to pay anywhere from Dhs50 to Dhs200 for an evening at one of the city's larger clubs. Finally, while there is a plethora of venues in Dubai, there is a clear-cut 'birds of a feather' mentality, meaning that clubbing is almost entirely segregated in the city, with few hedonists venturing outside of their cultural clique. At its worst this 'stick to your own'

The best Venues

For alfresco thrills
360° (see p208); **Chi Club** (see p207); **Tamanya Terrace** (see p211).

For simple pleasures
Jimmy Dix (see p207); **Rock Bottom Café** (see p207).

For the world's best DJs
Peppermint Lounge (see p211); **Trilogy** (see p209); **Apartment Lounge & Club** (see p208).

Arts & Entertainment

policy can translate to pure racism disguised by members-only policies. Certain bars, predominantly old-school pubs patronised by Western expats, will block the admittance of anyone they feel is 'unsuitable', claiming you have to be a member to enter. While many bars' licences do depend on operating such a system, if you are white you are likely to breeze through unhampered. Maddeningly, there is little that can be done short of boycotting such establishments, and arguing with the bouncer is liable to yield nothing more than laryngitis.

The scene in Dubai is constantly evolving. Many new bars and clubs open after the quiet period caused by long hot summers and by the month of abstinence that is Ramadan (which falls at the end of summer, and sees the city's clubs fall silent; *see p176*). Bars that weren't open at the time of publication but are expected to make a big impact are the **Asia Bar & Nightclub** at the Raffles Hotel, the reopening **Blush** next door at Wafi and the footballer-friendly **Embassy club** at Grosvenor House. There's also **iBO**, the city's most alternative-minded club that closed its doors in 2007 for the Dubai Metro development, but is expected to reopen before the start of 2008.

To keep up to date with the city's nightlife scene, pick up a copy of *Time Out Dubai* magazine or visit www.timeout.com/dubai.

Off the beaten track

Dubai is overloaded with swanky, Swarovski-filled establishments, but head into the older parts of town and you'll uncover some real diamonds. Mostly based around the Rigga area of Deira and Bank Street in Bur Dubai, a clutch of Russian, African, Arabic, Indian and Filipino clubs offer an alternative to Westernised hangouts. These bars are usually located in two- or three-star hotels and are often home to a joyously unpretentious atmosphere, great live bands and some of Dubai's more interesting characters.

Club Africana

Rush Inn Hotel, Khalid Bin Al Waleed Road (Bank Street), Bur Dubai (352 2235). **Open** 9pm-3am daily. **Credit** AmEx, MC, V. **Map** p330 H4.
Housed deep within the confines of the notorious Rush Inn Hotel, Club Africana is one of Dubai's best-kept secrets. The house band is a 15-strong Congolese collective who lay on freeform African rapping, harmonising and soliloquising to heart-stopping, jaw-dropping effect. Visit at 1am and the bar is invariably packed, a throbbing sinew of electrified energy. Alternatively, pop along at around 11pm for a couple of hours of laid-back African tunes.

Maharlika's

President Hotel Dubai, Trade Centre Road, Karama (334 6565). **Open** 6pm-3am daily. **Credit** AmEx, MC, V. **Map** p333 H7.
Maharlika's is one of Dubai's finest live music venues – presuming, that is, your favourite tunes come from Filipino cover bands. While lots of venues offer this kind of thing, Maharlika's does it with unashamed style, drawing a huge crowd every night of the week. The bands change occasionally, but the theme remains the same: a six- or seven-piece Filipino band heavy on guitars and lithe young women with syncopated head-banging. Expect to hear Led Zep's 'Stairway To Heaven', the Cranberries' 'Zombie' and some choice Guns N' Roses. Requests are most welcome.

Moulin Rouge

Broadway Hotel, Deira (221 7111). **Open** 6pm-3am daily. **Credit** AmEx, MC, V. **Map** p331 L3.
The Rouge – no relation to the famous Parisian club – is a paean to multiculturalism. Where else in the world can you sip Belgian lager in a French-inspired, *Eastenders*-style nightclub while scantily clad Slavs blast you with Arabic, French and English songs? Expect a royal variety show of dancers, singers and mime artists.

Rasputin's

Al Khaleej Holiday Suites (227 6565). **Open** 7pm-3am daily. **Credit** AmEx, MC, V. **Map** p331 K3.
Rasputin's is an expansive Russian club that really gets going in the smallest of hours. The band clearly dines from a varied musical menu, with everything from traditional Turkish to old-school Arabic and soft-rock standards tickling their fancy. In truth, the staggeringly attractive dancers could be reciting the telephone directory with a voice like a laryngitis-struck bullfrog and most of this club's clientele would still be captivated.

Arts & Entertainment

Peanut Butter Jam at **Garden Rooftop** – a showcase for local talent. *See p208*.

Bur Dubai

DJ bars/clubs

Chi Club
Al Nasr Leisureland, near the American Hospital/ Lamcy Plaza, Oud Metha (337 9470/www.lodge dubai.com). **Open** 7pm-3am daily. **Admission** varies. **Credit** AmEx, MC, V. **Map** p329 J3.
Once a dilapidated meat-market of a club, the Lodge was overhauled in early 2007, transmogrifying itself into a plush and incredibly spacious four-roomed venue. The gargantuan garden area is hugely popular during winter months and benefits from an adventurous booking policy. Inside there's an all-white room that hosts hip hop, funk and soul while the lavish VIP area is home to champagne-wielding celebrities – ex-boxer Chris Eubank is a regular. Make sure you get down early though as the queues can be horrendous.

Jimmy Dix
Mövenpick Hotel Bur Dubai (336 8800/ www. moevenpick-hotels.com). **Open** 6pm-3am daily. **Admission** free. **Credit** AmEx, MC, V. **Map** p329 J3.

Cast from the same no-frills mould as the Rock Bottom Café (*see right*), Jimmy Dix attracts an up-for-it throng, out to drink themselves silly. Although the poorly ventilated scarlet interior gives the impression that one is trapped in the lung of a chain smoker, the decent cover band and resident DJ can whip up an (admittedly subdued) storm with their airings of old school pop, rock and lightweight dance. Jimmy Dix is also worth a visit for the intermittently excellent Laughter Factory comedy nights, which are held monthly.

Rock Bottom Café
Regent Palace Hotel, World Trade Centre Road (396 3888/www.ramee-group.com). **Open** noon-3am daily. **Admission** free. **Credit** AmEx, MC, V. **Map** p331 J5.
Although it's officially a bar and restaurant rather than a club, Rock Bottom only really comes alive as other bars kick punters out. Something of a cattle market, RBC still pulls in an impressive crowd with its proven blend of Bullfrogs (a highly potent cocktail that utilises all the white spirits plus the magic of Red Bull) and a resident DJ and live band, who pump out the pleasers until closing time. There's even an in-house shawarma joint for dancers with the munchies.

Apartment Lounge & Club.

Live music venues

Garden Rooftop
Pyramids, Wafi City, Oud Metha Road (324 7300/ www.waficity.com). **Open** 8pm-midnight Fri & Sun (closed summer). **Admission** free. **Credit** AmEx, MC, V. **Map** p329 J3.
Situated between two other bars (Seville's and Carter's, both perfectly fine drinking joints in their own right) lies the Rooftop; a combination of fake rocks and real grass, with a sunken volleyball court in amphitheatre style that doubles as a music venue. On Fridays throughout the winter, this alfresco venue hosts Peanut Butter Jam, at which a variety of local bands peddle their wares to a crowd lounging on luminous beanbags. The atmosphere is terrific, even if the bands vary greatly in quality. If you're more of a blockbuster buff, the Rooftop hosts Movies Under the Stars every Sunday during the winter months with screenings of mainstream classics. *Photo p207.*

Theatrium
Royal Ascot Hotel (359 2341). **Open** Show starts 9pm daily. **Admission** Dhs400. **Credit** AmEx, MC, V. **Map** p330 H4.
Some people will find this extravagant nightly production very funny, especially when the dancers don shades and rainbow Afro wigs and gyrate to 'By the Rivers Of Babylon' by Boney M. At other times there's flamenco dancing, matadors and a brilliant magician who makes his assistant disappear and reappear at various darkened corners of the old amphitheatre. Unfortunately, the food is seriously lacking in magic, so the whole package doesn't quite justify the hefty price tags.

Deira

DJ bars/clubs

QD's
Dubai Creek Golf & Yacht Club, Garhoud Road (295 6000/www.dubaigolf.com). **Open** 6pm-2am daily. **Admission** free. **Credit** AmEx, MC, V. **Map** p329 K3.

Nestled in the grounds of the recently spruced-up Dubai Creek Golf & Yacht Club, QD's is a must-visit during the winter months. A classy open-air affair, this wood-decked bar offers superb views across the Creek, pizzas cooked by a wood-burning oven and all the shisha you can smoke. The regular DJ can be a bit hit-and-miss and the food is nothing to shout about, but if you can block out his musical mistakes, watching the sun crash down beyond the Creek with a cocktail in your hand is almost as good as it gets.

Jumeirah

DJ bars/clubs

360°
Jumeirah Beach Hotel (406 8744/www.jumeirah beachhotel.com). **Open** 4pm-2am Tue-Sat. **Admission** free. **Credit** AmEx, MC, V. **Map** p336 E1.
Situated at the end of its own pier, and overlooking the Burj Al Arab (*see p50*), 360° offers panoramic views of Dubai's ever-expanding coastline. With comfy sofas, excellent shishas and a decent cocktail list, it's a brilliant, if very expensive, venue. Head down on a Friday night and the bar is transformed into a hedonistic, electronic playground as the best in local and international talent take you from sunset to 2am. Make sure you're on the guest list on Friday and Saturday nights by logging on to www.platinumlistdubai.com, otherwise it's a case of you're not on the list, you're not coming in. As long as the weather's bearable, a visit is a must.

Apartment Lounge & Club
Jumeirah Beach Hotel (406 8000/050 748 4883/ www.jumeirahbeachhotel.com). **Open** 9pm-3am Tue-Sat. **Admission** free. **Credit** AmEx, MC, V. **Map** p336 E1.
A two-roomed club that opened at the end of 2005, the Apartment is ever-popular thanks to its forward-thinking music policy and lavish lounge. Thursdays plays host to eclectic DJs while Fridays are reserved for hip hop, R&B and soul, and are usually packed. The doormen can be a little strict, but have at least one girl in your group and you should be fine.

Boudoir
Dubai Marine Beach Resort & Spa, Beach Road (345 5995/www.dxbmarine.com). **Open** 7.30pm-3am daily. **Admission** free. **Credit** AmEx, MC, V. **Map** p332 D8.
This swanky, wannabe Parisian club ranks as one of the most exclusive venues in the city. Boudoir attracts a predominantly Lebanese crowd and if you want to get past the door staff, you should be dressed to impress and preferably in a couple. Different nights play host to various music genres, but they all come to a halt when a bottle of bubbly is bought. Yes, that's right, they celebrate the arrival of champagne by cutting the music out.

Panoramic views of the Dubai coastline fuel **360°**'s hedonistic nights.

Trilogy
Souk Madinat Jumeirah, Jumeirah Beach Road (366 8888/www.trilogy.ae). **Open** 9pm-3am daily. **Credit** AmEx, MC, V. **Map** p336 E1.
Dubai's undisputed king of the nightclub scene, this three-floored monster is always full at the weekends and attracts big-name DJs on a regular basis. The highlight at Trilogy has to be the rooftop bar, which offers a stunning view of the Gulf and hosts intimate midweek nights and weekend VIP bashes. Be careful when you try to find it though: you can get lost in the labyrinth of back rooms and dancefloors inside. *Photo p204.*

Live music venues

JamBase
Souk, Madinat Jumeirah (366 8888/www.madinat jumeirah.com). **Open** 7pm-12.30am Sat, Mon-Fri. **Admission** free. **Credit** AmEx, MC, V. **Map** p336 E1.
JamBase is the best venue for nightly live music in the city, although it's hardly up against strong competition. The furniture here is artfully angular, the decor is calculated art deco chic, and the

food, with dishes inspired by the southern US states, is very tasty too. The in-house jazz and blues band is one of Dubai's finest.

Malecon
Dubai Marine Beach Resort & Spa, Beach Road (346 1111/www.dxbmarine.com). **Open** 7pm-3am daily. **Admission** free. **Credit** AmEx, MC, V. **Map** p332 D8.
Malecon is a funky-enough salsa spot with an in-house Latino troupe and blue walls that have been graffitied to the max. A restaurant in the early evening, the smaller hours sees the dance floor get some action as a regular collective of merengue maniacs cut some rug. Malecon sometimes hosts house DJs.

The Marina

DJ bars/clubs

Buddha Bar
Grosvenor House West Marina Beach Dubai, Dubai Marina (399 8888/www.buddha-bar.com). **Open** 8pm-2am Sat-Wed; 8pm-3am Fri. **Credit** AmEx, MC, V. **Map** p336 B1.

Arts & Entertainment

Despite the incongruous setting – a large statue of a monk, who may or may not be Buddha himself, and a bar serving countless alcoholic concoctions – Buddha Bar is a chic and only slightly pretentious bar-cum-lounge club that also serves good, albeit expensive, Asian food.

Live music venues

DMC Amphitheatre
Dubai Media City, off Interchange 5, Sheikh Zayed Road (391 4555/www.dmc-communityguide.com). **Open** varies. **Map** p336 B2.
An expansive outdoor area set in the middle of the city's media enclosure, the Amphitheatre comes complete with real grass and its own lake. In recent years it has hosted a number of one-off events including Destiny's Child, Mark Knopfler and Roger Waters.

Tamanya Terrace
Radisson SAS Hotel, Dubai Media City (366 9111/www.radissonsas.com). **Open** 5pm-2am daily. **Credit** AmEx, MC, V. **Map** p336 C2.
Located at the heart of Dubai Media City, the open air Tamanya Terrace is a hive of activity every night of the week during the cool weather thanks to media types talking shop. There's also a good range of live music at the bar, with regular performances from jazz, house, soul and hip hop acts.

Sheikh Zayed Road

DJ bars/clubs

400 Club
Fairmont Dubai, Sheikh Zayed Road (332 5555/www.fairmont.com/dubai). **Open** 10pm-3am Thur, Fri. **Admission** free. **Credit** AmEx, MC, V. **Map** p333 G9.

The 400 holds exactly 400 occupants, all of whom, it would seem, have had run-ins with plastic surgeons in the recent past. High on frills but disappointingly low on musical thrills, it's a super-exclusive hangout where the rich and the famous go to see and be seen.

Peppermint Lounge
Barajeel Ballroom, Fairmont Dubai, Sheikh Zayed Road (050 552 2807/www.fairmont.com/dubai). **Open** 10pm-3am Fri. **Admission** varies. **Credit** AmEx, MC, V. **Map** p333 G9.
Peppermint Lounge should be an easy place to hate: it has a higher than average number of posers sporting sunglasses, queues longer than a Dubai traffic jam and bouncers with all the charm of Secret Service interrogators. But once inside the plush Barajeel Ballroom, all pretensions seem to be left at the door. The glamorous, up-for-it crowd is whipped into a frenzy by a host of international DJs playing electro, house and trance, and the dancefloor houses people more interested in dancing than seeing what their reflection looks like. A must-visit, if you can stick around long enough to get past the velvet rope.

Zinc Bar & Club
Crowne Plaza Dubai Hotel, Sheikh Zayed Road (331 1111/www.ichotelsgroup.com). **Open** 7pm-3am daily. **Admission** free. **Credit** AmEx, MC, V. **Map** p333 G10.
A Sheikh Zayed Road venue that is popular with flight crew, Zinc has a large central bar, separate dining area and a set of excellent resident DJs. The decor is metallic chic, but the general atmosphere is more down-to-earth than other venues on the strip. An unabashed crowd-pleaser, Zinc's residents supply a soundtrack of mainstream chart hits with the occasional inoffensive dance track thrown in. The venue also hosts monthly Laughter Factory comedy nights.

International DJs and an up-for-it crowd: **Peppermint Lounge**.

Arts & Entertainment

one luxurious guest rooms

two unforgettable dining

three tranquil spa facilities

fore! world class golf course

...reasons to experience The Montgomerie, Dubai

Find serenity and total relaxation at The Montgomerie, Dubai - a haven of indulgences in an exclusive setting. Luxurious guest rooms, a championship golf course, unforgettable dining and a host of leisure activities create the complete getaway for you to abandon your senses.

Isn't it about time you experienced the full Monty?

Active Dubai

Spectator Sports

Wherever sports champions go in Dubai, their legions of fans will follow.

Dubai Tennis Stadium hosts the annual **Dubai Tennis Championships**. *See p220.*

It certainly says something about Dubai's irrepressible ambition that despite having a climate that's not at all conducive to sporting events for half the year, it's rapidly becoming one of the top destinations on the planet for spectator sports.

The city's social calendar revolves around its sporting competitions, from the hugely popular **Dubai Rugby Sevens** and **Dubai World Cup**, for which thousands of sports fans and socialites fly in every year, to the slightly more sedate (by comparison) golf, tennis and water sport championships.

Since few international sports stars or teams actually reside in Dubai, exhibition matches and major sporting events with astronomical prize money are used to draw in the big names, with the warm winter weather, futuristic facilities and lavish hospitality providing extra incentives. Indeed, celebrities of the sporting variety are the most regularly spotted famous faces around town – whether they're playing, partying, founding sports academies or buying up residences on the Palm. Those who have graced the sports field while over here include Dubai resident Henrik Stenson, who made the city proud with his win against a stunned Tiger Woods and Ernie Els at the **Dubai Desert Classic** in 2007; current world tennis number one Roger Federer, who breezed his way to success for the fourth time at the **Dubai Tennis Championships** in 2007, and top-seeded Justine Henin, who held her nerve to claim the US$1 million **Dubai Duty Free Women's Open** in the same year.

Other stars simply want a break from the harsh northern European winter, and a growing number of British football teams choose to hold training camps, practise matches or 'bonding' holidays here. David James, Sol Campbell and Ashley Cole are among the host of players recently spotted in 'training' in Dubai's nightclubs, while retired heroes such as John Barnes, Steve McManaman and Paul Gascoigne have all enjoyed the chance to play at the semi-regular Dubai Masters Football Cup.

Dubai Desert Classic.

Golf

The shining jewel in Dubai's golfing calendar is undoubtedly the **Dubai Desert Classic** (*see p219*). This professional tournament is a respected fixture on the PGA Tour, luring world-class players like Colin Montgomerie, Darren Clarke, Mark O'Meara and Ernie Els to the wealthy emirate, in pursuit of prize money totalling more than US$2.4 million.

Golf is big business in Dubai, and the city now boasts no fewer than seven premium courses, with six more in the pipeline. The Desert Classic has been staged at both the **Emirates Golf Club** and the **Dubai Creek Golf & Yacht Club**, while various courses in the city enjoy the attention of stars in need of a practice session before the main event. Since security is consistently low-key, it's perfectly possible to come away with treasured autographs and photos. The **Jebel Ali Golf Resort & Spa** (883 6000) hosts a curtain-raiser to the Desert Classic in the guise of a nine-hole challenge match, while the Classic itself is well attended, drawing many amateur residents who play the same world-beating courses all year round – and who will probably be even more encouraged by Emirates Golf Club member Henrik Stenson's 2007 win. Besides the hangers-on (possibly more interested in the all-you-can-drink corporate hospitality), the tournament also enjoys its fair share of legitimate golf fans, happy to chase around after the pros.

Ultimately, if Dubai has been good for sport, then sport has also been extremely kind to the emirate, primarily as a highly effective marketing tool for the tourism sector. Pictures of Tiger Woods teeing off atop the Burj Al Arab helipad or Anna Kournikova trying on jewellery in the Dubai gold souk have bounced around the world, securing TV pictures and excellent publicity. Appearance cheques may have changed hands (rumour has it that Woods was paid US$1 million just to turn up for the 2007 Dubai Desert Classic, which perhaps helped to sweeten his loss), but there have been no complaints about value for money.

And whereas in the past the local sporting public hasn't taken full advantage of these chances to observe big names at close range, crowd figures fortunately seem to be ever increasing. The most recent Dubai Tennis Championships, Dubai World Cup and Dubai Rugby Sevens were all able to claim record attendance numbers.

Horse & camel racing

Holding its own in several sports, Dubai really pulls ahead of the chasing pack in the equine arts. Known these days as the new international centre for horse racing, the emirate can boast the unrivalled excellence of the Maktoums' Godolphin operation (*see p220* **Horse power**). Although the royal family's private stable has proved itself on tracks around the world, it's still a special experience to watch the planet's best horses strut their stuff on home turf.

Each year the emirate hosts the world's richest horse race, the US$6 million **Dubai World Cup** (*see p219*), as well as the two-month long **Dubai International Racing Carnival**, established in 2004. In 2007, the World Cup meeting was attended by a record-breaking 70,000 people, and Invasor, owned by Dubai's HH Sheikh Hamdan bin Rashid Al Maktoum, took World Cup victory to become the 45th winner of the Racing Carnival. A total of 200 horses from around 20 countries, representing over 70 trainers, were invited to compete at the Dubai International Racing Carnival in 2007.

Active Dubai

a spectacular golf course

FOUR SEASONS
GOLF CLUB
Dubai Festival City

Whether an avid golfer or diner you're destined to succumb to the dining choices
on offer at Four Seasons Golf Club.
Savour in the authentic Italian Cuisine and the dramatic interiors at the chic
Milanese-influenced Quattro. Enjoy a multi-cultural dining experience at the
contemporary Blades. Unwind at the casual Spikes and pamper your taste-buds with an
eclectic mix of international delights or grab a quick satisfying bite at The Tee Lounge,
located under the Club's striking spiral glass atrium.
Your discerning dining choice will be enhanced by Four Seasons' signature service, par excellence.

Phone: 04 6010101 Email: restaurants.dub@fourseasons.com
Visit: www.fourseasons.com/dubaigolf

The 2007 Cup also saw the announcement of important news for the future of the event. Until recently, the Nad Al Sheba track (*see p87*), which stages races on dirt and turf, has been the focal point and flagship facility for racing in the UAE. But a huge redevelopment of the entire Nad Al Sheba area is now planned to create a luxurious horse racing city named Meydan, set for completion by 2010. The news also rattled fans of golf – whose affordable Nad Al Sheba golf course closed in the summer of 2007, and rugby, as the project is likely to spill across land currently used by Dubai Country Club and the Dubai Exiles Rugby Football Club – home to the city's famous Rugby Sevens tournament since the 1970s.

The horse racing city will be shaped like a falcon, feature a one-kilometre long grandstand to host up to 60,000 race fans, a hotel, more than ten restaurants and the Godolphin Gallery and Museum. A canal will run from Dubai Creek to the racecourse and to mark its launch, the Dubai World Cup's prize money will almost double in 2010 to around US$10 million.

Wherever it's held, the World Cup will certainly retain its unique character, and continue to be the place to rub shoulders with the great and the good of the city. Indeed, there's as much action off the track as on it, not least at the Fillies & Fashion event, which has generous prizes for the best-dressed ladies. But racing in Dubai is about far more than one big day in the sun. The Dubai International Racing Carnival features 55 races (20 on turf, the rest on dirt) over a ten-meeting, nine-week period, leading up to the World Cup at the end of March. However, the bad news for visitors who like to indulge in a flutter is that betting in the UAE is strictly illegal. Instead, prizes are on offer for correct predictions of race results.

The crowd is all eyes at the world's richest horse race: the **Dubai World Cup**. *See p215.*

Fast and furious action on **Dubai Autodrome**'s three-mile track.

As well as Nad Al Sheba, there is currently a sand and oil surface racing track at Jebel Ali (call 347 4914 for details), turf racing at Abu Dhabi (02 445 5500) and another dirt track at Sharjah (06 531 1155). No visit to Dubai is complete, though, without witnessing another type of racing – the nearby camel track, also in Nad Al Sheba. The days of local residents climbing aboard one of these 'ships of the desert' for a gruelling trip across the sands to Abu Dhabi or Al Ain may be long gone, but camels remain revered in many Middle Eastern societies. Racing camels are a breed apart, and the strongest and fastest specimens change hands for millions of dirhams. The **camel racing** season in Dubai starts in November and runs through to April. Admission is free to the races at Nad Al Sheba, which usually begin on Thursdays and Fridays at 7am and are over by 8.30am (timings are later in Ramadan). For more information, *see p177*.

In response to international criticism that children as young as five were being illegally press-ganged from the subcontinent into becoming jockeys, 2006 saw their replacement with robots. Yes, robots. Merely half a metre high and weighing just over two and a half kilos, the robots look like a box with a dangling whip, decorated to suit the owner's taste. Each robo-jockey is controlled via a joystick and a computer screen, allowing the person in charge to operate the jockey from his car alongside the racetrack.

Motor sports

Bahrain may have beaten Dubai in the race to host Formula One Grand Prix racing in the Middle East (and Abu Dhabi will also be a host city from 2009), but the emirate has trumped its competition with the opening of the region's first fully integrated motor sports facility. Located a short drive out of town along the Emirates Road, the **Dubai Autodrome** (367 8700) boasts a world-class 5.3km (three-mile) motor racing track, an international-standard pit lane complex and a grandstand able to accommodate more than 5,000 spectators.

The Autodrome-based Aston Martin Phoenix racing team won the November 2006 MotorCity GT 500 in the International Federation of Cars (FIA) GT Championship, with the team's duo of Andrea Piccini and Jean-Denis Deletraz at the wheel. Consisting of two DBR9s and several high-profile drivers, including Sheikh Maktoum bin Hasher Maktoum Al Maktoum, Phoenix races across Europe, Asia, the USA and Middle East.

Away from the relative comforts of the tarmac, the Emirates Motor Sports Federation organises several high-octane events including the UAE Rally Championship, the 1,000 Dunes Rally and the Emirates Autocross Championship. Dubai traditionally stages the final leg of the FIA Middle East Rally Championship, usually in December, and also hosts the **Desert Challenge** (*see p219*), a renowned local rally-driving event held over

Sporting calendar

The oppressive summer heat forces anyone with any sense to retreat into air-conditioned comfort from June to September, so Dubai's sporting line-up is effectively squeezed into an eight-month period: nearly all events fall between October and May, with plenty of high-quality action for spectators to watch. Stars like Tiger Woods, Frankie Dettori and Roger Federer are among those who have visited Dubai in recent years. The dates below are subject to change; we advise you contact the organisers closer to the time. For more on sporting events, *see pp175-181*.

September
The UAE football league: The season kicks off at the end of September 2007 and ends in May 2008. Dubai teams include Al Wasl, Al Nasr and the mighty Al Ahli.
Visit www.goalzz.com for a fixture list.

October
Camel racing: The season kicks off at Nad Al Sheba, with races every Thursday and Friday. Season ends April 2008.
Contact Nad Al Sheba Club (336 3666).
UAE Desert Challenge: Expect to see 4WDs, motorbikes and trucks tearing up the desert.
Contact UAE Desert Challenge (266 9922/ rallyuae@emirates.net.ae).

November
Horse racing: Another season of floodlit racing gets underway at Nad Al Sheba, ending mid April 2008.
Contact Dubai Racing Club (332 2277/ info@dubairacingclub.com).
Dubai Rugby Sevens: Sixteen international teams and several social outfits compete over three days and odd-shaped balls for various plates and shields. Rowdy fun for all from 29 Nov to 1 Dec 2007.
Contact Promoseven Sports (321 0008/ www.dubairugby7s.com).

December
Offshore Powerboating: The Class 1 World Powerboat Championship combines with a festival of local and international musicians, in a celebration of the great outdoors. Held from 29 Nov to 1 Dec and 6-8 Dec.
Contact Dubai International Marine Club (399 5777/www.dimc-uae.com).

January
Dubai Marathon: It's not only about winning; register to run the city circuit of just over 42km and help raise money for research into sight restoration and blindness. Also on offer is a 3km fun run and 10km road race. The race is due to take place on 18 Jan 2008.
Visit www.dubaimarathon.org for more information.

February
Dubai Tennis Championships: The world's top male and female players battle it out in the intimate Dubai Tennis Stadium. Day-long sunshine and non-British finalists guaranteed. The championships begin in late February and end in the first week of March.
Contact Dubai Duty Free (216 6444/ www.dubaitennischampionships.com).

March
Dubai Desert Classic: Expect immaculate greens and the greatest swingers of the day at this PGA European event. Such stars as Colin Montgomerie, Ernie Els and Mark O'Meara are sure to attend; autograph-hunters and hospitality-freeloaders alike will find plenty to satisfy.
Contact UAE Golf Association (380 1777/ www.dubaidesertclassic.com).
Dubai World Cup: Dubai hosts the highest-stakes horse race in the world at Nad Al Sheba. Visiting celebrities, free-flowing bubbly and ridiculous hats are the order of the day.
Contact Dubai Racing Club (332 2277/ www.dubaiworldcup.com).

Justine Henin won the **Dubai Tennis Championships** in 2007.

five days in October. The Desert Challenge dune-bashing affair consistently attracts many of the world's leading drivers and is also the final round of the FIA Cross Country Rally World Cup and the Federation of Motor Sports (FIM) Cross Country Rallies World Championship.

Tennis

While most Dubaians relish the city's home-grown sporting calendar – the masses turn up to watch the clash of expat veterans at the boisterous Dubai Rugby Sevens – it would be great to see the British & Irish Lions up against the Qantas Wallabies on the rugby pitch here. Dubai's Tennis Championship, however, really does bring the sport's premium racketeers to town. Top tennis players such as Venus Williams, Anna Kournikova, Boris Becker and Tim Henman have all taken part in the annual back-to-back WTA and ATP tournaments under the umbrella of the Dubai Tennis Championships (*see p219*). Both men's and women's world number ones – Roger Federer and Justine Henin – took the honours in 2007 and should be back to defend their titles in 2008.

The action unfolds at the purpose-built stadium in Garhoud. Many spectators take pub grub and liquid refreshment at the **Irish Village** (*see p133*) between games; the restaurants of the Century Village on the other side of the stadium also lay on lunch deals. While the players flock to Dubai to take full

Roger Federer, a Dubai Tennis Champion.

Horse power

Few success stories in the world of sport can rival that of **Godolphin** (www.godolphin.com), the racing stable established by the Maktoum royal family. But while it has ruled the flat-racing roost for much of the past decade, Godolphin retains an air of mystery thanks to the closed-door policy of its Dubai and British stables, as well as the royal profile of its owning syndicate.

From humble beginnings in 1994, Godolphin – named after one of the three founding stallions of modern thoroughbreds – has grown to become a revolutionary force in racing around the world, with Dubai at its epicentre. Legend tells of the Godolphin Arabian, an 18th-century horse who ended up in England and won everything in sight before going to stud. Here he enjoyed still greater success, with leading sire titles in 1738, 1745 and 1747. And Godolphin's success lives on; it's thought that over

70 British Classic winners have had a strain of the famous horse in their pedigree.

The Dubai-based operation chalked up their first local winner at Nad Al Sheba in 1992. Since then their records have been matchless: Godolphin has won Group One races in no less than 11 countries, while Frankie Dettori, Godolphin's retained jockey, can claim 470 wins from 1,463 rides. The stable also bred the great Dubai Millennium, unleashed to win the race seemingly made for him – the Dubai World Cup 2000 – when he beat an international field by more than six lengths. Tragically, the horse, still commonly regarded in Dubai as the best ever, died just a year later after succumbing to grass sickness.

Frankie Dettori finished last on Discreet Cat in the 2007 Dubai World Cup race, but the chances of Goldophin notching up more wins in the future are very high indeed.

The Sir Nai'ir Dhow Race organised by the **Dubai International Marine Club**.

advantage of the city's magnificent hospitality and attractions (not to mention a healthy purse), it's also true that the general public has been a bit slower to show its enthusiasm, with early rounds routinely played out in front of thin crowds. However, crowd numbers are growing every year, and the final rounds attract packed houses. Home-grown players are also treated to an encouraging reception, even if expats tend to save the most rousing cheers for stars hailing from their respective home countries.

Water sports

Dubai plays host to the finale of the **Class 1 World Powerboat Championship**. The emirate is the base of the appropriately named **Victory Team** (www.victoryteam.ae), one of the most successful Class 1 outfits in the sport. A string of world titles, records and trophies have been secured since the championship was formed in 1989, with throttleman Saeed Al-Tayer earning a place in the record books as the first Arab to win a hat-trick of Class 1 championships in 2001. February sees Dubai host an **International Sailing Week Regatta**; the only event of its kind, this growing spectacle pits ten- to 17-year-olds racing in optimist and laser categories, and pulls in over 100 competitors from 14 nations each year. Dubai also hosts

the region's biggest annual boat show in March, at which manufacturers from all over the world display all manner of seacraft, from lightweight jet skis to luxury cruisers and yachts. For details of this year's races, *see p219* **Sporting calendar**.

The **Dubai International Marine Club**, based at Le Meridien Mina Seyahi Beach Resort & Marina hotel (*see p63*), is the body responsible for the growth of water sports in the UAE. It organises various meets each year to promote jet skiing, traditional rowing sports and dhow sailing, as well as races for catamarans and lasers. Venues include the Mina Seyahi, Dubai Creek, Abu Dhabi, Ras Al Khaimah and Fujairah. Because many of these races take place some distance from Dubai, spectator numbers are generally low. Nonetheless, the competitive sailing season in the UAE (from October to May) is keenly contested. The crowning highlight of the dhow sailing season is the 60-foot **Sir Bu Nu'air Dhow Race** from the island of the same name to Dubai, which takes place during May – the third and final race of the 60-foot category and the final race of the water sports season. The 58-nautical mile race attempts to recapture the glory of the pearling fleet as it struck for home at the height of the pearling trade. In recent years, fields of over 90 dhows have crossed the finishing line.

Continental GT
An expression of absolute refinement

A shape that evokes legends, Bentley Continental GT Coupe is engineered to challenge speed. Powered by a 6.0-litre, 12-cylinder, twin-turbocharged W12 engine, this sporting coupe simply wakes up and lunges towards the horizon.

Participation Sports

Dubai isn't all about taking it easy. With futuristic facilities, warm waters and a legion of sporting enthusiasts, it's the ideal place to work up a sweat.

Never a city to aim anywhere but astronomically high, Dubai is well on track to becoming a global sporting hub. While it already has world-class golf courses and horse racing tracks, and an autodrome ready and revving for the arrival of Formula 1, the development that is sure to secure its globe-conquering status is the awe-inspiring **Dubai Sports City** (*see p30*) part of the ongoing and mind-boggling Dhs18 billion Dubailand development.

Like the other 'City' projects (including Media, Internet and, soon, Horse Racing), the Sports metropolis takes a theme, adds a few million dirhams, some of the world's leading architects and outrageously ambitious vision. This 50 million-square-foot development will be a combination of academies and training facilities, entertainment and leisure. In terms of training facilities, it will house the Manchester United Soccer School Facility, open permanently in 2008; an International Cricket Council Global Cricket Academy, the first of its kind in the world; a world hockey academy, again a world first; a Butch Harmon School of Golf (that's the guy who trained Tiger Woods); rugby training facilities, and four major stadiums which will attract big international, local and regional events like the Gulf Cup. The largest stadium will be a 60,000-seat multi-purpose indoor/outdoor arena for football, rugby and athletics. There will be a 5,000-seat hockey stadium, a 30,000-seat cricket stadium and an indoor arena for events like trade shows and concerts.

If you like the sound of that – so much, in fact, that you wouldn't mind living among it – there will be a number of villas next to the golf course, with a development called Victory Heights and a group of 900 luxury villas in a residential community for families placed in and around the golf course. Very handy for practising your swing.

Bowled over: the **International Cricket Council** has relocated to Dubai.

Where to...

...catch a helicopter ride

If you've got a head for heights, book a helicopter flight with **Aerogulf Services** (220 0331/www.aerogulfservices.com). With helicopters departing from 7am to 7pm, a sunset flight past the iconic Burj Al Arab is one of those experiences that should be at the top of everyone's must-do list. Prices range from Dhs3,175 for a 30-minute flight to Dhs6,100 for one hour.

...go kayaking

Desert Rangers (340 2408/www.desert rangers.com) will provide an instructor and all the equipment you need for Dhs300; the rest is up to you. Kalba on the east coast is your best bet for some hard-core kayaking: spend the three-hour trip speed-paddling through mangroves, disturbing flocks of exotic birds as you pass.

...go sandboarding

Until someone decided that the desert was a prime snowboarding slot, sandboards were the weapon of choice for those looking for semi-vertical kicks. **Net Tours** (266 8661/www.nettoursdubai.com) run sandboarding trips departing from Dubai that cost Dhs275, which include dune bashing, camel riding and light refreshments.

...jump out of a plane

It's only when you get back to terra firma and have stopped screaming into your exceptionally patient instructor's ear that you realise just how exhilarating the last 45 seconds of free-fall have been. All for just Dhs850 per person, including land training,

jumpsuit, instruction, 20-minute flight – and a parachute, at the **Umm Al Quwain Aeroclub** (06 768 1447/aeroclub@emirates.net.ae).

...kill crabs

For Dhs260, **Lama Tours** (334 4330/www.lama.ae) will take you over to Umm Al Quwain from Dubai for this rather bloodthirsty expedition, involving spearing hundreds of crabs as you wade through mangroves, and then eating them on your return.

...pull off a grind

Head down to the **Wonderland Theme & Water Park** (324 1222) in Garhoud for some mild to terrifying skateboarding ramps or to just watch gnarly boarders flaunt their tricks. A three-hour pass costs Dhs25. Full equipment including boards, knee and elbow pads and different-sized helmets can be hired from Dubai Desert Extreme (336 9007), who have a shop on site.

...ride a fun boat

Hailed as the 'new jet ski', fun boats are outboard engines that require more throttle than their noisy sisters – and which of course involve more 'fun'. Rides cost Dhs250 per 30 minutes, Dhs400 per hour. Call **Nautica 1992** (050 426 2415) if you're intrigued.

...try surf-skiing

Dubai's surf-skiing fanatics meet every Friday morning near Kite Beach to plough to the Burj and back. They're extremely welcoming and always happy to talk newcomers through the basics (call **club captain Wayne Randall** on 050 813 3207 for more details).

While it is hoped that in the near future the city can lure events such as the ICC Cricket World Cup, the Twenty 20 Cricket Series and the Hockey World Cup, Sports City is also about championing the local sports scene. It will house facilities to encourage all manner of athletic pursuits, from extreme sports (think rock climbing, rollerblading and kiteboarding) to high-octane thrills like karting and dune buggying. Expect the Sports City extravaganza to come to fruition first with the opening of the Ernie Els golf course to the public – around the end of 2007.

If all that seems too grandiose to be true, just take a look at **Ski Dubai** (*see p235*). People still smirk at the idea of skiing and snowboarding in the desert, but Dubai's indoor slope has been

doing a roaring trade ever since it opened in September 2005. Holding over 6,000 tonnes of snow, it's the third largest indoor snow dome in the world and its Mall of the Emirates location makes it a great spectacle post-shop.

Dubai has long been a golfer's paradise, with several outstanding courses impressing even the pros that flow into the city for its **Desert Classic** tournament (*see p215*). New courses springing up in Dubai have taken the emirate's total to no fewer than seven different venues, including the **Four Seasons Golf Club** (*see p231*), which opened directly after the 2007 Dubai Desert Classic and incorporates the Robert Trent Jones Jr-designed Al Badia golf course, as well as the region's only TaylorMade Performance Lab, for scarily precise computer

Shoot to thrill at **Dubai Archers Club**.

generated swing analysis. Even with the 2007 closure of Nad Al Sheba, one of the city's most popular greens, it remains entirely possible to camp down in a five-star hotel a few miles from the airport and a three iron from one of Dubai's prestigious fairways.

An active life in Dubai doesn't necessarily require spending a small fortune in clubs, kit and green fees. Thanks to its cosmopolitan population and pleasant climate, the city offers a wealth of sports and games to be played in the great outdoors. The presence of thousands of workers from the subcontinent means that cricket is played widely and with great enthusiasm, both at an organised level and with impromptu games staged on patches of waste ground around the city every Friday. Football – which boasts a multicultural amateur expat league as well as a domestic professional league – is popular, while the city's beach culture ensures that all water sports have a healthy following, including the relatively new activity of kitesurfing: initiates to the sport will find tanned Dubaians performing aerial tricks at dawn along the emirate's pristine shoreline.

Archery

Dubai Archers Club
Dubai Country Club, Al Awir, off the Ras Al Khor road south of Dubai (050 881 7366). **Meets** 4pm-6pm Sat, Thur, Fri. **Price** Dhs50. **No credit cards.** **Map** p329 L5.
Archery enthusiasts meet here three times a week for target practice. All standards are welcome and the entry fee includes equipment hire.

Bowling

Al Nasr Leisureland
Behind the American Hospital, Oud Metha (337 1234). **Open** 9am-midnight daily. **Price** (Entrance fee) Dhs10; Dhs5 under-10s; Dhs7/game (includes shoes). **Credit** MC, V. **Map** p329 J3.
Markedly less plush than other lanes in town, but licensed – meaning that Al Nasr pulls in bowlers thirsty for a beer. Group bookings are taken but you must fax reservation details through to 337 6832.

Dubai Bowling Centre
Next to Century Mall, Al Barsha (339 1010). **Open** 10am-midnight Sun-Wed; 10am-2am Thur, Fri. **Price** Dhs17/game Sun-Thur; Dhs20/game Fri. **Credit** AmEx, MC, V. **Map** p336 D1.
Aside from the 36 lanes of undisputed bowling fun, there's an enormous games area full of the usual arcade games, pool tables and five-puck air hockey (believe us, it's a real challenge). There's also a soundproofed room that contains a full drum kit that you're free to bash away on.

Boxing

Le Meridien Dubai
Airport Road (282 4040). **Open** 8pm Sun, Tue. **Price** (1hr lessons) Dhs40 non-members; Dhs25 members. **Credit** AmEx, MC, V. **Map** p329 L2.
Train with Iraj Dor at the Fitness Club.

Climbing

Climbing's abuzz in Dubai. Hone your skills in the city first, and then take to Ras Al Khaimah's rocky terrain afterwards.

Pharaoh's Club
Wafi Pyramids, near Wafi City Mall, Oud Metha Road (324 0000). **Open** 7am-11pm Sat-Thur; 9am-9pm Fri. **Price** Dhs50/1hr class. **Credit** AmEx, MC, V. **Map** p329 J3.
Assuming that you don't suffer from vertigo and that you like scaling inanimate objects, there's no better place than Pharaoh's – the UAE's only climbing wall. It scales 50ft (15m) and includes a boulder cave about 11ft (3.5m) high and a 5ft (1.5m) overhang. If you need some chill time after your climb, then check out Cleopatra's Spa, which is also based at Wafi City.

Active Dubai

exclusive leisure
DUBAI GOLF

Dubai - a modern, dynamic city basking in year round sunshine and home to some of the world's finest golf courses.

Emirates Golf Club The Majlis championship course is host to the PGA European Tour sanctioned event, The Dubai Desert Classic, and has been voted one of Golf Digest's '100 Best Courses outside the USA', whilst The Wadi by Faldo is an exhilarating and challenging new golfing design for the region.

EMIRATES
GOLF CLUB DUBAI

Dubai Creek Golf & Yacht Club with its stunning championship course, is the finest 18-hole golf resort in the UAE and has been voted one of Golf World's 'Top 100 Must Play Courses'

Experience exclusive leisure today - Experience Dubai Golf.

DUBAI CREEK

Emirates

Emirates Golf Club – T:+9714 3802222, E:egc@dubaigolf.com
Dubai Creek Golf & Yacht Club – T:+9714 2956000, E:dcgyc@dubaigolf.com
Central Reservations – T:+9714 3801234, E:golfbooking@dubaigolf.com www.dubaigolf.com

Get yourself behind the wheel with **Desert Rangers**.

Cycling

Dubai Roadsters
Wolfi's Bike Shop, between 2nd & 3rd Interchange on Sheikh Zayed Road (339 4453/www.wbs.ae).
Open Varies. **Price** *Rides* free. *Bike hire* Dhs100 per day. **Credit** MC, V. **Map** p326 C3.
The Dubai Roadsters meet every Sunday and Tuesday evening at 7.30pm at Nad Al Sheba. There's also a two-hour meet for slightly more experienced riders every Friday at 5.30am (6am in winter) from the Lime Tree Café on Jumeirah Beach Road for two to four hours of cycling.

Dune bashing & dune buggying

Dune bashing doesn't involve attacking anything – it's one of the most popular pastimes in the UAE. While there are plenty of tour companies offering organised trips into the sands, if you want to do more than just get jostled about in the back seat, then try a desert driving lesson. Or if you're tough enough to feel the sand flying in your face and can cling on to a wildly juddering steering wheel, have a bash at dune buggying. With only the odd bemused camel as spectator, you can roar through sand and scrubland at breakneck speeds, slalom round shrubs and scream like a banshee all the while. Tailor-made for adrenalin junkies.

Desert Rangers
Dubai Garden Centre Building, Sheikh Zayed Road (340 2408/www.desertrangers.com). **Open** Varies.
Price *4WD* Dhs1,500/person (based on 2 people). *Own vehicle* Dhs1,000. *Dune buggying* Dhs375/half-day. **Credit** AmEx, MC, V.
The prices quoted above include transport, drinks, headgear and insurance.

Fencing

Dubai Fencing Club
Quay Health Club, Mina A'Salam hotel, Madinat Jumeirah (366 8888/www.dubaifencingclub.com).
Open *Advanced classes* 7pm Sat, Wed. *Beginners & advanced classes* 7.40pm Mon. **Price** (1hr session) Dhs45 non-members; Dhs35 members. **Credit** AmEx, DC, MC, V. **Map** p336 E1.
The head coach of this popular club is Mihail Kouzev, who represented Bulgaria in the Pentathlon World Championships. Fencers of all ages and standards are welcome.

International Fencing Club of Dubai
Metropolitan Hotel, Sheikh Zayed Road, Interchange 2 (343 0000). **Open** 7.30pm Sat, Mon, Wed. **Price** Dhs35/class; Dhs300/12 classes. **Credit** AmEx, MC, V. **Map** p328 G5.
Learn fencing (foil and sabre) or brush up your expertise at the International Fencing Club of Dubai with Master Zahi El Khoury, a former world championship finalist and Arabic champion.

Active Dubai

Putt in style at **Four Seasons Golf Club**. *See p231.*

Fishing

Dubai is an ideal place to boost your ego by snagging a few queen fish or barracuda (then, not so grandly, flinging them back in the water again). Reliable sunshine, calm seas and good fish can be found throughout the year, including the noble sailfish whose numbers are now protected by a conservation effort based in Abu Dhabi, despite the best efforts of illegal trawlers to plunder all and sundry. Prime months are considered to be January to March and advance bookings are highly recommended. And be sure to find a few friends keen to don waders too – chartering a boat can cost a packet.

Art Marine
Jumeirah Beach Hotel, Pavilion Marina, Jumeirah Beach Road (348 0000/www.artmarine.com). **Open** (for trips) 7am-6pm daily. **Price** Varies. **Credit** AmEx, MC, V. **Map** p336 E1.
Art Marine run one of the biggest operations in Dubai and offer a friendly, flexible service. There are various boats available for hire (which will take six-12 passengers per fishing trip), and multiple fishing lines ensure you're trawling for sharks while drifting for kingfish and catching some rays.

Bounty Charters
Dubai International Marine Club, Le Meridien Mina Seyahi Beach Resort & Marina, Al Sufouh Road, Jumeirah (050 552 6067). **Open** by advance booking only. **Price** Dhs2,000/4 hrs; Dhs2,400/6 hrs; Dhs2,600/8 hrs; Dhs2,800/10 hrs. **No credit cards**. **Map** p336 B1.
South African Richard Forrester, a veteran sailor of the region's waters, takes the helm at Bounty Charters. His 11m (36ft) Yamaha Sea Spirit game fishing boat can be booked in good time for tailor-made fishing trips all year round (up to six people).

Club Joumana
Jebel Ali Hotel, Sheikh Zayed Road, Exit 13 (past Interchange 7) (883 6000/www.jebelali-international.com). **Open** 8am-noon, 2-6pm daily. **Price** Dhs1,750/4 hrs; Dhs3,000/8 hrs. **Credit** AmEx, MC, V. **Map** p336 A2.
Club Joumana has one boat, the streamline Kingfish, which holds a maximum of seven people per fishing trip. Full- and half-day excursions are available, with an experienced and friendly crew on hand to steer you to the better spots; prices for both durations includes drinks, snacks and tackle.

Dubai Creek Golf & Yacht Club
Opposite Deira City Centre mall, Garhoud (205 4646/www.dubaigolf.com). **Open** (for trips) 7am-6pm daily. **Price** Dhs2,550/4 hrs (8am-noon, 1-5pm & 7-11pm); Dhs2,850/5 hrs (7am-noon & 1-6pm); Dhs3,150/6 hrs (6am-noon & noon-6pm); Dhs3,550/8 hrs. **Credit** AmEx, MC, V. **Map** p329 K3.
The club's own 10m (32ft) single cabin yacht, Sneakaway, is available for trips for up to a maximum of six people. The price includes tackle, bait and fuel as well as a good supply of soft drinks. If you prefer something a bit racier, you can hire the Princess sports boat.

Ocean Explorer Fishing Charters
Le Meridien Mina Seyahi Beach Resort & Marina, Al Sufouh Road, Jumeirah (399 3333/www.lemeridien-minaseyahi.com). **Open** Fishing trips depart 8am-noon, 2-6pm daily. **Price** Dhs2,000/4 hrs; Dhs2,400/6 hrs; Dhs2,600/8 hrs; Dhs2,800/10 hrs. **Credit** AmEx, MC, V. **Map** p336 B1.
Tackle, bait, and water are included in the price of these regular trips to some of the best fishing grounds in the Gulf (maximum six people), but you'll be asked for a 50 per cent credit card deposit. Look out for the World development on your way out to sea; fishermen in the know will opt for a sundowner at Barasti Bar (*see p135*) afterwards as it overlooks the Gulf.

Golf

An explosion in the numbers of visiting golfers means facilities here are constantly improving, although costs are constantly going up too. There are currently six new courses under construction throughout the emirate, including Ernie Els' course – 'The Dunes at Victory Heights' in Dubai Sports City, and the Tiger Woods Dubai, which will weave its way through an 80-suite boutique hotel. Courses justify their high prices by citing the extra expense built into green fees here – millions of gallons of desalinated water are needed daily to prevent the desert reclaiming these modern oases. Bookings for tee times for several clubs listed below can be made through a central reservations office on 380 1234 or online at www.dubaigolf.com. The UAE Golf Association (380 1777/www.ugagolf.com) is the governing body for the sport in this country. Affiliate yearly membership is Dhs200 and entitles players to reductions on green fees, lessons and merchandise at all UAE clubs.

Arabian Ranches Golf Club

Arabian Ranches, Emirates Road off Interchange 4 by the Autodrome (366 3000/www.arabian ranchesgolfdubai.com). **Open** (Room reservations & golf) 24 hrs daily. **Price** Dhs545 Sat, Thur, Fri; Dhs470 Sun-Wed. **Credit** AmEx, MC, V. **Map** p336 B2.

In association with Nicklaus Design (and formerly known as the Desert Course), this 18-hole par 72 grass course is (paradoxically) out in the desert, and the brainchild of golfing hero Ian Baker-Finch. Part of a bigger residential complex, the course boasts a floodlit driving range, putting and chipping greens and par three pitch and putt facilities.

Club Joumana

Jebel Ali Golf Resort & Spa, Sheikh Zayed Road, Exit 13 (past Interchange 7) (883 6000/www.jebel alihotel.com). **Open** 7am-4.50pm (last tee-off) daily; 5pm-darkness for twilight golf. **Price** *Non-resident* 9-hole Dhs150 Sat, Thur, Fri; Dhs140 Sun-Wed. Dhs275 Sat, Thur, Fri; 18-hole Dhs255 Sun-Wed. *Cart fee* 9-hole Dhs35. 18-hole Dhs55. *Club hire* 9-hole Dhs65/set. 18-hole Dhs120/set. Dhs25 for 50 range balls. **Credit** AmEx, MC, V. **Map** p336 A2.

A nine-hole, par 36 course, with superb views of the Gulf, a salt-water lake and the colourful presence of preening peacocks. The facilities include a driving range, 27-hole putting green and indoor swing room. There are also a variety of coaching packages to choose from depending on whether you are a virgin swinger or hardened pro; five 30-minute lessons start at Dhs675.

Dubai Country Club

Al Awir, off the Ras Al Khor road south of Dubai (333 1155/www.dubaicountryclub.com). **Open** 8am-6pm daily. *Driving range* 8am-8.30pm daily. **Price** Dhs90/game, plus Dhs60 for a piece of artificial turf. **Credit** AmEx, MC, V. **Map** p329 L5.

Dubai's first golf club opened in 1971 and is still a popular option, although the competition gets noticeably stiffer on an annual basis. The club boasts 18- and nine-hole courses on sand; players buy and then carry a piece of artificial turf to play off, except for on the 'browns' (sand equivalents of greens), which are brushed regularly to ensure a smooth roll. Players must wear flat-soled shoes.

Dubai Creek Golf & Yacht Club

Opposite Deira City Centre Mall, Garhoud (295 6000). **Open** 7am-2.40pm (last 18-hole tee-off) daily. **Price** Dhs600 non-members, Dhs550 UGA members Sat, Thur, Fri; Dhs550 non-members, Dhs460 UGA members Mon-Wed. Includes shared cart & bucket of range balls. **Credit** AmEx, MC, V. **Map** p329 K3.

Smells like team spirit

If you're in town for long enough to pick up a strip, there's a plethora of social team sports played across the city. Leagues are generally well-structured with a timetable for both training and games, and there are some superb social events at full-time. If **football** is your thing, take a look at the Dubai Amateur League (www.dxb.league republic.com), which has 22 teams across two divisions. Seven-a-side games are held during the summer. If you're looking for a **women's team**, check out the women's league, which hold their matches at the pristine Jebel Ali pitches (email dubaiwf@ hotmail.com for more information). If you're more of a **netball** person, get in touch with

Donna Meyrick (dmmadge@gmail.com), who runs the Dubai league. Games are held at the emirate's only two netball courts, located at the Dubai Rugby Football Club.

Rugby is also extremely popular. The Dubai Rugby Football Club has a men's and women's team (331 1198). For something different, see what the **Dubai Rowing & Sculling Club** offers (www.dubairowingandscullingclub.com), who are based at Le Meridien Mina Seyahi Beach Resort & Marina. Or perhaps the **Dubai Hockey Club** is for you (www.dubaihockey club.com). If you can ice skate, why not have a go at ice hockey? Get in touch with the **Mighty Camels** (www.dubaimightycamels. com), who are sure to give you a few pointers.

www.poloclubdubai.com

DUBAI POLO CLUB

Come to see, or be seen.

Dubai Polo & Equestrian Club is the perfect destination for everything equestrian, and a lot more besides. Ideally located at Arabian Ranches, the Club is spread over 68 acres of majestic desert landscape. From polo, show jumping and dressage to horse riding and desert hacking, everything horse lovers could wish for is here. With 336 stables, 25 paddocks and international-standard polo, jumping and dressage arenas, this is truly a haven for horse lovers.

Away from the playing fields, the cool, Spanish-styled Clubhouse offers ample leisure and business facilities. Relax with friends or colleagues in one of four stylish lounges, dine at the exceptional restaurant, cool off in the crystal clear pool or pamper yourself at the spa. Exclusive membership options are now open ....

EMAAR

Dubai Polo & Equestrian Club, P.O. Box : 7477 Dubai, Tel : +971 4 3618111, Fax: +971 4 3617111, E-mail: info@poloclubdubai.com

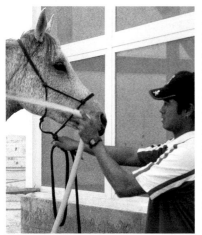

Horsing around at **Jebel Ali Horse Riding**.

The front nine of this luxury 18-hole, par 71 course was redesigned by local legend Thomas Bjorn. The par five 18th crowns this stunning course in the centre of the city. Luxury villas line the avenue leading to the landmark Creekside clubhouse, a towering building in the guise of a traditional sail. The meandering road also passes the 225-room Park Hyatt Dubai hotel (*see p51*).

Emirates Golf Club

Sheikh Zayed Road, off Interchange 5 (380 2222/ www.dubaigolf.com). **Open** 6am-3pm (last tee-off) daily. **Price** Dhs525. Non-members should book 18-hole sessions at least three days in advance through the Central Reservation Line (380 1234) if booking from other countries. **Credit** AmEx, MC, V. **Map** p336 B2.
Home to two fine courses and a Bedouin tent-inspired clubhouse, this is the most eye-catching golfing facility in the region. The 6,493m (21,302ft) Majlis course – the first grass facility in the Middle East – is home to the Dubai Desert Classic (*see p215*). Since 1996 it has been complemented by the 6,517m (21,381ft) Wadi course, which features 14 lakes and numerous bunkers. Both are par 72 courses and make good use of the natural rolling desert terrain to ensure a serious test for players of all abilities. Many experts consider this to be the premier club in Dubai.

Four Seasons Golf Club

Al Rebat Street, Al Badia (601 0101/www. fourseasons.com/dubaigolf). **Open** 6am-9.30pm daily. **Price** Dhs665 Sat-Thur; Dhs625 Sun-Wed. **Credit** AmEx, MC, V. **Map** p329 L3.
Al Badia golf course is the focal point of this Dubai Festival City golfing wonderland. Designed by Robert Trent Jones II, the 18-hole championship course has a desert oasis theme, and boasts a golf academy. *Photo p228.*

Montgomerie

Emirates Hills, Sheikh Zayed Road, off Interchange 5 (390 5600/www.themontgomerie.com). **Open** 6.30am-sundown (last tee-off) daily; twilight game 2.30pm-nightfall daily. **Price** Dhs675 non-members, Dhs495 UGA members Sat, Thur, Fri; Dhs675 non-members, Dhs420 UGA members Sun-Wed. *Twilight round* Dhs370 non-members, Dhs325 UGA members daily. **Credit** AmEx, MC, V. **Map** p336 B2.
The Montgomerie, designed by Scottish Ryder Cup star Colin Montgomerie, covers more than 200 acres of undulating links-style fairways. With 14 lakes and the small matter of 72 bunkers to avoid, drive placement is key here. Look out for the 13th hole and what is claimed to be the largest single green in the world, covering a staggering 5,394sq m (58,000sq ft). Less competitive golfers who simply want to practice will enjoy the Academy by Troon Golf, which boasts a state-of-the-art swing studio, a nine-hole, par-three Academy course, short game area, putting greens and 'dummy' fairway – all floodlit.

Horse riding

Jebel Ali Horse Riding

Jebel Ali Golf Resort & Spa (883 6000). **Open** *Oct-June* 7am-6pm daily. **Price** Dhs100/1hr adults & over-5s. **Credit** AmEx, MC, V.
Learn to ride around the paddock here, or, if you're a fully trained rider, head out to the desert around the hotel complex for a Dhs150 session.

Hot air ballooning

Amigos Balloons

(289 9295/www.amigos-balloons.com). **Open** (Pick up) 4.45am daily (depending on the weather). **Price** Dhs780/person or Dhs2,500 for a private balloon flight for two people. **Credit** AmEx, MC, V.
Take a trip over the desert spotting wildlife and cruising over villages and the oasis, followed by breakfast. Although the departure site isn't in Dubai itself, they'll drive you to and from the nearby Sharjah desert.

Karting

Dubai Autodrome

Off Sheikh Zayed Road, at Interchange 4 (367 8700/ www.dubaiautodrome.com). **Open** Varies. **Price** Dhs100/15-min session. **Credit** AmEx, MC, V. **Map** p326 B4.
This is a Federation Internationale de L'Automobile (FIM) sanctioned 5.39km (3.35miles) circuit, with six different configurations. It also has a race and driving school and a CIK-approved karting track. One day it may host Formula 1 racing, but for now you can go on one of their pro-karts that hit up to speeds of 100kmph (62mph). Children from seven years to 12 can also go karting, and there are special karts designed for them.

Active Dubai

desert palm
Dubai

LOCATION

A city of contrasts where outstanding modern architecture and soaring skyscrapers are juxtaposed with residential villas and traditional Arabic homes and then, a verdant retreat like Desert Palm. Your chauffeur meets you at the airport on arrival and escorts you to Desert Palm via a private luxury car, to begin your modern Arabian experience.

RESORT LEISURE FACILITIES

4 Full-size Championship Polo Fields
Polo Viewing Pavilions
Spa, Water Experience and Juice Bar
Infinity Swimming Pool
Private Business Centres and Meeting Room
Bar and Lounge
Rare- Wood-fired and Game Restaurant
Extensive International Wine Cellar
Poolside Cafe, Gourmet Market, Bakery,
Delicatessen, Gelateria
Wedding Pavilions

RESORT SERVICES

Airport Transfers
In-Room and In-villa Dining
Laundry, Dry Cleaning and Valet Services
In-room Personal Business Centre _ IDD
Telephone, Wi-fi Internet
DVD Library and IPod Music selection
Multi-lingual Staff
Concierge Service
Dedicated Butler Service in 'Villa Layali'
Facilities for Events, Weddings, Private Parties,
Conferences, Corporate Retreats

RESORT EXCURSIONS

Golf on World-class Courses
Flying Micro Lites over the Desert
Indoor Snow Skiing
4WD Adventures
Quad Bikes and Dune Buggies
Sky Diving and Bird Watching
Water Sports: Scuba, Sailing, Fishing, Waterskiing
Helicopter, Boar and Dhow Tours of Dubai
Horse and Camel Riding and Races
Shopping Expeditions and Art Gallery visits
Souk Exploration and City Tours

Postal Address: PO Box 103635
Dubai
United Arab Emirates
Phone: + 971 4323 8888
Fax: + 971 4323 8053

Reservations: reservations@desertpalm.ae
Information: info@desertpalm.ae

Take to the skies with **Umm Al Quwain Aeroclub**. *See p224.*

Emirates Kart Centre

Near Jebel Ali Golf Resort & Spa (050 559 2131/ www.emsf.ae). **Open** 2-10pm. **Price** Dhs100/30min session. Booking in advance is recommended. **No credit cards.**.
Go-kart around this custom-built 800m (2625ft) track with karts capable of 70kmph (43mph).

Kitesurfing

North Kites

Al Bahar showroom, Jumeirah Beach Road (394 1258/050 455 8976). **Open** 9am-9pm Sat-Thur; 4-9pm Fri. **Price** Dhs250/lesson, incl equipment. **Credit** AmEx, MC, V. **Map** p334 A15.
North Kites sells the boards and kites you need to start the sport; it also offers lessons and can give you details of other instructors.

Paintballing

Pursuit Games Paintball

Next to Wonderland Theme & Water Park, by Garhoud Bridge (050 651 4583/www.paintball dubai.com). **Open** 10am-10pm daily. **Price** Dhs75/2hr session, incl 100 paintballs; Dhs30/extra 50; Dhs50/extra 100. Discounts available for group bookings (minimum six people, 30 to take over the whole park). **No credit cards. Map** p329 K3.
This is a fenced-off 'zone' of desert scrubland, with strategically placed barricades to create choke and vantage points. Groups are divided into opposing

teams before being given protective overalls, face masks, 'guns' and paintballs, followed by a safety demonstration. The organisers claim they will open any time of the day or night to accommodate visitors.

Parasailing

Parasailing is a top way to see some aerial views of Dubai, and is far cheaper than a balloon ride, helicopter flight or skydive. All sports also now use special boats with a launch pad on the back, if you don't fancy racing along for miles before leaving the ground.

Nautica 1992

Based at the Habtoor Grand Resort & Spa (050 426 2415). **Open** 10am-5pm daily. **Price** Dhs200/single 15min flight; Dhs300 tandem (with weight limit). **Credit** AmEx, MC, V. **Map** p336 B1.

Quad biking

Quad biking is the ultimate way to zoom around the desert in the UAE (and be a right nuisance on normal roads). Head out to Big Red (*see p83*), an area of huge dunes made from red sand on the Dubai-Hatta Road, and pay around Dhs100 for an hour of engine-revving fun. There are no helmets included, however, and the area can get pretty busy – so watch out for hidden sharp falls on the other side of dunes and other bikers.

Active Dubai

Make a splash off the coast of Dubai.

Blue Banana

(369 7378/www.bluebanana.ae). **Price** Dhs395/hr.
Credit AmEx, MC, V.
Blue Banana will pick you up, deliver you to the
desert for quad biking and take you home again.
Minimum age 16. No driving licence required.

Sailing

Bluesail

*Dubai Creek, Bur Dubai, opposite British Embassy
on Al Seef Road (397 9730/050 506 8348/
www.bluesailyachts.com).* **Open** 9am-5pm daily.
Price Dhs4,000 to charter a yacht for half a day;
Dhs6,000/8 hrs. **Credit** AmEx, MC, V. **Map** p331 J4.
The highest qualified RYA sailing school in the
Middle East offers power and sail training for all lev-
els, from novice through to RYA Yachtmaster.
There are 42ft (13m) sail yachts available for char-
ter and corporate events.

Dubai Offshore Sailing Club

*Jumeirah Beach Road, by Miraj Gallery, KFC &
Hardees (394 1669/www.dosc.ae).* **Open** 8am-1am
daily. **Price** Dhs25 non-members (who must be
invited by a member); Dhs1,600/16hr private course;
Dhs1,000/16hr group course. **Credit** AmEx, MC, V.
Map p328 F5.
This non-profit club is typically abuzz with eager
sailors. Recognised by the Royal Yachting
Association, the DOSC offers courses all year
round in optimists, lasers and toppers (the Friday
and Saturday Cadet Club is popular with younger
enthusiasts). There are races held every Friday,
mooring facilities are provided and the club fronts
a full social calendar.

Scuba diving & snorkelling

It's possible to dive and snorkel all year round
off Dubai, but it should be noted that the dive
sites off the east coast of the UAE (*see p284*
Fujairah), are widely regarded as superior in

terms of visibility and marine life. Most Dubai-
based diving outfits organise trips to the east
coast (about two hours' drive away). You can
pick up snorkels, masks and fins at the dive
centres listed below, or find less expensive
flippers and face masks in the shops of any
Jumeirah beachside hotel.

Al Boom Diving

*Near Iranian Hospital, Al Wasl Road. (342 2993/
www.alboomdiving.com).* **Open** 10am-8pm daily.
Price *PADI Discover Scuba Diving experience*
Dhs550. *Scuba Diver course* Dhs1,500. *Open
Water course* Dhs2,000. **Credit** AmEx, MC, V.
Map p332 E9.
Al Boom is a five-star PADI dive centre offering
courses from beginner to instructor level, as well
as daily diving and snorkelling trips in Dubai,
Fujairah and Musandam.

Emirates Diving Association

*Heritage and Diving Village, Al Shindagha (393
9390/www.emiratesdiving.com).* **Open** 8am-4pm
daily. **Price** (Annual membership) Dhs100.
Credit AmEx, MC, V. **Map** p330 G3.
If you are already a trained diver, join EDA to
receive newsletters and information about diving in
the UAE, as well as trips abroad.

Pavilion Dive Centre

Jumeirah Beach Hotel (406 8827). **Open** 8am-
9.30pm daily. **Price** *PADI Discover Scuba Diving
experience* Dhs275. *Open Water course* Dhs2,050
(over 5 days). **Credit** AmEx, MC, V. **Map** p336 E1.
This accredited National Geographic PADI dive
centre can have you exploring a real shipwreck off
the Dubai coast in no time at all.

Scubatec

Sana Building, Karama (334 8988). **Open** 9am-
1.30pm, 4-8.30pm Sat-Thur. **Price** *PADI Discover
Scuba Diving experience* Dhs450. *Open Water course*
Dhs1,700. **Credit** AmEx, MC, V. **Map** p329 J2.
Scubatec is an accredited PADI dive centre that
offers diving charters.

Shooting

Jebel Ali Shooting Club

Near Jebel Ali Golf Resort & Spa (883 6555/ www.jebelali-international.com). **Open** 1-9pm Sat-Mon, Wed-Fri. **Price** Dhs150/30min lesson. **Credit** AmEx, MC, V.

A 30-minute drive from Dubai's centre, this is a great place to pulverise clay pigeons in peace. Full coaching is available, but make sure you keep your earphones on when you pull that trigger.

Ski & snowboarding

Dubai Ski Club

Ski Dubai, Mall of the Emirates (344 9897/www. dubaiskiclub.com). **Open** (Meeting) 5-7pm Sat; 10am Tue. **Price** (Membership) Dhs300. **Credit** AmEx, MC, V. **Map** p336 D2.

With nearly 900 members, the club organises races and social events, and membership allows you reduced slope fees and regular special offers on equipment, and even holidays.

Ski Dubai

Mall of the Emirates (409 4000/www.skidxb.com). **Open** 10am-midnight daily. **Price** (Introductory ski & snowboard lessons) Dhs130; Dhs175 subsequent lessons. (Free skiing or snowboarding) Dhs150/2hr session; Dhs130/2hr session children. **Credit** AmEx, MC, V. **Map** p336 D2.

Who wouldn't come to the desert and go skiing? One of Dubai's craziest ideas has been one of its biggest hits. After nearly two years, Ski Dubai is a firm favourite among tourists and expats alike, especially during the steamy summer months. For one incredibly low price you can hire all the necessary equipment, while on Mondays a DJ plays sounds to the freestyle session.

Speedboating

Bluesail

Dubai Creek, Bur Dubai, opposite British Embassy on Al Seef Road (397 9730/050 506 8348/www.bluesail yachts.com). **Open** 9am-5pm daily. **Price** (50ft/15m powerboat) Dhs200-Dhs2,500/hr. **Credit** AmEx, MC, V. **Map** p331 J4.

Go on Bluesail's 'Speed Boat Blast' or, alternatively, take the RYA Power 1 and 2 courses.

Surfing

Although many don't think of Dubai as a surf destination, the city does have its own gang of dedicated boarders. Umm Suqeim beach is the only spot where the tide hits the coast, due to all the offshore development in the Gulf. Check out www.surfersofdubai.com – this site has links to the security cameras at the Burj and therefore shows when the waves are ripe. The site also has links to where you can hire boards from.

Surf Dubai

By the Burj Al Arab, Jumeirah (050 504 3020/ www.surfingdubai.com). **Price** Dhs175/90min lesson; Dhs150 under-12s. **Credit** AmEx, MC, V. **Map** p336 E1.

Beginner's boards are provided and there are normal boards available to rent by the hour (Dhs50, or Dhs200 for the whole day). To organise a lesson you need to sign up to the mailing list on their website and look out for their regular forecasts.

Wakeboarding & waterskiing

Extremely in vogue at the moment in Dubai, wakeboarding is like a cross between snowboarding, waterskiing and surfing.

Dubai Water Sport Academy

Dubai Marina, Marina Walk (050 303 9700). **Open** 6am-7pm daily. **Price** Dhs150/15 mins. **Credit** AmEx, MC, V. **Map** p336 B1.

The Academy boasts qualified instructors for monoski, barefoot, wake and kneeboarding.

Nautica 1992

Based at the Habtoor Grand Beach Resort & Spa (050 426 2415). **Open** 10am-5pm daily. **Price** Dhs150/20 mins. **Credit** AmEx, MC, V. **Map** p336 B1.

Wakeboard School

Al Jazeera Hotel & Resort, Al Ghantoot (050 768 9504/www.thewakeboardschool.com). **Price** Dhs100/20 mins. **Credit** AmEx, MC, V.

Set in an ideal 4km-long saltwater channel on the UAE's largest private beach, the Wakeboard School is run by local champion Tom Ellis and is just 20 minutes drive from Jebel Ali.

Escape the sun – head to **Ski Dubai**.

Active Dubai

Sunset with taste.

MAYA
modern mexican cuisine

Relaxing at the rooftop bar at modern Mexican restaurant Maya is one of Dubai's defining moments. With amazing views, smooth grooves and cool cocktails, life does not get much better than this. During the warm winter months, it's the perfect social setting before, after or instead of dinner. Your sofa and sunset await. Maya Mexican cuisine with a modern twist.

For reservations call Jane at Le Royal Méridein Beach Resort & Spa Dubai on +971 (4) 316 5550

Health & Fitness

Whether you're looking to work out in a first-rate gym or be pampered by therapists boasting A-list clients, it's all here for the taking.

Double the pleasure, at **Talise** spa's honeymoon treatment room. *See p248.*

Beach clubs

Providing you're in Dubai during the cooler months – September to the end of May – you're likely to be blown away by the quality of the city's private beaches, most of which are set in hotel grounds. There may not be mile upon mile of sand, but what there is is pristine. Spending the day on a hotel beach can be costly if you're not an in-house guest, but it's an experience that you shouldn't miss out on, even if it's just for one day. You'll be waited on hand and foot while you lie on your sun lounger. And with the sun setting quite early, at around 6pm, it's worth waiting out to watch it disappearing behind the horizon.

Hotels cater to different budgets and requirements, so whether you're looking for the most luxurious and sophisticated or the most family friendly and good value, there'll be something to suit. Your dirhams will buy you access to the beach and swimming pool; some hotels include lunch. Water sports and spa treatments will incur an additional charge.

Outside the hotel grounds, you may find yourself chauffeured around unfinished landscaping. Dubai is permanently under construction, which can either be unsightly or interesting, depending on your point of view. There are some public beaches, but these aren't as impeccably looked after as those at hotels. For those on a budget, there are a couple of non-hotel beaches open to the public – Jumeirah Beach Park and Al Mamzar – where you pay a nominal fee. Both tend to get busy, particularly on Fridays, when most shops don't open until at least 4pm, and on Saturdays, but they do have maintained public conveniences, kiosks and sun loungers.

Club Joumana

Jebel Ali Golf Resort & Spa, Sheikh Zayed Road, Exit 13, past Interchange 7 (883 6000/www.jebelali-international.com). **Open** 9am-6pm daily. **Admission** *(Non-members) Sun-Thur* Dhs120; Dhs60 concessions. *Fri, Sat* Dhs200 incl lunch; Dhs100 concessions. **Credit** AmEx, MC, V. **Map** p336 A2.

About a 30-minute drive from the centre of Dubai, Club Joumana is known for its extremely friendly staff and unbroken peace and quiet. Miles from the bustle of the city centre, here you might choose to stretch out and doze on the club's lush lawns or engage in a variety of water sports available from the private beach. Activities include waterskiing, windsurfing, banana boating and sailing (catamaran and laser), while boat and fishing trips can also be organised. Back on dry land, Club Joumana boasts four floodlit tennis courts, a glass-backed squash court and a badminton court. There are also two fresh water pools, a sea water pool and a children's pool. Nearby is a par-36 nine-hole golf course and practice facilities. Make sure you get there as soon as it opens at the weekend (Friday and Saturday), as sometimes people are turned away from 10am due to the place's popularity.

Club Mina
Le Meridien Mina Seyahi Hotel, Al Sufouh Road, Jumeirah (399 3333/www.lemeridien-mina seyahi.com). **Open** 9am-7pm daily (members only Fri, Sat). **Admission** (Non-members) Dhs200 incl lunch; Dhs100 concessions. **Credit** AmEx, MC, V. **Map** p336 B1.
One of the trendier clubs in town, Club Mina's private beach stretches for about a kilometre and hosts many of the city's beautiful people whenever a powerboating race comes to town. If you can't beat 'em, join 'em; the relaxed beachside Barasti bar (*see p135*) is a terrific place to chill out. Club Mina's reputation for swank is borne out by excellent facilities, with three large swimming pools and two smaller shaded pools for children.

Dubai Marine Beach Resort & Spa
Dubai Marine Beach Resort & Spa, Beach Road (346 1111/www.dxbmarine.com). **Open** 8am-sunset daily. **Admission** (Non-members) Dhs200; Dhs100 concessions, incl lunch. **Credit** AmEx, MC, V. **Map** p332 D8.
The resort, a favourite with the occasional supermodel, features two pools, a kids' pool, a private beach and a tennis court; non-members can only book the court for tennis lessons.

Habtoor Grand Resort & Spa
Habtoor Grand Resort & Spa, Dubai Marina (399 5000/www.grandjumeirah.habtoorhotels.com). **Open** 7am-6pm daily. **Admission** (Non-members) *Sun-Thur* Dhs200; Dhs175 concessions. *Fri, Sat* Dhs225; Dhs150 concessions. **Map** p336 B1.
This is a busy beach club with three pools, one of which is a children's pool with a slide. If you're feeling energetic, there's beach volleyball, two floodlit tennis courts, two squash courts and water sports galore. You can have a break from the children by enrolling them in the junior Jungle Club for a few hours. If you need a bite to eat, there are plenty of restaurants to choose from.

Hiltonia Beach & Pool
Hilton Dubai Jumeirah Hotel, Al Sufouh Road, Jumeirah (399 1111/www.hilton.com). **Open** *Beach* 7am-sunset daily. *Pool* 7am-8pm daily. **Admission** *Sun-Thur* Dhs130. *Fri, Sat* Dhs180; Dhs55 4-16s. Under-3s free. **Credit** AmEx, MC, V. **Map** p336 B1.
There's no shortage of things to do here: water sports include parasailing, kayaking, jet-skiing, knee-boarding and fishing trips. Or you could just lie next to the pool and beach in order to show off a bronzed bod when you get home. As you'd expect

from a Hilton hotel, there's an emphasis on luxury; the pools are surrounded by landscaped gardens and there's a fairly pleasant beach.

Jebel Ali Golf Resort & Spa
See p237 Club Joumana.

Jumeirah Beach Park
Jumeirah Beach Road (050 858 9887/349 2555). **Open** 7am-10.30pm daily (women-only Mon). **Admission** Dhs 5 or Dhs20 per car. **No credit cards**. **Map** p334 A15.
There aren't that many facilities at the beach, but if you're after some relaxation, pack up your beach bag, grab a sun lounger and chill out for the day. This is one of the cheapest beaches in town, meaning that it is always busy. There's also a café selling junk food, a barbecue area, a children's playground and changing rooms.

Al Mamzar
Al Mamzar Creek, by the Sharjah border (296 6201). **Open** 9am-6pm daily. **Admission** Dhs5; Dhs30/ family of 4. **No credit cards**. **Map** p331 K1.
If you don't fancy the crowds at Jumeirah Beach Park, head for Al Mamzar. It doesn't have a café by the beach, but shower facilities and kiosks are dotted along the coast. There are sun loungers, but these tend to be in the main areas, so if you want a quieter spot, take a beach mat and camp down for the afternoon. As with everywhere in Dubai, Friday is busy, but if you venture out to Al Mamzar during the week, you should enjoy some peace and quiet. The beach is a good size, unlike at some hotels, so should you want to take a walk along the sand, this is the place to do it.

Oasis Beach Club
Oasis Beach Hotel, Al Sufouh Road, Jumeirah (315 4034/www.jebelali-international.com). **Open** 7am-8pm daily. **Admission** (Non-members) *Sun-Wed* Dhs85. *Thur, Fri* Dhs140; Dhs50-Dhs70 concessions. **Credit** AmEx, MC, V. **Map** p331 B1.
There are many sports facilities on offer at this lively club, which tends to attract a young, active crowd with lots of families. There is a floodlit tennis court, beach volleyball and water sports including windsurfing, wakeboarding, waterskiing, banana boat rides and snorkelling. A large pool with a swim-up bar and the Coco Cabana beachside restaurant make for a lively and relaxed atmosphere. Non-guests at the hotel can apply for 'Neighbourhood Privilege Club' membership. This is free and entitles holders to ten per cent discount on food and drink at the weekend (Friday and Saturday) and 20 per cent discount during the week.

Pavilion Marina & Sports Club
Jumeirah Beach Hotel (348 0000/www.jumeirah beachhotel.com). **Open** 7am-10pm daily. **Admission** (Non-members) Dhs400 (incl Dhs100 food voucher); Dhs200 concessions (incl Dhs50 food voucher). **Credit** AmEx, MC, V. **Map** p336 E1.
This upmarket beach club is popular with families as there are so many activities to choose from. If

Sheraton Jumeirah Health & Beach Club.

you're after water sports, then windsurfing, water-skiing and kayaking are available, plus banana boat rides and yacht charters, while if you simply feel like lounging by the water, there are four pools. Those who like their sports to be land-based can book themselves in for a few sets of tennis or practise their putting on the mini driving range. If you feel like a break from the little ones, simply pack them off to Sinbad's Kids' Club.

Ritz-Carlton Beach Club

Ritz-Carlton Dubai Hotel, Al Sufouh Road, Jumeirah (399 4000/www.ritzcarlton.com). **Open** 6am-10pm daily. **Admission** Dhs300-Dhs500; Dhs150-Dhs300 concessions. **Credit** AmEx, MC, V. **Map** p336 B1.
Despite the mess of construction edging closer and closer to this haven of tranquillity, the Ritz-Carlton Beach Club is still a spectacular place. For starters there is a 350m (120ft) stretch of private beach as well as vast landscaped gardens. Facilities include four floodlit tennis courts, a grass football pitch, two squash courts, pitch and putt golf and a comprehensively equipped gym. Personal trainers are on hand to answer any fitness questions, and classes available include power yoga and women-only 'aerotennis', a cross between aerobics and the racket sport. The spa now features two women-only treatment rooms, taking the overall total to ten, with a range of appealing options stretching from Balinese-style massage to Scentao hot stone therapy. Water sports can be organised on request for an additional cost.

Sheraton Jumeirah Health & Beach Club

Sheraton Jumeirah Beach Resort, Al Sufouh Road, Jumeirah (399 5533/www.sheraton.com/jumeirah beach). **Open** 7am-10pm daily (no pool lifeguards after 7pm). **Admission** (Non-members) *Sat, Fri* Dhs125. *Sun-Thur* Dhs100; Dhs50 children; free under-6s. **Credit** AmEx, MC, V. **Map** p336 A1.
As well as two swimming pools, two floodlit tennis courts and two squash courts, the club has a gym packed with the usual array of bikes, steppers, rowing machines and treadmills. Add in volleyball,

a range of water sports and a sauna and steam room, and you won't run out of things to do in a hurry. Or you could just treat yourself to a hot-stone massage (50 mins, Dhs310) or a vitamin facial (60 mins, Dhs425) at the Armonia spa.

Health clubs

There are gyms and health clubs galore in Dubai, with lots of hotel fitness centres vying for the local market as well as hotel guests. Many of the hotels sell day passes, which allow you to use their gym, pool and beach facilities. While the cost of this adds up if you're living in the city, it might be worthwhile if you're on holiday. Since most of Dubai has sprung up in the last five years or so, the gyms and spas are all pretty new, with modern equipment and trendy decor. The conservative local culture means that lots of gyms are for men or women only or that there are separate gyms. You normally find, at the very least, that there are separate saunas and steam rooms. Often if there is one gym, there will be women- or men-only times, so it's worth ringing ahead before you go along to check you can work out when you want to. If you're looking for professional instruction in a gym, you might not find it here. Staff tend to be unqualified, so it's worth asking about qualifications before you book a personal training session.

Aviation Club

Garhoud (282 4122/www.aviationclub.ae). **Open** 6am-11pm daily. **Admission** Dhs150/day; Dhs300/wk; Dhs900/mth. **Credit** AmEx, MC, V. **Map** p329 K3.
Home to the prestigious Dubai Duty Free Tennis Open and one of the few clubs to establish itself on the Deira side of the Creek, the Aviation Club is an incredibly popular option. An extensive upgrade was completed mid 2005 to ensure it remains at the forefront of the fitness scene, including the construction of separate spas for ladies and men and additional group exercise studios. It boasts an impressive list of facilities, namely ten floodlit tennis courts, a swimming pool with 25m (82ft) lap lanes, two squash courts, a dedicated spinning studio, a sauna, a steam room, plunge pools and a fully equipped gym. The club's aerobics studio continues to be the biggest and busiest in Dubai, hosting several fat-busting classes a day.

Big Apple

Jumeirah Emirates Towers Boulevard mall, Sheikh Zayed Road (319 8661/www.jumeirahinternational. com). **Open** 6am-11pm daily. **Admission** *Gym* Dhs60; Dhs530/mth. *Classes* Dhs35. **Credit** AmEx, MC, V. **Map** p328 H4.
Tucked away in the lower levels of the Jumeirah Emirates Towers, the Big Apple is a highly polished chrome and steel affair, the epitome of modern urban

Active Dubai

japanese restaurant & lounge

dubai marine - beach resort & spa
pobox 5182, jumeirah - dubai - uae
tel. +971 4 3461111 - fax +971 4 3541023
w w w . s h o - c h o . c o m

fitness centres. It lacks swimming, sauna or steam room facilities, but is armed to the teeth with state-of-the-art equipment, meaning you probably won't find yourself hanging around to use the treadmill or stepper. Aerobics classes cover everything from body pump to spinning and in the winter there are a couple of outdoor sessions on offer. If you fancy a fitness overhaul, book yourself in for an assessment and personal training session or two. One session is enough to deliver your own training regime.

Bodylines

Al Bustan Rotana, Garhoud (705 4119/www.albustanrotanahoteldubai.com). **Open** 6am-10pm daily. **Admission** *Sat, Fri* Dhs75; Dhs50 concessions. *Sun-Wed* Dhs100; Dhs30 concessions; *Thur* Dhs100; no concessions. **Credit** AmEx, MC, V. **Map** p329 K2.
Bodylines offer exceptionally good value day passes and aerobic-type classes for both members and non-members. The gym here is basic, but adequate for a workout, and it doesn't get too busy. Other facilities include two squash courts, three floodlit tennis courts, and both adult and children's swimming pools on the roof. You might also want to relax in their sauna, steam room or outdoor Jacuzzi after your workout. **Other locations:** Towers Rotana, Sheikh Zayed Road (312 2556).

Club Olympus

Hyatt Regency Hotel, Deira Corniche (209 6802/www.dubai.regency.hyatt.com). **Open** 6am-11pm daily (incl pool). **Admission** (Non-members) Dhs100. **Credit** AmEx, MC, V. **Map** p331 J1.

Friendly, professional staff attract a varied clientele to this city centre club. Classes range from aerobics to yoga, while also on offer is a gym and running track, which circles the two floodlit tennis courts. A pair of squash courts, an outdoor swimming pool, a sauna, a steam room, a Jacuzzi and a splash pool complete the line-up of facilities. The outside deck is particularly popular in the cooler winter months.

Colosseum Muay Thai Health & Fitness Club

Montana Building, Zabeel Road, Karama (337 2755/www.colosseumuae.com). **Open** 6am-midnight Sat-Wed; noon-10pm Thur, Fri. **Admission** Dhs50. **Credit** AmEx, MC, V. **Map** p331 J5.
Those into martial arts tend to be fanatical, so if you can't live without a few kicks while on holiday, Colosseum is a dedicated martial arts centre. The club boasts five boxing studios, an outdoor swimming pool, sauna and Jacuzzi. On the class front, karate, Thai boxing, aikido and kick boxing classes are available.

Dimension Health & Fitness Club

Metropolitan Hotel, Sheikh Zayed Road, Interchange 2 (407 6704/www.habtoorhotels.com). **Open** 6am-midnight daily. **Admission** *Gym* Sat-Thur Dhs50; Fri Dhs60. *Classes* Dhs30-Dhs35. **Credit** AmEx, MC, V. **Map** p328 G5.
The Metropolitan is one of the older complexes in Dubai, but Dimension packs a well-equipped gym with an assortment of free weights and Nautilus equipment. Its 25m (82ft) outdoor swimming pool is

Actively alternative

Mall joggers

A community spirited shopping mall may sound like a rather doubtful prospect, yet the Mall of the Emirates (*see p145*) seems to be on its way to becoming one since the management organised a walking group that traverses the mall daily. The mall's spread over a whopping 6.5 million square feet (600,000 square metres), so it's more than big enough for a calorie-burning stroll – a great alternative to a boring treadmill during the hot summer months. The group doesn't run, as the concrete floor can be detrimental to your long-term health, but if you fancy a 30-minute fast-paced walk in the dead heat of summer, get yourself down to the mall one morning (and make sure you have your credit card ready in case you want to do more than just window shop afterwards).

Nordic walking

It sounds unlikely, but you can now go Nordic walking in the desert. The sport sprang up in

health-conscious Finland in the late 1990s and you will now see everyone from children to grannies walking around Helsinki with poles. To the uninitiated it looks strange, with people walking with sticks that look like ski poles, but this new exercise offers a whole host of health benefits. Those looking for a painless path into exercise will love the fact that your workout is as easy as a walk in the park, but much more effective. Instead of just exercising your legs, the poles force you to work out your upper body too, which takes some pressure off the knee joints and helps you burn an average of 400 instead of 280 calories an hour. If you want to have a go at Nordic walking, contact Deborah at Stride For Life – the only qualified coach working in the UAE – on 050 657 7057. Or visit www.strideforlife.com.

one of its main attractions, although there is also a Jacuzzi, steam room and sauna. The studio offers various classes, including fencing and yoga. The Dimension Club is something of a one-stop shop, offering Indian and Chinese-style massage to those too tired to pump more iron. Worth a trip just to check out the dated 1970s-looking lobby.

Dubai Creek Golf & Yacht Club

(295 6000/www.dubaigolf.com). **Open** 6am-9pm daily. **Admission** *Membership* Dhs300/mth. **Credit** AmEx, MC, V. **Map** p329 K3.

The state of the art health club situated inside the plush Dubai Creek Golf & Yacht Club is a consistently popular choice and it's easy to understand why – members can enjoy great views of the Creek while working out. If you have never used a gym before then the Creek is a great bet, with a professional fitness instructor on hand to guide you through the equipment. After something more idle? A one-hour massage is competitively priced at Dhs100 for members. Once you've put in the hours at the gym, relax and refuel in one of the Creek's eateries.

Dubai Ladies Club

Jumeirah Beach Road, near Jumeirah Beach Park (349 9922/www.dubailadiesclub.com). **Open** 8am-10pm daily. **Admission** *Membership* Dhs1,500/mth. *Classes* Dhs35; Dhs360/12 classes. **Credit** MC, V. **Map** p334 A15.

Dubai Ladies Club is more than just a gym; it's a community centre. There are plenty of aerobics classes to choose from alongside other options including yoga (indoors and outdoors), tae kwon do, tae-bo and aqua aerobics. The club's facilities include squash courts, tennis courts, basketball courts and beach volleyball, some of which are for members only, while others are available for a nominal charge. Prices are reasonable.

Dubai World Trade Centre Apartments Club

Sheikh Zayed Road (306 5050). **Open** 7am-10pm daily. **Admission** *Sat-Thur* Dhs60. *Fri* Dhs85. *Classes* Dhs30-Dhs40. **Credit** AmEx, MC, V. **Map** p333 G10.

In addition to a decent gym, there's an outdoor swimming pool, four tennis courts, a basketball court, squash courts, a steam room, a sauna and a Jacuzzi to be found at this Sheikh Zayed Road club. Also on offer are some martial arts and dance classes.

Fitness First

Ibn Battuta Mall (366 9933). **Open** 6.30am-10pm Sat-Thur; 9am-9pm Fri. **Admission** Dhs100. **Credit** AmEx, MC, V. **Map** p336 A2.

Fitness First has finally arrived in town. In addition to the Ibn Battuta branch, there is a Fitness First outlet in Uptown Mirdif, which unlike the Ibn branch has a pool. More branches are planned, one on Sheikh Zayed Road and another at Dubai Festival City. Members can choose from a host of classes and can also take advantage of the saunas and steam rooms. **Other locations**: BurJuman Centre (351 0044); Uptown Mirdif (288 2311).

Fitness Planet

Al Hana Centre, Al Dhiyafah Road, Satwa (398 9030). **Open** *Mixed gym* 6am-11pm Sat-Wed; 6am-10am, 4-10pm Fri. *Women's gym* 7am-9pm Sat-Thur. **Admission** (Non-members) Dhs40; Dhs225/10 visits. **Credit** AmEx, MC. **Map** p333 F8.

The emphasis at this busy gym is on free weights and resistance machines, so expect to see some serious bodybuilders and weightlifters. For women who might find the mixed gym a bit intimidating, there's a separate women's area, Fitness Planet Hers, on the mezzanine level. Facilities include a Jacuzzi, steam room and sauna.

Griffin's Health Club

JW Marriott, Deira (607 7755/www.marriott.com). **Open** 6am-11pm daily. **Admission** *Sat, Fri* Dhs77. *Sun-Thur* Dhs99. *Classes* Dhs30. **Credit** AmEx, MC, V. **Map** p329 K1.

There are two squash courts, an outdoor swimming pool, a spa and Jacuzzi and a gym with a separate cardio room at this reasonably priced health club. Classes include aerobics, spinning and step.

Health Club & Spa

Shangri-La Hotel, Dubai, Sheikh Zayed Road (405 2441/www.shangri-la.com). **Open** 6am-midnight daily. **Admission** *Sat, Fri* Dhs220. *Sun-Thur* Dhs180. *Classes* Dhs40. **Credit** AmEx, MC, V. **Map** p335 F12.

Despite this club's upmarket location, this is a distinctly average hotel-based gym. However, the off-peak membership rates are reasonable enough to make it worth a punt. If you prefer group exercise sessions to gym workouts, then get yourself along to one of the many hatha yoga, martial arts and salsa classes on offer here.

Lifestyle Health Club

Sofitel City Centre Hotel, Port Saeed (603 8825/www.accorhotels.com). **Open** 6.30am-11pm Sat-Thur; 8am-8pm Fri. **Admission** *Gym* Dhs50. *Classes* Dhs30. **Credit** AmEx, MC, V. **Map** p329 K2.

This hotel-based club stretches over three floors: the reception, two squash courts, sauna and steam room are on one level; the gym and aerobics studio on the next; and an outdoor swimming pool and floodlit tennis court are on the roof. The gym is packed with resistance and cardiovascular machines; different aerobic classes are held each day in the studio.

Natural Elements Spa & Fitness

Le Meridien Dubai, Garhoud (702 2430/www.dubai.lemeridien.com). **Open** 6am-10pm daily. **Admission** Dhs150. *Classes* Dhs50 non-members; Dhs25 members. **Credit** AmEx, MC, V. **Map** p329 L2.

Besides a gym with some free weights and cardio machines, there's also a 25m (82ft) lap outdoor pool, three tennis courts and a Jacuzzi and steam rooms. There's also a separate ladies' gym, and the Power Plate – for those who want to end up with a stomach that's as flat as Madonna's (it's a favourite of the diva). Aerobic classes are mainly held in the evenings.

Nautilus Academy

Al Mussalla Towers, Khalid Bin Al Waleed Road (Bank Street), Bur Dubai (397 4117). **Open** 6am-11pm daily. **Admission** (1-mth pass) Dhs825 men; Dhs715 women. **Credit** AmEx, MC, V. **Map** p330 H4.
One of Dubai's best-equipped gyms, fielding all manner of Nautilus machines (as you might expect) and cardiovascular equipment, this fitness club falls right in the heart of the city. Increasingly popular, Nautilus no longer sells day passes as a rule but will sometimes makes an exception on quiet days to short-term visitors. Separate studios exist for spinning classes and aerobics, as well as two squash courts. There is also a small outdoor pool, a steam room, a sauna and a Jacuzzi.

Nautilus Fitness Centre

Crowne Plaza Hotel, Sheikh Zayed Road (331 4055). **Open** 24 hrs daily. **Admission** Dhs70 per day; Dhs800 1-mth pass. *Classes* Dhs35 members. **Credit** AmEx, MC, V. **Map** p333 G10.
The focus at this centre is on Nautilus fitness training techniques, but there are also free weights and an array of cardiovascular machines. The long list of aerobics classes stretches from yoga to belly dancing – for those who want something a bit more exotic. Other facilities include a squash court, table tennis, a sauna, a steam room and an outdoor swimming pool.

U Concept.
See p244.

Pharaohs Club

Wafi Pyramids at Wafi City Mall, off Oud Metha Road (324 0000/www.waficity.com). **Open** 7am-10pm Sat-Thur; 9am-9pm Fri. **Admission** Dhs450 1-wk pass; Dhs1,200 1-mth pass. *Classes* Dhs30 non-members; Dhs20 members. **Credit** AmEx, MC, V. **Map** p329 J3.
Still one of the most prestigious clubs in Dubai, Pharaohs offers members luxurious surroundings and an impressive array of facilities. There are well-equipped gyms for men and women. Steam rooms, plunge pools and Jacuzzis are also provided, as well as a large swimming pool and a separate pool in which, with a flick of a switch, you can attempt to swim against the tide. The club also boasts a climbing wall, three floodlit tennis courts, two squash courts and a comprehensive range of fitness classes.

Radisson Health Club

Radisson SAS Deira Dubai Creek Dubai, Deira (222 7171/www.deiracreek.dubai.radissonsas.com). **Open** 24 hrs daily. **Admission** *Sat, Fri* Dhs55. *Sun-Thur* Dhs55. **Credit** AmEx, MC, V. **Map** p331 J3.
What makes this gym stand out is that it is one of only two 24-hour gyms in town that we know of (the other being Nautilus Fitness Centre; *see above*), meaning that you've got absolutely no excuse not to fit a session into your busy schedule. If, however, you like group exercise classes, this isn't the place for you as none are available. Facilities include an outdoor swimming pool, a tennis court, a squash court, a steam room and a sauna.

Shapes Wellness & Spa

Dubai Knowledge Village (367 2137/www.shapeshealthclub.com). **Open** 6am-9pm Sat-Thur. **Admission** Dhs35. **Credit** MC, V. **Map** p336 C2.
A great gym for men and women who are trying hard to lose the lard. The owner, Sam, doesn't believe in treadmills which he thinks are tedious, so there are lots of interesting classes available to help you achieve your weight-loss goals; these include inch-loss callanetics, salsa and belly dancing. The word on the street is that those who come here regularly are much slimmer in a matter of months. There's a separate female gym and a steam room to unwind in after class.

Taj Palace Hotel Health Club

Between Al Rigga Road & Al Maktoum Road, Deira (223 2222/www.tajhotels.com). **Open** 7am-11pm daily. **Admission** *Gym* Dhs70. *Pool* Dhs50. *Membership* Dhs500 women, Dhs600 men for 1-mth. **Credit** AmEx, MC, V. **Map** p331 L3.
Equipment here is modern and membership prices are reasonable; both of which combine to make it a good choice for anyone after a gym in Deira. The gym is mixed and there's an outside swimming pool, a sauna, a steam room and a Jacuzzi. If you want to stop for some authentic Indian cuisine after your workout, make sure you try the excellent Handi restaurant (*see p108*).

Active Dubai

U Concept

Village Mall, Jumeirah (344 9060/www.uconcept6. com). **Open** 6am-9pm Sat-Thur. **Admission** Dhs300/personal training session. **Credit** AmEx, MC, V. **Map** p332 D9.

An ultra-trendy members-only gym, U Concept creates personal training and nutrition programmes with the busy professional in mind. If group exercise is your bag, however, then you best give U Concept a wide berth, as group classes aren't part of their philosophy. Sports massage and therapy is also available, as well as private yoga and pilates classes. *Photo p243.*

Willow Stream Spa & Health Club

Fairmont Dubai, Sheikh Zayed Road (311 8800/ www.fairmont.com). **Open** 6am-midnight daily. **Admission** Dhs200. *Classes* Dhs30-Dhs40. **Credit** AmEx, MC, V. **Map** p333 G9.

This medium-sized gym offers one of the best views in town. There's nothing more awful than working out in a basement of a building with no natural light, so here the windows have been fitted all the way round the gym, making it possible to watch the planes fly by outside. If you're not a plane spotter, there are also plenty of TVs to keep you occupied and entertained during your workout. The day pass includes the use of a steam room and sauna and there's a separate gym available for women. Group workouts, bums and tums, step, hatha yoga and hip hop are all on offer.

Spas

Holidays in Dubai normally revolve around five-star hotels, so it's no surprise that there's a spa culture. Whether you've come here for some upmarket relaxation time or are travelling on a budget, you shouldn't miss out on a spa session. Not all spas are located in hotels; with Dubai's huge Indian population, some interesting ayurvedic treatments are available in small centres around the city. As well as the usual facials and massages, you can also find a plethora of alternative therapies. You should find the service excellent; the only difficulty is deciding which spa and salon to plump for.

1847

Boulevard at Jumeirah Emirates Towers, Sheikh Zayed Road (330 1847). **Open** 9am-10pm daily. **Cost** *Massage* Dhs220/hr. **Credit** AmEx, MC, V. **Map** p328 H4.

One for the gents, 1847 offers a range of high-end services from shaves and facials, to manicures, pedicures and massages.

Other locations: Grosvenor House, West Marina Beach Dubai (399 8989).

Akaru Spa

Aviation Club, Garhoud (282 8578/www.akaru spa.com). **Open** *Men's spa* 10am-10pm Sat, Fri. 2-10pm Sun-Thur; *Women's spa* 10am-10pm daily. **Cost** *Massage* Dhs230/hr. **Credit** AmEx, MC, V. **Map** p329 K3.

This pleasant, warmly decorated spa offers all the usual suspects of facials, massages and body wraps, but for pure, lulling, dream-like ambience plump for one of their signature packages. We particularly like 'relax', which consists of a body scrub, aromatic body massage and a facial. At Dhs475, it's an expensive indulgence – but a wonderful one. Akaru uses Decléor, Thalgo and Nickel products, which are exclusively for men.

Alasalla Spa

Dubai Ladies Club (349 9922/www.dubailadies club.com). **Open** 9am-10pm daily. **Cost** *Massage* Dhs280/hr. **Credit** AmEx, MC, V. **Map** p334 A15.

The treatments available here are Arabian-inspired and specifically for women. Choose one of their many hammam sessions; once you've indulged, you'll want to go back again and again.

Amara

Park Hyatt Dubai (602 1660/www.dubai.park. hyatt.com). **Open** 9am-10pm daily. **Cost** *Massage* Dhs350/hr. **Credit** MC, V. **Map** p329 K3.

Amara is set in the Park Hyatt Dubai's Moroccan-style hotel and is probably the trendiest spa in the city. If your environment matters to you as much as your treatment, book yourself in here and it's unlikely you'll be disappointed. Each of the treatment rooms comes with a private courtyard and outdoor rain shower. After your session, you'll be treated to herbal tea and dried fruits in the courtyard and given some relaxation time before having to leave. The good news is that you can pay to hang out longer. The spa exclusively stocks Anne Semonin's herbal-based products and also uses local organic brand Shiffa, as well as the exclusive Carita brand.

Angsana Spa

Level 2, Marina Walk, Dubai Marina (368 4356/ www.angsanaspa.com). **Open** 10am-10pm daily. Last booking 8.30pm. **Cost** *Massage* Dhs330/hr. **Credit** AmEx, MC, V. **Map** p336 B1.

Angsana's signature treatment is the Dhs450 Angsana massage, which consists of a two-hour pummelling with oils that combines Asian and European techniques. Facials cost from Dhs280 and massages cost from Dhs330.

Other locations: Arabian Ranches (361 8251); Montgomerie Golf Course (360 9322).

Aroma Spa

Dubai Marine Beach Resort & Spa, Jumeirah Beach Road (304 8081/www.dxbmarine.com). **Open** 9am-9pm daily. **Cost** *Massage* Dhs280/hr. **Credit** AmEx, MC, V. **Map** p332 D8.

Guests staying in the secluded chalets at the charming but well-worn Beach Resort & Spa will likely be the sort of folk who appreciate some private downtime. This low-key spa boasts 11 qualified therapists who use upmarket Guinot and Espa beauty products. There are three treatment rooms where visitors can enjoy relaxing massages, facials (from Dhs290) and body treatments.

Assawan Spa & Health Club

Burj Al Arab Hotel, Beach Road, Jumeirah
(301 7338/www.burj-al-arab.com/spa). **Open**
6.30am-10.30pm daily. **Cost** *Massage* Dhs550/hr.
Credit AmEx, MC, V. **Map** p336 E1.
This lavishly decorated club is located on the 18th
floor of Dubai's iconic landmark, providing spectacular views of the Gulf. There are separate male
and female areas boasting a total of eight spa treatment rooms, a sauna, a steam bath, a plunge pool, a
Jacuzzi and a solarium. Espa and La Prairie facials
are offered, as well as wraps, massages and hot
stone treatments. Don't expect all this to come cheap
– a one hour basic massage will set you back Dhs550
– but if you're seeking a truly once-in-a-lifetime
experience then this is the place to head. Non-guests
can also book treatments here (minimum duration
two hours), subject to availability.

Caracalla Spa

Le Royal Meridien Hotel, Al Sufouh Road, Jumeirah
(399 5555/www.leroyalmeridien-dubai.com).
Open 9.30am-9pm daily. **Cost** *Massage* Dhs300/hr.
Credit AmEx, MC, V. **Map** p336 B1.
This spa is normally only open to hotel guests and
members of the Caracalla Club. Other visitors and
residents can book treatments if there are any free
slots, but such is the popularity of this venue that
this is rare indeed. Dedicated steam and sauna
rooms plus a Jacuzzi serve both men and women.
Treatments available include the one-hour 'well-
being' (face and body) massages and exotic facials.

Cleopatra's Spa

Wafi Pyramids by Wafi City Mall, off Oud Metha
Road, Bur Dubai (324 7700/www.waficity.com).
Open *Women's spa* 8.30am-8pm daily. *Men's*
spa 10am-10pm daily. **Cost** *Massage* Dhs325/hr.
Credit AmEx, MC, V. **Map** p329 J3.
For the ultimate in spa treatments you can't go far
wrong with the luxurious Cleopatra's. As the name
implies, the whole facility has an Egyptian theme;
larger-than-life statues outside Wafi Pyramids give
way to a far more sophisticated and visually stunning
interior. The usual facials, massages and wraps complement some very different treatments. Among these
is the gorgeous aroma stone massage, in which the
body is massaged with hot energy-filled 'batu' stones
from Indonesia, and exotic oils. Ayurvedic treatments
are also offered, as is ionithermie – a detox and slimming treatment to tone muscles and smooth the skin.

Comfort Zone Spa

Paris Gallery, BurJuman Centre (359 5334). **Open**
11am-9pm Sat-Thur; 3-9pm Fri. **Cost** *Massage*
Dhs250/hr. **Credit** AmEx, MC, V. **Map** p331 J5.
Comfort Zone offers a wide range of treatments
to rejuvenate your skin and relax a weary body.
Try their Dhs350, 90-minute hydratherapy facial
that deeply cleansers and instantly plumps
your complexion. Comfort Zone's your best bet if
you want a break from shopping til you drop.
Other locations: Deira City Centre (294 4000).

Akaru Spa.

Assawan Spa & Health Club.

Active Dubai

TOMATOES, ONION & GARLIC
THAT CAN ONLY HAVE BEEN GROWN BY
NATURE'S MOTHER HERSELF.

A new kind of Italian eatery.
A menu of fabulous authentic ingredients, cooked to perfection!
Bring some friends!

sanaBontà
WHOLESOME GOODNESS IN ITALIAN

LEVEL B1. UNIT 2. THE GATE BUILDING. DUBAI INTERNATIONAL FINANCIAL CENTRE. 04 4250326

Elche Natural Beauty Retreat

Villa 42, Street 10, behind Jumeirah Plaza (349 4942/www.elche.ae). **Open** 10am-7.30pm Sat-Thur. **Cost** *Facial* Dhs325/hr. **Credit** MC, V. **Map** p332 D9.

This idiosyncratic spa offers organic skincare treatments for women by trained Hungarian therapists. Herbalists hand-pick the ingredients, and the company's founder, Ilcsi Molnar, a beautician and herbalist, makes up the lotions and potions. Organic beauty products are still catching on in Dubai, so Elche is a find for boho babes on their hols.

Elixir Spa & Health Club

Habtoor Grand Resort & Spa, Dubai Marina (399 5000/www.habtoorhotels.com). **Open** 8.30am-10pm daily. **Cost** *Massage* Dhs320/50mins. **Credit** AmEx, MC, V. **Map** p336 B1.

The Habtoor's spa boasts five treatment rooms, a dry float room and a tanning booth. The spa menu offers something for both men and women, with massages starting from Dhs320 (with most around Dhs400) and facials from Dhs450.

Givenchy Spa

One&Only Royal Mirage Hotel, Al Sufouh Road, Jumeirah (399 9999/www.royalmiragedubai.com). **Open** *Women-only* 9am-1pm daily. *Mixed* 1-9pm daily. **Cost** *Massage* Dhs280/hr. **Credit** AmEx, MC, V. **Map** p336 C1.

The magnificent Health & Beauty Institute at the Royal Mirage Spa covers an area of 2,000sq m (21,500sq ft), divided over two levels. On the upper floor, the formal Givenchy Spa has separate areas and opening times for women; the rest of the time, it's mixed. It features 12 treatment rooms including an exclusive suite for private consultations, a resting area and a Givenchy boutique. The lower floor boasts an authentic oriental hammam with a traditional heated marble massage table, plus two steam rooms and two private massage rooms. The institute marries contemporary decor with the hotel's Moroccan-fort theme, to great effect: this is arguably the most heavenly escape in Dubai. Two Jacuzzis, a whirlpool and a plunge shower are also available.

Grand Spa

Grand Hyatt Dubai (317 1234/www.dubai.grand. hyatt.com). **Open** 9am-9pm daily. **Cost** *Massage* Dhs300-Dhs350/hr. **Credit** AmEx, MC, V. **Map** p329 K3.

This modern and tasteful candlelit spa stocks luxurious New York brands June Jacobs and Bella Lucce. Well-trained therapists perform skin-enhancing facials (from Dhs420) and massages. It's worth noting that prices for treatments are higher for bookings made after 3pm.

H2O Male Spa

Jumeirah Emirates Towers (391 8181/www.jumeirah emiratestowers.com). **Open** 9am-11pm daily. **Cost** *Massage* Dhs300/55mins. **Credit** AmEx, MC, V. **Map** p328 H4.

H2O provides a range of therapies for men, including manicures, pedicures, tanning, waxing, facial therapy and massage. For something different, however, give the flotation pool (Dhs300) and Oxygen Lounge (Dhs75-Dhs300) a try. The first is a unique relaxation treatment involving an hour inside a salt water tank, floating in privacy while listening to soothing music – said to be as refreshing as eight hours of deep sleep. And in case you didn't feel refreshed enough after that, just give the Oxygen Lounge a go. Muscles are eased on the active massage Cosmos chairs, while the user is treated to a dose of pure oxygen and 3D films.

Natural Elements

Le Meridien Dubai Garhoud (702 2550/www. lemeridien.com/dubai). **Open** 8am-10pm daily. **Cost** *Massage* Dhs350/hr. **Credit** AmEx, MC, V. **Map** p329 K2.

Natural Elements is a modern spa that offers a good selection of day packages. Facials start at Dhs275. Make sure you factor in enough time to indulge in their steam room afterwards.

Retreat Health & Spa

Grosvenor House Hotel, near Le Royal Meridien, Dubai Marina (317 6762). **Open** 9.15am-8.30pm daily. **Cost** *Massage* Dhs300/hr. **Credit** AmEx, MC, V. **Map** p336 B1.

The Retreat Spa is an intimate affair with separate areas for men and women. If you like Swedish massages, this is the place for you. Facials start at around the Dhs300 mark.

Ritz-Carlton Spa

Ritz-Carlton Dubai Hotel, Al Sufouh Road, Jumeirah (399 4000/www.ritzcarlton.com). **Open** 6am-10pm daily (massages 9am-8pm daily). **Cost** *Massage* Dhs400/50mins. **Credit** AmEx, MC, V. **Map** p336 B1.

The heady Balinese theme at the Ritz-Carlton Spa is a well-executed concept, running throughout the decor and artwork and extending to the treatments, which include a Balinese Boreh massage and a Pumpkin and Cinnamon Body Glow. There are a total of ten treatment rooms and a salon dedicated to hair and beauty treatments, as well as a Jacuzzi, sauna and steam room. European and Arabian-inspired treatments are also available, such as the Chocolate Indulgence.

Royal Waters Health Spa

Al Mamzar Centre, Sharjah Road, Deira (297 2053). **Open** *Women-only* 10am-8pm Sat-Thur. **Cost** *Massage* Dhs250/hr. **Credit** AmEx, MC, V. **Map** p329 L1.

Less formulaic and certainly less glamorous than most hotel-based spas, the high-tech Royal Waters will offer uneasy spa-virgins a more intimate experience that is in no way intimidating. Treatments available include Eastern and Western massage and slimming treatments. The spa also contains a swimming pool, sauna and steam rooms.

Active Dubai

Willow Stream Spa.

SensAsia Urban Spa

First Floor, The Village, Jumeirah Beach Road (349 8850/www.sensasiaspas.com). **Open** 10am-10pm Sat-Thur; 12.30-9pm Fri. **Cost** *Massage* Dhs250/hr. **Credit** AmEx, MC, V. **Map** p332 D9.

An exotic Eastern-style spa for women who prefer their shops, services and spas to be far removed from a hotel lobby, SensAsia is the cream of the crop of non-hotel-based spas in town. Its treatments, such as the excellent Dhs260 Sunset Sparkle, which includes a body massage and finishes with a glitter cream, are guaranteed to take you from downbeat to diva. The place may lack the extra swimming pool and fitness facilities, but it's a women-only affair and has a small relaxation area if you want to unwind for a little longer.

Solesenses Spa

Le Meridien Mina Seyahi Beach Resort & Marina (318 1904/www.lemeridien-minaseyahi.com). **Open** 9am-9pm daily. **Cost** *Massage* Dhs250/hr. **Credit** AmEx, MC, V. **Map** p336 B1.

Solesenses offers a wide variety of skincare and body treatments, many of which use Clarins products. One-hour facials cost from Dhs280.

The Spa at Hilton

Hilton Dubai Jumeirah (318 2406/www.hilton.com). **Open** 9am-6pm daily. **Cost** *Massage* Dhs250/ 55mins. **Credit** AmEx, MC, V. **Map** p336 B1.

This is a small health club rather than a full-on spa, but the menu is impressive. Pick from a range of Phytomer massages, facials and body treatments. Men aren't left out either and can choose a tailored facial and massage. It's worth booking yourself in if you're staying at the hotel or close by, but it's not a destination spa as such. A 60-minute facial will set you back Dhs330.

Spa at Shangri-La

Shangri-La Hotel, Sheikh Zayed Road (343 8888/ www.shangri-la.com). **Open** 10am-10pm daily. **Cost** *Massage* Dhs260/hr. **Credit** AmEx, MC, V. **Map** p335 F12.

When compared with some of the bigger players on the Dubai spa scene, the Spa at Shangri-La won't dazzle; the treatment rooms are quite small

and some are carpeted making them feel old-fashioned. But if you're staying at this hotel or on the Sheikh Zayed Road, it's a good-enough bet, with Asian-inspired therapies, a big outdoor swimming pool, Jacuzzis, plunge pools, saunas and steam rooms to indulge in. Try the Dhs300 chi balance massage – 60 minutes of rebalancing the flow of energy within the body with acupressure and oils. Facials start from Dhs380.

Taj Spa

Taj Palace Hotel, Al Maktoum Street, Deira (211 3101/www.tajhotels.com). **Open** 7am-10pm daily (last booking 8pm). **Cost** *Massage* Dhs275/hr. **Credit** AmEx, MC, V. **Map** p331 L3.

Three different styles of basic massage are available at this atmospheric and relaxing spa – Balinese, Ayurvedic and Swedish. Friendly staff will happily recommend appropriate in-depth treatments to achieve the desired effect, and facials and various acts of delightful pampering are also available. As well as separate saunas and steam rooms, the spa also features a swimming pool and a Jacuzzi.

Talise

Al Qasr, Madinat Jumeirah (366 6818/www. madinatjumeirah.com/spa). **Open** 9am-10pm daily. **Cost** *Massage* Dhs475/50mins. **Credit** AmEx, MC, V. **Map** p336 E1.

True to the Madinat philosophy, Dubai's most recent spa is built around a labyrinth of paths and waterways, courtyards and studios. Guests of the resort will enter the spa onboard a silent *abra* or water taxi, a relaxing experience itself. Otherwise, you should head for Al Qasr hotel until you see signs to the spa. Regardless of your method of arrival, though, the landscaped gardens and sculptured scenery soon set the tone for a serious blissout session. Many different treatments are on offer to rejuvenate tired travellers, from massages with exotic oils to the more scientific healing and wellness therapies. The Talise Pure Awakening is the signature treatment at this superior spa and includes a massage, foot acupressure and eye therapy for Dhs475. Both facials and massages start at Dhs465 for 50 minutes. *Photo p237.*

Willow Stream Spa

*Fairmont Dubai, Sheikh Zayed Road (332 5555/
www.fairmont.com).* **Open** 6am-midnight daily.
Cost *Massage* Dhs320/hr. **Credit** AmEx, MC, V.
Map p333 G9.

High-quality treatments are the name of the pampering game at the sublime Willow Stream Spa, which covers just under 4,000sq m (40,000 sq ft). As well as separate whirlpools, saunas and steam rooms for men and women, it also boasts two large outdoor swimming pools, positioned to catch the morning and afternoon sun respectively. There is a wading pool for children and a lounge that is open to all. After a few hours here, you'll forget that you're in a city. As for treatments, guests can enjoy a vast range of seductive options, including everything from the Back Stress Buster to a Sea Salt Body Scrub, as well as facials, skin treatments and waxing. All in all, this is a friendly and unintimidating spa, perfect for those who aren't regular spa-goers.

Package deals

If you want to be pampered with the full works, you've come to the right place. Dubai's work hard, play hard residents are spoilt for choice when it comes to spas. Treatment prices vary but are comparable with European costs these days. The best way to get your money's worth is to book yourself in for a spa package; this is normally cheaper than paying for the same treatments individually. Here are some of the best packages in town:

SensAsia Urban Spa

For listing, *see p248.*
Once you've dragged yourself away from the designer boutiques, smooth away the guilt here with a Blissfully Unaware massage (Dhs595 for 140 minutes). Choose your oil, then enjoy SensAsia's signature Hot Stone massage, a blissfest that concludes with a 60-minute Aromatherapy Associates facial to soothe dry skin. Afterwards, take a seat in the relaxation room for some tea and a plate of fruit, which should revive you just enough to drift back to reality.

Talise

For listing, *see p248.*
If you've been indulging too much in rich food and caffeine, the sumptuous Talise spa has just the tonic in its detox package (Dhs910 for 120 minutes). The treatment starts with a dry skin brush exfoliation before your body is enveloped in a warm marine mask. For ultimate relaxation, it's a sensation that can't be beaten. Next up, a luscious lotion is applied to create silky, smooth skin. The body ritual is then followed by a facial – specifically targeted to the customer's individual needs and concerns. You'll leave feeling radiant, refreshed, rejuvenated – and inspired to take better care of your bod. Talise Spa is out of this world, so if your credit card can take it, book yourself in.

Willow Stream Spa

For listing, *see above.*
Want it all? The Ultimate Body Bliss (Dhs920 for 180 minutes) at the Willow Stream Spa delivers a sea-salt body scrub, relaxation massage and customised facial. The scrub will leave your skin positively sparkling; the 90-minute massage will revitalise you and the Phytomer facial will leave you glowing like an A-list star. Make sure you take your swimming costume so you can chill out in the bubbling Jacuzzis afterwards.

Akuru Spa

For listing, *see p244.*
Those in need of deep relaxation should get themselves down to this spa for the appropriately named Relax Package (Dhs475, 150 minutes). After a creamy body scrub, you can jump in the in-room shower before enjoying the aromatic massage with Decléor products. Your therapist will de-stress you further with a scalp massage and reflexology. By the end of the session, you will probably have caught up on some sleep, so wake up slowly on the wicker loungers in the relaxation room, while herbal tea and a fruit plate are served up.

Amara

For listing, *see p244.*
One for the boys. This upmarket spa has created the Clubhouse (Dhs890 for 180 minutes), a refreshing peppermint scrub followed by a massage and reflexology by therapists the A-list stars request. This package is out of this world and will leave you feeling a million dollars. Once you're completely blissed out, you can take time to enjoy the private courtyard attached to the treatment room. Then do the clubhouse thing and get waited on hand and food at the Terrace bar overlooking the flash yachts on the Creek.

Active Dubai

Le Méridien Abu Dhabi has undergone a spectacular refurbishment of its 234 rooms; bringing together a complete new look with state-of-the-art facilities, such as interactive TV and high speed Internet.

The Meridien Village boasts a unique selection of 15 restaurants and bars featuring exotic cuisines from around the world surrounded by a splendid view of lushes' gardens.

Whether you are seeking sanctuary from city life, looking to recharge your batteries, or simply wanting to indulge in a serious pampering, at Eden Spa we offer massage therapies, facials, body and hydro bath treatments, hand and foot care and customized treatment packages. Our steam room, sauna rooms, Jacuzzi, Aquamedic pool and Turkish Hammam are guaranteed to soothe and relax the most tired and stressed minds.

For further information and reservations, call +971 2 644 6666 now, or e-mail us at meridien@emirates.net.ae or log onto www.abudhabi.lemeridien.com

Le **MERIDIEN**
ABU DHABI

كم ٩
كم ٢٦
كم ٤٠
كم ٥٨
كم ١٠١
كم ١٣٩

Dubai
Al Sharjah
Ajman
Umm Al Quwa
Ras Al Khaima
Al Fujeirah

The UAE

Getting Started

Take a short break from the frantic pace of Dubai to explore the other attractions the UAE has to offer.

Although it was the British who brought the seven emirates of Abu Dhabi, Ajman, Dubai, Fujairah, Ras Al Khaimah, Sharjah and Umm Al Quwain together as the Trucial States, it was the late Sheikh Zayed Al Nahyan – the much-mourned former leader of Abu Dhabi, whose death in 2004 brought dignitaries here from all over the world (*see p14* **Sheikh Zayed, architect of the UAE**) – who cemented the name of the United Arab Emirates. The country was formed in 1971 and, buoyed by the collective strength of this union and the foresight and fortunes of Abu Dhabi in particular, each emirate has since gone on to grow in status.

The UAE is situated on the south-eastern tip of the Arabian peninsula. To the north-west is Qatar; Saudi Arabia is to the west and south and Oman to the south-east and north-east (for map, *see pp322-323*). It goes without saying that Dubai leads the way in terms of accommodating and

entertaining tourists, but away from the glitz lies the wider UAE's tapestry of sun-drenched beaches, cool mountain escapes and bustling cities rich with cultural experiences. Just short of two hours south of Dubai is the capital, **Abu Dhabi** (*see p253*) and, closer still, to the north, there are unexpected pockets of quiet reflection amid the chaos of **Sharjah** (*see p268*). Adventure abounds further north in the wild reaches of **Ras Al Khaimah** (*see p277*), while superb snorkelling and diving is on offer at **Fujairah** (*see p284*) and along the east coast.

Be warned, however, that public transport remains fairly primitive here. Buses are as cramped as they are economical, and rarely would you see a tourist aboard one. Nonetheless, the government's determination to build smooth, efficient highways is paying off. Our advice if you're heading out of Dubai is take to the wheel of a 4x4 on short-term hire and explore the UAE's delights at your own speed.

A road with a view: the **Abu Dhabi Corniche**.

The UAE

Abu Dhabi

Spurred on by a heady dose of sibling rivalry, the nation's capital is plotting to become the Gulf's cultural hub.

Less than 50 years ago the entire emirate of Abu Dhabi was a near-empty desert populated by Bedouin tribes and small villages. Its initial elevation to economic prominence was the result of pearl cultivation until global recession, coupled with a thriving pearl industry in Japan, put paid to that and relegated Abu Dhabi to the position of poorest emirate.

But the discovery of huge offshore oil reserves in 1958 and the subsequent rule of Sheikh Zayed totally transformed its fortunes. As recently as 30 years ago the capital city was still short of a reliable electricity supply and roads. Now its expanse of highways are heavy with traffic, and the whole city is embarking on a process of development that (along with neighbouring Dubai) is almost unprecedented in modern times.

BLACK GOLD

Having noted that the island stood as a natural stronghold – and also offered fine fishing – the Bani Yas Bedouin tribe settled in Abu Dhabi in the 1760s. They dubbed the region Abu Dhabi ('Father of the Gazelle') and would thereafter lead a largely unchanged existence for nearly 200 years. Legend tells that the city owes its unorthodox name to gazelle tracks found by a wandering party of Bedouin hunters. The nomads followed the tracks into a shallow inlet of the sea only to discover that they emerged again on the shore of the facing island and ended at a spring of fresh water. They quickly returned to their base in the Liwa oasis and reported the discovery to their leader, Sheikh Dhiyab bin Isa, who decreed that the island should thereafter be known as Abu Dhabi in honour of their guides.

The discovery of a freshwater well encouraged the ruling Al Nahyan family to relocate from their home in Liwa to Abu Dhabi, securing the city's first steps on its rise to prominence. And the good times continued through the 1800s, as residents grew prosperous from the seemingly endless supply of pearls that were found off Abu Dhabi's lengthy coastline. Then came the aforementioned worldwide pearl recession and Abu Dhabi's subsequent decline, which forced potentate Sheikh Shakhbut bin Sultan to investigate other potential sources of revenue. Somewhat fortuitously, he granted

drilling rights to the British – who had been present in the region since 1892 in the role of overseers of a protectorate – and the search for oil began.

In 1958 huge offshore oil reserves were found; Abu Dhabi became the first of the Gulf States to export oil in 1962, earning an estimated US$70 million per year throughout the 1960s. Today, roughly two million barrels of oil are exported from the United Arab Emirates every 24 hours. Current estimates suggest this will continue for the foreseeable future.

The British left the Gulf region in 1971 and the seven factional emirates united to form the UAE, declaring Abu Dhabi the provisional capital. Sheikh Zayed Al Nahyan was welcomed as the new state's first president, and duly returned to power every five years before his death, when his son, Sheikh Khalifa bin Zayed bin Sultan Al Nahyan, assumed control. In 1996, the word 'provisional' was dropped from Abu Dhabi's title, making it the official capital city.

THE TOURISM CARD

When the government declared it wanted to turn Abu Dhabi into a tourist destination, some people scoffed. After all, why go to Abu Dhabi when the ultimate tourist city of Dubai is just down the road? Yet more than US$100 billion-worth of developments are being built over the next five years, including a reported 50 top-end hotels and a new airport that can process up to 20 million passengers a year. And if the emirate's ambitious plans work out, there's no reason that the new airport shouldn't be tested. Plans have been unveiled for entire communities to be created on **Al Reem Island**, **Lulu Island** and **Al Raha Beach**, as well as reconstruction work and new facilities all over the city's main island. Five-star hotels, golf courses, restaurants, spas and parks are going to be rising up all over the emirate.

The most intriguing project is **Saadiyat Island**, and in a noisy statement of intent the four main buildings in the island's cultural sector have been designed by four of the world's leading architects: Frank Gehry has designed the world's largest **Guggenheim** gallery; Japanese designer Tadao Ando has created a Zen-concrete **Maritime Museum**, while Frenchman Jean Nouvel's **Classical**

Abu Dhabi

Ras Laffan

Khor Laffan

A R A B I A N

G U L F

Port Zayed

Free Port Zone

Jazirat Bu Ash Shu'um

Carpet Souk

The Club

Iranian Souk

Dhow Harbour

AL MEENA

Le Meridien Abu Dhabi

Al Diar Capital Hotel

Abu Dhabi Mall

Sheraton Abu Dhabi Hotel & Resort

Cemetery

Mosque Gardens

Beach Rotana Hotel & Towers

Cemetery

Le Royal Meridien

SAADIYAT BRIDGE

Millennium Hotel Abu Dhabi

Al Ain Palace Hotel

AS SALAM ST

QASR EL BAHR

Lulu Island

Volcano Fountain

Capital Gardens

Madinat Zayed Shopping Centre

Al Noor Hospital

Gold Souk

SEA PALACE ROAD

Clock Tower

Crowne Plaza Hotel

MADINAT ZAYED

Police Station

EASTERN RING

AL ITTIHAD SQUARE

Fotouh Al Khair Centre

AL DHAFRAH

AL HOSN

Cemetery

Old Fort & Al Hosn Palace

Cultural Foundation

Grand Mosque

Bus & Taxi Station

NEW AIRPORT ROAD

AL MANHAL

Al Muhairy Centre

Central Hospital

AL WAHDAR

SHEIKH RASHID BIN SAEED AL MAKTOUM STREET

Al Mahnal Palace

HAZAA BIN ZAYED ST

ZAYED THE FIRST STREET

Flagpole

Breakwater

Municipality

AL KHALIBIYAH

Khalidiya Garden

AL KARAMAH

National Theatre

Marina Mall

Khalidiya Children's Garden

Municipal Market

AL TABBIYAH

MUSSALA EL EID

Khalifa Gardens

Hilton Abu Dhabi

Cemetery

AL KHALEEG AL ARABI STREET

Ministry of State

Mushrif Palace

Ras Al Bateen

Emirates Palace

Police Station

AL BATEEN

AL ROWDAH

Bateen Palace

Race Track

SAEED BIN TAHNOON ST

Dana Ladies' Beach

AR RAS AL AKHDAR

InterContinental Abu Dhabi

BAINUNAH STREET

SULTAN BIN ZAYED STREET

Khor Al Bateen

Hideriyyat

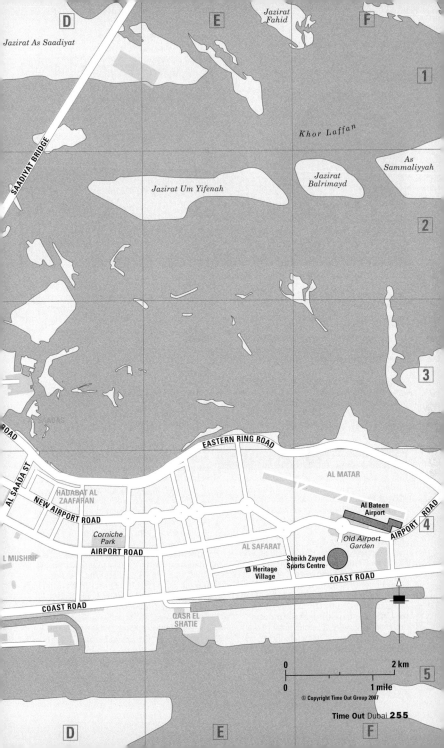

D

Jazirat As Saadiyat

E

Jazirat Fahid

F

1

Khor Laffan

As Sammaliyyah

SAADIYAT BRIDGE

Jazirat Um Yifenah

Jazirat Balrimayd

2

3

EASTERN RING ROAD

ROAD

AL MATAR

AL SAADA ST

NEW AIRPORT ROAD

HADABAT AL ZAAFARAN

Al Bateen Airport

AIRPORT ROAD

4

Corniche Park

AIRPORT ROAD

AL SAFARAT

Old Airport Garden

L MUSHRIF

Sheikh Zayed Sports Centre

Heritage Village

COAST ROAD

COAST ROAD

QASR EL SHATIE

0   2 km

0   1 mile

© Copyright Time Out Group 2007

Time Out Dubai **255**

D

E

F

5

Get the royal treatment at **Emirates Palace**. *See p262.*

Museum, and Zaha Hadid's **Performing Arts Centre** are two entirely contrasting yet incredibly inventive buildings of their own.

At its heart though, Abu Dhabi remains a traditional Middle Eastern city, which means it's advisable to watch your behaviour even when just passing through. Overt drunkenness and lasciviousness should be confined to private places, and revealing outfits are best avoided, especially during Ramadan. Gone are the days when such offences would result in jail time, but too much skin on show will still attract slack-mouthed stares from pretty much everyone you meet.

Sightseeing

Just east of Abu Dhabi next to Al Maqta Bridge on the Airport Road you'll find **Al Maqta Fort**. Now some 200 years old, the fort was originally built to keep bandits away from the city's riches. Another fortification to have witnessed great change is Qasr Al Husn, or the **White Fort**, which stands on the corner of Khalid Bin Al Waleed and Al Nasr Streets (map p254 B3). Built at the end of the 1700s, it once served as the official residence of the rulers of Abu Dhabi, but is now open to the public. Residents will tell you that Abu Dhabi is the cultural heart of the UAE, and the **Cultural Foundation** takes pride of place. The only facility of its kind in the region, it hosts temporary art exhibitions and local performances, between visits from inter-national artists such as the British Philharmonic Orchestra; expect dinner theatre, amateur dramatics, opera and the occasional touring ballet group.

To realise just how far the city has come in such a short space of time, get a glimpse of the past at the **Dhow Harbour**, still worked by doughty craftsmen, and the **Heritage Village**, a faithful representation of a small nomadic camp.

Follow this with a tour of the grandiose **Emirates Palace** which, like Dubai's Burj Al Arab, is often referred to as a seven-star hotel as it offers a lot more than your average five-star. The Palace offers guided tours, largely in an attempt to prevent huge numbers of sightseers from wandering around its cavernous interior unchaperoned. Tours cost Dhs100 and it's advisable to book in advance, as they're very popular. Alternatively, if you only want a quick look around then you're better off just turning up and going for one of their lavish afternoon teas instead.

Arabia is famous worldwide for its racing thoroughbreds, its ancient bloodlines and the passion with which the Emirati people hold the equestrian arts. The breeding of winning horses is a serious business, and the **Golf & Equestrian Club** (02 445 5500; map p254 C4) holds races every Sunday from November to April. In a surprisingly efficient use of space, there is a par-72 golf course located within the racetrack, which closes two hours before the racing begins. Non-member green fees for 18 holes are Dhs230 (Saturday to Wednesday) or Dhs240 (Thursday and Friday). More fun, but less prestigious, is a round at **Al Ghazal Golf Club** (02 575 8040), an 18-hole sand course chiselled into land alongside the airport. It's open to anyone – even transit passengers with a few hours to kill. Non-member green fees for 18 holes are a mere Dhs100.

The city also boasts a pleasant network of **parks**. In the centre of the city is **Capital Gardens** (map p254 B3), an assortment of manicured lawns gathered around a central pond – known to erupt into aquatic action whenever the mood takes it. Refreshments come courtesy of vending machines and a small cafeteria. The **Corniche Park** (map p255 D4), found on the east side of the island, is a haven for birdwatchers and anglers. Picnic tables are popular on warm winter evenings, and it's always well lit and clean. **Khalidiya Garden** (map p254 B4) doesn't have a cafeteria, but does offer vending machines and lawns like billiard tables. For a quiet stretch, the **Old Airport Garden** (map p255 F4), next to the ice-skating rink, has swings for the kids, is beautifully ornamental and manages to remain tranquil. Trainspotter types might even fancy a gander at one of the largest flagpoles in the world (map p254 A4), which resides at the end of Abu Dhabi's breakwater.

Cultural Foundation

Opposite Etisalat building, Airport Road (02 619 5223). **Open** 8am-2pm, 5-9.30pm Sat-Thur; 5-8pm Fri. **Admission** varies. **Map** p254 B3.

This vast centre for the arts is proof of a very real desire to stimulate artistry in a land where so much energy is put into making cold hard cash. As you might expect from a building with such a noble purpose, there's a hushed atmosphere throughout the network of corridors and arched courtyards. The summer months excluded, the Foundation fills its lecture halls with residents drawn to international acts – primarily musicians, but speakers and actors too. The Foundation publishes a wealth of Islamic texts and is home to the National Archives.

Dhow Harbour

Al Bateen (no phone). **Admission** free. **Map** p254 B2.

Visitors can watch craftsmen using the maritime skills that served the UAE for centuries to build traditional boats. For the most part, the craftsmen are happy to talk about their work.

The Gehry effect

Eyebrows were raised in the summer of 2006 when the Guggenheim Foundation announced it would be opening its largest museum on an island just off the coast of Abu Dhabi.

Frank Gehry, the celebrated architect in charge of the project, talks about the venture and the future of the city:

'They have the resources to do things that you can't do in other places and that's a great opportunity. There's no western country that can afford to build all these museums at once. In a place like New York, they build into various industrial spaces but here they're all going to be in one district and that's what's exciting about it. Physically and financially it probably couldn't be done anywhere else on the planet.

'There's a great opportunity for infrastructure to be designed here rather than just engineered. It could be really special. It's not been done anywhere in the world since the 19th century. It's never happened in contemporary times, perhaps the odd bridge here and there that's beautiful, but they have an opportunity here to make a statement and not just with individual buildings, but as an entire coherent city.

'Since they've built megalomaniac places like the Emirates Palace, people assume they are only doing that, but it's not how the current leadership's talking. They're trying to establish Abu Dhabi and the UAE as a cultural centre that has world connections. I don't think there's another Arab country that has done that as seriously.

'The people here are very intelligent and their intentions are very honourable. They have the resources so it's natural that they want to establish themselves in the world culture. They're certainly establishing themselves in the world's economy, but they're looking at culture too and that's rare – it's something that should be supported by everyone. It's really about more than just building places like the Emirates Palace. What they don't want here is a repeat of Dubai.'

The UAE

Beaches & islands

Some of the city's five-star hotels have their own stretch of sand, varying in size, which non-guests can use for a charge of somewhere between Dhs80 and Dhs100 for a day pass. Sadly, the best bit of beach in the city is attached to the Emirates Palace and is strictly for hotel residents only.

As an alternative, Abu Dhabi has several public beaches and there are scenic (if rugged) stretches around the peninsula (up past the InterContinental Abu Dhabi), but without facilities like changing rooms and shops. Otherwise, the best public beach is **Al Raha**, easily the most convenient in terms of amenities and refreshments. For a little more privacy, women can avoid the male of the species altogether at **Al Dana Ladies' Beach**.

There is no need for the more adventurous tourist to stop at the shore, however. Abu Dhabi is unique among the emirates in its wealth of islands. Over 200 of them, varying in size and level of habitation, lie just off the coast. Small wonder that hopping from island to island is one of the emirate's more popular pastimes. If you don't own a boat you can hire one – with captain – from a hotel beach club. This is the safer option in any case, as the water is dangerously shallow in places, and would-be captains must be able to navigate the treacherous dredged channels.

The large island opposite the corniche is **Lulu Island** (map p254 A3), a man-made landmass that's famous for having been built with no real purpose in mind. Depending on what you read, it was destined to become a Fun Island theme park, a wildlife reserve or an entertainment complex. Now it appears that it will be filled with housing, and is due to be linked to Abu Dhabi by a number of bridges and tunnels. Slightly further out is **Saadiyat Island** (map p255 D1).

Motor about three miles (five kilometres) south of Abu Dhabi and you'll come to **Futaisi Island**, an inhabited island, some 15 miles (40 kilometres) square, which is privately owned by Sheikh Hamad bin Hamdan Al Nahyan. Home to old quarries from which stone for Abu Dhabi's forts was once dug, the island is now a tourist retreat and nature reserve. Here you can rent a chalet and ride horses. Some 240 kilometres west of Abu Dhabi, near Jebel Dhanna, is **Sir Bani Yas Island** (*see p263*), a nature reserve where various conservation programmes run.

There are many other small, uninhabited bits of green dotted around out to sea, but still within easy reach of the city. Popular outcrops include **Bahraini**, **Cut** and **Horseshoe**, but all are good for a day's exploring and secluded sun-soaking. You'll often find a cluster of windsurfers taking brief respite on Surf Reef, gathering themselves amid the swirling offshore breezes.

Al Dana Ladies' Beach

Just past the Hilton Abu Dhabi, Corniche Road (02 665 0129). **Open** noon-6pm Sat-Wed; 10am-6pm Thur-Fri. **Admission** Dhs10. *Parking* Dhs5. **Map** p254 A5.
A totally man-free environment, Al Dana beach offers a cafeteria and swimming pool. It is typically open until dusk (around 6pm).

Al Raha Beach

Past Umm Al Nar roundabout. **Admission** free.
A clean and relatively recent beach development, Al Raha is one of the city's favourite suntraps. A small section is cordoned off for women only, but the rest is accessible to all. There's a small cafeteria selling snacks and soft drinks.

Restaurants & cafés

In terms of entertainment, Abu Dhabi can occasionally feel like the city that fun forgot, but thankfully there are some very good restaurants here. Although the superior (and licensed) restaurants are almost all within five-star hotels, there are familiar fast-food outlets and some charming independent restaurants down many of the side streets.

Art Cauldron

Al Falah Street, opposite Navy Gate (02 644 4309). **Open** noon-4pm, 6pm-midnight daily. **Main courses** Dhs30-Dhs45. **No credit cards.** **Map** p254 C3 ❶
Not located in a hotel – and therefore not permitted to serve alcohol – this Bohemian basement hideaway has a lot of atmosphere and great decor. It serves an inventive international menu and portions are plentiful.

Bice

Hilton Abu Dhabi, Corniche Road (02 681 1900). **Open** noon-3pm, 7-11pm daily. **Main courses** Dhs40-Dhs60. **Credit** AmEx, MC, V. **Map** p254 A4 ❷
There's a fine line between paying too much for simple Italian food and seeing wonderfully simple Italian food ruined by over-fussiness. It's a line that's walked pretty well at Bice. Polished oak floors, beautifully crafted chairs and a splendid in-house pianist define a setting that is rich in atmosphere; the food is of the highest quality and the menu has some great vegetarian options. Bice also has one of the best wine cellars in the city.

Al Fanar

Le Royal Meridien Abu Dhabi, Khalifa Bin Zayed Street (02 674 2020). **Open** 12.30-3pm, 7.30-11pm daily. **Main courses** Dhs40-Dhs60. **Credit** AmEx, MC, V. **Map** p254 B3 ❸

Say what you like about revolving restaurants, but the views from up here are excellent. The food too is also first-rate, and Al Fanar's popular Friday brunch affords diners the opportunity to drink an unlimited amount of champagne, ensuring the room *really* begins to spin.

Finz

Beach Rotana Hotel & Towers, next to Abu Dhabi Mall, north end of Ninth Street (02 644 3000). **Open** 12.30-3.30pm, 7-11pm daily. **Main courses** Dhs60-Dhs80. **Credit** AmEx, MC, V. **Map** p254 C2 **④**
If you have a hankering for seafood, there are few places better in the entire country than this excellent restaurant. From a comfy vantage point in this spacious and beautifully designed eatery you can peer into the large open kitchen and see the staff preparing your meal, while in the other direction you are able to enjoy sea views.

Mezzaluna

Emirates Palace, Corniche Road (02 690 8888). **Open** noon-midnight daily. **Main courses** Dhs150-Dhs200. **Credit** AmEx, MC, V. **Map** p254 A4 **⑤**
While most of the restaurants at the Emirates Palace are overpriced and underwhelming, this Italian is excellent. From the complimentary appetisers to the sabayon dessert prepared at your table amid flames, the meals here are usually difficult to fault. If you're determined to eat at the Emirates Palace, this is your best bet.

Rodeo Grill

Beach Rotana Hotel & Towers, next to Abu Dhabi Mall, north end of Ninth Street (02 644 3000). **Open** 12.30-3.30pm, 7-11pm daily. **Main courses** Dhs60-Dhs80. **Credit** AmEx, MC, V. **Map** p254 C2 **⑥**
With its dark wooden furniture and grand green leather chairs, you could easily mistake Rodeo Grill for an elegant English gentlemen's club rather than Abu Dhabi's best steakhouse. The cuts are the finest you'll find in town, the wine list is impressively eclectic and the chocolate soufflé a triumphant volcano of decadence. Recommended.

Sayad

Emirates Palace, Corniche Road (02 690 8888). **Open** 12.30-3pm, 6.30-11.30pm daily. **Main courses** Dhs150-Dhs200. **Credit** AmEx, MC, V. **Map** p254 A4 **⑦**
There was a point when Sayad was becoming the Middle East's equivalent of the Ivy, as celebrities such as Will Smith and Jamie Foxx dined here while in town. Accordingly, the price is A-list, but despite the grand setting it's not horribly overblown and the seafood is excellent. From the rich foie gras to the delicate Canadian lobster salad with mango and watermelon, the menu is classy throughout and when the bill arrives, it's on a big wave of white chocolate dotted with truffles in a gesture almost as grand as the price.

Soba

Le Royal Meridien Abu Dhabi, Khalifa Bin Zayed Street (02 695 0450). **Open** 1-3.30pm, 7-10.30pm Sat-Wed; 1-3.30pm, 7pm-midnight Thur; 7pm-midnight Fri. **Main courses** Dhs40-Dhs60. **Credit** AmEx, MC, V. **Map** p254 B3 **⑧**
Everything in this Japanese restaurant, from the decor to the dessert menu, stylishly fuses the

Fish to fry: **Finz** is the best seafood restaurant in the city.

The UAE

modern and the traditional. Coloured glass, light wood and geometric patterns are offset by floaty white curtains and pretty screens, which give a hideaway feeling to what is essentially a fairly narrow ground-floor room. There is a resident DJ, but the sound is so unobtrusive as to be almost forgotten at times. Whether you want to share sushi, grab a quick bowl of noodles or tackle towers of tempura with a group of friends, you'll find your corner here.

Talay
Le Meridien Abu Dhabi, north end of Sheikh Zayed Second Street (02 644 7800). **Open** 12.30-3.30pm, 7-11.30pm daily. **Main courses** Dhs50-Dhs60. **Credit** AmEx, MC, V. **Map** p254 C2 ❾

Talay is the pick of the restaurants located in Le Meridien's picturesque Culinary Village, and its traditional take on Thai food is best enjoyed at one of their beachside tables – even though you'll have to arrive early to be sure of securing one. Try the signature tom yam seafood soup, with its squid, shrimp and serious chunks of oyster mushroom deftly seasoned with coconut milk and lemongrass.

Pubs & bars

By 2015, it seems likely that Abu Dhabi will be a great after-dark city, but for the time being you'll have to get on the road to Dubai for a place to party. Many of the city's bars are currently little more than depressing dives, but as more hotels open over the coming years, nightlife options will increase rapidly. That said, there are a still a few places that are worth visiting if you're looking for somewhere to go out in the capital.

Captain's Arms
Le Meridien Abu Dhabi, north end of Sheikh Zayed Second Street (02 644 7800). **Open** noon-1am Sat-Wed; noon-2am Thur; noon-1am Fri. **Admission** free. Credit AmEx, MC, V. **Map** p254 C2 ❶

The Captain's Arms generally meets with the approval of expat punters, although this may have less to do with the nautical theme and more to do with the cheap pints available during happy hours – hours that stretch well beyond 60 minutes. During the cooler months, a pretty, if diminutive, terrace is the busiest place in town.

Heroes
Crowne Plaza Abu Dhabi, Hamdan Street (02 621 0000). **Open** noon-2am Sat-Wed; noon-3am Thur-Fri. **Admission** free. **Credit** AmEx, MC, V. **Map** p254 B3 ❷

An expat favourite, this American-style diner/sports bar is busy most nights and is a fair shout if you're after drinks and huge portions of comfort food – the giant spare ribs are the biggest served to man since the bronto-ribs that tipped over Fred's car in the opening credits of *The Flintstones*. Regular drink deals and a monthly comedy club, the Laughter Factory, ensure Heroes usually has a convivial atmosphere with barstools full of people

happy to talk the night away. A DJ plays all the oldies on Thursday nights and the band does passable renditions of Nirvana, Aerosmith, the Beatles and the Red Hot Chili Peppers.

Jazz Bar
Hilton Abu Dhabi, Corniche Road (02 681 1900). **Open** 7pm-midnight Sun-Fri. **Admission** free. **Credit** AmEx, MC, V. **Map** p254 A4 ❸

Home to one of the better bands in town, the Jazz Bar is understandably popular with the city's more sophisticated drinkers. The candlelit tables cannot be pre-booked, and often fill up early, and it's rare that the place doesn't get busy later in the evening. It's not cheap by any means, but if you're after a classier place to drink than the average pub and want live music then the Jazz Bar hits the spot.

Oceans
Le Royal Meridien Abu Dhabi, Khalifa Bin Zayed Street (02 674 2020). **Open** noon-1am Sat-Wed; noon-3am Thur; noon-1.30am Fri. **Admission** free. **Credit** AmEx, MC, V. **Map** p254 B3 ❹

Technically it's a restaurant, but they put on the odd good night here in the small bar area, usually on a Thursday. There's a wood-decked outdoor terrace and, if the right DJ is playing it attracts a decent crowd. It's also next door to Sax, so you can flit between the two.

Rock Bottom Café
Al Diar Capital Hotel, Meena Street (02 678 7700). **Open** noon-2.30am daily. **Admission** free. **Credit** AmEx, MC, V. **Map** p254 B2 ❺

A quick perusal of this bar's clientele and you'll be in little doubt as to why it is so named: the live entertainment oscillates between an ear-splittingly loud band and a DJ playing run-of-the-mill tracks to a dancefloor full of unsuspecting tourists, touchy-feely ladies and denim-clad bikers. It's the kind of place that only ever springs to mind at around 1am when you're trying to think of somewhere that serves alcohol and is still open.

Sax Restaurant Club
Le Royal Meridien Abu Dhabi, Khalifa Bin Zayed Street (02 674 2020). **Open** 7pm-2.30am Sat-Thur; Fri 7pm-3am. **Admission** free. **Credit** AmEx, MC, V. **Map** p254 B3 ❻

Low-lit and relatively snug, Sax is a good shout if you're after a meal with live entertainment. After 10pm it's usually packed with the well-dressed set drinking excellent cocktails.

Trader Vic's
Beach Rotana Hotel & Towers, next to Abu Dhabi Mall, north end of Ninth Street (02 644 3000). **Open** 12.30-3.30pm, 5pm-12.30am daily. **Admission** free. **Credit** AmEx, MC, V. **Map** p254 C2 ❼

The food is more miss than hit, but the cocktails at this Polynesian-themed grog house are out of this world. The Tiki Puka Puka, for example, is a legendary potent rum-based headspinner. A grass skirt-wearing band plays most nights and keeps the crowds happy. Thursday nights are packed.

Iranian Souk.

Shopping

You won't want to be traipsing around the streets of the city if it's hot, and there's little you'll be missing anyway. Many of the shops sell little more than cheap junk and badly counterfeited goods. For serious shopping you're better off heading to the two modern malls: **Abu Dhabi Mall** (or City Centre Mall as it's also known) and the newer **Marina Mall**. These similarly sized American-style shopping centres offer quick and easy food courts, cinemas, and wares ranging from domestic goods to designer labels.

But by far the most interesting (and hectic) shopping experience in the capital is at the **Iranian souk** located in Port Zayed and the **carpet souk** off Mina Road (map p254 B2). The Iranian souk sells goods fresh off the boats which arrive from Iran arrive every three or four days. On sale are all manner of carpets, ornaments, terracotta trinkets and the like. Haggling is regarded as a kind of sport in these parts, so you should indulge in a round or two as much to pass the time as to procure bargains. The souks are your prime source of traditional knick-knacks as well as the predictable range of Celvin Kline shirts and

Hogo Boos aftershave. Expect to find all the market favourites: cheap shoes, bags, clothes and toys, and it's not too expensive if you haggle hard. The fake watches, however, look the part (some amazingly replicated), but stop working very soon after you buy one, so are best avoided, while many of the pirate DVDs are terrible quality or else in Mandarin or Russian. The box sets of TV shows, however, are usually perfect. Dozens of shops and stalls open at seemingly random times between 8am and 11pm, depending on the enthusiasm of the owners. Far more predictable is the afternoon siesta, which ensures all trade stops between 1.30pm and 4pm. Most shops will appear rather dingy and dirty on the outside (and also inside) but there are plenty of bargains to be had.

Abu Dhabi Mall
North end of Ninth Street (02 645 4858). **Open** 10am-10pm Sat-Wed; 10am-11pm Thur; 3.30-11pm Fri. **Map** p254 C2.
Connected to the Beach Rotana Hotel & Towers, this large shopping centre keeps attracting bigger and better brand names to complement an already solid range of outlets. It hosts mainstream names including Tommy Hilfiger and Guess as well as gems like Pull and Bear and Kenneth Cole, a cinema and a noisy food court.

The family-friendly **Beach Rotana Hotel**.

Marina Mall

The Breakwater (02 681 2310). **Open** 10am-10pm Sat-Wed; 10am-11pm Thur, Fri. **Map** p254 A4.
Thanks to a recent expansion, the Marina Mall has vastly improved in quality with an increasing number of designer brands finding residence here. The prices are the same as those in other major cities around the world.

Where to stay

Beach resorts

Beach Rotana Hotel & Towers

Next to Abu Dhabi Mall, north end of Ninth Street (02 644 3000/www.rotana.com). **Rates** Dhs950-Dhs1,260 double (excl 16% tax). **Credit** AmEx, MC, V. **Map** p254 C2 ①
Probably the most family orientated of the top hotels in the city, the Beach Rotana is connected to Abu Dhabi Mall, meaning shopaholics don't have far to walk. It's wonderfully elegant inside, with a welcoming lobby and rooms that are spacious and stylish. The premium rooms have luxury bathrooms with Jacuzzis and rain showers. The beach is small, but there's a children's pool as well as an adult one and the obligatory swim-up bar. A first-rate gym is on site for those who want to keep up their fitness regime while away from home.

Emirates Palace

Corniche Road (02 690 9000/www.emiratespalace. com). **Rates** Dhs1,700 double (excl 16% tax). **Credit** AmEx, MC, V. **Map** p254 A4 ②
If you've ever wondered what sort of place you can build for US$3billion, then this is the answer. Far from mere hyperbole, this really feels like an actual palace, with luxury that regularly accommodates royalty. Rooms have plasma screens as standard, while the top-of-the-range accommodation comes with a room for your bodyguard and a private butler to take care of your every need. The beach and pool areas are outstanding, but room service can be slow and not all the in-house restaurants are worth the price. Even if you can't afford to stay here, it's worth a visit for afternoon tea. *Photo p256.*

Hilton Abu Dhabi

Corniche Road (02 681 1900/www.hilton.com). **Rates** Dhs575 double (excl 16% tax). **Credit** AmEx, MC, V. **Map** p254 A4 ③
Set in a fine location overlooking the Gulf, the majority of the Hilton's rooms have been renovated over the last couple of years. Guests enjoy unlimited access to the beach club, which sports a private stretch of sand and pleasant spa. The hotel is also home to some of the better food and drink outlets in Abu Dhabi.

Le Meridien Abu Dhabi

Tourist Club area, Sheikh Zayed Second Street (02 644 6666/www.lemeridien.com). **Rates** Dhs900-Dhs1,600 double (excl 16% tax). **Credit** AmEx, MC, V. **Map** p254 C2 ④
This pleasant hotel is situated by the beach and centred around the tranquil Meridien Village, a stretch of greenery with a variety of excellent alfresco food and drink outlets. There's an on-site spa centre that offers traditional Turkish hammam treatments, but the nightclub, Gauloises, can be a depressingly sleazy experience.

Al Raha Beach Hotel

Al Raha Beach, Shahama city (02 508 0555/ www.ncth.com). **Rates** Dhs1,300-Dhs1,600 double. **Credit** AmEx, MC, V
Set apart from the cluster of hotels in the city centre by a 15 minute drive, the Al Raha Beach Hotel is a five-star property that is unique in Abu Dhabi for the fact that it has a number of two, three and four bedroom beach villas. These can be rented for either a short holiday or a longer stay, and are wonderfully decorated. There's also a lovely infinity pool with views of the Gulf, as well as the UAE's largest nightclub, Enigma, which isn't particularly good.

Sheraton Abu Dhabi Hotel & Resort

Corniche Road (02 677 3333/www.starwood. com/sheraton). **Rates** Dhs850-Dhs1,300 double (excl 16% tax). **Credit** AmEx, MC, V. **Map** p254 B2 ⑤
Although best as a business hotel, the Sheraton does have a pleasant outdoor area set among palm trees, with pools for children and adults, a private lagoon and a small beach. The rooms are modern in decor and are fully equipped, but they tend to be on the small side. Nevertheless, it's a functional five-star with some good bars and restaurants on site, including a popular Italian restaurant and sophisticated, but quiet cocktail bar.

Special reserve

Only 30 years ago there was nothing but sand and volcanic mountains on what is now known as **Sir Bani Yas**, the largest island in the UAE, 240 kilometres (150 miles) from Abu Dhabi. Then along came Sheikh Zayed bin Sultan Al Nahyan, who had decided to set aside the island as a conservation area.

The idea was to protect the endangered Arabian oryx and sand gazelle and for a small community to live among these animals on the island, but the project evolved into something far more ambitious. An impressive mix of over 60,000 animals now call the island their home. Three artificial plastic-bottomed lakes were built and over 6,000 acres (15,000 hectares) of trees were planted, including 3,000 olive groves cultivated for local markets. Using the underground natural springs on the island (Sir Bani Yas translates into 'the place where the water stands'), the Sheikh ensured arid land became a hydro-powered isle that generated its own water and electricity.

A boat whisks you from Sir Bani Yas jetty at 8.15am to a haven of landscapes that smack of the savannahs of Africa. A kaleidoscope of browns and greens confronts you, strikingly offset by fuchsia-pink bougainvillea. But this being the UAE, the conservation park and important agricultural research centre is by no means a basic hippy affair. Home to no fewer than three Bedouin-style palaces (one

of which comes with its own helipad), the park also boasts an ornate lift for those unable, or unwilling, to make the ascent to the viewing point.

The tour itself needs reworking: after clambering in and out of the minibus for the umpteenth time, trudging from one lot of gazelle poo to the next to take another photo of (yet more) buck, you may feel as worn out as the languid llama, which are too hot to even spit at you. Each animal does, however, have its own idiosyncratic charm: the dhabis (spangled-legged deer that gave the emirate its name) are so adorable, it's difficult to refrain from popping one into your bag; the Oryx are challengingly elusive; the emus, with ears resembling cigarette burns, appear constantly perplexed; and the majestic giraffes parade their patchwork patterns with great pride. If you are lucky, you may even pass a school of dolphins en route.

Apart from reclaiming acres of dry land, some of the plantations are part of food growing experiments, which test new ideas and find species that show the maximum tolerance for the emirate's arid climate. And those who chose to make the island their home have found a refuge and staging post with a safe anchorage, excellent fishing and treasured pearling beds in the Gulf nearby.

Keen conservationists and curious tourists alike will enjoy a trip to this crown jewel of the Arabian waters. Refreshments come in the form of cold drinks and sandwiches with the crusts cut off, and what the guide lacks in command of the facts, she makes up for with her sunny personality.

Danat Resort Jebel Dhanna
02 801 2222/www.ncth.com. **Tours** 8am-12.15pm Thur, Fri. **Cost** Dhs100.

The UAE

One&Only
Royal Mirage
Dubai

Dubai's most romantic beach resort

The Palace   *Residence & Spa   Arabian Court

For reservations or more information please contact
One&Only Royal Mirage, PO Box 37252, Dubai, UAE. Telephone + 971 4 399 99 99   oneandonlyroyalmirage.com
*Member of The Small Leading Hotels of the World

City hotels

Crowne Plaza Abu Dhabi

*Hamdan Street (Fifth Street) (02 621 0000/
www.crowneplaza.com).* **Rates** Dhs450-1,550
double. **Credit** AmEx MC, V. **Map** p254 B3 ⑥
Centrally located, the Crowne Plaza is in prime position for those who want to take full advantage of
Abu Dhabi's shopping activities, although it's a little dated by today's standards. The Roman-style
rooftop pool is a major plus for visitors, while the
popular basement bar Heroes (*see p260*) offers entertainment for the evenings.

Le Royal Meridien Abu Dhabi

*Khalifa Bin Zayed Street (02 674 2020/
www.lemeridien.com).* **Rates** Dhs450-Dhs900
double (excl 16% tax). **Credit** AmEx, MC,
V. **Map** p254 B3 ⑦
Arguably the top business hotel in the city, this
plush 31-storey building resembles an ordinary city
skyscraper in all respects bar the revolving Al Fanar
restaurant (*see p258*) that slowly slides around the
roof of the building. Suites in the Royal Tower are
excellent, while the rest of the hotel's rooms are more
than adequate. The Meridien also has an impressive
number of restaurants and bars onsite, although the
Illusions nightclub is best avoided.

Millennium Hotel Abu Dhabi

*Khalifa Bin Zayed Street (02 626 2700/www.
millenniumhotels.com).* **Rates** Dhs800 double
(excl 16% tax). **Credit** AmEx, MC, V.
Map p254 B3 ⑧
The Millennium is a central hotel with large rooms
overlooking both the capital gardens and the corniche,
offering great views whichever side of the building
you are in. The decor is a nice mix of dark woods and
marble and competent staff conduct their business
with unobtrusive efficiency. The hotel is popular with
business travellers as well as B-list stars. It has a boutique feel and a modern gym and pool to while away
a day in before you hit the town. Then again you could
stay put enjoy a leisurely meal at the hotel.

Resources

Hospital

Al Noor *Khalifa Bin Zayed Street (02 626 5265).*
Map p254 B3.

Internet

Street Net Café *Abu Dhabi Mall, north end of
Ninth Street (02 645 4141).* **Price** Dhs15/hr.
No credit cards. **Map** p254 C2.

Police station

Police HQ *Sheikh Zayed First Street (02 446
1461).* **Map** p254 A4.

Post office

Central post office *East Road (02 621 5415).*
Open 8am-8pm Sat-Wed; 8am-6pm Thur.
Map p254 B2.

Tourist information

Ministry of Information & Culture, near police
station, Airport Road (02 444 0444/info@
abudhabitourism.ae). **Open** 7.30am-2pm Sat-Wed.
Map p254 C3.
There are plans to move the tourist office to the city
centre; contact the Ministry for up-to-date details.

Getting there

By car

From Dubai, Abu Dhabi is a straight drive of 150km
(95 miles) down the Sheikh Zayed Road. The road
turns into Airport Road as you enter Abu Dhabi,
and the city (where the roads are on a grid system)
is fairly easy to navigate.

By bus

Minibuses that leave from Bur Dubai bus station
cost between Dhs15 and Dhs20. Despite the set
timetable drivers usually just wait for the bus to
fill up before they set off, meaning seating is often
rather cramped. The minibus will drop you off at
the bus station in the centre of Abu Dhabi from
which cheap local taxis are available.

By taxi

The journey from Dubai to Abu Dhabi will cost you
Dhs220 to Dhs250 if you flag a taxi down in the
street, but make sure the seatbelts are working, as
the journey down the Sheikh Zayed Road to the capital is not always the best advert for road safety.
You're probably better off with Al Ghazal Express –
an Abu Dhabi-based taxi operator – who will come
to collect you in Dubai and take you to the capital for
a flat fee of Dhs150 (the return journey, oddly, is
Dhs225). It's a cheaper set fee and the cars are far
superior, in terms of both comfort and safety, than
standard Abu Dhabi cabs. Bookings can be made by
calling 02 444 5885 directly, which is cheaper than
going through a hotel. If you're travelling alone, you
could take a shared taxi from Bur Dubai bus station
at a cost of Dhs50. The taxi waits until there are four
passengers before departing, so you could be sat
waiting for anything from ten minutes to an hour.

Al Ain

The UAE's third city is a sleepy place where
very little happens, although it can be a
pleasant place for a weekend break. About
160 kilometres (100 miles) east of Abu Dhabi
and the same distance south-east of Dubai,
Al Ain is a 90-minute drive from either, but
there are also domestic and international flights
to Al Ain International Airport (03 785 5555).
Despite being sparsely populated, it's a large,
sprawling city that appears to be home to
around half the world's roundabouts.
　　The UAE's **Natural History Museum** (Al
Khubaisi, 03 761 2277) and **Al Ain Museum**

The UAE

Al Ain: a green and pleasant land. *See p265.*

(Zayed Bin Sultan Street, 03 764 1595) together house the country's largest collection of historical artefacts, and although they're hardly presented in the most engaging manner, it's a good place to investigate if you're interested in what conditions were like in the UAE before they struck black gold. The nearby **Al Ain Zoo & Aquarium** (Zoo roundabout, by the traffic police HQ, 03 782 8188) is the biggest zoo in the country.

Don't be tempted by the **Hili Fun City** theme park – it's a wasteland of decay and decrepit rides, the vast majority of which are, according to the signs, 'permanently closed due to safty (sic) reasons'. If, however, you're a location scout hoping to make a movie set in a children's theme park following the apocalypse, then you're in luck.

The best time to visit Al Ain is in the winter, when time can be spent exploring ancient archaeological sites and the hot springs in the Jebel Hafeet mountains. Jebel Hafeet is also the site of archaeological finds that date back to the end of the fourth millennium BC. The hills around here are pockmarked with caves, which can be explored by adventure groups. The elevation of the land makes Jebel Hafeet a good few degrees cooler than both Dubai and Abu Dhabi, meaning it's bearable even in the height of summer.

Al Ain Rotana Hotel

Zayed Bin Sultan Street (03 754 5111/www.rotana. com). **Rates** Dhs400-Dhs750 double (excl 16% tax). **Credit** AmEx, MC, V.
The low-rise Rotana boasts a stunning swimming pool and modish, nicely turned-out rooms. Tennis courts, a well-stocked gym and superb massage facilities are further draws. This is the classiest hotel to be found in the city.

Hilton Al Ain

Follow signs from city centre to Sarroj (03 768 6666/www1.hilton.com). **Rates** Dhs450-Dhs900 double. **Credit** AmEx, MC, V.

This good-value branch of the Hilton empire has large, comfortable rooms that are equipped with balconies on which you can take your time to grapple with the generous breakfasts. Sink-in armchairs, bouncy beds, myriad satellite channels and speedy room service make this a good option if you're after a lazy weekend.

InterContinental Al Ain Resort

Near Al Ain Mall, Ernyadat Road (03 768 6686/ www.ichotelsgroup.com). **Rates** Dhs350-Dhs700 double (excl 16% tax). **Credit** AmEx, MC, V.
A sprawling complex that's the focal point of the Garden City's social life in the evenings, the InterContinental hosts a series of good outlets and clean, functional rooms. Popular with families for its network of swimming pools and the laid-back attitude of the staff, this is a fine hotel to stay in.

Liwa

Liwa – the famed fertile crescent of the nation and the gateway to the Empty Quarter – should be on everyone's list of places to experience in the UAE. Only three hours by car from Abu Dhabi, Liwa's desert scenery and rugged terrain is a world away from urban living. The oasis features plenty of freshwater pools and date plantations and is home to the Bani Yas tribe – the Bedouin ancestors of Abu Dhabi's ruling family.

Sightseeing

Don't look to Liwa if you're in the mood to let your hair down – it is no party place. What it offers is a welcome respite from busy, bustling city life; visitors head here for the grand silence that echoes off the expanses of the Empty Quarter and the beauty of the vast dunes that roll into the distance. When you visit, take a drive around the series of villages, stopping off at points of interest such as the remarkably well preserved fort and the oasis of **Qatuf** which – for those who have read *Arabian Sands* – is where Sir Wilfred Thesiger camped during his visit to Liwa back in 1947. The wells that Thesiger mentions in his book are still here, right by the mosque.

You can't leave Liwa without experiencing the magisterial beauty of the desert. The star attraction here is **Moreeb Hill**; at 358 feet, it's the country's biggest sand dune and plays host to the annual Moreeb Dune Championship for cars and motorbikes. The intrepid or foolhardy (delete as appropriate) can attempt to scale the shifting sand mound in a 4x4. If that sounds a tad too intimidating, more sedate camel and horse treks can be organised through the **Liwa Hotel** (02 882 2000) at dawn and dusk, as well

as belly dancing shows out in the sands and desert camping. For desert safaris, try Off Road Adventures (www.arabiantours.com).

Where to stay

The four-star **Liwa Hotel** (02 882 2000/ www.ncth.com) is your only option and it's not a bad one. The 66-room resort overlooks the Rub al Khali desert and is surrounded by some of the highest sand dunes in the world. Spacious, well-equipped rooms are arranged around a sun-drenched pool and provide stunning vistas of the infinite dunes rolling out to the horizon. Facilities include four floodlit tennis courts, a volleyball court, a swimming pool, saunas, a Jacuzzi and a steam room. There's also a children's pool and playground area to keep the hotel's younger residents entertained. A selection of decent restaurants and bars – including an evening terrace for shisha – complete the food and drink choices. During the sizzling summer months, the hotel has some excellent offers.

A luxury five-star retreat – Qasr Al Sarab – is due to open in the Empty Quarter in 2009, thereby increasing accommodation options deep in the desert. When completed, the hotel will offer 150 rooms, 60 villas, a spa and an observatory from which guests can watch the sun rise and set over the desert.

Getting there

From Dubai, head 135km west along the Dubai-Abu Dhabi highway until you reach the Mafraq turning. Go straight towards Tarif and turn left 23km later when you see a sign for Dhafrah and Shah fields. Drive south following signs for Hmeem on the edge of Liwa. Turn right and head for the villages and oases. For more detailed directions and a map, visit www.ncth.com.

Liwa.

The UAE

Northern Emirates

Get out of the hustle and bustle of Dubai and explore the rest of the country.

It sometimes seems that while Dubai happily hogs the tourist limelight, the rest of the country recedes in its shadow, but these other emirates do have plenty to offer. When you've had your fill of bars, clubs and malls, can't stand to look at another Lamborghini and feel the need to escape the rising dust from gargantuan construction sites, it's time to take a road trip to the northern emirates. There you'll find more local culture than Dubai can muster, including graceful mosques in **Sharjah**, historical dhow yards in **Ajman**, pristine beaches in **Umm Al Quwain** and the dramatic Hajar mountain range in **Ras Al Khaimah**.

The further north you travel, the more preserved local traditions are. In these areas you'll find Emiratis sitting in seaside cafés drinking Arabic coffee, local women gathering in henna parlours gossiping about their husbands and bustling souks in which

merchants hold fast to the stalls their fathers owned in the 1950s. And while these northern states could use a sprinkle of Dubai's fairy dust to take away the grit and grime, they have an endearing sense of disorder about them. They're itching to be noticed and demanding to be explored.

Sharjah

In certain areas, you'll find multi-domed, intricately carved mosques bordering tree-lined, manicured lawns and artificial lakes, but most of Sharjah's neighbourhoods are, unfortunately, depressingly beige and cramped. However, as the undisputed cultural capital of the UAE (at least until the Guggenheim and Louvre open in Abu Dhabi), Sharjah's commitment to the arts is highly commendable. In spite of being home to the strictest laws in the UAE (it's the only

Anything London can do... **Eye of the Emirates** at **Qanat Al Qasba**. *See p270.*

dry emirate), Sharjah's thriving arts and culture scene has continued to attract and enthral visitors. With such landmarks as the **Heritage Area**, which includes the **Islamic Museum**, **Bait Al Naboodah**, **Souk Al Arsa** and **Qanat Al Qasba**, the emirate has preserved its history and traditions, rendering it the ideal destination for tourists who are keen on learning a thing or two about the UAE. Make time for the harrowing trek on the perma-clogged Dubai-Sharjah Road – this emirate's worth the effort.

History

Sharjah's roots lie to the north of its modern location, in and around what is now the emirate of **Ras Al Khaimah** (*see p277*), which replaced the ancient capital of Julfar as a local trading hub some time in the 17th century. Sharjah grew as a competing power to Ras Al Khaimah, with things coming to a head in 1814, when Sultan Ibn Saqr, a former Ras Al Khaimah ruler, seized Sharjah and declared it a separate sheikhdom. He then annexed Ras Al Khaimah to his new base, following the sacking of the city by a British expedition in 1819.

Thus began a game of chess, in which Ras Al Khaimah would move in and out of Sharjah's fold several times. Sharjah became signatory to the 1820 General Treaty of Peace between the British and nine local Arab sheikhdoms. Despite the British installing a garrison in the region and a political agent in Sharjah, different factions continued to feud. In 1835, the British became more active, signing a treaty to create a six-month truce with the principal sheikhs during the pearling season. This was renewed for ten years in 1843. In 1853, a 'perpetual maritime truce' was signed, giving the area the name the 'Trucial Coast'. By 1893, the British had effectively turned the Trucial Coast into a protectorate, even though the British flag did not fly anywhere other than from its military bases and agents' buildings. However, the swings back and forth of family politics did not end under British dominance: coups in Sharjah took place in 1951 and 1965, and there was an assassination only months after the British withdrawal in 1971. An attempted coup in 1987 was ended by consultation between the ruling families of all the emirates. Despite the intrigue, Sharjah grew rapidly from the 1960s onwards. It has become today a major trading hub and manufacturing base despite, or perhaps because of, the oil that has helped Abu Dhabi and Dubai to prosper so dramatically. Sharjah's trading history still stands it in good stead at present, though it has also been aided by investment from Saudi Arabia.

Sightseeing

Sharjah was bestowed the title Cultural Capital of the Arab World by UNESCO in 1998; cynics may well dispute the difficulty of achieving such status, yet the emirate proves the naysayers wrong. Several galleries face on to Arabic Calligraphy Square, a haven of artistry that seems miles away from the industrial part of Sharjah. It's also worth an educational stroll around the Heritage Area, a complex of old buildings and renovated structures clustered just a minute's walk from Rolla Street taxi stand. You can either pay a fee to visit each museum in the Heritage Area, or you can opt for the Dhs15 pass that gives you access to all the sights for a month. Sharjah also hosts the spring **Sharjah International Art Biennial**. The 2007 event, included works by Lutz & Guggisberg, Dan Perjovschi and Marjolijn Dijkman.

Archaeological Museum

Halwan District, off Cultural Square (06 566 5466). **Open** 9am-1pm, 5-8pm Sat, Mon-Thur; 5-8pm Fri. **Admission** Dhs5.
This large museum presents local archaeology beautifully. Stretched across several halls loaded full of audio-visual wonder, man's first and subsequent steps across the Arabian Peninsula are documented in chronological order. Clear displays of finds from Sharjah's many Stone Age, Iron Age and Bronze Age sites sit alongside lovingly wrought models of the emirate's first houses. Touch-screen computers provide images from the museum archives and also educational games for children.

Art Museum

Al Shuwaiheyn, behind the bazaar, close to the waterfront (06 568 8222). **Open** 9am-9pm Sat-Thur; 3-9pm Fri. **Admission** free.
Paintings, documents and maps, dating back to the 18th century and taken from the personal collection of the ruler of Sharjah, sit alongside occasionally awful abstract art. The permanent collection is brightened by an active programme of exhibition exchanges with international museums. The museum is home to the Sharjah International Art Biennial, held in spring (usually April) every odd-numbered year. There is a handy coffee bar here, and basement parking.

Bait Al Naboodah

Al Shuwaiheyn, between the waterfront & Al Hosn Avenue (Bank Street) (06 568 1738). **Open** 8am-8pm Sat-Thur; 4-8pm Fri. **Admission** Dhs5.
Built in 1845, the Al Naboodah family home was inhabited until the 1970s, but then very quickly fell into disrepair. However, in the early 1990s, the Sharjah government declared the home a historical building and began renovations. Today, it's an excellent example of the simplicity of traditional life in the emirate, even for the wealthy.

The UAE

Desert Park & Arabian Wildlife Centre

Sharjah Airport Road (direction Al Dhaid), Interchange 9 (06 531 1999). **Open** 9am-5.30pm Sat-Mon, Wed-Thur; 11am-5.30pm Sat; 2-5.30pm Fri. **Admission** Dhs15; under-12s free.

This impressive educational and research facility houses the most important captive breeding centre for endangered species in the whole of the Middle East. There's a charming public zoo in the centre, plus an innovative natural history museum (06 531 1411) and an excellent children's education park. More than 100 species of animal roam the various recreated habitats, while in the vast indoor aviary thousands of birds swoop mere inches above your head.

Heritage Area

Al Shuwaiheyn, between the waterfront & Al Hosn Avenue (Bank Street) (no phone). **Open** 8am-8pm Sat-Thur; 4-8pm Fri. **Admission** varies.

Around the courtyard of the former home of the Al Naboodah family, the buildings of the Heritage Museum are a fascinating example of traditional UAE architecture. Inside, you'll find displays of old clothing and heritage items. For the modern-day equivalent, check out the nearby Al Arsa Souk, an alley packed with antiques and jewellery.

Al Hosn Fort

Al Hosn Avenue (Bank Street), Heritage Area (06 512 9999). **Open** 9am-1pm, 5-8pm Sat, Sun, Tue-Thur (Wed afternoon women & children only); 5-8.30pm Fri. **Admission** free.

Al Hosn Fort was built in 1820 by Sultan Ibn Saqr, the first of the Qawasim sheikhs to make Sharjah his capital. The fort was the political centre of the emirate until it was demolished in 1969 to make way for the modern buildings that now typify the city; only two walls and a 12m (40ft) tower were left standing. Original 19th-century structures were renovated in 1996, and the rest of the complex was rebuilt to its original design; the fort now houses a museum, with a series of exhibition rooms surrounding the central courtyard. Inside are weapons, coins, jewellery and information about the pearl trade of old.

Islamic Museum

Al Gharb, off Al Hosn Avenue (Bank Street), Heritage Area (06 568 3334). **Open** 8am-8pm Sat-Thur; 4-8pm Fri. **Admission** Dhs5.

Along a narrow lane behind Arabic Calligraphy Square you'll find the old wooden door of Sharjah's single-storey Islamic Museum. This houses an important collection of rare Arabic manuscripts, a major Islamic mint exhibition featuring silver dinars and dirhams from the Abbasid and Umayyad periods (from the sixth century AD), plus archaeological artefacts from the Islamic era. Particularly fascinating are navigational instruments used by ancient Arabic seafarers and an extraordinary 'upside down' map of the world that was drawn 1,000 years ago by Sharif Al Idrisi.

Maritime Museum

Al Gharb, off Al Hosn Avenue (Bank Street), Heritage Area (06 568 3030). **Open** 8am-8pm Sat-Thur; 5-8pm Fri. **Admission** Dhs5.

This tribute to the emirate's booming pearl trade in the 19th and early 20th centuries will have maritime enthusiasts captivated. You'll find every imaginable artefact relating to the pearl industry, including the handmade dhows used to take the divers out to sea.

Museum for Arabic Calligraphy & Ornamentation

Al Gharb, off Al Hosn Avenue (Bank Street), Heritage Area (06 569 4561). **Open** 8am-8pm Sat-Thur; 4.30-8pm Fri. **Admission** Dhs5 adults, Dhs10 families.

Walk west to the large defensive tower that's visible from Al Hosn Fort, turn north into Arabic Calligraphy Square, and you'll find this intriguing museum. The galleries are filled with beautiful works by Arab, Persian and Turkish artists, while the calligraphy and ceramics studios, in the cool of winter, host students developing their ideas.

Shops & souks

For a change from the modern malls, immerse yourself in local culture with a trip to the traditional souks at the Ar-Ruba flyover end of the Corniche Road. In the single-storey

Qanat Al Qasba

It's only fitting that Sharjah, the country's cultural hub, would build a destination like Qanat Al Qasba. Described as a 'premier cultural, leisure and entertainment destination', it's a collection of bookstores, a theatre, an exhibition hall and the highest Ferris wheel in the region – the **Eye of the Emirates** (*photo p268*). The wheel's 42 air-conditioned cabins give visitors a chance to get a bird's eye view of Sharjah and the Qanat Al Qasba complex, which sits next to the Al Khan Lagoon off Al Taawun Road.

Despite its numerous shops, cafés and bookstores, Qanat Al Qasba feels deserted during the day. At night, however, the centre comes alive with expats and Emiratis alike, who file in for a relaxed evening at one of the many cafés. Although it's a valuable addition to Sharjah's arts scene, tourists in search of authenticity might be disappointed by how mainstream and commercial many of Qanat's concerts are. But it's still worth a visit, offering a good opportunity to mingle with the locals. *For more info, visit www.qaq.ae*

vegetable souk opposite the oil supply post, the date stall – with produce from Iran, Iraq, Saudi Arabia and the UAE – provides the best value for money: a kilogramme of sweet sticky Saudi dates costs around Dhs10. You might be surprised at the rather high prices of other fruits, but with the local climate as hot as it is, most of the produce has to be imported.

On the opposite side of the road is the **fish souk** (5-11am). Here, dhows berth and offload their catch direct to around 50 fresh fish shops facing the quay on Khalid Lagoon. Further up the corniche is the fantastically comprehensive **plant souk**, and behind this flea market of flora lies the **livestock souk** (follow signs for 'Bird and Animal Market' on the Corniche Road), offering cows, sheep and goats from Somalia and Pakistan, as well as young bulls that will be fattened in Fujairah for fighting or, more accurately, butting. With chickens running around and Bedouin boys driving pick-ups with goats in the back, this is a more accurate example of modern UAE country ways than any number of heritage museums.

From here, walk through to the poultry pushers of the **bird souk**. Another long, slim building, this souk is lined with shops selling every kind of bird imaginable, including pheasants, peacocks, baby ostriches, song birds and parrots. Be warned, though: many birds are in the sort of cramped conditions that you may find unpleasant to witness.

Blue Souk
Al Majaz, Corniche Road, close to Khalid Lagoon. **Open** 9am-1pm, 4-11pm Sat-Thur; 9am-noon, 4-11pm Fri.
Also known as Souk Al Markazi, the Blue Souk is set in a huge green space dotted with fountains, looking much like a cross between a European central train station and a mosque – a perfectly atrocious example of Sharjah's modern, wedding cake-style architecture. The crème brûlée colours of the interior and fiddly wrought iron don't help to dispel that image, but you're here to browse the architecture, especially as the souk is fully air-conditioned, allowing for proper browsing even in the height of summer.

There are around 600 shops in the Blue Souk, making it the largest single wholesale and retail market for handicrafts and textiles in Arabia. It is not an Arab market in the true sense: the vast majority of goods sold are Indian in origin. And don't expect to find genuine antiques. If you are told that what you are looking at is over five years old, be very careful. But if you find a shopkeeper you are comfortable with, sit down, drink tea and bargain away to your heart's content.

There are, in effect, two identical souk buildings, connected by bridges. The ground floor of the building nearest the lagoon is mostly taken up with gold, textiles, perfume and camera shops; the one further

away sells finished clothes and electronics. Look out for wooden furniture from Jaipur in Rajasthan, Iranian and Pakistani carpets and handmade textiles. Highest quality pure silk Nepalese pashminas should cost less than Dhs250, and you can get Indian pure wool pashminas for around Dhs100. Among the best bargains are the 1.5m (5ft) chain-stitched rugs from Kashmir – you should be able to pick one up for approximately Dhs150.

Sahara Centre
Al Nahda Street (06 531 6611). **Open** 10am-11pm Sat-Thur; 2-11pm Fri. **Credit** MC, V.
Sharjah's mall mania manifests itself in the snake-like sprawl of the Sahara Centre, with hundreds of shops coiling along the underbelly of the first floor. While Dubai's usual suspects are all featured, there are a clutch of more interesting independent stores. The biggest attraction is probably the indoor Adventureland (06 531 6363) on the second floor, which boasts two thrilling roller coasters (one for teens and one for kids), Wacky Racer mini dodgems and a Log Jam water ride. And if in all the excitement you've worked up an appetite, you can stuff yourself silly at the food court.

Sharjah City Centre
Al Wahda Street (06 533 2626). **Open** 10am-10pm Sat-Thur (Carrefour 9am-midnight); 2-10pm Fri (Carrefour 9-11.30am, 1.30pm-midnight).
This mall has the same Lego-like colour and feel as Deira City Centre in Dubai (in fact, it's owned by the same company), but with less variety of shops. Its Carrefour is similar to its counterparts in Dubai, and huge enough to sell absolutely everything, and there's a Magic Planet to keep the kids happy.

Souk Al Arsa
Al Gharb, off Al Hosn Avenue (Bank Street), Heritage Area. **Open** 8am-1pm, 4-8pm Sat-Thur; 5-8pm Fri.
Not only is this souk one of the oldest in the UAE, it's also one of the most widely used. UAE nationals from all over the Emirates come here to shop for jewellery and traditional clothes in the many outlets. Due to recent renovations, the souk looks a little contrived, and since the shopkeepers are well trained in the art of ripping off tourists, a little bargaining goes a very long way. And thankfully, the shops here contain a plethora of local artefacts worth haggling for.

Souk Al Majarrah
Corniche Road, next to Masjid Jamila Mosque. **Open** 9am-1.30pm, 4-10.30pm daily.
Souk Al Majarrah is a gorgeous structure, with a vaulted ceiling and Corinthian columns styled, in part, on the most beautiful souks of Damascus and Aleppo in Syria. The shops cater exclusively to Arab women's and men's fashions, notably selling *abayas* (cloaks), handbags, shoes and perfume. The only shop not selling some form of fashion is Mujezat Al Shifa Honey (06 565 8707), where you can pick up 500g jars of Afghani-Pakistani lotus honey for Dhs50.

Where to eat, drink & stay

Coral Beach Hotel

Coral Beach roundabout, Beach Road (06 522 9999/ www.coral-international.com). **Rates** Dhs1,050 double. **Credit** AmEx, MC, V.

With its coastline dominated by massive ports, Sharjah seems an unlikely place for a beach resort. A small and slightly cranky four-star accommodation option, Coral boasts an excellent private beach (actually a man-made cove). There's also a large raised swimming pool overlooking the beach, a 'rockery' for kids, slides and a circular 'bar' area (this is Sharjah, though, so no alcohol is served). A second pool is right outside the hotel, in reasonably extensive gardens.

Marbella Resort, Sharjah

Al Buheira Corniche Road, beside Hotel Holiday International (06 574 111/www.marbellaresort.com). **Rates** Dhs690 junior suite; Dhs1,150 master suite. **Credit** MC, V.

Built to look like a Spanish seaside village, Marbella Resort is an odd but pleasant hotel to find on Khalid Lagoon's shores. Junior and master suites are scattered around the manicured grounds, separated by well-maintained gardens and towering palm trees. The hotel boasts two outdoor temperature-controlled pools, two tennis courts, a couple of squash courts, a free daily shuttle to Dubai and the typical recreational facilities you'd find at any hotel, including a billiards table and a gym. Rendezvous Restaurant, the hotel's all day dining venue, prepares a breakfast and lunch buffet. The food here is generally good.

Radisson SAS Sharjah

Ahmed Bin Darwish Square, Corniche Road (06 565 7777/www.sharjah.radissonsas.com). **Rates** Dhs805 double. **Credit** MC, V.

The Radisson SAS may be getting on a bit, but its pyramidal blue-glass-and-cream cladding hides what is still one of the loveliest (and largest) atriums in the world, where you'll find Cappuccino's café. But the whole atrium is filled with calming noise from what lies inside: an indoor arbour, or, as the hotel likes to call it, a 'tropical rainforest'. A meal on the decking downstairs in the Calypso Café is charming (and overlooks a stream inhabited by happily waddling ducks), even if the food is the usual hotel fare (fish and chips, Dhs50; mezze, Dhs50). There's a very 1970s-looking beach, with wooden parasols dotted along a little curved bay.

Sharjah Rotana Hotel

Al Khaleej Square, Ar-Ruba flyover (06 563 7777/ www.sharjahrotana.com). **Rates** Dhs517 double. **Credit** AmEx, MC, V.

A clean and functional four star, the Sharjah Rotana is a proven respite from the maelstrom of the city outside. The Al Dar Restaurant on the first floor serves decent Western food, including sandwiches, salads and steaks, with the piped jazz music fitting in nicely with the place's general plasticky feel.

Resources

Hospitals

Al Dhaid Hospital *Al Dhaid, 50km (30 miles) inland from Sharjah (06 882 2221).*
Kuwaiti Hospital *Kuwait Road (06 524 2111).*
Al Zahra Private Hospital *Opposite the clock tower, Al Zahra Square (06 561 9999).*

Internet

Radisson SAS Sharjah, *Corniche Road (06 565 7777).* **Open** Call for information. **Price** Dhs30/hr.

Police station

Sharjah Police Station & Traffic Police Headquarters *Abu Tina (06 598 2222).*

Post office

Central post office *By Municipality roundabout, Al Soor (06 572 2219).* **Open** 8am-8pm Sat-Thur; 5-9pm Fri.

Tourist information

Sharjah Commerce & Tourism Development Authority *Off Ar-Ruba Road, towards the Corniche (06 556 6777/www.sharjah-welcome.com).* **Open** 7.30am-2.30pm Sun-Thur.

Essentials

It is illegal for women to wear clothes that show their upper arms or too much leg, or to be in a car with someone who is not related to them (this is mainly aimed at stopping prostitution). Alcohol is strictly illegal anywhere in Sharjah, including its enclaves on the east coast. Unlike Dubai, English isn't spoken everywhere – a few words in Arabic go a long way (for more on language, *see p39*).

Getting around

Metered taxis are slowly being introduced into Sharjah. However, there are still a number of unmetered cabbies operating, who are prone to ripping travellers off. Fares within Sharjah cost about Dhs10. Sometimes drivers won't take your custom if they don't understand you or don't want to go in your direction. If you're stuck, Delta Taxis (06 559 8598) will pick you up.

Getting there

By car

Sharjah is clearly signposted on Dubai's major roads. The easiest option is to cross Garhoud Bridge and continue north straight along the freeway to Sharjah.

By bus

Buses leave from the Deira taxi stand near Al Nasr Square whenever the bus is full (normally every 20-30 minutes). They cost Dhs5 and stop anywhere en route to Sharjah's Rolla Square.

By taxi

From Dubai you can take any of the usual metered cabs for roughly Dhs20 from Deira, Dhs40 from Bur Dubai and Dhs60 from Jumeirah. However, if you get an unlicensed cab you can haggle for a cheaper price. You have to return to Dubai in a Sharjah taxi, the majority of which are metered nowadays, although drivers remain famously erratic.

Ajman

At a grand total of 260 square kilometres, Ajman is the smallest of the emirates, and doesn't get much of a chance to leave an impression. Sandwiched between conservative Sharjah and sport-obsessed Umm Al Quwain, Ajman has a rich history. When, in the mid 18th century, the seafaring Qawasim tribe took control of the lower Gulf coast, the tiny coastal strip of Ajman fell under their sway. But soon after they destroyed the Qawasim fleet at Ras Al Khaimah in 1819, the British declared Ajman independent, leaving power firmly in the hands of the Al Abu Khurayban clan of the An-Naim tribe. Ajman was signatory to British Trucial treaties of 1820, 1835, 1843 and 1853, and became subject to the Residency of the Gulf in 1892.

Vestiges of this era remain in several locally built *burj* (defensive towers) which dot the coast, and the large and well-renovated 18th-century fort, now inland at the centre of the city – ask for Dowar Al Hosn or Al Hosn roundabout. Alternatively, at the roundabout before the Kempinski Hotel Ajman, look for the Ajman Chamber of Commerce building on your right-hand side. Turn right here and continue straight over the next roundabout. The fort is on the left and houses the **Ajman Museum**. Fishing has always been the main industry in the emirate; traditional fishing vessels can still be seen all along the coast. Ajman port, located on the northern side of the creek a few kilometres from the town centre, has been transformed into a major dhow-building centre and important dockyard. But, without oil resources, Ajman has been largely dependent on federal money for its development since joining the United Arab Emirates in 1971.

Still, hundreds of companies are being incorporated at Ajman Free Zone and Ajman Industrial Area which means the population grew from around 80,000 in 1992 to around 250,000 in 2005, and continues to grow at a fast rate. Indeed the expansion of Dubai, Sharjah and Ajman now means that the emirate is part of a coastal conurbation that starts at Jebel Ali in Dubai and ends at Ajman's northernmost border with Umm Al Quwain, with rent here cheap compared to in neighbouring areas, many people now live in Ajman but work in Sharjah or Dubai.

Ajman Museum

Al Hosn roundabout, Aziz Street, by Central Square (06 742 3824). **Open** 9am-1pm, 5-8pm Sun-Thur; 4-7pm Fri. **Admission** Dhs4 adults, Dhs2 under-7s.
Displays depicting weird and wonderful medical and religious practices give a fantastic if eerie insight into life as it must have been led for centuries among the coastal Bedouin. It isn't a large collection, but it certainly delves deeper than most displays of so-called heritage. There is also a working wind tower in one corner of the fort, under which one can sit to feel the breeze that's created by the traditional design.

Ajman Souk

Sheikh Rashid bin Hamid Road. **Open** 9am-1pm, 4-11pm Sat-Thur; 4-11pm Fri.
There's nothing more indicative of Ajman's commitment to its heritage than its old souk. This gorgeous structure, of modern Islamic design, houses a number of local merchants keen on promoting and selling Ajman's many offerings. Here you can buy carpets, bags, shoes, *abayas* and dancing white bears covered with lights. Be prepared to haggle.

Dhow Yard

Ajman Coast Road, past the Coral Beach Hotel. **Open** varies.
Set at the northern end of the creek, this impressive yard is rumoured to be the world's largest dhow-building hub. The craftsmen here still use traditional and somewhat rudimentary tools to build these 60ft monsters. Even if you aren't a fan of ships, a trip to this yard is a people-watcher's dream.

Where to eat, drink & stay

The emirate's most luxurious resort is the five-star **Kempinski Hotel Ajman** (06 745 1555/www.ajmankempinski.com). Prices start at a bargain Dhs699 during the summer season, which explains why German and Russian tour operators regularly make block bookings here. Guests tend to stay within the hotel confines and sun themselves happily on the private beach, which is in truth far more inviting than the stretch of sand called Ajman Corniche.

There's little else to do in Ajman besides topping up your tan and eating, and the Kempinski offers decent restaurants: for Italian there's **Sabella's Trattoria & Pizzeria**, while **Bukhara** does some great North Indian food. There is also a lovely veranda café, the 24-hour **Café Kranzler**, where you can sit out just metres from the sea. **Hai Tao** is the Kempinski's Chinese outlet, but for a meal that's equally good but

The UAE

costs less (albeit in considerably more basic surroundings) try the **Blue Beach Restaurant** (06 745 1524) halfway down Ajman Corniche, on the opposite side of the road to the sea. The delightful family running the place hail from Shanghai, and specialise in food from that area. For a boozy option, head to the **Outside Inn** up the road from the Kempinski (*see p273*), which sums up everything appealing about Ajman. Perched right on the beach, the bar's outdoor terrace is just a stone's throw from the water, making it the perfect place to unwind, watch the sun set over the Gulf, sample the excellent, well-priced food (try the seafood platter) and engage in some idle chit-chat.

Close by is the four-star **Coral Suites Ajman** (06 742 9999, www.coral-international. com/suites). Although it doesn't have its own private beach, you can use the facilities of the Coral Hotel, around 15 minutes away by foot. Rooms here used to cost just Dhs100 a night in low season back when the hotel was called Safir Dana Resort, but since the hotel was bought out by Coral, prices have risen dramatically and the cheapest room is now priced at Dhs450.

The **Ajman Beach Hotel** (www.abh ajman.ae, 06 742 3333) hasn't raised its prices much in recent years, but its restaurant and bar complex is full of Russian and Chinese 'entertainers', which usually sees guests only staying for a few hours. If you do want a full night's sleep, it will cost Dhs550 for a double room (including tax). The beach is uninspiring, but the hotel's an acceptable choice if other places are fully booked. The booking policy is erratic to say the least; hotel staff are reluctant to accept bookings over a fortnight in advance, and can be brusque and unhelpful on the phone.

Resources

Post office

Central post office, near Lulu supermarket/National Bank of Abu Dhabi (06 742 2257). **Open** 8am-8pm Sat-Thur; 5-9pm Fri.

Tourist information

Ministry of Information & Culture, nr Kempinski Hotel Ajman, the Creek end of Arabian Gulf Street (06 744 4000/www.uaeinteract.com). **Open** 7.30am-2pm Sat-Wed.

Getting there

By car

From Dubai, get on to Sharjah's Ar-Ruba Street by turning left underneath Sharjah Gate Square. Cross Khalid Lagoon, and then at the Khaleej Square roundabout turn left to the coast. The Ajman/Sharjah border is at the Coral Beach Hotel roundabout, just by the sea.

By bus

Dubai Transport buses leave for Ajman from the Deira taxi stand (near Al Nasr Square). They cost Dhs7, and leave when full.

By taxi

Metered taxis from Dubai to Ajman Corniche cost Dhs40-Dhs50 from Deira, Dhs60-Dhs70 from Bur Dubai and Dhs80-Dhs90 from Jumeirah.

Umm Al Quwain

Umm Al Quwain is hardly a bustling metropolis, but does offer an impressive array of sporting activities. Sailing enthusiasts stop by here on their way to Musandam, Oman; since the emirate has no reclamation projects in the works, its waters are cleaner and clearer than Dubai's and Sharjah's.

For those interested in natural landscapes, Umm Al Quwain has unspoilt desert dunes, and the largest mangrove swamp on the west coast of the UAE, where many bird species live. It isn't uncommon to find fervent birdwatchers crawling through the mangrove, hoping to spot rare Arabian species. For adventure junkies, the **Emirates Car & Motorcycle Racing Club** (Ras Al Khaimah Road, 06 768 1166, www. motorplex.ae) has full drag, motocross, autocross and even supercross tracks. Every Thursday and Friday night at 6pm from September to May (the drag race season) upwards of 15,000 people come to watch local teams compete in some of the world's fastest cars. On the other side of the road, the **Umm Al Quwain Aeroclub** (06 768 1447) is another thrill-junkies' dream. Here you can skydive from 9am to sunset daily. Tandem jumps cost Dhs850, while qualified jumpers can have a go from as little as Dhs90 (plus an extra Dhs40 for parachute hire and Dhs25 for packing); a parachute student's 'accelerated free fall package' is Dhs8,000 and includes ten jumps. Opposite the Aeroclub is the **Umm Al Quwain Shooting Club** (06 768 1900). You used to be able to shoot everything from Uzis to AK-47s here, but in 2003 the federal ministry in charge withdrew these licences across the UAE; you're now limited to single- and double-barrelled shotguns and .22 rifles. You can shoot these daily, except Wednesdays, from 1pm to 9pm (Friday 2.30-9pm). It's a good idea to have some form of ID to hand.

For chutes rather than shots, head a bit further up the road to **Dreamland Aqua Park**, a popular destination for families with water babies and fun seekers. The nearby **Umm Al Quwain Fort** (06 765 0888) is a far more calming experience.

Dreamland Aqua Park

Umm Al Quwain-Ras Al Khaimah road (06 768 1888). **Open** 10am-7pm daily. **Admission** Dhs80; Dhs50 4-11s; free under-3s. **Credit** AmEx, MC, V.
Although at times it might resemble a downtrodden holiday camp, there are enough flumes, swimming pools and crazily-attired chute fans in Dreamland to keep even the biggest kid happy. The super-fast, four-way flumes are great fun, while the vertiginous pink slide – offering unparalleled, if uninspiring, views over Umm Al Quwain – is a must-do. There are plenty of rides for the kids as well, while the well-stocked pool bar is the perfect place in which to sit back and bask in the sunshine.

Khor Al Beidah

For those unable to make it on to Al Siniyah Island (*see below*), Khor Al Beidah, on Al Ittihad Road, also northeast of the city, is a great place to observe Umm Al Quwain's wildlife.

Al Siniyah Island

Located just two kilometres north-east of the Umm Al Quwain peninsula, what might look to you like sand dunes and sparse scrubs is actually a bird watcher's paradise. This reserve is protected by the local government, so you may have trouble getting in, but if you do, you'll spot an impressive number of bird species and deer.

Umm Al Quwain Fort

Al Lubna Road, Old Town (06 765 0888). **Open** 8am-1pm, 5-8pm Sat-Thur; 5-8pm Fri. **Admission** Dhs4; free under-16s. **No credit cards**.
Very similar to other forts in the region, but with better access to rooms and walkways, Umm Al Quwain Fort has a well-laid-out jewellery collection, an in-depth weaponry display, plus a couple of rooms showing material from the Ad-Dur archaeological site. Most interesting of all, however, is the amazing story pinned to a wall of one of the towers. It relates (if you can decipher the slightly obscure English) the story of the murder of ruler Ahmed bin Ibrahim Al Mualla by his cousin-servant in 1929, and how the people of Umm Al Quwain punished the murderer by burning him alive inside the tower.

Where to eat, drink & stay

The **Flamingo Beach Resort** (06 765 0000, www.flamingoresort.ae) is one of those odd, desolate coastal resorts on the lower Gulf that brings to mind the Eagles' 'Hotel California'. Still, it has good service and is reasonable value for money – for Dhs400 you get a double room and the opportunity to lounge around a large, open grassy space with a pool and a bar that offers incredibly cheap booze. No food is served after 10pm but, as the concierge says, 'liquor is 24 hours'. The hotel also offers an unusual pastime: crab hunting. For Dhs125, you get taken out to the creek by motor launch for a couple of hours of night-diving along the shores of Al Siniyah Island. The trip includes snacks and dinner; the staff will barbecue your catch on the beach.

Another option is the **Umm Al Quwain Beach Hotel** (06 766 6647, www.uaqbeach hotel.com), which has poolside chalets of one to three bedrooms that are wickedly close to the beach. This simple hotel doesn't pretend to be any more glamorous than it is; it's a straightforward three-star beach resort with mediocre outlets and 1980s-inspired decor. The hotel is usually fully booked, no doubt by a

Umm Al Quwain.

Ras Al Khaimah's layered landscape takes in desert, mountains, coastline and greenery.

Dubai set looking for a more rustic experience. Chalets start at Dhs650 for a one-bedroom chalet, rising to Dhs1,500 for three-bedrooms.

Behind the Aeroclub is another lodging option, the **Barracuda Hotel** (06 768 1555, www.barracuda.ae) although it's not one we'd recommend. Firstly, it's expensive, at Dhs450 to Dhs750 (depending on whether you choose old or new ccommodation); secondly, the smell of sewage on the tide is well-nigh unbearable.

Don't feel obliged to stay in Umm Al Quwain at all. If you've got this far, you probably came by car, and there are only a few more kilometres to drive north until you reach the more attractive **Bin Majid Beach Resort** or **Al Hamra Fort Hotel** (for both, *see p278*).

Resources

Hospitals
Umm Al Quwain Hospital *Opposite National Bank of Dubai (06 765 6888).*

Post office
Central Post Office *(06 765 7001).* **Open** 8am-2pm, 4-10pm Sun-Thur.

Tourist information
Ministry of Information & Culture *Off Abu Bakr Al Siddiq Road (06 765 6663/ www.uaeinteract.com).* **Open** 7.30am-2.30pm Sun-Thur.

Getting there

By car
Take the Dubai-Sharjah Road and keep going north until you hit UFO roundabout (so-named because of the concrete, UFO-shaped building on one side), then take the second exit towards Cultural roundabout. From the roundabout, take the second exit. Filter right at the next major junction, take the third exit left, and head straight for about 20km (12.5 miles) until you hit Umm Al Quwain roundabout. Turn left to go into town, or head 15km (9.5 miles) straight on to reach the Aeroclub.

By bus
Dubai Transport buses leave for Umm Al Quwain from the Deira taxi stand near Al Nasr Square. Buses cost Dhs10, and depart once they are full. To return, take a taxi (around Dhs60).

By taxi
A metered taxi from Dubai to Umm Al Quwain town centre costs around Dhs180 from Deira, Dhs200 from Bur Dubai and Dhs240 from Jumeirah. Ras Al Khaimah taxis (they wait behind Deira bus station) will be cheaper. Be sure to haggle.

Ras Al Khaimah

Tucked away at the northern tip of the UAE lies the country's most underdeveloped emirate, Ras Al Khaimah (RAK). You won't find the ultra-modern skyscrapers, malls and bars that Dubai and Abu Dhabi are decked with, but you will be struck by a cultural authenticity that the rest of the emirates lack. Ras Al Khaimah abounds in archaeological sites, historical structures and natural beauty.

This emirate boasts a thoroughly documented historical background – an honour the rest of the Emirates can't claim. Ras Al Khaimah's schizophrenic landscape – a combination of a desert, a mountain range, a coastline and fertile land – made this area perfect for settlement, and the emirate's many settlers left behind bucketloads of pottery, graffiti and structures as evidence of their stay. So while the rest of the UAE is breaking world records, Ras Al Khaimah is quietly revelling in its rich history and beautiful landscape, which no amount of oil money could create.

Ras Al Khaimah's history dates back to the Ubaid Period (5000-3800 BC). While most of Europe was still in the grip of the Stone Age, the Ras Al Khaimah locals buried their dead accompanied by painted beakers, spouted jars, incised stone bowls and personal ornaments, suggesting a highly sophisticated society.

Named Julfar by the 12th-century Arab explorer Al Idrisi, the region then fell under the power of the Kingdom of Hormuz, the growing island-empire based in the sea straits separating the Musandam – in modern-day Oman – from Persia. Its flourishing wealth did not go unnoticed: the Portuguese invaded the Empire of Hormuz in 1507, sacking tributary cities along the east coast of Oman and taking Hormuz itself in 1514.

Constantly harried by local tribes, the Ottomans and their Omani vassals, not to mention the Dutch, British and Persians, the Portuguese were finally ousted in 1622, leaving a tumult of competing powers and navies. Julfar increasingly lost importance as first Safavid Persia, then the Al Yaruba Omani Empire took loose control of the area. Eventually it was abandoned, with the centre of trade moving four kilometres (2.5 miles) south. The new town was named Ras Al Khaimah, which literally translates as 'the head of the tent'. This became the home base for a local tribal confederation known as the Qawasim. The decline in Omani power in the area allowed Qawasim sailors to take control of the trade along the Gulf, Musandam and northern Omani coasts – as well as of commerce in the Indian Ocean. The Qawasim declared the independence of Ras Al Khaimah and the growing town of Sharjah from the Omani empire in 1749.

With the collapse of the world pearl market in the early 20th century, Ras Al Khaimah, like all of the towns of the lower Gulf, fell into abject poverty. Limited oil production from 1969 onwards helped matters, but while Ras Al Khaimah sought to remain independent from the Federation of United Arab Emirates (lasting for 44 days after the other emirates signed on 2 December 1971), joining a federation backed by Abu Dhabi's oil reserves was really the only option. The emirate received a boost with the

discovery of the offshore Saleh oil field in the 1980s and has since worked hard to develop export industries in cement and ceramics. Despite this, it remains far poorer than Abu Dhabi or Dubai, and thus maintains its reputation as Arabia's 'Wild West'.

Sightseeing

The creek, Khor Ras Al Khaimah, cuts the city of Ras Al Khaimah into two sections, connected by a single bridge. In the west, the original old town houses the **National Museum** and a number of souks, while the newer Al Nakheel district serves as the commercial and business zone, with a few hotels and the new Manar Mall.

Mountain Extreme

(07 227 1735/www.mountain-extreme.com).
A team of professionals offer tourists the opportunity to explore Ras Al Khaimah's rugged beauty. They offer hiking trips, overnight camping trips and a host of other sport-related activities. If you're at all keen on exploring this emirate, we highly recommend you get in touch with these burly men. They know what they're doing.

National Museum of Ras Al Khaimah

Old Town (07 233 3411). **Open** *June-Aug* 8am-noon, 4-7pm daily, except Tues. *Sept-May* 10am-5pm daily, except Tues. **Admission** Dhs2; Dhs1 children. Permission to take photos Dhs5.
From the Umm Al Quwain highway, head straight towards old Ras Al Khaimah at the first (Clock Tower) roundabout. Go left at the second roundabout and the fort is a few hundred metres away, on your right. Past the rather sullen guards, you'll find a lovely tree-lined courtyard with pearling, fishing and pottery-making exhibits – and the most detailed labelling in Arabic and English of any of the northern Emirati forts. Most interesting are the reproduction paintings of the first British naval expedition of 1809. Depicting the attack on Ras Al Khaimah, they are accompanied by text promoting the thesis of Sharjah's current ruler, Sheikh Dr Sultan bin Mohammed Al Qasimi, that the Qawasim weren't responsible for piracy in the area (read the cited references and make up your own mind). Silver tribal jewellery and a Baker Rifle, the British army's first standard-issue rifle, are also on display.

Ras Al Khaimah Shooting Club

Khuzam Road, first right after walled Ruler's Palace (07 236 3622). **Open** 3-9pm daily, except Mon.
Marksmen used to come to this club from far and wide, as the RAK Shooting Club is the best such public facility in the UAE. They once shot the likes of M16s, AK-47s and 9mm Browning, but these big boys' toys were spirited away when regulations changed in June 2003. This leaves shotguns available for skeet and trap shooting at a cost of Dhs60 for 25 cartridges – a whole Dhs15 cheaper than at the Umm Al Quwain Shooting Club.

The UAE

Scaling the Hajar heights

Ras Al Khaimah's landscape is as rugged and dramatic as Dubai's is flat, with the **Hajar Mountains** dominating the show. For many, the challenge of scaling these rocky beauties and admiring the sunrise of the Gulf's most striking landscape makes it well worth the snail's pace hour-and-a-half jeep ride up the mountains from RAK. It isn't just the landscape that brings adventure seekers to these cliffs, it's also the promise of scaling a range that's so dramatic it looks more like cartoon mountains than the real thing.

The best time to trek the Hajar range is early morning, sometime around 6am or 7am. If you're awake early enough, you'll have time to make coffee and watch a rarely seen sunrise come up behind the sinister-looking mountains. But once you're mentally awake, it's time to strap on your hiking gear and brave the steep trekking paths other mountain enthusiasts have set before you.

There are paths to suit all trekkers, including the ultra-lazy, but it's best to assess your strength before you hit the mountains. It's also a good idea to hook up with trekking experts Mountain Extreme, as they know the Hajar range better than most. The company has an office in RAK and will take care of your trekking itinerary.

If you opt for an overnight stay (which we highly recommend), you'll be driven to the campsite at Shihi village, where you'll watch the sunset turn the rocky mountains into a golden volcano-like landscape – a sight not to be missed. Come dawn, they'll prepare breakfast and get you hyped up for your trek, which takes you past valleys, fossils embedded in the cliffs and Bedouins whose ancestors roamed this range for centuries. While the rest of the UAE offers spectacular experiences, none are as beautiful or as awe-inspiring as a day spent trekking here.

Mountain Extreme Eco-adventures, *Ras Al Khaimah (07 227 1735/ www.mountain-extreme.com). Overnight treks cost Dhs1,000 per person, with a minimum of four people.*

Tower Links Golf Club

Khuzam Road, opposite walled Ruler's Palace (07 227 9939). **Open** 7am-8.30pm daily (last tee-off 8pm). **Rates** for UGA members Dhs325 Sat, Fri, Dhs270 Sun-Thur; non-members Dhs375 Sat, Fri, Dhs320 Sun-Thur (incl golf cart & bucket of balls). Tower Links Golf Club consists of an impressive 18-hole floodlit course, clubhouse, academy, restaurant, bar, gym and a spa. Designed by the American Gerald S Williams and built by Hydroturf, Tower Links is unusual in that it abuts the huge mangrove reserve sited at the base of Ras Al Khaimah's creek. Consequently, the grass used on the course is not the usual bermuda, but an entirely new, specially saline-tolerant species called paspalum. The course is such good value for money, it attracts Dubaian swingers.

Where to eat, drink & stay

Bin Majid Beach Resort

Umm Al Quwain-Ras Al Khaimah coast road, just before RAK Ceramics (07 244 6644/www.binmajid. com). **Rates** (incl breakfast, lunch & dinner) Dhs550 double. **Credit** AmEx, MC, V.
This four-star beach chalet hotel is peaceful, but it does have a ramshackle air about it that suggests the Costa del Sol, circa 1975. You'll find several bars, coffee shops, an 'Indian' nightclub and what must be one of the smallest hotel gift shops in the world, at about 2.5m (9ft) wide.

Al Hamra Fort Hotel

Umm Al Quwain-Ras Al Khaimah coast road, 25km (15 miles) from Dreamland, 20km (12.5 miles) from Ras Al Khaimah centre (07 244 6666/ www.alhamrafort.com). **Rates** Dhs800 double. **Credit** AmEx, MC, V.
With distinctive wind towers on top of its villas and two kilometres (1.25 miles) of private beach, unique for the area, this hotel is a hidden gem. Enjoy some water sports, before having a drink at the delightful covered bar outside, or visit the Italian and Arabic restaurants indoors. It's well worth dropping in to take afternoon tea in the lobby café (Dhs14 for two), even if you're heading further north. Ask about villa rates.

Hilton Ras Al Khaimah

New Ras Al Khaimah, by the bridge (07 228 8888/ www1.hilton.com). **Rates** (incl breakfast & tax) Dhs825 double; Dhs1,525-Dhs3,875. **Credit** AmEx, MC, V.
The Hilton's five stars hang by a thread, but even if decor is cheap and cheerful, the service is by and large efficient and friendly. The food is pretty good too, and there is a great wood-panelled bar called Havana for unwinding after a hard day's wander.

Hilton Resort & Spa

Ras Al Khaimah (07 228 8888/www1.hilton.com). **Rates** (includes tax) Dhs1,050 double standard chalet. **Credit** AmEx, MC, V.
The Hilton Resort & Spa opened in December 2006 to much applause from UAE residents, who

Hilton Resort & Spa in Ras Al Khaimah.

regularly take weekend breaks away from the work hard, play hard city of Dubai. The resort is more than your bog standard hotel, only offering chalets, most of which are a stone's throw away from the beach. At the time of publication, the spa had yet to open its doors, but leisure-wise there are plenty of watersports available if you want to keep active. Those seeking a peaceful retreat, however, will find it here. Pack some novels, lounge round the pools and take a candlelit dinner by the sea.

Khatt Springs Hotel & Spa
Al Jazeera road, opposite RAK Ceramics (07 244 6666/www.khatthotel.com). **Rates** Call for information. **Credit** Call for details.
If pummelling, pressing and being pampered like a princess (or prince) is your idea of heaven, book yourself into the Khatt Springs Hotel & Spa where one of the Gulf's most sophisticated spas is merely an elevator ride away. Aside from the comprehensive spa, there are natural healing springs to help soothe and rejuvenate your weary soul. At the time of publication the hotel was closed for renovations, although the spa is open for business. Management plan to have the hotel open again by late 2007.

Al Nakheel Hotel
Al Muntasir Street, opposite Dubai Islamic Bank, Al Nakheel (07 228 2822). **Rates** Dhs170 double. **Credit** MC, V.
Not the most salubrious establishment in town, but definitely the quirkiest; Al Nakheel has the northernmost bar in the Emirates. It rejoices in the name Churchill's, and is a hangout for expat Brits, Omani oilmen and Filipino workers. Rooms are grubby and bare, but the hotel's cheap and friendly.

Resources

Hospitals
Saif bin Gusbash Hospital *Nakheel area (07 222 3555).*
Shaam Hospital *Oman Street on the border of Oman (07 266 6465).*

Post office
Central Post Office *(07 233 3517).* **Open** 8am-9pm Sun-Thur.

Tourist information
Ministry of Information & Culture *Off King Faisal Road (06 765 6663/www.uaeinteract.com).* **Open** 7.30am-2pm Sat-Wed.

Getting there

By car
Take the Dubai-Sharjah road and keep right on going north until you hit UFO roundabout (named after the concrete, UFO-shaped building

Watch this space

This wild northern emirate may look rough and underdeveloped today, but it'll soon be home to the Middle East's first commercial space port. **Space Adventures** (www.space adventures.com), the only company to have sent laymen to space, is collaborating with the local authorities to construct a port from which sub-orbital space flights will be launched. The vehicle, Explorer, will be able to take up to five people to an altitude of almost 100 kilometres in space. There is no confirmed completion date for the space port, but don't expect Explorer to get off the ground before 2011.

on one side). Take the second exit to Cultural roundabout and, once there, take the second exit again. Filter right at the next major junction, and take the third exit left. Head straight past Umm Al Quwain (at about 20km or 12.5 miles) to the first roundabout (perhaps a further 46km or just under 30 miles). Continue straight ahead for Ras Al Khaimah old town or, for the newer side of the city, keep going and turn right two roundabouts later to cross the bridge.

By bus

Dubai Transport buses to Ras Al Khaimah leave from the Deira taxi stand near Al Nasr Square, but they won't set off until they're full; you'll pay Dhs20. To return, take a Ras Al Khaimah taxi, which should cost around Dhs90.

By taxi

A metered taxi from Dubai to Ras Al Khaimah town centre will cost about Dhs200 from Deira or maybe Dhs230 from Jumeirah. Ras Al Khaimah taxis can be found waiting behind Deira station, and should cost somewhere around Dhs80 post-haggle.

Musandam

At the most northern part of Oman sits the Musandam peninsula. Jutting out into the Strait of Hormuz, it is flanked on either side by the warm waters of the Arabian Gulf and the Gulf of Oman. Although the mountain panoramas are breathtaking, what makes Musandam worthy of the excursion is its large variety of marine life, which is attracted to the deep ravines and cool waters. Dolphins, turtles, reef fish and the occasional hammer-head shark have all been spotted by divers and snorkellers.

Formed during the Cretaceous and Miocene ages 1,850 million years ago, this craggy and unspoilt peninsula pushes itself out of the extreme north of the Sultanate. Originally just part of the Zagros Mountain range, the peninsula was split from them by earthquakes and volcanic activity to form the Hajar mountain range (*see p278* **Scaling the Hajar heights**). The Strait of Hormuz, the 60-kilometre-wide (37-mile) passage between the Zagros and Hajar ranges, is of critical importance to Oman, with 90 per cent of all the Gulf's oil trade passing through this area. Up until 15 years ago, no tourists were allowed into this imposing high security area because of its strategic military position.

Sightseeing

Belonging to Oman, Musandam's 'Fjords of Arabia' are best reached by hiring a boat from the port in Khasab. Be prepared to haggle to get the right price for your 30-minute ride to **Telegraph Island**. Even in the height of summer, a trip here is idyllic and you can always slip over the side for a quick swim. Secluded azure bays, frolicking dolphins, excellent snorkelling and quaint local villages at the foot of rugged mountains that plunge directly into the sea are just some of the sights that await you. You can also plan a longer trip and camp out on a beach.

It is not possible to rent diving gear in Khasab, so come fully equipped or book a diving trip ahead of time through **Khasab Travel & Tours** (266 9950/www.khasabtours.com). A half-day dhow trip (9am-1pm or 1-4pm) costs Dhs150 per person (without lunch); a full-day trip (9am-4pm) is Dhs200 per person. An overnight trip on a luxury dhow (for a minimum of ten people) costs Dhs1,000 per person, but the price is negotiable. You can also rent a 4x4

Diving in

With the rocky Hajar Mountains rising directly from the sea, Musandam's Omani enclave to the north of Dibba is not only stunning, but presents marvellous diving opportunities. With sightings of all sorts of sharks, eagle rays, coral, scorpion fish and sunfish, this is as good as diving gets.

The Caves

The main chamber of this limestone cavern recedes about 20 metres (65 feet) and its ten-metre (33-foot) depth makes it ideal for less experienced divers. Take a torch.

Al Boom Diving Club *Le Meridien Al Aqah (09 204 4925/www.alboomdiving.com).*

Ruqq Suwayk/Ras O'Shea

If you are going to catch a notoriously rare sight of a whale shark in the United Arab Emirates, then the advanced divers' paradise of Ruqq Suwayk is the place where it's going to happen.
Khasab Travel & Tours *(00 968 830 464/www.khasabtours.com).*
Al Marsa *(06 544 1232/050 462 1304/www.musandamdiving.com).*

from the same company at Dhs300 for half a day. Tours need to be organised before going to Khasab, as availability is far from guaranteed. But if it's diving trips you're after, you need to contact **Extra Divers** (00 968 2673 0501/www.musandam-diving.com) located at the Golden Tulip Hotel in Khasab. They're the only dive centre in the area, so they have a complete monopoly over the business, but they're honest divers and prices are very reasonable. A single dive costs Dhs170, but if you aren't a certified diver and you don't want to miss out on the marine life, snorkelling costs Dhs100.

Once back in port, drive to the top of **Jebel Harim** mountain for breathtaking views and temperatures that become some eight degrees cooler as you approach 2,000 metres (7,000 feet) in altitude. You can continue past the military dome on the summit for a little way, but must return on the same path as no access is allowed through the checkpoint at the bottom of Wadi Bih.

Where to eat, drink & stay

Golden Tulip Hotel
Khasab coastal road (00 968 2673 0777/www. goldentulip.com). **Rates** Dhs573 single; Dhs668 double. **Credit** AmEx, MC, V.
The Golden Tulip Hotel is nestled conveniently on the coast as you make your way into Khasab. The 60 rooms here are compact but clean, and there is also a swimming pool, a restaurant and a bar.

Khasab Hotel
Khasab coastal road (00 968 2673 0271). **Rates** Dhs235 single; Dhs350 double; Dhs700 apartments (4 people). **No credit cards.**
For many years the only hotel to greet you in the Musandam was the Khasab. It has 58 rooms and the service is genuine and friendly. There are also six apartments, each of which sleeps six people. The hotel restaurant is refreshingly old-fashioned, serving food that is basic but tasty, and the hotel can also sometimes arrange a rental car for you – check when making your reservation.

Resources

Tourist information
Omani Consulate *Off Khalid bin Al Waleed Road, Bur Dubai, Dubai (397 1000).* **Open** 7.30am-2.30pm Sat-Wed.

Essentials

Visa regulations
Gaining a visit visa to enter Oman seldom causes any problems, usually taking no more than about ten minutes (depending on your

nationality) at the Omani border post or at Khasab Airport; but don't forget your Omani car insurance, as you will need to show proof of coverage. The major issue is being allowed to re-enter the UAE: any single-entry visit visa is cancelled when you cross the border. This trip is therefore only possible if you come from one of the 33 countries eligible for a visit visa on arrival back in the UAE; it's best to check with **Dubai Tourism & Commerce Marketing** (223 0000, 7.30am-2.30pm Sun-Thur) to find out whether this applies to you.

Getting there

By car
It takes just over 2hrs to reach Khasab from Dubai, depending, of course, on how quickly you drive. For the most part the scenery is rewardingly picturesque and worthy of a few photographs on the way.

By plane
There are no direct flights between Dubai and Khasab, although you can fly via Muscat with Oman Air. Contact the airline's Dubai office on 351 8080 for details.

Fjord focus: the **Musandam Peninsula**.

The UAE

Airline flights are one of the biggest producers of the global warming gas CO_2. But with **The CarbonNeutral Company** you can make your travel a little greener.

Go to **www.carbonneutral.com** to calculate your flight emissions then 'neutralise' them through international projects which save exactly the same amount of carbon dioxide.

Contact us at **shop@carbonneutral.com** or call into the office on **0870 199 99 88** for more details.

CarbonNeutral®flights

East Coast

Hike in the hills, explore historic forts or relax at the beach on the UAE's beautiful east coast.

Coastline, greenery and a mountain backdrop – **Fujairah** has it all.

Dubai inevitably tops the itineraries of most visitors to the UAE. Some adventurous souls make it to Abu Dhabi, and a few discover the cultural capital Sharjah, with its souks, museums and heritage areas. But if anywhere really demands a couple of days of your time, it's the strikingly beautiful east coast, which is less than two hours' drive from Dubai and – for the time being at least – relatively undeveloped.

Whether it's a weekend camping break, a morning spent snorkelling around **Snoopy Island** (from a certain angle it looks like the cartoon canine), an in-depth diving course or simply the opportunity to sample a simpler, more relaxed pace of life after the ever-frantic Dubai, a trip through the rugged **Hajar Mountains** and down to the Gulf of Oman makes for a peaceful retreat.

Fujairah was part of Sharjah until 1952, and its relatively newfound independence means it's the only emirate to be located entirely on the east coast (with its coastline therefore on the Indian Ocean, rather than the Gulf). Cascading down to the Indian Ocean from the interior, bisected by wadis and scattered with hamlets

and towns, the Hajar mountain barrier lends Fujairah a landscape that's unique within the UAE. The humid climate also means that there are farms and green fields dotting the coastline, in addition to a littering of fascinating forts and archaeological sites.

It comes as no surprise that the emirate has become increasingly popular with tourists, who flock to Fujairah to enjoy the diving opportunities and more sedate lifestyle. While **Fujairah town** itself is perfectly pleasant, if you're short of time it's best used as a base to visit the inviting hot springs of **Ain Al Gamour**, or to explore **Khor Kalba**, a village on a tidal estuary that's home to one of the oldest mangrove forests in Arabia and an abundance of bird life. The ruined houses at **Wadi Hayl** and the T-shaped tomb of **Al Bithnah** are also well worth a visit, and if you venture north to **Dibba** and the border of the Musandam peninsula (*see p280*), you will be rewarded with some of the finest and most remote beaches in the whole of the UAE, and will get to enjoy such world-class diving sites as **Khor Fakkan** and **Al Aqah**.

Fujairah

The golden sands and coral reefs – home to
fabulous patterned fish – off the coast of
Fujairah make it ideal beach holiday territory.
Throw in the surrounding hillsides scattered
with mysterious ancient forts and watchtowers
and a thriving city centre crammed with
character, and you have an utterly charming
package on offer.

Fujairah was part of the Qawasim sheikhdom
based in Sharjah, until the local Al Sharqi
branch of the Qawasim gained some autonomy
in 1903. The British recognised Fujairah as
independent from Sharjah in 1952, but it isn't
local politics that gives Fujairah its distinct
atmosphere. With the Hajar mountains running
parallel to the east coast from Al Ain to Ras
Al Khaimah, Fujairah has always been cut off
from the rest of the UAE: the first all-weather
road through the mountains only opened in
1975. Despite new high-rises along the main
drag, the city is mainly a one-storey sprawl
that seems to be in a different time zone to
the rest of the country.

Fujairah is the second busiest refuelling
port in the world, and it is common to see
hundreds of ships queuing up offshore, which
unfortunately means that some illegally empty
their holds out at sea before heading to the
Gulf to upload more oil. This has clearly had
a detrimental effect on the wildlife in the area,
but the fishing remains excellent. Aside from
sea trawling and the variety of water sports
on offer, Fujairah is a prime place to watch
birds en route to Africa and Asia.

In the pleasant winter season, the stretch of
beach between the Hilton and the Khor Kalba
area takes on a Mediterranean feel as crowds
gather on Friday afternoons to watch the
ancient (and bloodless) Portuguese sport of
bull butting. More humane than bullfighting,
the sport sees a winner determined after two
big bulls have butted each other about in a
head-to-head duel.

On your drive to Fujairah, if you keep going
straight after Manama, after 20 kilometres
(12.5 miles) you'll find the **Friday Market**.
Although its name suggests otherwise, it's
open daily and sells countless carpets, plants,
pottery and fresh fruit, and presents a perfect
opportunity to put your haggling skills to the
test. Make sure that you don't get fleeced: none
of the items on sale at the market are antiques
and few are worth much. The most expensive
goods are the Iranian silk and wool carpets,
although the eye-catching designs may not
be to everyone's taste. You can also stop for
street snacks, such as roasted corn-on-the-cob,
for next to nothing.

Produce galore at the **Friday Market**.

Fujairah Museum & Fort

*Head inland & follow signs from Coffee Pot
roundabout, Al Gurfa Street (09 222 9085).*
Open 8am-6.30pm Sat-Thur; 2.30-6.30pm Fri.
Admission Dhs3; children free. Free guided
tours available on request. **No credit cards.**
For the budding archaeologist and those intrigued
by history, Fujairah is a gem. One of the town's main
tourist attractions, the museum houses a fabulous
collection of archaeological remains – taken from
local sites – which easily rival those in Sharjah's prestigious Archaeological Museum (*see p269*). The
downside is that several displays don't have explanations in English. Nearby is the Fujairah Fort – a
strategically located mud brick structure, which
appears to grow out of the hill it stands upon. Built
in 1670, the castle consists of three major parts and
several halls and towers, surrounded by the old
Fujairah. With slots for keeping watch and its prime
location overlooking the coast, it was a great vantage
point for defending Fujairah from attack. Although
the fort was fully renovated in 2000, it still retains
much of its original character.

Where to eat & drink

Near Coffee Pot roundabout (just before the
Hilton Hotel) is Al Owaid Street, which takes
you towards the shoreline where you'll find

the teapot-shaped **Fujairah International Marine Club** (*09 222 1166*). It houses a Thai restaurant and the **Armada Bar** (09 222 0969, 11am-1.30am daily) which serves excellent pub grub to an eclectic clientele of UAE nationals, expats, dive-centre workers and crew from visiting boats. The Hilton (*see below*), meanwhile, boasts a smattering of dining venues including the alfresco **Sailor's** (10.30am-midnight daily), which overlooks the sea. Sailor's serves soups, salads and sandwiches at reasonable prices (mains around Dhs30) but it's the sublime beachfront setting that draws the punters in.

Where to stay

Fujairah Youth Hostel
On the left-hand side of Al Faseel Street, parallel to the Corniche (09 222 2347). **Rates** (Bed in dorm room) Dhs50; Dhs35 members. **No credit cards**.
For those on a truly tight budget, this no-frills option is your best bet. It's a tatty, tired place in need of some serious care and repair, but if you're just looking for somewhere to bed down cheaply for the night, it does the job. While there is no café onsite, there are a few reasonable eating options just over the road.

Hilton Fujairah
Just off Coffee Pot roundabout, Al Gurfa Street (09 222 2411). **Rates** Dhs600-900 single/double. (Summer rates start from Dhs350.) **Credit** AmEx, DC, MC, V.
The Hilton is a charming retreat, where delicate fountains surround a shady courtyard and spill into mosaic-lined swimming pools. The hotel has a private stretch of beach, while the bar and beach huts lend a Mediterranean feel. Having been refurbished a few years back, the 102 rooms are clean and attractive. Staff are friendly and competent, and the hotel can arrange jet-skiing, windsurfing, waterskiing, fishing and diving trips.

Resources

Tourist information
Ministry of Information & Culture, off Jerusalem Road (09 222 4190). **Open** 9am-2pm, 4-8.30pm Sat-Thur.
Make the Ministry of Information your first port of call for any additional information you need.

Getting there

By car
The 130 kilometre (80 mile) drive from Dubai to Fujairah via Al Dhaid is a rewarding one, taking you

Fujairah Fort – strategically located on a hill overlooking the coast.

through deep desert and mountain villages. From Dubai, take the E11 towards Sharjah in the direction of Sharjah Airport. Then take the E88 in the direction of Dhaid. This takes you through rolling dunes until you come over the crest of a hill to find the oasis of Al Dhaid stretched before you. Go left at the first roundabout in the town, then right at the next roundabout towards Manama. Keep going straight on. After 20 kilometres (12.5 miles) or so, you'll dip down towards the Friday Market. Further on through the mountains lies the nondescript town of Masafi (Ras Al Khaimah's mountain enclave), best known for its mineral water production. The first junction you come to takes you left (north) to Dibba at the northern tip of the UAE's east coast before the Musandam peninsula, or right (south) to Fujairah town and Kalba at the Oman border, passing via the small townships of Diftah, Blaydah and Al Bithnah.

By bus

Buses to Fujairah go every 30 minutes from Deira taxi stand, near Al Nasr Square, and cost Dhs25. Oddly, you can't return to Dubai by bus – you have to take a taxi instead.

By taxi

A journey to Fujairah city in one of Dubai's metered cabs will cost roughly Dhs200 to Dhs250. In Fujairah, you can pick up taxis from the Karachi Darbar side of Plaza Cinema roundabout. A local taxi (taking up to six people) will cost around Dhs100 for a journey back to Dubai.

Khor Kalba

Not much further south than Fujairah is the UAE's most southerly village, Khor Kalba, home to the oldest mangrove forest in Arabia. Bird life here is particularly plentiful. The Khor Kalba conservation area supports a distinctive ecosystem and is the only place in the region where you can spot two of the rarest birds on the planet: the Khor Kalba white-collared kingfisher (kalbaensis) and the Sykes's warbler. But even if you aren't keen on hiding out for hours with binoculars in hand, the area's natural beauty and peaceful environs make it well worth a visit.

To get there from Fujairah, follow the signs towards Kalba, which is only about ten kilometres (six miles) away. Head straight through the town and you will soon see the swamps on your left. When you see a track, veer off to the left, and follow it until you come across a bridge onto the sandy area. Tracks along the shore are suitable for four-wheel drivers, but under no circumstances drive over vegetation or close to the waterfront. If you want to spend a longer time wallowing through the mangrove forest, arrange a canoe tour with Dubai-based **Desert Rangers** (*see p90* **Tour operators at a glance**). The knowledgeable guides can take you through the tranquil forest

and give you more information on the different species of wildlife you encounter.

Just a few kilometres south of Kalba, and inland from the coast, the tiny Fujairan village of **Awalah** sits on the north side of a wadi that runs from east to west. Sitting atop a terrace overlooking the wadi is a mud-brick fortified house dating back to the 19th century. The building covers the western corner of an Iron Age fortified enclosure, which still boasts visible defensive walls more than 2.3 metres (seven feet) thick and up to 60 metres (200 feet) long, preserved in places to almost 1.5 metres (five feet) above today's ground level.

Ain Al Gamour

For a rejuvenating dip, head to the hot springs at Ain Al Gamour, surrounded by a lush oasis of trees and vegetation. Strong, steaming bubbles, in which you can immerse yourself, feed a small pool near the parking area. This little haven can be reached by driving south past Kalba, keeping an eye out for the Adnoc service station. Pass the roundabout for the main road up into the mountains and take the next turn right onto a graded track 1.3 kilometres (0.75 miles) later. After some 2.5 kilometres (1.5 miles), take the next fork left and follow the signs for Ain Al Gamour.

Al Bithnah

In the Hajar Mountains, 13 kilometres (eight miles) outside Fujairah, sits the historic village of Al Bithnah. Notable mainly for its ancient fort and important archaeological sites, it was once a stopover for trading caravans from the Far East. The village can easily be reached from the Fujairah-Sharjah road, while if you drive through the village and the wadi you will access the fort, which used to control the main east-west pass through the mountain. What was used as a burial chamber from approximately 1350BC to 350BC is now known as the T-Shaped Tomb, or the Chambered Tomb. It has had to be sealed off and covered to protect it from the elements, but the **Fujairah Museum** (*see p284*) provides fascinating information about this famous archaeological site.

Wadi Hayl

Wadi Hayl is situated among some of Fujairah's most startlingly beautiful scenery, and is home to an abandoned village and arguably the best-preserved mountain fort in the whole country. This is a short off-road trip, and as such is perfect to link with a short break to the east coast.

All tanked up

There's a staggering array of marine life in the UAE, so get tanked up, strap on those fins and prepare to get wet in the following aquatic hotspots. What's more, visibility on this coast can reach 20 metres (65 feet), making it an ideal place for learner divers and snorkellers. If you require a bit of training before you head out, check out the centres listed on page 234.

Dibba Rock

This small sloping island is swamped with hard and soft coral. It's a 20-minute boat ride from Al Aqah Beach and offers dives ranging from three metres (ten feet) to 14 metres (46 feet). There's very little current here, so it's perfect for open water divers. As well as turtles, there are bags of moray eels, putterfish, boxfish, moses sole, clownfish, lionfish and pipefish – which are closely related to seahorses.
Scuba 2000 *Al Aqah Beach (09 238 8477/www.scuba-2000.com).*

Martini Rock

A favourite among east coast dive instructors, this underwater outcrop is ten minutes by boat from Khor Fakkan harbour and renowned for its range of corals. You can expect to see teddy bear corals and whip corals, as well as nudibranchs – marine snails decked out in rather garish colours. Suitable for learner divers, Martini Rock is also somewhere you can participate in night dives.
Divers Down Khor Fakkan Dive Centre *Oceanic Hotel (09 237 0299/www.diversdown.ae).*
7 Seas Divers *Near Khor Fakkan souk (09 238 7400/www.7seasdivers.com).*

Snoopy Island

The only shore dive along the coast, Snoopy Island is perfect for divers with their own equipment. Expect to see big mouth mackerel, moral eels, colourful anemones, funny-looking parrotfish and, if you are lucky, black tip and even guitar sharks (which are, in fact, rays).
Sandy Beach Diving Centre *Al Aqah Beach (09 244 5555).*

The UAE

It's easy to get there. From the outskirts of Fujairah, jump on to the Masafi-Fujairah road from the roundabout and go less than a kilometre west, looking left for signposts opposite the police station to Hayl Castle or Palace (22 kilometres/13.5 miles from Masafi). Two-wheel drive cars can easily reach the fort by turning left towards the quarry (the signpost reads 'Al Hayl Palace 4km') after turning off the main road. Four-wheel drives can continue straight on through the eerily abandoned village of Hayl.

The village's ruined houses and terraces follow the watercourse and its tributaries. You should keep an eye out for the hundreds of 4,000-year-old petroglyphs – depicting animals, horses and riders – that cover boulders on either side of the wadi. Bear right at the fork at the end of the track after the village and you will find the fort (some call it a fortified house) perched on an isolated outcrop. The fort has been dated to between AD1470 and AD1700, although much of today's structure is not thought to be more than about 100 years old, when it doubled as the palace of Sheikh Abdullah bin Hamdan Al Sharqi. It is built with natural materials – stone and mud-bricks mixed with straw and has wooden floors. There is a watchtower on the hill behind, and numerous ruins of smaller houses surrounding it. The main track continues past the fort and, although it doesn't lead to any other specific areas of interest, it's an attractive drive. If you're feeling particularly adventurous, you can leave the track at any point and explore further up one of the side wadis.

Getting there

By car

The simplest way to get to explore the south and west is to start at Fujairah itself (see p284). To pass through breathtaking mountains and incredible tunnels, head east from Dubai to Hatta (see p83). Pass Hatta's main roundabout (with Hatta Fort Hotel on your left) and 2.8km (two miles) further on take the next tarmac left towards Huwaylat and Munay. The twisting road from here on in is a lovely drive. After 11km (seven miles), take the second exit left at the Huwaylat roundabout towards Munay. After nine kilometres (5.5 miles), at Munay, turn right, down on to the motorway heading east. This takes you past mountain strongholds and through one of the country's most impressive feats of engineering in the shape of the 1.2km-long (just over half a mile) Gillay tunnel.

The road then snakes down through Wadi Moudiq on the other side of the Hajar mountains to Kalba's first roundabout – just follow the coast north (left) past the swamps to Kalba and on to Fujairah. If you get lost anywhere along the coast don't be afraid to ask the (older) locals.

Khor Fakkan

Halfway between Khor Kalba and Dibba, this popular holiday coastal town at the base of the Hajar Mountains is also known as 'Creek of the Two Jaws'. Attracting a steady stream of divers, the second largest town on the east coast is popular for the inland trip getting there and its charming harbour, as well as for the fact that it is by far the cleanest town in this region.

Wide streets, well-tended gardens and a palm-lined corniche make it a pleasant place to wander, even if there are few attractions worth visiting. If you're low on vitals and need to hit the shops, the covered souk by the container terminal at the far south of the port is perfect for fresh produce. Known as Chorf to Venetian jeweller Gasparo Balbi in 1580, Khor Fakkan has the remains of a Portuguese fort, most likely destroyed during hostilities when the Persian navy invaded the east coast in 1623 under Omani Sheikh Muhammad Suhari's command. According to the German traveller Carsten Niebuhr, Khor Fakkan belonged to a sheikh of the Qawasim by 1765, and today the town is another east coast enclave belonging to the Qawasim emirate of Sharjah. Khor Fakkan's most notable inland sight is **Wadi Wurrayah**. Guaranteed to provide cool, shady, watery relief from baking temperatures and blazing sun, its waterfall is an area of natural beauty spoilt only by graffiti and litter left by misguided visitors.

The entrance to Wadi Wurrayah is off the main road that runs north between Khor Fakkan and Dibba. There are therefore two sides from which you can approach the entrance to the wadi. Travelling north up from Fujairah, then from the roundabout at the Oceanic Hotel in Khor Fakkan, continue for almost five kilometres (three miles) and make a U-turn just beyond the third roundabout. Double back on yourself for 700 metres (slightly more than a quarter of a mile) before taking the tarred road off to your right. If you're coming at it from the opposite direction, from Dibba, then the turning will be on your right, around 2.4 kilometres (1.5 miles) from the Badiyah roundabout. This tarred road continues straight, forking after roughly five kilometres (three miles). At the fork you can take either road, as they join up just over a kilometre further on. The turning not to miss is in the second major dip in the wadi, one kilometre (half a mile) after the forked roads join up again. 4x4s can turn right into the wide wadi bed at this point, but normal cars should keep to the left and follow the tarred road for just under three kilometres (two miles), at which point you'll have a great view from above the waterfall. You can park

Fujairah Rotana Resort & Spa. *See p290.*

and climb down from here, but be careful: the gravel can often be dangerously loose.

If you are following the 4x4 track, the wadi gets quite narrow and twists and turns between high stony walls. The surface is quite rough and the going will be pretty slow for the next few kilometres. There is a fair amount of vegetation along the edges that adds to the atmosphere and when the wadi opens out, you'll find the deep, all-year-round pool, fed by the waterfall. Inevitably, the size of the waterfall depends on the season, with it becoming little more than a trickle in the hot and humid summer months.

Where to eat, drink & stay

As it is part of the emirate of Sharjah, no alcohol is served in Khor Fakkan.

Khor Fakkan Youth Hostel

Opposite Oceanic Hotel, follow signs from northern roundabout, Coast Road (09 237 0886). **Rates** (4-bed room) Dhs50; Dhs35 YHA members. **No credit cards.**

A charming and cheap alternative to the Oceanic Hotel, with many visitors using the 32-bed hostel as their base while making the most of the Oceanic's dive centre. The hostel is squeaky clean, has kitchen facilities and is run by a charmingly efficient Filipino called Rudy. If you are a single woman and it's appropriate, Rudy will happily give you a separate room.

Oceanic Hotel

Near Khor Fakkan dam, follow signs from northern roundabout, Coast Road (09 238 5111). **Rates** *Oct-May* Dhs690 single/double. *June-Sept* Dhs575 single/double. **Credit** AmEx, MC, V.

At the top end of the quality scale, the Oceanic tucks into a knoll of rock on the Indian Ocean. It has a funky, if musty, 1970s kitsch feel, mature gardens, a great swathe of white-sand beach and a good diving centre, while the area around the Oceanic is best for shelling. Rates are reasonably high, though you can negotiate outside high season.

Bidiya

The tiny village of Bidiya's biggest claim to fame is that it is home to the oldest and smallest mosque in the UAE. The whitewashed **Bidiya Mosque** dates back to 1446, predating the Portuguese invasion of the area by more than 50 years and representing a unique feat of engineering for its time, with four small domes supported by a central pillar, stone carvings and special shelves for the holy Qur'an. Also known as Al Masjid Al Othmani, it sits at the side of the main Khor Fakkan-Dibba road (about 38 kilometres or 24 miles from Fujairah) and, unusually for mosques in the UAE, can be visited outside prayer times if accompanied by a guide. It's also worth a short hike up the mountain to take in the view and look at the two watchtowers perched behind the mosque.

The new Dubai?

Compared to Dubai, Fujairah was very late out of the tourism starting gate, but is now making up for lost time, with its authorities keen to lure Dubai's visiting millions to its relatively unspoiled beaches.

International hotel chains have been snapping up key coastal locations. Hot on the heels of the recently opened **Fujairah Rotana Resort & Spa** and **Hotel Jal Fujairah Resort & Spa**, Germany's Iberotel is set to open its US$180million Miramar Al Aqah Beach Resort in late 2007 and its Royal Miramar Resort in 2009. Between them, the two Iberotel properties will add nearly 700 rooms to Fujairah's growing tourism industry. Also due to open in 2009 is the 320-room Radisson SAS Al Aqah Beach Resort and the 200-room Mina Al Fajer Resort.

The development set to create the biggest splash is the US$817 million Al Fujairah Paradise; the east coast's answer to projects such as the Palm (Dubai), the Pearl (Qatar) and the Amwaj Islands (Bahrain). The luxury resort is expected to open in Al Aqah in 2009 and will feature 1,000 five-star villas (owners will be able to lease them for short periods) as well as a 250-room hotel and a shopping mall. With mountainside restaurants, yachting cruises, cable cars and artificial lakes, the resort is expected to deliver some Madinat-style fantasy to the area.

With its attractive jagged coastline of aqua blue waters and pristine beaches drenched in sun, it seems a certainty that Fujairah will soon be attracting large numbers of tourists. The fear, of course, is that it will lose the very qualities that attract people there in the first place. It's worth enjoying the coast's simple charms in the next couple of years, before it becomes completely unrecognisable.

Al Aqah

Situated 16 kilometres (ten miles) from Khor Fakkan and 18 kilometres (11 miles) from Dibba, there's something for tourists at both ends of the spectrum at Al Aqah – famed for its beach. Moneyed holidaymakers can be pampered in the five-star **Le Meridien Beach Resort** or its new neighbour the **Fujairah Rotana Resort & Spa** (*09 244 9888*). Meanwhile, outdoorsy types will appreciate

the faded charms of the **Sandy Beach Motel** – not least its proximity to Snoopy Island (*see p287* **All tanked up**).

Where to eat, drink & stay

Fujairah Rotana Resort & Spa

From Dubai, head east towards Sharjah, through Al Dhaid to Masafi, then take the Dibba Road & follow the signs for 35km/22 miles (09 244 9888/ www.rotana.com). **Rates** Dhs600-Dhs1,200 double; Dhs850-2,000 suites. (Special summer rates available.) **Credit** AmEx, MC, V.

Despite having only opened its doors in Spring 2007, the Rotana group's first east coast venture has already established itself as a popular weekend retreat for peace-seeking Dubaians and foreign tourists. Compared to the imposing Meridien hotel next door (*see below*), the Rotana is a sleek low-rise affair; all of its 250 rooms and suites boast ocean views, and the best rooms open straight onto the hammocks and umbrellas of an excellent private beach. The swimming pool is huge and squarely aimed at families – it's not ideal for lengths. For more strenuous exercise, head for the sea. One of the Rotana's major strengths is that sports, including waterskiing, kayaking, wind surfing and snorkelling, are available free of charge. The alfresco dining at Waves offers a seafood-heavy menu of well-rendered classics and skilful touches of fine dining, while the Tabu bar specialises in cocktails. *Photo p289.*

Le Meridien Al Aqah Beach Resort

From Dubai, head east towards Sharjah, through Al Dhaid to Masafi, then take the Dibba Road & follow the signs for 35km/22 miles (09 244 9000). **Rates** Dhs555-1,150 single/double, depending on season; Dhs3,000 suites; Dhs12,000 Royal Club room. **Credit** AmEx, MC, V.

Love it or hate it, you can't miss the colossal glass and concrete construction jutting out of its remote setting between the mountains and the Indian Ocean. Le Meridien would blend in perfectly on the Dubai coastline, which explains why critics say that this uncompromising structure looming up unexpectedly is incongruous here. As a guest, though, you can't dismiss the impressively spacious rooms, with their spectacular views of the ocean and the Hajar mountains. The services and facilities (which include a beautiful beach and several good restaurants, including the alfresco Baywatch Village, stylish Thai eatery Taste, a health club and a nightclub) also make the place worthy of each and every neutron of its five stars.

Sandy Beach Motel

Head east from Dubai towards Sharjah, through Al Dhaid to Masafi, then take the Dibba Road & follow the signs for 35km/22 miles (09 244 5555). **Rates** Dhs460 single/double; Dhs690 single chalet; Dhs920 double chalet. **Credit** AmEx, MC, V.

Squatting in the shadow of Le Meridien, the simple Sandy Beach Motel is a favourite among divers and expats who want to get away from the glitz and glamour of Dubai. With mature gardens, a lovely beach and one of the best dive centres in the area, the motel is a serene sanctuary, with its faded decor setting it worlds apart from the big hotel chains. Arguably, Sandy Beach's greatest attraction is the fact that it is located directly opposite Snoopy Island, an outcrop in the ocean so-called because it very vaguely resembles the shape of the cartoon dog reclining on top of his kennel. The area around the rock is great for snorkelling and diving, though the dive centre at the motel also offers more technical dives in the Omani waters of the Musandam. The restaurant is basic, with the best dishes tending to be those that include grilled fish from local markets.

Dibba

Described by some as the most beautiful part of the whole country, Dibba is steeped in a rather volatile history. A walk through the old part of town, paying special attention to the ornate doors of the compounds, is one of the highlights of a trip here. You won't come across many Westerners in town, which lends an even more special feel to your adventure.

There are actually three different Dibbas: Dibba Muhallab (also called Dibba Al Fujairah – belonging to Fujairah), Hosn Dibba (belonging to Sharjah) and Dibba Bayah (Oman). There are no border posts here and it is possible to cross into any part of the conurbation without hindrance – just don't have a car crash in Dibba Bayah without Omani insurance. The three Dibbas share an attractive bay, fishing communities, Portuguese fortresses, wadi waterfalls and exceptional diving locations.

To access an appealing beach, well known for camping, snorkelling and picnics, follow the coastline until you reach the tiny Dibba port ('Mina Bayah' in Arabic) on the far northern edge of the town, just a few hundred metres from the Globe roundabout. An active fishing harbour, here you can see the day's catch spread out on the ground, and the air is loud with people bartering. If so inclined, you can charter a fishing boat or dhow from here for a short trip. Once past the port, continue along the main road away from town and then take the sandy track that forks right, bringing you towards a stretch of beach by the mountains in the very corner of the bay, which makes for a calm setting, especially when compared to Dibba's former battle-filled years.

Before the coming of Islam, no state had ever been able to control the tribes of Arabia. The Persian Sassanids, Byzantium and even the Southern Arabian states all tried but failed. The final battle in the AD633 Ridda Wars (Wars of Apostasy) ended this tradition of complete independence from external powers.

Many Arabian Bedouin tribes had sworn their personal allegiance to the Prophet Mohammed, so when he died in AD632, so did the Bedouin allegiance. By refusing to accept the leadership of Mohammed's successor, his father-in-law Abu Bakr, they were challenging outside control – as they had done for hundreds of years. But now they were also challenging Islam, and Abu Bakr was having none of it. The huge battles at Dibba (there are 10,000 gravestones in a cemetery here) marked the end of the Muslim reconquest of Arabia, the beginning of state control from Mecca (located in modern-day Saudi Arabia), as well as the beginning of Islamic expansion beyond this point.

Where to eat, drink & stay

Holiday Beach Motel
Head east from Dibba towards Khor Fakkan for 5km/3 miles along the coast road (09 244 5540). **Rates** Dhs450 studio chalets; Dhs550 single chalets; Dhs750 double chalets. **Credit** AmEx, MC, V.
Although the hotel is at the ramshackle end of the quality spectrum, with its chalets overlooking a distinctly underwhelming expanse of grass and a basic pool, it's a superb base for diving. The Maku Dive Centre (09 244 5747/www.makudive.com), run by great instructors, comes highly recommended. The four-day PADI Open water diving course costs Dhs2,350, with substantial discounts for group bookings. (Note that children must be over 11 years of age.) The motel has Arabic and Indian nightclubs open daily until 3.30am, but, as with most clubs on the east coast not located in five-star hotels; both border on the tacky.

Hotel Jal Fujairah Resort & Spa
(02 244 9700/www.jalfujairahresort.ae). *Due to open in late 2007.*
Located just to the south of Dibba and boasting its own private beach, this new five-star hotel offers 257 spacious rooms, all of which boast sea views. Refer to the hotel's website for up-to-date room rates and information on facilities.

Getting there

By car
The easiest way to get to Dibba is to head east from Dubai towards Sharjah, through Al Dhaid to Masafi, then take the Dibba Road and follow the signs for 35 kilometres/22 miles.

By taxi
To travel directly to Dibba, Dubai's taxis will charge Dhs250 to Dhs300 depending on your pick-up location. When travelling back to Dubai, in the unlikely event that a local cabbie won't take you all the way, make your way to Fujairah town and you will have no problem getting a taxi from there.

The UAE

Directory

timeout.com

The hippest online guide to over 50
of the world's greatest cities

Directory

Getting Around

Arriving & leaving

By air

Dubai International Airport

Switchboard 224 5555/ flight information 216 6666/ www.dubaiairport.com.

One of the most highly acclaimed airports in the world, DIA is currently undergoing an elaborate and extravagant expansion programme (scheduled for completion late 2007). This includes a new terminal (the airport's third) exclusively for Emirates airline flights.

Almost all major airlines arrive at Terminal 1. Here the Dubai Duty Free (224 5004) is the last port of call for the purchase of alcohol before entering Dubai's 'hotel-only' licensing restrictions (*see p301* **Customs**). Airport facilities include internet and banking services, shops, restaurants, business services, bars, pubs, a hotel and a regular raffle that gives you the chance to win a luxury car. Tickets cost Dhs500, but odds are favourable as there is a draw every time 1,000 are sold. The smaller Terminal 2 caters largely for charter flights, cargo and commercial airlines from Iran, and the CIS (former Soviet Republics such as Belarus, Moldova, Armenia, Ukraine and Georgia) countries. There is also a plush VIP terminal known as Al Majlis.

A card-operated E-Gate enables those who carry the relevant 'smart card' to check in and travel unhindered, using nothing more than their fingerprints for identification.

To and from the airport

DIA is in Garhoud, about five kilometres (three miles) south-east of the city centre. If you're staying at one of the big international hotels, you'll get a complimentary **shuttle bus** or **limousine** transfer to and from the airport.

Otherwise, **taxis** are the most convenient and practical form of transport. There is a Dhs20 surcharge on pick-up from the terminal (instead of the usual Dhs3). This means that the journey from the airport to the city centre costs around Dhs30, while the return journey is Dhs13 or so. It takes about ten minutes to get to Bur Dubai, while Jumeirah and the hotel beach resorts are about half an hour away.

There are bus links to and from both terminals every 20 or 30 minutes for around Dhs3, although timings are somewhat erratic and routes can be lengthy. Route 401 goes from the airport to Al Sabkah bus station and the 402 goes to Al Ghubaiba, running through the centre of the city. From Deira station, located opposite the Al Ghurair Centre on Al Rigga Road, the numbers 4, 11 and 48 will take you straight to Terminal 1, as will the 33 and 44 from Bur Dubai. Fortunately, all buses are air conditioned. Call 227 3840/ 800 9090 or visit www.rta.ae for more details.

Airport parking

There are short- and long-term parking facilities available at the airport. Tariffs range from Dhs10 per hour in the short-stay car park to Dhs120 per day for up to ten days in the long-stay.

Airlines

All airlines operating regular flights into DIA are listed on the airport website; some of the most popular are listed below. Note that some airlines ask you to reconfirm your flight 72 hours before departure, and that cheaper tickets will often incur a penalty fee for alteration or cancellation.

Air France *Information 602 5400/www.airfrance.ae.*
British Airways *Reservations & ticket sales 307 5777/8000 441 3322/www.britishairways.com.*
Emirates *214 4444/ www.emirates.com.*
Etihad Airways *02 250 58000/ www.etihadairways.com.*
Gulf Air *271 3111/3222/ www.gulfairco.com.*
KLM *319 3777/www.klm.com.*
Lufthansa *343 2121/ www.lufthansa.com.*
Qatar Airways *229 2229/ 221 4210/www.qatarairways.com.*
Royal Brunei *Information 351 4111/ticket sales 316 6562/ www.bruneiair.com.* (No alcohol served on board.)

By road

The UAE is bordered to the north and east by Oman, and to the south and west by Saudi Arabia. Road access to Dubai is via the Abu Dhabi emirate to the south, Sharjah to the north, and Oman to the east.

There is no charge for driving between emirates, but travel to or from Oman or Saudi Arabia requires you to show your passport, driving licence, insurance and visa. Crossing the Oman border costs Dhs30 per person for those with UAE residency and Dhs60 for those on a visit visa. Before you travel, it is worth checking www.omanaccess. com/explore_oman/visa1.asp,

Directory

for the latest visa requirements. Your car is likely to be searched: carrying alcohol is prohibited. All the highways linking Dubai to the other emirates and Oman are in good condition. Ensure your vehicle and the air-conditioning are in good working order, as it is inevitably hot at most times of the year, and the drive through the Hajar Mountains to Muscat, the capital of Oman, takes approximately five hours. Check with **Immigration** (398 0000) before you leave for any important changes in travel policy. For traffic enquiries, contact RTA (800 9090, www.dubaipolice.gov.ae). *See also right* **Navigation**, *p297* **Driving** and *p298* **Motoring menaces**.

By sea

There are boats to Dubai from Iraq and Iran; journey time is more than two days, and costs around Dhs580 return. For schedules and details you should contact the **Dubai Ports Authority** (881 5555/www.dpa.co.ae). Alternatively, if you're travelling north, you can call **Rashid Port** (345 1545), which operates sea routes to Port Bandar Abbas and Port Bandar Lankah in Iran, and Port Umm Qasr in Iraq.

Navigation

Thanks to its modern highway system, it's fairly easy to get around most of Dubai. However, in some places the existing infrastructure has struggled to cope with the growth of the city, most notably the Garhoud and Maktoum bridges spanning the Creek and the Shindagha tunnel underneath it. During rush hours (7-9am, 1-2pm, 5-8pm Sun-Thur), serious tailbacks can develop. A third bridge, Business Bay, opened in March 2007, and two more bridges are under construction, which, it is hoped, will help to ease congestion.

Despite the relatively good road system, Dubai can be a dangerous place to drive in. There are high numbers of road accidents and deaths, caused largely by speeding and poor lane discipline. Many drivers tailgate, chat away on their mobiles and do not use their indicators or mirrors (*see p298* **Motoring menaces**).

The easiest way to get around is by taxi (*see below*). **Water taxis** or *abras* (*see p297*) are also available on the Creek, but won't help you get around the whole city. Dubai's public buses (*see right*) are not tourist friendly, and are primarily used by people unable to afford cars or taxis.

The biggest problem with getting around Dubai, though, is the lack of an accurate system of street names. Some of the larger roads and streets are known by their name, but most are just numbered. This means your destination is usually identified by a nearby landmark, typically a hotel or building. *See also p299* **Addresses**.

Public transport

Buses

The public bus system is rarely used by tourists, due to the convenience of taxis. The service is extremely cheap but routes can be convoluted and timings erratic.

Timetables, prices and route maps are available from the main bus stations of **Al Ghubaiba** in Bur Dubai (342 11130) and by the **gold souk** in Deira (227 3840). You can also call the main information line (24 hours, 7 days a week; 800 9090) or visit www.rta.ae.

Should you brave a bus trip, try to have the correct money since change for larger notes is rarely available. All bus stops are request stops. Eating, drinking and smoking are not allowed on board; the front three rows of seats are reserved for women. Passengers without tickets are liable for prosecution.

Monthly bus passes can be purchased for Dhs95 (only valid on certain city routes) or you can purchase a rechargeable pre-pay card. These are available from the depots at **Al Ramoul** and **Al Qusais**.

Taxis

Official taxis are well-maintained, air-conditioned and metered. Fares are Dhs1.6 per kilometre (0.3 miles) with a Dhs3-Dhs3.50 cover charge depending on the time of day. The two biggest companies are

Making tracks

In an attempt to fix Dubai's severe congestion problems, the government is in the process of constructing a Dhs15.5 billion state-of-the-art Metro system. There will be two separate routes: the red track that will stretch from Rashidiya to Jebel Ali (with future plans to extend the track all the way to Abu Dhabi) and the green track from Al Nahda Street to Healthcare City. The project is to be completed in two stages, the red line being finished in September 2009 and the green line in March 2010. Until this time, the construction of the Metro will continue to cause traffic confusion, with detours and roads seemingly changing direction every day, particularly in the area surrounding the BurJuman Centre.

Directory

Dubai Transport Company (208 0808) and **National Taxis** (339 0002). Unofficial taxis are best avoided, as they tend to be older cars with poor air con and they may rip you off. If it's the only option available, be sure to agree on a price before entering the car. Taxi drivers usually have a reasonable grasp of English, so you shouldn't find it too difficult to explain where you want to go.

If you're in an outlying area of the city you should consider booking a taxi by calling 208 0808. Fares for longer journeys outside Dubai should be agreed in advance (there is also a 12-hour service available, with petrol and driver included).

Drivers have a reputation for being honest, so if you leave something in a taxi, your driver might find a way to return it to you. Failing this, call the company you used and give the time, destinations (to and from) and taxi number and they will do their best to help.

Water taxis

Abras are water taxis that ferry both Dubai workers and tourists across the creek for Dhs1. The boats run between 5am and midnight, carry about 20 people and take just a few minutes to make the crossing from Bur Dubai on the south bank of the Creek to Deira on the north, or vice versa. *See also p75.*

Driving

People drive on the right in Dubai. A vehicle licence may be secured at Dhs320 for the first registration, which is thereafter subject to annual renewal – following a road-worthiness test – at a charge of Dhs370. Driving licences issued by some overseas governments may be used to obtain a Dubai licence.

Seatbelts are compulsory in the front seats and highly recommended in the back. In residential areas, the speed limit is normally between 40 kph (25 mph) and 80 kph (50 mph). On the highways within the city it is 100kph (60mph); outside the city limits it's 120kph (75mph).

Although there are, in theory, fines and bans for a whole series of offences, in practice the enforcement of these is pretty erratic. While you may have to pay up to Dhs1,500 if you're caught going through an amber or red light, don't expect much in the way of road rules or driving etiquette if you venture out by car. *See also p296* **Navigation** and *p298* **Motoring menaces**.

Traffic fines & offences

A comprehensive official traffic police website (www.dubai police.gov.ae) lists details on licence requirements, contact numbers and fines for offences. All offences are listed under Kiosk Locations and Violations.

There is a zero-tolerance policy on drinking and driving. If you are caught driving or parking illegally by the police, you'll be issued with a *mukhalifaa* (fine). If caught by a speed camera you'll normally be fined Dhs200. When hiring a car, it's routine to sign an agreement of responsibility for any fines you may incur. You can check whether you've racked up any traffic offences on www.dubaipolice.gov.ae or call 800 7777. Fines can be paid online, or at the Muroor (Traffic Police Headquarters), near Galadari Roundabout on the Dubai-Sharjah road.

Traffic accidents

If you are involved in a serious traffic accident, call 999; if it's a minor collision, call the police

on 398 1111. If you do not report scratches or bumps to the traffic police, insurers will almost certainly reject your claim. Third-party vehicle insurance is compulsory.

If the accident was a minor one and no one was hurt, move the car to the side of the road and wait for the police to arrive. If there is any doubt as to who is at fault, or if there is any injury (however slight), do not move the car, even if you are blocking traffic. If you help or move anyone injured in an accident, the police may hold you responsible if anything happens to that person.

Breakdown services

There are two 24-hour breakdown services, the **AAA** (Arabian Automobile Association) (800 4900/www.aaauae.com) and **IATC Recovery** (International Automobile Touring Club) (800 5200/www.iatcuae.com). If you are driving when the car breaks down, try to pull over on to the hard shoulder. The police are likely to stop and will give assistance. If you're in the middle of high-speed traffic, it will be unsafe to get out of the car. Instead, use a mobile to call the police from the relative safety of your vehicle. Other breakdown services (not 24-hour) include:

Ahmed Mohammed Garage *050 650 4739.*
Dubai Auto Towing Service *359 4424.*

Vehicle hire

Most major car-hire companies have offices at Dubai airport (15 companies have 24-hour outlets there) and five-star hotels. Before renting a car, check the small print, and especially clauses relating to insurance cover in the event of an accident, as this can vary considerably from company to company.

Directory

Drivers must be aged over 21 to hire a small car, or 25 for a medium (two-litre) or larger 4x4 vehicle. You'll need your national driving licence (an International Driving Permit is best, although it isn't legally required). You'll also need your passport and one of the major credit cards. Prices range from Dhs77 per day for a small manual car, to Dhs1,000 for something like a Lexus LS430. Motorbikes are not available for hire in Dubai.

Autolease *224 4900*.
Avis *224 5219*.
Budget *224 5192*.
Cars *224 5524*.
Diamond Lease *220 0325*.
Europe *224 5240*.
Fast Rent A Car *224 5040*.
Hertz *224 5222*.
Patriot *224 4244*.
Thrifty *224 5404*.
United Car Rentals *224 4666*.

Fuel stations

At the time of writing, the cost of petrol was Dhs6.25 a gallon; so you should expect to pay around Dhs70 to fill a two-litre car. There are 24-hour petrol stations on all major highways. Most petrol stations also have convenience stores selling snacks and drinks.

Parking

Many areas in the city centre have introduced paid parking in a bid to reduce congestion. Prices are reasonable (Dhs1 or Dhs2 for a one-hour stay, depending on location), but this hasn't made it easier to secure a parking space. Paid parking areas are operational at peak times (generally from 8am to noon and 4pm to 9pm), and it's free to park there outside of these hours and on Fridays or public holidays. If you park illegally or go over your time limit, the penalty charge is Dhs100-Dhs150. Generally your car hire company will pay the fines for you and

Motoring menaces

The UAE has one of the world's highest death tolls from road accidents per capita, and if you drive along one of Dubai's highways, it isn't hard to see why. Few people adhere to traffic regulations, and speeding, undertaking and use of the hard shoulder are frequent occurrences. All cars sold in the UAE have an audio warning when speeds exceed the 120kph (75mph) speed limit – but many of the country's fast-living roadhogs simply have them illegally removed.

Bizarre manoeuvres such as reversing around roundabouts because drivers have missed their turning, or indicating right and then turning left are not unusual sights. One of the most unpleasant things you're likely to experience is extreme tailgating, with many motorists driving up behind you until they virtually touch your bumper in a bid to get you to move over and let them pass. If you're unable to move because the lane next to you is occupied, it's not unheard of for the driver behind to attempt to overtake by squeezing into the gap between your car and the central reservation.

Many resident expats pay that little bit more and opt for a large, sturdy vehicle such as a 4x4 purely on the grounds of personal safety. This is something you may wish to consider when hiring a car.

charge them back to you at the end of your lease.

Particular black spots include the warren of streets in 'old' Bur Dubai, the stretch of Sheikh Zayed Road between the Crowne Plaza and Shangri-La hotels and most of Deira. Parking in shopping malls is nearly always free, but if you visit them on a Thursday or Friday evening expect huge queues and delays, particularly at Deira City Centre mall.

Most hotels have extensive parking facilities for visitors, including valet services.

Road signs

Road signs are in English and Arabic, which makes matters easier for Western visitors, but the sheer scale of the American-style highway system (up to five lanes on either side at some points) means you have to stay alert, especially at the junctions on Sheikh Zayed Road that have multiple exits.

Walking

Due to the intense heat and humidity, an outdoor stroll is simply out of the question between the months of June and September. Even waiting for a bus or a taxi can become an ordeal after five or so minutes in this sort of weather. Unfortunately, the city is simply not designed with pedestrians in mind; certain areas lack pavements and the sheer size of some highways can mean waiting up to 20 minutes just to cross – unless you're prepared to gamble with your life. It is not uncommon for pedestrians to find themselves having to take a taxi just to get to the other side of the road. In pleasant weather, the best places to take a walk include Bur Dubai's 'Little India', the Meena Bazaar, the gold and spice souks of Deira and the stretches of sandy beach in Jumeirah and Umm Suqeim.

Resources A-Z

Addresses

Dubai is not divided into postcodes. While street addresses are slowly being introduced to the city, at present all official locations are simply given postbox numbers. The majority of roads are numbered, but not identifiable by anything other than nearby landmarks. Any resident here will happily point you in the direction of the Ritz-Carlton or the Jumeirah Beach Hotel, but few will know an actual address. Taxi drivers know most of the significant landmarks, but it's always worth carrying a map with you just in case. The most common reference points are hotels, shopping malls, restaurants and some of the bigger supermarkets such as Spinneys and Choithrams.

It's not a bad idea to invest Dhs45 in a copy of the *Dubai Explorer Street Map*, which is available from all bookshops (*see p148*), or any Emarat petrol station.

We've included a number of useful city maps at the end of this guide; *see p321-336*.

Age restrictions

You must be aged 18 to drive in Dubai (21 to rent a small car, 25 to rent a large one) and to buy cigarettes, although the latter does not appear to be vigorously enforced. In restaurants and bars you must be 21 to drink.

It is illegal to buy alcohol from an off-licence without a licence. Issued by the Police Department to non-Muslims holding a residence visa, these are valid for one year only, but are easily renewable. Alcohol can only be bought from two legal suppliers, a+e and MMI. *See p139* **Authorised alcohol**.

Attitude & etiquette

A cosmopolitan city with hundreds of different nationalities, Dubai has a well-deserved reputation for being tolerant and relaxed. It is, however, a Muslim state and must be respected as one. Most 'rules' concerning cultural dos and don'ts are basic common sense and courtesy, with particular respect needing to be shown for Islam and the Royal Family.

General guidelines

In formal situations it is polite to stand when someone enters the room and to offer a handshake to all men in the room on entering. Only offer your hand to an Arab woman if she does so first. It is courteous to ask Muslim men about their family, but not about their wives.

You may find yourself addressed by a title followed by your first name by expat workers – for instance, Mr Tom – and it's not unusual for a woman to be referred to by her husband's name – Mrs Tom.

While the last ten years have seen attitudes relax, avoid offending locals with public displays of affection and flesh. This is particularly true during Ramadan (when everyone is expected to dress more conservatively) and at the Heritage Village, but in nightclubs you won't find dress codes any different to those in the West. Topless bathing is not allowed, even on the private beaches, and sometimes women are asked not to wear thongs. Be respectful about taking photographs and always ask for consent. Communication can at times be frustrating, but patience is crucial in a nation where time holds a different significance and civility is paramount.

For further information contact the **Ministry of Information & Culture** on 261 5500 or the **Sheikh Mohammed Centre for Cultural Understanding** on 353 6666 or at www.cultures. ae. *See also p308* **Religion**.

In terms of getting by on a day-to-day basis, 'information', 'expansion' and 'efficiency' are buzzwords in Dubai. While the range of personal services can sometimes astound, the all-too-common collapse in communication can also astonish. There is a tendency to be keener to help than actually having the capabilities of carrying it through, with telephone conversations often leaving you more confused than when you started.

Far less harrowing is using the internet (*see p305* **Internet**) where countless sites offer straightforward facts and advice for tourists. In this guide, contact websites have been given in addition to the telephone number wherever possible.

Business

Dubai has been incredibly proactive in its bid to establish itself as the business hub of the UAE. Every effort has been made to welcome new business and its corporate care is the envy of the rest of the world. Dubai's booming economy is aided by low labour costs, minimal taxes, free zones, a secure convertible currency and a liberal community.

This safe environment has attracted international interest on a scale unrivalled elsewhere. The city's main economic activities are non-oil trade, oil production and export, and, more recently, tourism.

Airport business centres

All passengers using Dubai International Airport can use these 24-hour facilities:

Airport International Hotel Business Centre

216 4278/www.dubaiairport.com.
Map p329 L2.
24-hour facilities comprised of five meeting rooms (capacity: six to 18 people), one conference room (capacity: 60 people), eight workstations, state-of-the-art communication systems and full secretarial and support services.

Global Link

Departures level, near Gate 16, Terminal 1, Dubai International Airport (216 4014 or 216 4015/ www.dubaiairport.com).
Map p329 L2.
This business centre provides passengers with six ISD booths, workstations, internet connection, fax and secretarial services.

Conference & exhibition organisers/ office hire

With large halls and spacious showrooms readily available in all the major hotels, Dubai is able to handle any seminar, conference or trade exhibition. Comprehensive facilities will typically cater for small meetings through to major

international conventions. Several public institutes have also been developed especially to host significant events, such as the **Dubai International Convention Centre** (332 1000/www.dwtc.com), which annually hosts GITEX, one of the top IT exhibitions in the world. Most of the city's hotels provide business facilities/ venues with all the necessary support services. Otherwise, the **Dubai World Trade Centre** or DWTC (info@ dwtc.com; www.dwtc.com) and **Dubai Chamber of Commerce & Industry** (DCCI) are two useful points of contact for services and recommendations.

Dubai Chamber of Commerce & Industry

Baniyas Road, on the Creek, Rigga, Deira (228 0000/www.dcci.gov.ae).
Open 8am-4pm Sun-Thur.
Map p331 K4.
The DCCI exhibition halls and auditoriums are large, flexible spaces developed to accommodate exhibitions, trade and social fairs, and new product launches.

Dubai International Financial Centre

Emirates Towers (362 2222/fax 362 2333/www.difc.ae). **Open** 8am-6pm Sun-Thur. **Map** p330 H4.
The DIFC is an onshore capital market designated as a financial free zone. It's designed to offer financial services and to support

new initiatives, with the focus on Banking Services, Capital Markets, Asset Management & Fund Registration, Reinsurance, Islamic Finance and Back Office Operations.

Dubai World Trade Centre

Sheikh Zayed Road, near Za'abeel roundabout, Satwa (332 1000/ www.dwtc.com). **Open** 8am-5pm Sun-Thur. **Map** p328 H4.
The DWTC incorporates the Dubai International Convention Centre. It comprises nine interconnected, air-conditioned exhibition halls covering 37,000sq m (14,285sq ft), which are available for lease either on an individual basis or in any combination of multiples.

Courier companies

The companies listed below provide freight-forwarding, domestic, logistical, catalogue packing and moving services. They also offer source and delivery services (meaning they will find what you want and deliver it). Open 24 hours a day, they can be contacted both by telephone and internet. They all accept major credit cards. The UAE postal service, EMPOST, offers an express delivery service known as Mumtaz Express (*see p307* **Postal services**).

DHL
800 4004/www.dhl.com.
FedEx
331 4216/www.fedex.com.
TNT
800 4333/www.tnt.com.

Hours

In 2006 the government working week changed from a Thursday/ Friday weekend to a Friday/ Saturday weekend. This was done to make the working week closer to that of the West. While some people still have a Thursday/Friday weekend, most residents in the UAE either have a Friday/Saturday weekend or they work a six-day week with only Friday off. Working hours during the day can also vary, with a few firms still operating a split-shift system (normally 8am-noon and 4-8pm), although this is becoming increasingly rare.

Licences

The basic requirement for all business activity in Dubai is a licence (commercial/professional/industrial) issued by the Dubai Department of Economic Development. To apply, contact the **Ministry of Economy and Commerce** on 295 4000/ www.uae.gov.ae.

Sponsors

The regulation of branches and representatives of foreign companies in the UAE is covered in the Commercial Companies Law. This stipulates that companies may be 100 per cent foreign-owned providing a local agent (UAE national) is appointed. These agents will assist in obtaining visas in exchange for a lump sum or a profit-related percentage. The exceptions to this rule are the free zones, where no local sponsor is required.

Translation services

There are dozens of different communities in Dubai, covering many languages and dialects, but English is widely spoken, particularly in a business context. If you need something translated into Arabic you can try one of the following. (Note: none accept credit cards.)

Eman Legal Translation Services

Room 104, 1st Floor, above Golden Fork Restaurant, Nasr Square, Deira (224 7066/ets@emirates.net. ae). Open 9am-6pm Sat-Wed; 9am-2pm Thur. Map p331 L3.

Ideal Legal Translation & Secretarial

Room 17, 4th Floor, above Al Ajami Restaurant, Al Ghurair Centre, Al Riwqa Street, Deira (222 3699/ ideal@emirates.net.ae). Open 8am-1pm, 3-7pm Sat-Wed; 8am-5pm Thur. Map p331 K3.

Lotus Translation Services

Room 411, 4th Floor, Oud Metha Office Building, Oud Metha Street, near Wafi Centre, Bur Dubai (324 4492/lotrnsrv@emirates.net.ae). Open 8.30am-1.30pm, 2-6pm Sun-Thur. Map p329 J3.

Useful organisations

American Business Council

16th floor, Dubai World Trade Centre, Sheikh Zayed Road (340 7566/www.abcdubai.com). Open 8am-5pm Sat-Thur. Map p333 G10.

British Business Group

BBG Office, Conference Centre, British Embassy, Al Seef Road (397 0303/www.britbiz-uae.com). Open 8.30am-5.30pm Sun-Thur. Map p331 J4.

Department of Economic Development

DCCI Building, Baniyas Road, Deira (222 9922/www.dubaided. gov.ae). Open 7.30am-2.30pm Sun-Thur. Map p331 K4.

Dubai Chamber of Commerce & Industry

DCCI Building, next to Sheraton Hotel, Baniyas Road, Deira (228 0000/www.dcci.gov.ae). Open 8am-4pm Sun-Thur. Map p331 K4.

Consumer

Although people flock to Dubai to shop, there are no statutory rights to protect consumers, except the right to recover the paid price on faulty goods. However, unless you are prepared to take it to court, exchange is as far as many stores will go. Tourists with consumer-related problems and enquiries can contact the **Department of Tourism and Commerce Marketing** (223 0000/ www.dubaitourism.ae). For complaints about purchased items, the **Emirates Society for Consumer Protection** in Sharjah (06 556 3888) may also be able to assist, while the **Dubai Economic Development Office**

(222 9922) will try to help people who have problems with expiry dates and warranties.

Customs

There is a duty-free shop in the airport arrivals hall. Each person is permitted to bring into the UAE four litres of alcohol (be they spirits or wine), two cartons of beer, 400 cigarettes, 50 cigars and 500g of tobacco.

No customs duty is levied on personal effects entering Dubai. For more extensive explanations on any duty levied on particular products, see the Dubai Airport website, which has links to the Municipality site: www. dubaiairport.com (224 5555).

The following are prohibited in the UAE, and import of these goods will carry a heavy penalty: controlled substances (drugs), firearms and ammunition, pornography (including sex toys), unstrung pearls, pork, raw seafood and fruit and vegetables from cholera-infected areas.

For further information on what you can and can't bring into the country, call the **Dubai Customs** hotline on 800 4410 or check out www. dxbcustoms.gov.ae. *See also p308* **Prohibitions**.

Disabled

Generally speaking, Dubai is not disabled-friendly. While things are starting to improve, many places are still not equipped for wheelchair access. Most hotels have made token efforts, but functionality still plays second fiddle to design, meaning that wheelchair facilities have largely been swept under the carpet. Those that do have some specially adapted rooms include the Burj Al Arab, Sofitel City Centre Hotel, Crowne Plaza, Emirates Towers, Hilton Dubai Creek,

Directory

Hilton Dubai Jumeirah, Hyatt Regency, Jumeirah Beach Hotel, JW Marriott, Oasis Beach Hotel, Madinat Jumeirah, Ritz-Carlton Dubai, Renaissance, One&Only Royal Mirage and Sheraton Jumeirah.

The airport and major shopping malls have good access and facilities, and some of the **Dubai Transport taxis** (208 0808) are fitted to accommodate wheelchairs. There are designated disabled parking spaces in nearly all of the city's car parks; to use them you'll need disabled window badges, though many able-bodied drivers fail to respect this.

Drugs

Dubai adheres to a strict policy of zero tolerance for drugs. There are lengthy sentences and harsh penalties for possession of a non-legal substance, and there have been several high-profile cases of expatriates serving time for such offences. Drug importation carries the death penalty, although no executions have been carried out in the last few years. But even association with users or importers carries a stiff penalty. For more information see the Dubai Police website at www.dubaipolice.gov.ae.

Electricity

Domestic supply is 220/240 volts AC, 50Hz. Sockets are suitable for three-pin 13 amp plugs of British standard design; however, it is a good idea to bring an adaptor with you just in case. Adaptors can also be bought very cheaply in local supermarkets such as Carrefour or Spinneys. Appliances purchased in the UAE will generally have two-pin plugs attached. For queries get in touch with the **Ministry of Electricity** on 262 6262.

Embassies & consulates

For enquiries about visa, passport, commercial and consular services as well as press and public affairs, contact your country's embassy or consulate. In Dubai, they are usually open 8.45am to 1.30pm from Sunday to Thursday. If you need to contact an official urgently, don't despair; there is usually a number on the embassy's answer service for help outside working hours.

Your embassy provides emergency legal services (the stress being on 'emergency', since it has no authority over the UAE legal system if you are caught breaking the law), consular and visa services, and educational information and advice. For a list of all embassies in Dubai log on to www.dwtc.com/directory/governme.htm.

For embassies abroad visit www.embassyworld.com. *See also p300* **Travel advice**.

Australia

1st floor, Emirates Atrium Building, Sheikh Zayed Road, between Interchange 1 & 2 (508 7100/www.austrade.gov.au). **Open** 8am-3.30pm Sun-Wed; 8am-2.45pm Thur. **Map** p328 G5.

Canada

7th floor, Juma Al Bhaji Building, Bank Street, Bur Dubai (314 5555/ www.canada.org.ae). **Open** 8am-4pm Sun-Thur. **Map** p331 J5.

France

18th floor, API World Tower, Sheikh Zayed Road, (332 9040/ www.consulfrance-dubai.org.ae). **Open** 8.30am-1pm, Sun-Thur. *Visas* 8.30-11am Sat, Fri. **Map** p333 G9.

India

Al Hamaria Diplomatic Enclave, Consulate area, near BurJuman Centre (397 1333/www.cgidubai. com). **Open** 8am-1pm, 2-4.30pm Sun-Thur. **Map** p331 J5.

New Zealand

15th floor, API Tower, Sheikh Zayed Road (331 7500/www.nzte. govt.nz). **Open** 8.30am-5pm Sun-Thur. **Map** p333 G9.

Pakistan

Khalid bin Waleed Road, near BurJuman Centre (397 3600). **Open** 7.30am-noon Sun-Thur. **Map** p331 J5.

Russia

Al Maktoum Street (223 1272). **Open** 11am-1pm Sun-Wed; 10am-noon Thur. **Map** p331 J3.

South Africa

3rd floor, Dubai Islamic Bank Building, Bank Street, Bur Dubai (397 5222/www.southafrica.ae). **Open** 8am-4pm Sun-Thur. *Consular* 8.30am-12.30pm Sun-Thur. **Map** p331 J5.

United Kingdom

British Embassy Building, Al Seef Road, Bur Dubai (309 4444/www. britain-uae.org). **Open** *Passports* 8am-1pm Sun-Thur (*collection* noon-1pm). *Visas* 7.30-11am Sun-Thur (*collection* 1-2pm). *General* 7.30am-2.30pm Sun-Thur. Hrs change during summer months; call for details. **Map** p331 J4.

USA

21st floor, Dubai World Trade Centre, Sheikh Zayed Road (311 6000/www.dubai.usconsulate.gov). **Open** (to public) 12.30-3pm Sun-Thur. **Map** p333 G9.

Emergencies

For **police** call 999, for **ambulance** call 998 or 999 and for the **fire brigade** call 997. The **coastguard** can be contacted on 345 0260 and there is also a **helicopter service**. If you dial 999 or 282 1111, in an emergency Dubai Police will send a police helicopter, which they guarantee will be with you within eight minutes.

See also p307 **Police**; *p303* **Health** for a list of hospitals.

Gay & lesbian

Homosexuality is, in effect, prohibited in the UAE and there are no gay cafés, bars or pubs. While there is a small gay community in Dubai, it is not centralised around a specific region and there is no official gay presence in the city.

Health

Dubai has well-equipped public and private hospitals. Emergency care for all UAE nationals, visitors and expatriates is free from the Al Wasl, New Dubai and Rashid hospitals. All other treatments are charged to tourists, so it's advisable to have medical insurance as well as travel insurance.

The **General Medical Centre** (349 5959) on Jumeirah Beach Road is open 8am to 7pm Saturday to Wednesday and 8am to 1pm on Thursday. Should you require further information call the **Ministry of Health** (MOH) on 306 6200 or the **Department of Health & Medical Services** (DOHMS) on 337 1160. Both are open during normal government hours, from Sunday to Thursday. For people whose countries have a reciprocal medical agreement with the UAE, further treatments are available.

With high hygiene and cleanliness standards, the likelihood of picking up an infection or virus is low.

Accident & emergency

All the hospitals below have 24-hour A&E departments, but only emergency cases at the A&E of public hospitals are seen free of charge.

Contraception & abortion

Most pharmacies prescribe contraception over the counter, with relatively few contraceptives requiring prescriptions. It is widely known (although officially illegal) that this includes the 'morning after' pill. The **American Hospital** has a Family Planning clinic (309 6877), and the **Canadian Hospital** (336 4444) offers

consultation and an 'alternative' to the 'morning after' pill. Abortion is illegal in the UAE unless recommended by a doctor who is concerned about the mother's survival. Written permission is needed from either the husband or guardian.

Dentists

Good dentists are readily available in Dubai, including orthodontists and cosmetic dentists, though prices can be hefty. For a 24-hour emergency dental service, phone 332 1444. **Dr Michael's Dental Clinic** (349 5900/www.drmichaels. com) and the **Scandinavian Dental Clinic** (349 3202) both come highly recommended.

Doctors

Most of the big hotels have in-house doctors, as do the majority of the hospitals. Alternatively there is the **General Medical Centre** (349 5959) or you can ring your local embassy for its recommendations (*see p302* **Embassies & consulates**).

Hospitals

The three main **Department of Health** hospitals in Dubai are listed below. For more information, visit www. dohms.gov.ae.

New Dubai Hospital

Opposite Hamria Vegetable Market, after Hyatt Regency Hotel, Deira (271 4444/www.dohms.gov.ae). **Map** p330 H2.

Rashid Hospital

Oud Metha Road, near Al Maktoum Bridge, Bur Dubai (337 4000/A&E 219 1000/www.dohms.gov.ae). **Map** p329 J2.

Al Wasl Hospital

Oud Metha Road, south of Al Qataiyat Road, Za'abeel (324 1111/ www.dohms.gov.ae). **Map** p329 J3. The following are five private hospitals in Dubai that have Accident & Emergency

departments. Note that all private health care must be paid for, including emergency care. Hospitals are required to display price lists for all treatments at reception.

American Hospital Dubai

Off Oud Metha Road, between Lamcy Plaza & Wafi Centre, Al Nasr, Bur Dubai (336 7777/www.ahdubai.com). **Map** p329 J3.

Canadian Hospital

Ground Floor, Gulf Towers (336 4444). **Map** p329 J3.

Emirates Hospital

Opposite Jumeirah Beach Park, next to Chili's restaurant, Jumeirah Beach Road, Jumeirah (349 6666/www. emirateshospital.ae). **Map** p334 A15. As well as an A&E facility, the Emirates Hospital has a 24-hr walk-in clinic (though you're required to pay Dhs200 for the first consultation).

Iranian Hospital

Corner of Al Hudeiba Road & Al Wasl Road, Satwa (344 0250/ www.irhosp.ae). **Map** p332 E9.

Welcare Hospital

Next to Lifco supermarket in Garhoud, Deira (282 7788/www. welcarehospital.com). **Map** p329 K3.

Insurance

Public hospitals in Dubai will deal with emergencies free of charge. They have good facilities and their procedures (including the use of sterilised needles and the provision of blood transfusions) are reliable and hygienic.

Medical insurance is often included in travel insurance packages, and it is important to have it unless your country has a reciprocal medical treatment arrangement with the UAE. While travel insurance typically covers health, it is wise to make sure you have a package that covers all eventualities, especially as for serious but non-emergency care you would need to attend a private hospital or clinic, where treatment can be expensive.

Directory

Opticians

See p171.

Pharmacies

There is no shortage of extremely well stocked and serviceable pharmacies in Dubai and no formal policy of prescription: all you need to know is the name of the drug you need. Normal opening hours are 8.30am to 1.30pm, 4.30pm to 10.30pm Saturday to Thursday and 4.30pm to 10.30pm Friday, but some open on Friday mornings as well.

A system of rotation exists for 24-hour opening, with four chemists holding the fort at any one time for a week each. For a list of the 24-hour pharmacies on duty, check the back of the local newspapers or visit www.dm.gov.ae. Alternatively, you can call the **DM Emergency Offices** on 223 2323: they will be able to point you in the direction of the nearest pharmacy.

Prescriptions

Most drugs are available at the pharmacies without prescription. In rare instances when this isn't the case, pharmacists dispense medicines on receipt of a prescription from a GP.

STDs, HIV & AIDS

To secure residency in Dubai, you have to undergo a blood test and anyone identified as HIV positive is not allowed to stay in the country. Tourists do not have to be tested, but should you become ill and have to be hospitalised, expect to find yourself on the next plane out if tested positive for HIV. Despite there being no official figures, it's widely accepted that there is a genuine problem with sexually transmitted diseases, due in part to the

large numbers of prostitutes working in the city.

Sunburn/dehydration

The fierce UAE sun means that heatstroke and heat exhaustion are always a risk. Sunglasses, hats and high-factor sun creams are essential, particularly for children, and the importance of drinking large quantities of water to stave off dehydration cannot be overemphasised.

Vaccinations

No specific immunisations are required for entry to Dubai, but it would be wise to check beforehand – a certificate is sometimes required to prove you are clear of cholera and yellow fever if you are arriving from a high-risk area. Tetanus inoculations are recommended if you are considering going on a long trip.

There are very few mosquitoes in the towns and cities, and since it's not considered to be a real risk, malaria tablets are rarely prescribed for travel in the UAE. If you are planning to camp near the mountains or explore *wadis* in the evening, cover up and use a suitable insect repellent. If in any doubt, consult your doctor before you travel to Dubai.

Polio has been virtually eradicated in the UAE and hepatitis is very rare.

ID

ID is necessary for car hire as well as entry into bars and clubs if the bouncers don't think you look over 21. Passports are the most requested form, so have copies made in advance. Plans are well underway to issue all UAE residents with 'smart cards', which are set to replace all other forms of identification (including driving licences, and

labour and health cards). This initiative began in 2005 with the issuing of cards to UAE nationals and will be introduced to expats by the end of 2007. Primarily being introduced to increase the speed and efficiency of services and provide a population census, it will link to all government departments and carry personal information like the individual's blood group, fingerprints and other biological characteristics. *See also p299* **Age restrictions**.

Insurance

While the crime rate in Dubai is exceptionally low, it is still worth insuring yourself before you travel. Travel insurance policies usually cover loss or theft of belongings and medical treatment, but be careful to check what is included, and any clause that might be disputed, especially if you're intending to take part in activities like desert off-roading and scuba diving.

Car insurance will be covered by any creditable, authorised car hire company and anyone holding a valid licence should be able to get insurance. However, do check whether you are covered for insurance for the Sultanate of Oman. Since many parts of the UAE have a 'porous' border, you may find yourself driving within Oman without warning (the road to Hatta, for example, will take you through Oman in several places).

Medical insurance is often included in travel insurance packages and it is vital to have it, since health care in private hospitals can be extremely expensive. Emergency care is available free of charge at the government hospitals (*see p303* **Health**). Be careful to keep all your documents and receipts of any medical payments you make, as you will have to claim them back later. For a list of insurance companies, check out www.yellowpages.ae.

Internet

Dubai is leading the way in the global movement towards an electronic government. Not only is it often the most efficient way of gaining information, but you can now seemingly do everything online, from paying a traffic fine to reporting a lost licence. The government organisation, Etisalat, controls the server and is the regulator of content. Consequently there is an element of censorship, with pornography, dating and gambling sites blocked, along with a few photography and social networking sites. If the network fails there can be no service at all for hours at a time, although thankfully this is uncommon. In the past, internet users in free zones have been able to bypass censorship, although this situation is expected to change in the near future so that nobody can bypass the proxy. VoIP (Voice over Internet Protocol) programmes, such as Skype, which allow you to make cheap or free calls over the internet, are illegal and cannot be accessed. You can contact Etisalat by dialing 101, or visit www.etisalat.com.

The EIM (Emirates Internet & Multimedia) kiosks provide public access to email, news and business information, enabling users to access the net from anywhere, irrespective of their email provider. Kiosks can be found in airport waiting areas, shopping centres and hotel lobbies and take various methods of payment. Costs range from Dhs5 to Dhs 15 an hour. Most hotels have some form of internet access and there are net cafés dotted around the city. For a list of internet cafés check out www.yellowpages.ae.

Coffee Bean Café
Aviation Club, Garhoud (282 4122). **Cost** Dhs15/hr. **Map** p329 L3.

Dubai Cafe.net
Sheikh Zayed Rd, near Emirates Towers (396 9111). **Cost** Dhs10/hr. **Map** p328 H4.

Giga Planet Network Café
Garhoud, near International School (283 0303). **Cost** Dhs5/hr. **Map** p329 K2.

Al Jalssa Internet Café
Bur Dubai (351 4617). **Cost** Dhs10 p/hr. **Map** p331 H5.

Language

Although Arabic is the UAE's official language, English is widely spoken and understood by nearly everybody. *See p39* **Mind your language** and *p313* **Language**.

Left luggage

There is a left-luggage storage facility at the airport. Costs are Dhs10 per bag per half day (12 hours) for a normal sized bag or Dhs15 per half day for an oversized bag.

Legal help

Dubai has strict laws, severe sentencing, no free legal aid and no equivalent of the Citizens Advice Bureau. Should you require legal help or advice, contact your country's embassy (*see p302* **Embassies & consulates**). Foreign embassies cannot override any law in the UAE and will not sympathise if you claim ignorance of those laws, but they can offer advice and support and give details of your legal status and options. Otherwise, contact the **Ministry of Justice** for advice on 295 0004. The government has also set up a **Department for Tourist Security** (800 4438), whose purpose is to guide visitors through the labyrinth of the law and to liase between tourists and the Dubai police.

For a full list of law firms, see www.yellowpages.ae.

Libraries

You must be a resident to borrow from Dubai's libraries, but most will be happy for you to browse or use the reading room, where there is usually a broad selection of English-language books. The **Dubai Municipality Central Library** allows the public to view its collections online, offering title searches, browsing and the capability to reserve books from home. Dubai Municipality has launched its new eLibrary, which allows registered members to read hundreds of books, magazines and foreign newspapers online. They can be contacted on 226 2788, or visit www.libraries.ae.

DM Library
Al Ras Street, opposite St George Hotel, near Gold Souk, Al Ras (226 2788/www.libraries.ae). **Open** 8am-9pm Sun-Thur. **Map** p330 G3.

Dubai Lending Library
International Arts Centre, opposite the Mosque, Jumeirah Beach Road (337 6480). **Open** 10am-noon, 4-6pm Sat-Thur. **Map** p332 D9.

Lost property

A few years ago theft in Dubai was extremely rare, but instances of bag snatching are becoming more common. If you are a victim of crime contact the nearest police station or report it to the special **Tourist Police** unit (800 4438), necessary for the validation of your travel insurance claims.

If you lose something, most unclaimed items are taken to a general holding unit known as **Police Lost & Found**, which can be contacted on 216 2542. If you have lost something on a bus or *abra*, call the public transport information line on 800 4848 and ask for Lost & Found. If you leave something in a taxi, get in touch with the relevant company (*see p297*).

Directory

The **airport** has a contact number for lost baggage (224 5383 for all airlines). To minimise the aggravation of losing important documents, always make a copy. Should you lose your passport, report it immediately to the police and contact your embassy (*see p302* **Embassies & consulates**).

Media

Despite the creation of Dubai Media City (complete with the slogan 'freedom to create'), the media in the UAE is still subject to government censorship, although direct clashes are rare as most organisations operate a policy of self-censorship. This means you'll never see anything that criticises the UAE royal families or the government, and there are no scenes of nudity in any films or TV programmes. While censorship is becoming more relaxed in some areas (many references to alcohol and images of bikini-clad babes are now allowed), it is unrealistic to expect objective political coverage in local newspapers. Most international publications are available here, although the black marker pen of the censors ensures that overtly sexual images are covered up.

Newspapers & magazines

There are four English language daily newspapers in Dubai: *Gulf News*, *Khaleej Times*, *Gulf Today* (Dhs2-Dhs3) and a free paper *7 Days* (Dubai's equivalent to London's *Metro*). All publish local and international news. *Gulf News* also publishes a free tabloid, *Xpress*, which comes out on Thursday. *The Times* and *The Sunday Times* are also available, although the Middle East editions are different to the UK version of the newspaper and they avoid subjects that

might be considered to be sensitive discourse in the region.

The city's magazine sector has become increasingly competitive in recent years and there is now a wealth of magazines published in Dubai. Monthly and weekly entertainment and listings magazines include *Time Out Dubai*, *What's On* and *Connector*. Lifestyle magazines include *Emirates Home*, *Viva* and *Identity* (interior decoration), *Ahlan!*, *OK Middle East* and *Grazia*. There are also free tourist magazines available in some hotels, although most of them are of dubious quality.

Radio

Dubai has five English-language stations, featuring a mixture of British, Canadian and Australian DJs. Sadly, the quality of programming is generally pretty low, with an over-reliance on chart music, too many advertisements and plenty of opportunities for unsubtle product placement.

Channel 4 FM, 104.8 FM
Modern chart, dance and R&B music.
City 101.6 FM
Part Hindi, part English.
Dubai Eye 103.8 FM
Bridges the gap between conventional music and talk radio.
Dubai FM, 92.0 FM
Government-run station that plays a mixture of older hits and contemporary chart music.
Radio 1 FM, 100.5 FM.
Modern chart, dance and R&B .
Radio 2 FM, 99.3 FM.
Easy listening.

Television

The Dubai government runs the English-language channel **Dubai One**, which shows a mixture of sitcoms, popular series and movies. Most residents and hotels have a satellite package of some form, with **Showtime** and **Orbit** among the most popular, thanks to offerings like ShowMovies, BBC Prime

and the Discovery Channel. Over the past couple of years, MBC has been making big waves as a free service with MBC's Channel 2 screening films 24 hours a day and MBC4 showing the latest TV series from the US. English Premiership football is screened on Showtime's ShowSports channel.

Money

The national currency is the dirham. At the time of going to press, UK£1 was equal to Dhs7.3. The US$ has been pegged to the dirham at a fixed rate of Dhs3.6725 since 1980. Bank notes come in denominations of Dhs1,000 (silver), Dhs500 (red), Dhs200 (blue), Dhs100 (red), Dhs50 (purple), Dhs20 (blue), Dhs10 (green) and Dhs5 (brown). There are Dhs1 coins and then 50, 25 and 10 fils, though you'll rarely use these lower denominations.

ATMs

Visitors will have no problems finding ATMs in Dubai. These are in every major hotel and mall, and on most of the busier streets. Most credit cards and Cirrus- and Plus-enabled cash cards are accepted. Check with your personal bank for charges for withdrawing cash overseas.

Banks

There are a number of international banks in the city such as HSBC, Citibank, Standard Chartered and Lloyds TSB, as well as locally based operations such as the National Bank of Dubai and Dubai Islamic Bank. Opening hours are normally 8am to 1pm Sunday to Thursday and 8am-noon Saturday. All banks are shut on Fridays. They offer comprehensive commercial and personal services and transfers, and exchanges are simple.

Bureaux de change

Rates vary and it's worth noting that the airport is the first place you can, but the last place you should, change your money. There are several money changers in the city centre (Bur Dubai and Deira) who tend to deal only in cash but whose rates (sometimes without commission) can challenge the banks', particularly with larger sums of money. Travellers' cheques are accepted with ID in banks and hotels and other licensed exchange offices affiliated with the issuing bank. There is no separate commission structure but exchange houses make their money on the difference between the rates at which they buy and sell. As this guide went to press, they were buying UK£1 at Dhs7.26, and selling at Dhs7.32. Below are some reliable bureaux de change in the city:

Al Fardan
Al Fardan Headquarters, Nasr Square, Maktoum Street, next to Citibank, Deira (228 0004/www. alfardanexchange.com). **Open** 8.30am-8.30pm daily. **Map** p331 L3.

Al Ghurair
BurJuman Centre, Halid Bin Walid Road, Bur Dubai (351 8895). **Open** 10am-10pm Sat-Thur; 2-10pm Fri. **Map** p331 J5.

Thomas Cook Al Rostamani
Next to Al Khajeel Hotel, Road 14, Al Nasr Square, behind HSBC bank, Deira (222 3564/www.alrostamani exchange.com). **Open** 9am-9.30pm Sat-Thur; 4.30-9.30pm Fri. **Map** p331 L4.
Phone this branch for details of the company's other locations.

UAE Exchange Centre
Ground floor, Mall of the Emirates. (341 3132). **Open** 10am-10pm Sun-Wed; 10am-midnight Thur-Sat. **Map** p336 D2.

Wall St Exchange Centre
Near Naif Police Station, Naif Road, Deira (800 4871). **Open** 8am-10.30pm Sat-Thur; 8-11.30am, 2-10.30pm Fri. **Map** p331 J2.

Credit cards/cheques

All major credit cards are accepted in the larger hotels, restaurants, supermarkets and shops. Acceptance of cheques is less widespread. Bouncing cheques is a criminal offence and can result in heavy fines – even, in some cases, a jail sentence. The UAE was slow to jump on the debit card bandwagon and no chip card service is available. A handful of the bigger chain stores accept Visa Electron and Switch cards; check with individual retailers.

Tax

Famous for its absence of direct taxation – meaning thousands of expat workers enjoy tax-free salaries – Dubai does have some 'hidden' taxes, such as the ten per cent municipality tax included in food and hospitality costs, and, for those with a licence, a sales tax on alcohol from off-licences (often a steep 30 per cent). There is no corporate tax except for oil-producing companies and foreign banks.

Opening hours

The concept of the Saturday/Sunday weekend doesn't apply in the Middle East, since Friday is the holy day for Muslims. The weekends used to vary enormously with people either having a Thursday/Friday weekend or a Friday/Saturday weekend. In 2006, the government working week changed to a Friday/Saturday weekend, making a more unified working week across the UAE. Unfortunately, there are no clear-cut rules when it comes to retail outlets. The most common shopping hours are 10am to 1pm and 4pm to 9pm for stand-alone stores, but shops in malls are open 10am to 10pm and often until midnight on the weekends. The exception is Friday, when some don't open until 2pm or 4pm.

Police

In an emergency call 999. If you just want information, www.dubaipolice.gov.ae is a good place to start. If you want to report something confidentially or think you have witnessed something illegal, there is a hotline (Al Ameen Service) on 800 4888 or go to www.alameen.ae.

Postal services

The Emirates post is run solely by Empost and works on a PO Box system, although a postal delivery service is planned for the future. All mail in the UAE is delivered to centrally located post boxes via the Central Post Office. With Dhs220 per year and an email address you can apply for a personal PO Box and will be notified by email when you receive registered mail or parcels. There is also a service that delivers parcels to your door for Dhs9.

Hotels will handle mail for guests and you can buy stamps at post offices, Emarat petrol stations, many supermarkets and greeting card shops. Shopping malls such as Deira City Centre, Lamcy Plaza and Mall of the Emirates have postal facilities. Delivery takes between two and three days within the UAE and from three to seven days for deliveries to Europe and the USA. The service can be irritatingly erratic so don't be surprised if sending something to your home country takes a little longer than expected. All postal enquiries can be directed to the **Empost** call centre on 600 599999, 8am to 8pm Saturday to Thursday. Alternatively, phone the **Emirates Post Head Office** on 262 2222, 7.30am to 2.30pm, Saturday to Wednesday.

Central Post Office

Za'abeel Road, Karama (337 1500/www.empostuae.com). **Open** 8am-11.30pm Sat-Wed; 8am-10pm Thur; 8am-noon Fri. **Map** p329 J3.

Prohibitions

The law is very strict with regards to the consumption of alcohol (other than in a licensed venue or a private residence), illegal drugs, gambling and pornography. Israeli nationals are not allowed into the UAE; however, following a recent change in policy, other nationalities can now enter the UAE with an Israeli stamp in their passport.

Religion

Islam is the official religion of the United Arab Emirates. Around 16 per cent of the local population is Shi'a Muslim and the remainder Sunni Muslims. Dubai is the most multicultural and therefore most tolerant of the emirates and other religions (except Judaism) are respected, but it is still a Muslim state. The faithful congregate five times a day to pray and you will hear the call to prayer being sung from local mosques all over Dubai.

Tourists need to be extra sensitive if they are visiting during Ramadan, the ninth month of the Muslim calendar, lasting approximately one month, when Muslims fast during daylight hours to fulfil the fourth pillar of Islam. Determined by the lunar calendar, the dates vary annually, moving forward by roughly 11 days each year. During this period, bars will not serve alcohol before 7pm and clubs are shut as no loud music or dancing is allowed. Eating, drinking or smoking in a public place during daylight hours is forbidden, though some restaurants erect screens to allow people to eat and drink in private. In 2007, Ramadan is expected to commence from

around 12 September (depending on the sighting of the moon) for 30 days. For details of how to behave, *see also p299* **Attitude & etiquette**; *p311* **When to go** and *p176* **Ramadan rules**.

Owing to its relative tolerance, Dubai has a variety of Christian churches and Hindu temples. For details of places of worship, see www.yellowpages.ae. The list below is a guide to non-Muslim places of worship:

Church of Jesus Christ of Latter-day Saints

395 3883.

Emirates Baptist Church International

349 1596.

Holy Trinity Church

337 0247.

International Christian Fellowship (ICF)

396 1284.

New Covenant Church

335 1597.

Saint Mary's Church

337 0087.

United Christian Church of Dubai

344 2509.

Safety & security

Although at odds with some perceptions of the Middle East, Dubai is actually one of the safest places in the world to visit. However, bag snatching and pick pocketing does seem to be on the increase, so, as with other countries, be vigilant and don't leave your belongings unattended. The other problem issues tend to be restricted to areas such as money laundering that don't tend to impact directly on the tourist or resident. Security is high and accommodation blocks and malls are well-manned by private guards. Nevertheless, it is always a good idea for the visitor to take out travel

insurance, and to follow the normal precautions to safeguard themselves and their valuables.

Study

Dubai has developed an extensive and respected education system in only 30 years. UAE nationals enjoy very high standards of free education, while expats tend to send their offspring to private schools and colleges. There are more than 100 of these, catering for all nationalities. If you wish to learn Arabic there are a number of language centres in the city, by far the most popular of which is the Arabic Language Centre.

Arabic Language Centre

Dubai World Trade Centre, Sheikh Zayed Road (308 6036/ info@dwtc.com). **Open** 8am-6pm Sun-Thur. **Map** p333 G10. Arabic courses for all levels are held on a termly basis throughout the year.

Telephones

The international dialling code for Dubai is 971, followed by the individual emirate's code: 04 for Dubai. Other area codes are Abu Dhabi 02, Ajman 06, Al Ain 03, Fujairah 09, Ras Al Khaimah 07 and Sharjah 06. For mobile phones the code is 050 or 055. Drop the initial '0' of these codes if dialling from abroad.

Operator services can be contacted on 100; directory enquiries are on 181 or 151 for international. Alternatively, consult the *Yellow Pages* online at www.yellowpages.ae, which in many cases can be quicker and less frustrating. To report a fault call 170.

Making a call

Until recently, Etisalat (www. etisalat.com) had a monopoly on telecommunications in the UAE, but 2006 saw the launch of rival company Du, which is

Directory

expected to offer some competition, especially within the mobile phone market. Local calls are very inexpensive and direct-dialling is available to 150 countries.

Cheap rates for international direct calls apply from 9pm to 7am and all day on Fridays and public holidays. Pay phones, both card- and coin-operated, are located throughout the UAE. To make a call within Dubai, dial the seven-digit phone number; for calls to other areas within the UAE, simply dial the area code followed by the seven-digit phone number.

To make an international phone call, dial 00, then the country code (44 for UK; Australia 61; Canada 1; the Republic of Ireland 353; New Zealand 64; South Africa 27, USA 1, France 33, India 91, Pakistan 92 and Russia 7), then the area code, omitting the initial 0, followed by the phone number.

Public telephones

There are plenty of public telephones, which accept either cash or phone cards. Phone cards for both local and international use are available in two denominations (Dhs25 or Dhs40) from most Etisalat offices, supermarkets, garages and pharmacies. Coin-operated phones take Dhs1 and 50 fils coins.

Mobile telephones

Dubai has one of the world's highest rates of mobile phone usage and practically everyone has at least one cellular phone. A reciprocal agreement exists with over 60 countries allowing GSM international roaming service for other networks in the UAE. There is also a service (Wasel) that enables temporary Etisalat SIM cards (and numbers) lasting 60 days

(or until your Dhs300 credit runs out) for use during your trip if your network is not covered, or if you do not have a GSM phone. Calls are charged at local rates with good network coverage. *See also p305* **Internet**.

Time

The UAE is GMT+4 hours, and has no seasonal change of time. So, for instance, if it is noon in London (winter time), it is 4pm in Dubai; after British clocks move forwards for BST, noon is 3pm in Dubai.

Tipping

Hotels and restaurants usually include a ten to 15 per cent service charge in their bills; if not, adding ten per cent is normal if not obligatory. Unfortunately this inclusive charge usually goes straight to the restaurant and rarely reaches the pockets of the people who served you, so if you're particularly impressed by the standards of service you've encountered, you will need to tip in addition to the inclusive total. It is common to pay taxi drivers a small tip, just rounding up the fare to the nearest Dhs5 being the norm. For other services (supermarket baggers, bag carriers, petrol pump attendants, hotel valets) it is usual to give at least a couple of dirhams.

Toilets

There are well-kept free public toilets in malls and parks, and most hotels will let you use their facilities free of charge. Petrol stations have conveniences but their condition varies. Toilets in souks and bus stations are usually for men only, and are often unfamiliar to Western visitors – a simple squat toilet set in the floor, with no seat or toilet rolls.

Tourist information

The Department of Tourism & Commerce Marketing (DTCM) is the government's sole regulating, planning and licensing body for the tourism industry in Dubai. It has information centres around the city, the most immediately useful being in the airport arrivals lounge (224 5252). Its one-stop information centres aim to answer any visitor queries, provide maps, tour guides and hotel information, as well as business and conference advice. Most of the larger shopping malls have their own centres providing visitor information.

Department of Tourism & Commerce Marketing
10th-12th Floor, National Bank of Dubai Building, Baniyas Road, Deira (223 0000/www.dubaitourism.ae). **Open** 7.30am-2.30pm Sat-Wed. **Map** p331 K4.

Visas & immigration

Visa regulations are always liable to change, so it is always worth checking with your travel agent or with the UAE embassy in your home country before leaving. Overstaying on your visa can result in detention and fines (a penalty charge of Dhs100 per day that you're over). Nationals of Israel are not permitted to enter the UAE. Your passport must have at least two months (in some cases, six) before expiry for you to be granted admission into the UAE, so do check before booking your flight. Nationals of the following countries will not need to obtain a visa before travelling to Dubai or the UAE; they will receive it upon arrival at the airport.

Americas

USA, Canada.

Asia

Japan, Brunei, Singapore, Malaysia, Hong Kong, South Korea.

GCC (Gulf Cooperation Council) countries

Saudi Arabia, Qatar, Bahrain, Oman, Kuwait, UAE.

Oceania

Australia, New Zealand.

UK

Citizens of the UK will be granted a free visit visa on arrival in the UAE: passports will be stamped with the visa as you pass through immigration at any airport in the UAE. Although the visa is usually stamped for 30 days, it entitles the holder to stay in the country for 60 days and may be renewed once for an additional period of 30 days for a fee of Dhs500.

Western Europe

France, Italy, Germany, the Netherlands, Belgium, Luxembourg, Switzerland, Austria, Sweden, Norway, Denmark, Portugal, Ireland, Greece, Finland, Spain, Monaco, Vatican City, Iceland, Andorra, San Marino, Liechtenstein.

To establish or confirm the permitted duration of your stay, you should contact the UAE embassy or consulate in your country at the addresses below. Failing that, the contacts given in **Travel advice** (*see p300*) will keep you up to date with the latest visa requirements – which seem prone to regular, unannounced changes.

UAE embassies abroad

Australia

12 Bulwarra Close, O'Malley ACT 2606, Canberra, Australia (2-6286 8802). **Open** 9am-3.30pm Mon-Fri.

Canada

45 O'Connor Street, Suite 1800, World Exchange Plaza, Ottawa, Ontario, K1P 1A4 (613 565 7272/safara@uae-embassy.com/ www.uae-embassy.com). **Open** 9am-4pm Mon-Fri.

France

3, Rue de Lota, 75116 Paris (4553 9404). **Open** 9am-4pm Mon-Fri.

India

EP 12 Chandra Gupta Marg, Chanakyapuri, New Delhi 110021 (687 2822). **Open** 9am-3pm Sun-Thur.

Pakistan

Plot No.122, University Road, Diplomatic Enclave, PO Box 1111, Islamabad, Pakistan (227 9052). **Open** 9am-3pm Sun-Thur.

Russia

Ulofa Palme Street, 4 Moscow – CIS, (2374060). **Open** 9am-4pm Mon-Fri.

South Africa

980 Park Street, Arcadia 0083, Pretoria, South Africa (342 7736/9). **Open** 9am-5pm Mon-Fri.

UK & Republic of Ireland

30 Prince's Gate, London SW7 1PT (020 7581 1281/embcommer@ cocoon.co.uk). **Open** 9am-3pm Mon-Fri. *Visa section* 9am-noon Mon-Fri.

USA

3522 International Court, NW Washington DC, 20008 (202 243 2400/New York office 212 371 0480). **Open** 9am-4pm Mon-Fri.

Multiple-entry visas

Multiple-entry visas are available to business visitors who have a relationship with a multinational company or other reputable local business, and who are frequent visitors to the UAE. This type of visa is valid for six months from date of issue and the duration of each stay is 30 days. Validity is non-renewable. The cost of such a visa is Dhs1,000. The visitor must enter the UAE on a visit visa and obtain the multiple entry visa while in the country. The visa is stamped in the passport.

96-hour visa for transit passengers

As a way of promoting Dubai's city tours, passengers who stop at Dubai International Airport for a minimum of five hours are eligible for a 96-hour transit visa which enables them to go into the city for that period of time. Passengers wanting to find out about this are advised to go to the Emirates Airport Services Desk in the airport arrivals hall prior to immigration to make a booking for one of the several tours on offer. You need a copy of your hotel booking (fax or email print out). The visa is US$50. This visa is available only to those travelling onwards from Dubai and not returning to their original country of departure.

Water & hygiene

The tap water in Dubai comes from desalination plants, and while technically drinkable, it doesn't taste great. Most choose to buy their drinking water, which costs only Dhs1-Dhs2 for a litre bottle; but do be wary of the ridiculous mark-ups at certain bars and restaurants. Outside Dubai, avoid drinking water from the tap – you might even want to use bottled water for brushing your teeth.

Standards of food hygiene are extremely high in Dubai, though caution should be shown if trying some of the smaller roadside diners. If in doubt, avoid raw salads and *shawarmas* (meat cooked on a spit and wrapped in flatbread). Outside the city limits, milk is often unpasteurised and should be boiled. Powdered or tinned milk is available, but make sure it is reconstituted with pure water. You may also want to avoid dairy products, which are likely to have been made from unboiled milk.

Weights & measures

The UAE uses the metric system, but British and US standard weights and measures are widely understood. Road distances are given in kilometres.

Average monthly climate

Month	Temp °C/°F	Rainfall (mm)	Relative humidity (%)
Jan	23/32	11	71
Feb	25/77	38	72
Mar	29/84	34	68
Apr	33/89	10	65
May	38/100	3	62
June	39/102	1	65
July	40/104	2	85
Aug	40/104	3	85
Sept	39/102	1	69
Oct	35/95	2	70
Nov	30/86	4	69
Dec	26/79	10	72

For links to see the latest satellite images of the weather conditions in the Middle East and Europe, go to http://www.uaeinteract.com/uaeint_misc/weather/index.asp.

What to take

Lightweight summer clothing is ideal in Dubai, with just a wrap, sweater or jacket for cooler winter nights and venues that have fierce air-conditioning. The dress code in the UAE is generally casual, though guests in the more prestigious hotels such as the Ritz-Carlton and the Royal Mirage do tend to dress more formally in the evening.

Since you are visiting a Muslim country, bikinis, swimming costumes, shorts and revealing tops should be confined to hotel beach resorts. Bars and clubs are really no different from those in the West, with tans shown off to the max. That said, visitors should dress conservatively when travelling to and from these venues. With such a wealth of shopping facilities, including some of the world's largest malls, there is precious little you can't get hold of in Dubai. Visitors can't buy alcohol from off-licences – so be sure to stock up at **Dubai Duty Free** (*see p147*) when you arrive at the airport.

When to go

Climate

Straddling the Tropic of Cancer, the UAE is warm and sunny in winter and hot and humid during the summer months. Winter daytime temperatures average a very pleasant 24°C, though nights can be relatively cool: perhaps 12-15°C on the coast and less than 5°C in the heart of the desert or high in the mountains. Local north-westerly winds (shamals) frequently develop during the winter, bringing cooler windy conditions as well as occasional sandstorms.

Summer temperatures reach the mid-40s, but can be higher inland. Humidity in coastal areas averages between 50 and 60 per cent, reaching over 90 per cent in summer – even the sea offers no relief as the water temperature can reach 37°C.

Rainfall in Dubai is sparse and intermittent. In most years it rains during the winter months, usually in February or March. Winter rains take the form of short, sharp bursts and the very occasional thunderstorm. Generally appearing over the mountains of the south and east of the country, these rumbling cloudbursts can give rise to flash floods, but on average rain falls only about five days in a year.

In terms of when to go, you really can't go wrong if you visit any time between November and March, as you're virtually guaranteed beautiful weather every day. June to September can be unbearably hot and humid during the day, although hotel bargain deals can still make it an attractive proposition. Also bear in mind when Ramadan is taking place (*see p308* **Religion**).

Public holidays

There are two different kinds of public holidays, those that are fixed in the standard calendar, and those religious days that are determined by the lunar calendar and therefore vary from year to year. The precise dates are not announced until a day or so before they occur, based on local sightings of phases of the moon.

The fixed dates are: **New Year's Day** (1 January), **Mount Arafat Day** (11 January), **Accession of HH Sheikh Zayed as Ruler of the UAE** (6 August) and **UAE National day** (2 December).

The variable dates are: **Eid Al Adha** – a three-day feast to mark the end of the haj pilgrimage to Mecca (January/February/March); **Ras al-Sana** – the start of Islamic New Year (February); **Mawlid al-Nabi** – the prophet Mohammed's birthday (May); **Lailat al Mi'raj** – the accession day of the Prophet Mohammed (September); and **Eid Al Fitr** – three days marking the end of Ramadan (October).

Women

The cultural differences between locals and expats in Dubai are obvious, and the traditional advice for women in any big city – catch taxis if you're unsure about the area, don't walk alone at night and so on – should still be heeded, but all women here tend to enjoy a high standard of personal safety.

Wearing revealing clothing in a public place will attract stares, some of simple condemnation and others of a more lascivious nature. That said, physical harassment is rare, as the local police are swift to act against offenders.

The traditional *abaya* (long black robe) and *sheyla* (head scarves) worn by Emirati women is something you are less and less likely to see on younger women, who tend to wear Western-style clothes in the city. The metal facemasks (burkha) are largely reserved for the more conservative women in rural areas. This development in itself goes some way to illustrate the

changing roles of women in the UAE. With the instigation of an education system available to women (female students now outnumber male) and the government's active encouragement of women in the workplace, attitudes have clearly evolved.

Dubai International Women's Club (DIWC)

Opposite Mercato Mall, Beach Road, Jumeirah (344 2389). **Open** 8am-5pm Sat-Thur. **Map** p334 C12.
This is a social club with around 150 members, which meets four times a month. The club organises charity events, not only in Dubai but also overseas.

International Business Women's Group

345 2282/www.ibwgdubai.com.
The IBWG is an organisation for women in the business world, and meets on a monthly basis to exchange ideas and offer advice. Call or check the website for details of forthcoming meetings. Alternatively you can log onto www.expatwoman.com for advice and information on meeting other female expats.

Working in Dubai

Dubai holds many attractions for prospective newcomers, especially the enticing tax-free salaries. If you are considering working in Dubai, it is worth visiting first to get a feel for the lie of the land. Dubai is a relatively small business community, so even a week's worth of well-planned networking can be fruitful in terms of making contacts – there is a real 'who you know' attitude here, so come armed with your best first impressions and plenty of friendly pushiness. There are also several employment agencies and recruitment consultants online to help you; try www.yellowpages.ae for a full list of Dubai-based agencies. While UK-based recruitment organisations can be hit and miss, companies like the South African-based ww.ananzi.co.za and local

giant www.bayt.com have earned themselves sound reputations.

To be able to work in Dubai, either an employer must sponsor you or your spouse must do so. If you managed to secure employment from home, the process of becoming a fully-fledged Dubaian is a little smoother, but it can still take some time. New recruits generally arrive on a 60-day visit visa. This entitles you to work for the stipulated period, while your employer gets the residency ball rolling with the Immigration Department. It's advisable to have several copies of your passport as well as plenty of passport photos for the numerous forms. Your employer should provide a comprehensive list of the paperwork required – check before you fly out in case you need to bring original education certificates or other proofs of qualification.

In order to gain residency in Dubai you'll also need to pass a medical test for HIV/AIDS, hepatitis and other infectious diseases. It is fairly standard to be offered extra medical insurance as part of your package, but once you have received your health card you are entitled to use any of the public hospitals in Dubai. Health Cards need to be renewed every year, residency visas and labour cards only every three years. For further general information and advice about setting up in business in Dubai, visit www.ameinfo.com *See also p299* **Business**.

Dubai Naturalisation & Residency Administration (DNRA)

Trade Centre Road, near Bur Dubai Police Station, Bur Dubai (398 0000/www.dnrd.gov.ae). **Open** 7.30am-7.30pm Sun-Thur. **Map** p333 H8.
The DNRA presides over procedures and laws related to expatriate entry to and residence in the United Arab Emirates (including tourist visas).

Further Reference

Books

For a full list of Arabic authors and bookshops, visit www.uaeinteract.com.

Frauke Heard-Bay
From Trucial States to United Arab Emirates
In 1971, the seven sheikdoms at the southern end of the Gulf, the Trucial States, formed the state of the United Arab Emirates; it was soon a member of the UN, OPEC and the Arab League. This academic volume examines the historical and social movements that have shaped the present-day UAE.

Denys Johnson-Davies (translator) and **Roger MA Allen** (editor)
Arabic Short Stories
A charming and insightful collection of tales from the Middle East.

Alan Keohane
Bedouin: Nomads of the Desert
This photographic portrait pays tribute to the tribal customs that survive among those who continue their annual journey across the desert. It's a very timely reminder of the importance of preserving the UAE's ancient traditions.

Edward Said
Reflections on Exile & Other Essays
Powerfully blending political and aesthetic concerns, Said's writings have changed the field of literary studies.

Language

Arabic is the official language of Dubai, and Urdu and Hindi are also widely spoken and understood, but English is the predominant language.

Some basic words and phrases are given below, listed in phonetics. Capitals are not used in Arabic, but are used below to indicate hard sounds.

With Arabic possessing so many different dialects and sounds from English, transliterating is never easy. We've opted to go for a mainly classical option. *See also p39.*

Getting by

Hello *marhaba*
How are you? *kaif il haal?*
Good morning *sabaah il khayr*
Good evening *masaa' il khayr*
Greetings *'as-salamu 'alaykum*
Welcome *'ahlan wa sahlan*
Goodbye *ma' 'is-salaama*
Excuse me *afwan*
Sorry *'aasif*
God willing *insha'allah*
Please *(to a man) min fadlak (to a woman) min fadlik*
Thank you (very much) *shukran (jazeelan)*
Yes/No *na'am/laa*
I don't know *lasto adree or laa 'a-arif*
Who?/What? *man?/matha?*
Where?/Why? *ayina/lematha?*
How much? *(cost) bekam?*
How many? *kam?*

Numbers & time

Zero *sifr*
One *waahid*
Two *itnain*
Three *talata*
Four *arba'a*
Five *khamsa*
Six *sitta*
Seven *sab'a*
Eight *tamanya*
Nine *tis'a*
Ten *'ashra*
Sunday *al-ahad*
Monday *al-itnayn*
Tuesday *al-talata*
Wednesday *al-arba'a*
Thursday *al-khamees*
Friday *al-jum'a*
Saturday *al-Sabt*
Hour *sa'aa*
Day *yom*
Month *shahr*
Year *sanah*
Today *al yom*
Yesterday *ams/imbarah*
Tomorrow *bukra*

Getting around

Airport *matar*
Post office *maktab al barid*
Bank *bank*
Passport *jawaz safar*
Luggage *'aghraad*
Ticket *tath karah*
Taxi *Taxi*
Car *say-yarra*
City *madina*
Street *share'h*
Road *tareeq*

Magazines

For the top events, meal deals and local listings, pick up a copy of *Time Out Dubai*. Free listings magazines are also distributed at various malls.

Travel

Dubai Explorer publish useful maps including *Off Road Explorer* and *Underwater Explorer*.
UAE Yellow Pages
www.uae-ypages.com.
Invaluable resources full of local listings.

Websites

www.timeoutdubai.com, **www.timeoutabudhabi.com**
For an insider's glimpse of what's happening, when and where in Dubai and the capital.
www.uaeinteract.com
Website of the Ministry of Information & Culture, with information on the UAE.
www.dubaitourism.co.ae
General tourist information.

Transport

www.dubaiairport.com
News from Dubai International Airport.
www.dpa.co.ae
Messages about water transport from the Dubai Ports Authority.
www.rta.ae
Bus timetables and schedules.

Index

Advertisers' Index

Please refer to relevant pages for full details

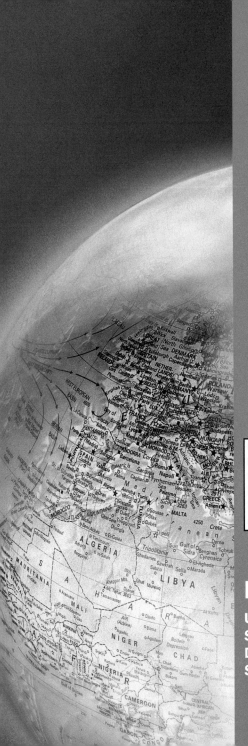

Major sight or landmark	...	░
Railway stations	...	░
Parks	...	░
Hospitals	...	░
Hotels	...	░
Area name	...	**AL RAS**

Maps

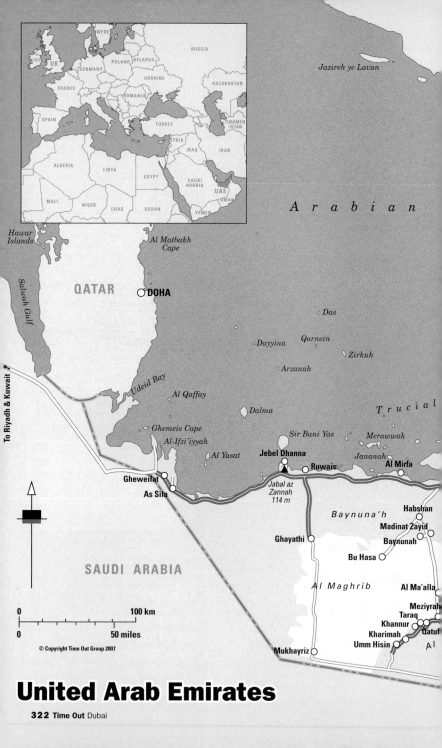

Hawar
Islands

Saluwah Gulf

Jazireh ye Lavan

A r a b i a n

Al Matbakh Cape

QATAR ⦿ **DOHA**

Das

Qarnein

Dayyina

Zirkuh

Arzanah

To Riyadh & Kuwait ↗

Udeid Bay

Al Qaffay

Dalma

T r u c i a l

Ghemeis Cape

Al-Ifzi'iyyah

Sir Bani Yas

Merawwah

Al Yasat

Jebel Dhanna

Jananah

⦿ Ruwais

Al Mirfa

Gheweifat

As Sila

Jabal az Zannah 114 m

Habshan

B a y n u n a' h

Madinat Zayid

Baynunah

Ghayathi ⦿

Bu Hasa ⦿

SAUDI ARABIA

Al Maghrib

Al Ma'alla

Meziyrah

Taraq

Khannur

Qatuf

Kharimah

Umm Hisin

Al

0   100 km

0   50 miles

Mukhayriz ⦿

© Copyright Time Out Group 2007

United Arab Emirates

IRAN

Jazireh ye Hormuz

Jazireh ye Qeshm

Jazireh ye Larak

Strait of Hormuz

Jazireh ye Kish

*Musandam
Peninsula*

Jazireh ye Forur

G u l f

OMAN

Ash Sham

Khaymah Cape   Rams

Ras Al Khaimah   Digdagga

Haffah Cape

Umm Al Quwain   Dibba   Rul Dibba

Hamriya   Idhn   Badiyah   *Fakkan Bay*

Ajman   Manama   *Jabal Adham*   Khor Fakkan

Sir Abu Nu'ayr   Sharjah   *1,128m*

DUBAI   Al Dhaid   *Gulf of
Oman*

See pp326-327   Al Awir

Al Haba   Mileiha   Fujairah

Fili

Ghanadah Cape   Al Liseli   Margham

Hatta

C o a s t   Al Samha   Al Faqa   Ash Shu'ayb

See pp278-285   Abjan   Al Haiyir

Sweihan

*Abu al
Jirab*   ABU DHABI   *At Khatam*

Saadiyat   Mafraq   Bani Yas   Al Saad

Al Khatam   Bu Samarah   Al Ain

Tarif   *Al Taff*   Ayn Al Faidah

Al'Arad

Al'Qua'a

Al Humrah   OMAN

Sabkhah

Al Khis

Jarrah   Je'eisah

Liwa   Hamim

At Rabbad

Umm a Zummul

To Muscat

Street Index

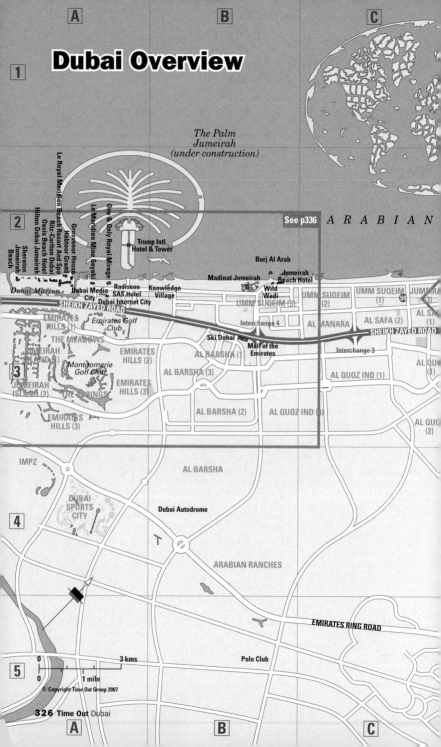

Dubai Overview

A   B   C

1

*The Palm
Jumeirah
(under construction)*

2   See p336   A R A B I A N

Le Royal Meridien Beach Resort And Spa
Le Meridien Mina Seyahi
Habtoor Grand
Ritz-Carlton Dubai
Oasis Beach Hotel
Hilton Dubai Jumeirah

Sheraton
Jumeirah
Beach

Grosvenor House
One & Only Royal Mirage

Trump Intl.
Hotel & Tower

Burj Al Arab

Madinat Jumeirah   Jumeirah
Beach Hotel

Dubai Marina   Dubai Media
City
Radisson
SAS Hotel   Knowledge
Village   Wild
Wadi

UMM SUQEIM   UMM SUQEIM   JUMEIRAH
Dubai Internet City   UMM SUQEIM (3)   (2)   (1)   (1)

SHEIKH ZAYED ROAD   59

EMIRATES
HILLS (1)   Emirates Golf
Club   AL MANARA   AL SAFA (2)   AL SAF
(1)

Interchange 4

THE MEADOWS

Ski Dubai   SHEIKH ZAYED ROAD   AL QU
(1)

3   EMIRATES
HILLS (2)   AL BARSHA (1)   Mall of the
Emirates   Interchange 3

JUMEIRAH
ISLAND (1)   Montgomerie
Golf Club   AL BARSHA (3)   AL QUOZ IND (1)   AL QU
(1)

JUMEIRAH
ISLAND (2)   EMIRATES
HILLS (3)   THE SPRINGS

EMIRATES
HILLS (3)   AL BARSHA (2)   AL QUOZ IND (4)   AL QU
(2)

IMPZ

AL BARSHA

4   DUBAI
SPORTS
CITY   Dubai Autodrome

ARABIAN RANCHES

EMIRATES RING ROAD

0   3 kms

5   0   1 mile   Polo Club
© Copyright Time Out Group 2007

A   B   C

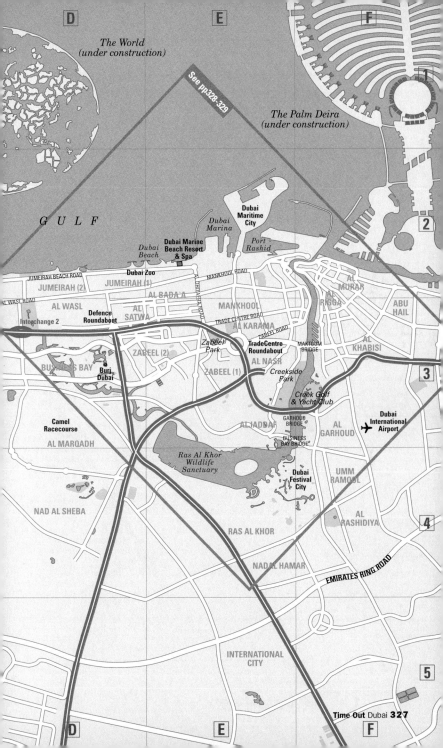

The World
(under construction)

The Palm Deira
(under construction)

See pp328-329

G U L F

Dubai
Maritime
City

*Dubai
Marina*

*Dubai
Beach*

**Dubai Marine
Beach Resort
& Spa**

*Port
Rashid*

Dubai Zoo

JUMEIRAH BEACH ROAD

JUMEIRAH (2)

JUMEIRAH (1)

MANKHOOL ROAD

AL BADA'A

AL MURAR

AL RIGGA

ABU
HAIL

AL WASL ROAD

AL WASL

AL SATWA

MANKHOOL

**Defence
Roundabout**

AL HUDAIBA ROAD

TRADE CENTRE ROAD

Interchange 2

AL KARAMA

ZABEEL ROAD

*Zabeel
Park*

**TradeCentre
Roundabout**

MAKTOUM
BRIDGE

AL
KHABISI

BUSINESS BAY

**Burj
Dubai**

ZABEEL (2)

ZABEEL (1)

AL NASR

*Creekside
Park*

*Creek Golf
& Yacht Club*

GARHOUD
BRIDGE

AL JADAF

BUSINESS
BAY BRIDGE

AL
GARHOUD

**Dubai
International
Airport**

**Camel
Racecourse**

AL MARQADH

*Ras Al Khor
Wildlife
Sanctuary*

**Dubai
Festival
City**

UMM
RAMOOL

NAD AL SHEBA

AL
RASHIDIYA

RAS AL KHOR

NAD AL HAMAR

EMIRATES RING ROAD

INTERNATIONAL
CITY

2

3

4

5

F

G

H

1

0   2 km

0   1 mile

© Copyright Time Out Group 2007

1 Hotels pp42-67

1 Restaurants & Cafés pp94-131

1 Pubs & Bars pp132-139

Port Rashid

See pp330-331

AL DAGHAYA

AL SHINDAGHA

AL SOUQ AL KABEER

AL MINA

AL RAFFA

AL KHALEEJ ROAD

Dubai Maritime City

2

ARABIAN

Dubai Dry Docks

AL MANKHOOL ROAD

MANKHO

GULF

See pp332-333

AL HUDAIBA

AL MINA ROAD

AL AUHID ROAD

AL DHIYAFHA

ROAD

3

Dubai Marine Beach Resort & Spa

AL WASL ROAD

AL BADA'A

BEACH ROAD

AL SATWA ROAD

Fairmont Dubai

Trade Centre

Dubai International Convention Centre

AL KIFA

2ND ZA'ABEEL RO

Dubai Zoo

JUMEIRAH

AL SATWA

Towers Rotana Hotel

Jumeirah Emirates Towers

54 63 87 89 92

17 22 25 27

Dubai International Financial Centre

See pp334-335

4

Dusit Dubai

Al Murooj Rotana

Jumeirah Beach Park

AL WASL

Burj Dubai

RAS AL KHOR ROAD (E 44)

SHEIKH ZAYED ROAD (311)

BEACH ROAD

5

JUMEIRAH

Safa Park

AL WASL ROAD

Al Safa Complex (Park'n'Shop)

Metropolitan Hotel

AL MARQADH

328 Time Out Dubai

F

G

H

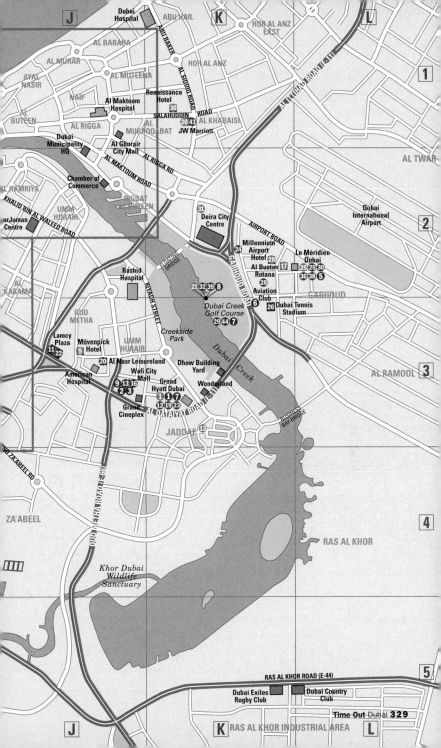

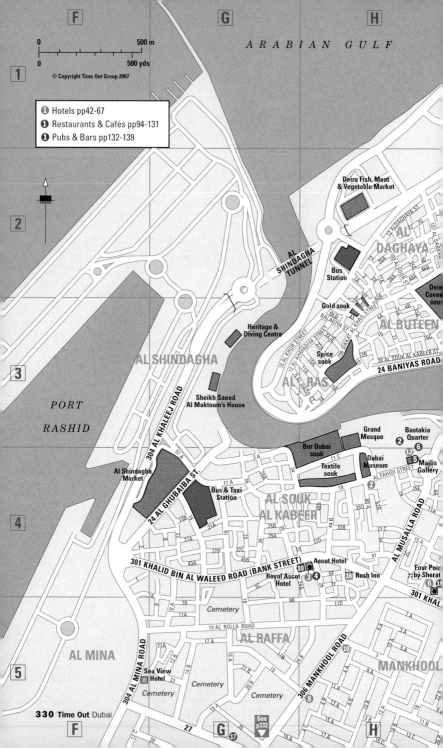

1

2

3

4

5

ARABIAN GULF

0   500 m
0   500 yds
© Copyright Time Out Group 2007

❶ Hotels pp42-67
❶ Restaurants & Cafés pp94-131
❶ Pubs & Bars pp132-139

Deira Fish, Meat & Vegetable Market

AL DAGHAYA

17 AL DAGHAYA ST

1 AL SABKHA

Bus Station

AL SHINDAGHA TUNNEL

Gold souk

OLD BALADIYA STREET

AL BUTEEN

Deira Covered souk

Heritage & Diving Centre

AL SHINDAGHA

10 AL KHOR STREET

17 AL AHMADIYA STREET

AL KHALEEJ ROAD

Spice souk

AL RAS

24 BANIYAS ROAD

PORT

RASHID

Sheikh Saeed Al Maktoum's House

304 AL KHALEEJ ROAD

51 A

Grand Mosque

Bastakia Quarter

❷ ❻

⑫

❺ Majlis Gallery

Bur Dubai souk

Dubai Museum

AL FAHIDI STREET

Al Shindagha Market

24 AL GHUBAIBA ST

Bus & Taxi Station

11 A

Textile souk

❷

AL SOUK AL KABEER

AL MUSALLA ROAD

301 KHALID BIN AL WALEED ROAD (BANK STREET)

Ascot Hotel

⑩❶ ❸❹ ⑯ Rush Inn

Royal Ascot Hotel

Four Points by Sheraton

❻ ❶

301 KHAL

Cemetery

15 AL ROLLA ROAD

AL RAFFA

⑩

306 MANKHOOL ROAD

MANKHOOL

AL MINA

304 AL MINA ROAD

Sea View Hotel

Cemetery

Cemetery

❽

See p333 ▼

⑰

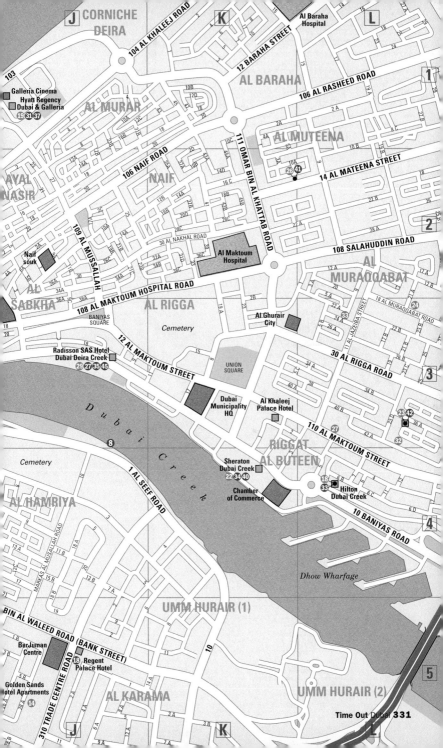

C   D   E

6

*Dubai
Dry Dock*

AL MINA

0   500 m

0   500 yds

© Copyright Time Out Group 2007

❶ Hotels pp42-67
❶ Restaurants & Cafés pp94-131
❶ Pubs & Bars pp132-139

7

Capitol Hotel ❹

305 AL DHIYAFHA RD

304 AL MINA ROAD

8

JUMEIRAH (1)

❼
❶ ❹
Jumeirah
Rotana Dubai

AL BADA'A

Dubai Marine Beach
Resort & Spa

38 47 60 12

Palm Strip

Jumeirah
Mosque

❺¹

*Dubai Open
Beach*

21 B AL HUDAIBA ROAD

Iranian
Mosque

9

❺⁰

Magrudy Centre

Jumeirah
Centre

Iranian
Hospital

The Village

Jumeirah
Plaza

304 AL WASL ROAD

306 AL SATWA ROAD

302 JUMEIRAH BEACH ROAD

Beach
Centre Mall

Sheikh Mohammed Centre
for Cultural Understanding

10

See
p335
▼

Dubai Zoo

C   D   E

A R A B I A N

G U L F

A

11

0   500 m
0   500 yds

© Copyright Time Out Group 2007

❶ Hotels pp42-67
❶ Restaurants & Cafés pp94-131
❶ Pubs & Bars pp132-139

12

A R A B I A N

G U L F

302 JUMEIRAH ROAD

Mercato Mall
49

Town Centre

311 AL UROUBA STREET

13

14

JUMEIRAH (2)

Jumeirah Beach Park
48

302 JUMEIRAH ROAD

304 AL WASL ROAD

15

JUMEIRAH (3)

334 Time Out Dubai

Majlis Ghorfat **A**
Um Al Sheef
313 ALATHAR ST

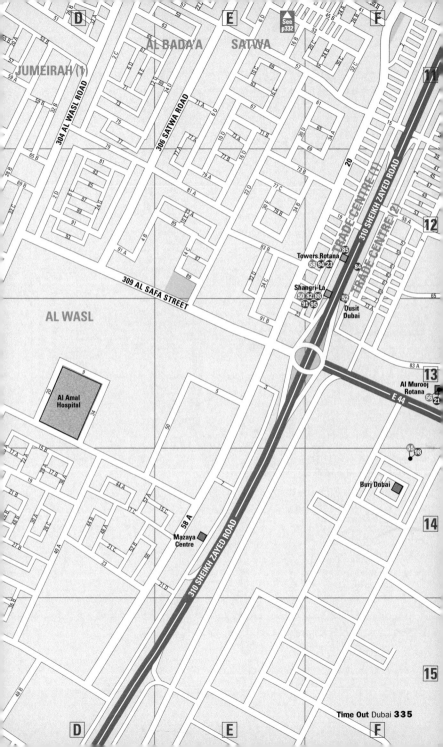

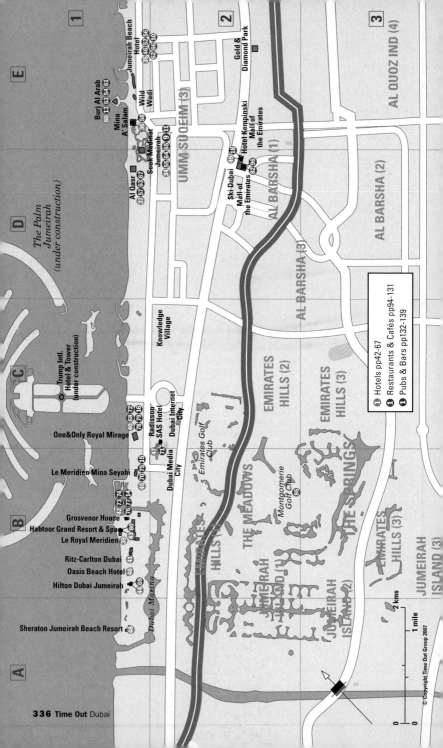

1

2

3

E

D

C

B

A

UMM SUQEIM (3)

AL BARSHA (1)

AL BARSHA (2)

AL BARSHA (3)

AL QUOZ IND (4)

AL QUOZ IND (3)

EMIRATES HILLS (2)

EMIRATES HILLS (3)

EMIRATES HILLS (1)

THE MEADOWS

THE SPRINGS

JUMEIRAH ISLAND (1)

JUMEIRAH ISLAND (2)

JUMEIRAH ISLAND (3)

The Palm Jumeirah (under construction)

Jumeirah Beach Hotel

Gold & Diamond Park

Wild Wadi

Burj Al Arab

Mina A'Salam

Souk Madinat Jumeirah

Al Qasr

Hotel Kempinski Mall of the Emirates

Ski Dubai Mall of the Emirates

Knowledge Village

Trump Intl. Hotel & Tower (under construction)

One&Only Royal Mirage

Radisson SAS Hotel

Dubai Internet City

Dubai Media City

Le Meridien Mina Seyahi

Emirates Golf Club

Montgomerie Golf Club

Grosvenor House

Habtoor Grand Resort & Spa

Le Royal Meridien

Ritz-Carlton Dubai

Oasis Beach Hotel

Hilton Dubai Jumeirah

Sheraton Jumeirah Beach Resort

Dubai Marina

1 Hotels pp42-67

1 Restaurants & Cafés pp94-131

1 Pubs & Bars pp132-139

65 46 52 66
62 64 10

60 13 53 54 61

38 58

34 55 60 65 9 11

57 59 63 67

49 45

82 86

40 68 72
78 79 16

47

71

70 75 51

45 70 74

42 73 74
76 77 14

39 43 80

41 50

46 69

44 69

48

2 kms

1 mile

0

0

© Copyright Time Out Group 2007